With Broadax an̶ ̶.̶.̶.̶o̶r̶a̶n̶a

A CENTENNIAL BOOK

One hundred books
published between 1990 and 1995
bear this special imprint of
the University of California Press.
We have chosen each Centennial Book
as an example of the Press's finest
publishing and bookmaking traditions
as we celebrate the beginning of
our second century.

UNIVERSITY OF CALIFORNIA PRESS

Founded in 1893

WITH BROADAX AND FIREBRAND

*The Destruction of the
Brazilian Atlantic Forest*

WARREN DEAN

University of California Press

BERKELEY   LOS ANGELES   LONDON

University of California Press
Berkeley and Los Angeles, California

University of California Press, Ltd.
London, England

First Paperback Printing 1997

Parts of chapters 10 and 11 were previously published in "Forest
Conservation in Southeast Brazil, 1900–1955," *Environmental History
Review* 9 (Spring 1985): 55–69. Reproduced by permission of the
publisher.

Library of Congress Cataloging-in-Publication Data

Dean, Warren.
    With broadax and firebrand : the destruction of the Brazilian Atlantic
forest / Warren Dean.
        p.   cm.
    "A Centennial book"—P.
    Includes bibliographical references (p.   ) and index.
    ISBN 0-520-20886-2
    Deforestation—Brazil—Atlantic Coast—History.   2. Rain
forests—Brazil—Atlantic Coast—History.   3. Man—Influence on
nature—Brazil—Atlantic Coast—History.   4. Atlantic Coast
(Brazil)—Environmental conditions—History.   I. Title.
SD418.3.B6D43   1995
    304.2'8'098109152—dc20   94-5681

Printed in the United States of America
9 8 7 6 5 4 3 2 1

The paper used in this publication meets the minimum requirements of
American National Standard for Information Sciences—Permanence of
Paper for Printed Library Materials, ANSI Z39.48-1984. ∞

This book is printed on partially recycled paper.

For Tom, Julie and Yun-ah

QUEM VIER DEPOIS, QUE SE ARRANJE.
Old Brazilian saying

The publisher gratefully acknowledges the contribution provided by the General Endowment Fund of the Associates of the University of California Press.

The publisher wishes to thank Jeffrey Lesser, who kindly offered to proofread this book and answer editorial queries.

Contents

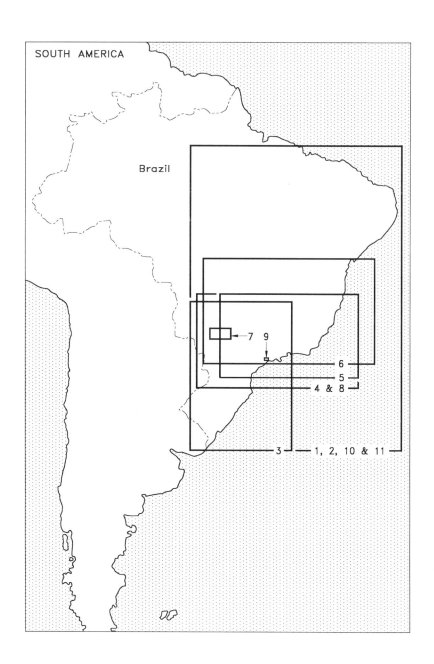

SOUTH AMERICA

Brazil

7 9

6

5

4 & 8

3 — 1, 2, 10 & 11

Maps

Foreword

This is a book about the *caá-etê*, the Brazilian forest. It is an innovative and powerful ecological history that sweeps across the whole expanse of Brazil's past, a cautionary tale that details what humans have wrought and destroyed and warns against the parallel destruction that seems all too imminent in the Amazonian region. Written with passion, irony, and clear but unromanticized love for its subject, it is a fitting capstone to a scholarly career in which concern for the human situation and social justice were combined with a consistent commitment to principle which reflected in Warren Dean's life and his work. This book had gone to press when he died in a tragic accident in Santiago, Chile, in May 1994. He was a historian of great accomplishment, at the fullness of his powers, and his death interrupted an important scholarly career in mid-stream.

The themes of Warren Dean's books are always large, always important. Any scholar can make a "contribution" by providing information on some topic "never done before," but the gift of recognizing the themes that are truly important, posing the appropriate questions, and designing the research strategies to answer them is not given to, or developed by, all historians. Warren Dean was one of the gifted. Each of his books provoked debate, each of his books caught the attention of the international scholarly community, because the underlying themes were always questions central to an understanding of the historical development of Brazil.

Above all, Warren Dean was interested in transitions—in the change from agrarian to industrial society, from slave to free labor, from economic boom to bust—and in the economic, social, and mental structures and actions that accompanied these transitions. In *The Industrialization of São Paulo* (1967) Dean addressed the problem of the social origins of Latin America's greatest industrial sector and its political role in Brazil prior to World War II. His study of the agricultural origins of industrial capital and the merging of planter and immigrant bourgeoisies shaped a generation of debate on these questions in Brazil. In the process of researching and writing that study, Dean published important and provocative articles on the attitudes of the agricultural elite in Brazil toward capital, land, and labor. This led him to his next book, a major study of Brazil's great question of the nineteenth century, slavery, and its implications for land distribution and labor recruitment, especially immigration. *Rio Claro: A Brazilian Plantation System* (1976), like Stanley Stein's *Vassouras,* still stands as a classic of its genre, a regional study in which large macro-historical themes were examined through the prism of local history. History for Dean was always human action and never determined by structures or contexts. In *Rio Claro* and throughout his work there was always room for the agency of subordinated peoples and classes. He explained the fall of of slavery like this: "The slave population, not the planters, at last brought ruin to the system of forced labor by refusing to participate in it, to the degree that repression became unendurably expensive." Only the availability of Italian rural proletarians as immigrant workers allowed the coffee plantation system to survive. The final lesson drawn from the experience in Rio Claro was the "futility of confusing private profitability with the advancement of society." This theme increasingly preoccupied Dean's concerns as his work began to move in new directions in the 1980s.

Quietly, almost alone among North American Brazilianists, he began to explore the relationship between society and the environment in Brazil. His research centered on the tragic history of rubber. Brazil held a virtual monopoly of rubber production in the mid-nineteenth century and then lost it, allowing Asian competitors to gain control of world markets. To tell this story demanded not only a knowledge of Brazilian politics and society and world economic structures but also a familiarity with botany, ecology, and a range of environmental sciences. To acquire that knowledge, Dean studied at the New York Botanical Garden, and in the 1980s he began to publish a series of articles that reflected his new interest in environmental history. *Brazil and the Struggle for Rubber* appeared in 1987, and with it Dean was recognized as the leading historian of the Brazilian environment, but not without creating controversy. Many in Brazil held that the failure to develop modern plantation rubber production in that country was due to the machinations of the colonial powers and the competition of the international marketplace, as well as local social and demographic factors. Dean's book shifted the emphasis to the ecological problems inherent in the relationship between *Hevea brasiliensis* and an indigenous fungus that made plantation organization and production in Brazil virtually impossible. Certainly no friend of colonial regimes or multinational corporations, Dean had simply reached an unconventional conclusion, and he did not hesitate to express an unpopular position. Such were his qualities as a historian.

With Broadax and Firebrand fully establishes Warren Dean's contribution to the developing field of environmental history. From the prehistoric formation of the land and the forest to the arrival of human inhabitants to the modern drive for development, the great Atlantic coastal forest and its destruction is the focus of Dean's concern. Against the backdrop of this subject he unfolds the history of Brazil, a history critical of exploitation driven at times by necessity, but often by unrelenting greed with little or no concern for the *mata*, the forest, symbol in Brazil of the backward, the undeveloped, the untamed. Many in this story bear responsibility— peasants, loggers, ranchers, coffee planters, industrialists, and the nation state itself. Dean is not the first to be critical of such exploitative behavior. Frei Vicente do Salvador, Brazil's first historian, wrote in 1627 that the colonists thought only of returning to Portugal and taught their parrots to say, "papagaio real, para Portugal" (royal parrot, back to Portugal), and would have taught their goods and chattels to do likewise if they could speak. Sérgio Buarque de Holanda, Brazil's great historian of this century, wrote in his *Raízes do Brasil* (1936) that the colonists wished to "pick the fruit without planting the tree." The present book turns this metaphor into a history.

The protagonists in this story are varied, Indians, missionaries, miners, developers, nationalists, cattle, trees, and even the "king of Brazil," the *saúva*, leaf-cutting ants; the heroes are a few scientists, idealists, and cranks. Around them all Dean has woven a complex story, describing with passion "a half-millennium of gluttony," and the curse of a forest that provided too much, too easily. This book details the tragic results of disregard in the past and warns against it in the present. It is a book about Brazil that has implications for much of the modern world. But Warren Dean was no armchair Cassandra. His influence and activity extended far beyond his publications, to the students trained by him in the United States and Brazil and to his colleagues at home and abroad. I still remember my first conversation with him at a meeting on colonial Brazil in Chicago in 1970. "Be careful," he warned, "the trouble with colonial historians is that they always believe the documents they read." It was sound advice and it underlined the healthy skepticism of sources he always maintained.

Warren Dean also led by example. His participation in a number of organizations working to uphold human rights during the dark days of dictatorship in Brazil, his actions on behalf of Brazilian colleagues and students, and his critical stance in regard to certain policies of his country all reflected his commitment to principle and his love for Brazil, its people, and its natural resources. Admired by students and colleagues, he made a major impact on his field and on those who came into contact with him. He was a "Brazilianist" in the best sense of the word, and none of his books more than *With Broadax and Firebrand* reflects his qualities as a man and as a scholar.

Stuart B. Schwartz
University of Minnesota

Acknowledgments

I wish to express my thanks to the John Simon Guggenheim Memorial Fund, the John Carter Brown Library, the Social Science Research Council, the Fulbright Commission–Brasília, and the Faculty of Arts and Science of New York University, all of which helped fund the research underlying this book. A part of the text appeared in the *Environmental History Review*, whose editors are thanked for permission to reprint. Parts of early versions of the text were presented in seminars at the Institute of Latin American Studies of the University of London and the Department of History of Duke University, as a McAlister Lecture at the University of Florida, a lecture at the Federal University of Rio de Janeiro, and in my graduate classes in the Department of History, New York University; the participants all have my thanks for their comments.

Many colleagues and students have assisted me with research leads, contacts, notes, and comments, especially Larissa Brown, Sueann Caulfield, Fay Haussman, Gloria Lacava, Jeff Lesser, Ghillean T. Prance, Richard C. Raymer, Raquel Rolnik, Kirsten Schultz, and Robert Wilcox. Readers of the portions or the entire manuscript who were good enough to provide me with comments—Scott Mori, Wayt Thomas, Stuart Schwartz, and an anonymous evaluator—were extremely helpful. Sarah Myers lent her superb editing skills.

Many Brazilians have generously made their facilities and knowledge available to me, among them Fernando Achiamé, Bias Arrudão, Keith Brown, Sérgio de Almeida Bruni, J. P. P. Carrauta, José Pedro de Oliveira Costa, José Augusto Drummond, Régis Guillaumon, Luciano Martins, Rodrigo Lara Mesquita, Cláudio and Susana Pádua, José Augusto Pádua, Judith Patarra, Marco Antonio Rocha, Arístides Arthur Soffiati Netto, Célio Valle, Orlando Valverde, Francisco Vinhosa, Mauro Victor, and José Sebastião Witter. Graduate students in my classes at the Federal Fluminense University, the Federal University of Paraná, and the University of

São Paulo provided inspiration as well. Gabriel and Clélia Bolaffi, Ana Veronica Mautner, Nancy and Tony Naro, Norman Gall and Catalina Pages, Climene Ruiz and Gicélia de Freitas, and Maria do Carmo Campello de Souza offered in addition hospitality and friendship, for which I am indebted for life. I thank my son and mapmaker, Thomas Dean, for carrying out a complicated task with dispatch and ingenuity. None of these persons, of course, bears any responsibility for errors or omissions that may persist in the text.

I owe my wife Elizabeth McArdle-Dean far more than I can express here. This enormous task could never have been finished without her support and understanding.

1

The Forest Evolves

Forêts vierges aussi anciennes que le monde.

Virgin forests as ancient as the world.

AUGUSTE DE SAINT-HILAIRE

We fly, seven thousand meters high, southward over the Brazilian subcontinent toward the city of Rio de Janeiro. It is early morning. The shadow of our 747 glides over the autumn mist far below. Through the plexiglass we see it encircled by a rainbow, an ethereal bird in a celestial gunsight. The mist dissolves, revealing the worn and ragged Archean shield of Minas Gerais, a confusion of crisscrossing ridges partitioned by the Serra do Espinhaço—the Backbone Range. To the west brown, sluggish creeks meander toward their encounter with the São Francisco River. To the east coursing streams rush toward the River Doce and the Atlantic Ocean. It is a landscape scarred by human striving. On the murky blue horizon the great reservoirs of the hydroelectric dams at Furnas and Três Marias are dimly visible. In the foreground stretch chalky-orange badlands, gashes carved by centuries of improvident mining, farming, and grazing. On flat bottomlands, here and there, cultivation persists. On fields recently plowed, the brick-red blush of fertile, iron-rich soils can be discerned. The highlands are in pasture, still green from the summer rains; soon they will wither, and then they will be fired to rid them of ticks and underbrush. Here and there are hillsides planted in eucalyptus trees, valued for plywood, pulp, and charcoal. Dirt roads careen through this chaotic patchwork, as though laid out by reconnoitering ants. Towns huddle in the valleys, glittering in the bright morning sun like jewels that have come unclasped and have scattered by the wayside.

Nothing about this humanized terrain is remarkable. The lofty traveler may even feel comforted in viewing it. These traces far from the Rhodian shore are manifestations of civilization, as we know it. An urbanized people took possession here five hundred years ago, and its numbers and its consumption of natural wealth have continuously grown: proofs of success, as we are satisfied to define it. From a height of seven thousand meters there is no sign that anything has gone awry, except for the badlands, hidden from those who travel the roads, which avoid the badlands, as though from shame.

At intervals below, however, the traveler descries verdant tracts of forest, not the orderly rows of planted woodlots but wild and irregular. One in particular is impressively large—two or three kilometers across. The traveler wonders how it escaped the civilizing ax and how long it has been left undisturbed. Woods like these are nearly all regrowths; very few date from before the European invasion, and all have for generations been logged and rummaged through for animals and plants for barter and sale. These patches are the last witnesses of the landscape that preceded civilization and its triumphs. Once, these hills were nearly submerged in a blanket of verdure, only the peaks breaking free in carpets of sedges and grasses. The streams would then have been nearly invisible under the looming trees. Through their boughs, the clear waters would have glittered in the morning sun. From a 747 flying back through time, the traveler would have looked out on an endless green carpet, flecked with the glory of entire trees in full bloom—the purple-pink of sapucaias, the white and red of copaíbas, the yellow of guapiruvus, the violet of jacarandás. Its original inhabitants called it *caá-etê*—the true forest, the undisturbed forest—a scene very like the Amazon, save for the ridges and bluffs.

What would Matthew Arnold have thought, looking down at this present tattered landscape? The depression that overcame him when he surrendered at last to the uttermost reality of natural selection and felt control slip away, and with it stewardship, hierarchy, righteousness—would it have lifted, if he could have observed from this height how completely the ignorant armies have defeated the sway of evolution, enthroning, in its place, entropy? Or would he, like the other passengers, tranquilized, already have slid shut the visor, settled back in his seat, and contented himself with his little box of disposable plastic into which an ersatz breakfast had been deposited, trying all the while to imagine what adventures awaited in the sweltering, sprawling, desperate megalopolis of Rio de Janeiro?

Is anything to be made of the transformations that have been worked on this great plateau by ten thousand years of human occupation? Why not try to write the history of a forest, of an endangered realm of nature, whose disappearance has occurred for the most part in a historical epoch?

Is a history of the forest possible? Maybe not. History is conventionally

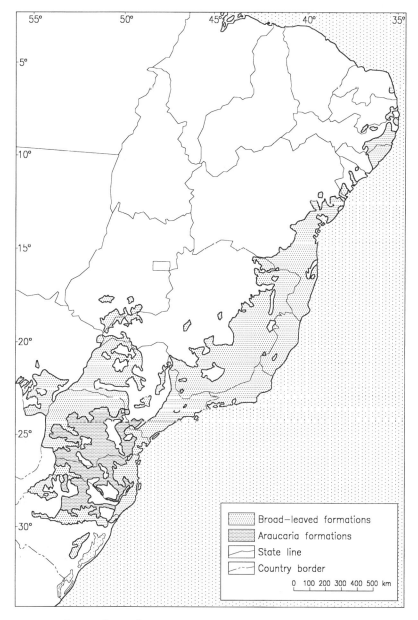

░░░	Broad—leaved formations
▒▒▒	Araucaria formations
	State line
— · —	Country border

0 100 200 300 400 500 km

Map 1. The Brazilian Atlantic Forest in 1500

about human ambitions, human satisfactions and frustrations. How can there be a telling of the "history" of other species when we must suppose that their actions lacked intention, beyond that of spawning and surviving? Other species on this darkling plain, it might be most comfortable to assert, cannot play any role in the drama of human history save that of scenery, even when the play is about the removal of the scenery. Nature, even when human ambition is directed against it, remains an object. The pathos of Sisyphus is entirely his; none pertains to his stone.

A kind of forest history has been written in North America in which the forest appears as raw material for the timber trade, nothing more. The forest is a living stockpile of wood. These accounts are thick with human intentionality, brimming with ambition sated, the stuff of drama and folklore, but in them the forests are unrecognizable in their entelechy, as societies composed of thousands of plant and animal species. These histories of a brief moment in the passage of nations through the "frontier" experience offer not an encounter with the natural world but a representation of a phase in the evolution of their business and technical organizations. In Europe, "forest histories" have been written that are rich in the sense of place as well as in human purpose and are careful in their accounts of the behavior and being of the life that constitutes them. Yet their matter, lamentably, is limited to the management of lopped and pollarded woodlots and macabre hunting preserves: concentration camps for the natural world, in fact, not the natural world itself. It could not be otherwise: On that continent there is "hardly a parcel of land that has not been turned over a thousand and a thousand times."[1]

Compared with the astonishing productivity, abundance, and variety of the tropical South American forests, neither North America nor Europe ever possessed so marvelous a history to tell. Their summer's leases have all too short a date; indeed, they were so frequently canceled during glacial episodes that their surviving life forms display, as their chiefest quality, superb resistance to cold and storms and a tenacious grasp upon their glacier-scoured soils. Alas, harsh climes discourage evolutionary novelty and experiment. Their forests huddle in timorous uniformity, vast stands of a score of different trees, or a dozen, or just a single species, and on their boughs, in their hollows, and amid their roots only a picket force of animals breed—and many of them with winter's cold flee southward or resign themselves to suspended animation.

The tales to be told of those starveling forests are of the endurance of desperate pioneers, not of the establishment of great cathedrals of life. So resistant and uncomplicated are they that all the devastation visited upon them by humans does not prevent them, unless they are covered over with asphalt, from reconstituting themselves. This circumstance attenuates the alarm that the sensible observer feels when watching a hundred-year-old forest of fir and spruce fall to the chain saw or go up in flame—by and by, it may return.

The same cannot be expected for the South American tropical forests, which most certainly can be obliterated but may prove impossible to reestablish on the sites from which they were removed. Hence the tragedy. The destruction of these forests is irreversible, within any sort of human time scale. What is lost when tropical forest is destroyed is not only greater in variety, complexity, and originality than other ecosystems, it is incalculable. For although cataloguing of the boreal forest is conceivable—and well advanced, in fact—cataloguing of a tropical forest is well beyond our resources, now or in the imaginable future. The disappearance of a tropical forest is therefore a tragedy vast beyond human knowing or conceiving.[2]

The history of the destruction of the South American forests is nevertheless a story to some degree accessible to our curiosity. History came late to nearly every other encounter of humans with wilderness. When Columbus first scanned the Antillean shore, ten thousand years and more of human occupation had already transformed it in ways unfathomable even to the most earnest efforts of archaeologists. Nevertheless, of all the tropical continents South America was the last to be invaded by humans, and human dominance of its forests was much less intense and of much shorter duration than that exercised in Asia, Africa, and Australia. Hence the Europeans confronted in their New World a nature more pristine than that which they encountered elsewhere in the tropics, and thus much more of the process of degradation has taken place in an era of written records. South America, then, is the forest historian's freshest battleground, where all the fallen still lie sprawled and unburied and where the victors still wander about, looting and burning the train.

Forest history, rightly understood, is everywhere on this planet one of exploitation and destruction. Humans reduce the natural world to "landscape"—domesticated surroundings trimmed and shaped to fit some practical use or conventional aesthetic, or else, more chilling still, to "space"—desert plains steamrollered and built upon to consecrate an extremity of species narcissism. Human interventions never quite realize human expectations. Their fields go plow sick, their pastures become coarse and woody, their cities collapse. The natural world, simplified, not in accordance with human desires but in response to their acts, is turned into a vast cosmopolitan weed patch.

Thus it is nearly impossible to write a forest history that conforms to a vision of what it is desired that the present become. The anchoring of events to dates and the insistence on chronology presume that penultimate and ultimate events foretoken a proximate, satisfactory resolution of the contradictions inherent in these events. Without this conviction—of the Second Coming, the realization of the idea of liberty, equality, and fraternity, the triumph of bourgeois hegemony, the inevitability of socialist revolution, the establishment of a new economic or political order—historians, even the "scientific" historians who sense a need to disguise their temptation to predict, lose the thread. What is to be made of a history that does not—cannot—make us rejoice in our prospects, that reflects so strikingly our improvidence and parasitism?

For humans, coexistence with tropical forest has always been problematic. Antagonism is not at any given moment a necessary part of the relationship, but forest "clearing" is not merely a dictate of cultural prejudice or pride or of improvident political and social arrangements. The aggrandizement of our species has been based upon the destruction of forests that we are ill equipped to inhabit. The preservation of forests must therefore be based upon something beyond the argument of cultural, environmental, or economic self-interest, perhaps upon a conception of self-interest that only a shrewder self-knowledge and a more profound and philosophical understanding of the natural world may be able to define. Many already view uneasily the proximate extinction of the forests of the world. Perhaps, to clarify such notions and respond to such concerns, a memoir of the destruction of a particular forest, shaming and damning though it be, may be a useful thing to have at hand. That, at least, has been the author's intention.[3]

On the eastern margin of South America there once stretched an immense forest, or more accurately, a complex of forest types, generally broadleaved, rain loving, and tropical to subtropical, stretching from about 8° to about 28° south latitude and extending inland from the coast about 100 kilometers in the north, widening to more than 500 kilometers in the south. Altogether the forest covered about a million square kilometers. This complex has been referred to as the Brazilian Atlantic Forest, related to the much larger Amazon Forest but distinct from it. Together, these two great forests formed a life zone distinct from and richer in species than those of the other tropics of our globe, situated in Africa and Southeast Asia. The Atlantic Forest was itself remarkably diverse, considering its relatively modest size. And it contained a remarkable number of endemic species—that is, life forms peculiar to it—even though it shared the same continental landmass with the Amazon Forest and was for long geological periods in partial contact with it.[4]

Forest occurred along this coast because of relief, wind patterns, and ocean currents. Along its length there rises, only a few kilometers inland, an imposing, almost continuous palisade, in some places nearly a thousand meters high. In the central and southern sectors of the coast there loom behind this first wall, in more or less parallel array, still higher mountainous chains, the result of plate upwelling more than a hundred million years ago. These chains add as much as another thousand meters of height to the coastal profile. Against these barriers a steady eastern trade wind blows during most of the year, laden with moisture from the warm equatorial sea. As the air current is lifted, it is cooled and must drop its moisture as rain, overall about 1,500 millimeters a year. The rains, however, are reduced in the Southern Hemisphere's winter, when the cool Falkland Current presses farther north along the coast. The eastern faces of these chains receive very high precipitation—more than 4,000 millimeters a year at some points along the coast. Inland, cloud moisture drops fairly sharply, and rainfall becomes more seasonal. Along the coast one winter month or another may experience less than 100 millimeters of precipitation, and even less may fall for three or four months in the rain shadow of the coastal ranges, so that the forest may not, in some places, transgress the more landward mountain peaks. Thus a vegetational gradient can be observed as one travels inland.

One still finds first, on bays and estuaries, where there is respite from the scouring of the waves, a shoreline of mangrove, whose stilt roots descend from their branches to the tidal waterside, fabricating soil and harboring colonies of caimans, fish, and mollusks. Behind this picket force, and also occupying lands behind the dunes that at points in the Northeast may soar to 90 meters, lie low thickets of *restinga*, a formation accustomed to sandy, nutrient-poor soil, bristling with cactus bushes, freestanding bromeliads, and stunted trees. Restinga stretches inland, in some places for 20 or 30 kilometers, on plains where geological upwelling produced, in serried rows, banks of Holocene fossil dunes. Behind this, on the piedmont, stands a majestic formation of rain-loving broad-leaved evergreens, 30 to 35 meters tall, with scattered emergent individuals up to 40 meters, resting on trunks 12 meters or more in circumference. Underneath the dizzying canopy, three or four more stories may be discerned, "forests layered on forests," the lower ones consisting of shorter broad-leaved trees, palms, bamboos, and giant ferns, tolerant of subdued light. Epiphytes and parasites festoon the branches, vines climb their trunks, and lianas curtain the spaces between.[5]

As the forest climbs the coastal cliff, it becomes noticeably less luxuriant. There the soil is thinner, and the hillsides offer easier access to sunlight and therefore less competition. Thus the trees are smaller, their trunks finer, and on the steepest hillsides one or two of the understories are absent. Above this somewhat distinct montane formation, along the coastal palisade, at the few points where the upwelling of offshore winds was constant and abrupt, what some have denominated a "cloud forest" was formed. On the sodden, thin, acid soils of these ridges, trees are dwarfen, their gnarled branches burdened with profusions of orchids and bromeliads that draw sustenance from the moist, nutrient-bearing clouds themselves. Mosses, lichens, and liverworts are even more favored—they cover branches and trunks with emerald green. The effect, glittering with droplets of dew and drowned in mist, is altogether unworldly. At the highest elevations, where winds blow mists away, moisture quickly drains from soils, and winter nights are harsh and often freezing, the tree line falters, and a montane flora appears, called *campo rupestre*, composed of peculiar endemic grasses, sedges, and forbs, most characteristically those of the family Velloziaceae. Some of the latter can still be seen clinging to the flanks of the dramatic granite outcrops that stud the lowlands, of which two—Sugar Loaf and Corcovado—have been photographed by millions of awed tourists.

In the intermontane valleys a highland forest occurred, somewhat lower than that of the coastal plain but structurally and floristically similar and nearly as impressive. Finally, on the landward faces of the massif, broad-leaved deciduous tree species that shed their leaves during the dry season become more and more common. Lianas and epiphytes are rarer along this axis, and tree heights are lower. Finally, the lease of the forest plays out along watercourses, where ribands of gallery forest, more open and studded with palms, snake westward in swaths up to a few hundred meters wide. In the southern highlands the Atlantic Forest acquires another character entirely. The primitive, hardy conifer, *Araucaria angustifolia*, dominates an open-forest formation in a region where frost is common. Because this species invades grasslands and cannot regenerate in place, some have considered these forests successional, destined over centuries, had humans not interfered, to be replaced by broad-leaved evergreens. Given the great range of latitude along which the Atlantic Forest spread, there was another gradient, one of temperature and insolation. Subtle changes could therefore be observed in the composition of the forest from its northernmost to its southernmost extension. Indeed, these formations interpenetrated. In the south the subtropical forest accompanies the warmer shoreline and penetrates the lowlands of the Paraná River. Conifers reappear along cooler mountain ridges, even as far north as 20° south.

Inland, where rainfall becomes too scarce and too seasonal to support forest, the savanna begins. This formation of widely spaced, low scrub woodlands and tall grasses is resistant not only to drought but also to fire, which occurs naturally across this landscape. The savanna, called *campo cerrado*—closed field—or simply *cerrado*, occupies an immense swath of the interior, almost a quarter of all Brazilian territory. North of the cerrado, penetrating in some places to the cerrado–forest border, is a thorn-bush scrubland, the *caatinga*—white forest—so called because its trees defend themselves against the prolonged droughts of the Northeast by seasonal leaf fall. Bleak, parched, and traditionally considered impractical to farm, relegated to an extensive sort of cattle raising, the cerrado and the caatinga form Brazil's *sertão*—outback—the antithesis of the lush and verdant Atlantic Forest.

Soil was less determinant than rainfall and temperature in the location of the Atlantic Forest. Except for the coastal dune lands, its soils have derived from parent granites, basalts, and gneisses that are ancient, highly weathered, and in consequence low in fertility. Abundant rain and warm weather have formed deep and clayey soils, iron-rich and therefore characteristically reddish. They possess little capacity to hold water or nutrients and yield them up only grudgingly to plants. In some forms they inhibit root penetration, and when exposed to sunlight and rain by cultivators they may become more acid, inhibiting further nutrient exchanges, freeing toxic aluminum, and bonding scarce phosphates to free iron molecules. Under these conditions, soil development depends in good measure on vegetational cover, rather than the reverse. The litter fall from trees is typically twice as heavy as that in temperate forests, and it is rapidly and continuously mineralized by termites, fungi, and bacteria. The deep shade of the forest provides ambient conditions for the formation of a fertile layer of humus. Thus the forest grows and spreads upon an organic, self-generated substrate. Nevertheless, soils are subtly influential in the array of species and the vigor the forest presents in a given location. Basaltic parent rock engenders a very deep, dark red soil that accommodates plants with high nutrient demands, whereas the leached, acidic coastal dune lands and interior mountain crests forbade their development. The soils of the cerrado characteristically contain free aluminum, toxic to plant species that have not invented defenses against it.[6]

Ecosystems are delineated by nature itself; therefore they are natural subjects—islands, lakes, or deserts, for example. The Atlantic Forest is such a subject. Although its great size, complexity, and variability have left biogeographers and ecologists groping for common designations of its components, its distinctiveness is unquestioned.

In this history little mention will be made of the forest's northernmost extension, above 13° south, or of the southern highland segment dominated by conifers. These are limits excusable only in practical terms; *ars longa, vita brevis*. Scattered and inaccessible sources, a multiplicity of political jurisdictions, immense distances, and budgetary constraints have lengthened the time needed to gather material for this truncated study far beyond what is normally expected of a sole, unassisted scholar. Perhaps these omissions will encourage other historians to study this vast natural realm more locally and more thoroughly. Meanwhile, the reader will not go far wrong in taking this central region for the whole, containing as it does more than seven-tenths of the area of the Atlantic Forest and having a history of human settlement in most ways typical of the rest.

This history of the Atlantic Forest is not a natural history; that is, it is not an account of the creatures of the forest and the relationships that obtain among them. It is, instead, a study of the relationship between forest and humans. The author's limited insight, training, and experience and the opacity and dispersion of many of the historical sources have at many points no doubt obscured numerous important interactions between humans and their natural environment. Even so, the intent has been to portray the Atlantic Forest as something more than an inviting stockpile of resources or a challenge to human ambition. Perhaps the study's failings will prove as inspirational to other historians as will its possible merits.

The tropical forest is an awesome place for humans. Although once, in our simian past, it was our niche, clearly we have been driven from this paradise. We make our way along its floor, stumbling between the legs of giants, much less dexterously than in open fields. Even in the dry season the morning dew falls in a steady drizzle, soaking the slippery litter and turning the earth to mud. Tangles of roots and vines slow our feet. Lianas, bristling with thorns, scrape our arms. To advance a kilometer is to clamber over fallen trunks a score of times or more. Along the streams, legions of blood-sucking ticks, mosquitoes, sand flies, some of them parasitized by microbes lethal to us hairless mammals—pursue relentlessly. Centipedes, scorpions, and urticating caterpillars dare us to touch them. Amid this chaos, this wreckage, these dangers, we peer upward at the distant light that filters wanly through the foliage. It is an unsatisfactory view, unlike the clear sweep of the horizon we enjoy in the grasslands. The life that teems in the canopy is beyond our ken. To reach that dizzying height, we require ladders, block and tackle, platforms—artifices hard to drag into the forest and harder still to erect.

The forest's gloomy floor offers our species few aesthetic attractions. Its denizens are solitary, ghostlike. Most of its birds are taciturn, their colors subdued. Most of its flowers are tiny, white or green, and unscented. Its tree trunks, spattered with the ocher, umber, and vermilion of lichens, are twined about with vines. Mosses and cacti droop from branches. Its canopy, fluttering in the wind that blows high above our heads, refracts the distant sun. A hundred shades of green shimmer and deceive our eyes. Although an artist may depict precisely this or that flower on the forest floor, the forest entire defies artistic skill. Neither paint nor photograph, no more than mere words, can capture the forest's enveloping, uncanny presence, its "plastic solidity." In the distance, howler monkeys roar their matutinal defiance at the emerald void. Then there is stillness. We hear only the vague hum of insects in the canopy or the rustle of the leaves—sometimes the fall of a branch "or, it may be, a strange sound that is inexplicable." Moisture forms constantly on our bodies, condensing from the humid ambient air. Eyeglasses fog over, as though in a shower stall. And sweat exudes from every pore on our skin. We must carry as much water in this water-drenched wilderness as we would in a desert.[7]

We are no longer nocturnal, if ever we were. But the forest comes alive only at night. Then is the forest filled with the screeches and screams and skirls of frogs, birds, and insects, engaged in a million dramas of chase, evasion, and copulation. Amid the clamor of the night forest we are blind without our flashlights, defenseless without mosquito nets and hammocks and campfires. The indigenes spend their nights in thatched cabins, a smoky fire always alight to ward off mosquitoes. Daylight brings joyful restitution of their autonomy.

The forest is no glen of idylls, of sportive dryads, nymphs and elves. These tree creatures are engaged in titanic, slow-motion struggles that we short-lived, frenetic humans cannot even sense. Far above our heads they batter each other for space and sunlight, grasp each others' branches, settle their seeds in the crotches of each others' trunks, scrape and penetrate each others' bark, engulf and strangle each other. In the night forest, above the animal din, one may hear a giant collapse when its burden of parasites overwhelms it, when its branches have been too effectively bored by termites, when its struggle is lost. Then the lianas may hold it up a little while longer, or they may cause the falling tree to drag its neighbors with it to the forest floor. In the rainy season, when thunderheads surge 18,000 meters high and wreak havoc on the canopy trees, humans caught in the forest, as well as its denizens, huddle in the folds of trunks, awaiting the end of the world. Then dozens of the giants may fall all at once, clearing the way for another forest generation to arise.[8]

We may visit the tropical forest, we may become artful in our extraction of the thousand and one rarities it offers, but we do not live in it, except in desperation. The Brazilian human forest "dweller" lives on its margins, beside watercourses or fields. There, where two or more ecosystems join, the hunter-gatherers are able to garner varied resources. When they place their dwellings in the forest itself, they open a broad, beaten-earth clearing, wide enough to avoid the peril of tree falls and to form a no-man's-land along which insect pests and reptilian predators can be spied out and destroyed. To live in the midst of the forest, the forest dwellers of necessity cut it down.

Botanists of the heroic age of taxonomy, cast loose into this marvelous and terrifying vegetable world, were struck dumb. Darwin found it "nearly impossible to give an adequate idea" of his emotions. Astonished at its strangeness yet unable to relate it to the nature he had found so amiable in England, his "reason" told him it was beautiful, "but the feelings do not correspond." Although he reported that his mind was elevated to "sublime devotion," it was clear that his god had not been in a contemplative mood when he created this nature. Perhaps it was even some other god. Von Martius, at once "exalted and uneasy" by his passage through the gloomy woods, admitted to "astonishment" at the Almighty, who "conjured in a wild and unknown tongue" a manifestation of power and majesty horrifyingly amoral, profligate, and tremendous. Perhaps this preference of the Europeans for a tamed nature ought not to prejudice us against the kind of nature they encountered. Their fascination, and ours, might be harder to arouse in a harmless milieu: "Pleasure in the sublime is always born of fear." So must it be if we are to appreciate the Atlantic Forest.[9]

It is hard to say whether it is appropriate to refer to the Atlantic Forest in the present tense. A certain amount of forest cover still exists in the region, and although most of it is identifiably secondary, some small patches of it may never have been cut down or burned by humans. Most of these bits, however, perhaps all of them, have suffered some degree of intervention, through selective logging, extractivism, or air pollution, so that it is impossible to say to what degree they resemble the forest that was there before the first humans arrived. These surviving stands display many of the characteristics of the primitive forest, but the worrisome doubt persists concerning the possibility that local extinctions have already occurred, that this forest is no longer exactly what it once was. Given the impossibility of restoring the original conditions under which the forest must once have grown, much less of managing its recuperation, an even greater doubt persists that it could be restored, even if its present-day human stewards willed it. Thus it may not be possible to represent the Atlantic Forest, except through analogy with that of the Amazon Forest or though imaginative reconstruction, based upon extrapolations of those relict patches that remain.

Even that which remains is in practical terms indescribable. It is immensely complex. A botanist can provide lists of its trees; in the most diverse patches of Atlantic Forest as many as eight hundred species are to be found—an extraordinary number, compared to the few dozens contained in the temperate forests of North America or Europe. Botanists also remark how unlike the floras of the tropical forests of Africa and Southeast Asia are those of the biotic realm of South and Central America. Although their families are mostly the same, and the bean, myrtle, mahogany, and sapodilla families provide many of the more common largest trees of both, most of the genera are different. The tropical forests of the New World lack, furthermore, that dominance characteristic of the Old World, in which a single family or a few families contribute a very great number of individuals or monopolize space in the canopy. In the Atlantic Forest, aside from the southerly conifers, canopy trees were not to be found in pure stands. Instead, the trees of each species were scattered, with no more than a few dozen mature specimens of each in a given hectare and some number of other species represented by no more than a single individual.[10]

At ground level there are few clues to the identity of canopy trees. Many are straight, smooth-trunked, and grayish. Exceptionally, some trunks display curious buttresses, great tail fin-like folds in their surfaces that give these trees the appearance of rockets about to lift off. Looking up into the canopies, it can be seen that some of the trees bear delicate fronds of compound leaflets, but the great majority possess simple, leathery, dark green leaves, the size of a human hand, elliptical, with smooth margins, often ending in a long, pointed "drip tip." Even forest dwellers have difficulty deciding the identity of a given tree, and they apply names that overlap several species, even several genera. Botanists must have flowers to identify a tree with certainty, but many of the trees flower very infrequently, at mostly unknown intervals of two, three, four, or more years. Thus does the protean forest present its curious human guests with endless riddles and confusions.

Trees of the Atlantic Forest that rose 35 meters or more, in its areas of lushest growth, might be a hundred years old, although some of very great girth could be much older, even a thousand years old. The eastern massif of South America is remarkably free of natural disasters—no earthquakes, vulcanism, or hurricanes disturb these shores—and so the dynamics of forest growth and succession depend upon subtler events like irregularities of rainfall and flooding and, for the rest, on the struggles among its creatures. The fortuitous collapse of trees undone by age, competition, or parasites opens clearings within which the forest is renewed. Indeed, the forest may be seen as a patchwork of clearings and more or less mature stands of trees, all at different stages of recomposition.

How long the process of recomposition might take is not known. Secondary forest, of a type that occurs when a clearing which has been burned for farming is abandoned, may reach a luxuriance approaching that of undisturbed forest in twenty or thirty years, but even at that age its dominant individuals are fast-growing softwoods, quite unlike those of mature forest and fated to disappear from the canopy at a later date. Clearings opened by storms might take a hundred years to reach a late successional state, identical to the neighboring forest. Even then, thick-trunked emergents will not have had time to become giants. Clearings made to accommodate ranching or large scale farming may prevent regrowth to such a state for a much longer time, perhaps forever.

Diversity is one of the signal characteristics of the forest. The extraordinary diversity of its trees—at one site in South Bahia 270 species were found in a single hectare—is matched by the diversity of other sorts of plants, especially epiphytes, parasites, and saprophytes, and of invertebrate animals. Ideal conditions for growth and reproduction—extended growing seasons, intense solar radiation, high temperatures, and generous and slightly seasonal rainfall—facilitate the abundance of life forms. Under these conditions, metabolic processes are accelerated, and growth is constant and rapid. The life forms themselves stimulate greater diversity by providing additional niches within which specialization proceeds with ever finer precision. A single tree canopy may shelter a thousand species of insects, and the Atlantic Forest as a whole may have sheltered a million of them, only a small percentage of which have been, or ever will be, named by scientists. The determined attacks of fungi and insects, specialized in preying on a single genus or species of plant, were especially deadly to clustered individuals; hence the prevalent scatteredness of tree species. An abundance of species implied that any given one would be at any place in the forest represented by few individuals—all species were, compared to those of temperate forests, rare species.[11]

The plants and animals of the Atlantic Forest were rare also in the sense that many of them were to be found in no other forest. Of its tree species, more than half were endemic. Another 8 percent were shared with the Amazon Forest. Several locations in the Atlantic Forest have been posited as the centers of endemism of birds, mammals, reptiles, and insects, containing numerous species that had not succeeded in expanding their range beyond its borders or that had found there a refuge when their former range became restricted—certain hummingbirds, tanagers, marsupials, sloths, tamarins, tree frogs, palm vipers, and numerous others are limited to the Atlantic Forest.[12]

Specialization implies improved efficiency, and the Atlantic Forest was indeed efficient in its capture of solar energy, in its absorption of nutrients from soil, rainwater, and atmosphere, and in its recycling and exchange of resources. The result was a plant biomass that in some places may have reached 600 tons per hectare and a capacity to generate perhaps 50 tons of biomass a year. None of the present-day relics of the Atlantic Forest have been observed to display so great a volume, probably because the most imposing stretches of this forest have been destroyed or selectively logged. By comparison, the forest's animal biomass was impoverished, despite its diversity. A hectare may have contained no more than a hundred kilograms of vertebrate flightless animals of all kinds.[13]

In the subtropical forest environment, the crude and generalized forms of association common in colder climates are replaced by subtler relationships. Competition tends to be relatively less important and cooperation more important. Evidence of the coevolution of plants and animals is abundant, in pollination and seed dispersal, even in plant defense. Some plants, for example, offer shelter and even nectar to ants that protect them from predation and that clip competing weeds away from their seedlings. The complexity of this forest, then, considered as a single system, is extreme. It cannot be regarded as more resilient than simpler systems, however. Indeed, the opposite may be true: Its complexity may render it more vulnerable to trauma. The integrity of the system may prove extremely difficult to maintain or to reconstitute, in the event of external intervention. For example, a very few species of root fungi, essential in the absorption of nitrogen by many of the canopy trees, may be destroyed in a human-made clearing, so that normal forest succession cannot thereafter take place. Perhaps it is of some relevance, in understanding the course of human settlement in the region of the Atlantic Forest, that neither humans nor their animal domesticates evolved correlatively in this milieu but came to it as strangers.

When and how did the Atlantic Forest come into existence—this luxuriance, this diversity, this arena where millions of life forms surge, contend, and agonize, purposelessly and incessantly? The pedigree of the tropical and subtropical forests is extremely ancient, though its evolution has been spectacularly swift and multifarious.

More than 400 million years ago, photosynthesizing, multicelled vascular plants began to attach themselves to the margins of the continents. Soon these organisms covered the rocky shores, slowed the course of the waters, formed soils, and advanced inland. Nutrient-absorbing rootlets formed, stems flattened into sunlight-capturing leaflets, and seeds replaced spores as agents of dispersal. Some 40 million years ago, some of them achieved a special kind of branching—no longer bifurcating, one branch became a main stem and then, as vessels developed to transport water upward and nutrients downward, a trunk. Thus they escaped ground-level competition for sunlight and gained a degree of immunity from insect predation. The first forests came into being. Arborescence, however, was also mortality: As these plants transformed themselves into trees, they abandoned, perforce, vegetative reproduction by root spreading. Upright at last, they had become, tragically as well as triumphantly, individuals—in their conception, their life struggles, and their dying.[14]

Meanwhile, South America, locked together with Africa, Antarctica, Australia, and India, remained far from tropic climes. Circling lazily around the South Pole for 300 million years, parts of this supercontinent suffered glacial deluge at least twice in that immense interval. In the region of the Atlantic Forest, a long, dry period followed, then one of intense igneous activity. Ancient outcroppings of weathered basalt all along the coast are testimony of that era. Then, some 110 million years ago, a fissure opened between the African and South American landmasses, by then sliding northward toward the equator—the beginning of the South Atlantic Ocean and of a distinct biotic zone.

It has been proposed that the first forests, dominated by the ancestors of our humble club mosses, whisk ferns, horsetails, seed ferns, and cycads, were rendered obsolete by an innovation that may have originated along those rift valleys, possibly in the region of the Atlantic Forest. There, certain plants turned to their advantage the evolution, among foliage-eating insects, of wings. Their mobility may have been at first only defensive, but their capacity to gorge upon plants was thereby greatly enhanced. In brilliant riposte, certain of the shrubs of the rift valleys, apparently those adapted to disturbed, arid environments, evolved special organs—flowers—that offered the flying insect a modest reward of pollen for undertaking the task of fertilization while prudently enclosing their seeds in a protective ovary. The innovation was immoderately successful. The flowering plants—angiosperms—were to carry the association to extraordinary lengths.

In the forests, the rise of flowering plants to dominance was gradual. For a long time, they were overshadowed by cycads and conifers. But the angiosperms, genetically plastic, fast growing, rapidly reproducing, and opportunistic, were the inheritors of the forest. They arrived at the canopy about 65 million years ago, at that fateful Cretaceous-Tertiary time boundary that marks the doom of so many life forms and the origin of so many others. As the ferns and their like declined, so did many of the early families of the angiosperms die off, to be replaced by new ones. The record is one of change, rapid radiation, and diversification. For 50 million years life forms of the Atlantic Forest evolved in place, suffering no further geological upsets.

The South American continent, sliding northward, shook loose from Antarctica. Grown warmer and wetter, its Atlantic coast became covered with a forest. The isolation of the new continent stimulated peculiar life forms. Few in species and relatively free of competition, its early land mammals evolved slowly and eccentrically from just three families—marsupials, ungulates, and xenarthrans, the latter an odd collection that includes sloths, armadillos, and anteaters. This was a history parallel to the Australian continent, where mammals also developed from primitive forms. Only much later do the vivacious rodents and primates appear in the fossil record, arriving perhaps over Atlantic island chains that are now submerged. In this independent realm of plant and animal life, a unique assemblage of endemic species and genera arose. Once again, as very anciently, before the collision of the continents had occurred, the biotic world was growing provincial and diverse.[15]

Two to four million years ago the South American continent took on its modern form. Along its western margin a tectonic ridge line broke out of the sea and welled up, as the continent collided with the Pacific plate, to form, quite suddenly, the towering Andes. The great shallow inland sea that had divided the landmass north and south was now blocked on one side and tilted toward the east, emptying itself to form the vast river basin of the Amazon. In the northwest, stepping-stone islands arose and offered communication with the northern continent; then they sank, and emerged again, this time creating an isthmus. The southern continent in consequence suffered an invasion by northern carnivores—representatives of the raccoon, dog, bear, and cat families, along with members of the deer, mastodon, horse, peccary, and camel families. These replaced a number of native forms.

During the same period, the globe began to suffer prolonged seasons of cold. At least four ice ages, perhaps as many as seventeen, have struck in this present geological period, called the Quaternary. In the south, in synchrony with those in the north, glacial sheets on the Antarctic continent grew thicker, and ice spread northward along the spine of the young Andes as far as modern Colombia. The ocean grew colder, and the chilly Falkland Current surged closer to the equator, so that the westerly trade winds carried less moisture to land and rainfall patterns were altered. Dry winds from the Andes blew silt over the plain: the beginning of the loess-thick Pampas, the rich grasslands of modern Argentina. Sea level fell more than 100 meters, extending the margins of the continents far out onto the continental shelf.[16]

The glacial intervals of the Quaternary lasted longer than did the intervals of warmth. Repeatedly the Atlantic Forest retreated, losing contact with that of the Amazon and possibly fragmenting as it sank into coastal valleys, then gradually reestablishing itself when warmth returned. Each of the advances and retreats of the Atlantic Forest may have transformed its species and their interrelationships. This instability has been put forth as an explanation for the superior diversity of Neotropical forests. Perhaps speciation was encouraged by phases of forest retreat into "refugia," on the ground that isolation is considered prerequisite to speciation. Present-day centers of endemism in the Atlantic Forest, in the region of the city of Rio de Janeiro, in South Bahia–northern Espírito Santo, and in Pernambuco mark, it has been hypothesized, the bounds of the forest refugia during the last, and possibly earlier, glacial epochs.[17]

Whether this model is correct or whether, more parsimoniously, Neotropical forest diversity may be seen merely as the result of its great extent and topographical variation or of phases of forest expansion, when it invaded new soils, reliefs, and climates, the image of the tropical forests has been transformed. No longer assumed to have reached their complexity through eons of climatic stability, they now appear to constitute some of the world's most disturbed environments. The genetic plasticity of organisms and their capacity to promote and control mutation have come to be cited more often; speciation seems to occur more constantly, species are presumed to be under much greater pressure to adapt, and the duration of species to the point of extinction is presumed to be much shorter. Each of the ice ages is thought to have provoked holocausts of extinctions, hordes of new species taking their places. The forest is thus a palimpsest of superimposed forms and relationships, reflecting evolutionary experience in complex and puzzling geographical patterns.

The last glacial period reached its height 25 to 18 thousand years ago; not until 12 thousand years ago did the South American glaciers retreat to their present sanctuaries atop the highest peaks of the Andes. In this instant of geological time, the Atlantic Forest rushed forward once again, to occupy a vast empire, 3,500 kilometers along the South American coast, and up and over the coastal escarpment as far as rainfall allowed. This most recent and continuing era has been perhaps more favorable for tropical forest growth than any previous interglacial period. Rainfall and temperatures rose higher than ever before during the Quaternary, and, fluctuating mildly, have at times reached levels even higher than at present.

Thus the modern Atlantic Forest evolved and came finally to occupy its historical boundaries, altogether like some remote, antique empire, its origins mythical, its dynasties extending over epochs, its splendor astonishing, its inhabitants luxurious, shrewd, and conservative in their exploitation of its bounteous resources, for millennia unchallenged and unchallengeable in its perfect and total dominion, yet at its foundation utterly brittle and vulnerable.

Meanwhile, on the grassland margins of the forests of Africa arose our hominid ancestors, wielding fire and stone weapons in their pursuit of game, spreading across Asia and Europe, becoming during the most recent glacial crises fully human in shape and intelligence, and setting out at last on a fateful odyssey of discovery, toward the Bering Strait and beyond, where that last hidden empire lay, ripe for conquest.

2

Humans Invade: The First Wave

Nosso povo viveu durante alguns milhares de anos aqui. . . .
Não tinhamos nenhuma escola de engenharia florestal aqui não.
Não tinhamos manejo de floresta.

Our people lived here for several thousands of years. . . .
We didn't have any school of forest engineering here. We didn't have
any forest management.

AILTON KRENAK

The resumption of the Atlantic Forest's expansion coincided with its discovery by humans, hunters who irrupted onto the South American plains
perhaps 13,000 years ago. Thus began a long period of interaction, with
results that are very difficult to assess—indeed, the assessments are as yet
little more than conjecture and may never be more than that. Only a limited amount of archaeological evidence has accumulated; it offers few clues
to settlement patterns, to cultural adaptations, or to the adequacy of these
first humans' exploitation of the environment. Still, the conjectures that
have been offered are, essentially, attempts to answer the most vital of
questions: Have any human groups, in particular migrating, invading human groups, ever attained an equilibrium with their natural environment?
Are these first discoverers of the New World to be counted among those
who managed that feat? How much disturbance of natural environments
was required in order to maintain the human presence? Was the Atlantic
Forest, when it was first descried by European navigators, entirely what it
would have been had they come upon an unpeopled shore, or was it already
transformed by this first wave of human invasion?[1]

The provenance and date of the arrival of humans in the New World
have come to be questioned lately. It still appears most probable that they
reached South America via the Isthmus of Panama, although there are
faint evidences of Asian and African contacts. There are datings at scattered sites as early as 50,000 years before the present, but they remain
controversial. All other sites indicate human presence began as the last

glacial episode was in retreat. Evidences of hunter-gatherers in the region of the Atlantic Forest are about 11,000 years old. Stone implements of that age are widespread in what was open country, at its southernmost reaches. Human remains 10,000 years old have been found in caves north of present-day Belo Horizonte, also in open country.[2]

For these first human immigrants, the forest was probably of little interest. It is apparent that they had come to the southern continent to exploit the game of the savannas—mainly large herbivores—and therefore they fanned out on the interior plains. They preferred to set up their camps near watercourses, which were wooded along their margins. Gallery forest offered shade and water and was the resort of animals attracted to these same resources. Thus humans occupied a familiar niche—the zone of encounter or "ecotone" between two biotic systems, each offering an array of resources for their prey as well as for the humans themselves. For these wandering hunters, the ultimate frontier was the coastal forest, which they approached from its landward, inner side. They penetrated considerable distances into the forest along streams, seeking rapids where fish might be easily caught. Aside from those forays, forested land was probably an unpromising dwelling place, because animals were scarcer there and harder to hunt.

In South America, as in North America, the era of glacial retreat was accompanied by the sudden extinction of megafauna. In the southern continent several genera of mammals suddenly disappeared—glossotherium, a large land-dwelling sloth; glyptodon, an ox-sized armadillo; toxodon, similar to rhinoceros; smilodon, the sabre-toothed tiger; the elephantlike mastodon; and horses. These were, undoubtedly, among the animals that attracted humans to the savanna. It has been hypothesized that in South America, as in every other landmass upon first invasion by humans, the disappearance of a number of species can be attributed to hunting "overkill." The intruders, euphoric at their good fortune, had perhaps lost the necessary prudence of those who exploit a resource they cannot enlarge. They had come upon a hunter's paradise—its prey so numerous that they appeared infinite and so unwary that stalking them was unnecessary.[3]

There is a contending thesis, that these creatures were made extinct by climatic change, but the South American plains had shrunk several times before during the course of mammalian evolution without, so it appears, producing that effect. The successive climatic changes had not been so severe as to eliminate the herbivores' grassland niche, it had merely been displaced; and at least a quarter of the continent remained well endowed with open range even as the climatic optimum approached. Nor were the defunct animal genera being replaced by newly arrived ones. Their niche simply became vacant, with what impact upon the savannas they had once roamed, one can only surmise. Had they played a role in spreading forest seeds to the plains? Had their grazing slowed the expansion of forest? Did their absence cause the extinction of plant species that might have depended on them to trample competitors, to spread their seeds, to loosen the savanna soil?

Archaeological traces of hunters of large animals of the savannas become rare after the first few generations of human occupation. Many sites are no doubt as yet undiscovered, or have vanished; yet those that are known were mostly abandoned, in the region of the Atlantic Forest, by 8,000 years before the present. The reduction in numbers of larger, slower prey seems to have caused a crisis among these first waves of invaders. The remaining species of savanna-dwelling herbivores may have had, or quickly acquired, an expedient fear of humans. Some, like the ostrichlike rhea, were too fast to catch without the invention of some new weapon; others were so small that they hardly recompensed the energy expended on their capture. Were more drastic tactics employed to harvest this hardy assortment of quick and wary survivors?

Hunter-gatherers did not disappear in the highlands. Archaeological surveys carried out recently at numerous hydroelectric dam sites have found their campsites all along the upland watercourses, usually at a distance of a few hundred meters from the streams, suggesting perhaps how far the gallery forests once extended. Their prey must have included several species of deer, monkeys, capybaras, peccaries, tapirs, pacas, rabbits, and coatis—all herbivores, small or middling sized. Some sites depended largely on giant land crabs. Fishing was undoubtedly a critical resource. Not all the rivers of the Atlantic Forest are productive, as local toponymy reveals: For every "River of Fish" there is a "Bad River" (Paranapanema). And fishing was largely seasonal in the highlands, because fish were difficult to capture in the rainy months of high waters. Yet some fishing sites provided abundant catches. As late as 1949 the fishery at Pirassununga, São Paulo, on the Mogi-Guaçu River, yielded 150 tons a year, a full ration of protein for more than 3,000 persons, and indeed the locale abounds in paleolithic remains.[4]

Judging from nineteenth-century accounts, it seems likely that early hunter-gatherers used fire to drive their prey and to sweep the plain of woody growth and replace it with tender shoots to attract scattered herbivores. Fire set in forests was perhaps even more efficacious. The invisible creatures of the canopy—monkeys, curassows, sloths, lizards—flee their protective cover and are easily killed. Frequent light burns of underbrush turns the forest into a hunting ground easily traversed and surveyed. How much was fire used against the forest? These invaders had arrived just as their preferred open-range landscape—their niche, in fact—had begun its retreat before the reinvigorated forest. Did human-set fires in woodlands as well as on the plains slow the forest's millennial advance, prolonging the isolation of the forest "refugia"? Fires set at intervals prevent restoration of the species of the primary forest and over a long period will very likely favor the vegetation of the grasslands and savanna, in their competition with forest, because they are formations naturally subject to fire and adapted to its influence. Thus humans acted as the ally of grasslands and savanna and may have won for it victories unearned.[5]

These are speculations of long standing, because evidence is mostly lacking. But generations of observers have wondered why such broad stretches of the continent were, at the time the Europeans invaded, treeless, because trees may easily be planted in many of these regions, where they flourish. The pampa, the grassy plain that extended from Bahía Blanca 2,300 kilometers north to the present-day city of São Paulo, is the largest and most intriguing of these anomalies. Were these humanized land-scapes? There are, in the region of the Atlantic Forest, traces of sites occupied by humans evidently practicing hunting techniques that were appropriate to open country, long into the "climatic optimum" of warmest and wettest weather, from 5,800 to 4,800 and 4,100 to 3,400 years before the present, when forest, not savanna, should have been present.[6]

Even though the Atlantic Forest was to a degree modified by the invasion of hunter-gatherers, it could not have been transformed as considerably as were forests on those continents occupied much longer by *Homo sapiens*. South America, after all, was the last continent discovered by humans, and their residence of 400 generations was brief, compared to 1,600 generations of fire-wielders in Australia and 4,000 generations in Africa. Some weight must be assigned to the relative lengths of these leases in considering how much influence humans may have exerted upon the Neotropics compared with the other continents and with the possibility or likelihood of coevolutionary developments. Not to do so seems a large oversight indeed. Is the relatively greater extent and diversity of species of the South American forests, for example, entirely a result of natural events transpiring in environments somehow dissimilar, or at least in part of much briefer human occupation?

With the decline of large game animals, some of the still-exploring humans moved to the lowland margin of the continent, for them the farthest reaches of their reconnaissance. The lowlands at the time were somewhat broader than now, because sea level still lay many meters below that of later times. Much of the shoreline was protected by reefs or sand spits, permitting the formation of tidal estuaries, in effect collection ponds for nutrients washed down by rivers and streams. There the explorers found mangrove swamps and, attached to the mangrove, mangrove oysters. A marvelously convenient economy—almost no energy or technique was needed to pluck protein from the trees! They camped in sheltered places, gathered the abundant mollusks, and tossed the shells over their shoulders. Soon vast mounds accumulated, of cockles, clams, mussels, and arboreal and mud oysters. These astounding monuments stretched up to 300 meters long and up to 25 meters high. Why were middens allowed to accumulate so grandly? Conspicuous consumption? Protection against predators? Windbreaks? Status? We can only conjecture. Along the coast, from Espírito Santo to Rio Grande do Sul, many hundreds of these shell mounds, called *sambaquis*, have been located, though weathered and covered by restinga vegetation. Many more once littered the coast, but some were lost through the action of storms and currents. Many more disappeared over the last 500 years as they were mined for lime that was used to make mortar for construction and, even though protected since 1961, for modern purposes such as airport runways.[7]

We know not how large were the human groups that accumulated these extraordinary middens, or how long they might have occupied a given site. One of the largest was estimated to contain 120,000 cubic meters of shells. At 50,000 shells per cubic meter, that would have provided a daily ration for 100 persons for 500 years. Probably, however, these sites were more temporary, the result of repeated abandonments and reoccupations, as local shellfish supplies were worked out and recuperated. The upper levels of some of the sambaquis contain juvenile specimens, a greater variety of shellfish species than that in the lower layers, and fish bones, barnacles, and sea urchins. Later sambaquis are smaller than earlier ones. These observations suggest that their final abandonment came as the most easily harvested or tastiest mollusks were growing scarce.

The oldest dated sambaqui was started about 8,000 years ago, but other, more ancient ones may now lie below sea level. The latest were abandoned about 400 years before the arrival of the Europeans. Thus shellfish harvesting remained viable in this region for at least 7,000 years, an extraordinary holiday from scarcity for cultures that left almost no sign of any technology more complicated than that needed to pry open an oyster. Their situation was perhaps not entirely prelapsarian, because a perceptible succession of cultures within the middens suggests that invaders may have wrested these valuable resources away from their possessors on more than one occasion—and additional, unsuccessful incursions may have at other times marred their exclusive enjoyment of the oyster flats. But clearly these people had little need to exploit the forest. Probably they gathered its wild fruits and medicinals; otherwise they lived with their backs to it, remote from their neighbors in the highlands.

During most of the sambaqui era, highland populations in the region of the Atlantic Forest persisted in hunting and gathering. Nevertheless, their uses of the forest resource was probably intensifying. Recent anthropological inquiries have shown how considerable is the plant knowledge of preagricultural peoples and how gradual is their shift from gathering plant materials to planting and tending them. They had many uses for plants, a number of them perhaps more important than foodstuffs—hallucinogens, stimulants, aphrodisiacs, cult objects, skin dyes, abortifacants, and so forth. There may have been in the region, then, some longer or shorter period during which naturally occurring useful plants were protected or spread by human agency. This is suspected in the case of *Araucaria*, which abundantly yield a seed of modest protein content. *Araucaria* was in southward retreat as the climate moderated during the whole of the period of human occupation, yet it persisted in clusters over wide areas invaded by the Atlantic Forest, assisted by human-set fires, perhaps, because it resists fire, and possibly spread intentionally, or accidentally, because caches of the nuts were commonly deposited by itinerant hunting groups. It may also be that the phenomenon of the *capão de mato*—the wooded islet—numerous in the sea of grasslands and so often commented upon by later botanical travelers, who thought their appearance both charming and paradoxical, may not have been an entirely natural formation. Contemporary hunter-gatherers deliberately plant valued trees in clusters, the more conveniently to harvest them, while culling those plants for which they have no uses. The resulting bowers, resorts of shade and recreation as well as extraction, may well have been spared from these hunters' periodic deliberate burnings of the grasslands.[8]

Maize found at a site in a gallery forest area in present-day Minas Gerais State has been dated at 3,900 years before the present. Thus farming was taken up several millennia after its adoption in the Andes and in Meso-America, suggesting a long phase during which gathered resources were adequate for a modest and itinerant human population. Several explanations have been proposed for the initiation of farming; climate change seems not to be a promising one. The climate of the region of the Atlantic Forest did not undergo any important change at the time. Agriculture seems more likely to have been the result of an increasing human population. No attempt has been made to estimate the population density of the Atlantic Forest region at the time that ceramics first appeared, nor does the archaeological evidence so far unearthed offer a basis for estimation. Density is rather a crude concept—it implies an economicist view of the natural world as merely land, an abstract factor of production rather than the complex biotic structure that it really is, and certainly was for hunter-gatherers. Perhaps there was no increase at all in human numbers in relation to surface area, but instead an irremediable dilapidation of the biota that had occupied portions of these surfaces and that these humans had been accustomed to extracting in the wild.[9]

Perhaps both of these hypotheses describe reality on the eve of the adoption of agriculture. The new regime may have retrieved wild plant populations from competing human groups, and it may have rescued them from local exhaustion or endangerment through too-intensive exploitation or through competing activities such as controlled burning. In either case the wild species were recouped by being transferred, as seeds or cuttings, outside their normal ranges. In effect humans became the principal dispersal agent of these plants, a circumstance that is suggestive of a peculiar form of coevolution. But human intentionality played a part in the process—there was selection and potentially hybridization, which ultimately distinguished human-managed plant populations, entirely dependent upon cultivation for propagation, from their wild congeners. The earliest cultivars of the first farming groups, in addition to maize, were native to lowland South America, mainly manioc (also called cassava)—a root crop, their staple in its several varieties—other roots of the genus to which yams belong, squash, pineapple, and peanuts.[10]

The adoption of agriculture utterly transformed the relationship of humans to the forest. What had been a residual resource, low yielding to hunter-gatherers, casually or accidentally burned when driving or attracting prey, now became their principal habitat. They found savanna soils too sandy, dry, acid, and aluminum-toxified to farm. Agriculture was much more viable on forest soils. From the beginning, farming in the region of the Atlantic Forest—indeed, throughout the lowland areas of the continent—required the sacrifice of forest. The technique was extremely simple: Near the end of the drier season the underbrush in a patch of forest, a hectare, more or less, was slashed, so as to dry it out, and the larger trees were ringed with stone axes. Then, just before coming of the rains, the area would be set afire, causing the enormous stock of nutrients stored in the forest biomass to fall to earth as ashes. A few of the largest trees that had resisted the fire would remain, scorched but standing. The rains washed the nutrients into the soil, neutralizing as well as fertilizing it. Planting was then carried out, with no tool save a digging stick. Forest that had never before been burned was not only marvelously fertile but also free of the seeds of invasive plants, and therefore little weeding was necessary.[11]

After two or three seasons—manioc requires eighteen months to reach maturity—the patch was allowed to return to woods. In regions of sandy and highly leached soil, abandonment was necessary because yields quickly declined, but in the region of the Atlantic Forest soils were generally fertile enough to permit longer cultivation. Abandonment of the cultivated patch was more likely to be caused by the invasion of weeds and pests. Weeds could be uprooted by hand, but there were no defenses against pests, which included, most formidably, the leaf-cutting ant. Abandonment also occurred when the village was relocated for reasons of sanitation, internal social conflicts, or insecurity in the presence of intervillage rivalry. All farming regimes represent a disturbance of a natural ecosystem. Indeed, they attempt to freeze natural succession at its earliest stage, introducing cultivated plants that in their wild state had been pioneer species. This kind of farming, called swidden or slash-and-burn, is the least intrusive, because it imitates the natural scale of disturbance and, rather than freezing permanently the process of succession, merely exploits it temporarily.

Secondary, or successional, forest, what the indigenes called *capoeira*—formerly planted land—that eventually reclaimed abandoned fields was similar in structure and composition to growth that naturally repaired canopy openings caused by tree falls. Tree regrowth repaired the soil by raising subsoil nutrients and dispersing them through leaf fall and by shading soil processes from direct sunlight and rainfall. Usually, farmers would not attempt a repetition of burning and planting in a given patch until the forest had grown back to a certain height. In practical terms, the delay was advisable to shade out completely weed growth and to restore the balance between pests and their ambient predators. It is uncertain how long this interval might have been in the region of the Atlantic Forest, but twenty to forty years seems probable.

Swidden was very economical of labor, but it was not artless. The burning itself was a dangerous and problematic task. Its timing required a sixth sense, lest it be done too far or too little in advance of the rains. It could not be too intense, lest it burn the shallow, fertile layer of litter and its organisms. Swidden did not imply the loss of skills already acquired because these farmers had to continue to hunt and fish. Proteins still had to be obtained from animal sources because manioc lacks them and even maize provides only a few of them. Swidden farmers could not replace wild game with domesticates because their fields were not adequate to provide forage for larger animals and they had no means of penning and protecting smaller animals or fowl. On the other hand, the planted patches, like any burned area, attracted game and thus served two purposes. To judge from observations of present-day swidden farmers, techniques slowly but continually improved. Shrewd associations of crops improved yields, speeded growth, and reduced infestations. The woodland fallow was not entirely abandoned but was tended, so as to exploit a variety of useful species common to secondary forest. Numerous "wild" trees were transplanted during the phase of cultivation and protected from competition as the forest recuperated. There were fruit bearers, among them guava, papaya, cashew, soursop, Surinam cherry, and—lacking an English equivalent because they were neither exported nor cultivated in the English-speaking tropics—*jabuticaba, grumixama, araçá, cambuçi, cambucá, sapucaia,* and *pacova;* fiber and seed-bearing palms; canoe-wood trees; and the prized genipap and annatto, which yielded black and red skin paints that also repelled insects and blocked the sun's rays.[12]

Slash-and-burn agriculture was stunningly reductive. Nearly everything live within the burned patches was reduced to ashes, and only the ashes were exploited. Perhaps the first farmers regretted this initial waste. There were, no doubt, episodes of burning that escaped control, as might happen occasionally in drought years on the wetter, windward side of the Atlantic Forest and more commonly in the drier, inland forest. Swidden farming, though more intensive than hunting and gathering, was more prodigal of the forest. It is likely that the interval allowed for woodland fallow was not long enough to restore the original forest to its fullest development. Under conditions of sufficient local human population pressure, it may not have been allowed even to reach its full potential height.

Agriculture, then, may have further reduced complexity and biomass over considerable areas of the Atlantic Forest during the thousand and more years it was practiced before the arrival of Europeans. To lend some concreteness to such an assertion, let it be supposed that farming was taken up by hunter-gatherers when their population reached 0.1 per square kilometer and that, in response to the success of the new regime, average density soon grew, in the highland regions of the Atlantic Forest, to 0.3 persons per square kilometer; that is, one per 333 hectares. John Hemming's estimates of highland populations in this area at the time of contact—about 0.4 per square kilometer—are consonant with this supposition, if the populations of agriculturalists then continued to grow slowly as techniques were refined. Suppose further that the nutritional requirements of this population could be satisfied by clearing annually 0.2 hectares per person (based on an average yield of manioc of 5 tons per hectare, more than half of it lost to animals and pests or wasted). Then, if these farmers cleared nothing but primary forest, they would have burned about 50 percent of it at least once during that millennium, even if they never allowed fire to escape accidentally or maliciously and never practiced fire drives of animal prey. It is more likely that they did not burn primary forest exclusively but concentrated their depredations along the forest edges and watercourses, especially at sites favorable for fishing. The result would have been patterned modifications of certain microenvironments within the upland Atlantic Forest.[13]

The upper levels of some of the sambaquis have been found to contain ceramics. It has therefore been suggested that one or another highland group already practicing agriculture, stumbling upon the lowland gatherers, may have decided to abandon their relatively onerous occupation for shellfish collecting. It may be, however, that the pottery was obtained through trade or through the capture of women from an agricultural group, because it was women who produced pottery. In either case, these shards show that there was some degree of temporal continuity between the sambaqui culture and those that replaced it. The appearance of agriculture along the coast appears to have been the result of a migration of various highland peoples. They were certainly attracted by the shellfish and fish resources of the estuaries, but they were already dedicated cultivators. There have been attempts to link them to groups found in the interior after the arrival of Europeans, but these connections remain uncertain. Several ceramic "traditions" appear briefly to have coexisted or succeeded each other.[14]

These earliest groups of agriculturalists were swept from most of the coast, almost as far as the Amazon, by another group, related culturally and linguistically to the Guarani of the Paraguay-Paraná river basins. This was the Tupi, who approached the region of the Atlantic Forest beginning about 400 C.E., perhaps from the direction of the Guarani hearth, although this is not firmly established. More than a thousand Tupi sites have been registered in Brazil, all along the forested coast to a distance inland in some places of as much as 500 kilometers. Their extraordinary success was due to an apparent command of navigation of interior waterways and the coast and to an invincible aggressiveness. Ritual warfare was the obsessive drama of Tupi existence. Their male-dominated culture was structured by warfare; its young men were not allowed to marry until they had captured either an enemy in battle or a redoubtable fellow predator such as a jaguar. Honors, additional wives, and chieftainship were bestowed only after further captures.[15]

It was mainly the Tupi whom the Europeans encountered in their first forays along the coast. Indeed, this group and their Guarani kinsmen, the most numerous and powerful inhabitants of the lowlands, engaged for nearly three centuries in an intensive cultural interchange with their invaders. The Europeans were to become almost entirely dependent upon them for the knowledge needed to exploit this alien environment. Unfortunately, however, European reports about the relationship of the Tupi to the environment are scattered, imprecise, and prejudiced.

How much pressure did the Tupi invasion exert upon the Atlantic Forest? Certainly far more than the indolent sambaqui dwellers. It is apparent, furthermore, that the Tupi increased in number once they arrived along the coast. Their first 500 years of residence in the lowlands were relatively serene. Villages were located where convenience dictated, commonly measuring 500 meters across, and they were built without defensive enclosures. By about 1000 C.E., however, competition for lowland habitat appears to have intensified. Villages, some of them grown to as much as 1,000 meters in diameter, were moved to defensible sites and were enclosed with palisades. Competition among the Tupi themselves became deadly. Our meager list of names for their subgroups is mainly a string of pejoratives that those Tupi closest at hand to the European invaders affixed to their neighbors. They divided repeatedly into warring factions, and the losers were often pushed into the highlands, displacing groups that were still hunter-gatherers or only incipiently agricultural. Because these regions were less productive than the coastal estuaries, the invaders, though introducing a more intensive form of environmental exploitation, were themselves reduced to a less abundant standard of living.[16]

Tupi farming in the lowlands was based principally on manioc. Protein-rich maize, which might have committed them to a more thorough dependence on agriculture but would also have demanded more of the nutrients of forest soils, was employed only as an alternative stock in concocting a much-appreciated fermented beverage. The Tupi cultivated smaller quantities of other carbohydrate-supplying roots and protein-supplying beans and peanuts. They do not appear to have intensified their agricultural practices in any radical way beyond those of their lowland predecessors. They gathered more than a hundred forest fruit species. Their exploitation of fish and shellfish was intensive, including mullet, which spawned in great number in coastal streams in midwinter, and at least twenty-three other species of saltwater fish, eight species of freshwater fish, crabs, cockles, shrimp, and manatee. They had not, however, learned to kill whales, which spawned in Guanabara Bay in great number in summer. They hunted deer, marmosets, turtles, crocodiles, monkeys, sloths, peccaries, agoutis, armadillos, capybaras, tapirs, pacas, and otters—among larger animals—while their children raided birds' nests, caught rats, lizards, land crabs, snails, and small birds, and foraged for insect larvae and honey. In October, when the winged forms of the leaf-cutting ants swarmed, they captured and roasted them by the thousands. Though varied and seasonally abundant, these sources of protein probably represented the critical factor in food supply. That is to say, the Tupi probably sensed shortages of game and fish sooner than shortages of their staple farm produce. This imbalance perhaps rescued the forest from reduction to an entirely secondary formation.[17]

The Tupi did not submit their neighbors to vassalage and tribute, which might have stimulated more intensive use of the land. Probably they could not, because the continental scale of the military field always permitted the defeated to escape bondage by retreating. Trade, another potential source of agricultural intensification, was carried on between the Tupi and interior regions only in a few superfluities—gemstones, live birds, rhea feathers, and possibly a few other goods. They maintained a network of trails whose traces were followed by some of the modern highways that scale the coastal palisade. The trails suggest a population of some density, but not necessarily a heavy trade. They seem more likely to have been principally strategic and migratory routes.[18]

The Tupi were able to produce surpluses for storage. The easiest method was simply to leave manioc roots in the ground after they reached maturity. Stocks thus preserved are safer from marauders and pests, though they begin to lose palatability and nutritive qualities after a few months. Indeed, soils may have been esteemed partly according to their capacity to store manioc. The Tupi also dried and smoked fish meal and roasted manioc meal. Evidently very large caches were maintained, because they were easily able to provision large Spanish and Portuguese fleets in transit with foodstuffs for the return voyage. Preserved fish and manioc may have represented a valuable stock-in-trade, but the Tupi did not consider them commodities. For them they were military stores. They were also consumed on convivial occasions when a single village might play host to several of its neighbors.[19]

The most spectacular cultural trait of the Tupi was anthropophagy. The capture of an enemy in battle was followed by an elaborate and sadistic ritual execution, which several villages might be invited to attend. The deceased was then barbecued and distributed among the guests. The celebrants thereby assimilated the strength and skill of the deceased. Indeed, the capture of jaguars was followed by the same ritual, in order to obtain the same benefit. Slow-moving animals such as sloths, on the other hand, were never hunted. The chroniclers dwelt upon the cannibal feasts with such gusto that they lately raised suspicions that these reports were a canard, intended to legitimize the European invasion by attributing to these "savages" the only sin that the Europeans themselves did not widely prac-

tice. The doubters seemed to be unaware, however, of the voluminous Jesuit dispatches, which mention the practice so frequently and circumstantially that it is impossible to disbelieve that the Tupi were indeed cannibals.
It is unimaginable that the missionaries, who already had overmuch to
complain of in regard to Tupi customs—nudity, polygamy, drunkenness,
gluttony, and refusal to attend their sermons, among others—would trouble to accuse them of an imaginary vice, which would certainly have further hindered their catechizing.[20]

The issue is relevant to this analysis because it has been hypothesized
that the consumption of human flesh was for the Tupi a necessary source
of protein. This would imply a very dense population indeed, one that
certainly would have already destroyed a great deal of its forest resources.
This hypothesis is untenable, however, in the case of the Tupi. As powerful
as they were along the coast, the Tupi were not hegemonic—their wars
were not like the Aztec "flower wars" that offered certain victory. Their
opponents, unlike deer or even jaguars, presented an even chance of dining
on them. Most important, the chronicles show that the Tupi had no
thought of maximizing the nutritional gain from their human meat supply. Far from it: They kept their captives alive for weeks or months,
awaiting the maize harvest, so that these gloating occasions might be accompanied by wassail and intoxication. What was fed the prisoner, then,
might well surpass the victuals he yielded. Evidently, cannibalism was
practiced not to provide sustenance but to promote the solidarity of scattered villages by channeling their vengefulness into a communal enterprise and embedding it in festivities, a practice to which the Europeans
themselves were much given.[21]

It does not seem that Tupi population levels reached the sort of ecological ceiling that might have exposed them to malnutrition, considering the
reports of astonished European observers, who uneasily witnessed the superior strength, vigor, and stamina of these "barbarians." The Jesuit Leonardo Nunes witnessed one terrifying display of this superiority: Seven
war canoes, each bearing thirty to forty Tupi, chased his caravel, which
was under sail, for three hours, paddling and firing off arrows the entire
time. It appears significant that protein-rich maize, beans, and peanuts
were not cultivated extensively in preference to manioc, suggesting that
fish and game resources supplied that requirement adequately.

The Jesuit Afonso Bras thought that warfare had the effect of checking
their numbers: "There are so many of them (even though the land is very
large) and so much do they multiply that were they not engaged in continual warfare among themselves, and if they did not eat one another, it seems
they would not fit on the land." The premature deaths of males, however,

more likely accelerated the rate of population growth, by increasing the ratio of gestating adults. Some tribes may have restored the balance of the sexes through female infanticide, but this appears not to have been the case among the Tupi, whose warfare did not have as an objective the kidnapping of females. Indeed, they were observed sometimes to execute female captives, even children, as well as men. What seems likely is that the Europeans arrived at a time when Tupi numbers were still growing, despite warfare, and Tupi conquest had not reached its fullest extent.[22]

It can be derived from sixteenth-century chronicles that each Tupi village housed an average of about 600 persons and controlled something less than 70 square kilometers of hinterland apiece, thus suggesting a population of about 9 persons per square kilometer. At that density, the lowland Tupi would have provoked, over the course of five centuries, considerably greater degradation of the Atlantic Forest than their highland neighbors. Assuming again the clearing of 0.2 hectares of primary forest per person per year, all of their domain would have been subject to burning within a space of only 55 years. Over the course of their millennium of occupation, they would have burned each patch at least nineteen times. A half-century represented an interval adequate to provide the conditions necessary to maintain the equilibrium of swidden farming, but it would not have been sufficient to restore the coastal forest to its original complexity and diversity.[23]

The need for defensible village sites and for control of productive estuaries and streams very likely caused the Tupi to exert a selective pressure on the forest, returning preferably to patches they had already burned rather than pioneering in more distant undisturbed forest. Tupi men were obliged to guard the women, who were the cultivators, when they went to the fields. This precaution suggests the danger involved in clearing patches too far from the village and suggests that villages may have expanded to unwieldy size for the sake of security. The social dominance of males may also have determined a preference for secondary forest: Although the soil of undisturbed forest was more fertile and freer of weed seeds and insects, it was harder to cut and more dangerous to burn. Males, who carried out the burning, would have chosen easier and safer secondary forest, even though the women, who planted and weeded, would have preferred invading undisturbed forest.[24]

Hostilities among the Tupi and their neighbors may therefore have patterned the attack upon the forest, with large areas of secondary forest, cut every twenty to forty years, surrounding densely populated estuarine sites that were highly productive of fish and shellfish. The spaces between allied villages of Tupi would be no-man's-lands, buffer zones, natively less productive than the occupied regions. These zones in the lowlands were mainly forest. Perhaps they were left undisturbed; perhaps not. The European invaders encountered a broad plain stretching north and south of the lower Paraíba River. This was the Campos dos Goitacases, a broad and deep barrier between the Tupi and their northern neighbors. Although it is usually presumed to be a natural formation, some of it was observed in the late eighteenth century to be returning to forest, in places where cattle were not set out to graze. One can imagine burning for the purpose of gaining a clear field of view and clear shots, an alternative defensive strategy to one based on ambush.[25]

Tupi pressures upon the forest were not entirely the result of utilitarian-rational urges to optimize output and labor or to enhance military security. There were also the imponderables of personal animosities and existential angst that divided villages or caused them to be abandoned. The Jesuit Azpilcueta Navarro complained that the Tupi moved their villages "every year"—or more frequently when they were drunk and set fire to their neighbors' longhouses or their own. He had witnessed such an episode just a few nights before: An entire village had gone up in flames, looking like "the day of judgment." Even though he exaggerated the impermanence of Tupi settlement, *taperas*—village sites destroyed or abandoned because of defeat in war, the exhaustion of local hunting or fishing resources, insect swarming, or internecine conflicts—were commonly encountered. Archaeological research shows clusters of sites only a few hundred meters distant from each other. It is clear that village sites themselves were a large consumer of forest. If occupation lasted on average ten years and taperas were always avoided in the choice of new locations, then, during the millennium of Tupi occupation, village sites alone would have claimed 18 percent of the area controlled by the average Tupi village. Even though abandoned sites were sometimes reoccupied, the claims on forest for mere living space, under the conditions of Tupi insecurity and bellicosity, were clearly not inconsiderable.[26]

Although Tupi agricultural practices appear not to have been more intensive than those of the lowland peoples they swept aside, their skill in food preservation may have been somewhat greater, a distinct military advantage because portable food supplies increased mobility and made possible the mounting of larger expeditions for longer periods. The chroniclers claimed that they would penetrate "a hundred leagues" into the interior to make off with a few captives. Indeed, warfare broke out in August, when they could be provisioned with fish meal from the annual mullet run. The Tupi incursions into the highlands, it might be supposed, would have had the effect of encouraging those nonagricultural groups they attacked to adopt agriculture, but it appears that they instead had the opposite effect, and perhaps they were so intended. Those on the defensive in forest warfare are forced to abandon their crops and ultimately are obliged to revert to hunting and gathering for survival. In such circumstances, the Tupi may well have reduced pressures on the forest along their highland borders.[27]

This suggests a more complex relationship between population density and agricultural intensification than that of simple cause and effect. Population density inspired warfare as well as cultivation; warfare, though it may have stopped the growth of the defeated, was most effectively waged by agriculturalists. Intertribal hostility, on the other hand, limited the array of subsistence techniques each group was able to undertake. Consider: The forest contained many more resources than any single group was aware of. Though each knew of the uses of hundreds of species, different groups knew uses for different species, and none could possibly know of more than a fraction of those thousands that were present. For example, it has been discovered that the Paumari, in northern Amazonia, do not eat mushrooms, although they are abundant in forest clearings. Their neighbors, the Yanomamo, do consume them. Because of intergroup hostility, this knowledge was not shared until modern ethnobotanists made it available to the Paumari. Might warfare not be regarded, then, as having been from the beginning a hindrance to the intelligent exploitation of human habitat?[28]

The hypothesis that the Atlantic Forest was much modified by the Tupi along the coastal plain during their thousand-year occupation is circumstantial, but it would help explain why the Europeans had so little to say about the forest when first they arrived. Sixteenth-century explorers and missionaries rarely suggest that the forest in any way intruded upon their affairs. Rarely did they report any difficulty in traversing it, and several of them, dispatched by the first expeditionaries, penetrated hundreds of kilometers with apparent ease. Evidently they followed a network of trails, signs of which have vanished. But how burdensome is the maintenance of trails in undisturbed forest—the continual collapse of trees, the constant regrowth of underbrush! Were these *peabirus* not passages through a countryside already much modified? Another piece of evidence: The earliest surviving land grants in the area of Rio de Janeiro, dating from the 1590s, nearly all describe the assigned locales as *matos maninhos*, apparently secondary growth; very few refer to *matos verdadeiros*—true forest, evidently a transliteration of Tupi *caá-etê*. Two or three thousand town dwellers could not, in forty-odd years, have accounted for so extensive a transformation.[29]

What perceptions did the Tupi evince in regard to their management of natural resources? Were their practices mediated by some sort of ideology—moral, ethical, or religious—that was deliberately conservationist or that might have tended to have that effect? This is obscure, because they produced no written texts before the European invasion, nor did the missionaries grasp the opportunity to help them transcribe their mental world after the conquest. Indeed, the Jesuits immediately identified the most popular cults as the work of the devil and deliberately distorted those few elements they found it convenient to incorporate into their catechesis. Although Tupi beliefs have persisted in the form of folklore down to the present, they have become reworked as they melded with European and African popular ideas of nature. Furthermore, collectors of native folklore have generally lacked ethnographic understandings of their possible meanings and seem often to have interpreted them according to their own preferences.[30]

It appears that the central figure in Tupi religious practice was Jurupari, a supernatural ancestor. Virgin born—his mother had been impregnated by the juice of a fruit—he had come to earth to establish a moral code that imposed male dominance over females. Accidentally, he killed his mother. He decreed polygamy, harsh punishments for female adulterers, and exalted male military prowess. Women were held to be impure because of menstruation, which rendered them vulnerable to evil influences. Menstruating women were not allowed to enter the forest. When wandering bardic priests made their periodic visits to a village, it was the women who were expected to confess their adulteries—to other women whom they had wronged. Men were awarded a happy hunting ground in the afterlife; whether women were expected to join them is not clear—they were never buried in the funerary urns that are characteristic of Tupi culture. Very likely Jurupari's cult represented an aggressive reaffirmation of male prerogatives that had been jeopardized when the Tupi first became dependent on female agricultural skills, evidences of which were to be found in women-centered households and the hunter's custom of presenting the kill to his mother. The cult may have been passed by the more northerly Arawak to the Tupi, and they in turn spread it to other groups as they took up farming. Clearly, Tupi society struggled with issues more fascinating than deforestation.[31]

The *pagé*—shaman—was Jurupari's priest. Pagés kept his sacred rattles and officiated at his rituals that were death for women to behold. The shamans also practiced healing, and in this capacity were the repositories of medical knowledge—more precisely, plant knowledge. Latter-day folk medicine evidently derives ultimately from a rich Tupi lore, of which the

European conquerors remained largely ignorant. Because the Jesuits identified their clerical competitors as servitors of the devil, they were not well positioned to learn from them what useful simples the forest might have in store, though they did come to attribute benefits to some native cultivated plants, such as pineapples and araucaria nuts. Tobacco, already cultivated, was the panacea of the indigenous pharmacopoeia. Its smoke was blown on the afflicted to drive away spirits; at the least it certainly drove away insects. It was represented to the Jesuits that smoking tobacco settled the stomach, a problem from which they suffered considerably, unused as they were to native foods. Though tempted, they abjured the habit for fear of appearing to defer to the wisdom of naked "infidels."[32]

Tupi hunters evidently experienced complex psychic interactions with their prey. They attributed souls to animals and identified profoundly with them. A hunter did not himself consume prey he had killed, for fear of the animal's vengeance. The honorifics a Tupi warrior earned by killing enemies were, much to the disgust of the missionaries, the names of animals. Frequently encountered in Tupi lore was Curupira, a spirit whose visible form was variously reported, usually as small in stature but very strong and with his feet turned backward; sometimes he rode a peccary. The Jesuits dismissed Curupira as merely another hobgoblin and succeeded in defaming him for succeeding generations of Brazilians. Lately he has been laid claim to by environmentalists as a symbolic protector of the forest, based upon the report of Couto de Magalhães, a nineteenth-century ethnographer, that Amazon Indians revered him in this guise. Perhaps it is useful to resurrect this version of the Curupira legend, to raise the consciousness of modern-day urbanites, though it probably distorts his real significance. The Jesuit José de Anchieta wrote in 1560 that the Indians made offerings in the forest to Curupira of feathers, arrows, and fans. Probably, Curupira was the spirit who ruled reciprocity in the chase. To be successful in hunting, it was necessary to restore something of value to the forest. Hunting lore, like medicine, is conservative: Hunters now propitiate Curupira, with *cachaça*—rum—and cigarettes.[33]

The few surviving notices of the rites that surrounded farm practice appear configured principally to stratify the sexual division of labor, rather than to conserve forest or regulate its use. Jurupari was held to have invented agriculture, appropriating what was far more likely to have been an ancestral woman's achievement. A legend attributed to a male hero the act (masturbation) from which germinated the first tobacco plant. The pagé practiced mummery and organized dances to increase yields and bring rain. The latter was his chief claim to eminence—*manda chuva*, or rainmaker, still designates a person of power and influence. The chroniclers of the first centuries of contact would no doubt have garnered other beliefs had they paid attention to the farmers, that is, the women. They did record, at least, a taboo upon the cultivation of peanuts by males.[34]

This is a meager body of evidence, but perhaps the search for conservationist regulatory mechanisms may be futile. The average Tupi was obliged to forage for approximately 60 grams of protein a day and to plant sufficient manioc to obtain a yield of about 2,800 calories a day. Taboos that limited his intake of these nutrients would have been life threatening. It was necessary to maintain the vigor that won battles, control over fishing sites and forest land, and dominance over his peers. Villages unsuccessful in these endeavors might have had need for conservationist viewpoints— limitations on fertility, on the hunt, and on forest burning, perhaps— because they had to retreat into a shrunken resource base. Those whose aggressiveness maintained their ranges intact would certainly have found such attitudes counterproductive. Even though warfare was in itself a check on the growth of Tupi numbers, it made possible not just maintenance but extraordinary expansion of their range during the millennium of their appearance in the archaeological record.[35]

The hunters who burst out upon the South American savannas some 12,000 years ago were participants in the final great act of human territorial aggrandizement. Fire and weapon-wielding humans had finally achieved cosmopolitan continental distribution. Once they had depleted the megafauna that had attracted them, they took up stations along the forest edge, where the encounter of two ecosystems encouraged fast-growing plants and attracted game. The forest was their antagonist, and fire was the means to penetrate it and slow its secular advance. At last some of the highland groups took up agriculture, possibly because their hunting and foraging resources were no longer sufficiently productive to support their numbers, though it is not clear which of these parameters had changed decisively. Perhaps both did; perhaps neither. Although it would be difficult to claim that military advantage caused the adoption of agriculture, that was the obvious outcome. Agriculture permitted denser populations, thereby enlarging the scale of warfare; it lessened the subsistence responsibilities of males, who then vied with each other to demonstrate prowess in battle; and it permitted the victualing of expeditionary forces, making possible long-range offensive campaigns. Once a group had taken up agriculture, it gained the power to take lands from those who had not. Agriculture in the region of the Atlantic Forest may have entrained, then, political, rather than demographic or economic, advantages.[36]

Swidden farming and unending warfare both intensified human pressure upon forest. The savannas were unsuitable to farming; therefore, the new subsistence regime implied a shift of population from one biome to another. Even though swidden required only small inputs of land and even though the population it sustained was ultimately limited by the supply of nonagricultural resources, over a long span of time farming was capable of reducing much of the forest to secondary growth. It seems unlikely that any of the lowland Atlantic Forest that was located on sites suitable to farming escaped clearance at least once during that phase of cultural development.

How shall this experience be judged? Do the first 10,000 years of occupation represent an equilibrium achieved by humans in relation to the natural environment? The record is not altogether unblemished. There is the initial disappearance of native megafauna, to be denied perhaps, or to be excused as miscalculation. And the hunter-gatherers seem to have burned the forest margin as well as the savanna, to stampede and to attract game. The sambaqui builders, on the other hand, dwelled in a sort of earthly paradise, from which resources could be plucked effortlessly and in which stocks, though not infinite, were at least capable of replenishing themselves if permitted a respite. The disappearance of these peoples remains a mystery—perhaps at last they overfished—but it is also possible that they lost their mudflats to more numerous and fiercer agriculturalists.

The prehistorical trajectory of the swidden farmers was intercepted by the arrival of the Europeans. What course might it have taken? The Meso-American and Andean experiences suggest precedents: generalization and intensification of agriculture, population increase, imposition of social castes and tribute, the rise of city-states, deforestation, and decline, repeated over several millennia. But these are speculations. All that is certain is that the Tupi in 1500 C.E. were capable of further expansion and had not yet exhausted the productive potential of their habitat.

The groups who gained control of the Atlantic Forest by the end of some years of human occupation demonstrated their talent for reversing vegetation history. The superior productivity of disturbed ground had attracted them when still they were hunters and gatherers; farming was a rationalization and an intensification of the disturbance cycle. Forest clearance for purposes of settlement, agriculture, communication, and warfare much enlarged the area of disturbance. One wonders if the talent displayed by swidden farmers was not, in fact, a specific vocation. Creatures that prey principally upon animals and plants whose habitat is disturbed ground, humans might also be considered an invasion species, just as those other species are that prey on humans, their crops, and their animal domesticates.

Naturally disturbed sites are often at the interface of two biomes—the ecotones. In human terms, are these naturally occurring zones not analogous to frontiers? The term "frontier," which historians in the United States have found so unavoidable, albeit ideologically distasteful, does refer to a physical reality. The frontier is most concretely, materialistically, and parsimoniously conceived as a relatively undisturbed ecosystem, one which exhibits a high potential for exploitation by the invading group. The forests of New England and the grasslands of the Great Plains were indeed frontiers when Europeans and their descendants invaded because they presented an array of resources that the invaders could instantly convert into abundant consumption, Walter Prescott Webb's "windfall." Where disturbance was already far advanced or technology inadequate to the potential harvest, the concept of frontier is evidently inapplicable. For Europeans, therefore, the Near East was no frontier, nor was Antarctica. There were humans on the other side of what has been designated frontier, a circumstance largely ignored by a certain historiographic tradition, but their subsistence techniques were much less disturbing than were those of the invaders. Where an ecosystem has already been degraded by human intervention, the interfaces between competing human groups are no longer spoken of as frontiers; instead, they are merely political borders and border struggles.

The region of the Atlantic Forest, then, presents two or perhaps three categories of frontier: that between the forest and the savanna, with gradually warming weather and increased rainfall favoring the forest, which detoxified the soil as it advanced and harbored the microclimates suitable for its further consolidation and development; that of the first wave of humans, who confronted the forest along its landward border and consistently allied themselves with the savanna; and that between the Tupi and their hunter-gatherer adversaries. The cast of characters was dramatically varied, but now another was to be added, and the plot itself was to be radically rewritten.

3

Humans Invade: The Second Wave

Os aruoredos sum muj mujtos e grundes e djmfimdas maneiras.

The trees are very many and large and of endless kinds.

PERO VAZ DE CAMINHA

One of the first acts of the Portuguese mariners who reached, on 22 April 1500, the forest-overladen shore of the South American continent at 17° south latitude, was to cut down a tree. Of the trunk of this sacrifice to the steel broadax they fashioned a rude cross, for them the symbol of the salvation of humankind. A mass was then celebrated beneath it, during which, to the satisfaction of the Portuguese, the indigenes who were gathered round aped their hand clasping and kneeling, albeit not their pious expressions. The moment has been engraved in the memory of every Brazilian who has completed grade school, through reproductions of a heroic painting commemorating the event by the nineteenth-century artist Victor Meirelles. Affixed to the wooden cross were the arms and boundary markings of the king, an unmistakable sign of the identity of aims and authority of state and church. This pretension to territory a wayward crew had barely glimpsed was based on a treaty that had been signed six years before by emissaries of the Portuguese and Spanish crowns, demarcating their respective spheres of influence over the non-Christian world by a meridian extending 370 leagues (2,200 kilometers) west of the Cape Verde Islands.[1]

The indigenes who fraternized innocently with them on that beach had no more idea than did the trees behind them what destruction this invasion would bring. This most momentous event in the history of humankind— the ending of millennia of separation of the two great population pools of the species—was also its most tragic. The chronicles of the discoveries are, beyond those of any other recorded episode in history, terrifying in their unreality. Unable to grasp intellectually the magnitude of their discovery, the Portuguese stumbled through half a continent, driven by greed and righteousness, unmoved by pity or even curiosity. The magnificent Atlantic Forest left them unmoved and uncomprehending. Again and again they entered it, to return with nothing but delirious reports of emeralds and gold. They wrought such havoc upon their brethren that, within a century, nearly all whom they had encountered were dead, their societies in ruins. This was the beginning, the foundation of settlement, of colonization and empire, of a transferred and imposed civilization.[2]

The fleet that made the discovery was, ostensibly, en route to the East, to India, which the Portuguese had for the first time reached by way of the Cape of Good Hope only three years before. Pedro Alvares Cabral, the captain of this second expedition, had set a course far from the African coast in hope of more favorable winds, so the landfall has the appearance of a chance event. Yet Portuguese charts had for a long time placed a "Land of the True Cross," an island approaching the dimensions of a continent, in approximately the position of this discovery. Indeed, True Cross—*Vera Cruz*—was the name Cabral bestowed upon the land, as soon as he set eyes upon it. The wooden cross erected on that alien beach, then, was also symbolic of the denotation that the Portuguese sought to fix upon it.[3]

Myths of fabulous islands and peoples that mediated the European encounter with this alien natural world influenced the Portuguese explorers but little. Their earlier imaginings of fantastical beings and places in the lands beyond the equator had been innumerable times rectified by long experience along the African coast. Sérgio Buarque de Holanda has shown how lacking they were in the paradisiacal vision, in any expectation of finding an earthly Eden. Portuguese "sobriety of the imagination" contrasted with the ready acceptance of portents and prodigies that drove the Spanish would-be conquerors ever forward. Portuguese empiricism was so pedestrian and narrow in its expressions that the explorers seem entirely out of place in that century of the "universal curiosity of the humanists."[4]

The account of Pero Vaz de Caminha, scribe of the first expedition, demonstrates this "resignation to the real and the immediate" that the modern reader finds so familiar. The encounter was entirely felicitous—both parties put aside their weapons and offered each other food and drink and mementos. The indigenes freely assisted the Portuguese to replenish their water, and, finally, they took up their musical instruments and danced together. Cabral turned aside the suggestion that a few of their new vassals be kidnapped, more out of practical than moral considerations: Such a measure, he opined, might prove less efficacious in acquiring a notion of their language and resources than the placement among them of two of their complement of *degredados*, banished convicts, whose death sentences

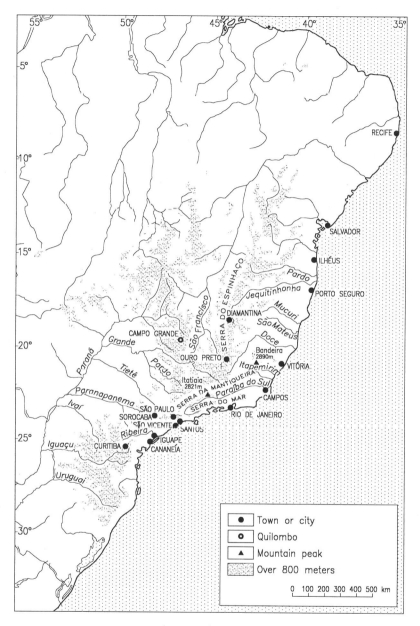

Map 2. Mountains, rivers, and towns of the Atlantic Forest

had been commuted to exile and who had been attached to the expedition for just such a purpose. The sailors refrained from molesting the women, though their resplendent nakedness wakened in them consternation. They "looked very closely" and admiringly at the depilated genitals of the women, who showed no unease thereat. Caminha, evidently recording this encounter almost moment by moment, was overcome by its charm—the inhabitants are in a state of innocence, they are without shame, without vices, without false idols. Aside from the growing of a few roots, which costs them little labor, they live from the fruits of the forest and the fish in the streams. Yet how baleful is the conclusion Caminha draws, in the same breath: Therefore their conversion to Christianity will be effortless—to reduction, to mortification, to wickedness, to the unavoidability of work.[5]

The expedition lingered idyllically in the bay of Porto Seguro. The captains took their ease in the shade of the trees. Crewmen cut down saplings for firewood and felled palm trees to extract their hearts. Their African voyages had somewhat accustomed the discoverers to this new, tropical environment. Their search for edible palms was evidently purposeful, and their identification of the native manioc was made, incorrectly but understandably, with the staple African yam. Their reconnaissance revealed nothing to them save woodlands, along the shore and on the hills behind, composed of large and imposing trees, filled with many sorts of birds. The indigenes offered them their feathered headdresses, more than mere tokens of esteem, because they considered them imbued with magical virtues. Cabral accepted them graciously, along with bows and arrows, songbirds, and monkeys.

The inhabitants displayed no adornments of gold or silver, the only circumstance that might have detained the fleet. One of the young men entertained aboard the flagship motioned to the captain's gilded necklace, and then landward, as if to say that there was gold in that direction, but then Caminha admits disarmingly that the gesture was thus interpreted, because "we desired it to be so." The fleet therefore set sail after only a week's delay. No garrison was stationed at Porto Seguro, only the two degredados, who whimpered fearfully as the last ship's pinnace heaved out into the surf. Two apprentices, evidently entertaining more favorable expectations of this paradise regained, or perhaps simply more afraid of the coming passage to the East, jumped ship and were not retrieved. The supply vessel, its goods unloaded and divided among the rest of the fleet, was sent back to Lisbon to report to the king. Cabral and his captains then pressed onward to India and its riches. Thus peaceably began the second human invasion of the Atlantic Forest.

This messenger ship, or perhaps the next expedition, in 1501, was the first to bring back samples of the earliest of Brazil's forest treasures. This was a dyewood, called *ibirapitanga*—red tree—by the Tupi, who colored their cotton fibers with it. The Portuguese called it *pau-brasil*, probably from *brasa*—glowing coal. At the first cut, the core of the trunk displays a golden brilliance, then turns a bright orange-red. When thrust in water it immediately becomes reddish violet. The large and growing European demand for dyes and inks had been satisfied by an Asian wood of the same genus, traded precariously through the Near East. Thus "brazilwood" was a word already applied in commerce. This tree of the Atlantic Forest (there were three distinct populations: one along the coast of Rio de Janeiro, centered on Cape Frio; another in South Bahia; the third in the north, centered on Recife) is a legume, *Caesalpinia echinata*. It prefers moderately watered environments, mostly coastal, though it can also be found in the highland, and it grows in secondary forest, so that it probably accompanied the Tupi as their numbers increased and might even have been encountered in stands of a certain homogeneity. The potential for a modest trade in this single species was therefore promising.[6]

Portuguese King Manuel sent forth a reconnaissance in 1501, under Gonçalo Coelho. Most notable for the presence on board of its pilot, Amerigo Vespucci, who dedicated the third of his famous letters to this voyage, this fleet may have reached as far as Patagonia. According to Vespucci's calculations, the meridian of the Treaty of Tordesillas, dividing Spanish and Portuguese territory, intersected the coast at about 25° south, at the mouth of an inviting estuary, where the Portuguese soon after placed a town they named Cananéia. Coelho's ships then visited Cape Frio and the Guanabara Bay and brought back more of the dyewood that was to make of the "conquest" a profitable enterprise.

There is very little record of how the brazilwood trade was carried out, but it is clear that this extractive product, like all the others the Portuguese dealt in, had its origin in native knowledge of the forest. The Portuguese certainly had no idea where the trees were to be found or how to identify them. Therefore the merchants left factors on the coast to barter for the wood. The Tupi, wielding European axes, or perhaps merely ringing and burning the bases of the trees, felled them, stripped the bark and cortex, and cut the trunks into shorter sections, weighing 20 to 30 kilograms, so that they could be carried on their shoulders over some distance to the landing places. The resources of the Portuguese crown were extremely limited and were at the time devoted almost entirely to the "enterprise of the

East," which appeared far more promising. Dom Manuel therefore let out the commerce of the new colony to a group of merchants, who were to dispatch at least six vessels a year to fetch brazilwood and whatever else they might find. In this they were assiduous: They appear to have collected about 1,200 tons a year in the first few years. The trade was wonderfully profitable, the king having helpfully closed the market to Asian dyewood. But excluded merchants soon pried open the monopoly, multiplying the number of vessels seeking the dyewood. Because these logs were sold to France, whose king saw no reason to respect the Portuguese-Spanish treaty line, interlopers from Honfleur, Rouen, and La Rochelle almost immediately appeared off the brazilwood coasts. The trade thus grew considerably in volume, especially because the French esteemed brazilwood and other trees of the Atlantic Forest as cabinet woods. The French factors also sometimes completed their cargoes with cotton. The ship *Pélérine* brought back 5.5 tons of cotton on its voyage of 1532, another sign of the scale and productivity of Tupi agriculture.[7]

In 1588, 4,700 tons of brazilwood passed through Portuguese customs, perhaps half of the true volume. The French clandestine trade in dyewoods was as well, or better, structured than that of the Portuguese—one chronicler of the mid-1550s reported observing 100,000 lengths of trunk stocked at the French colony at Rio de Janeiro. There was also intermittent smuggling by Spanish and English vessels. Taken all together, these merchants may have caused the removal of 12,000 tons a year.

In 1605, the Portuguese crown, alarmed at reports that wasteful cutting and stockpiling might "come to finish off and lose it all," regulated cutting and created forest wardens. The penalty for poaching was death. By 1607, brazilwood was again a monopoly, whose concessionaires were authorized to import only 600 tons a year—an invitation to continued smuggling. Perhaps the market had been flooded. It was not the case, however, according to a royal commissioner sent to investigate, that the tree was in danger of commercial extinction. Considering that an average annual sixteenth-century volume of 8,000 tons implied the cutting, porterage, stockpiling, and lighterage of about 320,000 25-kilogram sections, several thousand indigenes would have been kept busy at the trade. It may be estimated that this tonnage required the logging of nearly two million trees during the first century of the traffic. This is an impressive quantity, and it should probably be revised upward to account for wastage and losses at sea. The natives themselves stocked logwood in anticipation of market demand that did not always materialize, and the fires they resorted to in felling the trees sometimes escaped their control. If an additional 20 percent of wastage for these and other losses is allowed, and if it is supposed that brazilwood was of average frequency in the coastal lowlands, say 4 per hectare of a harvestable 50-centimeter diameter, then the brazilwood trade, in just the first century, affected 6,000 square kilometers of the Atlantic Forest.[8]

Frequently, the return voyages also brought back native slaves. This practice was first recorded in 1511, when the ship *Bretoa*, loaded with dyewood at Cape Frio, included in its cargo 36 slaves, 10 male and 26 female, even though the owners had forbidden the crew to traffic in them. The practice must have been common thereafter—the earliest Portuguese name for the harbor at São Vicente was Porto dos Escravos, Port of Slaves. The first royal charters sanctioned this pernicious habit, granting the holder the right to import a certain number of slaves, duty free. The Portuguese had long been dealing in slaves on the African coast, supplying labor to their island colonies and to plantations in the Algarve and southern Spain. The natives brought back to Lisbon were probably intended not as field slaves, however, but as curiosities, freaks, to exhibit or to sell to nobles, like monkeys or parrots, except that they were also valued as sexual objects. These slaves were acquired under the same pretext as that employed in the kidnapping of Africans: They were *resgatados*, captives rescued from other indigenes. The Tupi obviously provided an abundant source for this stock-in-trade, and the Portuguese could congratulate themselves for having performed a humanitarian act in snatching their captives from the barbecue grill.[9]

The readiness of the Tupi to engage in barter with the Europeans was motivated in considerable measure by a desire to conserve effort, expand their subsistence base, and avoid some of the dangers of the forest. European steel knives and axes were tools that much reduced their labor, because they eliminated the tiresome chore of flaking stone and tempering wood, and in use they lessened the time needed to fell trees and carve canoes by a factor of about eight. In addition, iron fishhooks opened a new manner of exploiting estuarine food resources. It is hard to imagine how gratifying their sudden entry into the iron age must have been, how transformative of their culture, and how disruptive of the forest. A Kaingang group resident in Paraná that had obtained steel tools only in the mid-twentieth century recalled that they no longer had to climb trees, once a very frequent activity, in search of larvae and honey. Death by falling from trees had been common—now they simply chopped the trees down. The Portuguese sought to keep the indigenes dependent on them for ironware and were to threaten repeatedly blacksmiths whom they suspected of apprenticing their Tupi relatives.[10]

On the other hand, the Tupi disdained to accumulate goods. The contempt expressed by one Tupi at the apparently limitless demand of the Europeans for dyewood was recorded by the French factor Jean de Léry:

"You French are great fools; must you labor so hard to cross the sea, on which (as you told us) you endured so many hardships, just to amass riches for your children or for those who will survive you? Will not the earth that nourishes you suffice to nourish them?"[11]

This insouciance by turns amused the Europeans, because it reinforced their sense of superiority, and infuriated them, because it limited Tupi demand for their products. Modern authors have frequently quoted this remark, in evident delight at encountering a nonacquisitive "other" who denied capitalist rationality. More important, for the Atlantic Forest, at least, is the evidence it offers that the Tupi were not conservationist in the sense of sparing natural resources for coming generations. It is probable that this absence of concern was not reckless but was based on a reasonable certainty of the adequacy of their resources and their ability to defend them against rivals. Unfortunately, their principal rivals were soon to be the Europeans, whose insatiable appetites were far more destructive than any of the weapons they shouldered.

The Europeans failed to understand, or avoided understanding, that, for the Tupi, barter was not merely a primitive form of commerce but a material token of an alliance, which included mutual aid in combat. Varying degrees of relationship and obligation were recognized, of which the closest was that sealed by intermarriage. Therefore, when they offered their nubile women to the Europeans—who had, of course, no women to offer in return—they were involving them in a deadly serious game, as important to them as was the pursuit of riches to the Europeans. Nevertheless, the responsibilities of kinship lay lightly on the foreign sons-in-law, out of guile perhaps, or out of ignorance of the implications of their participation in these exchanges. In either case, they exploited their position as thoroughly as possible to extract from the intervillage warfare a maximum quantity of trade goods. The Europeans had their own reasons to participate in intervillage warfare and even to stimulate it, because it was a means to the end of scouring their rivals—Portuguese or French—from the coasts and because it augmented the harvest of slaves.[12]

The Tupi also readily captured for their insatiable guests live animals and pelts. In addition to dyewood, the 1511 manifest of the *Bretoa* shows 23 parakeets, 16 felines, 19 monkeys, and 15 parrots; that of 1532 of the ship *Pélérine*, 3,000 skins of "leopards, etc.," 300 monkeys, and 600 parrots. One can hardly imagine the cost to the Tupi of these exotic trade goods. The killing of a jaguar was a risky adventure, not merely because of its great strength and ferocity but also because its spirit was considered especially vengeful. The carcass of the dead animal therefore had to be decked in fine plumage, exactly like that of a human adversary. The women were put to imploring its forgiveness: The men of the village had set snares for animals they might eat; the jaguar had fallen into the trap out of carelessness and the men had had to kill it for fear of its anger. The French factor who witnessed this ceremony and then purchased the skin may well have raised his eyebrow at these tendentious representations, which were indeed not much different from those the Tupi were accustomed to address to the spirits of their human enemies. One wonders further what was the impact upon the Atlantic Forest of the continual extermination of thousands of its largest predators.[13]

The Europeans fancied parrots because of their novelty and brilliant plumage as well as their ability to imitate human speech. Indeed, according to one myth, they were transfigurations of the fallen angels who accompanied Lucifer in his fall. The natives shared this fascination. They kept the birds and traded them among themselves for their feathers, with which they adorned themselves on sacred occasions. Again, the prior existence of a barter trade was essential to Portuguese exports. Indeed, some of the parrot species were native to palm groves of the interior savanna, more than a thousand kilometers distant. The shorebound factors whiled away their lonely enlistments by teaching the parrots to speak Portuguese (it was later a wry colonial saying that "the well-spoken parrot goes to Portugal"). The most beautiful and rarest species were valued by the Tupi as equal in value to two or three human captives. Considering that the Tupi acquired captives at the risk of life and limb and that by bartering them away they forwent the glory of bashing in their heads and appending another honorific to their names, that was an impressive price indeed. Of the parrots mentioned by the chroniclers, there are two that are mysterious. The anapuru, the rarest and most costly of all, was described by the chronicler Fernão Cardim as "very large" and "very beautiful," its feathers displayed "almost every color in great perfection, to wit, red, green, yellow, black, blue, brown, rose, and with all these colors its body is spotted and sprinkled." This does not appear to be a secondhand description, like some of those the chroniclers offered of fanciful creatures. Cardim, and perhaps Gandavo, appears to have seen it. Another, the arara-una, or black parrot, was described by all the chroniclers, from Cardim through the eighteenth century, as indeed a black bird. Thereafter, following Linnaeus, who confusingly applied the specific name *ararauna* to the canindé, which is quite unmistakably blue, the common name has adhered to that or to other blue parrots. Were these now unidentifiable birds the first extinctions brought about in the Atlantic Forest by the European invasion?[14]

Even though brazilwood fueled a very modest trade compared to that of the Portuguese in the Indian Ocean, it brought notoriety to the newfound Land of the True Cross—King Manuel had rather casually seen fit to rename it Holy Cross—such that throughout Europe it was soon being called Brazil. The pious were greatly dismayed that so seemly and inspirational a name should have fallen into desuetude. It must have been the work of the devil that that divine tree whose dye and virtues had stained "all the sacraments of the church" had lost currency in favor of another tree whose dye stained common, material stuffs. Capitalism as the devil's work and capitalism triumphant, but more substantial indignities to clerical precepts lay in the offing. The first coat of arms of the colony displayed a compromise—an ibirapitanga from whose topmost limbs sprouted a cross. The name applied to the inhabitants of the country was, and remains, *brasileiros;* hence all Brazilians, upon reflection, appear to be engaged in the office, or trade, of dyewood logging, a peculiar and poignant designation now that dyewoods have long disappeared from commerce and the tree itself has become quite rare in its native habitat, surviving perhaps more in the form of specimens planted patriotically in public squares and parks.[15]

The brazilwood trade was most intense northward along the coast from Porto Seguro because the trees native to the southeast were less esteemed. The convenience of the Guanabara Bay nevertheless encouraged logging there, as did the remoteness and isolation of Cape Frio, which appealed to clandestine French loggers. In 1534 the crown, considering the trouble it was put to to clear the coasts of foreign competitors, declared all brazilwood trees royal property and the logging of them subject to concession, measures that remained in effect for more than three centuries.[16]

The repeated and flagrant incursions of the French obliged the Portuguese crown to dispatch punitive expeditions. But the lure of dyewood, so important to the merchants of Rouen and Honfleur, offset the new danger. The French, in addition, were more acceptable to the Tupi as trading partners, because they took no slaves and were generous in their supply of tools and weapons, even cannons. Furthermore, several Spanish expeditions, including that of the world-girdling Magellan, sent to explore the coast beyond the Portuguese claims, had landed and provisioned on the Brazilian coast, to the displeasure of the Portuguese king. He might well have allowed his colony to slip away, were it not for his hope that, like the Spanish claims, it also might contain gold. The first expeditionaries who penetrated the interior emerged with tales of booty—precious stones and gold—lost along the way. The forests they slashed their way through were of no interest to them, an alien and irrelevant living world. A fanciful geography was concocted: a "Golden Lake" in the center of the new continent whence flowed the two great rivers of the Amazon and the Plate. There, it was imagined, the precious metals would be found. Surely all the lands to the east of this lake must belong to Portugal.

Wishing to believe these accounts, the king sent in 1531 a large force under the command of Martim Afonso de Souza to establish a base camp somewhere near the southern extremity of the Portuguese claim, nearest to the rumored realms of Andean riches. They entered Guanabara Bay, where de Souza set up a fortified camp and sent a party inland to reconnoiter. They returned in two months, having penetrated 115 leagues, probably to the northwest. The "great king" they brought back with them was happy to confirm that there was gold and silver on the Paraguay River. De Souza, easily convinced when the subject was his "greatest desire," quickly set sail southward and made landfall at Cananéia. In the vicinity he encountered a few Portuguese and Spanish residents, who were willing to enter the interior, assuring him that they would return in ten months with 400 slaves loaded with gold and silver. De Souza decided, instead, to dispatch eighty of his own men to find the Inca empire.

The expedition set sail again, expecting to rendezvous with the exploring party to the north, at another, more secure harbor. De Souza then came upon an island covered with nesting frigate birds and boobies. He ordered a skiff to be launched, so that he and some of his officers might land on it and take their sport. They killed numerous birds, with which they filled the skiff. Contentedly they pulled back to the ships, but then they felt, blowing over them from the crest of the island, a sudden hot wind, that seemed "like naught but fire." Observing that the flags on the topmast of their ships were waving in a contrary direction, they were overcome by a fear that the baneful wind might visit a fever upon them. Therefore, reported the chronicler, "As soon as I returned the captain to his ship, I returned to the island and set it on fire."[17]

This depredation, so casually performed, no doubt a reaction to horrors experienced on the African coast, is a kind of talisman that reveals an entirely pragmatic attitude toward the natural world: When in doubt, burn it. These were hearts ruled not by wonder or panic but by caution and thoroughness. The Portuguese soon decided, in fact, that the Brazilian coast, quite unlike that of Africa, was governed by "good airs" and that there was no need to fear along it the scourge of malaria. One cannot help wondering if the site of this episode was Queimada Grande (Great Burned) Island, where boobies and frigate birds still nest. Partly tree covered although the object of repeated burnings, it is one of the few ecosystems in the world whose dominant species is now a reptile, *Bothrops insularis*. This extremely venomous snake preys on birds, so its poison must act almost instantly. Had de Souza and his men only known of the real dangers on that pleasant little island.[18]

De Souza's destination was a few kilometers north, the "Port of Slaves" that had already been the frequent resort of ships passing to and from

Europe. The Tupi, perhaps in consequence, called it Temiuru, from their word for provisions. De Souza renamed it São Vicente, after the patron saint of Lisbon. From one point of view, it was a favorable beachhead. It was not much disputed by rival tribes because the estuary was not very productive, though the silting of its streams and its innumerable sambaquis showed that that had once been so. On the other hand, it was an extremely difficult point from which to attain control of the interior, for here the coastal escarpment, rising to almost 900 meters, begins only a few kilometers from tidewater. De Souza waited in vain for his expeditionaries—they never returned. Nevertheless, succored by a Portuguese who had fathered a numerous brood of mestizo warriors, this first town survived. Within a few years a second port, called Santos, had been founded nearer the entrance to the bay, and two other towns, Santo Antônio da Borda do Campo and São Paulo, had been placed atop the escarpment. This hasty extension of a precarious outpost on the highlands was apparently the result of a desire to penetrate the gold-bearing regions as soon as possible.

A second beachhead of the Portuguese invasion of the Atlantic Forest was established only three years after São Vicente. This was on the Bay of Espírito Santo, somewhat below 20° south latitude. There the colonizers were attacked almost as soon as they landed, and they endured constant warfare even after they retired to a more defensible site on a bay island. Meanwhile, another European nucleus was beginning to form on the west side of Guanabara Bay, where French factors first ingratiated themselves with the Tupi and then the French crown attempted to found a regular settlement. At the same time, far inland, more than a thousand kilometers up the Paraguay River, the Spanish installed a settlement at Asunción, where they encountered a dense population of cooperative Guarani. From that base they hoped to launch an attack on the vaguely reported empire of the Inca.

In 1534 the Portuguese king, impatient at the failure of his explorers to bring back riches, decided to reduce the cost of colonization by bestowing proprietary rights upon certain of his courtiers willing to undertake the expense of settlement and defense. Brazil was sliced into parallel coastal strips, called captaincies, and charters were emitted, granting the donataries, as the courtier-proprietors were styled, powers thought sufficient to the task. Martim Afonso de Souza received one of these grants, centered on São Vicente, and nine others intersected the Atlantic Forest from north to south. The captaincies eventually proved impractical, because the resources of most of the donataries were insufficient to the task. News of the Spanish discovery of a mountain of silver at Potosí, in modern-day Bolivia, rekindled the king's enthusiasm for his vast Neotropical realm. A royal governor was dispatched in 1549 to establish a capital at Salvador, on the Bay of Todos os Santos, to strengthen the colony's defenses and to supervise the efforts of the donataries.

The migration of plants and animals is an intermittently occurring phenomenon in the natural world; indeed, the migration of humans, at least before the invention of agriculture, may be seen as merely one more such event. The first human invaders of the New World had carried with them a meager baggage of stone weapons and were accompanied only by their hunting companion, the dog. Although this was armament enough to have devastating impact on those few New World species that became their favorite prey, eventually it was the human invaders who had to discover productive environments on a continent that was largely inhospitable. The European invasion of the New World differed from the first invasion in that this second wave had already taken up agriculture. Its cohorts therefore possessed a considerable array of domesticated species that they might with advantage bring with them. They were also capable, to a degree, of evaluating the biotic resources of the native agriculturalists they encountered, either to trade in them or to cultivate them in their homeland.

The other critical characteristic of the second invasion was that the Europeans were not merely migrating to a new environment, they also intended to maintain contact with the old one. From this point of view, the colony of exploitation and the colony of settlement—what the Portuguese from the beginning distinguished as *conquista* and *colônia*—did not much differ. Both had to trade with the metropolis in order to survive and, indeed, in order to justify the expense of implanting them in the first place. Therefore this second invasion implied the replacement sooner or later of a desultory barter between a native population desirous of iron weapons and willing to ransack its forests for stocks in trade and a bemused and ignorant band of interlopers satisfied with an unpredictable flow of exotic collectibles.

Alfred Crosby showed that colonization has been, historically, an essentially ecological phenomenon, in which the colonizers direct a broad and critical process of plant and animal dispersal. Invaders who arrive with their own biotic resources possess a great advantage, in that transferred species escape from pests and predators with which they have coevolved. In the new environment, therefore, they tend to swarm. It is difficult to imagine how the Europeans could have so quickly achieved such widespread hegemony in the New World had they not commanded an army of plant and animal domesticates. Indeed, in the region where nearly all these domesticates originated, the Near Eastern–South Asian continental heartland, European imperialism was faltering and superficial. On the other hand, in the tropical regions, where the Europeans could not introduce their temperate-zone domesticates, it was necessary to transfer, in the main, species from the Old World tropics, a conquest by proxy that proved a good deal more complex and problematic than their colonial settlements in temperate climes.[19]

That the Portuguese intent was to conquer and transform this territory and not to submerge themselves in it or allow themselves to surrender to its native cultures is evident in their limited appreciation of its vegetation and animal life. They recognized and reported gross differences between the tropical environment and that of the familiar North Atlantic: It was always warm, there was no winter, the rains were abundant and seasonal, the forests were ubiquitous and filled with mists, their trees were very tall and evergreen. They compiled lists of potentially exportable species—mainly fine logwoods, a few medicinals, birds of plumage or speech, and fur-bearing animals. Occasionally they accepted reports of marvelous beasts or were taken with the metaphorical qualities of some of the curiosities they encountered—the passionflower, for example, which the Jesuits represented to the natives as symbolic of Christ's death and resurrection. Their lists were neither lengthy nor detailed, however. As conquerors, they were largely immune to that curiosity concerning the natural world contemporaneously awakening in Europe.

Their initial attitude toward this strange shore was unreceptive, even dismissive. The encounter at Porto Seguro had included exchanges of foods. This was the only awkward moment of that idyllic interlude, yet it was telling, for neither group appreciated the other's cuisine. Indeed, the Europeans soon took to characterizing the native diet as inferior (even though the physiques of the Tupi were noticeably more imposing than theirs!). Although the chroniclers hazarded a taste of the native fruits, they did not find them "as good as those from home." Exile may be expected to produce such sentiments, even in missionaries whose practice of horticulture was efficient and painstaking. But the effect was to lessen the intrinsic value of the Atlantic Forest, to hinder the domestication of wild species that native peoples had not troubled to cultivate, and to delay or prevent the arrival in Europe of the seeds of a number of Neotropical plants—some native to temperate highlands and more nutritious than any Europe possessed—that might well have been acclimated with advantage to the starveling hamlets of Portugal. Maize did make the transit quickly, but many other plants never arrived, and so their names remain strange to the European ear, untranslatable and exotic in the psychic as well as the botanic sense.[20]

The Portuguese invaders did see the point, however, of effecting transfers to Brazil from the tropical forest regions of the Old World and were, among all the Europeans, the best placed to do so. Some of the semitropical Old World domesticates they sent to Brazil—bitter oranges, lemons, sesame, and rice, for example—had already been acclimatized in Portugal. But others of the transfers were of tropical African and Asian origin—yams, bananas, coconuts, ginger, and okra, for example—which the Portuguese had already brought to their offshore colonies of São Tomé, Madeira, and the Cape Verde Islands. The Portuguese thus became the dispersal agents in Brazil for a tropical flora that was alien to them, implanting it in another natural realm that they thought of as their conquest. Perhaps it is not so easy to decide that the conquerors were in this regard the humans

A few of the crops introduced to Brazil from the Old World tropics were welcomed by native peoples, especially bananas. And a few Neotropical species found their way to Africa, most notably manioc, which became a staple as important there as it was in the South American tropical lowlands. Other root crops, peanuts, pineapples, and a number of fruits also spread in Africa, apparently not through official channels, at a time when Portuguese colonies on the mainland were nothing more than fortified slave warehouses.

Because Portuguese colonists longed to consume familiar foods and because their compatriots at home could not be expected, at least in the short run, to esteem inordinately, and therefore to pay inordinate sums for, native tropical products that the Tupi might cultivate, it was necessary to introduce crops from the Old World already appreciated in Portugal. Thus the expeditionaries came bearing seeds and leading domesticated animals from the homeland. With the settlement at São Vicente the biotic conquest of Brazil began in earnest. Although earlier reconnoitering had casually introduced a few exotic domesticated animals and plants, de Souza appears to have deliberately brought a variety of Europeanized domesticates "for the experience of what the land would yield." On the São Paulo plateau, a cool habitat was found suitable for Mediterranean crops: quince, fig, apricot, peach, pear, date, and pomegranate trees; garden vegetables such as cabbages, onions, cucumbers, melons, rape, dillweed, roses (for medicinal rosewater); and—essential for the practice of the faith—grapes and wheat.[21]

Of all the colonial crops—that is, those planted to return an export surplus to the metropolis—the most valuable and viable was sugarcane. Cultivated in India centuries before and planted throughout the Mediterranean, it was for the Portuguese a major export to northern European markets. Probably it had been brought to Temiuru even before de Souza's expedition. There has always been the small mystery that he ordered the building of a sugar mill before there appears to have been any cane to grind. It is likely that some earlier, unrecorded mariner had brought it from Madeira or from São Tomé, where there were already 60 mills, intending it merely as a subsistence crop because cane need only be squeezed to render an agreeably sweet juice.[22]

These introduced domesticates they planted in burned fields, employing much the same techniques as the Tupi and benefiting from the astonishing initial fertility of the forest biomass that had been reduced to ashes. Fruit trees reached maturity more quickly than in Portugal, and cereal seeds yielded five or ten times as much grain. Although sugarcane had to be manured on Madeira and São Tomé, that was unnecessary in Brazil, where in some places the cane could be cut year after year without replanting. Furthermore, the abundant coastal rainfall obviated tiresome irrigation. Most important, the introductions were free of the diseases and parasites that plagued them in the places whence they had been transported. Even though these introductions were discovered to be gratifyingly easy to cultivate, the necessity for cultivation remained. Domesticated plants had undergone modifications that rendered them uncompetitive in natural environments, and the Atlantic Forest, continental in scale and tropical in diversity and competitiveness, was not itself easily invaded. Therefore these introductions, unlike those on many an oceanic island, did not result in a replacement of native flora beyond the bounds of the burned and planted fields.

De Souza's order to construct sugar-grinding mills in São Vicente implied the impressment of a slave work force similar to those already employed on the sugar plantations of the Mediterranean and the Atlantic islands. This decision has apparently left no traces of its assumptions or justifications, yet it displays on its face a cruel opportunism, an intent to reduce the "conquest" to nothing more than a site of primary extraction. For the history of the world economy, the implications of this decision were profound. Thenceforward, for the next three hundred years, the Portuguese slave-plantation model was copied in English, French, and Dutch territories throughout the tropical and semitropical New World, in behalf of an intensely exploitative colonialism. In Brazil the installation of a large slave population was to render impracticable the replication of the peasant base of the Iberian Peninsula.

For the Atlantic Forest, the dangers were immense, because a society based on forced labor was heedless of its environment. Those who commanded the trade were transient and improvident: "Of those who came none has love for this land. . . . All want to act in their own behalf, even if it is at the cost of the land, because they expect to depart it." Not only were the short-lived slaves only briefly attached to the soil, they were, whenever possible, strangers to it. The essence of the plantation, in addition to an exotic domesticated plant, was an exotic work force. Indigenous captives were traded among coastal towns, not only because intermittent warfare resulted in localized gluts in the slave market but also because increased distance from their homeland reduced the likelihood of escape. Those who planted sugar were to see in the forest nothing more than an obstacle to the realization of their ambitions. Those who came increasingly to occupy the fringes of the plantation economy—backwoods squatters—were impelled to exploit the forest recklessly and improvidently. The conservation of natural resources was to prove irrelevant in a society in which the conservation of human life was irrelevant.[23]

Native slave dealing now became a large-scale enterprise, for it had as its purpose the stocking of local plantations, not of the salons and palaces of Portugal. Upon the defeat of the French colony at Rio de Janeiro in 1560, the west side of the Guanabara Bay was also turned over to sugarcane. The Tupi who had allied themselves with the French were bound into slavery. A trade in captives then developed among the coastal towns. But indigenous slaves were rebellious; they refused to work and escaped easily into the forest, whence they could be retrieved only by other indigenes. They were therefore very unsatisfactory laborers, and they were accorded a low value in trade. Only in the Northeast, at Recife and Salvador, were coastal planters prosperous enough to bid African slaves away from the Atlantic island colonies. But in the less well capitalized and less efficient Southeast, native slaves remained a necessity.[24]

The result was an intensification of warfare. At São Vicente and São Paulo the acquisition of slaves by "rescue" diminished sharply by the 1580s. By then the area for many leagues around those towns had been cleared of enemies suitable for impressment. The settlers themselves had meanwhile acquired the capacity for offensive warfare in the forest as their second, native generation reached maturity. They began eagerly to invent excuses to penetrate far into the interior to make war, for the real purpose of capturing slaves. These *saltos*—assaults—ranged farther inland, upriver from Porto Seguro and from the mouth of the São Mateus River, down the Tietê River to the Paraná, and, by the turn of the seventeenth century, westward across the Paranapanema—reaching ultimately to the end of the Atlantic Forest and the beginning of the interior savanna. Out of São Paulo alone there were at least twenty such expeditions by the year 1600. From Asunción, meanwhile, Spanish punitive expeditions penetrated eastward and northeastward, up the Ivaí and to the mouth of the Tietê. These incursions, in addition to providing a labor force for the colonies, were beginning to define geopolitical borders.[25]

The destruction of the interior population was facilitated by the activities of the missionaries, who arrived at São Vicente and Espírito Santo by 1550. They were appalled by the bellicosity and strangeness of the Tupi, who were on the "path to perdition": All they thought of was drinking, dancing, making war, and "cooking human meat." The Jesuits combated the cults of the Tupi to destroy the power of their competitors, the shamans, who exalted the virtues of virility and bravery, attributes utterly inappropriate to a conquered caste. The Jesuits also desired to assert the separation of the divine and the natural. They chose to identify the Christian god with a remote and cultless spirit, Tupã, the Thunderer, and they vilified the forest spirits, whom they characterized, indiscriminately, as devils. Thus the Atlantic Forest became the abode of the devil, a convenient metaphor for those who feared it and intended to eliminate it.[26]

It was the Jesuits' purpose to convert the indigenes not merely to Christianity but to the passivity and dependability of a Portuguese peasantry that would accept perpetual wardship and all the indignities that were its marks—flogging, personal service, sexual submission, and labor in the fields. To attain this goal, it would be necessary to put an end to the indigenes' itinerant and extensive exploitation of the forest. How closely, in their minds, farming was identified with Christianity may be seen in the exhortation of the Jesuit Diogo Jacomé to his colleagues in Coimbra: "This vineyard lacks grapes because there is no one here to fell the surrounding woods and to prune it; you are the pruners, and you are sorely missed here." For a time, repelled by the Tupi and delighted by reports that the Guarani, a large interior tribe, were settled farmers who did not practice cannibalism, they sought permission to depart into the interior. Later, other Jesuits were to achieve that goal, but in the 1550s the Portuguese governor was seeking to avoid giving the Spanish a pretext to close the frontier, which the Portuguese had so easily penetrated. Obliged to remain on the São Paulo plateau, the Jesuits, alleging the impracticality of preaching to numerous tiny, scattered villages, lured the Tupi and whatever other groups they could contact to the vicinities of the Portuguese towns. The missionaries or their proxies therefore undertook *entradas*—entries— from São Paulo, Rio de Janeiro, and Espírito Santo. These were numerous and parallel to the saltos of the slave catchers, encompassing nearly all the region of the Atlantic Forest, and they gathered in as many as two or three thousand at a time. The "descent" of these "lost sheep" who were willing to accept a new religion, or perhaps simply hoping to obtain protection from their neighbors, was usually problematic—it was often necessary for the proselytes to fight their way through on the *descida*—descent—to the coast, a struggle that cost many lives.[27]

Within the pale of European settlement, the new arrivals were settled in *aldeias*—villages—where they were to live, abandoning the "promiscuity" of the longhouse and adopting the nuclear cottage and ceasing slash-and-burn farming. The aldeias obviously represented a tempting source of bound labor for the colony. Although the Jesuits opposed white demands that natives be enslaved, their long-run intentions toward them differed little from those professed by the lay settlers. Both desired to turn indigenous males into farmers and to reduce tribal people to the status of a tenanted peasantry. In the short run both made heavy demands on them for unpaid labor. The Jesuits employed aldeia inhabitants for as much as three days a week as personal servants and missionary construction laborers, porters, and farmers; they supplied them to government authorities for public works; and they leased them to settlers for months at a time. Indeed, the governor had to insist that such contracts be limited to three months. The labor requirement, from the point of view of both Jesuits and settlers, furthermore, offered more than the opportunity to profit and enjoy leisure. It was also an adequate means to break the Tupi and their neighbors, a deliberate intent to destroy a culture and reshape it immutably into a subordinate caste.[28]

Within a decade, the inconstancy and rootlessness of the Tupi had quite discouraged the priests. One of their leaders, Manuel da Nóbrega, exasperated by the Tupis' incorrigible cannibalism and polygamy and jealous of the influence of the shamans, called for a war of conquest. Only when the Tupis had been roundly defeated would they cease their constant fighting and wandering, and only then could they be fixed to lands "that are enough for them" and indoctrinated in the faith. Another Jesuit, José de Anchieta, believed that their indoctrination would last only as long as "there is someone to make them live in subjection and fear." Still another, Pero Correia, advocated withholding iron tools from those who refused Christianity. The tools, by shortening their workday, enabled them to spend all their time getting drunk and plotting wars. By withholding them, "they will suffer hunger, and hunger is war day by day, and in a short time it has to conquer them." He had seen villages where the natives had no iron, and there "hunger was so great among them that they died of hunger and would sell a slave [*sic*] for an iron wedge . . . and they also sold their sons and daughters." The ferocity of the proposal is matched by its impertinence, because it was the Tupi women, not the quarrelsome men, who farmed.[29]

Nóbrega's appeals were heeded. The campaigns against the French were prolonged until the mid-1570s, in order to crush all Tupi resistance through the lowlands surrounding Rio de Janeiro, from the Bay of Angra dos Reis to Cape Frio. A six-year-long offensive on the São Paulo plateau, begun in 1590 under Jerónimo Leitão, is said to have destroyed 300 villages, killing or capturing their inhabitants, to the number of 30,000. This was possibly an exaggerated report—assuming a density of 0.4 inhabitants per square kilometer in the highlands, it implies the clearing of 75,000 square kilometers—yet some not much lower figure is entirely possible, because entradas often returned after six months in the forest with one thousand or two thousand captives in train. In the social collapse that followed, indigenes desperate for food sold their children and even themselves into slavery. Nóbrega found it necessary to counsel the notaries who recorded such sales that the Bible prohibited a person's selling himself and that, unless it was ascertained that the seller was the parent of a child offered for sale, the notary placed his conscience at risk.[30]

Although slave trading and the hardship of the plantations brought death to the Tupi and their neighbors, the destruction wrought by the introduction among them of Old World infectious diseases was greater still. European and Asian cities had gathered together, over several millennia, human settlements large enough to permit many species of microbial parasites to evolve dependent, for their dispersal, on human contact alone, without the agency of animal vectors. The cities, especially the ports, where population concentrations were largest and where disease agents were most efficiently transported, had come to serve as reservoirs for these parasites, which gradually accommodated themselves to their hosts, displaying, over many generations, a reduction in virulence. Human populations came to consist mainly of survivors of earlier epidemics; they were the bearers of antibodies that helped protect them against reinfection. Thus infectious disease episodes gradually became endemic, typically striking children, who had not experienced prior exposure.[31]

The cities of the New World, compared with those of the Old World, were newer, fewer, and more scattered, and none were ports fed by seaborne commerce. Microparasites therefore lacked a favorable ambience for transmission directly from host to host, and thus these human populations held in store for the Europeans no retributive surprises, with the possible exception of syphilis. It was possible for the chronicler Pero Magalhães de Gandavo to report from Brazil, evidently thinking only of the state of health of the Portuguese invaders, that "this province is without contradiction the best for the life of man than any of those of America, because it is commonly of good airs and very fertile, and in fine manner delightful, and agreeable to the human eye." Its healthfulness he attributed "to the winds that generally course over it . . . because they all proceed from the sea, they arrive so pure and filtered that not only do they do no harm, they recreate and increase the life of men." A serenely contradictory reporter, Gandavo a little farther on blamed the winds, now blowing from the interior and infected by their passage over "the rot of the grasses, trees, and swamps," for the generation in Brazil of "many venomous animals and creatures . . . in such abundance that it would be a long story to name them all."[32]

Transferred across the Atlantic, Old World infectious microparasites acted with renewed and horrifying virulence. The entire native population of the New World was utterly susceptible, experiencing death rates that greatly surpassed those of even the worst plague epidemics of Europe and Asia. The impact of disease has been unmistakably charted at every point of contact between Europeans and indigenes. Most poignant is the state of entire ignorance in which these events transpired. Measles, smallpox, respiratory diseases, and possibly malaria carried off millions of New World inhabitants during the first century of contact. Indeed, the charnel resumed whenever and wherever susceptible peoples were contacted by neo-Europeans.

In the region of the Atlantic Forest the saltos of the slave traders and the entradas of the Jesuits intensified the exposure of the native population to infections. The aldeias acted as foci of epidemic outbreaks. In 1576, for example, the priests at Espírito Santo reported that 75 of the 160 natives they had lured to their aldeia had "departed this world to live in the other, happy one." Although the indigenes suspected danger in the proximity of whites, the missionaries were oblivious, claiming that baptism would prolong their lives. They frequently expressed satisfaction at the deaths of backsliders and relief at the deaths of converts. Bitterly aware that it was only a question of time before all their acolytes reverted to their old ways, at least the latter, they reasoned, had been saved. The epidemics spread far beyond the pale of Portuguese and French settlement, as aldeia dwellers fled back to their hearths and as the interior villages they infected were in turn depopulated when their inhabitants routed in panic. Entire villages were destroyed at once, as Indians, too weak to hunt or dig for manioc or keep their fires lit, died of starvation as well as disease.[33]

Along the coast from São Vicente to Cape Frio, wave after wave of disease ravaged the Tupi; they were reduced by 1600 to some four or five thousand, a horrifying decline of 95 percent in a century. The upland forest very likely experienced a similar scale of depopulation. The few survivors were those who had been prudent enough to avoid all contact with the

Europeans, either by abandoning agriculture entirely and breaking up into small hunting bands or by demonstrating a ferocity so terrible that the Portuguese feared to enter their territory. Of these the most successful survivors, at least for another century or so, were the Aimoré, reported in 1587 as living "like brute animals," without shelters but so "wild and so fugitive in nature that they cannot be pacified, not even to captivity like other Indians." These remnants were insignificant in numbers and were obliged to maintain a wide no-man's-land between them and the nearest neo-European settlement.[34]

Of all the weapons loaded in the caravels of the Europeans, none was as effective as their diseases in overcoming the resistance of New World peoples. Indeed, epidemic disease is the key to understanding the course of European imperialism in the New World. In the other tropical regions of the globe, all of which had been linked by trade and conquest since the emergence of agriculture and cities, the seaborne approach of Europeans did not have this result. For two and a half centuries, the invaders controlled no more territory on the Asian and African coasts than that secured by the range of cannon shot. Because Asian and African disease resistance was even more complete than that of the marauding Europeans, the latter had no opportunity to repopulate the landscape as they pleased with an exotic human stock of colonists and captives and domesticated stocks of animals. It is astounding that the reality of a densely populated New World scourged by suddenly introduced diseases was denied not only by those who witnessed it but also by all their descendants, for more than four hundred years, in an endless chain of complicity that enabled the neo-Europeans to claim the inheritance of an empty land, a boundless "frontier."

Preliminary to the enterprise of appropriation, the Portuguese monarch applied to the new colony his concept of the ownership of nature. In the act of dividing Brazil into captaincies in 1532, the crown presumed itself to be the legitimate possessor of everything on the South American continent east of the line of demarcation, by right of conquest, even though its effective control extended at the time over a single enclave, a few kilometers in radius, at São Vicente. The charters it issued to the donataries and the instructions it delivered to the royal governor bestowed the power to distribute rights of ownership over an abstract entity, *terra*—land. Comprehended implicitly in this concept was the entire biotic world that inhabited it and the substrate upon which it depended. In these acts the crown made note of the eventual presence of certain accidental features of this abstract possession, because it reserved to itself, in addition to brazilwood trees, the ownership of mines of precious metals and gemstones, and it subjected to special adjudication private claims to watercourses and to riparian sites for the placement of water mills, used to grind sugar. It ignored, however, the potential prior claims or even the presence of the indigenous inhabitants.

Indigenous views of the ownership of nature do not appear to have been inquired into by the chroniclers. It seems likely that the Tupi thought of the forests as belonging to the spirits and animals that inhabited them, or at least as belonging as much to those beings as to them, even though at some level their wars were certainly a struggle over the exclusive possession of natural resources. Their views, in any case, would have been considered irrelevant. The crown denied that the natives retained any legitimate rights to the space they occupied, although the governor and the donataries from time to time conceded, as a grace, limited tracts to be occupied by the aldeias and overseen by the missionaries. Commentators on colonial land policy, immersed as they have necessarily been in a Eurocentric vision that subsumes reality to categories of "discovery," "conquest," "pacification," "civilization," and "salvation," have found nothing remarkable in this single, astonishingly arrogant stroke of expropriation, although it is evidently one of the most magnificent in all of history.

As it happened, the crown had at hand a precedent for the confiscation and alienation of land. A Portuguese law of 1375 had asserted the authority of the crown to seize private lands that had fallen into disuse. Rural crises and epidemics had caused large areas in the countryside to be depopulated. These were designated *terras devolutas*—reverted lands—reverted, that is, to the crown, which thereby asserted its original ownership. They were then distributed as *sesmarias*—portions—with the principal condition that the grantees have the means and will to work them. In Brazil, these concepts of original crown possession, usufruct, and potential reversion to the crown all suited the purposes of colonization. The donataries, the governor, and the municipal councils were therefore all authorized to issue grants of land, subject merely to the condition of effective occupation. Pretendants who alleged prior services to the crown were preferred. In addition, sesmarias were granted to missionizing orders, inasmuch as their activities were considered of value to the colonizing effort. Jesuits, Franciscans, Benedictines, and others thus came to be owners of forest, along with individual magnates, and like them depended on forced labor.[35]

By 1600 the human relationship to the Atlantic Forest was transformed, principally because most of its original human inhabitants had disappeared and because the number of invaders was insufficient to replace them. Along the coast, after a century of constant warfare, enslavement, and epidemics, only seven of the donataries had managed to install any sort of settlement; the crown had consolidated four of them. That of São Tomé was abandoned to its native inhabitants after two invasion attempts in the 1550s. Only twelve Portuguese settlements had been awarded the status of *vila*—town. Several settlements were already decadent. Altogether, in the southeastern captaincies only fifteen sugar mills were operating, six each in Santos and Rio de Janeiro and three in Espírito Santo.[36]

The plan of the Jesuits to construct a society based upon aldeias was a demographic failure; the aldeias did not expand in number or population, even though new recruits were fitfully attracted or herded into them throughout the century. By 1600 some twenty-one aldeias were associated with the Portuguese settlements in the southeastern captaincies. In Espírito Santo, five were around Vitória and as many as six more were scattered along the coast. Two were near Rio de Janeiro, three were near São Vicente. Surrounding São Paulo there had been twelve Tupi villages when the Portuguese arrived, but these had been consolidated as the indigenes died off—only six remained by 1600.[37]

The population of Portuguese-controlled Brazil in 1600 may have amounted to less than 65,000. Fewer than 10,000 of these residents were Europeans or mestizos. Their area of effective occupation may have extended over 16,000 square kilometers, calculating about 4 persons per square kilometer, including the town populations. The surviving native population inhabiting the area of the Atlantic Forest beyond the Portuguese pale is entirely a matter of speculation, but it may be that it had nearly disappeared within a radius of 300 kilometers of the coastal towns, as the result of entradas and saltos, the spread of infectious disease, and the flight of its population to areas farther in the interior. Beyond these zones, native populations were preagricultural or had abandoned agriculture to maintain their mobility. Willem Glimmer's expedition of 1598–1602 to the headwaters of the São Francisco River offers a vivid report of an abandoned countryside, where "in these solitudes," only wandering bands were to be found "with impermanent dwelling-places, who along the way take no care of seeds." This diminutive population of hunter-gatherers reverted to the practices of their more remote ancestors, subsisting for the most part on the kill of prey that preferred the forest margin, far in the interior, where the cerrado met the Atlantic Forest.[38]

Control of the coast was not yet secure a century after the Portuguese had first asserted their claim, even after expulsion of the French from Rio de Janeiro. Smuggling and pirate attacks occasionally threatened the ports. The struggle for the north coast, stretching to the Amazon, had only just begun, and Portuguese encroachment to the south of Cananéia would embroil the colony—indeed, the independent successor states—in intermittent warfare for a further century and a half. The violent colonial rivalries of the first century were therefore only a foretaste of growing threats to the realm of nature.

The catastrophic native population decline that followed upon the sixteenth-century European invasion and the demographic insignificance of Portuguese immigration granted the Atlantic Forest a respite, after ten thousand years of hunting and gathering and a thousand years of swidden farming. Forest remote from adequate harbors or lacking in brazilwood was left in peace. A period of vegetational and faunistic recomposition began. In a few places this is verifiable. The first Portuguese settlement on the highlands was abandoned because the proximity of forests rendered it indefensible. The town of São Paulo, founded on a hill in the midst of a broad, open plain, by 1587 possessed "more woods than aught else," and the townspeople were commanded to cut down the trees within and along their stockades. Similar orders were given to the inhabitants of Rio de Janeiro in 1620 and 1624.[39] Firebrands and broadaxes would have to keep at bay an advancing forest that the Tupi had maintained in a secondary state, and the neo-Europeans would struggle to prevent its penetration into areas that had long before been denuded of forest cover and had stabilized in open prairies.

The Atlantic Forest was still almost entirely unknown and unremarked. An immense natural reality, in plain sight of the invaders, was still a century and more away from discovery.

4

Estrangement: Depopulation and the Regrown Forest

*Neste país tudo é vergonteas novas e espinhosas cujo fruto
é imperfeito, que são os mamelucos.*

*In this country all is new and thorny shoots whose fruit
is imperfect, which are the Mamelukes.*

FRANCISCO PIRES

The depopulated Atlantic Forest gained over much of its extent a respite from the pressure of human necessities and cravings. But during the course of the seventeenth century it also became a reality farther and farther removed from human understanding. The Portuguese invaders improvidently destroyed a considerable cultural achievement, one that they were only dimly aware of and failed almost entirely to appreciate: the capacity of its native inhabitants to survive in its midst. An ecosystem may be seen as an information storehouse, containing both genetically programmed and learned information accumulated by its species, relevant to their survival and reproduction within it. The humans of the Atlantic Forest, like all its other creatures, had stored up, over twelve thousand years, their own stocks of information. Each group had attached names to hundreds of species for which they had found some use and in regard to which they had learned habitats, seasons, habits, and relations with still other species. Because the resources and experiences of each village differed from those of its neighbors, thousands of the species of the Atlantic Forest had been catalogued in the memories of its human inhabitants. Only oral tradition preserved this culture. Once the indigenes were removed from their habitats, all this information inevitably began to deteriorate, and the forest became strange and without human purpose.

The first generation or two of Portuguese invaders had depended entirely upon indigenous understandings of the Atlantic Forest. The Tupi hunted, planted, and cooked for the expeditionaries and cured their ills.

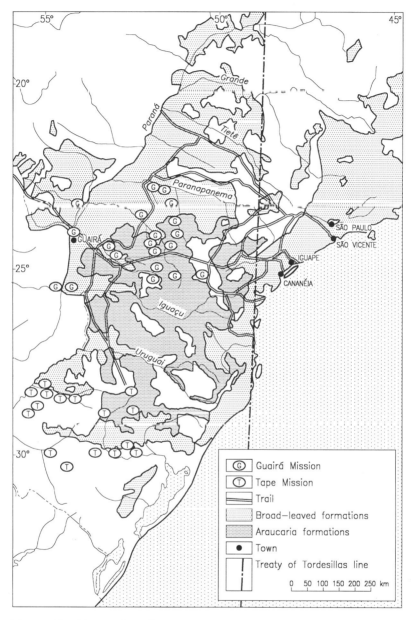

Map 3.   Bandeiras, 1580s–1640s

So dependent were the Portuguese that they were reduced on occasion to bartering their stocks of knives and fishhooks, not for trade goods or slaves but for manioc. The invaders could not navigate confidently in the forest; they needed guides. "The Indians are like beasts of the forest," they reported enviously, "because they enter the forest to hunt, naked and shoeless, with no fear at all." During this interval the invaders rarely dared to penetrate the forest in search of slaves; instead, they acquired them through dealings with natives to whom they applied the same name as that they used in their African trade: *pombeiros*—referring to the pigeons set loose to lure others back to the cote. Truly, as an English interloper remarked, the indigene was "a fish in the Sea and a Fox in the Woods, and without them a Christian [was] neither for pleasure or profit fit for life or living."[1]

Some of these first Portuguese did indeed find native ways attractive, or at least they accepted the necessity of learning them. Deserters, degredados, and factors had no choice: They slung their arms on the post of the longhouse and became apprentices, suspended in hammocks, wreathed in sacred tobacco smoke. They learned from their native wives and brothers-in-law to make snares, to distinguish animal cries, to treat snakebites, to find wild fruits, and to set fire loose in the forest. The historian Capistrano de Abreu, commenting on a report sent to the king by a certain Fróes, one among the first wave of deserters and degredados, who had had to adopt native subsistence techniques and culture, observed that "within a few years a man in those conditions became morally a mestizo." Indeed, Fróes was, temporarily at least, not a mestizo but an indigene.[2]

The mestizo generation spawned by the degredados was culturally indigenous, Tupi-speaking, knowing of the forest and of the means to exploit it. This expertise did not, however, endear them to latterly arrived Portuguese-born colonists, who called them *mamelucos*—Mamelukes. This outlandish term was probably derived from *membi oca*—(mother's) child of the house. Mamelukes may seem an opprobrious term, considering the history of Moorish conquest of the Iberian Peninsula and continuing conflict thereafter with the Ottomans, yet it was one that suggested grudging respect, as well as recognition of their utility to the colonial polity. Portuguese imperialism, however, remained uncertain concerning the status that should be awarded a social group intermediate between whites and submissive, protoservile indigenes. The children of the first generation of unions between Portuguese and Tupi did not accept the status of peasants, much less that of slaves. They resisted baptism and were indifferent to the brand of illegitimacy. They went about naked and did not hesitate to abuse the priests when their impositions annoyed them. Characteristically, the Jesuit Francisco Pires applied a horticultural metaphor: They wanted pruning and grafting.[3]

That the ways of the natives were attractive to the degredados and their colleagues, and not merely a necessary evil, can be seen in their resistance to Jesuit demands that they put their clothes back on, abandon their Tupi wives, and attend mass. The Portuguese inhabitants had come "to be almost like the Indians, because being Christians, they live in the manner of heathen." Their defiance, and that of the deserters from the French outposts at Rio de Janeiro and Cape Frio, suggests how superficially felt were the moral compulsions of European Christianity and how dependent were the churches on the state to exact compliance from the "faithful." The result had been a further decay in the church's moral authority: Its effort to impose monogamy on Portuguese society had been successful only to the degree that open relations were punishable by lay courts. Thus concubinage was, in practical terms, available only to those who controlled the courts—the nobility and the rich. But the Atlantic Forest beckoned any Portuguese who was adventurous enough to cross the pale to ignore the injunctions of the church on this score, as on many others.[4]

A few of the deserters and degredados were even found to be taking part in cannibal feasts, no doubt those that crowned the successes of their brothers-in-law. The custom was abandoned by the Tupi themselves, however, possibly before the end of the sixteenth century. It does not seem likely that they had been moved by the appeals of the missionaries. No one has tried to explain the case, but the demands of the Portuguese for forced labor had vastly increased the value of live prisoners and, probably as a result, had transformed the hierarchy of prestige and enhanced temporarily the survivability of those tribes that collaborated most closely in the slave traffic. By the early 1600s the new contingents of indigenes filtering into São Paulo, Espírito Santo, and Rio de Janeiro were increasingly Guarani and other indigenes who had never practiced anthropophagy. Thus one of the most picturesque forms of human aggressiveness and status seeking disappeared, commemorated only in the chronicles of a few dozen or so brazilwood traders and clerics.

It was not long before the squaw men and their mestizo offspring were rounded up and subordinated to a colonial enterprise that had little use for their knowledge of the Atlantic Forest or for their potential role in the integration of European and indigenous techniques. Rio de Janeiro and São Paulo continued to receive quite small but significant flows of migration— adventurers from the Spanish colonies and even from other countries in western Europe, as well as from Portugal. A few of them were women, imported deliberately so as to avoid the genetic absorption of the whites. A society of castes thus became possible, as the more ambitious and dominant white males, shrewd enough to preoccupy themselves with finding favor in the eyes of Portuguese authorities, sought white marriage partners and thereby distanced themselves from the ordinary run of European colonists as well as from the Mamelukes and indigenes. The mestizos consequently passed through a triage: Those recognized by their white fathers continued to be called Mamelukes, but those unrecognized were referred to, without euphemism, as "bastards" and were subject to slave labor, much the same as natives. Gradually, over the course of the seventeenth century, no doubt as a sufficient number of white offspring were born, the designation Mamelukes fell into disuse, and mestizos were all called bastards. The royal officials did not hesitate to bestow privileges on the colonial whites, not only in response to their own racial and social prejudices but also as an efficient means of assuring their control over the colony—through a minority that would be, without their backing, unlikely to retain its privileges.[5]

Among the measures instituted by the crown to delineate a caste society were those that segregated neo-European and native residences and defined the city as the proper domicile of whites. Just as those indigenes being converted to Christianity and subjected to Portuguese control were separated from those still recalcitrant or hostile, and placed in aldeias, so were the Portuguese separated from the aldeia dwellers. At first whites lived in aldeias, but by the beginning of the seventeenth century they were forbidden to build their houses within them. In part this prohibition sought to eliminate the advantage that whites resident among the indigenes might gain in claiming their labor. But it also sought to avoid the dissolution of Christian whites in the surrounding native culture. Indigenes who attempted to "pass" as mestizo were repeatedly expelled from the towns. And in 1583 the municipal council of São Paulo forbade visits by whites to aldeias "to drink and dance after their manner."[6]

   This was a first attempt at defining, in the Atlantic Forest, the city as synonymous with "civilization," endowing it with the instruments of command while relegating what was native and barbarous and properly repressed to the villages. It required that the whites, and mestizos perhaps as well, separate themselves psychically from the villagers, suppressing their desires for conviviality with them. This separation had evident noxious social consequences, but it represented as well an insistence on the separation of white society from nature itself, an impulse buried deep in the culture of the Mediterranean, where seven thousand years of plowing and sheep raising had left little more than a desert to despise. In the colonial setting this estrangement was to work dramatically and powerfully, limiting the diffusion of forest knowledge from the huts of the aldeias while exalting ignorance of it among the dominant caste.[7]

The colonial government continued to sponsor aldeias, in order to assure that natives who came more or less voluntarily to live on the neo-European side of the frontier would occupy fixed homesteads, each consisting of a single male and female. This was problematic, not only because the indigenes had never made it their habit to remain in fixed abodes but also because, lacking a sense of property, they raided the larders of whites whenever they pleased. The aldeia was therefore a training ground for learning respect for property as well as acceptance of the European definition of work and reverence for the Christian god. For most of the colonial era, missionaries—usually Jesuit or Franciscan—were in charge of the aldeias. Intermittently, however, they were taken over by civil administrators, whenever secular anger at clerical monopolization of this tempting labor pool resulted in their temporary expulsion or loss of legal control. The lands granted the aldeias were continually encroached upon by whites, until finally most of them ceased to be self-sufficient. The populations placed in them were heterogeneous, and new groups were installed from time to time without granting the existing inhabitants any say in the matter. The colonial authorities certainly had no intention of assisting native peoples to preserve any trace of their culture; indeed, they would have found the idea both repellent and impolitic. The Jesuits nevertheless continued for practical reasons to catechize in a pidginized version of the related languages of the Tupi and Guarani. In this *Lingua Geral* they also preached to tribal peoples of other language stocks.[8]

The inhabitants of the aldeias were subjected to labor tribute, applied to the point of beggaring them. The newest of these recruits to civilization continued to suffer disastrously from periodic epidemics. On several occasions they were uprooted and moved elsewhere, to suit the convenience of the authorities. In São Paulo the aldeia was principally a means of keeping occasional labor close at hand; in Rio de Janeiro and Espírito Santo, where African slaves were more easily obtained for that purpose, aldeias more often served to extend the frontier. Most of the towns in the eastern and northern districts of the modern state of Rio de Janeiro were originally aldeias, as were many of the coastal towns to the north and south of Vitória. Over time, despite occasional fresh levies of forest dwellers, the aldeias lost their identity and blended with the rest of the impoverished settlements of mestizo villages, just as the colonial authorities would have it.[9]

Another effective measure in the establishment of a caste society was the manner in which sesmarias were bestowed. The abundance of unoccupied land, in the aftermath of assaults and epidemics, made it possible for any free person to squat on unclaimed land. This became a general practice, unrecognized by crown law, though authorized in custom as *posse*—possession. As long as the posse was pacific—as long, that is, as neighbors mutually accepted each others' claims, there might be a considerable delay in the submission of a petition to the municipal council or to the governor to turn the posse into a sesmaria. This was a precarious solution, however, and was usually due to the squatter's relative lack of influence or funds to pay certain officially required charges and unofficially solicited emoluments. The squatter's claim was strengthened by his local prominence, which might include public office—in the courts and the militia, for example—or commerce or previous landownership and did not exclude bullying and sharp or corrupt dealing. The sesmaria—which was the only legal form of gaining ownership of unoccupied land and which in itself constituted title—was therefore a principal distinguishing mark of a person of influence, repute, and wealth. It was not, however, the initial or effective step in acquiring control of land or even the final step.

In Portugal the policy of royal land grants had been intended to stimulate peasant production for the supply of the towns; in Brazil it was bent to the purpose of encouraging the search for gold and gems or, failing their discovery, the production and export of sugar. Pretenders to sesmarias who, in evidence of their worthiness, at first emphasized loyal services to the crown or their descent from the first settlers, later came to emphasize their ownership of slaves as proof of their capacity to increase exports. Thus a dominant class arose whose ownership of land was a form of privilege, conquered through local prepotence and confirmed through royal connivance. Landownership under this regime did not achieve the quality of a market good, even though notarial registers show that it was sometimes bought and sold for money. What was always at stake in any land dealing was the intangible of local power and status, variables that were necessarily local monopolies or, if not monopolized, then the object of violent contention.

The first grants of land were modest, on a European scale of property holding, perhaps because of the straitness of the colonial pale and the difficulty of defending it from waves of indigenes bent on restoring their rights. Initial cessions of a hundred hectares or so, however, soon gave way to much larger grants, characteristically for what in Portugal would have been considered vast estates, a quarter of a square league (1,089 hectares) at a minimum, but most often for a full league (4,356 hectares—more than 43 square kilometers)! A royal order of 1698, evidently issued to curb abuses, limited sesmarias to a maximum of three square leagues, considering that amount to be as much as "a *morador* [white or putatively white head of a settler household] can cultivate." Evidently such grantees would have been men possessing numerous slaves and enormous ambition, which the crown was willing, or obliged, to try to slake. There were occasionally even larger grants, and the richest and most powerful of the local notables struggled with the donataries to acquire holdings the size of principalities. João Raposo Bocarro, a crown officer and militia captain, was the recipient of a seventeenth-century grant of six square leagues. Perhaps the most arrogant of all the notables who sought possession of the Atlantic Forest, however, was Salvador Correia de Sá, whose uncle had captained the extermination of the French colony on Guanabara Bay. Appointed governor, he crowned numerous military and commercial exploits with the confiscation, in the name of the king, of a group of sesmarias that were successors to the failed captaincy of São Tomé, which he awarded in 1652 to himself and his sons, in recognition of their rights as legitimate heirs, a total of 1,300 square kilometers, to which the king was persuaded to add, in behalf of one of the sons, the title of Count of Assumar.[10]

Unfortunately for the tranquility of the colony and its government, land grants were normally bestowed in conditions of utter imprecision and confusion. The king, the donataries, the governors, and the municipal councils made no effort to coordinate their grants, so that the same territory might well have four apparently legal owners—or more, because municipal and captaincy limits might overlap and grants might be awarded to several pretendants in succession. The sesmarias never clearly specified boundaries and sometimes not even locations. This was much to the advantage of the most ruthless of the pretendants, who then felt authorized to expand their claims as they might. Although the grants contained provisions calling for demarcation to be carried out by the grantee, this was usually omitted or marred by fraud and incompetence. Under these circumstances, sesmarias were hardly more secure than posses, and maintaining them continued to be a matter of the fine tuning of the greed and suspicions of powerful neighbors. Kinship therefore became an almost indispensable means of battening the fires of hostility, and endogamy consequently became an overwhelming preoccupation among them. Insecurity of property certainly diverted the minds of local notables who might oth-

erwise have entertained disloyal sentiments long before the final break of
the colony with Portugal in 1822, but it was a costly royal stratagem, if
such it was, because it abdicated authority over what was supposedly the
object of the entire colonial adventure: the land itself. The absolutist state,
in this tropical version, appears in this respect miserably accoutred
indeed.[11]

One of the principal reasons for the astonishing scale of the sesmarias was
the technique adopted for the exploitation of the forest and its soils. This
was an adaptation of the indigenes' slash-and-burn regime, which included
acceptance of maize and manioc as staple crops. Because newly burned
forest soils were immensely fertile and slash-and-burn obviated the need
to cultivate the fallow, the plow was abandoned. This represented an enormous saving in labor, veritable liberation for the Portuguese settler who
owned no slaves. Slash-and-burn, as it was carried out by native populations with densities of less than 0.5 persons per square kilometer in the
highlands and less than 10.0 in the lowlands, had been indefinitely viable.
Portuguese colonization, however, implied a more intensive exploitation
of forest soils because both the government and the church were preoccupied with permanently fixing rural population and because the settlers
were preoccupied with confining slave workers in order to exploit them
more effectively. Furthermore, now there were urban residents to be fed,
principally in the government seat of Rio de Janeiro, where a few thousand
officials, clerics, soldiers, prisoners, and construction slaves were stationed.
And there was, in addition to all this, the necessity of providing a surplus
to the metropolis, which implied an expanded cultivated area, both to supply the demand and to provide subsistence for those engaged in the trade.[12]

The invaders made more intensive farming practicable, at least in the
short run, by introducing, very early on, domestic animals from the Eur-
asian biotic realm. Pigs, chickens, sheep, goats, and especially cattle offered
a meat supply with very little additional labor input. Of these, pigs probably provided the most substantial addition to the agricultural regime. Able
to defend themselves from predators and to subsist on what they could
root out from secondary forest, becoming in the process somewhat feral,
pigs probably supplanted certain wild animals, such as tapir and deer,
in the vicinity of settlements and probably influenced as well the dispersal and survival of forest flora. Thus the contribution of pork to the neo-
European diet ought to be to some degree discounted, in that pigs were
also competitors of animals that might otherwise have been hunted and in
that they slowed the regrowth of the secondary forest on which farming

depended. Pigs, nevertheless, were preferred by small farmers, because they were easy to raise and herd to town markets.[13]

Cattle were introduced first to São Vicente, possibly with the expedition of Martim Afonso de Souza in 1532, from the Cape Verde Islands, where the Portuguese breed, free-ranging and weighing 200 to 300 kilograms, had already been acclimated. Some were driven up the coastal palisade to São Paulo, and others were taken by ship to Rio de Janeiro. At São Vicente pasturage was very limited, but on the São Paulo plateau and on the lowland plain around Guanabara Bay grass was abundant, more than the Portuguese could remember anywhere in their homeland. There were no competitors for this niche, because no large mammals had grazed these plains since the extinctions of the Quaternary. Nor were there any reports, at first, of diseases or parasites. They required no care—they did not have to be stabled nor, in a climate that provided fresh grass twelve months of the year, did they have to be supplied with fodder. They multiplied rapidly: "each year they bear fruit," marveled one of the Jesuits, "without any work at all." Although jaguars came to fancy cattle, and natives sometimes killed them, their numbers soon filled the available grassland.[14]

The insertion of cattle into the slash-and-burn regime was, however, problematic. Slash-and-burn cultivators did not build fences, because their clearings were too ephemeral. Although in native practice the tempting manioc plots lured wild game, domestic animals were annoying intruders. At the edges of the towns, where few of the settlers owned cattle, the animals became a source of conflict. Owners often neglected to brand them, so that damages were difficult to assess. The incompatibility of grazing animals with slash-and-burn and the absence of any need for associating them in the farming regime—because the plow had been abandoned and forest ashes offered more abundant and much more convenient nutrients to the farm plot than did animal dung—generally led quickly and fatefully to separation of the two systems. In the Northeast cattle ranching was soon banished to the sertão, where savanna offered an adequate, if not optimum, environment for a breed of animals resistant to drought and a diet of coarse grasses and thornbush. There were at least 500 ranches in the northeastern interior by 1700.

Beyond the town limits, pastures were formed. The Jesuits were granted a plain, called Santa Cruz, to the west of Rio de Janeiro. This they drained and installed some 20,000 head, all on a single vast pasture. The herds satisfied not only the city's voracious demand for meat but also, not unimportantly, the demand of the sugar mills. The average mill employed, as draft animals and as the motive force for the grinding rollers, perhaps a hundred oxen, whose life expectancy was no more than two years. Hides were a profitable by-product of this business: In 1709 Brazil shipped 110,000 hides to Lisbon, most of them from Pernambuco and Bahia. Cattle raising in the Rio de Janeiro region pressed eastward along the coast where patches of grassland were to be found, as far as the mouth of the Paraíba do Sul River. There stretched the former no-man's-land between Tupi and Goitacá groups, a marshy plain more than 5,000 square kilometers in extent, which came to support many thousand head for the Rio de Janeiro market. Cattle raising, in this latter area of especially tangled land disputes, and probably quite generally throughout similar regions of the Atlantic Forest, was an enterprise especially accommodating to squatters because it established the claim of prior "use," essential to the acquisition of title, without requiring an investment in improvements. It is apparent that the confusion and violence of the sesmaria system stimulated the spread of ranching in preference to farming, perhaps even in the absence of potential demand.[15]

In the Southeast horses and pack animals were hardly used during the first two centuries of colonization. The slaving expeditions and the movement of goods, even of goods of little value by weight, were carried out entirely on foot, where river transport was impractical. Horses were to be found mainly in towns; the first mention of donkeys dates only from 1635. The waste of human effort was extraordinary, almost incomprehensible, especially considering how little effort was devoted to cultivation or animal raising. Possibly the explanation lies in the higher nutritional requirements of horses, which may have been difficult to satisfy on native grasslands (an explanation that implies widespread transformation of the range in the period since the Quaternary extinction of native horses). As long as the forest remained, in the interior, largely intact and the locations of grassy clearings too scattered and imperfectly known, long-range explorations on horseback remained impractical. Villagers would have found it difficult to employ donkeys in the presence of the unfenced clearings characteristic of slash-and-burn farming.[16]

The introduction of iron implements made possible another kind of intensification of slash-and-burn. The ax made it much easier to choose primary forest over capoeira, because the labor of cutting down trees was much reduced. The hoe made possible larger cultivated plots, from perhaps 1.0 to 2.5 or 5.0 hectares per worker. The use of the hoe meant that the inevitable invasion of weeds did not necessarily bring about the immediate abandonment of a field. It also meant that second-growth forest was at less of a discount because of its likely infestation with weed seeds. The hoe permitted cultivation for prolonged periods and permitted the burning and exploitation of less-developed second growth. The extension of the period of cultivation, however, was critical for the stability of the swidden farming regime and disastrous for forest regeneration. Most trees in tropical primary forests require for their development association with mycorrhiza—fungi that take up residence in their roots, thereby assisting in the uptake of minerals. Too long an exposure to direct sunlight destroys these creatures. This simple tool, the hoe, was thus potentially capable of eliminating the Atlantic Forest permanently.

Grantees of sesmarias amounting to a thousand or more hectares could be found not long after begging for another, as a "remedy for my poverty" on the grounds that their lands were "tired." It seems impossible that so few inhabitants could have exhausted so much forest so quickly, had it been primary. Even the Jesuits, presumably the most effective managers and less driven to expand their holdings for the sake of expansion, applied for a new sesmaria, only twenty years after receiving one at Carapicuíba, alleging that those lands were "already tired and turned into open fields without any woods."[17]

The rapid expansion of the area occupied by neo-Europeans in the 1600s points to a ruthless dilapidation of forest resources. The Paulistas (that is, the inhabitants of São Paulo) and their dependents and slaves by 1650 totaled perhaps 15,000. Their settlements extended 250 kilometers along the valleys of the Tietê and Paraíba do Sul rivers, an expanse that is evidence that the chronicler Gabriel Soares de Souza was correct in remarking, in this case apparently with approval, that "In regard to the fertility of the land, I say that many times the newness of a farm is worth more than the property, so that they maintain themselves with little patrimony." His observation was not only well taken, it is central to the understanding of the construction of a peculiar, extractive form of capitalism, in which the capital stock is entirely *in natura*, existing prior to neo-European occupation, and is quickly dissipated, reducing the population to the level of subsistence. Dare we call this capitalism, or is it capitalism in reverse? The astounding improvidence of the neo-European adaptation of slash-and-burn agriculture, utterly beyond the conception of the miserable Portuguese peasantry, whose households might be obliged to make a living from a single hectare yet be expected to pass it on from generation to generation, its productivity undiminished, has been ever since the wonder and horror of foreign observers.[18]

The customary size of the sesmaria suggests a measure of population density and of the speed of forest clearing. Each sesmaria was the abode of the grantee and a modest retinue, consisting of his kinsmen, free dependents, and slaves. Wheat-growing estates in São Paulo employed, over the course of the seventeenth century, an average slave work force of about 25, with the largest work forces reaching 110 at midcentury. If the average estates occupied sesmarias of half a square league (2,178 hectares—assuming a minority of smaller estates and an ongoing degree of division through inheritance) and if the free inhabitants on such estates averaged another 20 persons, then population density within the neo-European settlements of the highland would have been about 2 persons per square kilometer, four or five times that of its former inhabitants. The slaves on these estates would have been capable of clearing and planting, at most, some 5 hectares each, or 125 hectares a year. This, according to an early eighteenth-century governor, they were commonly required to do. So wasteful a cycle, he pointed out, did not leave sufficient time for forest regrowth, when the sesmaria was only a quarter of a square league—indeed it would not, for then clearing would be finished in just 8 years.[19]

Even half a square league was insufficient to guarantee stability, especially when one considers that at least some part of each sesmaria would probably be too steep, sandy, or marshy to be farmed. Grantees along Guanabara Bay, in fact, complained that much of their land was bogs. It seems likely, however, that farm practice was normally somewhat more conservative than that suggested by the governor, because the rate of occupation of the São Paulo highland and the Rio de Janeiro lowland was slower than what might have been observed if he were correct. If subsistence and wheat clearings were maintained for at least three successive harvests, then a perhaps sufficient 24 years would elapse between burnings. It is also likely that the first Portuguese towns, built upon prior Tupi settlements, were attacking mostly secondary forest, perhaps only partly regrown, a practice the indigenes would have avoided. Pretendants to sesmarias very likely exaggerated the rate of exhaustion of their soils, the better to support unfounded demands for additional land grants. However, in most cases pretendants were already squatting on lands for which they were petitioning, sometimes for more than a generation. Under those circumstances, then, it is not so surprising that soil exhaustion often set in soon after the grant was made. In any case, the regrowth of forest was generally retarded, not only by domestic animals but also by the demand for firewood, construction materials, and tools. Process heat was expended liberally in the making of bricks and tile and in the baking of lime, used in mortar and the surfacing of walls. Thus even the largest sesmarias might practice a predatory and unstable form of slash-and-burn cultivation.

The consolidation of the Portuguese colony took place during a period of extreme uncertainty concerning the independence of the metropolis and the survival of its empire. The Portuguese throne became vacant in 1578 and was occupied two years later by Philip II of Spain. Dutch merchants, also Philip's subjects, thereby gained access to the Brazilian sugar trade, which they largely financed. But when the Dutch declared independence they were excluded. In retaliation they made war on the Portuguese tropics, capturing Pernambuco, Angola, El Mina, the Cape of Good Hope, Ceylon, the Japanese trading posts, and the spice islands. They were, by 1650, dislodged from Angola and Pernambuco, but the rest of their conquests were permanent, and the Portuguese Asian empire was all but extinguished. The Dutch carried off to the Caribbean the secrets of sugar making, diverting much European trade from Lisbon. Portugal, meanwhile, had been struggling to regain its own independence and was finally successful in 1640. Fearing a return of the Spanish and the loss of his remaining possessions, however, the Portuguese king was obliged to accept subordination to the growing power and interests of the British, then engaged in crushing Dutch naval power.[20]

Even while the crowns of Portugal and Spain were united, an independent administration was maintained in the Portuguese colonies, so that the treaty line of Tordesillas continued to divide the South American continent. But unification rendered the frontier more permeable. The trails that had long connected the Guarani with the coast between Cananéia and São Vicente remained in use; indeed, inhabitants of São Paulo kept up considerable contact with the Spaniards of Asunción and shared a common point of view regarding the necessity of dominating the natives and curbing the Jesuits.

Along the coast, at Recife, Salvador, Espírito Santo, and Rio de Janeiro, sugarcane, introduced nearly a century earlier, had not yet been joined by any of its coevolved Old World parasites or pests, save for a few weedy grasses, rats, and other domesticates—cattle, goats, and pigs. Sugar became the only sizable economic activity linking the region of the Atlantic Forest with the metropolis, except for brazilwood logging. Yet output rose only modestly: by 1600 it reached 10,000 tons; by 1700 it totaled about 19,000 tons. Assuming a yield of 50 tons of cane per hectare and an extractive rate of 3 percent by weight, by 1700 sugarcane fields would have occupied about 120 square kilometers. This would have been land taken from forest, because sugarcane was thought to be cultivable only on forest soils. The governors exerted themselves to distribute the best lands to sugar planters, uprooting subsistence farmers when necessary. The planters, as itinerant as swidden cultivators, took no care to maintain soil fertility, preferring instead constantly to dun the authorities for sesmarias in primary forest. One request for a sesmaria in Rio de Janeiro, for example, complained that the land then held by the pretendant became "tired" after just two crops, because none of it had been in "virgin forest."[21]

It may be calculated that by 1700—some 150 years after export of sugar achieved commercial scale—canefields would have done away with some 1,000 square kilometers of the Atlantic Forest, assuming nearly steady growth and abandonment of "tired" canefields to subsistence or pasture after an average of fifteen years. This was a modest depredation; indeed, it represented less than half the area of the present-day municipality of Rio de Janeiro. Sugar production also consumed forest in the form of firewood, burned under the vats in which the cane juices were crystallized. It appears that about 15 kilograms of wood were burned for every kilogram of sugar produced, hence an average 210,000 tons of secondary woodland and bay-side mangrove forest was cut each year for this purpose. In addition, the mills required wood ash to purge the sugar of its impurities; the mangrove of the bays was preferred for this material. Estimating 200 tons of fuel-wood per hectare, the mills would have consumed another 1,200 square kilometers over 150 years—a contributing factor, along with associated cattle raising and brick and tile making, to the prevention of forest re-growth around many estuaries. Sugar planters on Guanabara Bay were complaining by the middle of the seventeenth century of shortages of firewood. Their preference for planting in undisturbed forests and the in-efficient use of firewood plantations was causing sugar cultivation to spread, by the late 1600s, eastward across the lowlands toward Cape Frio.[22]

Wheat would not set seed in the lowlands, but, introduced to the semi-tropical plateau of São Paulo sometime after 1609, it flourished there. The Portuguese nostalgia for their staple cereal—sacralized in the ceremony of the mass—and the inability of Portugal to raise a surplus created a consid-erable market, extending as far as the Northeast. At its height, in the mid-1660s, Paulista wheat output may have reached 2,600 tons. The trade was carried out despite extremely high transport costs. Native porters brought the flour down the escarpment in 30-kilogram panniers, a cumbersome procedure that doubled its price in Santos and killed even more of the indigenes. Gradually a colonial trade in exotic foodstuffs was continuing to modify the environment of these slowly expanding enclaves.[23]

Sugarcane and wheat cultivation and cattle raising were all carried out with slave labor. In the Southeast the slaves were mostly native, obtained through an expansion of slave raiding by Paulistas. Although the inhabi-tants of Rio de Janeiro and Espírito Santo extended their settlements along their coasts, the Paulistas, already perched on a highland plateau, all of whose rivers flowed inland toward the Paraná, exhibited a preference for penetrating the interior. The entire forested zone, from about 16° to 26°

south latitude, became their area of operations. After 1600, with most of the native agriculturalists of the region between the Grande and Paranapanema rivers dead or fled, the Paulistas turned their attention farther southward and southwestward, to the region occupied by present-day Paraná and Santa Catarina. In the Atlantic Forest's southwesternmost extension, a region called Guairá, along the Paraná River, were concentrated fairly dense populations of Guarani and other tribes. Since the 1550s, Jesuits under the authority of the Spanish governor at Asunción had been extending a network of missions among these peoples. By the 1620s there were thirteen missions, of which the farthest east were located near the mouth of the Paranapanema River.[24]

Against the villages of Guairá the Paulistas mounted waves of assaults, or entradas. Their forces were organized into military companies called *bandeiras*, whence the jingoist neologism *bandeirantes*, suggesting flag bearers or pioneers. Each expedition was composed of a hundred or more whites and Mamelukes and as many as a thousand native auxiliaries. Their leaders were specialists in their trade—Tupi-speaking, skilled at arms, excellent foragers and hunters—and they preserved a part of their heritage for grotesque purposes. These were wars officially sanctioned, for which the entire male population was drafted. Just causes were invented for the sake of appearances, usually retaliation for incursions that might have occurred years before. The entradas were carefully planned, with caches of supplies set up by advance parties, sufficient stocks of powder and chains, and rear guards that planted a food supply to feed the captives on the return to the city. The raiders marched overland or sailed down the Paranapanema or Tietê River. Either journey lasted months and took its toll of the raiders themselves. One bandeirante complained petulantly in 1607 of the 240 native soldiers he had "spent" in the forest looking for more natives to enslave—a death rate of three a day. Generally short of supplies on the return, the impatient raiders murdered infant captives, the old, and the infirm. Once the assaults had destroyed all accessible native villages, they were then directed against the Jesuit missions, enslaving indigenes who had already been baptized. By 1640 all this ruthlessness had netted, out of an original population that may have numbered 150,000, perhaps 60,000 captives, of whom about half may have been sold to the sugar planters of Rio de Janeiro.[25]

In São Paulo many of the captives, exposed to contagious diseases, soon sickened and died. The return of each bandeira was therefore followed by another epidemic. The consequent labor shortage was justification enough for another assault. The depopulating of Guairá was followed by raids even farther westward, upon the mission area of Itatim, on the headwaters of the Paraguay, and southward, upon the missions of the Tape region, in present-day Rio Grande do Sul. The indigenes in the Tape, however, were armed, and the Paulistas, suffering the disadvantage of overextended supply lines, were defeated there in 1641. This was not the end of the bandeiras: Some of them, contracted by the governors and donataries of the Northeast, were kept at work putting down indigenous rebellions for another generation. In the Southeast assaults were by then limited to the capture of modest-sized bands of hunter-gatherers, no doubt already refugees from more coastward zones. These raids, also justified as the only available "remedy for their poverty," supplied only local markets. Quite a few of these later captives were members of tribes that had earlier collaborated in the capture of the sedentary Guarani and now met the same fate.[26]

It seemed bizarre even to contemporaries that the Spanish king allowed the Brazilian colonials to exterminate immense numbers of natives, whom he presumably supposed to be equally his vassals, for a result so ephemeral and trifling as a few thousand tons of sugar. Indignant petitions were addressed to the crown to employ these bravos instead in the campaign against the Dutch invaders. Indeed, they were conscripted for that purpose, but they did not heed the call. The disjuncture between the interests of the Spanish crown and his feckless Brazilian subjects reflects further upon the efficacy of imperial governance. It is apparent that, as with land titles, crown officials were unable to impose royal authority when the most urgent presumed interests of the colonists were at stake. Repeated royal prohibitions of Indian slavery, each time quickly and abjectly canceled, are proofs enough that, whatever it may mean for the theory of imperialism, the empire was founded rock solid upon the immediate and predatory desires of the neo-European colonists.[27]

The colonists nevertheless found it advisable to employ euphemisms when setting down in notarial records their putative rights of possession. Thus they were described as "administered" persons, as persons "obligated to service," or as "pieces of service" (a "piece" was a sort of standard laborer-unit—a concept that the Portuguese had already applied to their trade in African slaves). Captives were sold and they figured in wills, and often so did their offspring. In this fashion they gradually were branded with the characteristics of chattel slaves. Their number, however, could not be stabilized, because heirs sometimes renounced their presumptive rights to the captives or their offspring and because the indigenes suffered so terribly from European-borne epidemics. They also rebelled and fled, apparently more commonly than did Africans.[28]

Whites who did not own slaves eventually mated with natives and Mamelukes, gradually forming a disinherited mestizo mass, subordinate to those who wielded social power and living—according to the devastatingly apt usage of the region—*a favor*, on favor. In the hierarchical order imposed upon them, these mestizos occupied a position above that of the African slaves, who soon began to take their places. Their status as free persons was eventually respected, because of the presence of this new stratum of the utterly dispossessed. Assimilated natives were finally more advantageously left unenslaved, like the Mamelukes, because they would be needed to defend the whites against pirates and unpacified tribes and, above all, against the kidnapped Africans, "who are many and fear only the Indians."[29]

The introduction of Africans to the region of the Atlantic Forest began by the 1550s. They were preferred for plantation labor because of their longer life expectancy and the habituation of African males to field labor. As kidnapped and displaced peoples, they were presumed less likely to flee, "because they have nowhere to go." Their price was as much as triple that of indigenous captives for these reasons and also because their supply was irregular and unpredictable until the late seventeenth century. Even so, they had by then supplanted native slaves in the northeastern plantations.[30]

The practical, empirically minded Portuguese did not lack a degree of curiosity concerning the natural realms they had conquered, but they appear to have concentrated nearly all such attention on their Asian colonies, perhaps because they more readily accepted information from silken-appareled Indian and Chinese savants than from the more botanically knowledgeable, but naked and illiterate, Tupi pagés. Not until the middle of the second century of colonization in Brazil did the altogether exotic and overweening Brazilian forests become a minor hobby of the Jesuits, who were by then able to consider it in isolation from its feared, but largely exterminated, human denizens. The drawings of Friar Cristóvão de Lisboa, resident in Maranhão in the late 1620s, of fish, birds, and plants, are the earliest to have survived. Simão de Vasconcellos, who lived in Bahia, took it as one of his purposes, in his chronicle written in 1663, to show that Brazil was not inferior to the other three quarters of the world, an idea that had grown venomously among the Europeans in the wake of their initial enthusiasm for what they had fancied to be a terrestrial paradise. The business of slaughtering and enslaving indigenes had necessarily been accompanied by a change of opinion concerning the positive qualities of their victims. This hardening of hearts toward their fellows the Portuguese and, indeed, the rest of the Europeans had then extended toward the habitat of the natives. Vasconcellos, however, was one of those who took walks in the woods and found there both solace and wonders. Those who "calumniated" Brazil, he wrote, were ignorant of it. Aristotle and the other classical authorities, who after all had not even known it existed, were of no use in reaching an understanding of its excellence.[31]

They had been wrong, for instance, in supposing that climates grew drier nearer the equator. Brazil was verdant, and it enjoyed favorable influences of the sun, moon, and stars, an abundance of fishes in its waters and birds in its skies, and every sort of terrestrial beast, just as the first chapter of Genesis had vouchsafed. Like every other chronicler, Vasconcellos rejoiced in Brazil's eternal spring, "which recreates the eyes and invites the spirit to praise the Author of nature, because without doubt it exceeds in this beauty all other parts of the earth." He had penetrated that verdure, climbing the coastal escarpment and entering the roiling clouds that obscured their heights, clambering past crystalline springs, breathing the "vapors and exhalations of the soil," then breaking free, upon the dizzying precipice, of the rains and winds and, looking down upon mists and rainbows, he felt himself bathed in "sunlight and tranquility," as though he were suddenly raised to another world, "exempt from time's jurisdiction, as if on the peak of Olympus, acclaimed by the poets." And then he had entered in the "immense forests" beyond, "glory and crown of all the universe, their feet in the ground, their canopies in the heavens, forming delightful woods, sylvan shades, the most agreeable in the world." There, "in the stillest summer weather," he had wandered, "in the interior of those forests whole leagues together, always under shade, without sight of the sun, as though in the freshest spring of Europe," wondering at "the monstrous thickness of the ancient trunks, the variety of precious species, of cedars, vinháticos, jacarandás, copaíbas, almécegas, bicuíbas," many of them entirely covered in flowers—red, purple, white, and yellow. All of this was incomparably finer than anything Europe had to offer.[32]

And this forest, dense and unbroken, was bountiful: Vasconcellos's list of the fruits of the forest is an incantation: mocuguê, sapucaia, pitomba, araçá, ibacurupari, ibanemixama, imbu, araticum, guti, caía, iapina, audá, ingá, juá, maçaranduba, murici, ibaraé, guabiraba, guabiroba. There were the cabreúva and copaíba trees, from which fragrant balsams were obtained and fashioned into many products. And of the "perfumed herbs and simples, their species are countless: nature deposited on these mountains a treasure of human remedies, known to few," more than would fit in the books of Dioscorides or his followers. Thus does "the verdure of the herbs and woods of Brazil . . . grace the earth, delight the eye, please the nose, sustain the herds, cure the men, raise the edifices, feed the hungry, enrich the poor: I know not what more bounty there were at the first creation."[33]

Vasconcellos's descriptions of the forest occupy, nevertheless, only a few pages of his massive work, whose principal object was to describe the "heroic mission" of his order to wrest Brazil from the power of hell, in whose dominion it had lain since the beginning of the world, some six thousand years before. These tidbits of nature appreciation are in fact rather repetitive, and they are sandwiched between immensely detailed narratives of the comings and goings of missionaries and the tribulations of their aldeias. These sketches and reports were amateur efforts that do not contradict the impression that the Portuguese authorities did not concern themselves overmuch, for at least two and a half centuries, with the astonishing biota of the splendid colony that had fallen into their hands. In contrast, the brief Dutch occupation of the northeastern captaincies, from 1626 to 1649, resulted in the publication of brilliant treatises on natural history, plant and animal collections, and a treasury of vivid and precise botanical and zoological drawings that are still of inestimable value to present-day biologists.[34]

Even though Portuguese scientific interest in its New World territories was slight, somewhat more attention was paid to economic botany in the aftermath of the loss of the Asian colonies. A quarter of a century after that calamity, the Portuguese diplomat Duarte Ribeiro de Macedo wrote a sagacious memoir on the subject. He had been told by a Dutch informant that the colony of their West India Company in Pernambuco had been undermined by the East India Company, which feared that the spice plants of Asia might be transferred to Brazil, thereby ruining their monopoly. Although Macedo seems to have been unaware of it, that stratagem had apparently been employed by the Portuguese at the time they evacuated the spice islands—pepper and cinnamon had been planted in the Amazon and the Northeast. But the Dutch had put pressure on the Portuguese government, no doubt while the recently restored monarch still lacked British protection, and these plants had been uprooted. A generation later the idea had to be reintroduced to Macedo when the British ambassador informed him that his country was introducing exotics to Virginia and suggested that the Portuguese do the same.[35]

Macedo undertook a study of the history of economic introductions, finding that some were indeed very recent—sweet Chinese oranges had arrived in Lisbon only in 1635—and that the royal prohibition on the planting of Asian spices in Brazil, decreed soon after the founding of Goa, had not been revoked. Even so, some exotics, notably ginger, had reached Brazil through agents unremembered and had acclimated well. He concluded that further transfers could easily be carried out. If successful, they might restore the lost Portuguese spice trade and also humiliate the Dutch, a very satisfactory prospect. Apparently the king had already been thinking along these lines. In 1671 he had permitted exports of Brazilian ginger, the sixteenth-century command to uproot it having luckily proved ineffective—another ineffective edict. When the burgers of Rio de Janeiro heard the news they paraded to the church and offered a Te Deum.[36]

There followed a period of intensive efforts to collect Asian species and acclimate them in Brazil. It was to prove a good deal more difficult, now that the Portuguese had lost political control and naval supremacy in the East. The Dutch company considered the transfer of its monopolized plant treasures as acts of war. In 1661, for example, they had sent an expedition to the Malabar Coast to attack the Kingdom of Cochin and uproot its cinnamon plantations, which competed with their own in Ceylon. Nevertheless, the Portuguese governor of Goa managed to collect all the desired seeds, except for cloves, which were too closely controlled by the Dutch in the Moluccas. There followed a decade of remittances, at first mostly unsuccessful but increasingly effective as improved ways of shipping were developed. Seeds were received in all the captaincies and given over to the Jesuits, who had already displayed a talent for introductions, especially at their garden in Salvador. Several of these new plants adapted well— jackfruit, mangoes, saffron, and camellias. Unfortunately, the plants that would have been of some assistance to the Portuguese trade balance— black pepper and cinnamon—did not. Black pepper would not set seed, and the gathering and processing of cinnamon proved a mystery. A Jesuit was sent in disguise to Ceylon to lure out natives skilled in the art, to no avail. These efforts continued until the 1720s, by which time new discoveries of gold and diamonds in Brazil had rescued the crown from insolvency and diverted the attention of Brazilian landowners.[37]

The replacement of native flora with another array of introduced plants of economic interest was evidently difficult for the Portuguese to achieve, partly because it was rather complicated—unlike the imperialist practices of more temperate climes, it involved transfers not from the metropolis but from other tropical colonies. Also, as in the case of the Dutch empire, parochial mercantilist interests interfered with the project. But it seems that success eluded these early initiatives as well because willingness to experiment was not intense.

The society that inhabited the Atlantic Forest, for all the destruction and disruption wrought by the European invasion, remained at the end of the seventeenth century to a considerable extent indigenous, both culturally and genetically. The vast highland, crisscrossed hundreds of times in the first two centuries by raiding parties, proselytizing missionaries, and gold-crazed explorers, witnessed an exchange of cultural elements and, beyond the boundaries of the towns, a sort of Indianization.

On the indigenous side of an osmotic frontier, adoptions of European culture were piecemeal—not entirely a matter of choice, yet selective. Natives who had been settled in aldeias or who had been slaves on wheat farms sometimes departed, even en masse. A few tribes that had experienced defeat at the hands of the invaders, most notably the Goitacases, who had in former times held off the Tupi in the coastal lowlands at the mouth of the Paraíba River, withdrew to the highlands and regrouped, subordinating or absorbing still other tribes in turn. In resuming forest residence these survivors added to their cultural store a knowledge of the Portuguese language and what one colonial governor called "artificial necessities," principally salt and iron implements, for which the headmen were sometimes ready to trade the village children, so dependent on them had they become. Those groups residing at distances sufficiently great to allow them a degree of security took up a few exotic domesticates—rice, oranges, bananas, and sugarcane; these in particular were hardy enough to survive in clearings that wandering groups might visit periodically. Animal domesticates were impractical—when offered pigs and chickens, they usually killed them immediately. Although the Portuguese authorities had kept the natives from learning how to smelt iron, conviviality with whites was sufficient to permit them to learn how to work it, so that they came to trade iron articles among themselves and to refashion them into weapons of greater utility, such as arrowheads. These artifacts and others were passed on to other indigenes who may never have set eyes on a white man.[38]

Meanwhile, native cultural elements, though repressed and despised by the dominant neo-Europeans, nevertheless persisted and suffused the neo-European pale. Even after two centuries of occupation, whites still constituted a small minority everywhere except in the cities of Recife, Salvador, and Rio de Janeiro. Many among the moradores, whom the governors considered fit for public office and patents in the militia, were genetically mestizo. Tupi-Guarani remained the lingua franca between indigenes and neo-Europeans, as well as among indigenes, and it was the language of women, the mother tongue in aldeias and rural neighborhoods, even though it left no trace in the documents of the era. It contributed thousands of words to Brazilian Portuguese, especially the lexicon of the natural world. The Portuguese bestowed, by analogy, the names of familiar European plants and animals upon some of the species of the Atlantic Forest, but the rest were received from the indigenes. Two-thirds of the common names of the trees of the Atlantic Forest and of nearly all of its animals are Tupi-Guarani in origin. Neo-Brazilians preserved the names of innumerable natural formations—geological, edaphic, vegetational—and of natural features—rivers, mountains, valleys, estuaries. Often modern-day Portuguese place-names are translations of the original Tupi. There were signs of the continuing vivacity of this lingua franca along the forest frontier, possibly into the middle of the nineteenth century. Well might contemporary indigenous representatives claim legitimate rights to a land they named.[39]

Submerged native cultural elements were not necessarily marginal, merely picturesque, or irrelevant to the colonial dynamic of domination and extraction. It is hard to resist the impression, for example, that the bandeiras represented an adaptation of the Tupi predilection for military adventures. The historian Jaime Cortesão expressed a sort of admiration for the capacity of the Paulistas to bend the native cultures to their purposes, assuming that the immense effort expended on capturing and enslaving Guarani was an economically rational effort to supply the labor demands of the sugar and wheat plantations. When one considers how paltry was the output of wheat and sugar compared to the massive depredation of the labor pool, one wonders if the point of capturing remote tribal peoples may have been not to put them to work but to gain through the capture itself the same sort of honor that dynamized Tupi society. Indeed, one of the Jesuit chroniclers, referring to the late sixteenth century, said as much: The Paulistas "lived by kidnapping Indians, and the profession of assaulting them was taken for valor; and that was what men were esteemed for." This would help explain why estate owners in São Paulo referred to their native retainers not as tenants but as *frecheiros*—bowmen! This immersion in a native set of values would not be unexpected, considering how outnumbered in these militarized societies were the white captains and lieutenants, how Tupi were their mestizo sergeants, and how un-European behavioral norms must have been on the wilderness trails and battlefields.[40]

By contrast, the crown's insistence that the bandeiras look for precious metals and gemstones was not only ignored, it was, until quite late in the seventeenth century, actively resisted. The Mamelukes who guided a mining specialist sent by the governor in 1607 murdered him on their return to São Paulo and scattered his specimens. They had come to the sensible conclusion that, if gold were discovered, they would be enslaved along with their captives. Meanwhile, the work that male mestizos and indigenes were customarily put to seems to have been those activities that they were fond of or at least inured to—hunting for subsistence, making and handling dugout canoes, and attacking their enemies. Even their service as porters appealed to their exaltation of endurance and physical strength. Tupi males may have labored in the fields of the plantations, thus breaking down the sexual division of labor—but domestic farm labor continued to be carried out by women and children, and males may have been persuaded to participate in the canefields only by disguising this labor as a form of *moti-ro,* or *mutirão* in Brazilian Portuguese, a festive collective work event.[41]

Other ineradicable folkways of seventeenth- and eighteenth-century neo-European settlers appear curiously unlike those of their peninsular forebears: the repeated division and relocation of villages, caused frequently by dissension among the inhabitants; and the uncertainty of their locations—some town sites were moved and moved again as local woodlands were exhausted. The bouts of collective work, as useful as they were in extracting labor from natives, irritated colonial authorities, who found it popular among whites and mestizos as well and regarded it as sporadic and no more than an invitation to drunken disorder. One might also speculate that the tardy diffusion, in the Southeast, of the use of pack animals might have been due to indigenous cultural resistance, because the characteristics of native pasture and of slash-and-burn agriculture do not entirely explain the nearly total absence of beasts of burden in rural areas. The additional labor inputs that the keeping of such animals would have required was surely less than the additional labor that their absence implied. Perhaps it may be asserted, without imposing a geographical or technological determinism, that at some level these cultural survivals, so paradoxical in a colonial regime supposedly capable and determined to impose the elements it preferred, were related to the persistence of slash-and-burn farming and the introduction by the neo-Europeans of techniques to extend it and thus to a peculiar relationship to the Atlantic Forest, one that was to last for yet another two hundred years, almost as long as the forest was to last.[42]

By the end of a second century of the Portuguese invasion, the colonial enterprise installed on the edge of the Atlantic Forest had much intensified. The genocidal assault on tribal peoples had extended over a much wider area, and a broad swath of forest had been left nearly empty of human occupants. The survivors of these forest cultures now served as a captive underclass. An English adventurer observed in 1650 the effects wrought upon those he observed in the towns: "most like Asses, dull and phlegmatic, *in servitutem nati,* and only fit for toil and drudgery," he remarked contemptuously; "neither can I believe what is reported of their fierceness, though all that is reported of their ferity I do." The area of neo-European settlement had grown only modestly, devoted to the extraction of an exotic plantation crop, sugar, whose cost in slave lives and in native forest was astonishingly disproportionate to the product. Humans within the Portuguese-controlled sector of the Atlantic Forest may have numbered 300,000, of whom perhaps a third were of Portuguese origin. Perhaps 20,000 lived in towns. Rural density continued to be quite low, perhaps 5 per square kilometer on the coast and 2 per square kilometer in the Paulista highlands, a total area occupied by neo-Europeans and their subordinates of about 65,000 square kilometers. Most of this area had been subtracted from the Atlantic Forest, though some of it had already been cleared and burned repeatedly by Tupi agriculturists. There were four times more cattle than humans, most of them spread out into the interior savanna behind Recife and Salvador, occupying perhaps another 65,000 square kilometers, calculating one head to five hectares of grassland or savanna.[43]

More than a century and a half after the Portuguese invasion, the geography of the colony's interior was still mythical, its great rivers still imagined to originate in a single great lake, somewhere in the foothills of the Andes. In its forests, inhabited by Amazons, were locked treasures of emeralds and sapphires. The later bandeiras of the Paulistas ranged immense distances, toward the headwaters of the São Francisco, Paraguay, and Amazon rivers, in search not only of ever scarcer indigenes but now also of gold. Small amounts of the metal had been found in streams in the hills surrounding São Paulo. The colonial authorities were desperate to locate gold, which would rescue the Portuguese crown from the disastrous effects of the loss of the Asian colonies and the loss of much of the sugar market to the Caribbean. At last, in 1690, one of the bandeiras struck gold. Alluvial deposits were found far in the interior, along the Spiny Range, beneath a hill they called Itacolomi. The Atlantic Forest was now to undergo a widespread and permanent invasion. The greatest gold rush in history was about to begin.

5

Gold and Diamonds, Ants and Cattle

*Nenhuma outra coisa mais desejo senão, que os meus vassalos logrem as
utilidades que lhes podem fazer alcançar um feliz negôcio.*

*No other thing do I desire more, than that my vassals obtain the means
that may enable them to gain a fortunate business.*

KING AFONSO VI (1664)

The great eighteenth-century Brazilian gold and diamond strikes were the
most important ever found in the colonial New World. From 1700 to 1800
a million kilograms of gold were officially recorded, and perhaps another
million evaded the royal fisc. Some 2.4 million carats in diamonds were
extracted, according to official records, and some unknown and inestimable
additional quantity was smuggled. The impact of this bounty upon the
colony was immense. At last large numbers of Portuguese arrived, perhaps
450,000 over the course of the century, imparting to the colony a stronger
European cast. Local population and resources flowed to the gold-bearing
areas, which were well in the backlands, along the inland frontier of the
Atlantic Forest. The mining sector was affluent enough to afford African
slaves—indeed, to cause their prices to rise. Colonial dependence on African captives thereby increased, and Africans and their descendants came
to share preponderantly in the tasks of interpreting and destroying the
Atlantic Forest. Nearly all the extracted mineral wealth was exported,
mostly to Lisbon, where it shored up the power and stability of the crown,
increased investments in agriculture, industry, and trade, and reawakened
the cupidity of Portugal's more powerful neighbors.[1]

With the discovery of gold, Brazil became far more strategic to Lisbon,
as may be seen in the decision of 1720 to elevate it from the status of
a governor-generalship to that of a viceroyalty. Convinced at last of the
inefficacity of the inherited captaincies, the crown abolished all those remaining by 1759. The transfer of the viceregal seat from Salvador to Rio
de Janeiro in 1763 was a sign of the royal desire not only to enhance control over gold and diamond shipments, by then in worrying decline, but

also to challenge Spanish possession of the left bank of the River Plate. The capture, in 1714, of the Spanish throne by the French Bourbons caused British-oriented Portugal's relations with its neighbor to grow thereafter steadily more conflictive. At stake in their rivalry over the River Plate was the capture of the clandestine trade with the silver mine of Potosí, in present-day Bolivia, and the strengthening of the Portuguese hold on the gold workings of Mato Grosso. To accomplish these objectives, the Portuguese crown diverted considerable colonial resources to new border settlements in Rio Grande do Sul and Santa Catarina and to forts constructed along the Mamoré and Paraguay rivers.[2]

It was inevitable that more numerous inhabitants, more intense economic activity, heightened governmental vigilance, and European rivalry would affect the integrity of the Brazilian forests. These pressures were not reduced when gold and diamond output began to slacken by midcentury, partly because mining for a long time hardly abated in response to lessening productivity. As the miners finally lost hope and took up farming and animal husbandry, however, they extended their range farther and farther into the as yet untouched forest. The eighteenth century, then, represents the beginning of an irreversible and cumulative trend in the exploitation of the Atlantic Forest.

Traces of gold may have been found as early as 1555 in the area of São Vicente, encouraging the king to believe that his new colony might soon equal the value of the Spanish territories, so enviably endowed with mines of silver. Not until 1597, however, are there documentary evidences of gold extraction in that captaincy. Throughout the seventeenth century there were scattered gold workings at many points along the Serra do Mar. Signs of some of this activity were until recently visible at many places in the highlands southwest of the city of São Paulo, in the hills surrounding it, and on the coast between Iguape and the bay of Paranaguá. Many other workings are known only through vague reports, and it may be conjectured that still others left no documentation. The royal tax of 20 percent on precious metals was adequate reason to evade the fisc, which confronted a scattered, transient, and inaccessible industry. The quite modest scale of this first century of gold exploitation, hardly comparable with the mines of Potosí or Mexico, whetted the appetites of king and colonial elite but provided meager revenues.[3]

These gold workings were all alluvial, found easily at first in creek beds. The ubiquitousness of minor deposits of this kind, along the escarpments and landward side of the Serra do Mar, gave rise to a special sort of frontier

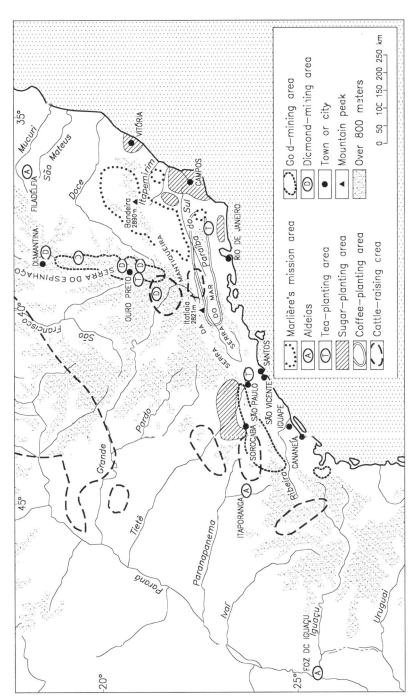

Map 4. The Southeastern Atlantic Forest, 1700–1850

penetration by prospectors, called *faiscadores* or *garimpeiros*. They specialized in their clandestine craft, and they acted most commonly in bands, for
mutual protection and survival, living partly off forest resources and
partly as slash-and-burn farmers. Prospecting was and remains to this day
widely engaged in, powerfully attractive to people who have been denied
the means of establishing land rights and for whom a single gram of gold
equals a week's wages. The illegality of prospecting and its extreme itinerancy suggest that these foragers did not much affect the forest, even
though that foraging population might have been as densely concentrated
as those of hunter-gatherers. Garimpeiros were careful to evade patrols or
would-be competitors, who would investigate the smoke of fires, the
mounds of refuse, and the sounds of domestic animals. The necessity for
self-sufficiency must have reawakened among them a curiosity concerning
forest resources, especially foodstuffs and medicinals. Nevertheless, prospecting, peculiarly focused on a single, nonrenewable, and abiotic resource,
was not an occupation likely to enhance appreciation of nature. Garimpeiros competed antagonistically with surviving tribal bands and with
frontier farmers, thereby limiting exchanges of information. Eventually,
however, many had to resign themselves to a farmer's life as the gold beds
played out.[4]

A few of the early goldfields were directly under government control,
notably the one opened sometime after 1608 by the first governor-general
of the southern captaincies and "administrator-general of mines," Francisco de Souza, on the great hill of Jaraguá that dominates the horizon
north of the city of São Paulo. Others in the region were exploited by
Jesuits. These workings benefited from the advice of contracted German
mining experts, like the one murdered by Mamelukes. Their principal innovation was the diversion of streams to wash alluvial beds. Royal
smelting houses were established to which it was required that all gold be
brought so that the "fifth" might be collected and the rest formed into bars
of certified weight. The works operated by the crown employed indigenous
captives as labor. Indeed, the prospect of golden riches caused the crown to
cast off all its scruples regarding the enslavement of indigenes. De Souza
rounded up 200 indigenes from Espírito Santo for his first venture in São
Paulo, and fifty years later another administrator of mines demanded that
the aldeias of São Paulo be scoured of their Indians to pan for gold at
Iguape. The king himself repeated this demand in 1664, requisitioning as
well, in behalf of the "fortunate business" of his vassals, the natives in
private households, to whom he referred unblinkingly as "your Indians."[5]

Having repeatedly stumbled across gold-bearing alluvia, the participants in the bandeiras were better prepared to recognize their signs when,

toward the end of the sixteenth century, they turned from slave raiding to officially encouraged gold exploration. Finally, in 1690, in territory a few hundred kilometers north of Rio de Janeiro that had already been criss-crossed by raiders who had returned repeatedly with tourmalines they took to be emeralds, the Paulistas discovered extremely promising gold deposits. Within a few years several very rich streams had been found, and by 1713 all the major strikes were already in operation. They were located in an arc along the Serra do Espinhaço from the modern city of Belo Horizonte to São João del Rei. Other scattered and lesser finds were made in Pernambuco, Sergipe, Bahia, and Espírito Santo. The date of the first discovery of diamonds is uncertain. These deposits, found farther to the north along the same ridge, centering on a town now called Diamantina, were brought to the attention of the king only in 1729, by which time several private fortunes had probably already been made.[6]

The attraction of gold and diamonds was so intense, in fact, that it took the crown a generation to impose a degree of authority in the region. The inflow of unruly and improvident prospectors from south and north caused starvation, epidemics, armed conflict, and, of course, the evasion of taxation and the diversion of much of the output to clandestinity. The government's overvaluation of its currency further stimulated this diversion. A smelting house was founded in Rio de Janeiro in 1702, but when, in 1719, it was proposed to set up another in Minas Gerais, a rebellion broke out that was repressed only with considerable force.

Nevertheless, the colonial authorities persevered. Town governments were set up, mining was more straitly confined to crown-awarded lease holdings; and the gold and diamond region, now known as Minas Gerais—general or widespread mines—was separated from the captaincy of São Paulo and its government lodged at Villa Rica de Ouro Preto—Rich Town of Black Gold. A smelting house began at last to operate in that town in 1726. A regiment was raised, to fight off interlopers as well as to control the miners. The port of Rio de Janeiro had twice to be defended against French pirates, and in the second assault, in 1711, the treasure was lost. The road from Rio de Janeiro to the mines was improved and embellished with toll gates, and stringent controls over residence and access were instituted. This last was an attempt to remove persons not directly engaged in mining so as to reduce smuggling, an impractical measure, because the remote mining district was constantly short of food and supplies. Military patrols, even though not very effective in interdicting the operations of garimpeiros or petty traders or the exit of contraband, nevertheless did hinder the penetration of new settlements farther east of the Serra do Espinhaço into the Atlantic Forest.[7]

At first, gold extraction was done by panning. Gangs of slaves were posted knee-deep in streambeds and set to scooping up gravel and water in flat, conical wooden basins, which they agitated and refilled until only the heavier gold flakes were left. It was Africans from the Gold Coast who showed their owners how to pan and who proved most adept at locating pay dirt. These workers commanded the highest prices because they were believed to be especially lucky or practicants of a gold-divining sort of witchcraft. Laborious and health-destroying panning—consider the pain of bare legs in cold water and bare back under scorching sun—by the 1730s was no longer profitable in many claims. Leaseholders turned to dredging larger streams with primitive scoops and diverting smaller streams in order to investigate their beds more thoroughly. That accomplished, placer mining was taken up—streams were turned against their banks. The degradation caused by mining was most intense in the gravelly floodplains and stream bottoms. It was remarked that the Sabará and Das Velhas rivers began to run muddy because of placer mining. Gold was also to be found on hillsides in certain kinds of clays, a meter or two deep, and in friable rock formations. On this kind of terrain, forest was burned down—a great deal of forest, enough in some places to eradicate swidden farming. Sometimes streams were played against hillsides, a technique called "carrying a hill in open cut," so as to wash down every clod of soil that might contain gold or to cause the collapse of a promising rocky outcropping. At Jaraguá, for example, steps about a meter deep were cut into the hillside, and diverted water was washed over them. Slaves muddled the mass that collected in a trench at the bottom, and the precipitates were carried by hand to another diverted stream, where they were panned out.[8]

Evidently these malign hydraulics required large amounts of freeflowing water, so that in the main they were attempted more readily on the east side of the Serra do Espinhaço; that is, the windward, forested face of the highlands, where rainfall was heavier and streams were larger and flowed year-round. In regions of pronounced dry season, where the forest was in the main deciduous, mining might be suspended until the rains returned. On the drier, leeward sides of hillsides, water was sometimes dammed, sometimes piped in, along aqueducts consisting of hollowed tree trunks. Some of these waterworks were quite ambitious—one extended for 48 kilometers. A few required tunneling as well as freestanding arches. It was therefore, as one contemporary claimed, "an axiom among these miners that a mountain of gold is worthless if there is no water"; and it appears that miners did avoid cutting down forest in the headwaters of streams they were exploiting—a rare conservation measure. Despite this preference for placer mining, in many places promising hillsides were "carried" *a seco*—that is, dry. This was a technique stupefyingly labor intensive: Shallow, funnel-shaped pits were dug by slaves who were provided neither wheelbarrows, carts, nor pickaxes. Fifty thousand to 100,000 baskets of earth might be carried off to obtain a single gold-bearing basket. One expert expressed his disappointment that such techniques were unable to shear away more than two meters of topsoil.[9]

A local savant, José Vieira Couto, surveying these depredations in 1799, considered the term "mines" quite inappropriate; he preferred the local term *lavras*—works. Oddly, the same word was applied to agriculture, *lavrar*—to farm—and *lavoura*—farming—an activity approximately as predatory in its methods and conception. Thus the very concept of work assumed the character of despoliation rather than that of production, construction, or conservation.[10]

The effect of this sort of mining was to replace forest with pockmarked moors. "On all sides we have under our eyes the distressing traces of the washings, of vast overturned terrain, and of mounds of gravel," reported the French botanist Auguste de Saint-Hilaire when he traveled the road north of Ouro Prêto in the second decade of the nineteenth century. Arriving at a valley "so somber, that compared to it the country through which we had just passed might be considered cheerful," he beheld hills covered with a grayish, sterile turf and, where the miners had stripped the earth of vegetation, a dark red smear of clay. A few years later, another botanist viewed a similar sight all along the road from São João del Rei to the camp of Santa Rita, a distance of about 15 kilometers: "a bald and deserted region, whose terrain is entirely overturned by excavations in the search for gold." These hills would at length receive a scraggly cover of *mata-pasto*—kill-pasture—and other tenacious weeds. Later, approaching Ouro Prêto along the Cocais ridge, he commented, "as far as the eye can see, the earth is turned over by human hands, so much has the dreamed-of profit excited the desire to work," and "wherever there is water, there is also a gold works." Alexander Caldcleugh, beholding another such area and "considering the many square leagues [he] had passed over," was astonished "that in so small a space of time as 120 years, there had been hands and industry sufficient to give the soil its present riddled appearance." The denudation of the hillsides caused sheet erosion, giant gullies—called *voçorocas*—silting of streambeds, and flooding that can still be found in the region but are by now so generalized and ancient as to appear to be natural features of the landscape.[11]

The area devastated by gold and diamond prospecting may be roughly estimated. Modern surveys of the region suggest that the Mineiros obtained perhaps a gram of gold from a cubic meter of gold-bearing material and overburden and that this layer averaged about 50 centimeters deep. Thus the total volume of gold obtained during the eighteenth century would have overturned 4,000 square kilometers of the Atlantic Forest region. This suggests the destruction of about 20 percent of the gold-bearing arc extending for 450 kilometers between Diamantina and Lavras, in a band that varied in width but averaged about 30 kilometers from the ridge line eastward and about 15 kilometers westward. The workings in that zone would have been concentrated along streambeds; thus the damage was done mostly to hygrophilic—that is, wet-seeking—plant associations. Along the inland slopes these would have been gallery forests, in some places the only local tree cover, in others the only nondeciduous cover available and hence a main defense against erosion and river siltation. This extensive intervention would have been easily accomplished by the available "hands and industry," because the gold and diamond work force must have averaged about 100,000, including garimpeiros, over the course of the century, so that each worker would have dug, sluiced, dredged, and panned a modest 200 cubic meters a year.[12]

The gold content of ores was commonly 21 to 22 carats, but ores of lower quality were baked with mercury. This source of pollution has not been investigated by historians or scientists. The amounts of mercury that may have been mined or imported and the amount that may have been employed and dispersed in the soils of this region of the Atlantic Forest over the course of a century are therefore conjectural but, judging from current very primitive practices in the Amazon, may have amounted to 100 tons, assuming no more than 10 percent of output was thus refined—with what effect on biota?[13]

The discovery of gold and diamonds greatly enlarged the neo-Afro-European population of the Atlantic Forest. By 1800 it totaled about 1,800,000, having multiplied six times over the course of the century, an annual gain of about 1.8 percent. In the mining region, half of the inhabitants were African slaves, and more than half of the remainder were persons of African or mixed African race. Meanwhile, the area within the neo-European pale did not grow proportionately. The neo-Afro-Europeans may have occupied by then 90,000 square kilometers of the southeastern segment of the Atlantic Forest, from Paranaguá to Caravelas. This represented a density of somewhat more than 10 persons per square kilometer, 2.5 times that estimated for 1700. In large measure this greater concentration can be attributed to the gold and diamond strikes. Official policy in the mining area discouraged the dispersal of settlements in order to prevent the evasion of gold, but more important must have been the diversion of about 40 percent of the labor force exclusively to mining. This mining-driven development of the internal market encouraged suppliers of food-stuffs, fuelwood, and handcrafts to concentrate near customers who settled their accounts in gold dust. Mining prosperity also permitted the growth of the parasitical primate city of Rio de Janeiro. By 1800 it was thronged with a population of perhaps 70,000—officials, soldiers, merchants, clerics, slaves, and hangers-on.[14]

Over the course of the eighteenth century, the requirements of the population of the mining region for foodstuffs, satisfied almost entirely by slash-and-burn farming, would have required on average the destruction each year of 600 square kilometers of forest. Much of this burning would have been repeated in secondary forest, convenient to towns and gold workings. The degradation of forest in these regions rendered swidden farming less and less viable, so that the densely populated zones came to be supplied from considerable distances. Ouro Prêto, for example, was provisioned largely by mule train from farms carved out of the ever-retreating forest, by 1800 as much as 100 kilometers distant. The higher density of population, however, encouraged the reduction of the interval between burning on farms in the vicinity of mines and the larger towns. This would have slowed the attack on primary forest, which otherwise might have lost two-thirds of its extent within the neo-European pale over the course of the century. However, secondary forest in these areas was thereby reduced to a quite immature phase of regrowth, and the likelihood was increased that it would not grow back at all. This modification, and the exploratory hydraulic and manual skimming of forest soils, suggests that eighteenth-century mining enterprise demanded much more of the Atlantic Forest than the first two centuries of subsistence farming and wheat and sugar plantations and that the degradation of much of the soil of the cleared areas was occurring to the point that the vegetation which grew back lacked many of the species that would have, in the absence of human interference, reconstituted the original forest.[15]

The itinerancy of slash-and-burn agriculture, once the despair of the missionaries, now became the target of the civil authorities, who saw in it the principal obstacle to the collection of taxes, to the increase of urban food supply, and, indeed, to the imposition of authority and social order. It was therefore one of the principal goals of the governor appointed to the captaincy of São Paulo in 1765, Luís Antônio de Souza Botelho, to impose village life upon its wandering and scandalously unsupervised inhabitants.

He created eighteen new towns and villages and offered generous incentives to settlers—tax exemptions, free tools, assumption of their debts, collection of sums owed them elsewhere for improvements—all in the hope that mestizos, acculturated indigenes, and mulattoes might be persuaded to "abandon the virgin forest" and take up "the plow and the cow"; that is, the stolidly fixed life of the Portuguese peasant. Indeed, under the authority of a royal order prohibiting settlements of fewer than fifty households, he ordered a certain amount of force applied to round up dwellers in "floating farmsteads" and would have used more had it been at his disposal.[16]

The governor sought to convert Paulista farmers to the use of the plow, a reform that would involve integrating draft animals and their manure into the cultivation of fields. The inhabitants had offered him their "universal opinion," however, that the soils of São Paulo were not suitable for plowing. This view he had come to realize—"in the light of a clearer and more careful experience"—was entirely false and justified only by the "negligence and laziness of the natives, and the facility with which the land sustains them at little cost." He therefore imported plows and experienced plowmen from Portugal to demonstrate this exotic technology, which might have transformed not only the productive regime but also the structure of society.

Pressure upon the Atlantic Forest would have greatly diminished had this reform been successful. But one can only imagine the incredulity of the mestizo horticulturalists when it was put to them that they should exchange a method of cultivation that interrupted their leisure for no more than 500 hours a year for another that would have burdened them with at least 2,000 hours of toil and was, in addition, unproven and unlikely to yield larger crops. It is not surprising that Souza Botelho's campaign proved no more successful than the missionary-led aldeias of the previous centuries. "All the fields around São Paulo," he wrote despairingly, "are without fruit, as are those of all the towns of the captaincy" because—and this is the phrase that immortalized his rule—they followed "the lure of the virgin forest." What was worse, "they abandon village dwelling and go after the forest, distancing themselves ever more from civil society, reduced to live sans mass or doctrine, becoming," in a phrase even more worthy of collective recollection, "familiars with the beasts."[17]

The governor sensed that colonial land policy had contributed to the preference for slash-and-burn. The excessive cost of land titles had placed them beyond the reach of mere cultivators and had concentrated them in the hands of court favorites. Small farmers were unable to regard their clearings as property, heritable or improvable. Furthermore, the sesmarias, awarded in immense tracts, encouraged itinerancy. Souza Botelho reasoned that if they were reduced in size to that which a peasant family might be expected to manage and if they were freely awarded, small farmers would accept the plow as a responsibility necessary to the maintenance of patrimony. The success of permanent agriculture also depended, he admitted, on the abolition of slavery, which had proved to be "the total perdition of this America." In these musings, Souza Botelho showed himself to be a committed collaborator of his superior, the marquis of Pombal, that enlightened despot whose ministry under José I, from 1750 to 1777, sought to make Brazil a more productive colony through accelerated assimilation, the introduction of European techniques, and the replication of European peasant society.

Souza Botelho well understood that Portuguese mercantilism and militarism contradicted his agricultural policies. His proposal to license textile factories that would have absorbed local cotton was turned down by Lisbon. He was directed instead to marshal the slender resources of the captaincy for the war in the south. He and his successors taxed small farmers voraciously, demanded labor to build forts, confiscated crops to feed the troops, and commandeered their houses for billets. Their tax farmers demanded payments in cash, while their treasurers delayed reimbursements for years. Worst of all, they impressed the householders' young men into military service. In his first two years in office, Souza Botelho conscripted almost 5,000 soldiers from an adult male population that could not have numbered more than 35,000. He also pursued for a decade a fruitless project largely his own, the fortification of Iguatemi, on the far-distant Paraguayan border. To that insalubrious and unpromising place he dispatched yearly convoys of hundreds of unwilling colonists up the Tietê River, to the increasing unease of his superiors, until finally, in 1777, a year after his dismissal from the governorship, Iguatemi was allowed to fall to the Spanish.[18]

Those who escaped the exactions of the authorities necessarily cut themselves off from intercourse with the towns. They also advanced into a forest utterly without security, to which fugitives from criminal justice had also fled and to which other criminals had been banished, a continuation of the judicial practice of banishment, thus converting the frontier into a sort of human dumping ground for degredados. Many of the expelled, however, were merely the unemployed of the towns. The governor of Minas Gerais impressed men accused of vagrancy into the militia and sent them to frontier posts, supposing it "more reasonable that the troop be composed of vagrants and miscreants than of hardworking men necessary for the cultivation of land." His successor, Antônio de Noronha, ordered convicts jailed in Ouro Prêto to choose *farda ou foice*—uniform or sickle—that is, to join a military levy to Rio Grande do Sul or his colonization scheme along the Doce River. The official designation of *vadio, vagamundo*—vagrant, vagabond—was laden with a special poignancy in that, by attaching a criminal penalty to a lack of employment, it relegated all the poor to a potential criminal state and obscured the evident origin of joblessness in the land monopoly that the government itself ratified. Nor did those expelled from the towns cease to be considered vagrants because they were obliged to squat on private or crown lands.[19]

The backwoodsmen entered an Atlantic Forest grown more luxuriant during the two centuries that human population had nearly disappeared in the interior. Along the eastern frontier of the gold-mining zone, as far as the seacoast, a distance of more than 200 kilometers, and northeastward from the diamond district, another 400 kilometers down the Jequitinhonha River, subsistence farmers could lay waste to undisturbed forest to form their fields of maize and manioc. In São Paulo there stretched beyond the seventeenth-century hamlets of Itu, Jundiaí, and Taubaté vast tracts of forest, and itinerant farmsteads were cleared where now stand the cities of Piracicaba, Botucatu, Rio Claro, and others, at the time beyond the reach of the governor's recruiting agents or tax collectors. Other subsistence farmers, occasional prospectors for gold as well, occupied the hilly lowlands southwest of São Paulo that were watered by the Ribeira River. All these racially mixed backlanders were coming to form a culture distinct from the Portuguese-controlled towns. Townspeople called them, disdainfully, *caboclos* or *caipiras*. Significantly, these are Tupi pejoratives, whose most likely meanings are, respectively, dwellers in a white man's house and fellers of forest.[20]

The forest frontier had also grown less hospitable to humans. Although mosquito-borne diseases of the Old World tropics may have been transferred very soon after first contact, sixteenth-century chroniclers continued to praise Brazil's "good airs," and it is only in the eighteenth century that references to *maleitas*—malaria and yellow fever—became frequent, indeed innumerable. By then the former had become endemic, as the slave traffic intensified and the rural population became more dense. Expeditions on the Tietê River had become perilous by 1800—on one expedition all the white and native crewmen were struck down by it. Malaria, introduced by the slave traffic, ironically stimulated its continuation because the Africans alone resisted its onslaught. Yellow fever was probably becoming endemic as well among primate populations, as infected mosquitoes bred in the bromeliad cups of the canopy, with unknowable influences upon the distribution of these animals and on forest composition and plant dispersal. These exotic scourges provoked contradictory reactions. On one hand, certain regions—the upper São Mateus valley, for example—acquired especially baleful reputations as malarial and were consequently long free of human occupation. On the other hand, it came to be the general belief that fevers emanated not only from swamps but also from the forest, so that much clearing came wrongheadedly to be carried out merely to *espantar as febres*—scare off the fevers.[21]

Into the same diffuse frontier entered escaped African slaves, who often formed and maintained independent communities, called *quilombos*, a word from the Kimbundu language meaning union or assembly. These settlements appeared in the highlands of Rio de Janeiro soon after the African slave traffic began there. In Minas Gerais, where the immensity of the forest beyond the pale made possible constant fresh escapes, new quilombos sprang up everywhere, often reappearing on the same sites. Today at least 20 populated places in Minas Gerais and numerous natural features still bear the name quilombo. The largest of them, occupying an area equivalent to more than 20 sesmarias, or 860 square kilometers, was Campo Grande, near the River Grande, in the municipality of Ibiá. In the mining region quilombo dwellers prospected quite successfully for gold and diamonds—thereby sustaining a powerful means of trade with the white-controlled cities.

Quilombos excited fear and anger among plantation owners and city dwellers, who soon hired slave catchers. By the mid-1860s, the professional *capitao do mato*—captain of the forest—mounted expeditions of a hundred or more slave catchers to destroy quilombos in the Rio de Janeiro highlands. On one occasion, the captains negotiated a reward scaled to the intensity of the planters' panic: two-thirds of the value of captives, excepting only the ringleaders, who were hung, and the children born free in the settlement. Early in the gold rush the authorities attempted to form aldeias—barracks, really—to recruit as militia against the quilombos, but the natives proved too scattered and wary. Unemployed town "vagrants" were then dragooned for the purpose.[22]

These same regions contained a few remnant native populations that had long before retreated inland. The expansion of the gold-mining frontier forced some of them to withdraw still farther. East of the Tietê, along the Paraná River, the Caiapó, a warlike tribe that may have continued to practice cannibalism, gathered in numbers sufficient to hold that bank against the neo-Europeans for a whole century. There they exploited the resources of the gallery forests that were the extreme limit of the Atlantic Forest and they farmed, incorporating bananas, rice, and chickens in their diet. Less numerous or aggressive groups were pushed toward the coast of Rio de Janeiro, Espírito Santo, and Bahia, where they came in conflict with other indigenous groups like the Caiapó or with mestizo backlanders. The wanderings of these groups now ended frequently in the acceptance of "reduction" into aldeias. As long as the Portuguese maintained the policy of isolating the gold region in order to lessen smuggling, the wilderness eastward toward the coast remained a safe haven. Within this region, the Goitacases, long before driven from the Campos area, defeated and absorbed the Coropós and then defended themselves against other invading groups. They remained on the lower Paraíba River for a considerable period, trading in honey, live birds, and clay pots. These survivors were often of the Gê language group—those whom the Tupi had dispossessed long before. Neo-European fear of the indigenes had largely turned to contempt. They called the Gê speakers *Botocudos*—a reference to the lip plugs worn by some—*Coroados*—referring to the tonsures worn by others—or simply *bugres*—a generic pejorative suggesting a status less than human and implying as well a degree of "detribalization," as the historian Mário Neme suggested, that rendered them featureless to the indifferent whites.[23]

Pombal was determined to acculturate these wanderers more quickly. In 1755 the enslavement of indigenes, the principal hindrance to this end, was once again declared illegal. Pombal also abolished legal discrimination against whites who married natives. Indeed, they were to be preferred in government employ and in granting land. He also forbade use of the pejorative term caboclo. Yet acculturation remained as problematic as it had been in the century of the bandeiras. Disease continued to destroy those who chose to cease resistance and enter the aldeias. The Jesuits, whose insubordination, untaxable wealth, and persistence in catechizing in the "barbaric" Tupi language, had angered Pombal, he expelled in 1759. Their successors were mostly Franciscans, missionaries authorized by their provincial to apply the lash and the stocks for every sort of infraction. The natives soon deserted, as indeed they had often done under the Jesuits. Constant pressure upon the aldeias by land-hungry settlers, by gold prospectors, and even by crown officials seeking their labor as porters, builders, or soldiers, also laid waste to many of them. "Thus," lamented Joaquim Norberto de Souza e Silva, a chronicler of the Rio de Janeiro aldeias, with eery ecological insight, "withered on native soil the indigenous plants uprooted in the shadows of their forests, while in them grow and prosper exotic plants." Indeed, he noted that, in aldeias on navigable streams, commercial logging for the Rio de Janeiro market did away with the shadows as well, depriving its native inhabitants of the last of their customary resources. Despite these depredations, a few aldeias persisted along the coast of Espírito Santo and Rio de Janeiro, and a few more were established in association with military garrisons on the eastern flank of the gold-mining region.[24]

The incorporation of indigenes was less violent along the caboclo frontier. The concept of caboclo now stood for a more complex cultural and racial mixture, with the addition of escaped African slaves, and their offspring by mestizos and natives, sometimes separately categorized as *cafusos* or *caburés*, the former possibly a Kimbundu term meaning defective, the latter another Tupi word, that for a small, brown forest owl. (Note how the languages of the subordinate peoples remained lively enough to characterize emerging social relations, encoding meanings that are by now long lost to the compilers of Brazilian dictionaries.) Cultural as well as genetic interchange took place among them: Caboclos were more successful than governors or missionaries in converting roving indigenes to neo-European customs or, more accurately, an Africanized version thereof, because they exchanged labor rather than demanding it. There is evidence, as well, that escaped slaves introduced the use of Portuguese among them. Indeed, at least one quilombo, that of Piolho, was officially tolerated in recognition of its function as a pacifier of neighboring tribes. "A fugitive black can accomplish more among the Indians than all the missionaries together—this has been proven since the discovery," commented Guido Thomaz Marlière, the most successful of the army's frontier agents. Whites considered this an unacceptable solution. In 1771 the viceroy stripped José Dias Quaresma, an indigene, of his patent of captain-major of an aldeia because he had married an African woman. The memorialist Joaquim Norberto de Souza e Silva, reporting this event eighty years later, heaped invective on Quaresma for this "scandal," emblematic of a life "entirely contaminated by vices."[25]

In some places near neo-European villages, indigenes were to be found taking up slash-and-burn farming, a sign that they were free of pressure from slaving expeditions and that some forms of peaceful interchange had been restored. Towns newly founded by Souza Botelho listed among their first settlers numerous natives, complacently identified as Guarani—a group still regarded as culturally superior to all the rest—and not as unworthy bugres. Meanwhile, the situation of many indigenes who had been captured as slaves was tending toward that of the peasant retainer, as may be seen in wills of the 1760s in Mogi-Mirim. There, natives described euphemistically as *administrados* were coming to be called *agregados*—

attached persons—suggesting a relationship that might include kinship or sharing of bed and board. The term was coming to be applied to persons in separate households but resident on another's land and therefore dependents, but not yet employees, because the implicit condition of their residence was generally the provision of occasional services, not steady labor, even though those services might be as onerous as the murdering of the landlord's enemies. This form of incorporation was indeed close to Pombal's ideal, with the natives assimilated—yet dispossessed. Thus the census also lists other natives, neither administrados nor agregados, as "without goods" and then, as though by way of explanation, as "red people, or Indians."[26]

Cultural exchange along the caboclo frontier followed curious paths, but it was evidently consequential. The botanist Johann Emanuel Pohl was entertained on a remote estate on the headwaters of the Jequitinhonha by African slaves playing on native trumpets, in so accomplished a fashion that he thought himself transported back to an Amazon village. Escaped slaves learned from the natives and taught them, in turn, magical and religious practices, hunting and fishing techniques, and remedies for snakebites, wounds, and illnesses. Shamanistic elements were incorporated in African religious ritual: the imbibing of the juice of jurema (*Pithecellobium tortum*), a hallucinogenic, for example. Another valuable acquisition was amansa-senhor—tame-the-master—some species of leadwort that acted as a soporific. Current Afro-Brazilian ritual has almost completely substituted native for African plant species. These shards of evidence suggest a reconstitution of some small part of forest knowledge that had been lost during the century of genocidal slave-raiding.[27]

Unfortunately, Africans, caboclos, and even many of the indigenes were all refugees on alien ground, and it is doubtful that they had retained intact the information their ancestors had accumulated. Collectively, however, their influence on the neo-European pale was strong. Portuguese continued to be enriched with Tupi names for plants and animals, and in the mining zone indigenous place-names continued to be applied. Hundreds of them survived, despite official efforts to substitute Lusitanian toponymy. Africanisms were applied to a few place-names and to geographical features (*murundu*—hill; *cafundó*—narrow pass), and the Portuguese received from them the vulgar names of a few common native species (*camundongo*—mouse; *caxinguelê*—another small rodent; *gongolô*—millipede; *marimbondo*—wasp). Brazilian Portuguese accepted a Kimbundu word even for the colony's most staple food (*fubá*—maize meal). Frontier hunting techniques can be seen to have been infused with indigenous beliefs regarding the guardian spirits of the forest. Caboclo hunters stripped off their clothing when they went hunting, apparently out of a sense that neo-European garb was offensive to the spirits or diminished their identity with their prey.[28]

The oppressiveness of colonial government was evidently self-defeating. Small farmers would not take up fixed abodes as long as proximity to authority subjected them to confiscation of their surpluses and their sons. Official malfeasance in the bestowal of land titles was certainly to blame for the "makeshift" appearance noted in Minas Gerais by John Mawe, who was unwittingly perspicacious in remarking that the farmers acted "as if the tenure by which they held their lands was about to be abolished." The white population refrained from providing any practical examples of intensive farming. At stake was the immigrant desire to overcome social disabilities in the more fluid setting of the colony. To preserve their eligibility for civil-service occupations, they eschewed all forms of manual labor. Many newly arrived Portuguese, eager to improve their station, "even though they were raised with a hoe in their hand," one governor complained, would no longer work "from the moment they set foot in Brazil" and, "if God gives them no more licit means of occupying their lives, they are wont to support themselves with thefts and fraud." The tendency of observers themselves exempt from picking up the hoe to characterize rural dwellers as indolent must be interpreted in the light of these petty struggles.[29]

Imagine, however, a different society in which none of these social and political arrangements existed. Would subsistence farmers have adopted more intensive methods? Even a just society would have confronted material, ecological obstacles to the use of the plow. The most daunting obstacle to agriculture, shaping its practice—indeed shaping an entire culture and restraining its development—was the competition presented by innumerable pests and plagues. The marvelous diversity of the Atlantic Forest included a remarkable array of invasive creatures eager to appropriate the harvests of the disturbed zones that were the farmers' burned clearings. The natural cycles of the forest permitted the occasional swarming of animals—rodents, for example, which multiplied prodigiously when bamboo fruited and, when the bamboo was exhausted, turned to field crops and stored maize. These were undoubtedly seasons of hunger for humans. Along with numerous species of rodents were numberless sorts of birds that were fanciers of fruits and grains.[30]

Infinitely more varied were the insects, of which by far the most relentless and frustrating were the leaf-cutting ants, called by the Tupi *saúva*.

Indeed, for native farmers these pests were the single most significant limiting factor: None of their staples was immune. The chronicler Gabriel Soares de Souza was in 1587 the first European to register the invaders' astonishment at the voracity of these ants. Capable of stripping a field of manioc in a night or two, invulnerable to any countermeasures, the leaf-cutters also severely hindered the transfer of European and African agricultural regimes.[31]

Soares de Souza's judgment on the leaf-cutters was also a lament for the colony of settlement: "If it weren't for them, many parts of Spain [Portugal was then united with the Spanish crown], would be emptied in order to populate Brazil, for everything that one might want will grow in it, but this damnation prevents it, so that men lose their taste for planting any more than they must in order to survive on the land." An accurate assessment, this—if an effective means had existed, during Brazil's first 450 years, to combat saúva, its agriculture, and consequently its history, would have been very different. That an insect can deflect human designs is an abhorrent idea, surely more abhorrent than the pest itself, because it questions the hegemony of our species. Yet consider the evidence.[32]

The ant genus *Atta* is extremely successful—it has spread throughout the New World tropics and semitropics. At least five of its species inhabit the region of the Atlantic Forest. Its success is due to an extraordinary adaptation: The ants consume exclusively a fungus, which they cultivate, in underground burrows. The fungus must be fed fresh leaves, which they harvest on the surface. Ant society is composed of large, strong-jawed soldiers, middling-sized cutters and gatherers, tiny fungus gardeners, and winged, sexual forms—the ephemeral male, which dies after mating, and the female, which immediately digs into the earth to give birth to the new colony. The ants' burrows are visible on the surface as mounds five to eight meters across, raised a half meter or so above the surrounding terrain. The position of the burrows may be off to one side of the mounds, and they may be much larger than the mounds themselves. Their entrances may be a hundred or more meters distant. The burrows penetrate as far as the water table; indeed, they may be 20 or 25 meters deep. Marvelously engineered to provide security and drainage, they form a bewildering network of passageways linking chambers wherein grow the grey, stringy shapeless fungal masses, kept at optimal humidity by the ants' choice of leaves of appropriate moisture content and by their careful wallpapering of the chambers with more foliage.[33]

In the forest, undulating files of saúva are occasionally to be seen, each one toting a snippet of leaf like a miniature parasol. In primary forest, however, the ants are but one of innumerable competing species, and their populations are contained. They are more common in regrown, immature forest and on bare ground. On ground that has been farmed for several seasons or has been turned over to pasture, ant colonies gradually increase in number as repeated burning drives away ant predators. The initial colonies dig deeper and deeper into the soil, multiplying chambers and extending their radius, and offshoot colonies form on unoccupied patches. Within five years an eighth of the area of a pasture may be covered by mounds. By that stage the lament of Toledo Rendon, an acute eighteenth-century colonial official, that the ants ate more grass than the cattle, might be approximately correct.[34]

Some plants have evolved a defense against *Atta*: their leaves contain substances toxic to the fungus. The ants will not cut leaves containing them, and even when such leaves are deposited at their entrances they refuse to drag them into their lairs. Unfortunately for humans, very few of the plants they had domesticated were to any degree repellent to saúva—quite the contrary—and hundreds of years of selection have yet to result in resistant plant varieties. In some locales, one plant or another will be rejected by the ants, but the reasons for this behavior are never clear. Almost nothing is known of the parasites and pests that contain *Atta* populations in undisturbed forest (and that may be reason enough to preserve it for study!). Observation is difficult—most of the leaf cutting is nocturnal—and of course the ants' habitat is subterranean. Indeed, that the purpose of the leaf cutting was to feed fungi was discovered hardly more than a century ago.

Of creatures that might be marshaled against the ants, few are persistent. Anteaters avoid leaf-cutters, unfortunately. Although other insects, most notably another ant, the cuiabana, have been unleashed against them by amateur improvers, they have all proved reluctant to confront *Atta's* soldiers when other prey is available. Only at one moment are the ants entirely vulnerable to enemies—when the winged sexual forms emerge above ground in spring, quickly to mate and burrow into the earth to form the new colonies. Then they are attacked by numerous predators—birds, lizards, frogs, and other insects, including other colonies of territorially defensive saúva, and by humans themselves. The thorax of the female ant, called *içá* or *tanajura*, was—and is—considered a delicacy, even an aphrodisiac, among mestizo country people. Unfortunately, it was a dish disdained by neo-European city dwellers and thus not marketable.[35]

Human countermeasures, until the twentieth century, were largely unavailing. The ants refused bait that might harm their fungal gardens. Detecting the location of immature nests only recently and still superficially buried in the soil was very difficult, and unearthing them was an excruciating task—the soldiers bit ferociously, and farmers, equipped only with hoes, were usually barefoot. Once the burrows were mature, their extraordinary depth rendered even the deepest hoeing or plowing ineffective. Colonial farmers tried to flood the burrows, generally unsuccessfully, because the tunnels were constructed so as to drain off rainwater. They tried to smoke them out by burning the leaves of plants that they had observed were refused by the ants. This was laborious and slow-acting and largely ineffectual, even with bellows, because the smoke could not reach the deepest chambers. As farmed areas spread and human destruction of the habitats of ant predators—birds, lizards, and frogs—intensified, so did infestation by saúva. In a sense, however, destruction of the saúva, to the extent that it was possible, was self-defeating, because the ants were certainly performing a herculean task of improving the mechanical qualities of the soil and transporting nutrients. A mature colony can churn up enough soil each year to cover a hectare to a depth of two centimeters.[36]

A lucky farmer might plant in a locale whose conditions disadvantaged the leaf-cutters for some undefinable reason, but the only environmental characteristics that were generally unfavorable to the ants were sandy soil or low, wet soil. *Atta* avoided wet land, because high water tables prevented them from deepening their burrows. This explains the concentration of agricultural and pastoral activities in the soggy Campos region and on the plain of Santa Cruz. It also explains why planting crops on river islands and floodplains—evidently advantageous, because the streams were nutrient laden—could be carried on permanently.[37]

The only other effective evasive maneuver was to cede old fields to the leaf-cutters and burn new patches of mature forest. As Soares de Souza noted, "in new clearings there are no ants to do damage to anything." The farmer could rely on an interval of two or three years of tranquil harvests before the ants appeared in large numbers. All the colonial observers of farming agree that the ubiquity of the leaf-cutters, their aggressiveness, and their resistance to any countermeasure that farmers were then able to devise or apply were a major cause of the persistence of swidden agriculture. Baltasar da Silva Lisboa, an energetic and knowledgeable colonial official who was for a long while the conservator of the forests of southern Bahia, complained of the ants, "which multiply in an astonishing manner; and the inhabitants, unable to extinguish them, turn to devastating the neighboring forests, whose soils turn equally sterile, becoming habitations of these most terrible enemies of agriculture." Silva Lisboa was inclined to believe that the farmers, who took no measures against the ants, were "indolent," yet the only measure he proposed, the introduction of sulphate of arsenic at the entrances of the tunnels, was certainly of slight effect.[38]

What would Brazilian agriculture have been like, if there had been no saúva? Would it not have attracted more European colonists, as Soares de Souza supposed? Would the attack on the Atlantic Forest have proceeded so rapidly? Slash-and-burn farming might still have continued because it would have remained the least laborious technique, but cleared fields would have had more value as pasture and arable, and the incentive to install more productive techniques, including the plow, would have been much greater. Instead, the presence of the leaf-cutters confirmed the impermanence of settlement inherent in slash-and-burn and intensified the "lure of the virgin forest."

The gold and diamond miners ate beef. Beef was the preferred source of protein in the neo-European diet, and the growth of a cash market caused cattle prices to rise and many a subsistence farmer to shift to ranching. Cattle converted and stored protein conveniently for the consumption of town populations. They could be raised on the frontier of settlement, where the land was cheapest and the grasses most nutritious, and then herded to market. Cattle raising therefore spread as far as the grasslands extending southwestward from the town of São Paulo and broadening into the Guarapuava plains, on the plateau west of the towns of Paranaguá and Curitiba. Although cattle could be driven immense distances over trackless prairie, the mining districts came to rely for their supply mainly on the savannas west of the Serra do Espinhaço and on those extensive and possibly anthropogenic patches of grasslands stretching along the north side of the Serra da Mantiqueira. To prevent the abandonment of the militarized settlements newly placed in Rio Grande do Sul to strengthen Portuguese claims, the crown reserved to that region a monopoly in the breeding of mules. Mule and horse drives thus became the main commercial link of the southern captaincies with São Paulo and Minas Gerais.[39]

On the unfenced range, cattle bred as they would. Those that survived were those that had stood off jaguars and had resisted the diseases and rigors of the shelterless plain. These "breeds"—curraleira, caracu, junqueira, crioula—offered no advantages to their human predators except rusticity; that is, they needed no human intervention to maintain their numbers. Intervention, in fact, was limited to yearly corralling for the purpose of castrating and branding. In some regions even this latter formality was omitted. Ranchers provided no fodder, so the dry season witnessed severe cattle mortality, and the survivors required several years to achieve market weight. The only dietary supplement provided the animals was salt. This nutrient, scarce in highland soils, was found in low concentrations in *barreiros*—dried lakebeds and riverbanks. There the cattle, in company with salt-famished wildlife, gouged slimy troughs with their tongues, an effect, according to one observer, very like that produced by surface scraping for gold. The crown found salt a convenient commodity from which to extract revenue. It declared a monopoly in its importation and sale, taxing it by weight on toll roads and closing down competing coastal salt pans at Cape Frio. Until the abolition of this vexatious regime in 1801, salt was only inadequately and intermittently provided to cattle, and salt-preserved meats and dairy products remained unnecessarily expensive.[40]

Cattle were vulnerable to vampire bats, to gadflies, and to the larvae that invaded the wounds they caused. Indirectly, the flies were another cause of forest encroachment. To escape them, cattle and horses habitually invaded forest margins, trampling their own clearings and transporting grass seeds in their hooves. The animals' principal scourge was ticks, ubiquitous in the grasslands, against which ranchers mounted no defense. Cattle suffered many kinds of intestinal parasites, some of which the first levies of the animals had no doubt brought with them from Portugal. The introduction of animal exotics was never as advantageous as that of plants. Because live animals, unlike seeds, inevitably brought their parasites with them, biotic escape had not been complete.[41]

The appearance of cattle on native grasslands and savannas was botanically a momentous event. The earliest observers "told marvels" about the pastures—how lush was the growth of the grasses and how quickly the cattle fattened on them. But a generation or two of grazing by a single species was enough to transform these edenic landscapes. Untended, cattle tended to overgraze the most palatable grasses, so that fields grew back in scrubby, noxious plants.

Against this transformation, ranchers had only one weapon, fire, which they applied unmercifully. Because grasses grew quickly with the spring rains, at a time when the cattle to consume them were fewest, the pastures were burned, to avoid the development of unpalatable woody growth. Burning was then commonly repeated over the course of the year, whenever grasses again grew tall and fibrous or when cattle ticks became too bothersome. Burning destroyed small animals—rodents, reptiles, armadillos, anteaters, insects, and ground-nesting birds—turning the prairies into a desert. Burning reduced inedible plant matter to ashes, thereby temporarily enriching the soil, if rain soon followed. But burning subtly damages soils and grasses. It destroys plants that spread horizontally to form mats, while it favors those that build tussocks, thus exposing bare ground, which causes erosion. Fire reduces soil permeability, thereby favoring plants that have superficial roots, less effective in recycling leached minerals and more quickly parched and inedible in the dry season. Saúva invade as these soils dry up, undertaking the unappreciated task of revolving their organic matter.

Burning, furthermore, removes soil nitrogen and soil bacteria that participate in nitrogen fixation, essential to animal nutrition. Degraded pasture then fills with ferns, with the weedy *sapé* grass, whose name was the Tupi for firebrand, and with *barba-de-bode*—goat's beard—another nutritionally valueless Graminea that exudes chemical defenses against competing plants and that, ironically, offers a habitat to ticks. Worse yet is the invasion of the pasture by innumerable poisonous plants that cattle, normally wary, will eat when famished. As the carrying capacity of pastures declined, the animals took more time to reach maturity. Herders, choosing among them the largest animals for slaughter, exercised a negative selective pressure, so that the breeds, such as they were, tended to degenerate.[42]

The deterioration of native pasture caused it to become, paradoxically, a scarce commodity. Therefore cattle spread out over forest land that had been farmed and was abandoned. These pastures were often called artificial, suggesting that they were planted to selected grasses, but that was never the case in the eighteenth century and was rare in the nineteenth. They were, instead, populated by whatever invasive native grasses found degraded farmland congenial. Exceptionally, grasses were sometimes planted on pasture near the cities and towns that were destinations of the cattle drives. Intended to fatten for market the cattle left lean by the exertions of the trail, these *invernadas*—wintering grounds—were often located where the available array of invasive weeds was entirely lacking in nutritional value. Near Rio de Janeiro and at points along the cattle trails, the scarcity of pasture was insistent enough to dictate the burning of forest, even primary forest, skipping the intermediate farming stage entirely.

Sometime in the eighteenth century, African grasses appeared in the invernadas and hayfields reserved for horse fodder near the city of Rio de Janeiro. They may have been introduced to the region of the Atlantic Forest in the straw bedding of slave ships. Guinea grass, pará grass, molasses grass, and jaraguá grass are species that in Africa occupy disturbed forest margins. For a century their African origin was obscure; indeed, it was in Brazil that they were first collected and classified by botanists. These accidental transfers continued, so that, by the late twentieth century, more than forty species of African grasses have been encountered in Brazilian pastures. Coevolved with grazing animals and companions of fire-wielding humans for a million years, they proved both palatable to cattle and fire resistant.[43]

Once arrived and acclimatized, these grasses were sometimes spread deliberately. Thus molasses grass was for a time called "Brother Luis's grass" in parts of Minas Gerais, in memory of a clerical benefactor. It is likely, however, that cattle themselves were the most common agent of dispersal. The African grasses were welcomed as more effective competitors with weeds on fire-managed pastures, but they were in fact a disappointing substitute. Compared to the varied native grasslands, pastures filled with a single exotic grass did not provide a balanced regime of amino acids and micronutrients. Deficiency diseases became common among cattle, especially in the dry season, when the grasses ceased extracting minerals from the soil. Some of the African introductions soon became an annoying presence in farmlands cleared from secondary-growth forests and therefore were another factor encouraging their abandonment to cattle. Still worse, some of these grasses were capable of invading areas of native campo, riverbanks, and even the forest itself.[44]

The cattle regime was remarkably unproductive. Degraded native and converted pasture permitted only a very thin cattle population, probably no more than one head for every 2 to 5 hectares. Worse, high mortality and slow growth to maturity prevented the rancher from bringing more than a tenth of his animals to market each year. At maturity, in 4 to 5 years, carcasses weighed 100 kilograms or less, so cattle raising provided at most 5 kilograms of meat per hectare per year—certainly less than hunter-gatherers could obtain on the same area left in native grasses or forest. Nevertheless, cattle raising grew to large proportions during the eighteenth century. In 1808, a year in which ranchers, encouraged by free trade, may have sold off an unusually large share of their herds, Rio de Janeiro exported 450,000 hides. This quantity suggests the exploitation of at least 36,000 square kilometers of grassland.[45]

The response of cattle raisers to the long-run tendency of range and animals to degenerate was ever to expand into new range, where there would be "neither weeds nor anything else that might kill the cattle." Thus cattle raising became approximately as itinerant as agriculture and, like agriculture, depended for its productivity on the degradation of primary ecosystems. Cattle raising, permanently extensive and expansive, everywhere prevented the reversion of abandoned farms to forest. Furthermore, the continual and aggressive use of fire presented a constant danger to forest margins, and in the dry season or during droughts it imperiled the forests themselves. Very likely they were a greater hazard than fires set by hunter-gatherers or by swidden farmers, because they were more frequent and on a much grander scale. It is no wonder that the geographer James J. Parsons believed that in the American tropics it was cattle raising, not agriculture, that represented the final, permanent result of human ecosystem transformation and that farming was merely an intermediate and temporary stage.[46]

The third century of the European invasion of the Atlantic Forest can be seen to have reduced considerably its extent. Mining, farming, and cattle fattening in the Southeast may have eliminated during the 1700s another 30,000 square kilometers of it. So broad, complete, and irreversible had forest removal in Minas Gerais extended during the eighteenth century that Karl Friedrich Philipp von Martius, the most distinguished of the botanists admitted to Brazil in the 1810s, was led to suppose that the gold and diamond region, southwestern Minas Gerais, and the region northeast of the city of São Paulo had never been forested but were natural grasslands. Von Martius failed to consult the rural folk, who made a clear distinction between natural campos and cleared forest land; his error continued to be repeated by European biogeographers a century later.[47]

A remarkable aspect of this expansion is that the rewards of these extraordinarily wasteful forms of natural resource exploitation had been for the neo-Europeans as exiguous as the waste had been immense. Thomas Lindley, visiting the coast near Porto Seguro in 1802, was astounded that "in a country which, with cultivation and industry, would abound with the blessings of nature to excess, the greater part of the people exist in want and poverty, while even the small remainder know not those enjoyments which make life desirable." Unaware of the ravages of internal parasites and fevers, he complained unjustly of the inhabitants' apathy and unnerving indolence. John Mawe, a sympathetic and curious observer, remarked wonderingly of Minas Gerais in 1812 that even families of means, possessing dozens of slaves, were usually to be found living "in the most wretched hovel that imagination can describe"—wattle and daub, dirt floors, with holes in the wall for windows, furnished with no more than a few plates and cups and sticks of furniture, with pigs their constant household attendants. Mawe supposed that slavery had taught the neo-Europeans to consider "all occupations servile" save gold mining, by then nearly futile, not imagining that their ancestors had arrived with that idea already fixed in their heads.[48]

Abysmal living standards in resource-rich Brazil astonished visiting Europeans, who were used to extracting much higher returns from a miserly menu of resources. The fall from riches to rags had evidently been vertiginous. What was the rationality of destroying forest resources to achieve so meager a result? Clearly, the forest had not been transformed into capital, at least not into capital locally accumulated. The government offices, forts, churches, and convents of Rio de Janeiro and the mining zone and a single unpaved highway connecting them were all of substance that can be said to have resulted from this century of exertion, which sacrificed so many lives and so much forest.

Of course, the point was to accumulate capital not in the colony but in the metropolis. Perhaps a survey of a century of improvements in the capital stock of Portugal would provide justification for the waste of resources that the Atlantic Forest had suffered, but that seems doubtful. Did some significant proportion of Britain's growing wealth derive from its evidently asymmetrical trade relations with Portugal, its financing of Portugal's colonial trade, and its resultant extraction of much of the coveted gold? If it did, then Mawe was observing the consequences of a relationship, rather than a contrast between two separate spheres, and the fruitlessness of the destruction of the forest may then be ascribed, as many have, to colonialism and to capitalism. The convenience of this explanation and the appeal it makes to a universal sense of justice may be all that is necessary to convince. Yet there is much evidence that regal authority was obeyed only when it suited the colonists. Colonial authorities, indeed, appear not infrequently more enlightened and progressive than their charges in regard to the exploitation of nature. There are other historical examples, furthermore, to show that colonies are not necessarily condemned to levels of capital formation lower than their metropoles, and resistance to the demands of imperialism may well be regarded as a historical dynamic as forceful and determinant in the formation of states and nations as imperialism itself.

At issue is the effectiveness and efficiency with which scarce resources are employed, the skill that goes into their transformation, and the validity of the uses to which they are put. Beyond that is the capacity to regard the natural world as something more than a disposable collection of utilities, a thing inherently valuable even when untransformed and unexploited. The Atlantic Forest was beginning its long journey to extinction. Its inhabitants still had nothing to show for it, and they had not yet even discovered it.

6

Science Discovers the Forest

En peu d'années, un petit nombre d'hommes auront ravagés une immense province et ils pourront dire "É uma terra acabada."

In a few years, a small number of men will have ravaged an immense province, and they will be able to say "It's a land that's finished."

AUGUSTE DE SAINT-HILAIRE

Nearly three hundred years had passed since the first Europeans had set eyes on the Atlantic Forest. A considerable part of it had been degraded by their descendants, whose demands had been few but devastating. The forest contained a tree from whose cortex a dye might be derived, it was the hiding place of gold and diamonds, and it overlay soils that were subjected to a primitive sort of farming and, in the final stages of their degradation, to a primitive sort of grazing. Through the dimly remembered lore of the indigenes, transmitted with difficulty to the caboclo and African fugitives from the colonial pale, some of the Atlantic Forest species had acquired names, and some names had been associated with uses. These scraps of empirical knowledge had almost no commercial application; indeed, they had not yet reached the attention of the colonial authorities. Thousands of the forest's species were yet unnamed even by the indigenes; thousands whose virtues were yet unknown. All this complexity was being destroyed before human intelligence might comprehend it. By the end of the eighteenth century, however, European scientific interest was coming to be directed more systematically to the natural world beyond its borders. The indigenous knowledge that the first invaders had contemptuously ignored was to be, at considerable cost, re-created and finally surpassed. The Atlantic Forest was at last to be the subject of *curiosity*.

The king's patronage was essential to this enterprise, and he provided it, once he became convinced that the slump in collections of the royal fifth on gold and diamonds was due not simply to smuggling but also to the decadence of the mines. Substitute sources of income had to be found. The colonies, furthermore, had to be tied more straitly to the metropolis. As the other European powers developed their tropical colonies, not only were the Portuguese losing their overseas markets but the metropolitan market was itself penetrated by their goods. Resuscitation of the imperial economy would require an enlarged fleet, more efficient and diversified colonial production, improved colonial infrastructure, and perhaps greater productive integration within the colonies themselves, at least in those sectors that supported export trade.

To employ science to achieve these ends was to confront the Atlantic Forest with the prospect of further devastation. But even though more intensive exploitation of forest resources might speed its destruction, more careful and considered exploitation might allow more of it to be preserved and the rest to provide sustained yields. The botanists and geologists of the turn of the nineteenth century, in the service of a ravenous crown, were certainly keen in their observation of the utilities of the forest, but they were voluble in their condemnation of waste and ignorance. The contradictory role of science and technology in the management of the Atlantic Forest begins here, with the awakening understanding of these civil servants that the forest would be managed or it would be destroyed. It is not difficult to discern in their efforts the beginning of conservationism in Brazil.

Although Portuguese natural sciences stood only at the periphery of the eighteenth-century European Enlightenment, they accompanied them and contributed significantly to them. In 1764 the marquis of Pombal appointed to Coimbra University Domenico Vandelli, a doctor of the University of Padua and correspondent of Linnaeus. Pombal reformed the university's curriculum in 1772, abolishing scholastic philosophy and replacing it with the sciences. Vandelli trained a generation of natural scientists, most of them Brazilians. He organized the botanical garden at the Ajuda palace and founded the museum of natural history, projects in which Pombal was deeply interested. Despite the resistance of the church and the aristocracy to these reforms, the crown endorsed them. Vandelli promoted his research by emphasizing the head start of the French and English in their colonies. These initiatives therefore went forward even after Pombal's fall. In 1779 the Royal Academy of Sciences was founded in Lisbon. It corresponded with other societies, encouraged collection and observation among amateurs in the colonies, and published their reports.[1]

Brazil's first scientific society held meetings in Salvador in 1759, under the protection of the viceroy, the count of Arcos. Studies of agriculture, flora, fauna, and minerals were planned, but none of them survive, if any were pursued. In 1772 another viceroy—by then the seat of colonial government had been transferred to Rio de Janeiro—the marquis of Lavradio, founded the Academia Fluviense, whose purpose was to study medicine, surgery, botany, and pharmacy. Its officers and principal members were members of the viceroy's military staff. At the inaugural session the pharmacist Antônio Ribeiro de Paiva complained that in Portugal the herbal trade was in the hands of ignorant merchants who often misidentified their wares, frauds that Paiva wanted to avert in Brazil. He had found a number of legitimate medicinals in Rio de Janeiro—very likely transferred by Jesuits, years before—yet the city continued to import inferior or mislabelled stuffs. Brazil, Paiva noted, was the habitat of the true copal of commerce, yet Portugal had been importing it. When a foreign visitor to Pernambuco who had obtained some locally passed it off in Lisbon as his discovery, he was granted a monopoly in its trade! Here was a shrewd exposition of the practical purposes that the academy might serve.[2]

The academy restored the former Jesuit botanical garden and appointed collectors, gardeners, and botanical artists, but its existence was brief. Lavradio promoted agricultural diversification and the search for useful native plants, but he was distracted by warfare in the south, and when he relinquished his office in 1779 his staff of scientific amateurs returned with him to Portugal. The new viceroy, Luiz de Vasconcellos e Souza, under instructions of the court, created a museum of natural history in Rio de Janeiro, but the modest collection of specimens donated by private individuals was housed in a mere shed—very likely the viceroy's enthusiasm was less than that of the crown. The academy was revived, during his term, as the Literary Society, literary in the sense of promoting written knowledge, scientific as well as humanistic. It too came to an end when Vasconcellos e Souza was replaced in 1790.[3]

What has come to be known in Brazil as "administrative discontinuity" was only one of the difficulties attending the implantation of the sciences. The Portuguese had permitted no institutions of higher learning in the colony save seminaries. Talented young men had to go to Portugal for training, where they were often pressed into the service of the empire. If they did return to Brazil, they were far removed from the encouragement of colleagues and barred from training a new generation. There were no public libraries in the colony, and printing presses were forbidden. The papers of local enthusiasts therefore had to be posted to the Lisbon academy for publication, and circulation of their discoveries within the colony was problematic. Indeed, many of the scientific projects sponsored in these years appear to have been withheld from publication and exchange, remaining secrets of state, as mercantilist in conception as the crown's economic policies. This is why it was so easy for Vandelli to appropriate samples from the magnificent Amazon collections of his protégé Alexandre

Rodrigues Ferreira, whetting the curiosity of his correspondents but dissembling their origin.[4]

Most disastrously, however, the sciences in Portugal were ideologically suspect. The subversive political and social conceptions of the Enlightenment were tangled with its scientific proposals, in the minds of the authorities no less than in the minds of the scientists. A conspiracy uncovered in Minas Gerais in 1789 was extremely alarming to the court and proved, indeed, to be the beginning of the long passage to independence. Two of the Brazilians implicated in that plot were members of the Royal Academy of Sciences, and other members and correspondents thereafter found themselves under a cloud. José Bonifâcio de Andrada e Silva and Manuel Ferreira da Câmara, both promising young scientists, were sent to northern Europe on study grants for eight long years, a mutually convenient arrangement that kept them from harm's way.[5]

Portuguese scientists, furthermore, were wont to correspond with French colleagues, because France was the locus of most of the innovation and resources in their fields. The palace abhorred the French, who were allies of their Spanish rivals and the source of anticolonial and egalitarian tracts, and these associations became anathema with the outbreak of revolution and the act of regicide. Vasconcellos e Souza's successor, the count of Rezende, closed down the reactivated Literary Society, supposing it to be subversive. When some of its members thereupon founded another without his sponsorship, he had them put in jail, where they languished for three years. In 1788 the botanist Felix de Avellar Brotero fled the Inquisition to Paris. The Brazilian-born abbot José Correa da Serra was obliged to exile himself twice to avoid its rigors: In 1786 he went to Paris, where he met Jussieu and Geoffroy Saint-Hilaire at the Jardin des Plantes; back in Lisbon in 1795, again under suspicion for assistance he rendered an exiled French botanist, he escaped to London.[6]

At this moment, Correa da Serra and the other young scientists came under the protection of a powerful courtier. This was Rodrigo de Souza Coutinho, a polymath of intellectual distinction and a charter member of the Linnaean Society of London. In 1796 Souza Coutinho became minister of colonies and navy. His strategy for coping with the French danger was to accelerate the absorption of foreign scientific knowledge, which he saw as a means not only of galvanizing the backward colonies but also of assuring their loyalty, by employing their university graduates in projects that were empirewide in conception and execution. Indeed, he wished to see the empire transformed into a federation of equals, and, in 1803, he urged the prince to transfer the throne to Brazil. Souza Coutinho ordered the release of the jailed fellows of the Literary Society and paid the fugitive

Correa da Serra to establish contacts at the Royal Botanic Gardens at Kew and report on British colonial products. He sent another potentially dangerous Brazilian, Hipólito José da Costa Pereira, to the United States, with a commission to inquire into every branch of production and report on improvements that might be adopted in Portugal and Brazil. Still another Brazilian student of Vandelli, Manuel Arruda da Câmara, received funds to collect specimens in his native Pernambuco, while another, Joaquim Velloso de Miranda, carried on unhindered with his botanical studies in Minas Gerais, despite the governor's distrust.[7]

Souza Coutinho also endowed the Brazilian priest José Mariano da Conceição Velloso, who had been botanizing for years in Rio de Janeiro, with viceregal funding. Velloso displayed in Lisbon the collection of botanical drawings made by his companions, notably Father Francisco Solano. This exhibit must have impressed Souza Coutinho, who issued instructions for the compilation of a flora of the entire empire. He appointed Velloso director of a new publishing house, which specialized in editing and translating a series of writings on improvements in tropical agriculture gleaned from other European colonies. Among Souza Coutinho's other initiatives were the establishment of the Royal Maritime, Military and Geographic Society, through which he intended to improve imperial communications, and his orders to found botanical gardens at Salvador and Belém.[8]

The period was propitious for the diversification of Brazilian agricultural exports because the colony's Caribbean competitors were wracked by warfare. First the American War of Independence, then the French and Haitian revolutions, and finally Napoleonic imperialism had caused the colonial powers to direct immense expeditionary forces to the region, nearly extinguishing its trade. Portugal remained for a time happily marginal to this unrest, and Brazil came to supply increasing amounts of sugar, cotton, rice, and tobacco to the European market. But this respite was not to last. England and France pressed the Portuguese court to choose sides: Souza Coutinho resigned in 1803 when his policy of promoting the economic development of Brazil to the potential detriment of peninsular interests was interpreted as coinciding too closely with those of the British, who were coming to regard Portugal as expendable. This was not incidentally a misfortune for the network of scientific researchers he had put in place.[9]

Napoleon persuaded Spain to allow him to invade Portugal as punishment for its failure to heed his demand for a continental boycott of British goods. The unfortunate country was already under English naval blockade, in reprisal for its promise to the French to apply the boycott. The prince regent, João, resolved to follow Souza Coutinho's recommendation of six years before and sailed to Brazil protected by the same British fleet that had been blockading his capital. He arrived at Rio de Janeiro in 1808, to the acclaim of the local elite. The Haitian Revolution had filled with dread even those Brazilians who had sympathized with the insurgents of Minas Gerais, and a conspiracy of mulatto workmen uncovered in Salvador in 1798 had revealed how precarious their own status would be were the legitimacy of the crown cast off. The regent's providential appearance therefore represented the most congenial outcome imaginable: Now Brazil was the seat of empire, its ports declared open to the world and all the mercantilist legislation that had hindered its development annulled, hurriedly replaced by decrees granting to prospective manufacturers guarantees, exemptions, subsidies, and favors for importing raw materials, contracting workmen, and installing machines.[10]

More than 20,000 courtiers, bureaucrats, and tradesmen soon found their way to the refugee court. Several thousand foreigners joined them— artists, craftsmen, military officers, merchants, and even scientists. Portuguese government was reconstituted in Rio de Janeiro. Rodrigo de Souza Coutinho, soon titled count of Linhares, became the regent's principal minister, entrusted with foreign relations and war. Although no Brazilian was included in his cabinet, it was evident that the king considered it imperative that the economic potential of Brazil be developed as far as possible. The army and navy needed gunpowder, so surveys were taken of nitrate deposits in northern Minas Gerais. It was recommended that the manufacture of potash be stimulated. Astoundingly, this raw material that had so many industrial applications, and that was so easily derived from wood ash, appears not to have been produced on any important scale. On the contrary, Brazil had been importing it! No datum better exemplifies the backwardness of the colonial economy or the wastefulness of its consumption of forest resources.[11]

It was apparent on all sides that quite small investments in techniques already widely diffused in Europe might greatly improve Brazilian production. Courtiers turned up their noses at badly made cheeses and butter, sun-dried meat, and preserved fish turned out in the colony, all of which might have become articles of export but instead suffered competition from abroad. Certainly, the colonial monopoly and taxes on salt had ruined the possibility of improvements in these articles. The convenient salt pans of Cape Frio were still unexploited. It was noticed that planters persisted in packing their sugar in wooden boxes, instead of barrels, which, although more difficult to make, would have reduced handling costs and were salable at their destination. Mercantilism may also have been the reason why

Brazil still shipped brazilwood as logs, rather than first converting it to dyestuffs, yet it was an Englishman, Luccock, who raised this issue, rather than any indignant Brazilian. The Portuguese court, undeterred, focused its hopes upon the natural endowment of Brazil, which it imagined to be limitless. Indeed, a decree of 1813 effusively proclaimed Brazil "this fortunate and opulent country . . . , especially favored in the concentration of riches otherwise scattered throughout the four corners of the world." As problematic as these suppositions were, they inspired extraordinary efforts to discover and catalog the natural resources of this exotic realm that had suddenly become the seat of empire.[12]

Unfortunately, French invasion had not only cut off Brazilian natural scientists from the center of their network of information but also caught scientists resident in Portugal in further embarrassments. Some of the liberals had welcomed General Junot at Lisbon's gate. Manuel Joaquim Henriques de Paiva, a physician of the royal household and son of the Paiva who had helped found the Academia Fluviense in Rio de Janeiro, was suspected of collaboration and stripped of all honors. Hipólito José da Costa Pereira had to flee to London, where he became an important propagator of liberalism to Brazil and, not incidentally, an instrument of British policy via a newspaper he published for distribution in his homeland. Vandelli himself, accused of aiding the French, escaped to England and only returned in 1815. Fascination with revolutionary principles, freemasonry, nationalism, or perhaps the Napoleonic ideal of the career open to talent probably disqualified from royal favor many who might otherwise have accompanied the wave of scientific discovery in Brazil. The French authorities contributed to their isolation with a display of scientific greed: The naturalist Geoffroy Saint-Hilaire, acting on terms negotiated for the evacuation of Junot's army from Lisbon, carried off many hundreds of the specimens amassed by Vandelli's students, including the Amazon collection of Rodrigues Ferreira.[13]

The crown, meanwhile, did not hesitate to install in its new court powerful instruments of investigation of the natural world: a printing press, a library, a medical school, a chemical analytic laboratory, a chair in agriculture (at Salvador), and a military academy, whose functions included civil engineering and mining. These institutions offered employment to local savants such as José da Costa Azevedo, lecturer in zoology and mineralogy, Leandro do Sacramento, lecturer in botany and agriculture, and Francisco Vieira Goulart, director of the chemical laboratory. The printing press began to turn out, among other useful publications, a journal called *O Patriota*, which regularly printed notices of agricultural improvements. Two important scientific institutions were created, a botanical garden and a museum of natural history. Both survived to become the parents of the modern Brazilian natural scientific network. The Botanical Garden, authorized in 1808, was one of the first initiatives of Souza Coutinho's ministry, but not the very first because it was attached—with an odd but not entirely inappropriate symbolism—to the new army-directed gunpowder mill. The museum, still functioning from the time of the Viceroy Vasconcellos e Souza, was closed soon after Souza Coutinho's untimely death in 1813 and its collections transferred to the new military academy.[14]

The museum reopened in 1818, through the influence of the Austrian Archduchess Leopoldina, married shortly before to Pedro, the son of the regent, now King João. She had been accompanied to Brazil by a brilliant retinue of Austrian and German natural scientists, including Johann Emanuel Pohl, Karl Friedrich Philipp von Martius, and Johann Baptist von Spix. The establishment of the Portuguese court had at last made hitherto forbidden Brazil accessible to European scientists. Numerous ambitious young botanists and zoologists voyaged eagerly to an unknown field of investigation, among them Auguste de Saint-Hilaire, who was given passage in the party of the duke of Luxembourg, appointed in 1816 ambassador of the restored French monarch. Saint-Hilaire was to collect, over the next six years, some 15,000 specimens of plants and animals, from the highlands of Goiás to the pampas of Rio Grande do Sul, and to publish, upon his return to France, some fourteen volumes of travel memoirs, botanical descriptions, and agricultural reports. Many other collectors—English, Italian, Bavarian, Prussian, German, Swedish, and French—followed his path, dispatched by botanical gardens, scientific societies, and museums. Still others were invited by the crown as technical experts, principally to revive the gold mines. The most energetic of the geologists, Baron Wilhelm von Eschwege, opened new lead, iron, and gold mines, installed water wheels and blast furnaces, projected maps, and published at least a dozen extensive reports on his travels and activities. Thus was rent the curtain that had been drawn over this immense natural realm.[15]

One of the charges of the Botanical Garden was to receive and acclimatize exotic tropical plants of economic interest. The Botanical Garden was intended to bring organizational perfection to the transfer of colonial crops, a critically important activity that had been carried on up to then empirically, even haphazardly. The consciousness of the continuity of this effort may be said to have begun during this period. Manuel Ferreira da Câmara, a mining specialist trained in Europe, later appointed by Souza Coutinho to be the first Brazilian-born intendant of the diamond district, demonstrated this in a report to the Lisbon Academy of Sciences in 1789. He reminded them of the Duarte Ribeiro de Macedo aide-mémoire of 1675, which remained in manuscript: The Dutch could have been defeated then, had the spice plants of the East been replanted in Brazil. What could be cultivated below the Tropic of Cancer, Macedo had prophesied, could be cultivated above the Tropic of Capricorn.[16]

The Pernambucan naturalist Manuel Arruda da Câmara, writing in 1810 in favor of the installation of a botanical garden in his province, offered an even more apposite critique of earlier colonial policy and of botanical understanding. How much blood, he lamented, would have been saved had the Portuguese transferred Asian spices when first they entered the Indian Ocean, instead of trying to conquer the region and hold it against its competitors. Arruda da Câmara was so bold as to exalt his homeland over the abandoned metropolis: Tropical countries, he commented, were far more fertile than Europe, which would be in a "mean and wretched" condition, had it not received citrus and other plants in the past. Even so, nowhere in Europe could cacao, coffee, or cotton grow. Thus did nationalism and botany mix, to invert the prejudice cherished by the peninsulars since the invasion. Prudently, however, Arruda da Câmara converted his gibe to flattery: If sterile Portugal could be made to bloom beneath the feet of a good king, how could fertile Brazil fail to flourish?[17]

Arruda da Câmara correctly supposed the transfer of tropical crops to be a difficult enterprise for the Europeans. Unlike their transfers to temperate North America, they were unfamiliar with the growing conditions of the plants they removed from Asia and Africa and with the environments of the places to which they brought them in Brazil. The Ajuda garden, the center of interchange of the seeds of numerous tropical species, was no longer accessible. Because the crown had not troubled to install botanical gardens in any of its African or Asian colonies, little practical information was available concerning the exotics that the Portuguese wanted to fetch from there. The royal decrees of July 1809 and July 1810, offering prizes and tax exemptions to persons introducing economic plants, appeared unlikely to have takers. As it happened, the Portuguese made up for their lack of a network by parasitizing French botanical endeavor—disreputable, perhaps, but a fair exchange for the sacking of the Ajuda garden.[18]

The prince regent quickly ordered the invasion of Cayenne (now French Guiana) in reprisal for the invasion of his kingdom and in fear that that little colony might soon be reinforced. Souza Coutinho directed the captain-general of Belém to effect its "total ruin," expecting that France would regain the territory at the next peace conference. Nevertheless, he was careful to order the removal of the nutmeg trees "that exist there and never have been obtained" by the Portuguese. The minister was in error on that point, but he was correct in regarding the botanical resources of the French governor's garden, charmingly named "La Gabrielle," the principal booty of the colony. Since the beginning of the eighteenth century, French botanists had expended considerable effort in diversifying the agricultural resources of Guiana, and La Gabrielle boasted not only nutmeg but also cinnamon and cloves, which the colony had come to export, and pepper, still experimental, along with breadfruit, starfruit, bilimbi, mangosteen, Tahiti gooseberry, soursop, custard apple, sapota (which provides sapodilla fruit and chicle), Surinam quassia wood (an insect repellent), and jalap (a purgative).[19]

Luckily, Souza Coutinho's ferocious instruction was thwarted by the commander of the victorious Luso-Brazilian-British expedition, who was persuaded by the French governor to spare La Gabrielle "in all its splendor." The Regent João received gratefully the seeds and plants forwarded by his Minas Gerais–born civil governor, João Severiano Maciel da Costa, who saw to it that the French gardener kept at his post. Another botanical garden was created at Olinda, directed, like the Belém garden, by a French exile brought from Guiana along with seeds from La Gabrielle. João began to delude himself that he might retain the territory, but the English opposed the expansion of Brazil's borders, and Guiana was returned to France in 1817. By then all the transfers had been carried out, including a Tahitian variety of sugarcane, which came to be called "Caiena" in Brazil.

The next great coup of the Portuguese was fortuitous. Most of La Gabrielle's exotics had been sent there from the botanical garden on French-held Mauritius. That garden, "Le Pamplemousse," had been organized by the energetic and appropriately named Pierre Poivre, who had conducted collecting expeditions across the length and breadth of the Indian Ocean. A Portuguese officer, Luiz d'Abreu, captured by the French and interned on Mauritius, effected his release and managed to steal some seeds before leaving the island. These he brought to Rio de Janeiro in 1809. They included more of the highly desired clove, cinnamon, and nutmeg; breadfruit, camphor, grapefruit, avocado, sago palm, and otaheite apple. His surreptitious remittance included mango as well, but that had been introduced more than a century before and was already widely planted in Rio de Janeiro. Abreu also brought back mammee apple, another example of a Neotropical cultivar arriving in Brazil via the East. Finally, he presented the king with *Roystonea oleracea*, a noble palm of imposing height that soon ornamented every aristocratic garden in Rio de Janeiro and still flanks impressively the central avenue of the Botanical Garden itself.[20]

Basking in the honors bestowed upon him for his audacity, Abreu wrote to a friend, Rafael Bottado de Almeida, a senator of the Portuguese colony of Macau, to request seeds of the tea plant. These arrived on a Portuguese man-of-war in 1812. They germinated and grew, but, because no one in Brazil possessed any experience of the cultivation and processing of tea and no one seems to have remembered Avellar Brotero's 1788 treatise on the subject, King João ordered that Chinese gardeners be contracted. Thirty of them arrived in 1814. They were successful enough at propagating the plants, and soon several dozen planters in Rio de Janeiro, Minas Gerais, and São Paulo took up cultivation. This was a remarkable achievement, for it was the first time that tea had been transferred outside East Asia, and it excited much curiosity in Europe.[21]

Some of these transfers, notably the spices, were merely repetitions of earlier remittances, first sent from Goa in the seventeenth century. Besides ginger, by then ubiquitous, there were pepper, cinnamon, and nutmeg plants surviving in Bahia, Rio de Janeiro, and Pernambuco. A shipment of pepper seeds from Goa, apparently intended for Ajuda, had been diverted and planted in Bahia in 1782. Further shipments of black pepper and cinnamon were made from Goa in 1787, 1788, and 1790. The governor of Goa reported in 1800 that cinnamon, which grew wild there, was beginning to be cultivated, no doubt under urgings from Souza Coutinho. This was rather a late adoption—it was already under cultivation on the Portuguese island of Príncipe, off the African coast. In 1802 the governor sent more seedlings of a variety of plants. There had also been remittances from the Ajuda garden, which had received seeds of tea, cinnamon, and camphor from England, sent by José Correa da Serra in 1797 or 1798. These were forwarded to Bahia, apparently, by 1800. Of these species, only black pepper came to be produced in quantity, mainly in Bahia, which nevertheless continued to be a net importer of the product.[22]

Along with plant introductions officially sponsored or known to the authorities, there were many others whose agencies are obscure. Saint-Hilaire found many temperate plants growing in highland São Paulo: strawberries, peaches, apricots, and chestnuts. Both he and Johann Emanuel Pohl, who passed through Rio de Janeiro in 1818, commented on the great variety of ornamentals transferred from Europe. Pohl also found chayote—of Central American origin—and jackfruit, rose apples, and soybeans—of Asian origin. Curiously, the local name for soybeans was "Angola peanuts," suggesting a transfer via Africa. Okra, African oil palm, yams, black-eyed peas, and castor beans—all of African origin—were also present. Castor oil, widespread as an illuminant, may have been brought to Brazil earlier via the Ajuda botanical garden, but it is quite likely that the others had been initiatives of Africans, slaves or freedmen. African potherbs such as *caruru* and *bertalha*, misnamed Jamaica sorrel and Ceylon spinach in English, were also widespread. The remittances of Abreu and Maciel da Costa had no sequel. An instruction, dated 1819, ordered the governors of Portuguese Asia and Africa and Portuguese consuls to remit seeds, which were to be given free passage through customs, but this was too late to have any effect. Within a year Portugal would undergo a revolution, and Brazil would begin to slip loose of the empire.[23]

These numerous transfers had no effect in diversifying exports. Although repeated introductions of spice plants failed in Brazil to result in an export trade, the French in Guiana, the Dutch in Java, the British in the West Indies, and Arabs in Zanzibar were all successfully cultivating cinnamon, cloves, and nutmeg. One can only speculate on the contrast. It cannot have been caused by the baneful institution of slavery, because the other European colonies also relied on forced labor. Official incentives were often counterproductive. They often guaranteed producers purchase of their output, but payments were delayed long enough to cause their bankruptcy. English merchants who financed trade between Portugal and its colonies represented another obstacle, because they opposed competition with British colonies. One finds, nevertheless, a shocking insouciance in the disposition of these botanical treasures that cannot well be attributed to external forces: João Barbosa Rodrigues, the late-nineteenth-century reformer of the Rio de Janeiro garden, blamed carelessness and vandalism for the loss of most of them. The leaves of the cinnamon and clove plants, for example, were, to celebrate religious festivals, stripped and strewn on the floor of the chapel of the Santa Casa.[24]

Rice proved, at least temporarily, the only exception to this unfortunate record. Introduced earlier in the north, it had become a domestic staple in the colonial diet. Its success as an export crop had little to do with official sponsorship, however; it was, instead, largely due to commercial promotion by a Rio de Janeiro miller, Manuel Luís Vieira. English merchants who had previously supplied Portugal did indeed attempt to shut down this upstart, but unsuccessfully. Vieira was granted a monopoly, but then his payments were long delayed and he was even jailed for four years. His example was nonetheless widely followed in Rio de Janeiro. By 1781 Portugal was able to bar Carolina rice; by 1789 Rio de Janeiro was exporting more than 1,000 tons, and São Paulo nearly equaled that amount soon after.[25]

Except for the mango tree, which possesses the admirable advantage of resistance to leaf-cutting ants, custard apple (*fruta do conde*—possibly a reference to the count of Linhares), jackfruit, and chayote, the fruits and vegetables introduced to the domestic market in these years were ignored by the populace. Possibly they encountered in Brazil pests or parasites at the time seemingly invincible, or perhaps the remarkable array of native fruits that indigenes had long before brought into partial cultivation rendered the Asian species superfluous. It is interesting to note, however, that some of the Brazilian plants sent to Goa were widely accepted in South Asian cuisine, notably cashews, papaya, Surinam cherry, passionfruit, and pineapple.[26]

Curiously, the domestication, improvement, and commercialization of native Brazilian species were not among the purposes listed in the decree reorganizing the Botanical Garden of Rio de Janeiro. Certainly the cultivation of hitherto wild plants was a much more complicated project than the simple transfer of already domesticated exotics. Portuguese naturalists were still ignorant of the Brazilian forests and their potential uses. Although they were ready to admit the superiority of the Brazilian climate and soils, they seem not to have much esteemed its native species. Nor did the colonials, according to Auguste de Saint-Hilaire, who lamented that "Brazilians are unfortunately accustomed to disdain all the benefits that nature has heaped on them." Even the patriotic Manuel Arruda da Câmara appears infected by the lamentable thesis of the inferiority of colonial nature, when he presumed that neither manioc nor peanuts could have been native to Brazil.

Among the European visitors, however, there were a few whose curiosity and sympathy overcame prejudice. Saint-Hilaire, an especially acute observer, pointed out that "European" fruits were the product of centuries of cultivation but that if wild varieties of those fruits were compared with wild Brazilian fruits, the latter were unquestionably superior. His writings include a remarkable treatise on useful plants, most of them wild, which he suggested for domestication—among them beverages, cordage, spices, and medicinals that might have come to compete with Asian species in the European market. Saint-Hilaire did not notice that the fruits that he thought wild were at least semicultivated by indigenes. Although the European travelers inquired occasionally of caboclos concerning the uses of plants they encountered, they seem to have been unaware that the ultimate source of this botanical lore was the indigenes. An exception was the shrewd and garrulous Baltasar da Silva Lisboa, who pointed out that indigenes had discovered uses for an enormous number of plants.[27]

The difficulty remained of drawing from tribal peoples and frontier settlers their knowledge of the resources offered by the forest. Their knowledge reached the cities and ports of Brazil in the form of a few artifacts
and trade goods, extracted from estuaries and forests. Rio de Janeiro was
itself in good measure still supplied with products collected in the wild,
sometimes by slaves, many of whom were professionals in their specialty:
fish and shellfish, firewood, hay (Para grass went wild in its new habitat),
charcoal, meat (of monkeys, armadillos, lizards, and birds), shells (for lime
baking), medicinals, cordage, basketry, and fruits. There was an export
trade in pelts and skins of jaguar, deer, otter, agouti, paca, snakes, alligators,
tapir, seal, and other animals, in feathers and plumes, in turtle carapaces,
and in falsified articles, such as "rhinoceros horn." There was a minor trade
in *drogas do sertão*—drugs of the interior—that included resins, essences,
flavorings, waxes, glues, gums, balsams, cordage, tow, fibers, tannin, spices,
dyes, and medicinals. Among them perhaps the most prized was the resin
of the copaíba tree, which provided the copal of the Mayas, highly regarded
as a vehicle for paints, as a digestive, salve, antitoxin, and presumed cure
for gonorrhea and elephantiasis, as well as a palatable fruit and the most
valuable of mastwoods. Many more wild products might have been gathered, had urban residents known of them or had they known how to
acquire them.[28]

Wild medicinals were extremely varied; indeed, the medicinal lore of
the indigenes was the only aspect of their culture that urban whites did
not disdain. The formidable maladies of the tropics frightened them into
acceptance of native vermifuges, febrifuges, remedies for yaws, venereal
disease, and, most elusive, antidotes for snakebite. All these in addition to
cures for pedestrian complaints—rheumatism, colic, endoparasites, diar-
rhea, hemorrhoids, skin eruptions, inflammations, infections, and nutritional deficiencies. Indigenes also possessed contraceptives and abortifac-
tants. Saint-Hilaire was especially careful to note the uses that were
claimed for these plants, but even he lacked the means to verify their effi-
cacity. One wonders if the Regent João was aware that the anda-açu tree,
which Joaquim Velloso de Miranda named *Joannesia princeps* in his honor,
was esteemed mainly as a purgative—the suspicions that the government
had harbored toward that Mineiro botanist may have been well founded.[29]

Only one of these remedies from the Atlantic Forest became an important article of foreign commerce, however. This was *ipecacuanha* or
poaia—ipecac, whose rhizome is an emetic. At the turn of the nineteenth
century Rio de Janeiro exported about four tons of it a year. Ipecac is an
inconspicuous plant that formed part of the ground cover of primary forest. Caboclos collected it as a cash "crop," generally pulling it up when it

was in flower, because it was almost impossible to identify during the rest of the year. This procedure, destructive because it prevented seeding, had eliminated easily reached occurrences of the plant in Rio de Janeiro, and the search moved to the highlands of Minas Gerais.[30]

Other plants were urgently sought in the Atlantic Forest: sarsaparilla, hemp, and cinchona. Sarsaparilla was considered a specific against syphilis. Several of its local species entered into commerce, but not much as an export, because the Amazon species were more highly regarded. Hemp was considered the best material for the manufacture of naval cordage, and vain attempts had been made since the 1620s to acclimatize it to Bahia and Rio de Janeiro. Unfortunately, the plant that provides fiber for cordage is a temperate variety, or species. By the 1780s it had finally been implanted successfully in Rio Grande do Sul and Santa Catarina; nevertheless, futile remittances of seeds to Rio de Janeiro went on. On the other hand, hemp's tropical congener, whose seed and leaf have hallucinogenic virtues, became very comfortably rooted in Brazil. This was another of the plants that arrived unsponsored. Because African names—*maconha, pango*—became attached to it, that may have been the route it took. The Atlantic Forest contained many plants that might serve for cordage. In the Rio de Janeiro region guaxima, a liana, and in Bahia piassava, a palm, were gathered wild to make rope. Hemp, however, was preferred, once its cultivation was assured.[31]

Cinchona had long engaged official interest. Correa da Serra seems to have sent seeds of it, or what he thought were such, from London; Vandelli had hypothesized that it existed in Brazil, because it bordered on the regions where the Spanish gathered it. Cinchona was a remarkable and historically decisive medical discovery, because it was a native plant truly effective against an introduced disease. Brazil had to buy it from Spain, whose merchants monopolized the trade; it was therefore both expensive and spoiled by the time it reached Rio de Janeiro. Numerous samples of supposed cinchona had therefore been sent to Ajuda. The quest for quinine was not a little like the quest for gold; indeed, it offered the advantage that a false product could easily be presented for sale, at least in local markets. A certain Pedro Pereira Correa de Senna was promised payments, in a royal decree of August 1808, for each delivery of Mineiro cinchona he provided the royal hospital. The bark he brought back was accepted as genuine by pharmacists in Rio de Janeiro, and Correa de Senna was awarded a knighthood of the Order of Christ and an annual pension of 438 milreis, a gratification he was apparently still receiving in 1830.[32]

Cacao was still being gathered wild in its native Amazon valley when Alexandre Rodrigues Ferreira was a witness to this excruciatingly laborious practice. It seems likely that cacao, cultivated in its native habitat, was vulnerable to coevolved parasites, so its officially stimulated transfer and cultivation on the forested coast of southern Bahia in the 1780s may be counted as a success of the period. Even so, it was not to become a significant export for another century and a half.[33]

Only two of the numerous wild products of the Atlantic Forest reached the point of cultivation and export during this period—cochineal and indigo. In one of the first sessions of the Academia Fluviense, in 1772, one of its members, Maurício da Costa, a military surgeon just returned from an assignment with the commission that was demarcating the border with Spanish territories, reported having observed a valuable curiosity. An officer of the Spanish border commission had pointed out to him a certain insect that was infesting an opuntia cactus at their feet. This, he remarked, was the cochineal, from which a red dyestuff was easily derived. The dye, the officer told him, was an important item of commerce in Mexico. Da Costa was immediately encouraged by his fellow academicians to locate specimens of cochineal in the neighborhood. This he soon accomplished. Apparently cochineal had never been noticed by the Tupi; nor had knowledge of its use diffused to the region of the Atlantic Forest. Soon many more reports of the presence of cochineal were reported from Santa Catarina and Rio Grande do Sul. The gardener of the academy succeeded in propagating several species of cactus upon which the insect was accustomed to feed. Another academician, José Henriques Ferreira, demonstrating familiarity with a number of French and Spanish treatises on the insect, carried out his own careful observations of its life cycle and suggested its proper classification.[34]

This discovery was the academy's only substantive achievement before it disbanded, yet it is one that justifies recalling its name. Cochineal became briefly an article of commerce, but then it disappeared from export lists, for reasons that are unclear. The English historian Robert Southey stated that it came to be adulterated and so fell out of favor with importers. The account of the discovery of the insect, which appeared in print only in 1814, refers mysteriously to the "same reason" that had caused the failure of other such initiatives. Distressingly, another effort at cultivation had failed.[35]

Indigo was the other native resource that was domesticated and exported, for a time a good deal more successfully than cochineal. This blue dyestuff, derived from numerous native species of *Indigofera*, widespread both in the New World and the Old World, had been recognized and used by indigenes. For a century and a half, however, the neo-Europeans made no attempt to exploit it. Nor had the Portuguese interested themselves in the Asian indigo trade, which competed with their own dyestuff, Azorean woad. Their English, French, and Dutch successors in India exported indigo and then transferred it to the Caribbean. The Spanish had found native peoples processing indigo in Central America and spread these techniques to Venezuela. By the early eighteenth century, Portugal was in the absurd position of having to import indigo from Spain. That the colonists and the authorities could for so long ignore a plant that everywhere "presented itself spontaneously to their eyes" seemed to José Mariano Conceição Velloso nothing but "inertia." Indeed, it appears that native knowledge of the indigo plant had entirely been lost to them, because it was a French surgeon who may have once resided in Guatemala who, in 1749, noticed the plant growing in Rio de Janeiro and tried to exploit it.[36]

Repeated experiments in planting and processing indigo were stimulated by the government's willingness to buy all that was offered for sale. By 1779 there were several hundred indigo works in Brazil, most of them in the captaincy of Rio de Janeiro, and they entirely satisfied Portuguese demand for the dyestuff. Warfare and revolution in the Caribbean presented the indigo growers a great opportunity; by 1796 Rio de Janeiro exported 85 tons of it, mostly for transshipment. Unfortunately, by 1818 the trade almost entirely disappeared. The fate of Brazilian indigo was common to that of its cotton and rice, the other sudden great successes of the time: The external market disappeared once the colonies of the great powers resumed operations. Certainly, mercantilism had not yet been dismantled, but the Brazilians were not able, apparently, to overcome this obstacle by offering cheaper or better products. The crown was aware of insufficient investment in indigo processing but did not offer effective means of matching or surpassing the techniques of the other colonies. Because the collapse of indigo was even more sudden and complete than that of Brazil's other new exports, a greater degree of technological backwardness may have played a role, as well as other factors. As in the case of cochineal, English observers complained of adulteration and poor quality. There is also mention of insect attacks and diseases, misfortunes common enough in tropical agriculture, even in temperate climates, when native plants are for too long grown in profusion.[37]

Conceição Velloso discerned the great advantage of the indigo trade, compared to plantation crops such as sugar. Though less profitable, crops like indigo were more available to "less powerful persons" and were "less complicated in their equipment, less costly in their operation, [and] much less destructive of the forests." The collapse of indigo was thus more than an incident in Brazilian commercial history, it was a symptom of the social domination that channeled resources to a single crop, typically one that placed the poor at a disadvantage in its production and that relied for its competitive advantage in foreign markets on minimal inputs of managerial skill and on the primeval fertility of the soils underlying primary forest. This was a failure that boded ill for the Atlantic Forest.[38]

A central concern of the crown, essential to the defense of empire and the increase of its trade, was the supply of ship's timber. Although boatbuilding was common all along the Brazilian coast, very few oceangoing vessels are recorded before the eighteenth century. For two centuries and more, most of the timber suitable for oceangoing vessels was sent to the royal shipyards at Lisbon (and so was firewood for the royal palaces!). This activity must have been ineffectively administered, despite the extraordinary abundance in the coastal forests of giant trees, whose wood was stronger and more resistant than any available in Europe, and despite the possibility of shipping the timber cost free as ballast. The royal yards continued to import from New England, while the crown received repeated intelligence of smuggling of Brazilian timber by the Dutch and English. The shortage of suitable wood was at times so acute in Lisbon that the shipyards were obliged to piece planks together, reducing thereby the strength of the vessels and obliging constant repairs.[39]

By the mid-1700s, however, a large shipbuilding industry had come to be organized in Salvador, at the arsenal and royal yards and in private shipyards. Men-of-war and merchantmen built in Bahia constituted, by the end of the century, most of the tonnage under the Portuguese flag. The timber for these ships was obtained in Pernambuco and Alagoas and in South Bahia, in the former captaincies of Ilhéus and Porto Seguro. There, unbroken stands of primary forest persisted into the late eighteenth century, even at water's edge, wherever Jesuit aldeias had survived or tribal peoples had resisted encroachment.[40]

Royal commands to conserve naval timber began to be issued in 1698, when sesmarias were forbidden in areas of naval timber reserve. Though few sesmarias were subsequently issued, logging became a tightly organized private industry. Although formally supervised by "guard-majors" and administrators, they were systematically suborned and thwarted by a small number of loggers, sawyers, and drovers, who decided, in effect, where and when timber would be cut. From 1795 to 1799, Rodrigo de Souza Coutinho issued a series of orders designed to conserve naval timber: Authority to cut hardwoods suitable for shipbuilding, referred to as *pau real* or *madeira de lei*—royal trees or woods-of-law—was reserved to the governors, who were provided with "judge conservators," exclusively charged with surveying, regulation, and licensing. Sesmarias in areas of naval reserve were to be canceled and compensated by the grant of land elsewhere. Those species of hardwoods of greatest value in naval construction were to be sold exclusively to the royal yards, at prices fixed by the governor.

The governors diligently executed these instructions. Surveys of timber reserves and means of transport were carried out, maps were drawn up, and tables of prices to be paid contractors or private landowners were devised. Some of the squatters within the zone might be permitted to remain, if they limited their activities to fishing or were willing to take up the duties of forest guards (this is a measure proposed by current-day environmentalists). Incendiarism was to be punished with prison. For perhaps the first time, the concept of primary forest entered the vocabulary of conservation: The governor of São Paulo, considering that the "public good" required a limit on the liberty of individuals to destroy "forever" forests that had taken centuries to form, prohibited the felling or burning of forests "that are called and are reputed to be virgin forests, even though in them few woods-of-law are to be found."[41]

Additional reserves were formed. In the captaincy of São Paulo, all the hardwoods of the forests between shoreline and the coastal escarpment were declared liable to royal expropriation, and five royal reserves were established and demarcated between Paranaguá and Santos. The surveys of these reserves by army engineers and the reports of the judge conservators appointed over the reserves record the state of the coastal forests at the turn of the nineteenth century; indeed, they offer more information than anything that had been written since 1500 concerning the distribution of tree species. Among those of most value for shipbuilding, tapinhoá was ranked in first place because it resisted marine parasites; others included sucupira, canela, canjarana, jacarandá, araribá, pequi, genipap, peroba, urucurana, and vinhático. The forests of Alagoas were esteemed for the misshapen timbers they supplied for ribs, prows, and keels.[42]

The surveys and reports indicate that adequate timber no longer existed for many leagues in the vicinity of the larger towns. A great deal of logging for boatbuilding had already occurred. At Iguape there were no longer any suitable trees within 60 kilometers of the bar. At Paranaguá the "woods easiest to remove have been removed because, besides the various shipyards that have been established on those rivers, . . . there are at present more than a hundred saws at work, whose lumber is exported to Rio de Janeiro [and] Bahia, which is the principal trade of this town." At Campos logs had to be hauled 3 to 9 kilometers to the coast. This selective logging, continued over centuries, suggests that many of the stands of coastal forest that are today represented to be "primary" and have been selected for protection as such had already been skimmed two centuries ago.[43]

Souza Coutinho's policies had been drafted in part by Baltasar da Silva Lisboa, a Brazilian judge who had studied natural science at Coimbra and knew intimately the forests of South Bahia. It was he whom the minister appointed judge conservator of that region in 1796. Prodigiously energetic and loyal to the crown, he was impelled by a commitment to the conservation of what he called "this sublime storehouse of Nature." The Supreme Being had displayed his partiality toward the Portuguese Empire by bestowing this wooden treasure upon it, suitable for the construction of a respectable navy. It therefore caused him great anguish that so much forest destruction had already occurred. Because the crown could not cease promoting agriculture, however, he foresaw the necessity of rationalizing forestry. His reports demonstrate a familiarity with hundreds of tree species of the coastal forest and their myriad uses. He measured growth rates and carried out experiments in thinning, stimulating regrowth, and replanting. He realized, however, that the harvest of forest trees would be delayed by fifty to a hundred years, and he came also to understand that Brazilian trees were "subject to very different physical laws, compared to Europe," each of them requiring specific and subtly different growing conditions. His studies suggested to him that

> the towering trees here support the small, and contribute to their periodic growth: The roots, which commonly scour the surface of the ground, do not damage those of new plants that are destined to replace the loss of the old, when they are cut or for one reason or another perish. Observation has confirmed that the trees do not increase in girth and relative height, planted apart from the woods of their natural existence, whether as seedlings grown from seeds, or saplings transplanted from those woods, to isolated terrain, even though fertile; . . . which can be proved by ocular inspection of the sucupiras, and other trees growing on open pasture and others which I ordered planted ten years ago in Mapendipe [and] which for the most part perished; and those that escaped are altogether defective for the use of the Navy.[44]

The knowledge that the trees of the Atlantic Forest would not grow back from stumps, that they could not be made to grow at all except within the forest, and that their growth was so slow that generations must pass before they could be harvested suggested that, unlike the forests of the temperate Old World, the replanting of native hardwoods in homogeneous stands was neither economical nor ecologically feasible and that the supply of ships' timber could be sustained only through the careful management of existing forests, including selective logging and encouragement of the regeneration of tree species of greatest value.

These realities were of no concern to the loggers and their allies, who were infuriated by the unaccustomed challenge to their mode of production. Neither the expulsion of caboclo squatters nor the forced transfer of natives to work the reserves was a matter of political consequence, because these were acts inveterately perpetrated by the rich and powerful themselves. But the expulsion of the rich and powerful was by no means easy. Souza Coutinho's orders also interfered with itinerant farmers who followed close upon the loggers, planting manioc and rice to feed the growing urban population and the suddenly expanding sugar and cotton plantations of the Northeast. Conflicts grew apace. Contractors sent by the government onto private property to remove needed timber took no care to avoid damage to other trees. Private owners were now required to obtain permission to fell hardwoods on their property, obliging them to travel to the provincial capital and subjecting them to still another occasion for graft. The governors applied taxes on the removal of timber by private owners, arbitrarily decided purchase prices of hardwoods, and then delayed payment.[45]

In South Bahia these measures did not remain long in effect. The loggers simply refused to supply the royal yards, and the monopoly of fine hardwoods was hastily rescinded. Against the visions of a mercantilist bureaucracy, opponents of Silva Lisboa's policies raised the principles of liberalism. The economist José Joaquim de Azeredo Coutinho asserted that government control simply caused landowners to destroy their forests as quickly as possible, "to free themselves of that onus, that kind of tribute . . . and the vexations caused them by all those who go to cut timber in their woods." Left to their own devices, Azeredo Coutinho supposed, landowners would preserve their forests, because it was in their best interests. It seems grotesque, two hundred years removed from these polemics, to observe, on one hand, a corrupt and authoritarian government defending the preservation of the Atlantic Forest in order to sustain its war-making capacity and, on the other hand, an equally corrupt, opportunistic, and slave-driving elite pledging its allegiance to the principle of free markets and claiming equally to be the forest's defenders.[46]

As strange as it might seem that Portugal was obliged to import wood from New England, it is stranger still that Rio de Janeiro, which by 1818 was buying most of its wood from far-distant Porto Seguro, nevertheless also bought wood from African, North American, and Swedish ports, whence it arrived for half the price of locally cut wood. This certainly demonstrated the improbability of realizing the other objective of the order of 1797—to sell Brazilian wood to other countries. One reason for this anomaly was that Brazilian logging was several centuries out of date. The sawing of timber was in many places still done by hand, nearly two hundred years after water-powered sawmills had been installed in English and Dutch colonies.[47]

It was not only along the coast that competition for forest resources resulted in shortages of timber, lumber, and even firewood. In the highlands, markets were more dispersed, transport much dearer, and naval woods entirely inaccessible. There were no royal preserves, and forests customarily went up in flames before any timber was removed. Observers of the time complain interminably of high prices for these products, of the necessity of bringing them long distances to town centers, and of the disastrous mismanagement of resources that permitted immense treasures in hardwoods to be set afire in order to plant a few seasons of manioc. These practices especially shocked the Europeans, unaccustomed to such waste and improvidence. Saint-Hilaire was amazed that the Brazilians had managed to destroy so much and yet continued the practice "with a strange perseverance" while refusing to consider the idea of replanting. In the Campos region he had seen vexing shortages of wood on the sugar plantations, although there was considerable land inappropriate for cane upon which fast-growing trees might be grown. He was astonished at how quickly a thin population could have ravaged such vast areas of Minas Gerais. Imagining that these losses would lead finally to the "imperious necessity" of changing the agricultural regime, nevertheless it would be eternally regretted that "these beautiful forests" would have been lost, "whose precious woods, managed with care, could have sufficed a long train of generations."[48]

Brazilian-born naturalists could be still more mordant in their view of forest destruction. The Mineiro José Vieira Couto, another of Vandelli's students, described the Brazilian farmer, "with a broadax in one hand and a firebrand in the other," practicant of a "barbarous agriculture," as one who

> gazes upon two or more leagues of forests as though they were nought, and hardly has he reduced them to ashes but he extends his view still further to carry destruction to other parts; he harbors neither affection nor love for the land he cultivates, knowing full well that it will probably not last for his children.[49]

These learned critics of customary farming methods did not explain them as a logical response to environmental limitations, as an efficient allocation of capital and labor, or even as a consequence of the impossibility of a poor family's acquiring legal title; instead, they agreed with Silva Lisboa in attributing them to "ignorance and barbarity" or to "sloth and ignorance." Although the Frenchman Saint-Hilaire and other foreigners did not exempt sugar planters from their criticism, Silva Lisboa and his Brazilian colleagues tended to limit their scorn to "the vagabonds, who devastate, ravage, and reduce to ashes the richest trees on water's edge." Likening these practices to those of the "ferocious savages, their first inhabitants" (and thereby maligning the indigenes as well), he lamented that the frontiersmen were quite unaware of the "great ends of Providence," which had bestowed such bounties on Brazil, and of the "incalculable loss to the State" caused by their "horrifying burnings," whose only purpose was to permit the "ruinous planting of manioc."[50]

In these texts, the wastefulness of the caboclos is boundless; they are capable even of felling a tree to save themselves the trouble of climbing it to pick fruit or dislodge a wild bee hive. Their farming is not regarded as useful. Manuel Ferreira da Câmara, by 1807 retired from the diamond intendancy, complained that his sugar estate in Bahia was surrounded by open country by then suitable only for maize or rice growing, because all the woods that might have fed sugar-mill furnaces were gone. But maize and rice were basic supplies for the towns, and their producers therefore filled an essential niche in the Brazilian economy. Another essayist who recognized the utility of small-scale farmers complained instead that they were also attempting to sell their produce for export, a grave matter, because it threatened the towns with hunger. It is likely that the writer, who called them "a mob of vagrants," was annoyed as well that this diversion of their energies upset the social hierarchy thought appropriate between small farmers and plantation owners, who presumed a right to monopoly of the export market.[51]

It is possible that the losses of forest resources was less than these writers believed. Critics of royal forest policy claimed that private owners had an interest in preserving woodlots, because they would always need fuel and lumber. John Luccock saw farms that maintained woodlots in the vicinity of Rio de Janeiro, and Saint-Hilaire found "virgin forest" not far from the city. Because much coastal land—indeed, most of it—remained to be given out in sesmarias, it is not even clear that the need for naval timber was as pressing as the government imagined. Although the crown waxed indignant at the continued cutting of brazilwood on private lands, it does not appear that it found any licensees willing to revive the trade on the Rio de Janeiro coast, where these dyewood trees were by then probably quite rare in accessible locations. Liberal theorists asserted that abolishing the monopoly in woods-of-law and brazilwood would be more likely to achieve higher output, with less waste of forest.[52]

How regrettable that the European-trained naturalists of the turn of the nineteenth century left behind only brief and colorless memoirs of their experience under the canopy of the Atlantic Forest. Full of complaints at the inconveniences of the road, the incomprehension and doltishness of the inhabitants, the difficulties of keeping their specimens and notes dry, rarely did they confide to their readers their sensations amid the silence and gloom of the forest giants. Only once did Saint-Hilaire hint at them, when he spoke of "that sort of religious terror that the view of virgin forests usually inspires." This remark he follows with an expression of his delight, upon emerging from woodland, in seeing the river and town of São João da Barra spread before him—how charming it appeared, after passing several hours enclosed in a tunnel of trees. James Wells admitted feeling "an imperceptible depression" in the "dark silent shades," followed by "elation" upon breaking out into the "fresh breezes of the campos, brilliant with flowers and bright-plumaged birds." Alfred Russel Wallace felt "relief" upon "again seeing the blue sky and feeling the scorching rays of the sun." Hermann von Burmeister, perceiving amorality in the struggles among the forest's creatures, thought they set the decisive example for the country's inhabitants, whom he judged false and oppressive of their fellows.[53]

John Luccock recalled a dramatic and emblematic episode. He had climbed to an aerie high in the Tijuca massif behind Rio de Janeiro, where a friend was clearing a lot upon which to build his house. His slaves, however, had not yet felled the trees that obstructed the view:

> Almost three hours were spent in cutting down tree after tree, each of which, falling against its neighbor, remained for the most part in an upright position. At length one large and hardwooded tree giving way towards the south, the rest, which had been upheld by it, followed. The effect was like drawing aside a curtain. In an instant there lay before us a complete view of the city of St. Sebastian, its bay, islands, shores and surrounding mountains, together with a wide expanse of ocean. The very slaves [sic] were struck dumb with astonishment, feeling the effect of beauty beyond description bursting unexpectedly upon them. The silence and the clamor which succeeded were both expressive; in various languages, used by the natives of three different quarters of the globe, the same sentiment was heard: "surely this is a goodly world which we inhabit."[54]

Just so: The creatures and vegetables of the forest might fascinate, one by one, each related to the other in intellectual exercises that filled the halls of vast museums, but the conjuncture was overwhelming and replaceable with more cheerful views, that is, landscapes—open, sunny, and anthropomorphosed.

The crown had clear purposes in patronizing natural science in Brazil: to enhance its revenues through increased exports and to improve imperial defenses through the local manufacture of war matériel. Buffeted by the turbulence of war and revolution, it made no effort to replace its despotic rule with a constitution or to end the injustices of colonial society. Slavery was abolished in Portugal in 1773, but there was no move to end it in Brazil, now that it had become the metropolis. On the contrary, the regent was persuaded in 1808 to declare war on the Botocudos—"by means of a written and published act, as is the custom among civilized peoples," sneered one foreign observer. This pretext for slave raiding was accompanied by temporizing over British demands to carry out his pledge to end the slave trade. The practice of bestowing vast sesmarias upon court favorites was intensified and remained as corrupt and unregulated as before, thus guaranteeing the perpetuation of large numbers of propertyless, itinerant swidden farmers. Did the natural scientists whom João welcomed to his realm sense any incongruity between his goals and those of the Enlightenment and liberalism, which promised the toleration of dissent and the free flow of information that were essential to the progress of science?[55]

Johann Emanuel Pohl, arriving exhausted one night in São João del Rei, was grateful to find a lodging house with a clean and comfortable bed, which he took to be a sign of civilization. When he flung open his window the next morning, however, he found himself looking into the eyes of a bloody, fly-encrusted head, affixed to a pike that was implanted in the town square, only a few meters away. This repellent spectacle had belonged to a slave who had killed his master. Pohl offers no reflection upon it, whether of distaste or sympathy. The violence and desperation of this country were unrelated to its flora and fauna, his only interest. The naturalists rarely maintained such punctiliousness in their observations of the underclass. Never did they attribute their indifference and apathy to the impossibility of acquiring title to the lands they improvidently fired. Saint-Hilaire, who affirmed his sympathy for the French Revolution, from which the majority of Frenchmen had "gained immensely" through the suppression of "the legal privileges that a favored class had enjoyed" and who perceived that the movement for independence in Brazil was little more than a counterrevolution carried out by a similarly favored class, nevertheless permitted himself to indulge in a "dream" in which he acquired a farm in Brazil, laid out a garden *à l'anglais* by cutting paths into the forest. The farm would be worked rationally, by slaves who, under his care, married, well nourished, provided with marks of his favor, would come to hold their master dear and love the land where their children were born. Then he would attract indigenes with little presents, teaching them to farm and catechizing them. The "former anthropophagus [*sic*]" would enter Saint-Hilaire's humble chapel "to pray for his enemies, and his daughter would at last know her shame." (Nakedness greatly upset Saint-Hilaire.) These expressions of paternalism differed from those of estate owners and the crown only in their ingenuousness and obliviousness of hidden menace.[56]

Attitudes such as these clearly reserved for scientific investigation a tutorial role, if not one clearly supportive of the status quo. Baltasar da Silva Lisboa, in contrast, represented a more forthright, or upright, position. An abolitionist who supported the extinction of the slave trade, he observed a logical connection between that institution and the lack "of respect and veneration for [nature's] inestimable benefits," which caused the Brazilian to "destroy cruelly and barbarously its marvels, not following and imitating its conduct." The Brazilian, observed Silva Lisboa, "was not less ungrateful, unjust, and destructive toward his own species in the manner of dealing with men who are his slaves," maltreating them "with punishments that appal all of nature." Here Silva Lisboa may be forgiven his romantic view of nature, considering his realistic appraisal of slavery. Another who approved the end of the slave trade was the savant Antônio Rodrigues Veloso de Oliveira, author of memorials directed to the court advocating sawmills, potash manufacture, salt pans, and other improvements. He proposed as well the immediate end of chattel slavery—a measure taken only in 1871—recognition of the right of slaves to free themselves with earnings, and the free grant of smallholdings to colonists, both freedmen and immigrants. Veloso de Oliveira was not, however, a conservationist, believing as he did that forests grew back within thirty years "with great perfection" and that the encouragement of the export of forest products "would disembarrass the land of importunate and until now useless woodlands." What might now be regarded as a misalignment between conservationist and progressive opinion among the Brazilian elite was not in the nineteenth century uncommon.[57]

The wave of scientific investigation and the plans for rational utilization of the Atlantic Forest had hardly crested when, quite suddenly, its patronage was withdrawn. King João tarried in Rio de Janeiro after the French withdrew from the Iberian Peninsula in 1814, possibly because he feared further political upheavals in Europe. In 1815 he declared Brazil a kingdom, coequal with Portugal and the tiny Algarve, hoping thereby to impress the congresses that were about to redistribute the spoils of war but also deluding his Brazilian subjects that Rio de Janeiro would remain the seat of empire. Five years more this idyll lasted, then, upon the outbreak of a rebellion in Lisbon, led by resentful liberals who desired rather contradictorily a liberal constitution and a restored mercantilist empire, João was forced to return to Europe. The Brazilian landholding elite, supported by the intelligentsia and convinced of its ability to maintain its position without Portuguese bayonets, rejected the demands of Lisbon and, having in their midst João's eldest son, Pedro, prompted him to declare independence on their behalf. He grasped the title of emperor and imposed his own constitution. The Portuguese garrisons were soon evacuated, and Portugal, through the self-interested offices of Britain, legitimized its colony's independence.

These dizzying political events, accomplished by 1826, modified considerably the relationship of Brazilians to the natural world they inherited. No longer subject to colonial tutelage, able to decide the terms of their material and intellectual exchanges with the rest of the world, able to redefine their social relationships to suit themselves, they were at last free to decide what they would do with what remained of the Atlantic Forest. It was not altogether surprising that they would choose to abandon the attempts to investigate it, to rationalize its use, and to conserve it, choosing instead to attack it with redoubled energy and enthusiasm.

7

The Forest under Brazilian Rule

*As divisões principalmente [das posses] só são firmadas, e respeitadas
pela arma de fogo desfechada d'emboscadas de traz dos grossos troncos de
nossas arvores seculares.*

*The boundaries principally [of posses] are settled and respected
by means of the gun fired in ambush from behind the thick trunks
of our centuries-old trees.*

JOÃO CALDAS VIANA, VICE-PRESIDENT
OF THE PROVINCE OF RIO DE JANEIRO (1843)

The new government, detached from its subservience to an exploitive and
distant monarch, found itself blessed with extraordinary resources and opportunities. Independence had been achieved at only a trifling cost in
blood. The propertied classes of every captaincy had accepted the legitimacy of the emperor and his constitution, thereby denying the oppressed
masses the occasion for a rising. Brazilian territory was thus preserved
whole, unlike the viceroyalties of the Spanish empire, which descended
contemporaneously into ferocious and seemingly interminable civil wars.
The country had inherited a modest but vital scientific and technical cadre,
and it was endowed with an immense territory, most of it still beyond
the neo-European pale, its potential value unknown. The intelligentsia,
having absorbed the social and political thought of the century of Enlightenment, though convinced of its right to rank and privilege, yet professed
its desire to bring the nation to a state of civilization equal to that of
Europe, through just and liberal laws, education, and institutional and
economic development.

It cannot be affirmed, however, that this intelligentsia conceived of the
independent nation as more than a state and citizenry secured by defined
political borders, occupying an agreed-upon geographical space. The idea
that it might be as well a community identified with the living world from
which its citizens drew their sustenance in perpetuity was altogether

muted, almost unidentifiable. Emílio Joaquim da Silva Maia seems to have been quite alone in equating the conservation of Brazil's forests with patriotism, asserting that it was the fitness of every work of nature to a specific place that inspires citizens to a love of their homeland. But this was a random, isolated view; nationalistic nature sentimentality was still three-quarters of a century in the future, and the romantic naturalism stylish in contemporary England found no echo in Brazil at all.[1]

The opportunity afforded by independence, a tranquil polity, and the reformist spirit of the times was dissipated. The empire was soon wracked by external and internal conflicts so tenacious that it appeared that its fate would be the same as that of the former colonies of Spain. Pedro became involved in the succession to the Portuguese throne and thereby was obliged to renounce his own. Under the succeeding regency, regional and partisan rebellions spilled over bloodily to mass uprisings. These conflicts were resolved under his son, the second Pedro, crowned in 1840, but Brazil's interference in the affairs of its southern neighbors continued, exploding in a war against Paraguay in 1865. Even though this violence ended in 1870, it enervated the empire, which fell twenty years later, leaving to the republic a legacy of reforms postponed or perverted, of government unable to gain control of its patrimony, to impose the rule of law, or to convert the mass of its population from servility to citizenry. These failures were to extort a terrible price from the Atlantic Forest, which was soon transformed from an occasional obstacle to the wealth that might be obtained from precious metals and gems to the very source of the wealth.

It is not surprising that the agenda of the notables who constructed the new state at first consisted primarily, indeed, almost exclusively, of personal and factional aggrandizement, because the capture of power was prerequisite to the carrying out of substantive programs. Nor is it surprising that their resentment toward the departed autocracy came to be directed against many of its rational policies, although it is remarkable how many of these policies were frustrated by mere indifference and incomprehension. In essence, however, the omissions of the new rulers exhibited neither procrastination nor incompetence: Independence offered the great landowners the opportunity to turn from resisting the dictates of central authority to molding them to its interests, and this was certainly the wellspring of their patriotism.[2]

The most important of the interests they wished promoted was the African slave trade. King João had been forced by the British to restrict slaving to Portuguese colonies south of the equator and to bind his government to eventual extinction of the trade. He had found it expedient to join the other European powers in an expression of opposition to it in principle. Now, with independence, Brazil might at one stroke forswear this retrograde commerce and thereby begin the task of eliminating slavery entirely under conditions that might yet permit the survival of the great estates, or at least of their owners as a class. By 1822 all other Western countries had forsworn the trade; only Portugal had not been converted—Brazil might have begun its national life unstained by that dishonor. Although Pedro himself professed to the British a desire to end the trade and although his closest advisors, most important of whom were José Bonifâcio de Andrada e Silva and his brothers, along with many other liberals attracted to the court, openly deplored slavery and wished to see it ended, they were unwilling to risk the positions they had so lately won by struggling for this great reform. Pressed hard by the British government, which might have bestowed considerable benefits in return, the emperor and his circle nevertheless temporized. Not until 1831 was a law abolishing the trade reluctantly signed; this was not enforced, however, until 1851. During that last half century of the traffic, as many as 1.25 million more slaves were imported, enough to fuel the plantation system until the waning of the nineteenth century.[3]

The impact of a slave agricultural labor regime upon the forested region of southeastern Brazil is impossible to calculate but not difficult to discern. The inflow of this great number in itself necessitated vastly larger areas of planted land for subsistence. These levies made it possible to exclude native itinerant subsistence farmers and small cash-cropping farmers from the export trade, which the planters reserved to themselves. They also made it impossible to attract to Brazil in any significant number free immigrant workers, the principal means by which the government had hoped to transfer the more intensive agricultural practices of Europe to the benighted emancipated colony. Most harmful were the techniques that were inevitable in the working of slave plantations. Constantly driven by a "labor shortage," of which the ultimate cause was the speculative expansion of plantings and the refusal of a slave labor force to work any harder or more carefully than the whip could stir them, the planters engaged in a form of agriculture so exploitative that it hardly deserves that appellation. Agriculture practiced by slaves was inherently predatory—it could not be intensified, and it expanded along a resource frontier until the resource was exhausted.

That this form of exploitation was allowed to persist, suppressing and distorting the employment of human skills for another sixty-six years until at last, fresh levies of slaves having been cut off and the last generation of them, born Brazilian and grown weary of procrastination, ceased to pick up their hoes and thereby forced the assembly to accept in 1888 the fait accompli, is the most terrible reflection upon the governing classes of the nation. Shamelessly, they retrospectively painted themselves as abolitionists from the beginning, claimed the entire credit for final abolition, and prided themselves that they had in timely fashion avoided civil war. On the backs of the freedmen and the denuded hillsides were scars enough to contradict their version of history. This choice to cling to slavery to the bitter end, if choice it may be called, demonstrated how dominant was the plantation interest and how independent it had been of the "absolute" despotism of the Portuguese monarchy. Indeed, the British government, supposedly awash in humanitarian sentiment, had retreated from its insistence on the abolition of the slave traffic as its condition for recognition of Brazil's independence when it reflected that such a measure might cause the empire to be overthrown and the provinces to break away. This it would have regretted extremely, because it desired to maintain on American soil at least one strong exemplar of the monarchical principle.[4]

Another of the planters' great concerns was to be released from every restraint upon their engrossment of public lands. The sesmaria system, a legal fiction that had legitimized the usurpation of royal patrimony, had proven over the whole of the colonial period a convenient vehicle to this end. During the eighteenth century, the crown had continued to issue these grants as a means of favoring the rich and powerful, with whom the crown identified and upon whom it relied to populate the vast colony, produce exportable goods, and defend its borders. The rich and powerful nevertheless found flaws in the system. The sesmaria had come to be limited in size, usually to no more than a square league (43.56 square kilometers) in regions fit for agriculture. To the rural notables, this seemed a paltry benefaction, and therefore they often stooped to claiming several sesmarias through front men or relatives. This was also a common practice among crown officials, who were disqualified from requesting grants but quite naturally considered their posts a means to securing them.

It was a major cause of the destruction of the Atlantic Forest that the government assigned no value to the land it so freely granted. Having consumed all the most promising primary forest in a given sesmaria, a grantee commonly sold it off for a trifle and asked for another, which he normally experienced no difficulty in obtaining. According to one late-eighteenth-century report from Minas Gerais:

> The facility with which sesmarias have been conceded has been
> very prejudicial, because the best forests have been burned, along

with those closest to populated places, which already [1780] feel
the lack of wood, firewood, and forage. . . . Besides this the farmers
practice no form of cultivation at all, because they carry it out
without improving their lands, it being infinite those that are abandoned, and that would certainly produce harvests in greater abundance than those of this kingdom [Portugal] were they improved.
That facility causes the patrimony of the captaincy of Minas Gerais
to be unstable; because the farmers, since the concession of new
lands is not made difficult, do not install the requisite improvements on those they possess, and abandon them for whatever
motives of fantasized convenience.[5]

Curiously, these practices differed only in their greater intensity and scale
from the itinerancy engaged in by the lower classes and excoriated by the
governors and the grantees themselves, ever avid to exploit a stable work
force. The result, according to the report, was that "there are in the same
captaincy hundreds of sesmarias conceded many years ago without the
slightest cultivation; and always the inhabitants go on asking for new
lands, without there being any necessity to concede them."

Despite the ease with which pretendants were awarded multiple sesmarias and the consequent low price of land, it was axiomatic that "landholding is the greatest wealth," because only land bestowed prestige, made
possible the accumulation of other forms of wealth, and exonerated its
holder from the many impositions of royal officials.[6]

Although the crown was unable to devise a substitute for the sesmarias,
it did seek increasingly to impose more stringent conditions upon their
concession. The decree of 1795, probably the work of Rodrigo de Souza
Coutinho, demanded the demarcation of all existing and future sesmarias.
(It had been the practice to omit from the petition all references to boundaries and area!) The decree also limited the size of sesmarias near towns
and along rivers, required the keeping of land registries, and created royal
judges to hear land disputes. The scarcity of surveyors in the colony, it was
alleged, frustrated the 1795 decree; it was abrogated a year later, much to
the satisfaction of the landowners, who also alleged insufficient funds to
pay for demarcation.[7]

Landowners had not the slightest desire that the state fix their boundaries and legitimize their land claims. They preferred uncertainty, the better to encroach upon public lands. But uncertainty led to violence, on a
scale that wracked the interior and challenged the authority of the crown.
That the landowners preferred bloodshed to the stability of clear titles
guaranteed by the state suggests a political system still more centrifugal
than feudalism. The sesmaria might be brandished in court by any and all

contestants in the primordial struggles of the countryside, but the effect was less than when firearms were brandished on the forest trail; consequently, it offered only a trifling advantage. Indeed, it appears that many of the sesmarias were obtained merely to extort a settlement from genuine settlers who might later appear. Therefore the licenses and bribes that it cost to acquire them were necessarily modest—according to Auguste de Saint-Hilaire, 100 milreis (at the time, 100 dollars, hence 43 cents a hectare). Even demarcation by a crown official, it would seem, added little to the security of ownership and therefore little to the value of a claim.[8]

The sudden transfer of the seat of royal authority to Rio de Janeiro had threatened these rural autocrats. Decrees were issued in rapid order to require confirmation of all sesmarias by the palace, to make foreigners (King João's minions) eligible for sesmarias, to eliminate the need for witnesses to establish the applicant's means to work a sesmaria, and to create in every judicial district the post of surveyor. The crown, far from intending to act evenhandedly, was under the necessity of compensating hangers-on for their loyalty under the hardships of the tropical court, and this compensation was often to take the form of land grants. Landowners in the captaincies could foresee that the court would outmaneuver them for the best lands.[9]

The granting of sesmarias was suspended in the midst of the political crisis that led to independence, and then it was abolished by the Constituent Assembly, unwilling as it was to allow this enormous source of patronage to pass to Pedro, who was already displaying considerable talent for arrogating power. There were several proposals at hand for the reformation of land grants. Indeed, the reformers of King João's era anticipated most of the proposals made in the 1880s—indeed, in the 1960s. Baltasar da Silva Lisboa wanted sesmarias not effectively occupied to revert to the crown and distributed to smallholders, in order to "abolish the unemployment of men and lands"; what generated citizens, he insisted, was property. Antônio Rodrigues de Oliveira coupled land reform to the abolition of slavery—freedmen should each be awarded a hectare or two, with clear title. The crown should honor owners who donated lands for that purpose with knighthood. After that, let the government take the place of private police—an immensely subversive idea. José Bonifâcio de Andrada e Silva proposed to delegates to the provisional government that uncultivated lands revert to national property and that sesmaria owners be allowed to retain only a quarter square league (10.6 square kilometers) of their grants, on condition that it be immediately cultivated. Squatters would be entitled to no more than the land they were cultivating plus a reserve of about 75 hectares. All owners would be required to leave a sixth of their property in forest or to replant up to that amount, if they had already cleared more. Henceforth, he recommended, all crown land should be sold, not granted, at 300 reis (30 cents) per hectare, a day's wages for a common laborer. Revenues from these sales were to be applied to colonization, both European and national. These proposals would have within a generation restructured Brazilian society. For precisely this reason they gained no hearing at all. They might also have prevented the forests of the new nation, victims, he said, of "ignorance and egotism," from being "reduced to the wastes and deserts of Libya."[10]

Unfortunately, for the next 27 years, the assembly avoided passage of any method of alienating crown lands to replace the sesmaria. Sesmarias continued, in fact, to be awarded exceptionally by provincial presidents if the pretendant was sufficiently powerful or incipiently rebellious, a practice unobtrusively authorized in 1829 by an administrative decision of the emperor. During this long interval, thousands of coffee plantations were established, and tens of thousands of discouraged gold prospectors fanned out in search of cattle pasture and slash-and-burn homesteads. The new properties were posses—claims based on the right of occupation, or squatting. These were astounding in their extravagance: Often they extended ten or twenty times the size of the royal grants of a single square league. Such a pretension was not conceivable for the ordinary backwoodsman, but it was incumbent upon the leader, or would-be leader, of a clan, one who invited his kinsmen with their agregados and their slaves to take part in the usurpation of public land on a scale grand enough to intimidate rivals, buy off officials, and establish a local preeminence that the imperial government would be obliged to acknowledge.[11]

Even more than the sesmaria, the posse was based on violence. The president of Rio de Janeiro admitted openly to his provincial assembly in 1840 that "it is known that to establish a posse, and keep it, . . . force is indispensable. He who lacks it is obliged to cede the land to another who is stronger or to sell it to someone who by means of the same force can retain it." Although he and other officials called for a legal remedy for this state of affairs, the assembly persisted in craven indecision until 1850, when it finally passed a law subjecting all crown lands to public sale. Posses before that date, no matter how large, were recognized, provided they were uncontested and were duly entered in the land registry. The execution of this law was nearly as much a travesty as was the preceding period of lawlessness. These claims were, like the sesmarias, set down in the land registry without demarcations. Squatters holding subsistence-sized plots were commonly too poor to pay the registration fee and therefore remained as precarious as ever. Usurpation went on as before, subject to numerous frauds to make it appear that occupation antedated 1850. No tax was imposed on privatized land, except for transfers, and even this was evaded by undervaluation.[12]

The imperial government never carried out an inventory of public lands. It was therefore reduced to inquiring of county councils whether any such existed within their jurisdiction. Cunningly, they invariably reported that all had disappeared. In the province of Espírito Santo, a region so unattractive to neo-European settlement in the nineteenth century that the imperial government had had to take on nearly all the tasks of populating it, including sponsored immigration and colonization, a rough accounting was possible. In 1888, the last year of the empire, a special inspector of lands and colonization found that even there invalid and illegal posses totaled almost 44 percent of all land claims.[13]

The empire's inability to control the public lands—indeed, its willingness to connive in their private expropriation at no cost to the expropriators—was a major cause of rapid deforestation. A nineteenth-century chronicler of Minas Gerais recognized the "terrible effects" of these policies:

> The grantees felled and burned the forest, failed to improve the land and when they lacked the space necessary for planting, they abandoned the sesmarias or sold them for little more than nothing and went to ask for another grant or laid claim to another piece of land somewhere else.[14]

This, he said, is why rural houses were so flimsy and temporary and why there were so many taperas to be seen in the province and why construction wood was leagues away from settlements. Thus the view was confirmed that soil was an expendable resource. Clearly it was pointless to attempt to conserve a farmstead that could be replaced at no cost. Nor could a farmstead that had already been worked fetch a price in the market equal to cleared frontier land. What then would be the point of trying to preserve its fertility? Under such conditions land, though the basis of political power and social prominence, was not patrimony. It is interesting to note that the peers created under the empire enjoyed their titles only during their lifetimes. The sons of the "coffee barons" were rarely ennobled, and those who were almost never resided on the same estate. Indeed, there is at least one case of a baron finding himself forced to emigrate to another province with all his slaves as his estate collapsed under him, very likely because of reckless management.[15]

Patriarchal application of inheritance law was a factor that stimulated the explosive expansion of the nineteenth-century frontier. Alida Metcalf has shown that fathers habitually favored sons-in-law and younger sons in their bestowal of their properties in an attempt to stave off as long as possible the inevitable transfer of control of the family and its resources to the younger generation. Sons-in-law, often immigrants valued for their commercial links and indubitably white skins, were even less likely than younger sons to challenge the authority of the aging paterfamilias. Elder sons were in subtle ways obliged or encouraged to move on and establish themselves along the frontier, remote from the family homestead. This manner of transferring land rights assured that proprietors, from generation to generation, remained strangers to the land, first outcasts and usurpers, then epigones and arrivistes.[16]

The third facility desired by the landed classes was the continued removal of the indigenes from their lands and their impressment into the work force as auxiliaries, if not as outright slaves. Portuguese monarchs had prohibited their enslavement several times, most resoundingly in a decree that took effect in the region of the Atlantic Forest in 1758. Missionaries were henceforth to have no authority over the indigenous aldeias. It being suspected, however, that the villagers would immediately disappear into the forest, governors were authorized to appoint civilian directors over them. Rare was the white who would take on such a responsibility unless he intended to exploit native labor to the fullest and connive in usurping their lands. In consequence, many of the aldeias along the Rio de Janeiro and Espírito Santo coasts had been nearly extinguished by the time of an enlightened decree of 1798 that devolved control of the aldeias upon their own leaders, a measure with slight effect, because Indian directors received scant hearing in the courts or the governor's palace.

The arrival of the Portuguese court had not marked a turn toward a more humane policy. The regent's declaration of war upon the Botocudos, who inhabited the highlands between the gold and diamond districts and the coast, was intended to encourage prospecting in the region, hitherto forbidden to settlement in order to discourage smuggling. It was being penetrated by prospectors hoping for one last lucky strike, and the crown was only too ready to oblige them. The Botocudos had survived in this entirely forested zone by avoiding agriculture, which would have exposed them to raiders, and by combatting intruders ferociously. They had acquired, indeed, an undeserved but useful reputation as cannibals, which now was to be employed against them. As they fought off the prospectors, they retreated eastward and thereby threatened the coastal settlements of Espírito Santo. They were also competing more fiercely with their rivals, the Coroados, peoples who had been formerly more sedentary and horti-cultural. Groups of Coroados were therefore obliged to "descend" for pro-tection to the neo-European pale. João's declaration was soon extended to other hunter-gatherers who were inconveniencing cattle ranchers moving into the patches of grasslands in the interior of São Paulo. These groups, some of them without any prior contact with neo-Europeans, were migrat-ing toward the coast from the interior, sometimes in search of the legend-ary land without evil.[17]

Aldeias were established to receive the captives brought in by the troops, to fix them in one place so that they might be catechized and made available for work on the lands of the whites. These aldeias were entrusted not to missionaries but to the same army commanders whose salaries were adjusted to the number of natives they killed or captured. Military posts were located alongside the villages, and whites were to be settled among the natives, to instruct them in trades and agriculture. As it turned out, the soldiers were usually mestizos or natives recruited from rival tribes whose vindictiveness was often personally inspired. The white settlers, on the other hand, were "vagrants, scoundrels most perilous to society," in the words of the governor, who saw an opportunity to scour his jails. These lumpen, unskilled in any craft, quickly scented opportunities to exploit native labor—even better, to exploit native sexuality, "to prey upon Indian women, practicing with them the greatest debauches."[18]

Indigenes were also captured by public-spirited citizens who mounted entradas into the forest. Those captured in this fashion were subject to enslavement for a term fixed in the declaration of war to ten years; soon afterward this was raised to twelve, then fifteen, years. For boys the term began only when they reached the age of fourteen; for girls, twelve. Local interpretation of the decree had it that the term began only after baptism was performed, a ceremony that might suffer some delay, very likely. Local interpretation also permitted the sale of these captives, who came to be called *kurucas*, to third parties. A kuruca fetched 100 milreis, at a time when an African slave sold for six times as much. Although the authoriza-tion to kill and capture was valid only against Botocudos and bugres, Coro-ados who gave themselves over to white protection were also taken captive: Two thousand were thus enslaved in Ouro Prêto in 1811. Within a week all the males of that group escaped and began a war to the death against their betrayers.[19]

Astonishingly, in 1813 the court appointed to this grim genocidal re-doubt an émigré French officer sympathetic to the indigenes, Guido Tho-maz Marlière. The remote and forbidding forest presented at first merely an occasion to prove his loyalty, but he soon found it to his liking and remained even after King João returned to Lisbon. He rose from command of one of the military districts to the rank of colonel, with responsibility for native pacification throughout Minas Gerais, by the time of his retirement in 1829. Marlière encountered a few missionaries already working in the region, notably Father Manuel de Jesus Maria. This priest's mother was an African, thus he, too, had good enough reason to prefer to distance himself from the disdain of the court. Marlière's strategy differed from that of prior waves of missionaries. He could not see why the tribal peoples should be "descended"; instead, he sited the aldeias well into the forest, remote from white settlements and close to available wild resources, especially fish-bearing streams. He ordered his troops to burn clearings and plant them, so that the first year's subsistence of his neophytes would be assured; then he attracted the forest dwellers with gifts of machetes and hoes.[20]

Marlière's continual preoccupation thereafter, as he informed his superior in 1825, was to ward off white settlers who sought to usurp native lands by plying them with liquor, setting loose cattle in their clearings, and deliberately exposing them to smallpox. In this struggle, the civil authorities had proved uncooperative:

> For thirteen years I have cried out to successive governments against the killers, oppressors, and invaders of the lands of the Indians; never have I received anything but evasive replies, offhanded investigations that reached no conclusion, orders that went unexecuted, and promises of regulations and directives that never came: Not one single murderer of Indians was ever hanged, oppression was not punished, not a single yard of Indian land was ever restored.[21]

Marlière's letters recount dozens of crimes practiced by government officials themselves—the buying and selling of children, the connivance of judges in claim jumping, the kidnapping of indigenes for the militia and for work on the roads, and theft and mayhem committed by his own soldiers. The missionary priest who was respected by the natives he called a "rara avis." One to whom he entrusted a school at a salary of 150 milreis a year promptly subcontracted the job to a deaf man for 50 milreis and pocketed the rest. Meanwhile, the authorities received petitions signed by hundreds of settlers, complaining that Marlière, a self-admitted non-Catholic(!), was misappropriating funds and was too easy on the Botocudos, who continued their old ways, stealing cattle and destroying crops, for which Marlière was slow in making reparation. A stronger hand, they claimed, was needed to restrain "men so barbarous."[22]

Marlière's network of aldeias grew to some two dozen by the end of his career, extending from the upper Jequitinhonha to the headwaters of the Pomba, a distance of nearly 600 kilometers, along a swath some 100 kilometers wide. At the high point of settlement some 10,000 Coroados and Botocudos lived in them. Similar efforts in Rio de Janeiro and Espírito Santo had settled several thousand more, under circumstances less gracious than those in Marlière's district. All suffered the same fate by the 1840s. Their numbers rapidly declined, as infections spread among them. Saint-Hilaire, who had visited a number of these villages and professed himself overcome with "pity and humiliation" at the sight, had predicted as much: Marlière was to have no successor, and his work, like that of all the other "civilizing agents," had "no other result than that of accelerating the destruction of those whom he wanted to make happy."[23]

Although King João came to understand that native rebellions were reactions to mistreatment and that the campaigns of pacification involved "murders and cruelties," he saw no other way of dealing with them than to intimidate them, even to destroy them. Those who brought about independence did not devise any measures significantly different from that of the colonial regime. José Bonifácio's "Suggestions for the Civilization of the Wild Indians," presented to the Constituent Assembly, drew the most contemptuous portrait imaginable of the native Brazilians: Vagabonds engaged constantly in robbery and warfare, with no religious or civil restraint upon their passions, they were given by nature to indolence, allowing their gardens to become overgrown. They refused to abandon the hunt, fearing that settled villages might not provide them sufficient fare for their "unmeasured gluttony." The most valiant and powerful among them vaunted their reputations as warriors; those who had made war on the Brazilians feared eventual retaliation. In addition to all this, the males refused to abandon their drink and polygamy, José Bonifácio complained, suggesting a contrast with neo-European society that was perhaps based more on the ideal than the reality. Even though he admitted that conflicts had grown inevitably from the past experience of slavery, land theft, frauds, military impressment, and generalized contempt, grafting on "all our vices and illnesses, while communicating none of our virtues and talents," still it was needful to recognize who they were, "so that we might then find the means to convert them into that which it suits us that they be[!]."[24]

The prescriptions that flowed from this analysis were unavoidably similar to past policies. Expeditions, which José Bonifâcio did not blush to call bandeiras, after the seventeenth-century slave raiders, should be sent into the forest with interpreters and priests, to persuade the indigenes to settle in aldeias. Aldeias should be under the supervision not of military officers but of missionaries. Army posts, nevertheless, should be mounted not far away, subject to missionary authority, equipped with a few small artillery pieces, perhaps. José Bonifâcio was as committed as any of Pedro's advisors to augmenting the work forces of the great estates, but he accepted glumly the reality that these latter-day converts to civilization could not be expected to perform as field hands; at most they might serve in auxiliary occupations, as mule drivers, fishermen, foot soldiers, woodsmen, or trailblazers. Clearly, however, the modest parcels of land assigned to their aldeias were not intended to keep them independent—one way or another they would eventually become wage earners subordinate to the estates.

These were indeed to be the general lines of policy pursued by the empire in the years following. Bandeiras were raised by provincial governors, while the minister of the empire advised "leniency and affability." Local notables were granted tracts of land where tribal peoples were resident on the grounds—not above suspicion of hypocrisy—that they would demonstrate to the natives the benefits of civilization. In 1831 the same liberal regency that "abolished" the African slave traffic finally ended the state of war against the Botocudos and bugres, ending as well the servitude of those who had been captured, insofar as the writ of the government extended over the interior, and declaring them wards of the state, under the care of orphans' courts. This same government pursued its decentralizing course by authorizing provincial presidents to carry on their own programs of pacification.

In 1843 the imperial government invited Italian Capuchins, already present in the country, to take in hand the pacification and settlement of tribal peoples throughout Brazil. Placed over the missionaries was a civil agency, the Service of Catechesis and Civilization, represented in each province by a director. Again, as at the beginning of the Portuguese invasion, recourse was had to a foreign religious corporation, this time one expected to be more submissive to regalist ascendancy than had been the Jesuits but not any more likely, one may surmise, to appreciate the forest environment from which their charges were to be extracted or the knowledge that indigenes had of it. The mission system did not entirely exclude a military option. In Espírito Santo, a string of garrisons was maintained along the coast. In São Paulo and Paraná, which was separated from São Paulo in 1853, a few militarized colonies, designed to withstand native attacks, were established at the extremes of the Atlantic Forest. Of these, the ultimate was placed at the mouth of the Iguaçu River, in 1888. The long-delayed law on public lands, passed in 1850, retained the colonial legal principle that all the national territory belonged to the crown by right of conquest, asserted three hundred and fifty years before when Cabral's crew pounded a wooden cross into the sand on the beach at Porto Seguro, extinguishing all prior indigenous rights.[25]

Although the formation of aldeias continued through the rest of the century, the missionizing zeal of former times, by means of which, as the director of São Paulo aldeias put it in 1862, "so many souls were conquered for religion, so many men for civilization, and so many hands for work," by midcentury "no longer glow[ed] in the Province." The aldeias were becoming obsolete, their role no longer of much economic value. By the 1840s the native-occupied zone of the Atlantic Forest had been reduced, in Minas Gerais, to the region between the Doce and the Jequitinhonha rivers, where Botocudos still ranged freely, sometimes attacking intruders. In the south, government explorations were now extending beyond the Paranapanema River to the Ivaí, and neo-European settlement, formerly confined to the grasslands near Curitiba, was now moving up the forested banks of the Tibagi and Iguaçu rivers. The neo-European frontier was advancing faster than in times past, and the invaders were impatient to have the indigenes removed. Native predation of cattle that had been set loose in their hunting grounds infuriated ranchers. The labor potential of these forest dwellers was of diminished interest. Neo-Europeans had always branded the indigenes as lazy, even as they enslaved them. But these last surviving groups were of still less utility than their predecessors. Their previous isolation had left them more susceptible to disease, so they died even more quickly; they had no experience of agriculture, sometimes not even of iron tools, so they could not be impressed into any steady labor. It was beginning to happen that whites who were offered native captives refused them, as troublesome and unproductive.[26]

The practice was therefore becoming more common to avoid the tiresome delays inherent in the founding of aldeias by simply murdering natives encountered on coveted land. This might be done at less risk now that the Brazilian market was adequately supplied with shotguns. The profession of native hunter was emerging, and the expression to "kill a village" was coming to have the contractual implications of any other task prerequisite to initiating farming, like to "clear a field" or "construct a mill." In São Paulo, these hunters became known as *bugreiros*. Provincial officials, despite the expiry of the declaration of war on the Botocudos, continued to authorize assaults and, indeed, led them: On one punitive expedition, sometime after 1838, near São Mateus, on the Espírito Santo coast, the military district commander returned in triumph with 300 ears. Other natives were employed in these forays, intensifying rivalries among them. Sometimes hired indigenes were turned against neo-European settlers, as a form of extortion, provoking demands that they be done away with entirely. The groups that collaborated did not gain special privileges thereby; on the contrary, the whites, having lost their fear of them, stole their lands all the faster.[27]

Here and there a few of the invaders sought to spare the forest dwellers, after the example of Marlière. In 1852 Teófilo Otóni, a visionary political figure, in disgrace at court for having participated in the liberal rebellion of 1842, exiled himself to the Mucuri River valley, where he put into action a plan to provide northern Minas Gerais access to the sea. He organized a riverboat and road-transport company, and, accessory to it, he founded a settlement on one of the Mucuri's affluents, at the site of the town that today bears his name. He called it Filadélfia, in homage to the principle followed in the Quaker colony of Pennsylvania of coexistence with indigenes. For perhaps the first time in Brazilian history, trailblazers in his employ were under instructions not to fire on the indigenes, even in response to their arrows. The Botocudos, indeed, initially attacked the road builders a number of times. But they were at last convinced by Otóni, who returned kidnapped kurucas, mostly women taken by soldiers as sexual slaves, that he meant them no harm. They then ceded some of their land to the company, and in return Otóni provided them with metal tools and saw to it that their remaining lands were duly registered.[28]

It was Otóni's intention that the Mucuri should be free of slavery, so he introduced German, Swiss, Belgian, and other immigrants, setting as a requirement that they bring cash savings with them and promising in return that the company would treat them as associates, not proletarians. Although he was frequently deceived by some of his immigration agents in Europe, who misrepresented the advantages the company offered or sent miscreants lately emerged from jail, the Mucuri valley prospered under this liberal regime of egalitarianism and mutual respect. Filadélfia grew to more than 4,000 residents, and the Botocudos, no longer warring among themselves, took up farming and traded with the townspeople. Otóni maintained peace among his settlers, the local garrison, and the natives largely through the force of his character and example. In 1862, however, political opponents in Rio de Janeiro forced him to sell his company to the imperial government and to withdraw.

This idyll then suffered fatal reverses. Conflicts between indigenes and neo-Europeans broke out and continued until 1873, when Capuchin priests established an aldeia, called Itambacuri, some 40 kilometers to the south of Filadélfia. Unlike the Jesuits, the Capuchins mixed neo-Europeans among the natives from the beginning, encouraging intermarriage. For twenty years the aldeia maintained a population of about 500 indigenes, and another 2,000 wandered in the vicinity, appearing at the mission on holy days. Here, too, periodic epidemics raged. Another aldeia in the vicinity had been destroyed by an earlier outbreak when, in 1890, Itambacuri was also struck by diseases introduced by refugees from a drought in the north. The indigenes were encouraged by settlers, who wanted to be rid of the Capuchins, to believe that the missionaries were poisoning them. They rose up in 1893, destroyed the mission, and returned to the forest. Some of them remained unreconciled and hostile, threatening the building of the railroad to Salvador, as late as 1909. The district pioneered by Otóni is now the poorest in the state.[29]

In São Paulo and Paraná, only six aldeias were established after independence, mostly upon the initiative of private persons. The longest lasting was that of João da Silva Machado, baron of Antonina, who in 1845 settled on his estate in present-day Itaporanga, in São Paulo, several hundred Kaingang whose lands had been stolen, joined by a number of Guarani. The baron invited a Capuchin to missionize and obtained recognition of the aldeia from the provincial government. He was also instrumental in the formation of the aldeia of São Pedro de Alcântara, on the Tibagi River, in Paraná. He actively defended his charges, who were attacked by bugreiros whenever they left his property. After the baron's death and the fall of the empire, claim jumpers besieged the estate, even though its title was secure and more than half a century old and even though the aldeia had been continuously directed according to law. By 1898 there were some forty squatters on the land. In 1910 an agent of the new Indian Protection Service recommended measures to restore the natives—he would have awarded them one-eighth of their original lands—but even this modest concession to justice was denied.[30]

By the end of the century, then, almost all of the Atlantic Forest's original occupants had been enticed or driven out of it. Permanent residence in the aldeias was the surest sign that conversion had been effected. Although the Jesuits had not allowed their charges to leave without permission, the Capuchins were satisfied to reel them in gradually, but the ultimate goal was to separate them definitively from the wild. In the aldeias, the Capuchins sought to turn them as quickly as possible into neo-European peasants. They were clothed, their nakedness representing to the whites not only sexual temptation and rejection of Christian prudery but independence of civilization. The Capuchins carried out instruction in Portuguese, and the natives learned to feel shame in the use of their own languages, reverting to them in the presence of townspeople only when drunk. They were encouraged to marry the whites and mestizos who had been settled among them. Legal marriage to natives was a novelty that excited the "curiosity" and often the "derision" of the townspeople when the priests brought bridal couples to the registry offices. By the end of this process of acculturation, the neophytes had no recollection of their ancestral ways and shared white disdain for their unpacified brethren. The aldeias of the Jesuit period, nearly a century untutored, had become "nominal," according to one director, "where, besides having no more than a few mestizos, who barely remember the existence of their antecedents, are so mingled with the present population that one could hardly distinguish them," their lands being "almost entirely occupied by intruders, some of them powerful."[31]

The disappearance of peoples native to the Atlantic Forest, at home in it, and empirically familiar with its utilities did not dismay the neo-Europeans. The natives had been "ungrateful, inconstant, disloyal, envious," according to Antônio Muniz de Souza, an outspoken but not untypical Brazilian nineteenth-century observer who wrote a memoir of his travels in the interior. They were, he insisted, by nature "lazy, disorganized, obedient to all the vices, principally the drinking of rum." Many other writers agreed with him. And yet Muniz de Souza recognized that the qualities exhibited by the indigenes were appropriate to an environment that they had been deprived of, while those they lacked were demanded of them by a society that was itself artificial:

> I have heard some men, who think philosophically, say that there is no life equal to that of the Indians, because they follow the order of nature. I do not doubt it; but only as long as they are not interrupted by us, or by our social order, which is entirely contradictory to the order of nature that they follow.

Indeed, he admitted, their present state of "continual misery" was owing to the circumstance "that we have taken from them a great part of their lands and forests," reducing their supply of game and other resources. In return, he complained that the neighbors of the indigenes had acquired their deplorable habits, "sloth" in particular, which was general throughout Brazil.[32]

Muniz de Souza was describing a rural culture that was clearly mestizo, in which indigenous elements were too adaptive to abandon and too useful for the invaders to ignore or evade. Even though the pacified natives had lost their lands and had been forced to conform to a more powerful social order, they had endowed it with elements of their own. Most certainly, the economy, apparently entirely a construction of the neo-European colony and its successor empire, was most curiously shaped, far into the nine-teenth century, even into the twentieth, by the practices and preferences of hunting and gathering peoples.

The fourth issue of importance to the landed interest was liberation from forest legislation that had been imposed since the earliest colonization. The royal prohibitions on the cutting of brazilwood and hardwoods suitable for naval construction negated in principle the rights of landownership in fee simple, even if they were in most areas impossible to enforce or easy to evade. The constitutional empire for a time preserved these monopolies. Local economic interests, already assertive before the Portuguese court evacuated Rio de Janeiro, moved under the new regime to undo them. In 1827 the responsibility for inventorying forest stocks and guarding against unauthorized cutting passed from the treasury council in Rio de Janeiro and the judge conservators to justices of the peace, elected authorities sub-servient to local landowners. A law of 1829 repeated the prohibition of logging on public lands but allowed county councils to grant licenses. In 1831 the forest conservatories were extinguished, thereby ending imperial supervision of surviving coastal forest that might have imposed a regime of conservation and forest renewal. The prohibitions upon the unlicensed cutting on private property of a reduced number of hardwood species, the madeiras de lei, nevertheless remained in place, though unenforced, until 1876.[33]

The imperial government remained for a time the monopoly buyer and exporter of brazilwood. The dyewood represented a modest but valuable source of foreign exchange, which was applied to the external debt and the costs of the fledgling diplomatic service. Unfortunately, it was a product altogether too easy to smuggle from dozens of minor ports along the for-ested coast. Official reports from the last years of colonial rule mention contraband apprehended or entering foreign harbors that was worth more than official sales. Revenues from this product therefore rarely reached the level of budget forecasts. The government tried to monitor brazilwood cutting by allowing it to be done only by landowners on whose properties the tree was known to grow. This measure proved unenforceable and was rescinded, followed by another that allowed cutting by contractors on pri-vate land and, under license, on public lands. Revenues, nevertheless, con-tinued to fall. In 1826 the director of the National Museum was requested to study extraction of the dyestuff, a sensible suggestion, even though sev-eral hundred years late. Unfortunately, nothing came of it, and dyewood exports collapsed with the invention of garish coal-tar dyes a few years later. The monopoly was finally abolished in 1859.[34]

Meanwhile, far in the interior, extractivism offered a means of exchange between those indigenes who remained in the Atlantic Forest, avoiding sedentarism and subjection, and commercial agents of the towns and ports. It is repellent to list, as one of the extractive products, humans, yet so they were, as they had been since the sixteenth-century bandeiras. Botocudos captured the children of rival tribes to sell them as kurucas to the neo-Europeans, at prices considerably below their resale value, apparently. The natives, it was admitted, possessed a varied pharmacopoeia, and they were a major source of medicinals. In return they obtained metal tools and weapons, cloth, foodstuffs, and cachaça, always cachaça. A few of these Atlantic Forest products were exported, principally sarsaparilla, false cinchonas, waxes, balsams, and ipecac. Of these, the most important was ipecac, whose alkaloid products were at the time valued as emetic, astringent, and diaphoretic.

Ipecac exports grew in volume from about 4 tons a year at the beginning of the century to about 25 tons by the late 1860s. By then, however, caboclos from Rio de Janeiro, where native stands of the plant had disappeared, had moved on to Minas Gerais, apparently lured as much by the hope of striking gold along the forest trails as by plant extractivism. Unfortunately for the forest, they cut roads that stimulated the inflow of a larger migration of swidden farmers. The ipecac trade did not long survive these interlopers because they culled the plant before it set seed, leading to its local extinction. The trade began to move to Mato Grosso in the 1830s. There it lasted more than a century, apparently because a more rational method of locating the plant was adopted: Instead of picking it in flower, the gatherers waited until it seeded. A certain bird (*Lipaugus vociferans*) that feeds on ipecac seeds and disperses them was then followed to ipecac patches. It does not seem that there was any attempt to cultivate the plant, although the idea was broached. As in the case of rubber and yerba maté, that feat was accomplished elsewhere, this time in India. This lack of initiative is the more to be lamented, because ipecac has recently come to be considered a specific against amoebic dysentery, bilharziasis, and even certain tumors.[35]

Indigenes and caboclos were assiduous hunters. The German naturalist Georg Freyreiss reported that many people hunted, spending days in the forest. They were seeking commercial as well as subsistence prey: animal pelts, live birds, fish, monkeys, flowers, bird feathers, butterflies, and other insects. Muniz de Souza raged at the hunters, whom he called "the first class of the idlers," but a jaguar pelt was worth 6 milreis, comparable to the value of a steer. Commercial agents bought them for export, sometimes to be sold as stuffed exhibits. In Nova Friburgo a resident taxidermist named Beschke bought monkey pelts, reportedly contributing to their local extinction by 1850. Raw materials were also gathered in the wild, for the confection of handcrafts for the town markets. Natives and caboclos, descendants themselves of natives made sedentary at some earlier time, or mestizos born of indigenous mothers, persisted in the traditions of indigenous artisanry that were of use to town dwellers: rush matting, cordage, basketry, and the tubular cane baskets that were used to extract the poisonous juice from grated manioc. The forest also provided tool handles, clogs, and other wooden implements.[36]

One of the headiest enthusiasms to overcome bourgeois Europeans was the collection of tropical flowers. Enthralled by the travel memoirs of scientists like Humboldt, von Martius, and La Condamine, they were avid exhibitors of inanimate trophies from the natural world—such objects as fossils, rocks, stuffed birds, and gems. They were even more eager to display to their intimates living collections of fragile flowers, which reeked of the exotic perfumes of the rain forest, hinted at dangers and hardships beyond imagining, and flaunted the owner's skill in horticulture. Steam packet-boats, Wardian cases, heated greenhouses, and railroads made possible these astonishing introductions. The highland region of the Atlantic Forest, with its chilly winters and intermittent seasonal rainfall, was an excellent source of these treasures, because its species would resist the uncertain and inadequate household heating systems of northern Europe and the erratic watering habits of novice gardeners. The hunt for flowering epiphytes—bromeliads, cacti, and, above all, orchids—thus became a large business, employing agents who followed upon that first generation of scientists whose drawings and dried specimens had awakened their commercial instincts. A single one of these firms imported 100,000 to 200,000 orchids a year.[37]

These incursions into the Atlantic Forest, utilizing it as a warehouse for the city dwellers of the coast, even for the urban sophisticates of the industrializing world, suggest a salutary homeostasis, a primary forest turned into an "extractive reserve," a concept recently made law in the Amazon. Native lands evidently were not in any sense reserved in the nineteenth century, yet the image of the indigenes as illuminati, sole possessors of the knowledge of the uses of the forest, capable of exchanging its products for money while preserving it whole, was already evoked in 1873 by the botanist José da Saldanha da Gama in a paper he delivered in Vienna, at an international congress of agronomists and foresters. Da Gama's observations were romantic, intended to charm learned foreign specialists while drawing a veil over the reality of the Brazilian interior. The natives, he informed them, were through this trade with the caboclos drawn to the "holy love of labor."[38]

The reality was the rapid invasion of the gathering trade by caboclos, who considered the indigenes merely an obstacle to direct access to the forest's resources and who had learned only too well the lesson that imme-diate profit maximization was achieved through minimizing labor inputs and suppressing whatever regard they may have conceivably felt for the forest that fed them. The epiphytes desired by the English, Belgian, French, and German commercial agents nested high on the branches of the Atlantic Forest's emergent trees. The only practical way of getting them was to cut the trees down. In 1853 the naturalist Hermann von Burmeister found many trees felled in what was left of primary forest in the region of Nova Friburgo, where he also noted the presence of one of the most beauti-ful of orchids, *Cattleya labiata*. These random cuttings were very likely for the orchid trade that Burmeister noted was organized in the region by a French resident named Pinel. The extraction of orchids, which were all indiscriminately and inaccurately termed "parasites" by the rural folk, went on in some areas until forest burning for coffee planting finally ended the trade. In southwestern Minas Gerais a single agent was said to have shipped more than 20,000 orchids of a single species, *Oncidium varicosum rogersii*. Eventually all the orchids in a given location might be removed. One county, abandoned by the gold prospectors years before, was roused in midcentury by the arrival of a foreign commercial agent who bought orchids for as much as 2 milreis apiece. Local residents went gaily into the forest with their axes, cutting down trees until orchids became so rare that they were no longer worth the agent's time; then, according to the botanist Âlvaro da Silveira, who related this story, the "exploiter of the caboclos" abandoned the "exploiters of the forest," and the county slumped back into apathy.[39]

More important to European collectors than the beauty, fragility, and exoticism of the epiphytes was their rarity. Rarity, to put it crassly, raised their price. This demand for rarity was another of the extractive trade's dangers. The caboclos evidently were paid according to rarity. What then if a dozen, or a hundred, trees had to be felled to find one specimen of the rarest? The caboclos were nothing loath; they would cut down a tree for a beehive or an animal. Charles Darwin, accompanying a hunting party near the city of Rio de Janeiro, had looked on in amazement while one of his rustic hosts chopped down a tree because a monkey he had shot in one of its branches had not fallen to the ground. Indeed, the monkey had been shot the day before, so that the meal to be gained from it was at that point problematic. If a tree's value was less than that of a putrefied plate of game, what was it worth in relation to an orchid that might fetch a week's wages? What then if all the specimens of a rare species were thus removed? In-deed, it was in the interest of the commercial agent that all of them should be found and brought him, leaving none behind for others. At the end of his season in the forest, he was not averse to guaranteeing his monopoly by paying the caboclos to burn down what remained of the forest. So concerned were Mulford and Racine Sarasy Foster, twentieth-century collectors of bromeliads for botanical gardens, that their rarest finds would be thus exploited by commercial agents that they often omitted locations from their field reports.[40]

By far the most valuable of the Atlantic Forest's extractive products were its hardwoods. Sawmill machinery became common at last in the 1820s; there were 53 sawmills in São Paulo by 1838. By the 1850s the Monlevade iron mill in Minas Gerais was making sawmill blades. There appeared a modest foreign demand for hardwoods, sold under the generic names of jacarandá, rosewood, or palisander and used in fine cabinetry. Hardwood boards sold for 280 milreis (150 dollars) a dozen, about the same price by weight as coffee. Mechanically operated saws also increased the merchantability of lower-valued species in the domestic market. They reduced construction costs as well, by as much as half, and stimulated shipbuilding.[41]

Commercial logging of hardwoods was carried on in river basins below the fall lines; this, in the region of the Atlantic Forest, was a quite limited area, because of the barrier of the coastal palisade. Many of the hardwoods were heavier than water, so they had to be rafted together with lighter woods to bring them to port, but bringing them down over falls or rapids was much more difficult. Along the narrow littoral, much of the primary forest had been burned down at least once in the three hundred years since the Portuguese invasion, the secondary forest that succeeded such an event would not contain mature specimens for a century or more after. Three hundred years of cutting trees employed in shipbuilding had rendered many of the best species scarce even in forests that had not been burned. Even in untouched forest, furthermore, only a few species were considered merchantable; these were never found in stands, always scattered in the remaining primary forest. All of these circumstances considerably increased costs and reduced the practicality of finding and bringing out hardwoods.[42]

It is not surprising, then, that tribal groups that had been settled in aldeias were able to insert themselves into the trade as woodsmen. They were entirely familiar with the terrain, skilled in recognition of tree species, and willing to work at tasks that were unsupervised and occasional. They also became sawyers; indeed, they specialized in that skill. The aldeia of São Pedro, on the lower Paraíba do Sul River, was one of the most important suppliers of fine woods to Rio de Janeiro. According to the Austrian botanist Heinrich Schott, the aldeia's lands were "extraordinarily

rich" in numerous valuable tree species, and he obtained many of his specimens there. Burmeister, who wandered through much of Rio de Janeiro
and Minas Gerais, found in that area the largest trees he saw in Brazil,
some 2.4 meters in diameter. It is notable that these aldeias—some, like
São Pedro, founded early in the seventeenth century—still had primary
forest to exploit. Even an observer as benign as Saint-Hilaire complained
repeatedly of the "improvidence" of the indigenes, yet they had preserved
for centuries what the neo-Europeans regularly destroyed as soon as they
beheld it. One can only speculate on the motives that led the indigenes at
last to exploit and sell the forest that had provided them game and gathered
resources for centuries.[43]

In the highlands, lacking all but mule transport, hardwood had little
value for landowners beyond their immediate needs. When a patch of forest had to be burned, its trees were rarely culled beforehand. Such useful
material might have been stored against future needs, but storage, it appears, was an even rarer practice, a circumstance that suggests that improvidence was more justly attributed to the neo-Europeans. Francisco de
Lacerda Werneck, a Rio de Janeiro planter, deplored the "greatest wastefulness [that] one finds among almost all the farmers, not only allowing
wood to rot on the ground, being able to bring and store it in warehouses,
but also setting fire to it with the greatest sang-froid, as though they were
practicing a heroic act." By the end of the gold boom in Minas Gerais,
hardwoods had become extremely scarce and expensive in the towns, because all primary forest had disappeared in their neighborhoods, an economic reality that was foreseeable and perhaps might have suggested an
opportunity for profit to more prudent and frugal farmers.[44]

Astonishingly, Rio de Janeiro imported mahogany from Jamaica, paying
considerably more for it than local fine woods. Saldanha da Gama was
taken aback to find jacarandá being used in Europe for the finest cabinet
work. The eminently bourgeois cast of mind that depreciates what is local
was evidently at work, no doubt making possible unnecessarily high profit
margins for English and French importers of Brazilian woods. The cost
to the new empire was not trifling, but neither was it great. Hardwoods
represented a very small portion of exports: All the extractive products
of the Atlantic Forest together amounted to less than 2 percent of them
by value.[45]

Independent Brazil, freed of mercantilist oppression, no longer a pawn advanced by a penurious Portuguese monarchy to save its game on the European chessboard, had decided to follow autonomous policies that would
permit it to prosper by accelerating the exploitation of its natural re-

sources, by intensifying, in short, the colonial extractive economy, but now in an era of free trade and rationalized agriculture. The Atlantic Forest was a principal asset, and the manner of managing it would not differ from times past.

Not every member of the elite approved this trajectory. Some must have agreed with José Gregório de Moraes Navarro, whose tract against the waste of forest had been published at the turn of the century by Conceição Velloso:

> They will say that this conduct of the Brazilians is very useful and advantageous because otherwise no profit could be taken from those immense woodlands, occult habitat of the wild beasts; the great variety of the trees and plants, their uses or virtues, could not be known. The rich treasures that the earth hides in its breast could not be discovered, the barbarous nations that were born to it could not be civilized, domestic and foreign commerce of those vast domains could not be increased. Finally, they will say that, according [to] our same principle, since the land is ever capable of the same production, it makes no difference that men for a time sterilize it because when they have no more new lands that voluntarily offer their natural products, after all the land is populated, after all the race of wild and venomous beasts is extinguished, after civilizing the peoples raised among the beasts, then they will make use of those means that necessity and industry may show to be more convenient to revive the earth's former fertility.

These were indeed the arguments frequently encountered in behalf of staying the course of the Brazilian economy. Nevertheless, Moraes Navarro wondered, "can they achieve all these advantages without depriving themselves of many others, that through their fault they are losing, and that their descendants will not be able, even if they wish, to repair?"[46] This was a question left, after political independence was achieved, quite unexamined. The state turned over to the great landowners, and to those who had the resources to become such, the right to convert the forest into cash as quickly as possible. The obstacles to the landowners' mastery of this vast stockpile—its indigenous inhabitants and the state as guardian of the national patrimony and protector of Brazilians born slaves yet future citizens—had been overwhelmed by their capture of the state and by their exercise of force in entirely unchallenged private jurisdiction. The Atlantic Forest was to pass through a new trial as its landowners shifted to a novel and drastic form of production. Largely abandoning the search for gems and precious metals, they became planters once again, adopting an exotic crop of enormous economic potential.

8

Coffee Dispossesses the Forest

*Consolemo-nos com a consideração de que a terra foi dada ao homem,
que as matas caem para estender o domínio da civilização.*

*We may console ourselves with the thought that the earth was given to
man, that the forests fall to extend the dominion of civilization.*

THEODOR PECKHOLT (1871)

The social policies mandated by the large landowners of independent, imperial Brazil guaranteed them a work force and title to whatever public land they chose to call their own. These policies could not guarantee, however, that the employment of the resources thus secured would generate capital; indeed, this authoritarian monopoly would in large measure frustrate their efficient utilization. In the interior were vast posses, inhabited by starvelings and ruled over by satraps whose stock of capital consisted of cattle and pigs and whose dwellings, clothing, and knowledge of the world were nearly indistinguishable from those of their peasants and slaves. Independence had not exorcised a critical colonial reality: Capital to transform these barrens into real wealth and power had to come from abroad, through the sale of goods that richer countries valued. Nearly everything that would be instrumental to that end was to be obtained in Europe. From these countries, as well, came the luxuries that signified status to a fledgling elite that had for fifteen years observed at first hand their consumption by its royal mentors and masters.

Independence had improved the conditions under which such transfers might be effected, because it banished the yoke of mercantilism, already shrugged off when the court had transferred to Brazil. The empire, indeed, had been forced by the British government to adopt a policy of free trade as a price of recognition. Although this treaty lapsed by 1845 and higher tariffs were then increasingly imposed, the government's eagerness to stimulate exports never flagged. The imperial government desired to enlarge trade because nearly all of its revenue derived from import duties. Imports were not only a convenient source of taxes, they were, given the

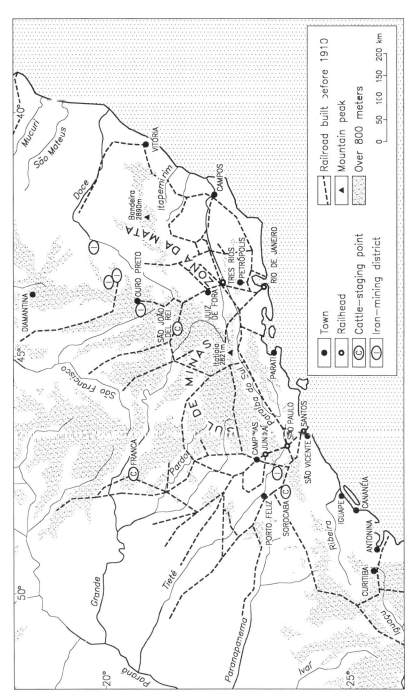

Map 5. The Southeastern Atlantic Forest, 1850-1920

weakness of the government, the only practical source. A small, easily monitored customs service collected revenues at a few controllable points. Applied to foreign manufacturers and merchants, the duties did not directly burden Brazilian citizens; indeed, they elicited greater loyalty from domestic artisans. Import duties, furthermore, could be levied in gold, thereby placing in the hands of the empire the means to meet payments on its foreign debt—a portion of the Portuguese debt, in fact—that it had been forced to assume by the British as another of the prices of recognition and that it imprudently magnified ever after. Foreign exchange also permitted it to import on its own account utilities, such as military equipment, to enhance its authority. Thus the goals of the landowners—those at least whose properties lay at some convenient distance from ports—and those of the independent government coincided. The empire, no different from its predecessor, had taken it as axiomatic that, the demands of the landowners having been satisfied, they would in return earn foreign exchange to cover the state's expenses.

Unfortunately for the landowning class and the state, the most coveted of the exports with which Brazil had long experience, gold and diamonds, could not be restored to prominence. The remaining deposits, much investigated during the king's sojourn in Rio de Janeiro, did not appear to hold great promise, at least not under prevailing technology. Baron von Eschwege, the most energetic specialist hired to revive the industry, foresaw the need for more capital-intensive methods. Despairing of the capacity of local notables to cooperate in large-scale undertakings because of "envy and distrust," he attempted to set up a milling works near Ouro Prêto with government backing. Eschwege failed, according to his account because he was besieged by a swarm of officials who blocked his every move. Eschwege was seemingly unaware that these persons were simply after baksheesh. The gold rush had given employment to numerous civil servants who now, as the gold washing gave out, were desperate to restore their incomes. The export "cycles" so characteristic of Brazilian economic history, in which a product is produced successfully for a time, even though inefficiently, relying on the bounty of nature, but then falls out of world trade as that bounty grows scarce and as more efficient techniques of production fail to be applied, is largely the result of the inability to join together capital and proceed to more intensive exploitation and to shake off bureaucratic parasitism.[1]

British capitalists rushed into this gap and formed a number of gold-mining companies. Most of them failed, but two were successful, applying the deep-shaft techniques of Cornish miners to the few important veins that had been located, at Gongo Soco, near Caeté, and at Morro Velho, near present-day Belo Horizonte. These operations together amounted to no more than a tenth of that achieved during the peak of the gold rush in the middle of the eighteenth century. Gold hunting went on in the far reaches of the Atlantic Forest, backed by moneyed individuals, and minor discoveries may have been here and there quietly exploited, because the empire was less effective than the viceroyalty in policing revenue sources, but the great gold rush was over. Many mining towns fell into decadence, their inhabitants wandering into the forest to resume slash-and-burn farming—while keeping an eye out, no doubt, for streams that looked promising. Indeed, it is likely that the nineteenth-century frontier was dilated as much by the continued hope of again finding gold and diamonds somewhere in the shade of the forest as by the extensiveness of agricultural practice, so that the lack of a gold strike may have been nearly as damaging to the Atlantic Forest as had the gold strike itself.[2]

Nor did the landowners or the government prove capable of pursuing further the acclimatization and development of any of the tropical crops upon which Portuguese and local Brazilian botanists had expended so much attention. The Botanical Garden in Rio de Janeiro and the museum of natural history rapidly fell into a state of near abandonment. Foreign observers remarked despairingly that the garden, enriched with so many exotic species, was nothing more than a public park where no botanical work was any longer carried out. Symbolic of the altered view of the new authorities is an order in the name of the just-acclaimed emperor written by José Bonifâcio de Andrada e Silva, by then no longer a practicing scientist but Pedro's closest political advisor. Sent to the keeper of the museum, it commandeered the stuffed specimens of toucans, "those that have very yellow throats," leaving only two for display, so that a feathered mantle might be confected in time for the enthronement. The assembled foreign dignitaries thus witnessed the exotic new dynasty's intent to ransack its native resources to consolidate its power. The mantle remains on display in the imperial museum at Petrópolis, an attestation to the priority of nation over nature.[3]

The most determinedly pursued and most innovative of the experiments begun at the Botanical Garden under the last Portuguese king was the attempt to acclimatize tea. The Chinese tea farmers brought all the way from Macau in 1814 to tend the plants and teach methods of processing the leaves continued to work assiduously at the garden. Visitors commented on the perfection of the plants, which were yielding six harvests a year, compared to four in China. One can hardly imagine the despair of these unfortunate immigrants, whose isolation and uprootedness were as extreme as any witnessed by the agitated nineteenth century. They remained at the garden for at least ten years. All during their employment, alienated and alone, they were suspected by the garden's director, Leandro do Sacramento, of deliberately withholding the techniques of processing. The confusion concerning their work was considerable: Darwin was surprised and disappointed to find that the tea, which he saw at the garden in 1832, neatly planted in straight rows, was an "insignificant little bush." The infusion produced by the green leaves, kindly poured for him by one of the gardeners, he found "scarcely possessed the proper tea flavor." At the time, the best botanical knowledge in the West believed that green tea and processed tea were derived from different species. It is entirely possible that the Chinese tea farmers were accustomed to drinking their tea green and simply did not know how to cure it so as to be acceptable to the Western palate.[4]

Sacramento seems to have given up trying to extract the "secrets" of tea processing from the Chinese, even before he retired from the garden's directorship. The tea plants, however, did interest at least a few landowners. It grew prodigiously even on indifferent soils. The product was extremely light in relation to its value and so might be transported even on the execrable mule trails that were most farmers' only connection to the ports. Although tea required careful tending, the work was light and, they expected, could easily be accomplished by the children of their slaves. The province of São Paulo imported a second group of Chinese presumed skilled in tea growing, and a number of important planters there took up tea, including José Arouche de Toledo Rondon, who wrote a memoir on its cultivation and preparation. There were also experimental plantings at the botanical garden in Ouro Prêto and in Santa Tereza, in Rio de Janeiro. Unfortunately, samples of tea sent to England in 1837 were not favorably received. Desultory experiments went on through the 1850s, and some tea continued to be offered in local markets. But Brazilian tea could not be exported. According to one contemporary specialist, it was more than twice as expensive as Chinese tea of the same quality. Very likely, with further effort, costs of cultivation might have been reduced and quality improved. The Belgian horticulturist Jean-Christian Heusser thought processing methods very defective and proposed fairly simple improvements. But these measures were not taken. Brazil was obliged to import most of its tea, and only a century later were immigrant Japanese colonists able to supply the domestic market.[5]

It is possible that the difficulties experienced in bringing new products to market were in part the result of unacknowledged imperial preferences. The British East India Company, an enterprise still monopolistic, clearly would have wished to maintain its control of the market, based on its Chinese source. By the 1840s British interests were involved in trying to grow tea in Assam; Brazilians have suspected that these may have interfered with the acceptance of their product. Economic rivalry was visible in the reaction of the French to the news that Brazil was cultivating tea: In 1838 the botanist D. M. Guillemin was sent to Rio de Janeiro to inspect these efforts and to carry off seeds to France, whence they might be planted in their own colonies. To his credit, he did bring with him various seeds in exchange, but none were of a comparable potential value. Whatever the commitments of European colonialism, at least American merchants, who possessed no tropical colonies and who obtained only a grudging share of the Chinese supply, might well have reflected on the absurdity of sailing past Rio de Janeiro to far-off Canton in quest of a product that Brazilians might have conveniently sold them. Instead, Rio de Janeiro went on importing some of the tea it consumed from the United States![6]

The region of the Atlantic Forest did experience for a time a revival in the export of its most traditional and least-improved crop, sugarcane. Rio de Janeiro's sugar plantations had gone into decline in the early eighteenth century with the discovery of gold, which increased the cost of replacements for its slave work force. Brazilian sugar had been driven from northern European markets when the Dutch, French, and English established plantations on their island colonies in the late seventeenth century. Thus Brazilian sugar exports suffered multiple disabilities, averaging little more than 10,000 tons annually by the 1750s, little more than half those of fifty years before. Exports rebounded late in the century as revolution and mercantilist conflict raged in the Caribbean and the Indian Ocean, raising prices and enticing merchants disposed to run the heightened risks of wartime trade. By 1800 Brazil sold about 24,000 tons of sugar.[7]

Sugarcane was raised in nearly every neo-European settlement in the region of the Atlantic Forest because *muscovado*—unrefined, molasses-laden sugar—was a staple and because cane juice was the raw material for the distillation of rum. There were hundreds, probably thousands, of small, primitive mills that satisfied a domestic demand considerably larger than the overseas market. As a plantation crop, grown on a large scale for export, sugar was important in scattered nodes along the wet coastal lowlands from Natal to Rio de Janeiro. Commercial sugar planting became marginally profitable in highland São Paulo as well, after the paving, in 1792, of the mule trail down the coastal palisade to Santos. Direct exportation was permitted from that port a few years later. Paulista production continued to expand; by 1836, 558 mills were operating there.[8]

Most of the sugar, and nearly all the sugar for export, was produced in oxen- or water-powered mills—*engenhos*—that integrated grinding and crystallization. Smaller mills were designated, somewhat pejoratively, as *engenhocas*, sometimes manually operated. Their product was commonly cachaça, not sugar. The cachaça of the engenhocas, distilled directly from cane juice, was judged superior to that of the engenhos, which was distilled from the liquor left over from the rendering. Labor forces on the large sugar estates were varied. In some areas, landowners worked their own slave gangs, which might number in the hundreds. In other areas, the owners allotted some of their fields to sharecroppers, who employed their families and a slave or two, set up wooden presses of their own, put on the boil whatever pots they owned that might serve to crystallize the juice, and turned over half their crop to the mill owner.[9]

The policy of the colonial government toward sugar and alcohol production had been, since 1681, apparently conservationist: No sugar mill could be built less than a half league (3.3 kilometers) from another, on the grounds that each mill's forest reserves had to be large enough to guarantee sufficient firewood for the boiling and crystallization processes. In Minas Gerais the construction of mills was, throughout the eighteenth century, forbidden without the governor's license, on the grounds that they diverted laborers from gold washing and led to dissolution and disorder. Despite these measures, hundreds of engenhocas operated during the gold and diamond rush. In 1802 Dom João signed another decree, insisting upon the utility of the earlier provisions even while admitting that they had been ignored. To prevent evasion in future, the requirement of a gubernatorial license was extended to all the captaincies. This may have been enforced to some degree. It was objected, probably with justice, that these were mere pretexts to maintain the privileges of the owners of existing mills and to relegate lesser cane farmers to a state of dependency. They were also an opportunity for informal exactions by crown officials: It appears, for example, that the governor of Espírito Santo took advantage of the 1802 decree to advance his private interests.[10]

The special, and contradictory, status of those sugar growers who were the possessors of mills is evident in the epithet that adhered to them: *senhoresde engenho*—lords of the mill. Imagine a technical contrivance as complicated as a mill as the demesne of a lord—a title that had everything to do with social status and nothing to do with ingenuity or enterprise. Pombal's decree of 1758, exempting the sugar planters of Rio de Janeiro from judgments for debt, epitomized and legitimized the feudal privilege of a colonial elite embedded in a regime otherwise relentlessly mercantilist. Undoubtedly, the intention was to protect the resources of those who were expected to generate the revenues of that regime. In 1807 and 1814 this economically retrograde measure was reaffirmed under Dom João, whose court supposedly leaned toward liberalism. In these decrees, at least, protection was limited to cases in which the total debt was less than the value of the estate. Apparently the crown sought to preserve revenue-producing plantations from fragmentation, under the unwavering assumption that small-scale operators would not export. Only in 1827 did the empire end restrictions on the building of mills and, in 1833, restore their liability to creditors.[11]

The late-eighteenth-century revival of sugar encouraged some landowners to install some of the improvements that had long been standard in the Caribbean. The transition to more efficient milling techniques was very gradual, however. Although the shifting of the rollers from a vertical to a horizontal position and the adding of a third roller had been introduced at least a century and a half before, these changes had not been universal. After foreign ironmasters set up shop in Rio de Janeiro, beginning in 1837, iron-plated or cast-iron rollers were mounted in many of the lowland engenhos and in a few in the highlands. Most of the mills were, at the beginning of the revival, worked with animal power; relatively few, by water. In 1818 a water-powered mill near the court was a curiosity worth showing a foreign visitor. The first mill with steam-powered rollers was built in 1816. Thereafter conversion continued and, at least in the Campos region, steam-powered mills were common by the mid-1850s. The "Jamaica train"—the placement in train of boiling vats graduated in size, more economical of fuel, seems not to have been widespread in lowland engenhos before 1800, even though they had been invented, probably in Brazil, by the 1650s. Thermometers, to gauge the readiness of the cane juices for crystallization, began to be imported in the 1840s. The use of bagasse—the spent stalks of the cane after milling—for fuel was unknown except in Campos, and there it was, even in the 1850s, incipient.[12]

Improvements in milling did not imply improvements in farming. Tahitian cane, brought in triumph from Cayenne, was rejected by most planters. Although this variety was faster growing, more wind resistant, and higher yielding, its stalks were thicker and very difficult to grind with wooden or iron-plated rollers. Cultivation was carried out in the same fashion as slash-and-burn subsistence farming. In some areas turned over to cane, the original or cattle-induced vegetation had been grassland; in others, especially in the area east of Guanabara Bay and in the highlands of São Paulo near the capital of the captaincy, only secondary forest persisted. But primary forest was burned and cleared where any was available, because it overlay the most fertile soils. The canes, planted in the ashes of whatever vegetation it replaced, was harvested after a year and allowed to regrow from its roots for two more harvests, then burned and replanted. This cycle was repeated for another turn or two, then the field was abandoned to the forest, at first for as long as it took for a modestly tall capoeira to form, perhaps twenty years. As prices rose, the fallow phase was shortened to as little as three years. This practice, however, lowered fertility, so that the planting cycles then also had to be shortened, perhaps to a single planting.[13]

Finally, after twenty or thirty years, the planter would lose interest, declare his land "tired," and petition for another sesmaria. Sugar growing therefore spread beyond the plain of Campos, northward into southern Espírito Santo and westward into the forested piedmont, and in the São Paulo highlands farther inland beyond Campinas. The prepotence of the lords of the mill may have been an impediment to the timely introduction of more intensive techniques. They certainly appear to have been less than amenable to instruction in the view of the indefatigable traveler Antônio Muniz de Souza, who encountered many of the sort who informed him

> that there is nothing in all the Macrocosm greater than his mills; that there is no better method, nor easier means to fabricate sugar than those they have adopted and employ, and finally they presume that there can be no manner or principles upon which these same methods could be reformed or modified, including the abuses and losses that still follow upon them.[14]

Brazilian sugar exports may have averaged 16,000 tons a year during the whole of the eighteenth century, rising to perhaps 30,000 tons by 1850. This suggests production for export of about 2.6 million tons over a period of 150 years. How large an area of the Atlantic Forest had to be cleared to produce 2.6 million tons of sugar? The extractive rate probably averaged no better than 3.5 percent, or 74 million tons of cane. Canefields yielded about 50 tons per hectare, so that canefields sufficient to grow that quantity would have occupied an average of 1,000 square kilometers. If planters persisted in cultivating their fields an average of 20 years, then clearing, over a century and a half, totaled 7,500 square kilometers. It seems likely, however, that part of this area would have been taken from second growth farmed in earlier times or else from fields, especially in the Campos region, that had been natural or indigenously created grasslands.[15]

Sugarcane also consumed forest as fuel for the boiling vats. There was much worry, mainly in the Northeast, concerning the mills' immense demand for wood. Fuel requirements were much reduced by the installation of the Jamaica train, from about 15 to about 5 kilograms of wood per kilogram of sugar. Because this improvement was still not universal, even by

1800, perhaps 7 kilograms is closer to fact. A demand for 18 million tons of wood over 150 years would have consumed about 900 square kilometers of forest, assuming that 200 tons of wood suitable for the ovens could be found in a given hectare. Much of this wood, too, would have been extracted from secondary forest or, in the beginning of the sugar boom, at least, from forest that was allowed to grow back over fallow. Nevertheless, there is evidence that primary forest was cut down for this purpose—sometimes it was burned down simply to make the extraction of firewood less troublesome![16]

These calculations suggest that sugar planting up to 1850 was not so destructive of forest that it had to be abandoned over any large area, even taking into account its extreme extensiveness. Nevertheless, there are a few notices of the abandonment of plantations because fuelwood had been exhausted. These were probably isolated cases. An average-sized engenho, such as might occupy a one-league-square sesmaria (4,356 hectares), typically produced less than 30 tons of sugar a year. The figures cited above suggest that no more than 18 hectares would have been needed to yield this output and that less than a hectare of woodland would have been cut down for firewood each year. Evidently, so limited a scale of sugarcane cultivation was entirely sustainable indefinitely, even if the shifting of fields was very frequent, and the explanation for the abandonment of these grants has to be found in activities other than sugar production for export.[17]

The grassy plains of Campos were exceptional. There, the lack of native forest may have exerted a real constraint on the expansion of sugar growing. Firewood had to be sent down the Paraíba River from São Fidelis and beyond, and probably down the Muriaé River, on the bank of which, some 80 kilometers from Campos, there is a place still called Porto Madeira—Port Wood. In 1844 a canal nearly 100 kilometers long was dug to Macaé, partly to bring firewood to the mills. The increasing use, by the 1840s, of bagasse in the mills of Campos was also related to wood scarcity. Nevertheless, bagasse had advantages, only slowly admitted, independent of the availability of firewood: It heated the boiling train faster and required less tending of the fire, and it eliminated the costs of felling, chopping, and transporting. Astonishingly, some sugar planters had been assigning their slaves the task of chopping entire trunks of forest giants into kindling for the furnaces! Bagasse revived the planting of Tahitian cane, whose woody stalks were especially suitable for stoking the boilers.[18]

Sugar planting demanded other, lesser, but not insignificant forest products. Wood was burned to produce ash to purify the crystalline sugar. Sugar continued to be packed in boxes, and certain trees were favored for this purpose, because they imparted no color or taste. Among them were jequitibá and tapinhoá, supposedly reserved for the use of the navy. Cachaça was put up in barrels, preferably of canela (*Ocotea* spp.). All of these were trees of the primary forest. Oxen brought cane from the fields and powered the smaller mills. Pasture had to be cleared to support them. As sugar fields replaced cattle in the Campos region and penetrated farther into forested land in the São Paulo highlands, these animals had to be raised at considerable distances from the plantations, in the Minas Gerais highlands, the Pomba River valley, or the savanna region of Goiás.[19]

Brazilian producers confronted an international sugar market that was only briefly favorable. Many competitors, among them European beet farmers, emerged following the crises of revolution and war that had provided Brazil its initial opportunity. The result was falling prices that made it difficult to install the costly new equipment that was reducing dramatically the costs of European sugar millers. In consequence, sugar growing in the southeastern Atlantic Forest by the 1850s fell into decline. The Campos district, blessed with rich alluvial soils, continued to specialize in sugar, supplying domestic urban consumers, but elsewhere planting was reduced in scale. As a cause of additional primary forest loss, sugarcane thus remained quite secondary for the rest of the century.[20]

The mountainous area above the imperial city of Rio de Janeiro had escaped commercial sugar planting, because it possessed only isolated ribbons of level bottomland suitable for the crop. But another tropical plantation product, one that held forth to the landowners of this problematic and still heavily forested zone the prospect of much greater rewards, was gaining their attention. The same withdrawal of foreign colonial competition that stimulated sugarcane had also encouraged a few landowners to experiment with a plant almost overlooked by officials of the crown and their botanical adjutants. This novel crop, coffee, was to become, in the first decades of the empire, the basis of Rio de Janeiro's export economy. Coffee, *Coffea arabica*, a small tree of the Rubiaceae family, native to the understory of southwestern Ethiopian highland forest, bore the caffeine-laden seeds so highly appreciated by European city dwellers. Its opportune appearance was to resolve brilliantly the quest for a product the new empire might exchange for the manufactures and luxuries of Europe. Just as the eighteenth century had been for Brazil the century of gold, the nineteenth was to be the century of coffee. But for the Atlantic Forest the introduction of this exotic was to pose a more intense threat than any other event of the previous 300 years.

Coffee's arrival in the region of Rio de Janeiro is obscure. Centuries before, it had been transferred from Ethiopia to Yemen, where it was brought under commercial cultivation. All the coffees later introduced to South and Southeast Asia and to the New World are derived from the two Yemeni varieties, now called tipica and bourbon. Seeds of tipica may have reached Brazil in the late 1600s, possibly via India, but the product was not then exported. What may have been a second introduction was carried out in 1727: The French had received coffee from the Dutch and had transferred it to French Guiana. A Brazilian army officer, sent there to negotiate a border settlement, surreptitiously removed to Belém do Pará a pocketful of seeds grown from these trees. There and in nearby Maranhão it soon became a modest article of commerce. A judge posted to Maranhão may have brought the first seedlings to Rio de Janeiro in 1752 or 1762. They were kept in the monastery garden of the Capuchins, but apparently they were looked upon only as ornamentals. When the explorer Captain James Cook visited Rio de Janeiro in 1768, he found that the city was still importing coffee from Lisbon.[21]

With the formation of the Academia Fluviense in 1772, Johan Hopman, a Dutch émigré who kept its garden, began to distribute the seeds of these trees and advice on tending them. The first recipients may have been two priests who owned farms in the suburbs. By 1779, when the Viceroy Lavradio turned over his post, coffee was still so unimportant that he overlooked it in his final report, even though he mentioned many other, even minor, crops. Meanwhile, the French had acquired the other Yemeni variety and brought it to their Indian Ocean island of Réunion, then called Bourbon. This variety also reached Brazil at some uncertain date. Possibly this was what was introduced in 1782, obtained directly from Cayenne by Bishop José Joaquim Justiniano. By 1790 a little more than a ton of coffee was produced for the local market. In that year its presence was noted by Manuel Ferreira da Câmara, who predicted that the soils of Rio de Janeiro would offer the best location for its expansion.

Considering that this plant became and remained for a century and a half Brazil's most important staple, Domingos Borges de Barros's rebuke, penned when coffee cultivation was but incipient, echoes ruefully:

> I do not know why we expend so much time, and paper, to know who commanded in such-and-such a battle, how many dead were left on the field; and none in transmitting to posterity the names of those to whom we owe such-and-such a plant; perchance is it of more interest to know who contributes to the destruction than to the conservation of the human species?[22]

For those wretches condemned by slavery to cultivate coffee for another seventy years, the anonymous heroes who implanted coffee would have appeared as destructive as any Napoleon or Wellington. Although coffee is decidedly a plant whose yields and quality can be increased through the careful treatment that family landownership and wage incentives can elicit, in Brazil it was to be raised and brought to market under the same conditions applied to sugar growing. Coffee came to be the product of the large estates granted in sesmaria while the Portuguese court resided in Rio de Janeiro. Indeed, coffee was the salvation of the colonial aristocracy. It was also the salvation of the tottering imperial court, which, beset by regional rebellions and hard pressed to pay the civil and military bureaucracies needed to establish the state, was rescued by the revenues from coffee that flowed into Rio de Janeiro's customhouse. For the empire, then, this trade was altogether fortuitous. Had the growing conditions of far-off, restive Recife, Porto Alegre, or São Luis been more favorable to coffee, centrifugal forces would have been generated that would have sundered Brazil. The empire therefore pampered the planters of Rio de Janeiro: They were its primary interest group and its financial mainstay.

In turn, the ecological desiderata of this Ethiopian plant set the physical limits to the reproduction of the plantation system and therefore to the stability of the empire. The coffee plant encountered in the province of Rio de Janeiro an environment adequate, if not ideal, for its cultivation. It requires heavy rainfall, from 1,300 to 1,800 millimeters annually, because it transpires continuously and, as an understory tree, has no mechanism for storing or conserving moisture. Subject to a dry season in its native habitat, it draws soil moisture from considerable depths, 3 meters and more, as a water reserve. Coffee was at first planted along the coast, where it may have suffered somewhat from salty ocean winds. It was soon moved to the somewhat cooler highland, where its temperature optimum of 20° C to 24° C is available. The more pronounced dry season of the interior is also favorable, because the onset of the rains is the main inducement to flowering and because simultaneous flowering promotes simultaneous ripening of the berries. The dry season, May through August, when the harvest is carried out, offered another competitive advantage, because it facilitates the open-air drying of the berries, a process that elsewhere had to be carried out in wood-fired ovens.[23]

The coffee tree is mesic; that is, it requires soils neither soggy nor parched. In highland Rio de Janeiro, the valley bottoms were poorly drained, so planting had to be done on dauntingly steep gradients—the "sea of hills" or "half-oranges" of the regional physical landscape. The Atlantic Forest had stabilized on them, over thousands of years of negligible human intervention, a shallow but moderately fertile, somewhat acidic soil. This material, and the biomass of the forest itself, might for a time supply essential nutrients.

This was precisely the danger to the Atlantic Forest: It was believed that coffee had to be planted in soil overlain by "virgin" forest. Capital and labor were too scarce to expend them in planting on soils less fertile. The coffee tree is a perennial—it takes four years to reach maturity and may remain productive for thirty years—so it might be imagined that, once implanted, coffee represented a promisingly stable and conservative agricultural regime. That was not so. On the plantations of Rio de Janeiro, senescent groves were not replanted but were abandoned, and new swaths of primary forest were then cleared to maintain production. Thus coffee marched across the highlands, generation by generation, leaving nothing in its wake but denuded hills.

Planters prized neither yield nor quality, but only the economizing of labor and capital and, not incidentally, their own managerial effort. This strategy, if such it could be called, rendered a product of only mediocre quality. Francisco Peixoto de Lacerda Werneck, one of the most important of the first generation of Rio de Janeiro coffee planters, a man who undoubtedly knew his neighbors well and certainly shared most of their prejudices, could not have been expressing anything but their common aspiration in paraphrasing them thus: "What I want is a lot of [coffee]; it gets a lower price . . . , but I take the same net profit, even though I don't have as much work." To this Lacerda Werneck responded acidly that if Brazilian coffee, sugar, and cotton were as well regarded as those exported from other countries, they would not be stranded for months and even years in Europe's warehouses awaiting buyers. Luckily, North Americans were less discriminating than Europeans. As the population and economy of the United States boomed, so more and more of its consumers could afford to indulge this habit, and the Brazilian empire became more and more tied to this single market.[24]

The choice of terrain upon which to plant was, as long as primary forest remained, a matter of vague empiricism. A reconnaissance was carried out to find tree species that were regarded as *padrões*—indicators—of superior locations for coffee groves. Lacerda Werneck's planters' manual, based on his own experience, offers insight into the practices of the more reflective of the estate owners and was apparently the most widely read, passing through two more editions after it first appeared in 1847. In it, he advised that hillsides should be observed in springtime, when many forest trees were in flower. Where jacarandá-tã was to be seen, or certain other species—he listed sixteen—the land was of first quality. These were all, like coffee, mesic, and they were all to be found only in primary forest. Other authors listed other trees, however, and not even Lacerda Werneck had accumulated sufficient experience to have been certain that the growing conditions of coffee exactly paralleled those of jacarandá-tã or any of the other padrões he mentioned. Lacerda Werneck also counseled against planting on south-facing hillsides, which he considered too cool; other authors with less logic rejected east- or west-facing hillsides. The thickness of the humus layer was regarded a promising sign: It was supposed to be thick enough for a man to sink in up to midcalf. (One wonders if any of the supposedly "primary" forest still to be found in the region exhibits humus thick enough to sink in up to midcalf, much less the "four palmas"—88 centimeters—mentioned by Inácio Accioli de Vasconcellos; perhaps modern-day investigators are overlooking a clear sign of prior human intervention in such sites.) It is likely that novice planters ignored even these few counsels and that they learned from experience, a school that cost the Atlantic Forest even more dearly than they.[25]

In other places and climes coffee was grown in shade, a practice that imitates its native habitat and appears to improve its quality. In Brazil, instead of preserving part of the native canopy, the entire forest was destroyed, in preparation for planting—save, here and there, a pau d'alho, garlic tree. These were left in place, because they were accepted as the surest of all padrões and thus might be displayed to an estate's potential purchaser as proof of the productivity of its groves. (And when coffee groves were ruined and abandoned, surviving pau d'alho trees comforted the cattle, because they exude a smelly secretion that wards off insects.) It is not clear whether disregard for shading coffee was a deliberate innovation. Apparently the earliest planters had little notion of how coffee was grown elsewhere and merely applied traditional techniques of slash-and-burn on a larger, more drastic scale. It was not until long after coffee growing in the Paraíba Valley had fallen into decadence that the question whether shading might have been a superior technique was seriously raised. Certainly clear-cutting and burning was the cheapest way of initiating production, and perhaps that was all the justification that was, or would have been, necessary.[26]

In the winter months of May, June, and July, gangs of roving woodsmen were hired to execute the task of clearing according to a system called *picarias*. Working upward from the base of the hill, they swung their axes against each tree in turn, chopping away until the trunk, still intact, groaned with the imminence of its collapse. An experienced foreman observed carefully the slope of the hill, the position of each tree, and the lianas—abundant in this sector of the Atlantic Forest—which tied each to its neighbor, and he supervised the cutting so that each tree was poised to fall in a precise direction. Upward climbed the woodsmen, hacking at another and then another trunk, ever higher, until the summit was reached.

Then it was the foreman's task to decide which was the master tree, the giant that would be cut all the way through, bringing down all the others with it. If he succeeded, the entire hillside collapsed with a tremendous explosion, raising a cloud of debris, swarms of parrots, toucans, songbirds, and, from the woodsmen, a shout of joy and relief. For if the foreman's choice had proved mistaken and only a few of the trees went down, then the hapless woodsmen would have had to descend among the tottering giants and finish them off one by one. Then it was not uncommon for the giants to wreak vengeance as they toppled:

> In its fall a branch catches against a neighbor and the cut trunk, finding a point of support, describes an arc; the woodsmen, who have their eyes nailed to it, avoid the danger by jumping to one side; but the trunk, colliding against another tree, changes direction, freeing itself of the branches that for a moment had held it fast, and propelled by its own weight falls with the speed of a thunderbolt. The foresight and dexterity of the woodsman avails him naught—he is crushed.

No wonder this job paid twice that of common day labor and entitled these rural freemen, above all their comrades, to at least a measure of respect and pride within that oppressive society.[27]

A few of the trunks thus felled were chopped into kindling for charcoal for the city market or were dragged away or pit sawed on the spot for construction materials. County ordinances usually required that trunks fallen over roads or into watercourses had to be removed. The rest were left to dry for a few weeks, then, in the chill of late August, just before the rains, all the forest slash was set afire. This was also work for the experienced and fearless. A burn of proper intensity was essential. One that scorched the humus layer was to be avoided, as was one so superficial that it failed to produce enough ash to neutralize the soil or left resident insects intact. If the woodsmen were unskillful, the fire might also overleap some areas, leaving them unburned. Beginning at midday, when the air was still, the woodsmen divided at the top of the clearing into two groups. Each descended along one of the margins, putting the slash to the torch as they went, rejoining finally at the bottom of the clearing. This was never work to assign the slaves, who, their captors were only too vividly aware, might easily trap them in the blaze.[28]

The desiccated vegetation leapt into flames with a roar, the popping of bamboo stalks, according to one observer, sounding like rifle fire, the rending of the trunks, like artillery. From the volcanic conflagration a whirlwind of smoke soared into the sky, carrying brilliant geysers of sparks. For many hours ashes fell like rain. The fire would go on for days, then it would smolder for many more, from its embers rising "spiracles of grey smoke, as if escaping through crevices from an immense furnace, hidden and burning beneath." At last the rains came, washing into the greasy muck of the humus and soil the nutrients released from the rich bed of ashes.[29]

Local ordinances also required that, before setting a fire, firebreaks be cleared and neighbors be advised. It is unlikely that, in the case of primary forest remote from towns, such barriers, which would have cost considerable additional labor, were much employed, especially if the field did not border on a neighbor's land. In any case, it was only necessary that the firebreak be four to six meters wide, quite insufficient to prevent accidents in tall forest. Fire therefore often escaped, especially in drier years. John Luccock witnessed such an accident near the city of Rio de Janeiro in 1816. Although half a square league had gone up in smoke, local residents did not appear much concerned, because the destruction had occurred on public land. In the interior, where rain was much more seasonal, fire regularly got out of hand: "If one wishes to clear a hectare, one destroys sometimes five or ten through the barbarous resort to fire," remarked a French coffee specialist who witnessed this "folly" during his visit to São Paulo in 1892.[30]

The destruction of forest was a matter of momentary regret for some of those who viewed it, but such feelings were quickly followed by others—pragmatic:

> However, upon contemplating the conscientious work carried out in the vicinity of Cantagalo, we feel reconciled to the devastation previously noted, principally upon thinking of the benefits that such a labor must provide, not only to its executors, but to all those who will come later to continue it, possessed by the same love of the land.[31]

—or weirdly pyrophiliac:

> The fire . . . is terrible, but it attracts us, because we feel the necessity of observing it close at hand. . . . Really, how beautiful is the fire of a great burn. . . . What a strange sensation. . . . It is distressing for some, in truth; for others it is a grandiose spectacle that awakens the feelings and sharpens the eye in the same way that we are taken when we see and hear the mass of an army that moves to the sound of a triumphal march.[32]

The fires of many clearings raised immense gray clouds of smoke. The Paraíba Valley must have appeared at the end of the dry season infernal, with hundreds of fires stretching its length and breadth. By midcentury, as the clearing of the Atlantic Forest for coffee accelerated, a yellowish pall hung over the province during these months, obscuring the sun by day and obliterating the stars by night. Travelers unused to this phenomenon were surprised at the haze that limited visibility from the hilltops and that shortened their breath and caused them a sensation of weariness. In August and September ashes from the interior fell on the city of Rio de Janeiro: "Such was the quantity of smoke that for days, and even months, the sun is almost entirely hidden or, if we saw it, it is red, almost as though we see it through smoked glass." Curiously, there were some in the city who could not accept the burnings as the cause, and it came to be debated formally in the learned Vellosiana Society why Rio de Janeiro experienced this yearly so-called dry fog. The botanist Francisco Freire Alemão commented that only those who had never witnessed the burnings could doubt that they were to blame, pointing out that the phenomenon appeared only when the wind blew from the north and that it ceased with the rains.[33]

The terrain, thus readied for the healing hand of man, resembled some modern battlefield, blackened, smoldering, and desolate. Most of the felled trees were only partly incinerated; they were left to rot with their stumps still in place and their trunks pointing down the slope. The work gangs assigned to planting the seedlings were then allowed to proceed in what was no doubt the least irksome fashion, working their way uphill. Thus were the groves aligned, on the most disastrous master plan imaginable. The rows straggled up the hillsides, guided by the forms of the fallen trunks. Down the rows came coursing the rains, forming gullies between them, carrying off humus and topsoil rapidly and efficiently. It was never the practice to swing the logs around to form barriers against erosion. On the contrary, trunks fallen crosswise were objects of fear and avoidance because, as the stumps and roots that held them in place rotted away, they were known to roll downhill, smashing coffee trees and crushing workers unfortunate enough to stand in their path. The French émigré Jousselandière claimed that eight of the slaves of a friend of his had been killed by a single rolling trunk. Only after the rains had begun to expose tree roots were halfhearted efforts made to pile up ridges to impede the runoff.[34]

Coffee planters, in their haste to set out their groves as quickly as possible, did not divide them into blocks. This would have been a waste of time, because they did not trouble to experiment with different seed sources, planting, or cultivation techniques or even to keep account of costs and yields by field. They did not bother to plant on the diamond pattern, though they were aware of the advantages. Many of them did engage, however, in the odd, counterproductive procedure of snipping off the tip of the seedlings' tap roots. They did not select their planting materials. Estates usually started off with coffee berries solicited from a relative or a neighbor. They were not chosen from trees that bore heavily or produced better-quality beans but were chance gifts or purchases that were received gratefully, whatever their provenance or pedigree. These heterogeneous berries were usually first planted in a nursery, a small patch burned out of the forest in order to provide the shade that this understory tree appeared to need in its first year or two of growth. Otherwise they were planted directly in the field, and the seedlings, as they germinated, were shielded with a few pieces of lath or maize stalks in the form of a lean-to. As the groves expanded, nurseries were eliminated, because the planter could now rely on adventitious seedlings sprung up here and there under the branches of mature trees, it seeming to matter little whether the source trees were productive or not.[35]

A normal planting density was 800 to 900 per hectare. This was remarkably few, compared to the modern practice of 3,000 to 5,000. The low density allowed trees to grow wide and tall, hampering the harvest, and it facilitated the invasion of weeds. Worst of all, it reduced yields per hectare. Had dense planting been the rule, forest clearing could have been greatly reduced in extent.

Cultivation was not carried out upon principles that were in any way conservative of the resource. Weeds began to appear in the freshly exposed forest soils of the new groves only as the trees reached maturity, at three or four years. Weeding was done with heavy iron hoes two or three times a year, as labor was available. The slave gang worked its way down the hillside, a procedure that facilitated vigilance, because the workers remained in straight ranks. It also speeded runoff of rainwater. The heavy hoe cleaved superficial roots, a morphological feature of the coffee tree, not noticed until much later, that supplies a considerable portion of the plant's nutrients. Trees unable to withstand this treatment were rarely substituted; dead trees were allowed to decay in place. Soil nutrients were infrequently recycled and never replaced. It was expected that the ashes and the humus layer would provide whatever the tree might need, for as long as the grove might last. Justus von Liebig's 1840 discovery of mineral nutrients was for many years unappreciated in Rio de Janeiro. Chemical analysis of the coffee tree's requirements was attempted only in the 1870s, and it was not connected to practice until much later. It was accepted, however, that "green manure"—that is, fallen leaves and stems—was beneficial, and it was sometimes heaped up under the trees at the end of harvest. This task the barefoot slaves must have been reluctant to undertake, because the mulch beds attracted rodents, and rodents attracted snakes. Often this green matter was not conserved at all, merely burned.[36]

The usual techniques of harvesting and processing lessened output and lowered quality. Slave field hands were assigned quotas and therefore indiscriminately stripped the branches of green, ripe, and overripe berries. Methods of drying, shelling, and winnowing the berries had to be puzzled out in the years following the introduction of coffee, a remarkable empirical process that adapted simple implements used in hulling rice, grinding maize, and shredding sugarcane. The drying of the berries was done under the sun, in the open air, because the harvest season was normally relatively free of rain. The drying terraces were of beaten earth; only in the 1860s were they lined with brick. Processing was laborious, contradicting the notion that labor was in short supply. Slave women, squatting on the dirt floors of storage sheds, sorted the beans. Hulling was done in large wooden pestles. Water power was soon applied to this task, and primitive mills evolved, in which the mortar-and-pestle units were set in tandem. By the early 1850s the first steam engines appeared in the leading county of Vassouras, but it is not known what sort of machinery they were attached to.[37]

Estate owners did not have the resources to put all their holdings into coffee production immediately, so the Paraíba Valley became a patchwork of coffee groves and primary forest as first the north-facing slopes, then less favorable sites, were fired and planted. The rapid senescence of the trees on their precarious perches increased the value of the remaining forest: "The wealth of a plantation consists, then, less in the great extension of its coffee groves, than in the lands available for the future planting of the rubiacea," as the naturalist Hermann von Burmeister put it. New entrants in the coffee business, therefore, preferred to buy lands farther up the valley, across the provincial border of São Paulo, or in the Zona da Mata, the Forest Zone of Minas Gerais most recently despoiled of its Indian population, where rose the headwaters of the Doce, Pomba, and Das Mortes rivers. Coffee arrived somewhat later in Espírito Santo, where growing and soil conditions were less favorable. Thus coffee cultivation spread extensively, and a considerable portion of the upland Atlantic Forest was transformed into a rolling sea of coffee trees.[38]

Coffee trees thus planted and tended usually began to fail within twenty years of maturity. Senescence marked the end of the productive life of the estate itself. When a grove became so decadent that it was no longer worth harvesting, it was occasionally coppiced, but this generally yielded only meager results. More often it was left in place, the trees were leased to firewood merchants, and grasses invaded, followed by cattle, very frequently under new ownership. Lacerda Werneck himself, the empiricist expert in coffee planting, willed his heirs a plantation "very old and sterile," in the words of his son, written in 1858, "from whose soil my father took all his fortune, but which he left completely ruined." Forest, therefore, was not reestablished. Years later, long after the trees had disappeared, barren hillsides oddly pockmarked, as though sites of artillery duels, remained as witness to the rapid passage of coffee along the Paraíba Valley. Finally, even these traces were erased by the cattle, whose plodding hoofs incised ribbonlike trails back and forth across the slumping hardpan of the mournful wastes.[39]

The first century of commercial coffee cultivation in the region of the Atlantic Forest—1788 to 1888—was also the last century of slavery. During this period, Brazil produced about 10 million tons of coffee, nearly all of it passing through the ports of Rio de Janeiro and Santos. Supposing that 700 kilograms was the average yield per hectare, and supposing that the average grove was economically productive for twenty years, then it was necessary to clear for this purpose some 7,200 square kilometers of primary forest, the equivalent of 300 million tons of forest biomass gone up in smoke. This area equaled nearly 18 percent of the surface of the province of Rio de Janeiro, where four-fifths of this coffee was planted. To this must be added the forest cleared for subsistence for the slave work force, which must have averaged 140,000 in number. Some unknowable portion of subsistence fields, possibly south-facing hillsides, may have been covered with primary forest.[40]

By the time of the collapse of slavery, lands thought adequate for coffee cultivation were nearly exhausted in Rio de Janeiro. How biologically unique were these zones of the Atlantic Forest? Unfortunately, this is not a matter that can be investigated retrospectively, although it is historically verifiable that few of its species were collected before it went up in smoke. Auguste de Saint-Hilaire thought the western zone of the Paraíba Valley harbored the most diverse vegetation he saw in all his travels through the Atlantic Forest. One may well wonder, therefore, whether some of its creatures, especially of the canopy, which shaded him and his fellow scientists but which they lacked the means to investigate, were already disappearing forever. It seems at least possible that extinctions were part of the price of bringing 10 million tons of coffee to market, even though the species whose types are warehoused in pickling jars and pressed sheets in the Jardin des Plantes and the Bayerische Botanische Gesellschaft have so far survived. These early investigators had neither the time nor the resources to do more than sample the life forms of the forests they traversed. Nearly all of them had kept to the same mule trails, they had for the most part avoided tall forests, which were too impenetrable and troublesome, and their expeditions were carried out after the assault on the forest had already begun. Among the botanists, only the Brazilian Francisco Freire Alemão grasped the opportunity presented by the destruction of forest: He hurried from felling crew to felling crew, to examine the downed giants they were extracting preliminary to burning the rest. But he was only one individual, barely able to study the trees themselves, much less their epiphytes and parasites. He lacked, furthermore, funds to collect and store everything he found or to publish his notes.[41]

It is sometimes put forward that the most rational exploitation of a natural resource is the most rapid, accompanied by the least expenditure of labor or capital, so that the resource may be transformed as quickly as possible into more capital, a better legacy to bestow upon posterity than the untouched resource. This argument smacks of self-interest, and the history of the Paraíba Valley demonstrates some of its weaknesses. The Atlantic Forest was undoubtedly, within the scale of time that concerned its expropriators, their creditors and brokers, and the imperial government, a nonrenewable resource. Its destruction in this locale was inevitable with population increase, no matter what crop was planted, whether for export or local consumption. Once cleared, however, the hills of Rio de Janeiro were also treated as nonrenewable, when they might have been defined otherwise. Had the planting of coffee been done with care, it might still be growing where first it was introduced, and much of the Atlantic Forest might have been spared for some other purpose or, in peace, for none.

Most of the resources acquired through the sale of coffee were not "accumulated," or "formed," as capital to equip the brawn of a future generation, but spent on goods at the time prized as luxuries, imported exclusively for the consumption of the families who owned these properties and these workers. The preservation of the coffee trade served as the main argument for delaying the abolition of slavery, an institution that even slaveholders were ashamed to defend on any other grounds. Brazil was the last country in the Western Hemisphere to bring this blight to an end. Coffee income captured in the customhouses of the imperial government was expended largely on the rail network that brought coffee to market; much of this investment was uneconomic once the serviced coffee estates went broke. Most of the rest of these resources went to pay the salaries of the military and the civil service, which by the end of the coffee cycle included many scions of decadent plantation families. When, as the Paraíba Valley's economy faltered, the empire experienced difficulty in maintaining the planters' living standards, they turned ungrateful and pronounced in favor of a republic. Coffee lured some foreign capital to the area, but nearly all of it was directly or indirectly in support of the trade itself, tendered only with the prospect of speculative and short-term returns larger than might be achieved in the countries of origin.

These reflections suggest that a resource policy designed for stability and renewability might have better served the longer-term political and economic well-being of the inhabitants of the southeastern Atlantic Forest, including the landowning upper class itself. A century after the introduction of coffee, Augusto Ruschi, Espírito Santo's great naturalist and environmentalist, mourned the result: "We shall never restore the climate and biotic soil conditions that we had." Even though it was on coffee "that the life of our people depends; on it that a good or bad government depends," still, he vowed, "we would give everything that we enjoy as the result of this coffee monoculture to be free of this undesirable intruder." The characteristics of the postcolonial society—its avidity for immediate profit, concentration of wealth, fixation upon vigilance and control, extreme empiricism, and entire disregard for what only in another hundred years an enlightened few would cherish as priceless natural wealth—bring to mind instantly how futile it is to raise such objections now, when the deed is done and no traces are left of it on the sere and yellowed hills of the Paraíba Valley.[42]

We who look back upon these events from a perspective of more than a century might imagine that sounder means to the same end have been devised by modern science, but that is not entirely the case. Although selection, breeding, planting, and cultivation of the coffee tree have been much rationalized, there is still no tool readier to hand than the matchbox for establishing a coffee plantation. Surviving primary forest, in the region of the Atlantic Forest or elsewhere in Brazil—or indeed in the rest of the tropical world—where any is found overspreading adequate soils, remains an immense temptation to any who would, at a profit, dispense to humankind its daily dose of caffeine.

9

Instruments of Devastation

E já não é raro encontrar se pequenas forjas cercadas de rijas de oligisto
em estado de completo abandono, por não terem nas vizinhanças florestas
que fornecem combustível.

And already it is not unusual to find small forges surrounded by
outcroppings of hematite in a state of complete abandonment, for lack
of forests nearby to furnish fuel.

FRANCISCO MAGALHÃES GOMES (1880)

The burning of forest to plant coffee groves was the principal, but not the only, cause of deforestation in the nineteenth century. The coffee trade induced population growth, urbanization, manufacturing, and the implantation of railroads. These indirect consequences of a feverish prosperity in a single export commodity exerted pressure over a wider area of the Atlantic Forest, the beginning of what now can be seen to have been irreversible losses to anthropomorphosed landscapes.

The human population of the Southeast region of the Atlantic Forest multiplied remarkably in the nineteenth century. Numbering about 1.0 million in 1808, by 1890 it reached 6.4 million. The urbanized portion of the population grew faster still: At the turn of the nineteenth century, Rio de Janeiro, though it was the viceregal capital, contained only 50,000 residents. The arrival of the Portuguese court doubled its numbers, and another 50,000 were added by the mid-1850s, despite the ravages of cholera and yellow fever. Thereafter growth was rapid: It was a metropolis of more than 500,000 by 1890. This multiplication of souls represented also a multiplication of stomachs. Given the voraciousness of traditional farming technique, the feeding of the Atlantic Forest's residents was becoming a heavy burden upon it. The trade in coffee and other export products made economical the installation, at last, of transportation more effective than pack-mule trails. This improvement, too, would increase pressure upon formerly inaccessible reaches of the forest. The larger population formed also a sizable market for iron tools, easily supplied by the rich and shallow ore deposits of Minas Gerais. The smelting and forging of these instruments was to intensify the industrial demand upon the fuel resources of the forest. The nineteenth century was thus in a number of ways a harbinger of troubles to come in the twentieth.[1]

The rate of population growth in the Southeast during the nineteenth century—2.25 percent a year—surpassed that of the gold- and diamond-rich eighteenth century. This was in part the result of an increased inflow of slaves. The British threat to the traffic made it an even more feverish and profitable speculation. In the forty years before the final abolition of the African trade in 1850, 3.1 million slaves were imported, more than nine-tenths of them to Rio de Janeiro. This was a rate eight times greater than that of the preceding three decades. After the end of the African traffic, the human flow shifted, as slaves and free persons were transferred or migrated south from the economically stagnant provinces of the Northeast. Throughout the period there were modest accretions through European immigration, principally of Portuguese, seeking urban opportunities, jobs on plantations, or plots in the few scattered frontier colonies established by the state and by private entrepreneurs. Considering the high mortality rates imputed to the nineteenth century, especially to slave populations, this continuing remarkable demographic increase must be attributed in the main to the wombs of Brazilian women, who heroically outpaced death by malaria, tuberculosis, enteritis, bilharzia, Chagas disease, snakebite, gunshot, and a thousand other ills and perils.[2]

This enlarged population was still quite unevenly distributed. A settlement frontier remained, beyond which tribal peoples survived in small bands and along which only a thin population of mestizo pioneers—fugitives from slavery, serfdom, or justice—and colonists chipped away at the forest margin. Most of Espírito Santo's interior remained in this state to the end of the century, and the eastern flank of Minas Gerais, bordering Espírito Santo, remained so seldom penetrated that the boundary between these two states was contested until the 1950s. São Paulo west of the Tietê and north of the Botucatu escarpment was shown on maps of the era as "unknown." The westernmost extension of the Atlantic Forest that occupied northern and western Paraná province—carved out of São Paulo in 1854—was still more mysterious, inaccessible, and rarely traversed by scouting parties.

Although the frontier continued to advance, populations within the neo-European pale were becoming fairly well concentrated: The province of Rio de Janeiro, which was more or less evenly settled by 1890, then contained 32 persons per square kilometer. How could swidden agriculture feed so dense a population, an increasing part of which consisted of urban dwellers and plantation workers who did not grow their own food? Productivity per unit of land cleared from primary forest was extraordinarily high, but surpluses for market had been traditionally modest. Even at the beginning of the nineteenth century, Rio de Janeiro was importing part of its food supply via coastwise shipping from ports as distant as Caravelas and Rio Grande and from Lisbon and the Atlantic islands. The city imported roughly 250 kilograms of foodstuffs per capita in the late 1810s; observers believed that this dependence on long-distance supplies increased over the course of the century. The greater density of rural population suggests that primary forest suitable and available for the growing of foodstuffs must have been growing scarcer, especially in the region surrounding the imperial capital. Farmers were now clearing *capoeirinha*—secondary formations that had been cleared many times before and that exhibited only a few hardy (and useless) tree species of unimpressive height.[3]

Traditional swidden farming yielded market surpluses that were not only scanty but also uncertain. Losses of standing crops to leaf-cutting ants were sometimes overmatched by the depredations of various mammals—armadillos, cotias, and peccaries—and by seed- and fruit-eating birds—among them maitacas, blackbirds, parakeets, parrots, and oropendolas. Grasshopper swarming was beginning to be reported, a perhaps unnatural phenomenon connected to the enlargement of fields devoted to commercialized food crops. Stored food crops were vulnerable to rats; chicken pens, to snakes. The vagaries of climate aroused yet more anxieties. Years in which rainfall was unusually abundant did not reduce crop yields, but dry years were invariably years of hunger. When rains did not appear soon after the burning season, the ashes simply blew away, their nutrients lost to the soil. Planting was then nearly useless, and farmers had to fall back on stored food. But food was difficult to store, except for manioc, which could remain in the ground. Drought years such as 1818, 1819, 1833, and 1876 were times of terrible hardship and very likely deaths from starvation in the midst of what seemed to outsiders a rain forest paradise.[4]

Vast prestige attached to the growers of crops for export; none, to the growers of crops for domestic consumption. Such had been the colonial scale of values, a scale not reordered by political independence. Indeed, it was reinforced by the newly won direct access to the imported manufactured goods that rewarded the planters' exertions. The result was a two tiered agricultural sector of *grande lavoura* and *pequena lavoura*—great farming and small farming—and perhaps a third tier of farming too marginal to yield surpluses or to find a route to urban markets. Planters were often imprudent enough to divert too much of their slaves' efforts to coffee, forcing them to buy subsistence crops from neighbors. Indeed, prices of foodstuffs rose faster than those of exports, tempting quite a few planters to stoop to growing rice and beans for sale. Those whose lands were unfit for coffee had few other choices and, indeed, might even count themselves fortunate if they were situated conveniently near the marketplace of Rio de Janeiro.[5]

The lower yields typical of lands cleared of capoeirinha led to expanded fields and reduced fallow. Remarkably, the plow was not generally adopted at this point. Even in fields where large tree stumps had long before rotted away, field workers resolutely wielded the hoe   for many more hours and days than formerly—and the average area under cultivation rose from perhaps one hectare to three to five hectares per worker. The interval between temporary abandonment of a field and burning for clearing also appears to have been reduced, from seven or eight years to four or five. Rotation was not introduced; instead, a single crop was planted until it failed. Nor was fertilization attempted. When, after a series of plantings and fallows, a field no longer grew back into secondary forest but supported only grasses, sedges, and ferns, it was abandoned to pasture.[6]

The farmer's departure was less abandonment than rout. The crisis in swidden farming rendered the smallholder extremely vulnerable to the invasion of cattle. As long as his fields were scattered in forest, difficult for cattle to penetrate, they were safe. But once the forest was several times cleared and degenerated to scrub and bush, marauding cattle were able to destroy his crops. Indeed, the farmer had to ward off his own pigs. As long as there was plenty of woodland, the pigs were content to root in them, but as the woodland disappeared, the farmer had to allow them to feed upon his corn and manioc. Reports of pigs being fed crops is a clear indicator of the diminution of forest reserves. The African grasses that had immigrated the century before were the bane of farmers, so hardy and resistant were they to the hoe. Fences were impractical to install around temporary fields. Fencing materials were lacking: Rot-resistant wood for fence posts had become scarce, climate and soils were not such as to cast large stones to the surface, and barbed wire was beyond the means of smallholders. The depredations of cattle were thus yet another reason for the supposed "lure of the virgin forest." Complaints to police and lawsuits were of no avail; with the disappearance of the protecting forest, the swidden farmer had to sell out, losing his improvements and much of the real value of the land as well. Once legally installed, cattle efficiently ensured that no sapling would thereafter arise to challenge their dominion.[7]

In the neighborhood of Rio de Janeiro abandoned fields were in great demand as seasonal pasture. Cattle driven from Goiás, São Paulo, Minas

Gerais, and Mato Grosso in the late winter months had to be fattened, or at least kept alive, for market. By the early 1880s, the municipal slaughterhouse was selling 120,000 carcasses a year. Each of these animals took up about half a hectare of grassland. Draft animals kept within the city were fed fresh grasses from suburban pastures. When John Luccock observed the business in the late 1810s, slaves harvested grass in suburban pastures, not with scythes but with machetes(!), and then baled and carried it on their backs five or six kilometers to town.[8]

The maintenance of capoeira was critical to the survival of small cultivators. Whether squatters or tenants, they needed substantial reserves in woodlots. Commonly the kitchen fire was kept burning all day long, for cooking—beans simmered for hours—for boiling clothing, for heating bathwater, for drying linens and clothing in wet weather, and for keeping the kitchen warm in winter. Small cultivators required firewood to process their cash crops: bacon, rope tobacco, cheeses, cachaça, soap, and manioc. Manioc had to be dried to evaporate its poison; it took nearly a kilogram of firewood to produce a kilogram of meal. Modern estimates suggest that rural families formerly consumed annually at least a ton of firewood per capita. Trees were not cut down for burning; that was green wood, which they would have had to store to dry out. Instead, the women of the family gathered fallen branches in capoeira. But when capoeira on their claim was exhausted, neighbors had to be asked for permission to gather in their woodlots—an imposition not readily granted, especially because it might lead to the surreptitious cutting of live wood. Eventually the women would have to collect wood without permission, another source of communal conflicts. In either case, more hours had to be spent each day trudging back and forth from the scattered woodlots, and capoeira experienced still another pressure, leading to its extinction.[9]

Farmers had to cut down live trees for building materials, fence posts, crating, hoe and axe handles, troughs, yokes, furniture, and many other utilities. The woodlot was also the source of lianas, used for cordage and in place of nails. When the capoeira had entirely disappeared and foraging had become impractical or dangerous, the family had to move on, selling out to larger operators, who sought the land only as pasture. Smallholders, it seems, never considered the alternative of reforesting with useful tree species before they came to such a pass. "Planting a tree is what no one, absolutely no one, thinks to be a thing connected to agricultural exploitation," complained the Mineiro botanist Âlvaro da Silveira at the turn of the century. Possibly poor farmers considered their land claims too precarious, or perhaps they viewed their farmsteads as transitory resources, just as plantation owners did. Thus the elimination of forest appears to have been an important factor in the paradoxical preservation of concentrated landholding even in the suburbs of towns and cities.[10]

The city was also a great consumer of firewood and of charcoal. Wood sellers and charcoal makers usually bought the lots they cleared, although sometimes they worked on contract. There was also a lively wholesale trade in wood. There does not appear to have been a monopoly in this product, as there were in other essentials supplied to Rio de Janeiro, so the rise in its price, which was faster than that of prices generally, may be attributed to local scarcity and consequent increased transport costs. An observer reported in 1888 that 500 carts of firewood were sold in Rio de Janeiro each day, suggesting (at 1.5 tons per cart) more than 270,000 tons a year. This was very likely an underestimate, because it implies a consumption of only half a ton per capita. Although city householders would have restricted their use of firewood in view of its cost, there was an important commercial demand for firewood. By 1882 there were 173 bakeries in Rio de Janeiro, along with 30 coffee roasters and 36 sugar refineries. Rio de Janeiro was not yet an industrial city, depending instead on imports from Great Britain and other countries for most of its manufactures, but the imposition in the mid-1840s of a degree of protectionism contributed to the emergence of a wide range of manufactories, in shipbuilding, woodworking, textiles, leather, paper, metalworking, construction materials, soap and candles, and other goods. Sixty smithies and foundries in 1882 were consuming much of the 12,000 tons of charcoal reportedly transported into the city annually. The city's 66 felt hat makers, 11 brick and tile works, 5 paper and cardboard makers, and 5 glass and china works required process heat, supplied by wood or charcoal. Steam engines were quite common by then: There were 22 boilermakers and engine-repair shops. Only reluctantly did engine operators employ expensive imported coal to stoke them; usually the fuel was wood.[11]

The preferred wood for many purposes, especially boiler fuel, was mangrove, which burned slowly and left no resin deposit. Mangrove swamp spread a half-kilometer back from the shores of Guanabara Bay. Valued even more highly for the tannin in mangrove leaves and bark, late colonial edicts had forbidden burning it before its bark had been stripped. This was, unfortunately, merely one more conservationist measure to which no attention was paid. Mangrove was cut at a furious rate. In 1890, 20 percent of the capital's firewood was mangrove; by then it was estimated that half of the mangrove on the bay had been eliminated. The effects of the removal of this critical resource were already noticeable: a decline in shellfish, which clung to mangrove roots, and in fish stocks, because fish bred among them. Birds and mammals that formerly preyed on these resources were disappearing as well. The silting of the bars of rivers that fed into the bay hampered transportation, which had once led to the hinterland as far as the coastal palisade. It also may have increased the risks of malarial fevers in the city because the mudflats were inundated by stagnant waters.[12]

Rio de Janeiro became in the nineteenth century a city of brick and mortar. Official and religious construction had been largely of locally quarried stone, whereas most of the poor, in town or country, lived in houses made of rammed or hand-formed earth or of wattle-and-daub, roofed with palm thatch. The introduction of fired bricks and tiles considerably increased demand for firewood. A kiln charge of 30,000 bricks, measuring approximately 63 cubic meters, which was enough to build a small house, consumed 18 tons of wood, or about 20 tons including the baking of the roof tiles. The dwelling's mortar and plaster were made from lime, which also consumed firewood, usually mangrove. Mangrove was most convenient to employ in making lime derived from oyster shells. Ancient kitchen midden mounds of the first coastal indigenes were mined for this raw material; otherwise the mudflats of the bay were scraped clean of shells. These were then piled with wood in alternating layers and set afire. This was an amazingly wasteful method—37 tons of firewood may have been needed to produce the 6 tons of lime needed for a small dwelling. Therefore, in a real, material sense, the brick dwelling was really made of wood. Supposing that by 1890 Rio de Janeiro contained 40,000 dwellings and structures of baked brick that had consumed on average 100 tons of firewood, then 4 million tons of wood had been burned to build the city, the equivalent of 200 square kilometers of secondary forest.[13]

The heaviest industrial concentration of nineteenth-century Brazil was located in Minas Gerais, where, amid some of the former goldfields, smelters and foundries were built to exploit immense superficial iron deposits, as much as 50 percent pure. Iron was first discovered in São Paulo as early as 1589 and was briefly exploited there in the early seventeenth century. By the 1740s African slaves, employing their own methods, were operating small forges in Minas Gerais. Iron and other manufactures were forbidden in Brazil by a decree of 1785, but this was canceled within a decade, as it became apparent that the colony would have to fabricate the weapons needed to invade Spanish territory and the tools needed to revive gold and diamond extraction. Not until the court descended on Rio de Janeiro, however, were positive measures initiated. Mills were constructed with government funds, and forests were reserved for their use in Minas Gerais, at Congonhas do Campo and Morro do Gaspar Soares, near modern-day

Belo Horizonte, and in São Paulo at Ipanema, near Sorocaba. The latter two possessed blast furnaces, but they were poorly designed. Most of their output came not from the blast furnaces but from small Catalan and Swedish furnaces. The mills operated fitfully, in the care of often incompetent managers, untrained immigrants, and careless slaves, for a number of years. They expended vast amounts of charcoal for each ton of pig iron. Ipanema, always unprofitable, was finally closed by the republican junta.[14]

These official initiatives were unimportant compared to the dozens, even hundreds, of African forges, called *cadinhos,* scattered in an arc southeast of the modern city of Belo Horizonte. Contemporary observations suggest an output that peaked in the 1860s at about 4,000 tons a year or about 180,000 tons during the empire. Their customers were several hundred smithies, foundries, and workshops, from Diamantina to the Paraíba River. All of these forges and workshops smelted their raw material with charcoal, usually charcoal baked in their own woodlands. Even blacksmiths, who were often itinerant, carrying their tools on muleback, passing from one backwoods forge to another, gathered their own firewood and made the necessary charcoal themselves. Charcoal, unlike firewood, could be burned green—indeed, moist wood was preferred because it burned more slowly. Therefore capoeira, which provided logs of modest diameter, was cut down to make it. Certain trees were avoided, so that surviving capoeira groves were charcoal-maker-selected formations. The wood was fired in *covas*—sod-covered pits. Firing 100 tons of wood resulted usually in no more than 6 tons of usable charcoal. Only late in the century did some of the forge masters begin to prepare charcoal in more efficient *medas*—earthen-mound kilns.[15]

Cadinhos had the advantage over Catalan forges in that they ran well enough with poor-quality charcoal, but, unfortunately, both consumed large charges of fuel, about seven tons for every ton of usable iron. The woodlands round about these forges were by then nearly all secondary forest, the original forest having been sacrificed to the search for gold. They can be supposed to have contained about 200 cubic meters, or 100 tons—taking the average density to have been 0.5 tons per cubic meter—of wood per hectare. Therefore at the high point in the mid-1860s, these forges required the clearing of at least 40 square kilometers a year, or more than 2,000 square kilometers from independence to the republic.[16]

It is usually supposed that the decline of these backyard forges occurred in Minas Gerais when railroads were installed, intensifying competition from imported ironware, yet it seems likely that scarcity of wood, which represented 70 percent of running costs, was critical. Forge owners counted on their woodlots growing back, just as they did when they practiced swidden agriculture, but they could not count on obtaining a stable tonnage of wood or the appropriate species from lots repeatedly cleared. Not only did the primitive methods employed in charcoal making waste enormous quantities of wood, but fumes from the pits and kilns also destroyed surrounding trees. It is not surprising, then, that a study of the iron region carried out in 1880 already found that the cadinhos were decadent. Francisco Magalhães Gomes observed that "in the places where charcoal is fabricated in pits, the forests, once populated with gigantic Bignonaceae, today are almost entirely devastated; they present only rachitic Solanaceae and mediocre euphorbs." Abandoned forges were surrounded by deserts, "only 60 years since the industry began to spread in Minas." Nevertheless, no one thought this a waste.[17]

Forge masters could not expect to resume business at any great distance from markets, because transport of their finished products became prohibitively expensive beyond 50 or 60 kilometers. Replacement of pits with earthen-mound kilns suggest increasing scarcity. Pits were tiresome to dig; they were economic only when they could be used several times. Therefore the shift to earthen-mound kilns is evidence that woodlots were shrinking and scattered. Observers recommended the obvious measure of replanting trees suitable for charcoal making. Only the forge master Jean Antoine de Monlevade appears to have taken this step.[18]

Nevertheless, iron making in Minas Gerais did not entirely disappear. Some forges procured charcoal at great distances. This became economic with the arrival of the railroads, which also solved the problem of distribution of the finished pig iron. Five blast furnaces therefore were built in the region in the last days of the empire and the early republic and exhibited a modest prosperity. Although their use of charcoal was parsimonious compared with the cadinhos, their suppliers persisted in employing primitive methods and continued to devastate annually dozens of square kilometers of primary and secondary forest.

The loss of capoeira to enlarged arable land and to wasteland must be considered a further misfortune for the Atlantic Forest, even though capoeira was itself an anthropomorphosed, degraded formation. By the late 1850s, naturalists had identified some of the critical ecological distinctions between primary forest, which they usually called *mata virgem*—virgin forest—and capoeira. The species of the latter required more sunlight, they noted, and their seeds were light, carried by winds and by birds. Yet it was only in capoeira that the tree species of the mata virgem, so highly prized as padrões, were likely to germinate and grow. Their seeds were infrequently produced and were usually the product of some complex interaction of pollinating and distributing agents. They were provided with large nutrient reserves for independent development and therefore were encased in protective shells, resistant to predators. The moist, temperate recesses of capoeira, as in the regrown windfalls of natural forest, facilitated the succession of mata virgem species. Perhaps succession to the point of their restored dominance occurred generally during the thousand-year reign of the Tupi, whose fallows may have lasted for generations. It was more likely to have occurred during the terrible native population collapse accompanying the second wave of invaders. These natural forest nurseries were the formations sometimes called *capoeirão*—high capoeira—to distinguish them from patches of secondary forest that had been more frequently subject to human pressures. But now these formations were becoming rarer. Capoeira patches became progressively impoverished, their nutrients and humus exhausted, and increasingly isolated from each other and from the relict primary forest.[19]

A few responses to the decline in primary-forest soils can be observed in nineteenth-century farming, implying much greater inputs of labor: A substitute for plow farming on poorly drained lowland soils were lazy beds, variously termed *leiras, valas, camalhões, torrões,* or *matumbos*—the last a Kimbundu word, suggesting that this was at least in some places another African contribution to the exploitation of the natural world. The piling up of soil from trenches to form rectangular beds was a technique usually intended merely to obtain drier soil for the planting of manioc, but it was superior to burning in that it incorporated nitrates and humus directly into the soil. It is not clear how widely it was practiced. Another intensive technique, possibly more common, was the temporary use of abandoned corrals, called *malhadas,* for horticulture. The floodplains of rivers, especially riverine islands, were sometimes cultivated, a practice that took advantage of nutrients deposited by the waters but perhaps was intended more to evade leaf-cutting ants, which could not establish themselves in soggy soils. The floodplains doubtless became less viable wherever placer mining and hillside coffee planting clogged streams with overburden and intensified the seasonality of watercourses.[20]

The persistence among the rural population of itinerancy, unendingly castigated by the authorities, was in considerable measure the work of the authorities themselves. Army recruitment, the scourge of the colonial government, remained a great burden upon the sons of small farmers. The empire was entirely unsuccessful in filling army ranks with volunteers or mercenaries and therefore scoured the countryside for young men lacking protectors. Although recruiting agents were supposed to impress "vagrants and miscreants," that tribe was probably too slippery to find or keep under lock and key. It was more often the unwary small farmer who was taken away. The empire, in fact, surpassed the viceroyalty in the arbitrariness of its military exactions: Smallholders, supposedly exempt from the draft, found themselves nevertheless forced to hire lawyers and bribe court officers to avoid impressment. Recruitment became in the hands of political bosses a weapon to eliminate voters of the opposition party; consequently, immunity was achieved only by a degrading fealty to those in power. Thus recruitment itself became a principal source of conflict within the rural community: "The men desert their dwellings and settlements and go to live in the most hidden of the forests, some not to be recruited, and others not to be obliged to rise against their own friends and relatives."[21] Impressment was a death sentence: The term was for sixteen years, and mortality in the holds of the vessels that bore them off to Rio de Janeiro was higher than in those of the slavers. Recruitment terrorized the poor, whose sons scattered to the four winds, and was still another reason for the churning of the rural population, for the attack on primary forest, and for ignorance of local soils, climates, and vegetation.[22]

The land law of 1850, the consummate expression of land policy under the empire, did not assist the smallholder to obtain title to his claim, even though that was one of its stated objectives. For many small squatters the cost of registration much exceeded their means. Others could not withstand the pretensions and impositions of those socially prominent claimants to vast tracts of public lands with whom they had to compete. Eventually, they came afoul of these usurpers, despite the protections embodied in the law, and they were given the choice of "selling" their claims or of accepting a place as agregados, paying a token rent in produce, and consenting to bear arms to protect the new owner against his slaves and political enemies. Otherwise, they were branded "intruders" and expelled by those among them who had yielded and accepted vassalage. Even these conformists would later be thinned out, as the forest was thinned out. For once the boundaries of the usurped estate were secure and the forest had been cut back, their presence was dispensable.[23]

Agregados were offered no incentive to intensify their cultivation. They commonly left their tenancies stripped and eroded: "Instead of improving the land, as is their duty, they ruin it with bad treatment and carelessness, living, as they are accustomed, more from the proceeds of the hunt and fishing, than from the care of the land."[24] Only in the vicinity of Rio de Janeiro, it appears, did landowners turn over parts of their estates to tenants in return for cash rents. The imperial capital was the country's only metropolitan market, and perhaps this is explanation enough for the rarity of tenancy. But the reluctance of the landlords also derived from the law that granted compensation to the tenants for improvements, whether the landlord wanted them or not. Instead of welcoming energetic and ambitious tenants, whose productivity might enrich them as well, landlords were commonly "averse to wealthy tenants" and expelled them! Thus even in those locales where capitalist tenancy might be expected to have taken hold, the tendency was for estate owners to keep management in their own hands and to rely on slave labor.[25]

Those driven from these estates in formation perforce turned toward the frontier and the primary forest; to remain in the settlements was to risk imprisonment as vagrants or worse, impressment. This acceptance of isolation, of every kind of hardship, and of frightful dangers among lawless neighbors often exiled to the frontier by the courts thus owed little to the "lure of the virgin forest." These pioneers did not break all ties with the settlements of the deforested zone. Along trails that sometimes followed only beachfronts or along streams traversable seasonally in dugout canoes, they traded in surpluses, mainly pigs, which rooted in the forest and could be walked to market. With the proceeds they bought what was essential— shotguns, shot, and powder, at least. They kept wayside "inns," commonly mere thatched sheds, catering to mule trains, offering them cornmeal, beans, and cachaça, as they had them to spare.

Disinherited caboclos do not appear to have been ideal conservators of the primary forest into which they were thrust. They continued to farm as they had on the coast, burning and planting for brief seasons. As their invasions penetrated farther inland, they reached forest that was subject to longer dry seasons, with trees that were more characteristically deciduous. Very likely, the yearly burning was turning more and more problematical: How to know, a hundred or more kilometers inland from the place where one was born, when to expect the onset of the rains or how intense a burn to set? Fire launched in dry forest easily spread and might destroy hundreds, even thousands, of hectares, instead of one or two. Less rational musings often preceded use of the firebrand. Observers alleged that incendiarism was a major, or the major, cause of fires, launched for spite, revenge, or boredom.[26]

This far interior margin of the Atlantic Forest was highly attractive to prospective cattle ranchers, who carried out a transformation of bordering grasslands swifter and more devastating than that imposed by farmers on woodlands. Mineiro ranchers crossed the provincial border into São Paulo early in the nineteenth century, invading the prairies near modern Franca, Araraquara, and Botucatu, in hope of exploiting the growing demand of

Rio de Janeiro for fresh beef and of Paulista sugar plantations for mill oxen. Ranchers burned the fields not once a year but repeatedly, seeking to prevent woody growth from taking over the field, to reduce the biomass to fresh, tender growth, and to destroy the numerous insects that harried their animals.

Their burning was amazingly widespread, because there was no reason to contain it: One could not have too much range in new grasses, and even if the fire spread to neighbors' lands, they would not have complained; on the contrary, they would have considered it a favor. In July 1864 the botanist Ladislau Netto, atop the Trinchete Ridge near the town of Pirapora, in Minas Gerais, saw fires extending over an immense area, the sky obscured by "a dense haze, giving a livid and somewhat sinister cast to the light of the day." In that season, the botanical collector was unemployed, unless he could find a dank gallery forest resistant to the flames. Explorers sent forth by the baron of Antonina in August 1846 to find a direct route to Mato Grosso from his Paraná estate climbed the Apucarana Ridge southwest of the present-day city of Londrina and found their gaze obscured by fires raging in the campos of Guarapuava and Curitiba, more than 150 kilometers distant. Each day for four days they mounted the ridge, hoping for a clear view; only on the fifth day, when rains had at last extinguished the flames, were they able to glimpse the Paraná River to the northwest and the border of the prairies to the southeast. This party, as it then headed toward the Paraná, came across several isolated grassland openings in forest. Each time, for no reason they thought worth explaining in their report, they set fire to them as they advanced![2/]

It is difficult to gauge how much damage this incendiarism did to the native grasslands. To the minds of those who practiced it, no damage was done at all, because the grass grew back lushly green, and the cattle grew fat upon it. Grasses, resilient and vigorous, most of their biomass preserved in underground rhizomes and roots and protected by the humus layer, were resistant to fires. Nevertheless, fire-induced changes in the grasslands gradually undermined their productivity, obliging the ranchers constantly to expand their range, migrating like the farmers to less-disturbed locales. The plants that grew back after repeated burning were called *macegas*, a pejorative suggesting low nutritive value and resistance to eradication. The foreign botanists who collected in "native" fields that were evidently fire managed ought to have pondered how much they had already been transformed from their state in 1500. Indeed, the frequent observations by explorers, including the Antonina party, of Indian burnings to drive game suggest that the grasslands had been for thousands of years an anthropomorphosed formation. This was probably not true of those campos, or *campinas* to be found on the crests of many ridge tops, where rapid drainage and thin soil had prevented the establishment of forest. These patches of grassland, the evolutionary sites of numerous curious endemic species, were as tempting to the ranchers as those of the valleys but were far more vulnerable, because wildfire had reached them rarely, perhaps never before.[28]

The repeated and frequent burnings of native grasslands constituted a severe threat to the interior, drier margins of the Atlantic Forest. Typically, the ecotone consisted of the gallery forests—long forest tentacles along watercourses—and of the capões de mato. They were vulnerable to invasion by fire, because their edges were penetrated by grasses. Cattle therefore wandered gladly into these shady refuges, to graze on ground cover, especially bamboo shoots, which they favored. Horses and mules also entered, to scrape bark from trees. Ranchers valued the soils of these forest patches, which were less likely to dry out in the winter months, when many of their animals died for lack of forage and when they were undertaking the long drives to market, so they often burned them down. This may explain the grasslands on red soils that Auguste de Saint-Hilaire was so surprised to find near Franca, one of the main staging points for the cattle drives from Goiás. Burning of forest for artificial pasture may have been carried out at other such points, such as Sorocaba, where 30,000 mules and horses were sold each year in a great market that required considerable pasture, and São João del Rei, where Mineiro herds were staged on their way to Rio de Janeiro.[29]

The spread of plantation agriculture and the growth of cities and towns can be seen not to have supplanted traditional forms of forest exploitation but to have intensified them, to have subjected them to pressure sufficient to destabilize and degrade them permanently. At the same time these processes encouraged the spread of traditional exploitation over much larger areas, to replace resources no longer available close to centers of export production and urbanization.

Even as the rapid improvements in maritime transport made profitable a great expansion in Brazilian plantation production, the continuing inadequacy of the country's internal transport determined the reproduction of traditional agricultural and pastoral techniques on the margins of settlement. Even so, the last third of the nineteenth century witnessed the implantation of the railroad and the steamboat. What were the implications of this large capital investment for the future of the surviving stands of primary forest?

Much of the southwestern Atlantic Forest had escaped clearing due to the extremely difficult topography over which it spread. Except for the narrow coastal strand, only a few kilometers wide from the Jequitinhonha River in the north to the Bay of Paranaguá in the south, it was inaccessible to loggers who otherwise might have made short work of much of it. The coastal palisades, furthermore, made communication with the interior nearly everywhere along the coast exhausting if not perilous. Where rivers cut through to the coast—the Ribeira, Paraíba do Sul, Itapemirim, Doce, São Mateus, Mucuri, and Jequitinhonha—their navigation was blocked by rapids discouragingly close to their mouths. On the highlands, criss-crossed by serried ridgelines reaching nearly 3,000 meters at Pico da Bandeira and Itatiaia, the rest of the rivers ran not to the coast but inland, to the São Francisco and the Paraná rivers. All of the tributaries of these great rivers were scarred with numberless cataracts, rapids, and falls.

The Tietê, the most direct route to the goldfields of Mato Grosso, measured, from the jumping-off place at the misnamed Porto Feliz—Happy Port—to its mouth, a distance of about 550 kilometers. It took a month of anxious steering, nightly layovers, and portages—61 of them—that required the unloading and reloading of canoes. The Tietê could be traversed only in the dry winter months, when fever was less likely and when low water improved the fish catch. Some crews died of starvation on return upriver in high water. But of course low water meant more portages and dragging of canoes over sandbars. Fevers on this river finally drove most traffic to an overland trail in the middle of the eighteenth century. The Portuguese army persisted nevertheless in the river route, to supply with cannon and shot the border forts in Mato Grosso. Swidden farming in the county of Porto Feliz, meanwhile, caused such destruction of the peroba and tamburi trees prized for canoe making that they had to be sought downriver and on the tributary Piracicaba River. A single trunk cost as much as a horse and saddle—this still in an era of exceedingly thin population and few sesmarias or officially recognized townships, suggesting how far clearing of the Atlantic Forest had already proceeded. The Paraná and the São Francisco are themselves both majestically navigable waterways, but both of them were blocked well before their exit to the sea by colossal waterfalls.[30]

These geopolitical fatalities were the bane of Brazilian generals and statesmen, who took up the task of trying to define and defend a long, uncertain interior border. The Atlantic Forest was itself a principal cause of unnavigable rivers. Most of them ran clear—the forest retained underlying soils so well that no cargo of silt was deposited in them. A few million years of scouring with suspended silt would have smoothed their beds to a desirable regularity. Eighteenth- and nineteenth-century deforestation did indeed quickly turn them all a turgid brown, heavy and dangerous as an avalanche, but now they ran so seasonally that they became impossible to navigate even with canoes. There were continued efforts to find more passable river routes—expeditions were sent up and down the Jequitinhonha, Doce, Paranapanema, and Tibagi, to no avail. The Doce, which led tantalizingly directly to the gold region, began to receive official attention when the court transferred to Rio de Janeiro. But it was as interrupted as the Tietê and lacked a port site at its mouth. The rivers were also notorious for fevers, which caused casualties worse than impressment or the slave traffic. Only the most insubstantial riverine trade persisted in a few essential items, fetched by canoe in convoys once or twice a year. The rivers were hopeless.[31]

For the first century and a half of conquest and settlement, overland transport was on foot, on footpaths no wider than a man's tracks. Often called roads, they were more appropriately referred to as *picadas*, literally, routes hacked or chopped out of the underbrush. They were for the most part inherited from the previous indigenous residents and served the needs of merely local trade and communication. The persistence of these paths explains the mobility of bandeira slave-raiding parties. Many thousands of kilometers of them must have disappeared, nevertheless, as epidemics swept away the native villages. Even so, it is suspected that some of today's railroads and highways follow their traces. The coastal "road" between Salvador and Rio de Janeiro, for most of its trace merely followed the beachfront, serviced at river crossings by ill-tended ferries. The footpaths were ignored by the authorities, except for those that led to ports, where taxes were collected and goods were shipped to Lisbon. Only with the discovery of gold was their presence noted, and then with disfavor, as potential conduits for contraband. Many of them were officially closed, and traffic was ordered to flow over a single path, which was subject to internal customs duties at checkpoints called registers. Even so, the closed routes no doubt continued to carry local traffic—and smugglers, too.[32]

It was not until the eighteenth century that mules replaced Indians as carriers of burdens. As long as the Atlantic Forest remained more or less intact, the lack of pasture, as well as the scarcity of goods of value to transport, rendered saddle and pack animals impractical. The gold rush changed those circumstances, opening sizable patches of abandoned goldfields to grassy invasion and providing a medium of metallic exchange for trade goods from all over the colony, indeed from all over the world. The crown decreed that mules could not be bred north of the Iguaçu River, so as to reserve an economic function to the otherwise disconnected border captaincies of Santa Catarina and Rio Grande do Sul. From there the animals were driven every year to the market of Sorocaba, and thence to Rio de

Janeiro and Minas Gerais. So many royal decrees were ignored that it may be wondered why this one was obeyed. Very likely the southern captaincies possessed a competitive advantage in their vast sweeps of native grasslands, which may have offered more nutritive pasture to horses and donkeys than the nearby campos of western Minas Gerais and Goiás.

A mule could be laden with about 130 kilograms and led 20 to 25 kilometers a day on mountain trails. Although ox carts were able to cover only half that distance, they were preferred on flat terrain. Solid-wheeled ox carts, pulled by 5 to 14 animals, weighed 1,000 to 1,500 kilograms and bore loads no heavier than their tare. The ungainly carts were able to negotiate the mud of the canefields, and they did not have to be unloaded at night, thus saving labor and keeping their cargoes from the damp. The drovers could sleep on top of the cargo, or under it when it rained. Oxen were less demanding of pasture, probably a consideration in degraded grassland. It was often proposed that these ungainly carts, which ruined the roads, should be replaced by light, spoke-wheeled vehicles, but the latter were to be found only in the cities until, it appears, the arrival of German immigrants.[33]

The first trail to the goldfields departed from São Paulo, because it was Paulista bandeiras who had come upon them. This route descended the Paraíba Valley, then crossed the Serra da Mantiqueira near Itatiaia, and headed northeastward over rolling, partly grassy country. Soon émigré prospectors and crown officials made their way from Rio de Janeiro by boat to the fishing village of Parati, then climbed the coastal palisade to join the Paulista route. This transit consumed more than seven weeks and exposed gold shipments to the danger of pirates. The governor therefore soon decreed that all traffic depart due north from Rio de Janeiro, up the palisade, across the Paraíba Valley, and over the Serra da Mantiqueira along the eastern foothills of the Serra do Espinhaço to Ouro Prêto. There were already farmsteads the entire distance, suggesting that unauthorized backland settlement either predated the discovery of gold or rapidly responded to this sudden economic opportunity. In 1733 all other roads to the goldfields were proscribed. The so-called New Road, somewhat less than 500 kilometers long, took three weeks by mule train. Towns grew up along it, and gradual improvements in surface and grade reduced travel time to about 18 days. Yet it remained, until the 1840s, unpaved and no wider than two mules might require to pass each other. This was the road followed by all the foreign scientists and technicians invited to Brazil by King João; their travel diaries collectively provide the modern reader a detailed picture of late colonial life, surpassed in verisimilitude only by their observations of the capital itself. Their accounts suggest a yearly passage of at least 75,000 mules at the end of the colonial period, laden with coffee, cotton goods, metalwares, cheeses, and other staples.[34]

The smugglers and traders who followed the numerous illicit trails to the interior defied viceregal efforts to "legalize" them by installing registers. For forty years they resisted completion of a road between Rio de Janeiro and São Paulo. Indeed, road taxes were so high that they discouraged passage of all but the most expensive luxuries. Nevertheless, in the last decades of the eighteenth century some of these revenues were devoted to improving transport. The trail to Santos, a dangerous ruin traversable only by men on foot, was several times rerouted and repaired in the eighteenth century, and it was paved in 1792 through local initiative. Although well engineered, it still accommodated only mules and horses. Even so, this improved trail at last opened the Paulista highland to direct overseas trade, almost two and a half centuries after the European invasion began. From its terminal at the town of São Paulo, more trails fanned out, following the dictate of colonial policy and the lure of gold: to the viceregal capital of Rio de Janeiro, to the southern border via Curitiba, to Porto Feliz at the head of navigation of the Tietê, to Goiás via Campinas, and to the southern region of Minas Gerais. This was only the merest sketch of an overland network. For the most part it was laid out in open country, where forests had been cleared many years before or where swaths of grassland penetrated the forest. Where the Atlantic Forest extended intact for any great distance, mule trails were too difficult to maintain, and footpaths remained the only passage to remote settlements.[35]

The arrival of the court did not much accelerate road building. The continued granting of sesmarias, the traditional means of stimulating private persons to clear mule trails, resulted for the most part only in more picadas. A new section of the road to Minas Gerais was built via an estate that eventually became the royal summer resort of Petrópolis. The prohibition on new trails to the gold district was canceled in 1816, and further incentives were offered to private builders. A trail was laid across the flatlands from the capital to the highlands via Vassouras, which was to become an important coffee-growing county. Guido Thomaz Marlière and the governor of Espírito Santo constructed a trail between Vitória and Ouro Prêto, but it did not draw traffic from the improved road to Rio de Janeiro. Maintained only by corvée labor from the aldeias—another reason for the scattering of the rural population—it soon fell into disrepair. Workers could not be hired in Vitória because, "full of panic terror" of the indigenes, they "never want to enter the interior." Another trail was built under government auspices from Minas Gerais to the mouth of the Itapemirim River, with the hope of finding gold along it. This hope fulfilled, the route was kept passable. Only gold and diamonds justified the maintenance of mule trails, and even these were no quicker than footpaths—for that reason the mails to Ouro Prêto were regularly carried on foot over parallel paths, not on the main mule trail. As long as the other products of the Atlantic Forest commanded low prices and were obtained mainly by extraction or predation, the network of land transport changed little from that laid out by the native peoples.[36]

The coffee trade at last supplied the necessary stimulus. By the 1840s government revenues were sufficient to pay for several well-engineered roads, covered with paving stones and wide enough for carts, connecting several ports with the most important coffee zones in the highlands. The roads behind Rio de Janeiro became a network, and the cliffs behind the coastal towns of Antonina, São Sebastião, Ubatuba, and Angra dos Reis were scaled. A paved carriage road was built to French engineering standards between Petrópolis and Juiz de Fora—possibly a political investment in the loyalty of the immense province of Minas Gerais. The road between São Paulo and Santos was widened and twice more reconstructed, and the section from the base of the cliff to the port was macadamized. At last a few bridges were built over the principal rivers: The first suspension bridge in Brazil spanned the Paraíba in 1857, at Sapucaia, and another crossed it at Três Rios by 1861. French roads had long been planted with trees, providing shade and a source of revenue that paid for their maintenance. This was proposed by foreign observers, among them Saint-Hilaire, though he also provided a reason why it might have been impractical: In so rainy a climate, trees had to be cut back from the roads to permit sunlight to dry them out. In fact, the saying went that "the maintenance engineer of Brazilian roads is the sun."[37]

These latter-day efforts at opening channels for the delivery of coffee to the ports were finally rendered obsolete by the construction of railways, and not a moment too soon: By 1860 export of coffee from all ports implied 1.5 million mule trips. The life expectancy of mules in the hill country was probably brief, requiring much replacement from the breeding areas in the South. Supposing that each mule was capable of three trips to the coast during the harvest season, the coffee crop must have required a herd of 500,000 animals. The feeding of these animals implied a vast area given over to forage—at a half hectare each, 2,500 square kilometers—within the southeastern Atlantic Forest. Even so, these constraints do not appear to have been critical, suggesting that the plantations were prosperous enough to pay the freight and that they had already burned away so much forest that pasture availability was not problematic.

The steam engine arrived in the region well before the first railroad tracks. The first steamboats on Guanabara Bay began service in 1821; soon the bay was crisscrossed by cargo and passenger vessels. Steamboats plied Espírito Santo Bay in 1826. Stream flow on the Paraíba River has become so irregular because of deforestation that it is hard to imagine that steamboats really operated on its middle course in the 1860s. In the same decade, steam service was introduced on the lower Doce and Mucuri rivers as far as their fall lines—unfortunately, not far from their mouths. By 1869 steamboats ran on the Ribeira River; to facilitate their passage, a channel was dug behind the town of Iguape, a project very soon regretted because the current thus accelerated nearly swallowed the town. Somewhat later, steamboats were in use on the Sapucaí and Grande rivers in Minas Gerais. Wood was used in the boilers of all these vessels; near the coast this was mangrove.[38]

The true revolution in transport and, consequently, in the relationship of humans to what remained untouched of the Atlantic Forest was the steam locomotive. Its introduction to Brazil came quite late in the century. The first line, finished in 1856, running from the north rim of Guanabara Bay to the base of the escarpment below Petrópolis, was little more than a toy of the capital's elite, who patronized it to escape summer fevers. In 1867, despite the economic uncertainties of the Paraguayan War, two truly consequential lines were completed, one from Rio de Janeiro to Três Rios, on the Paraíba, the other from Santos to Jundiaí, the terminal that was to scour the coffee grown on the new plantations of the region known as the Paulista West. Both were 1.6-meter lines, well engineered—indeed, in the case of the Santos railway an engineering marvel. In another ten years, spur lines fanned out into the Paraíba Valley and toward the coffee plantations of the Zona da Mata—Forest Zone—of Minas Gerais, east from Rio de Janeiro to Cantagallo, and west from Jundiaí to Campinas and beyond, most of this on narrow-gauge tracks. Curitiba was connected to the coast at Paranaguá only in the mid-1880s, and two short lines were built out of Cachoeiro, in southern Espírito Santo, about the same time.[39]

The railroad was an immense leap forward in a landscape untrammeled by any tracks save those of human feet and the hooves of mules, cattle, and horses. Whereas these creatures had perforce avoided forest transits, the locomotive was indifferent: It sought only the flattest grades and the most direct traces; the clearing of forest was a minor expense. The Atlantic Forest was now directly in the path of what was taken for progress in the nineteenth century. The pressures that immense troops of mules placed upon grasslands now slackened somewhat. But forest clearing was to accelerate, now that this instrument of frontier penetration had become available. Plantations of a certain age lost their value more quickly, as lower transport costs increased the speculative value of prime coffee lands over the horizon. The frontier was to push forward faster than ever before, as access to the ports became possible. The railroads were also to make demands of their own on the forest, because they required great quantities of crossties, for which hardwoods of the primary forest were preferred. Although the rail lines that ran to the ports burned imported coal, those of the interior usually burned wood. Wood cutting thus became a sizable economic opportunity for owners of land along the rails.

The potential impact of the railroad upon the Atlantic Forest was predicted by Gustavo Schuch de Capanema, a planter and amateur natural scientist, in 1858, well before the first line had climbed the coastal palisade. The enthusiasm for railroad building, he warned, was misplaced, given the kind of agriculture to which Brazil was addicted:

> Our railroads, instead of being useful to us, will come to be prejudicial. Around our capital we see nothing but hills covered in capoeiras; their primeval forests disappeared, and so have the farms that replaced them: today the land is exhausted and unproductive, and anyone who wants good harvests travels far to find virgin lands. The coffee groves near the seacoast, which even twenty years ago were profitable, are today despised, and no others grow there; only in the highlands is production excellent, but within a few years it will be necessary to abandon the tired soil there too, to search for a more remote fertile zone, so that the rail lines will have to cross many leagues of fallow terrain to find cargo only at their extremity and to link population centers, which will in their turn be deserted when the railroad extends beyond them, and they cease to be the emporiums of a cultivated region.[40]

Capanema thus foresaw that railroads would promote the perpetuation of extensive, itinerant agriculture and accelerate forest destruction. They would be not a means of progress but "an instrument of devastation." Is this paradox the reason why economic historians are unable to assign to the railroad any sizable share in the growth of nineteenth-century economies?

More than the plantations had been transformed by the growing of an exotic crop esteemed by the inhabitants of far-off industrializing countries. The indirect results of the coffee trade also had their costs for the Atlantic Forest. The accelerating growth of urban as well as rural populations, the demand for increasing quantities of foodstuffs, fuel, ironware, and other goods, all of them produced by means unchanged from earlier times, exerted intense pressure on woodlands. Nevertheless, the expansion of the coffee front was at first contained by the inadequacy of primitive transportation. When coffee profits made possible the installation of rails, the breakthrough was at hand: Coffee could be planted in the farthest reaches of the Atlantic Forest and fetched from there at an acceptable cost.

As it turned out, the railroad was not the only novelty witnessed by the Atlantic Forest in the last years of the century. Slavery was finally extinguished in 1888, the empire was exchanged for a republic that proposed several consequential environmental reforms, vast levies of European peasants were lured to the coffee plantations, a real market in land came closer to reality, several more technological marvels were imported and adopted, capital accumulated in the cities, and, most interestingly, among significant numbers of the elite a consciousness spread and deepened that generations of waste had to be brought to an end and that resources of the forest and soil had to be employed more efficiently and conserved for the general good. A long delay in the application of scientific knowledge was coming to an end. Institutions were being formed and reformed to apply this knowledge to agriculture and industry. What remained of the Atlantic Forest was to be the subject not merely of examination but of responsible concern, if not yet of effective management.

10

Speculation and Conservation

*E como não sentir-se-á o homem pequeno diante desta gigantesca
majestade esmagadora? E como furtar-se-á ele de ser orgulhoso quando
se lembrar que basta um aceno de sua mão para destruir toda esta
obra de uma quase eternidade?*

*And how shall man not feel himself small before this gigantic overwhelm-
ing majesty? And how shall he stifle his pride when he remembers that a
wave of his hand is enough to destroy all this work of nearly an eternity?*

ALBERTO LOEFGREN

The overthrow of the aged and ailing emperor in November 1889 was accomplished by a barracks mutiny, led by a general of inchoate ideology and
fulminant ambition. Amid the succeeding political strife and rebellion, an
opportunist elite erected a republic that was even more exclusionary than
the empire. The partisan political competition that the direct intervention
of the emperor himself had kept operational was replaced by a monolithic
party, the Republican, that united in each of the states (the former provinces) its dominant economic interests. The social power of the great landowners, legitimized under the empire by the grant of titles of lifetime nobility, was now confirmed by patents in the national guard. The right to
vote was defined even more narrowly, and voting, for those few of the
lower class authorized to exercise that function by the rural "colonels,"
consisted of a public expression of loyalty in return for an election day run
of the town bars and whorehouses.

The planters had witnessed with indifference the expulsion of the imperial family because Princess Isabel, the heir apparent, had signed in her
father's absence in May 1888 the "Golden Law" of final abolition. This
long-overdue measure was not accompanied by compensation to the owners; their loyalty to the throne thereupon evaporated. The Republicans had
regarded abolition as prerequisite to the achievement of the Comtian highest stage of political development, but they had taken no part in the abolitionist struggle, which was the work of the slaves themselves, their mulatto

brethren, and a fraction of the free white townspeople, acting as individuals or in concert. The elitist conveners of the Republican government viewed the ex-slaves and mulattoes with nothing but antipathy and relegated them to the lowest ranks of the new social order.

For the Atlantic Forest, this mundane shift in political fortunes with its uneventful perpetuation of the social order was not without lasting consequences. The Republicans stitched on the new national banner the positivist motto "Order and Progress." This was not an empty gesture: Both of these pitiless goals were pursued deliberately, in accordance with the Republican elite's view of its own best interests. "Order" was taken to mean discipline in behalf of social hierarchy and the rights of property. "Progress" meant the heedless application of imported technology in behalf of the same. The rapid elimination of unremunerative vegetation was a defining mark of both.

The constitution promulgated in 1891 transferred to the states the public lands formerly belonging to the central government. In the region of the Atlantic Forest these were still extensive, including all of Espírito Santo north of the Doce River, much of the eastern part of Minas Gerais bordering Espírito Santo, the northwestern quadrant of São Paulo—three-eighths of its territory—and the western half of Paraná. These states in turn passed statutes recapitulating the imperial land law of 1850. São Paulo's statute of 1895 put up the public lands for sale, stipulating that no purchaser could claim more than 500 hectares of forest. The 1850 law had recognized squatters' claims established after the abolition of sesmarias in 1823 and registered by 1856. The 1895 São Paulo law extended this measure to claims occupied thereafter, but limited them to 1,000 hectares of forested land. Even this well-bureaucratized state government evaded its responsibility to carry out a cadastral survey of its lands. Consequently, few land titles in São Paulo derive from purchase; they are nearly all based on claims originally established by squatting.[1]

Nearly all of these claims were fraudulent or outrageously exaggerated. Fraudulent claims to public lands—many of them overriding legitimate squatters' rights—were legalized on a vast scale as the state governments proved largely impotent to prevent the appropriation of public property. The art of private expropriation—*grilagem*, from *grilo*, the cricket, which hops over the claims of others—became a profession. Purloined watermarked official paper, counterfeit tax stamps, and quill pens were employed to feign transactions anterior to the state laws, subterfuges that civil servants were nearly always willing to condone or indeed conspire in. Monteiro Lobato, a novelist and publicist who wrote of these deeds with no little trace of admiration for the picaresque, cites the case of a *grileiro* who "persuaded" a notary to copy a title in his registry as 22 instead of 2 leagues of land and had the copy certified by a judge's clerk, who did not trouble to compare it with the original. The grileiro then had a lawyer friend borrow the original and "lose" it. When the lawyer was properly jailed for this offense, the grileiro helpfully appeared with the certified copy and had him released. Twenty-two square leagues amounted to 950 square kilometers, a quantity suggestive of magical realism perhaps, yet other instances are documented of still greater presumption: The Medeiros clan began in 1881 its campaign to legitimate claims along the Paranapanema River amounting to 1,750 square kilometers![2]

Because paper, ink, stamps, and the services of counterfeiters—"alchemists" in Lobato's terminology—who could artfully age and sew these documents into notarial books were readily available to the less scrupulous among the impetuous new bourgeoisie, it usually happened that such papers were only one of the instruments necessary to establish a claim. The complaisant state abdicated, in effect, its duty to establish property rights and acted only feebly in behalf of their maintenance. Every hectare might have several illegitimate yet insistent pretendants. The courts decided these disputes on the basis of political prominence and even of prowess in combat. Large landowners kept *capangas*—hired gunmen—not only to intimidate their workers but also to assassinate unaccommodating neighbors. "The dissention over the boundaries of the supposed properties always end in murders, looting, and reciprocal depredations," lamented Antônio Mariano Azevedo, a naval lieutenant sent to explore the Tietê valley.[3]

Frontier disputes were somewhat mitigated within the formal political organization of the local branches of the Republican party and rather more through the personal influence of the colonels. Arranged marriages and fictive kinship ties—godparenthood at baptisms and weddings—were also designed as much to resolve estate borders as to accumulate capital. The outcome of all these struggles and maneuvers was the buying out or expulsion of the great *posseiros*—those claimants to vast territories who had migrated into the frontier nearly a century before and installed cattle and poor relatives and hangers-on, unconnected to the coastal markets save for yearly exchanges of steers for salt and gunpowder. They were overrun by a class of profit-oriented planters, mostly of urban background, who purposed to put their holdings into production as quickly as possible. The caboclo frontiersmen who had lived *a favor* of the posseiros found themselves further reduced to the status of employees, their tenure more precarious, their functions yet more marginal.[4]

It is important to observe that throughout this struggle, what was truly at stake was not land, or property, although that was how the struggle was defined then by its participants and even now by its historical interpreters. The prize was in fact the living biomass of the trees—which was to be reduced to ashes—the litter of the forest floor, the humus underneath, the microbial and insect life that inhabited these strata, and the nutrients contained in the soil horizon below that. These living, organic, and mineral resources were all that the land contained from which profit could be extracted. "Fertility" is nearly as reductionist a concept as "land" or "property," yet it too is evidence of human pettiness and ignorance. These immensely complex and abundant biotic realities were nevertheless vulnerable and evanescent. When they were exhausted, the land lost nearly all its value. By the time such properties were reduced to cow pasture, title was already established for a generation or more, but even had titles been still insecure, who would have risked death to usurp or defend degraded cow pens?

Several states imposed land taxes, not only for revenue but also to stimulate intensified farming practices. The collection of these taxes did not prove to be a remedy against the consolidation of the latifundia—tax levies were arbitrary, there were too few collectors, and they exhibited the same venality as notaries and court officers. The taxes raised little revenue and raised it from those who were politically the most vulnerable. Minas Gerais's tax on "unproductive" land was an important cause of deforestation, as landowners circumvented it by burning down forest to simulate farming or ranching activity.[5]

The republic therefore gobbled up in a few decades nearly all that had remained in public hands of the Atlantic Forest. All this was done a century after the first calls for land reform, calls that grew more frequent as the nineteenth century wore on. The emancipation of the slaves was not accompanied by compensation to the freedmen for years of unpaid labor (a thought unimaginable to the statesmen of the empire) in the form of land grants. The elite well understood that, to attract the European settlers they so longed for, it would be necessary to make homesteads easily available, yet there were only token establishments of official colonies in places near town markets, where small farmers might prosper. Nearly all the immigrant colonies of the late nineteenth and early twentieth centuries— brave, starving little hamlets, abandoned to their fates—were placed in the most problematic of forest climes, at the farthest extreme of transport, their task to be that of advancing the neo-European pale in regions where no sane Brazilian farmer would risk himself. Thus the rugged and relatively unfertile highland forests of central Espírito Santo were cleared and cultivated by handfuls of immigrant Germans and Italians, beginning in the 1870s, efforts that achieved only hardscrabble livings.[6]

The inability of pioneer caboclo subsistence farmers to transform their squatters' rights into titled property and to shift to smallholding production of cash crops like coffee accelerated the destruction of the Atlantic Forest. Inevitably, smallholders on the remote frontier would have continued to practice swidden farming. Surely a waste of forest, yet a slow-working one that doubled back frequently upon secondary growth, which, as long as the population remained dispersed, was allowed to grow back. The new class of expropriators coveted great fortunes, made at a single stroke, and this called for the immediate clearing of immense stands of primary forest for coffee. The value of the coffee crop was far greater than any alternate crop grown for the local market—one official report, for example, showed that coffee output per hectare was seven times the value of that of rice, an important commercial crop grown on the Paulista coast around Iguape. The rapid increase in value of land planted in coffee was another reason for speculation. The speculator typically invested in planting only a modest advance, paid to a sharecropper, who brought his own slaves to the property and was also allowed to interplant subsistence crops and sell the first year's coffee harvest. At the end of four years, the grove reverted to the owner, who could sell it for several times his initial outlay.[7]

The expectations of investments doubled, tripled, quadrupled in value within four years fueled an astonishing expansion of primary-forest felling. São Paulo was the locale of this frenzied development. Coffee reached the state in the 1790s when planting began in the western reaches of the Paraíba Valley and along the coast at Ubatuba. By 1817 there were commercial plantings in the region of Campinas, a hundred kilometers inland from the provincial capital. Not until the rail line of the English company reached Jundiaí, however, did exports reach a significant level. By 1872 Santos exported 20,000 tons. Coffee growing fanned out northwestward, following the spread of primary forest toward the Paraná River. The rail lines, soon easily financed by the coffee planters themselves, accompanied this clearing, extending from the railheads at Jundiaí, and Campinas. Planting doubled in the decade after abolition, and by 1900 there were 650 million coffee trees in the state. It may be estimated that by that date 10,000 square kilometers of the state's forest had already been felled to accommodate this first century of planting.[8]

This new coffee region, the Paulista West, came into production as the Paraíba Valley and the Zona da Mata of Minas Gerais fell into terminal decadence. The region lay over ancient eruptive formations, a rolling topography that produced deep, well-drained, and moderately fertile soils. This was a far more promising environment for coffee than had been the easily eroded "half-oranges" of the Paraíba Valley. The more marked seasonality of rainfall in the region, the effect of its remoteness from the coast, offered the advantage that the flowering and consequently the ripening of the berries took place in a shorter period. The harvest could therefore be conducted with fewer passes through the groves, economizing labor. The more pronounced winter dry season, furthermore, followed the harvest and made the drying of the berries a faster and more secure operation. Although the coffee plant was unable to store water or reduce its rate of transpiration in the absence of rain, therefore suffering stress in drought years, the profundity and porosity of Paulista soils permitted it to vegetate adequately.

The coffee plant was at risk in this new area of cultivation from freezing temperatures that occurred at intervals of sixteen to nineteen years. A half hour at 0° C is sufficient to kill the plant, if the ambient air is still and humid. In fear of these disasters, planters always located their groves away from bottomlands, which consequently were sold at much lower prices than hilltops and hillsides. This practice repeated the experience of the Paraíba Valley, where the principal concern had been to avoid the soggy soils that are inimical to the plant's root development. Fortunately for the planters, the flatter topography of the Paulista West better suited upland farming and permitted survival of the groves for longer periods. The effect upon primary forest was the same, however: Hillside formations were the first to be destroyed. The bottomlands did not necessarily survive much longer; they were soon used to plant rice and other subsistence crops.[9]

The most valued soils of the Paulista West, diabases so rich in ferrous oxides that they appear to be *terra roxa*—purple earth—were only slightly acidic and contained more of the nitrogen, potassium, and calcium needed to form the berries than had been available on the hills of the Paraíba Valley. A considerable number of the early groves were successfully planted on soils that had already been given over to sugar, cotton, and subsistence crops earlier on. Most of these forest soils were capable of supporting coffee plants without fertilization for at least the first twenty years of their growth. But soil erosion often undermined production, despite the region's flatter profile, because planters continued to plant uphill and down. This was a pattern easier to hoe than contours and was therefore preferred, even though the advantages of contouring were not unknown. First to disappear was the humus layer, exceedingly valuable for its organic content and its porosity. It was calculated that coffee groves lost three-quarters of their humus content over the first twenty-two years of their growth. The acidity of the humus blocked the tendency of soil phosphates to fuse with free iron and aluminum. Fortunately, phosphorus was taken up by coffee only in small amounts, but adding phosphates was useless unless humus was present, because iron and aluminum were abundant. Aluminum and iron compounds caused laterization on soils that tended toward clay—the characteristic "hardpan" of weathered subtropical soils. Humus also harbored microbial agents that passed nitrogen to the coffee plant's roots. But humus was a legacy of the Atlantic Forest, irreplaceable under the conditions of Paulista plantation agriculture.[10]

Paulista planters did not attempt to shade their coffee trees, a practice that would have been risky in this drier inland climate because of yearly water deficits—shade trees would have competed for soil moisture. The planters had to pay for this deviation from the natural conditions of their domesticate: Unshaded groves were sooner senescent, they had to be weeded more frequently and aggressively, their yield fluctuated wildly from year to year, and the product was of lower quality. But large-scale investors did not count these disadvantages for much compared with the higher early output that unshaded trees normally yielded. "Santos" coffee, most of it lower grade, encountered an ample demand in the world market. Furthermore, the trees were to some extent self-shaded: The technique had become established of planting six to eight seeds or seedlings in each hole and allowing the most vigorous three or four to grow. Each *pé de café*—"foot of coffee"—was in fact a cluster of intertwined plants. Although coffee groves planted nearer the equator in Colombia, Costa Rica, and Java were all shaded, like the wild trees in southwestern Ethiopia, the Brazilians were in effect carrying out a massive unconscious breeding experiment, selecting for drought and sun tolerance.[11]

Burning and clearing broad swaths of primary forest also had the effect of separating the coffee plants from potential pollinating agents. The earliest planters in the Paulista West made much of the *bafo da mata*—breath of the woods—that they imagined was the cause of increased yields in those of their groves that were nearest the tree line. Possibly these coffee plants benefited from the higher humidity and more even temperatures present within the forest microclimate. It is probable, however, that their flowers were more likely to be visited by the forest's bees and other pollinators. Luckily, the domesticated coffee plant is mostly self-pollinating; even so, the presence of insect pollinators can increase yields by 10 or 15 percent. The entire removal of forest cover therefore may have cost the planters lowered yields, because the keeping of domesticated bees on plantations was quite rare. Self-pollination was thus another characteristic for which the planters were unconsciously selecting: Wild trees have been observed to be as much as 60 percent cross-pollinated. The possible advantages of restoring that characteristic have not yet been given much thought.[12]

The commercial and practical success of unshaded and unpollinated coffee trees—according to the lights of those who directed the enterprise—unfortunately had dire consequences for primary-forest survival. Had they considered native or introduced pollinators and had they exercised any conscious program of breeding, forest preservation might have been regarded as economic, and the area and labor force devoted to coffee might have been significantly reduced. Although some of the early advocates of shading proposed leaving some of the trees of the original forest in place to serve as shade trees, in the fashion of cacao planting in southern Bahia, a practice that would have avoided burning as well, this was not done. Slashing and burning forest for the purpose of laying out coffee groves therefore proceeded in São Paulo into the twentieth century, through-out the state and over the border into Paraná, until all the Atlantic Forest that overlay what were presumed to be adequate coffee soils was entirely consumed.

The Republican government facilitated the other requirement of this transformation: It paid the passages of European immigrants willing to sign work contracts on the coffee plantations. More than a million of them—Italians, mostly, but also Spaniards, Portuguese, and others—ar-rived between 1888 and 1914, attracted as well by the news that slavery had finally been done away with. They were provided groves to tend and paid in piecework, and they encouraged their relatives and friends to join them. Despite several years of crisis caused by overplanting after 1900, the inflow of peasant workers continued, drawn by the reports of easily grown subsistence crops and wages high enough to assure an easeful retirement in the homeland. These free passages represented a considerable transfer of resources from the rest of the country and from the rest of the citizenry to a single sector for the benefit of a small number of landowners, all in the hope of eventually raising state revenue from export taxes. This hope was indeed realized: Coffee came to supply three-quarters of the budget of the state of São Paulo, and coffee paid for much of Brazil's imports. The coffee trade also paid for and determined the traces of an enlarged railroad network, which by 1917 extended over nearly 6,000 kilometers in São Paulo. These were economic triumphs so dramatic that the means by which they were achieved seemed beyond criticism.

And yet criticism did accompany this extraordinary expansion of planta-tions and growth of population. Scattered, at first inconsequential, expres-sions of dismay and mistrust were heard among the directing elite from the beginning of the country's independent existence. It is remarkable that the person considered most responsible, after Dom Pedro I himself, for the political and constitutional form of the monarchy, José Bonifácio de An-drada e Silva, was a Coimbra-trained geologist who had studied forestry at Brandenburg and had served as director of reforestation of the Portuguese coast until the French invasion. This experience was incorporated into his recommendations to the delegation sent to the Cortes and to the Constituent Assembly that landowners be required to keep forest reserves on their holdings. No attention was paid to this sensible advice. The legislature of the new empire, unable to produce any sort of land law for twenty-eight years, was still less concerned to preserve forests.[13]

Inquiry into the state of the empire's natural resources was, nevertheless, officially patronized, reviving the modest viceregal tradition of applied scientific societies. The Auxiliary Society of National Industry was formed in 1825, and the Brazilian Historical and Geographical Institute was established in 1838, both officially sponsored. The former advocated intensive farming techniques and carried out some further introductions of exotic plant domesticates; the latter compiled and published geographical documentation that revealed the interior to the urban elite. These were institutions that enjoyed long and productive life-spans—the institute still exists and was the model for similar ones in all the provinces. At mid-century, a Conservative ministry came to power that engineered several reforms, including the effective abolition of the slave trade. As was frequently to occur, the reformist spirit was paralleled in civil society. Several additional scientific and technical societies were simultaneously established. In 1849 the Imperial Brazilian Horticultural Nucleus was formed by a Rio de Janeiro seed importer. The Vellosiana Society, which counted as members active science enthusiasts from the southeastern provinces, began its meetings in 1851. A Fluminense (referring to the province of Rio de Janeiro) Agricultural Society dates from 1854. And in 1858 the Scientific Dais of Rio de Janeiro, a dissident offshoot of the Vellosiana Society, began to publish its sessions.[14]

Members of these societies—traveled, educated, and accomplished—gave expression to awakening fear of environmental damage caused by more than a century of intensified economic activity and denser population. Slash-and-burn farming was constantly worried over; the agricultural improver Gustavo Schuch de Capanema published reflections on the deforestation that read very much like his contemporary George Perkins Marsh in the United States. Drought repeatedly caused elevated food prices in the towns, angering the middling sort of town inhabitants, those who owned no rural property of their own. It became commonly believed that forest clearing was itself the cause of drought. At the time this was an impressionistic supposition, but it is now asserted on fairly solid scientific grounds: The forests of the Amazon coast transpire vast amounts of water, which easterlies carry farther into the interior. The removal of coastal forests therefore implies a drier inland climate. In the Southeast, by the late nineteenth century the interior margin of the Atlantic Forest had in many places been reached. This was, even without human intervention, already a zone of longer, more intense, and less predictable winter dry seasons. By midcentury it could also be observed that rivers that had once run clear and steadily the year round were now charged with the muddy runoff of the plantations; at their mouths sandbars formed that made impossible their navigation even by dugout canoes. Critics also worried that forest clearing increased temperature extremes, an assertion for which they had some evidence, because the Royal Academy of Lisbon had collected and published observations of Rio de Janeiro's temperatures in the 1780s.[15]

The supplying of firewood to the towns was probably an even more critical aspect of the survival of their inhabitants: The five tons or so of firewood that each town family consumed annually was essential to its well-being. Every household task and many domestic industries required the continual burning of wood in the kitchen or backyard stove. As capoeira was felled and replaced by pasture, the towns became more and more remote from their sources of supply, brought to them by donkey trains that themselves increased the demand for forage. One observer compared the towns of Minas Gerais to a tree commonly called *solitária* because nothing grew for twenty paces around it—evidently a case of what now would be called allelopathy. By midcentury proposals to replant and protect woodlots were becoming, if not frequent, at least common. Indeed, there are claims that this was done in a few places: A memoir of 1823 remarks that a municipal council in the district of Rio das Mortes, in Minas Gerais, was driven by the scarcity of wood to "the extreme necessity" of planting pine trees. These reformers apparently ignored what would have been a less troublesome improvement—the redesign of their stoves for better thermal efficiency. Even so, because the arrangements of their kitchens were beneath the notice of the literati, it may be that the traditional brick stoves still to be seen in some rural houses do represent improvements over those of earlier times.[16]

As the woodlands in the vicinity of the cities retreated, so did game animals. The botanist Francisco Freire Alemão noted in 1845 the disappearance or rarefaction of dozens of species in woodlands in the vicinity of Rio de Janeiro that he considered to be still primary forest. Missing entirely were peccaries, tapirs, deer, jaguars, tamarins, and woolly spider monkeys—the latter two now on the endangered list—and several birds, including the now endangered jacutinga. The possibility of certain animals "not associated with the civilization of man" disappearing entirely was already foreseen by a few observers.[17]

Of more immediate consequence was the appearance of pests and plagues that were beginning to attack the coffee groves of the Paraíba Valley. Tropical domesticates normally enjoyed near immunity from parasitism for some considerable period after their transfer to an exotic locale—indeed this was the strategy, entirely unconscious, that made possible the worldwide spread of the plantation system. Unfortunately, by the 1860s that halcyon interval was coming to a close in Rio de Janeiro. This might have been predicted, because coffee is a member of a cosmopolitan family, Rubiaceae, with which many Neotropical predators had coevolved. A few native insects were coming to adapt to the immense feast that had been set before them. One was a nocturnal butterfly whose larvae were leaf eating; another was a nematode that infected roots, shriveling the trees. These were both considerable disasters that contributed to the decadence of coffee in the Paraíba Valley. Although Brazilian scientists at the time were able to do no more than identify the causes of these calamities, their intervention was desperately sought by planters. This was the first time that the self-sufficient and self-satisfied plantocracy had found itself asking scientific experts for help. As exotic pests and plagues joined the list of dangers to coffee, scientists were to gain still greater respect.[18]

More unease was caused by increasing dangers to human health. Nineteenth-century Rio de Janeiro was an unsanitary city, attacked repeatedly by pandemic cholera and yellow fever. Some thought that the disappearance of surrounding primeval forests, especially the mangrove that had once ringed the bay, had somehow provoked these disasters. One of the theories extant was that trees attracted lightning, which purified the atmosphere or perhaps, lacking trees upon which to ground itself, provoked atmospheric disorders that inhibited normal precipitation.[19]

None of these speculations had any important consequences during the first forty years of the empire. It was, instead, another belief, that deforestation of watersheds caused the drying up of springs, which impelled the first official attempt at conservation. This initiative was undertaken in 1862, as the increasing precariousness of the environment of the capital persuaded the imperial government to invest a modest level of resources in a program of reforestation. From the days of the Portuguese king's residence in Rio de Janeiro, the capital city had suffered acute crises of water supply, especially during droughts. An aqueduct, completed early in the 1700s, tapped springs that rose from the Tijuca massif, fronted by the dramatic promontory of Corcovado—Humpback—that loomed a thousand meters high over the city. As the population grew, this source became insufficient, despite the further extension of pipelines, and increasingly erratic.

Blame was laid on deforestation of the watershed, carried out for charcoal making and, late in the century, for coffee planting. In 1817 further felling of trees had already been prohibited in that watershed and, soon thereafter, appraisals were ordered for the purpose of its expropriation. Only in 1856, however, were a few properties at last acquired on Tijuca and the adjoining Paineiras hill. In 1862 these were given over to administrators under instructions to replant forest cover. This was in the Brazilian experience an astonishing novelty. Some sporadic replanting had already been carried on in the area, but this effort was to be carried on steadily until 1891. The person principally credited was a local landowner named Manuel Gomes Archer, who lived in the forest for most of this period and administered the Tijuca forest until 1873, supervising a work force that included a foreman and a dozen or so slaves who planted and tended the trees and a number of forest guards who prevented logging, hunting, or the removal of any plants. Archer has become a mythically heroic figure to the inhabitants of Rio de Janeiro—indeed, to all Brazilian environmentalists. The massif was reforested and effectively protected for posterity, a magnificent and inspirational living endowment that still survives.[20]

Archer's work and that of his successors were probably determined as much or more by the desire of the city's elite for a woodland retreat in the highlands, free of the threat of yellow fever, which had become endemic in the urban center by the 1850s. The Tijuca massif was first settled in the time of King João by a brilliant coterie of French expatriates, exiles or deserters from the court of Napoleon such as the prince de Montbéliard, the comte de Gestas, and the court artist Nicholas Antoine Taunay. Soon they were joined by other foreigners and the city's wealthiest residents, including the count of Bom Retiro, minister of the interior, who issued the order to reforest. Few of their houses were expropriated, although some of those that were purchased by the state were turned over to government officials, possibly a form of favoritism. A large work force was kept busy extending the water-supply system and maintaining a road network within the forest. Therefore the carriages of the wealthy rode smoothly on macadamized roads, and their picturesque chalets were connected by the 1860s to a piped water supply and to the city's gas network. Archer's labors hence were intended not to restore the forest primeval but to enhance a parklike, planned landscape. His technique was to plant in the shade of existing trees and then, when the seedlings were well rooted, to cut the old trees down! Although he was directed to plant native trees, he also introduced exotic ornamentals, including dracaena, pandanus, jackfruit, and eucalyptus. He was also sent orders occasionally to supply seedlings from his nursery for the public gardens of the city. The rate of tree planting was morose in the extreme—in some years amounting to one or two trees a day per worker.[21]

Archer abandoned his work at Tijuca after more than a decade, invited by the emperor to take up the reforestation of Petrópolis, the imperial summer capital. Tijuca was turned over, in 1874, to Gastão d'Escragnolle, a descendant of another of the patrician Frenchmen who also kept his residence within the forest. His work force was diverted from tree planting to embellishing existing groves, building grottoes, belvederes, fountains, artificial lakes, and bridges. Most of these improvements were named for members of Escragnolle's family. The effect is even today altogether charming, but while this work was going on, deforestation and charcoal making was continuing on the other hills surrounding the city. Escragnolle died in 1887; two years later another aqueduct was inaugurated, bringing a much larger water supply from the more distant Tingu Hill. Archer returned to the direction of the Tijuca forest briefly in 1890 and planted more trees than had Escragnolle in fourteen years.

It is unlikely, however, that much of the forest now found on the heights behind Rio de Janeiro was planted by Archer or his successors. All the planting done between 1862 and 1892, when the administration of the forest was divided among several offices by the republican government and reforestation seems to have ceased, amounted to 127,000 trees, whose long-term survival was not reported, although a publication of 1890 suggests that there was considerable destruction already in the three years between Escragnolle's death and Archer's return. For an area of 32 square kilometers, this represented only 20 trees per hectare, assuming half of them reached maturity. Therefore, most of the trees on the massif must have grown back naturally.[22]

This modest but highly visible experiment in reforestation was not only an indication of the awakening consciousness of the urban elites to the precariousness of their artificial environment and the need to manage it in behalf of social tranquillity and indeed of their own comfort, safety, and health. It was also a small sign of the state's reviving will to manage the natural environment. This was nevertheless an awkward beginning. It had been carried out by amateurs whose methods were altogether empirical and who were subordinate to an undifferentiated and mostly unconcerned bureaucracy. Gradually, these circumstances were to change. By the turn of the century, a number of specialized government agencies had been created with specific responsibility for resource management. Their staffs, a cadre of scientific and technical professionals, were destined to confront conservationist and environmentalist issues.

Brazilian scientists and technicians over the course of the nineteenth century set themselves the task of reintegration with the European intellectual community. Indeed, their renewed contacts with European technological advances evoked in them a fierce desire to close a widening gap in knowledge and skills. The Brazilian commissioners sent to the Universal Expositions of 1855 and 1862 observed the improvements in agriculture and forestry, not only in the industrial countries but even in their tropical colonies with which Brazil directly competed. These exhibits portended a future that might be either prosperous or disastrous, depending on Brazil's ability to accompany these improvements. Indeed, Brazil's very domestic market was at stake. How could it be, they wondered, that a country still largely and exuberantly forested was importing lumber from the Baltic states and North America? The commissioners had brought with them an assortment of hoes, axes, and billhooks that represented their country's agricultural technology. These they displayed shamefacedly, resigned to the Londoners' and Parisians' pity and disdain.[23]

Transfer of Western scientific knowledge was essential to the success of the institutions to which these returning delegates were appointed. To this end, collaboration with distant and often indifferent foreign colleagues was necessary, a difficult challenge. Fewer European scientists visited the country after independence. Hardly any intended to instruct or even to collaborate with their local counterparts. Saint-Hilaire had been an honorable exception, a collector who offered numerous specimens to the National Museum and mentioned Brazilian work respectfully. More often they denigrated the institutions they visited. Brazilians trained in Europe encountered on their return social isolation and official incomprehension. Their European correspondents not uncommonly expropriated the information that Brazilians sent them, sometimes without acknowledging their priority. A genus published by Freire Alemão, for example, was given a new name three years later by the French botanist Tulasne, even though he had been sent a copy of the Brazilian's description. When the great botanist Karl Friedrich Philipp von Martius formed a team in Bavaria to publish a flora of Brazil, he invited no Brazilian members, even though Pedro II subsidized the project.[24]

After 1876 Brazilian scientists would remember with some degree of bitterness the triumph of the British Royal Botanic Gardens at Kew, which obtained viable seeds of the rubber tree from the Amazon, leading to the plant's acclimatization and cultivation in British Southeast Asian colonies. Even so, collaboration with the European scientific network was usually available when requested. Seven years earlier, Auguste Glaziou, the emperor's landscaper, had planted seedlings at Santa Tereza of the precious cinchona, from which quinine was derived. They had been donated by Kew, which had obtained them at considerable cost and trouble from the Peruvian highlands only a few years before. This was quite a remarkable gift, considering that it has been claimed that the intent of the British botanical network was imperialist and therefore monopolistic.[25]

Brazilian science characteristically did not draw upon the stock of knowledge of the natural world possessed by indigenes or mestizo frontier people. This may seem a remarkably obtuse lapse of curiosity, but it is easy to understand, given the cultural gap between them. The scientists were appalled at the wastefulness of the slash-and-burn farming they practiced and were quite sure of the reason for their adherence to traditional ways: "No one is unaware of the supreme ignorance of the greater number of our farmers," the director of the National Museum complained in 1859, expressing a general opinion. Such people could hardly be imagined as a source of useful knowledge.[26]

Furthermore, because the European scientists who visited Brazil were wont to treat the indigenous people they encountered much as they did the herbarium and zoo specimens they collected—indeed, on at least one occasion the remains of Indians massacred in ambush were purchased for a museum, and on another a Botocudo couple were packed off to Europe as living scientific souvenirs—it would have been difficult for them to have conceived of the native peoples as keepers of higher knowledge or to have sought practical, empirical information from them. Again Auguste de Saint-Hilaire was exceptional in asking backwoods people the uses to which they put the plant species he collected, but there is no sign that these intimations were ever put to the test in France (or anywhere else— right up to the present!).[27]

Only European knowledge was valid, in the eyes not only of the self-confident Europeans but also of the still psychically colonized Brazilian scientists, struggling for a secure footing within the elite classes of the empire. One wonders whether they lost more than they gained—or, at times, accomplished more harm than good. Consider, for example, the French pharmacist Alexandre Brethel, who in 1862 settled in the frontier town of Carangola, in Minas Gerais: The numerous letters he sent back to family and colleagues in Brittany over the course of a long and prosperous career reveal no interest at all in Brazilian medicinals. Quite the contrary, his stock-in-trade was medicines imported from France, upon which his social position as well as his business depended. For more than forty years he dispensed in good conscience to a large rural clientele the remedies of Western science, among them laudanum and arsenate of strychnine![28]

This is not to suggest that the information amassed by frontier people was infallibly more adaptive or scientifically verifiable than that of the European collectors. One is struck by the relative absence of what might be called environmental awareness among the folk, at least as can be deduced from the anecdotal collections of folklorists. Instead, there are indications that faulty observation, pious superstition, greed, and not an insignificant amount of hostility toward their natural environment partly determined their actions within it. The taboo against the hunting of the bird called João de barro, for example, derived from its supposed refusal to work on its ovenlike clay nest on Sundays or holy days; thus they called it the "Catholic bird." The army officer sent to investigate the grotto of Maquiné, later to be recognized as one of South America's most important archaeological sites, found that his guides were eager to invade it, to bear off the treasure of gold and diamonds they supposed were hidden there. On occasion, an individual tree would come to be venerated as having healing powers, possibly an African introduction. More common was the belief in the possibility of ridding oneself of diseases by transferring them to trees—a string that had been tied around the ill person's neck was removed by a relative and affixed to a tree trunk while a litany of prayers was recited. These, and the belief that a sufferer of venereal disease might rid himself of it with acts of bestiality, are among those few recorded in which the natural world enters into the consciousness of the folk.[29]

The scientific establishment gained somewhat more solidity after the Paraguayan War, which ended in 1870, beginning a period, like the reformist early 1850s, of crises of inflation and urban epidemics. A reform cabinet was installed whose principal political achievement was passage of the law of free birth. A census was taken—the first in the empire's history—and a civil registry of vital statistics was organized. The metric system was imposed, not without opposition from the folk, which suspected short weights. Naturalization requirements were eased. A newly created Public Works Office began drawing maps, work that was expanded in 1874 when a Geological Commission was founded, under the North American Charles Frederick Hartt. A school of military engineering on the French model— the Polytechnic—was founded, as were a school of mines and several secondary schools of agriculture. An undersea cable to Europe was authorized, railroad subsidies were increased, and river-valley exploration was carried out in Minas Gerais and São Paulo.

The Brazilian Acclimatization Association was founded in 1872, a curious imitation of the movement originating in France that proposed to test the adaptability of European biota, including humans, to their tropical colonies. This society also proposed, however, to study the practicality of the

domestication of native species. Its members included such notables as André Rebouças, an engineer, abolitionist, and timber entrepreneur; Auguste
Glaziou, the emperor's Swiss landscaper; João Martins da Silva Coutinho,
an intrepid public servant who reported on agricultural conditions
throughout the empire; Gustavo Schuch de Capanema; Joaquim Monteiro
Caminho, lecturer in botany and zoology at the Faculty of Medicine; and
the viscount of Rio Branco, the prime minister himself. The association
stimulated a considerable number of transfers from Europe and even more
interchanges among the provinces, although most may have been of ornamentals. Brazilian consuls and naval vessels were instructed to forward
seeds, and a few direct transfers were carried out independent of the European scientific network: Liberian coffee was brought directly from Africa.
Curiously, the association discussed the utility of the wild-growing Pará
rubber tree in the very month that its seeds were delivered from the Amazon to the Royal Botanic Garden at Kew. That momentous transfer was
noted for the first time, only a few months after it was achieved, in the
Revista de Horticultura, another initiative of the 1870s, edited by a seed
importer who assiduously followed Kew's newsletters.[30]

The most impressive achievement of this early phase of reformation in
the natural sciences, however, was that carried out at the National Museum by Ladislau de Souza Mello Netto. The museum had languished for
fifty years after its grudging restoration by João VI. The government had
been interested only in its mineralogical section, expecting it to locate new
deposits of gold and diamonds. The museum's equipment, however, had
been diverted to the medical school, and the mint and its herbarium had
largely disappeared, the remaining specimens left in disarray and unclassified. It had come to serve mainly as a warehouse for Egyptian and Etruscan
rarities that had come to it by chance. All this changed radically as the
result of somewhat unkind remarks about its state that were published by
Louis Agassiz. Netto, a French-trained botanist employed at the National
Museum, took advantage of the government's embarrassment to extract
from it a greatly increased budget for the institution and the directorship
for himself.[31]

Netto's initiatives included nearly every idea that now inspires economic botanical research in the Neotropics. He had participated in an exploration of the upper São Francisco River during which, like Saint-Hilaire,
he had inquired into the uses of the plants he encountered. In the far interior of Minas Gerais, he noticed, each inhabitant was his or her own pharmacist or veterinarian. He wanted these native remedies tested for efficac-
ity and had already proposed, in a lecture presented to the French Botanical
Society in 1865, that the Botanical Garden of Rio de Janeiro receive and

acclimatize them. He was concerned about the possibility of extinctions through burning of grasslands and forest and advocated the study of this problem. Significantly, Netto included in the published version of this lecture the response of the distinguished Charles Victor Naudin—that forest reserves be created in each province to safeguard useful forest species. Netto collected wood samples as well as herbarium material and regarded taxonomy as essential to the practical task introducing useful species to commerce. This could only be done in Brazil, he observed, because the collections he had studied at the Jardin des Plantes were defective, often missing flowers, seeds, fruits, or roots. Under his direction, the museum added sections in paleobotany, paleontology, and anthropology. Netto inaugurated courses in botany and agriculture, which, he complained, lacked audiences unless the emperor attended. Netto created a Brazilian network of correspondents, including the eminent immigrant scientist Fritz Müller, Darwin's first public advocate; Charles Hartt; Henri Gorceix, head of the School of Mines; and Hermann von Ihering, whom he persuaded to resign his post at Jena to come to Brazil.[32]

The hapless Botanical Garden of Rio de Janeiro achieved no comparable budget enlargement. Subordinated to the Imperial Fluminense Agricultural Institute, a school founded in 1860 that was, like other such institutions of the time, little more than a demonstration farm and orphanage, it was limited to the acclimatization and dissemination of exotics. This was undertaken energetically by its director, Karl Glasl, who planted novel varieties of coffee, cotton, tobacco, and sugar. He also tried to interest planters in bamboo, teak, eucalyptus, and albizzia. At the same time, a few planters, notably in the Paulista West, were coming to accept more intensive farming practices. The publishers of the 1878 edition of Francisco de Lacerda Werneck's manual of maxims on the art of coffee planting appended a remarkable appreciation of several of these notables. Its author, Luiz Correa de Azevedo, deplored the casual empiricism of Lacerda Werneck's generation and extolled the more careful techniques of, among others, José Vergueiro, whose São Paulo plantations had been the scene of the first, ill-fated attempt to regiment northern European workers to plantation labor. Agricultural improvement was also instigated by a few foreign agents, such as John James Aubertin, superintendent of the British-owned São Paulo Railway, in whose interest it was to promote the cultivation of cotton in Brazil during the blockade and military occupation of the Confederate States of America.[33]

The Agricultural Institute and the National Museum initiated the publication of the first journals in their fields that would enjoy the continuity necessary for the accumulation and transmission of scientific knowledge.

These and other works published in the 1870s demonstrated a broadening familiarity with the theories of Liebig and Darwin and the emergence of ecological concepts. The phrase "the economy of nature" began to appear, along with tentative theories of plant succession, habitat preference, community, and seed morphology.[34]

The Constitution of 1891 reserved to the states the right to levy export taxes. This was of immense advantage mainly to São Paulo, which was thus enabled to spend its revenues as it pleased. On the whole, its priorities were shrewdly drafted. The solidly incumbent Republican party of this most prosperous state was aware of the hazards that plantation agriculture and metropolitan city growth presented for the viability of the economy and its own monopoly of power. The state motto, *Non ducor, duco*—I am not led, I lead—a provocation to the rest of the federation, had to be made good: Beyond speculation and the main chance, the Paulista Republicans pursued modernization and rationality. To the degree that their legitimacy rested upon this commitment, they could not entirely ignore the damage to the natural environment that their developmental policies had set loose.

This was all the more so because they involved real economic harm to much of the city middle classes, afflicted with inflation, the competition of immigrants, and the importunities of indigent freedmen. This growing, increasingly better trained group was also inconvenienced by the deterioration of the capital's environment—its microclimate, influenced by accumulations of brick, tile, stone, and asphalt, was seemingly hotter in summer and drier in winter, and this they attributed increasingly to deforestation. The disappearance of wildlife from the center of the capital provoked some citizens to form a Fish and Game Club, to prevent the killing of vultures, songbirds, and other useful species. They managed to gain the passage of a state law, apparently directed covertly at Italian immigrants— whose custom of hunting birds for food was one of many that the native middle class despised—forbidding the killing of any bird during mating season.[35]

Railroad excursions revealed to the city middle class the extent of irreversible damage that was taking place in the countryside. The journalist Euclides da Cunha, traveling to São Paulo from Rio de Janeiro in 1901, wrote his essays, "Makers of Deserts" and "Among the Ruins," in which he described the endless piles of firewood stacked along the right-of-way and the eroded and barren hillsides, where gullies and exposed bedrock gave witness to coffee plantations abandoned a generation earlier. Newly awakened to these bitter results, the middle classes were vituperative in their criticism of the planters and railroad directors who had inflicted them and the government officials who had countenanced them.[36]

The state government therefore contracted technicians and scientists—some of them hired away from the federal government—trained in the best foreign academies, to create or renovate state institutions that might accelerate economic growth or overcome obstacles to it. While still a province of the empire, the state had created its own Geological and Geographical Commission under the North American Orville Derby. Its purpose was to explore its remaining unclaimed public lands and assist the placement of rail lines. Attached to this agency was a Botanical Section; by 1896 it was installed in the wooded Cantareira hills north of the capital. This was the state's first forest preserve, and, like Tijuca, its main purpose was to guard the watershed of the streams that were piped to the city's reservoir. Quite soon after the republic was declared, the state took over the Agronomic Institute that had been founded at Campinas in 1887. It was intended that this first true agricultural research station improve coffee and forage crops and diversify the rural economy. One of the tasks of its German director, F. W. Dafert, was to establish a wine industry, which the elite supposed essential to attracting Italian immigrants. The Paulista Museum was built in 1895 at Ipiranga, just south of the state capital, at the site where Pedro I had declared independence: both an affirmation of the state's primacy in nationhood and a challenge to its venerable rival in Rio de Janeiro. Public health specialists were enlisted to eliminate the scourges of bubonic plague, smallpox, cholera, and yellow fever endemic in Rio de Janeiro, Santos, and São Paulo. The evil sanitary reputation of the state had to be overcome before immigrants or foreign capital could be lured in great number. Laboratories for the production of vaccines were established in 1892 in São Paulo and in 1900 in Rio de Janeiro. The former eventually became the world-famous Butantã Institute, specializing in the production of anti-snake venom serums. Snakebite, a by no means uncommon cause of death in the countryside, thereafter held somewhat less terror for uneasy Italian laborers.[37]

The scientists employed by these new institutions undertook their tasks loyally, but their very mandate of efficiency caused them to raise the banner of conservation. The concept of structural contradiction seems here altogether applicable. Public servants, members of an emerging middle class, often of immigrant origin, they came to experience a conflictful relationship with the governments that employed them, dominated as they were by the great landowners whose speculative urges, wasteful managerial techniques, and jealousy of their rights of property were to form barriers to the implementation of conservationist policies. A great struggle was to be joined, of uncertain outcome.

The most effective of the first generation of Paulista scientists was Alberto Loefgren, a Swedish botanist who had arrived with a collecting expedition and was contracted to direct the Meteorological and Botanical sections of the Geological and Geographical Commission. Enchanted with the unspoiled nature of the region, he turned down an invitation to return to a research post in his native land, saying that in Europe all there was to study were the "pallid mummies" of the gorgeous plants he studied live in Brazil. Loefgren was immensely energetic and effective, collecting in all the state's varied ecosystems, organizing a large herbarium, publishing his findings in numerous articles in Europe and Brazil, and translating important works in botany and ecology, including Eugenius Warming's study of the Minas Gerais cerrado. Practical in his endeavors, he imported numerous plant domesticates and assessed hundreds of native plants for their potential as planted forage, medicinals, and industrial raw materials. His studies of economic tree species and his calculations of rainfall and temperatures led him to believe that deforestation was causing climatic change and that reforestation was the necessary and unavoidable remedy.

By 1899, through the force of Loefgren's arguments and his connections with the landed elite, his Botanical Section was redesignated the Forest and Botanical Service, elevated to the same rank as the commission. It was charged with the "conservation, better exploitation, and reforestation of the forests." Loefgren began to campaign for a national forest code, national parks, and a national forest service. He was perhaps the first to note the phenomenon of the "hollow frontier," pointing out that the advancing line of settlement left behind "exhausted and unproductive terrain that constantly increases in extent." Permanent settlement, he argued, required forest; grassland was the abode of nomads. A national forest service could guarantee the conservation of forests necessary to protect watercourses, soils, and microclimates, and it might end the need for wood imports, eventually making possible its export.[38]

Loefgren inspired the celebration of the first Arbor Day in Brazil, which took place at Araras, in 1902, in the presence of the state president and vice-president. He failed, however, to persuade the legislature to take any more concrete measures to protect the state's remaining primary forests. There were two obstacles to his proposal and to others put forward in Rio de Janeiro and Paraná at the time. First, there was the difficulty that the states had been unable to demarcate public lands and continued to permit this patrimony to fall into the hands of unscrupulous grileiros. Loefgren naively believed, or pretended to believe, this to be merely an administrative matter, to be resolved by a cadastral survey, rather than the sinister political game it was. Second, because there were no public preserves in São Paulo save Cantareira, conservationist state law would have to apply to private forests. The colonial prohibition of felling on private lands— madeira de lei, that is, primary forest hardwoods—was altogether a dead letter after independence and was formally abrogated in 1876, the victim not only of the general disregard of landowners but also of liberal ideology and the revolution in naval construction. The republican state could not be convinced to reestablish so discredited a monarchist policy. Liberal prin- ciples were, as ever they are, selectively applied: In 1903 the planting of new coffee groves was prohibited by law, in a vain intervention to boost coffee prices.[39]

Nor would the government expend funds to buy back its former prop- erty in order to set up state or national forests, as Loefgren observed was being done in the United States and wished to see established in São Paulo. As a last resort, he therefore proffered advice to landowners concerning the conservative exploitation of their woodlands. The growth of the urban, railway, and industrial markets for lumber and fuelwood, he noted, pre- sented planters an opportunity for rational exploitation of an ancillary re- source. Loefgren presumed that on most estates the best timber on the most accessible terrain would already have been destroyed to plant coffee and other cash crops and that most of the remaining timber would consist of species that were not merchantable. It was therefore necessary that the landowners replant with more valuable species. Although he did not spec- ify, it appears that he had in mind the planting of hardwoods. This was clearly uneconomic, because trees of the primary forest were too slow growing to be profitable, and it was impractical, because the edaphic condi- tions under which these species were capable of growing were entirely unlike those of cleared farmland.[40]

The restoration of the Atlantic Forest, it was only dimly understood, or reluctantly admitted, by conservationists like Loefgren, was more or less impossible. There were, as Loefgren well knew, many planters who allowed a part of their estates to remain in forest, not only for future exploitation but also as woodlots. They removed timber from them as they needed it or found a market for it, but they could not manage them as they had heard was done in Europe or North America because, unlike the woodlots of those cold climates, this forest was not composed uniformly of a few hardy, fast-growing species, uncomplicated in their pollinating, seeding, and fruiting habits, undemanding in their nutritional requirements, and mostly competitive, rather than cooperative, with the rest of the forest's inhabitants. Re-creating a northern pine or broad-leaved forest needed lit- tle management; re-creating the Atlantic Forest would have required near omniscience and a life-span of centuries. The woodlots of even the most prudent of the planters, therefore, all degenerated gradually—the finest woods were removed one by one, and the canopy became more open as other young trees were smashed when their elders were felled. At last, as useless trees and lianas sprang up, the purpose of the woodlot vanished, the plot was burned, and coffee, maize, or pasture grass was planted.[41]

Loefgren, nevertheless, was an effective provocateur. His calls in Paulista newspapers for conservation of forest resources were seized upon by the censorious middle classes. They were especially annoyed at the rising retail prices of lumber and firewood in the midst of a coffee economy that was suffering, after 1900, extreme depression, the altogether predictable result of the furious expansion of planting of the 1890s. Especially appreciated were Loefgren's criticisms of the railroads, which, as foreign exchange became scarce, were shifting from burning coal to burning wood. These complaints were echoed even by planters, who had come to count on sales of wood as a hedge against declining coffee prices. The region of Ribeirão Prêto alone had more than 300 sawmills in 1903, most of the output of which went to the railroads. The railroads, however, were trying to extort from the hard-pressed planters cut rates for their inventories, which some counties were now taxing as revenues from coffee fell. Planters also had a long-standing grievance against the railroads because of the fires that live coals from their locomotive smokestacks caused in fields, coffee groves, and woodlands. Some plantations had been forced to keep permanent fire brigades.[42]

The railroad companies were obliged pay some attention to these complaints, if for no other reason than to fend off further regulatory legislation. Certainly their demand for wood was very great. At the turn of the century they were consuming half a million cubic meters of wood a year; by 1910, in addition to 300,000 tons of imported coal, they required 2.4 million cubic meters, the equivalent of 80 square kilometers of forest. In addition, there was the need for crossties: 1,500 per kilometer, which had to be replaced every six years. The state of São Paulo consumed an average 1.5 million crossties annually in the decade after 1902. For this purpose forest hardwoods were often used, but woods of the cerrado were coming to be preferred—marking the first attack upon that formation for industrial purposes. Track maintenance was costing the state about 20 square kilometers of forest a year. Although the rail networks of the other southeastern states were not growing as fast as that of São Paulo, their demand in this period was at least as large, so that 200 square kilometers a year were being consumed by transport requirements, not including the areas destroyed by accidental fires. This loss was considerably less than that caused by household and industrial consumption, but it was novel and very visible.[43]

In 1904 Antônio Prado, president of the Paulista Railroad, the most prosperous of the Brazilian-owned lines that fed into the São Paulo Railway, hired Edmundo Navarro de Andrade to install a forest reserve. It is not clear whether the purpose was to still the company's critics or simply to find suitable employment for the 23-year-old Navarro. A godson of Veridiana Prado, dowager of the clan, he had been packed off to Portugal to try for a degree in agronomy after he had been expelled from the military academy and had shown slight talent for a literary career. Antônio Prado, one of dona Veridiana's sons and a minister of agriculture under the empire who had been instrumental in founding the Agronomic Institute and in promoting immigration, may have chosen the lackluster Navarro merely on the urgings of his mother. Amazingly, the young man sprang into action. He set up several experimental stations at Jundiaí, Campinas, and Rio Claro, where he painstakingly tested nearly a hundred native and exotic tree species under varied soil conditions to determine which produced the most useful fuelwood the fastest.[44]

The result of these trials, already evident by 1906, was a clear victory for trees of the genus *Eucalyptus*, native to Australia and nearby islands. This was not an unexpected discovery; Loefgren had already recommended eucalyptus in 1903. A specimen of *E. gigantea* had been planted in the Botanical Garden of Rio de Janeiro as early as 1825, and by the early 1870s dozens of other species, including the hardy and multipurpose *E. globulus,* were planted in Rio Grande do Sul and Rio de Janeiro from seeds brought from Uruguay, where it was first introduced in 1853, and also directly from Australia. These early plantings, however, were for sanitary and medicinal ends. Eucalyptus absorbs water in great quantity; it had the capacity therefore to dry up standing water, thereby reducing mosquito populations. Its aromatic oils were also held to have disinfectant and healing qualities. Navarro's purposes were different, and his methodology was far more focused and scientific than his predecessors'. This was very necessary because there are some 450 species of eucalyptus, of varied requirements and qualities. His experimental plots therefore quickly became the source of information for other railroad companies and for those planters prescient enough to foresee the end of their native woodlots.[45]

Navarro organized, during his long administration of the Paulista Railroad's forests, 17 reserves occupying 175 square kilometers. He toured Australia and nearly every country to which eucalyptus had been transferred, seeking to learn everything possible about the genus and the optimal methods of cultivating it. He published several treatises on eucalyptus growing that went through numerous editions and that, had they been translated from Portuguese, would have established him as the world's leading expert on the subject. In 1911 Navarro took over from Loefgren the Forest and Botanical Service, which ominously dropped "Botanical" from its title. Navarro turned the agency into a eucalyptus nursery—in one year distribution surged from an average 25,000 seedlings a year to 250,000. Unfortunately, Navarro's emphasis was exclusively on the diffusion of eucalyptus. Botanical studies that might have established the industrial and medicinal values of native forest were halted. Loefgren's herbarium disappeared.[46]

Navarro gave up the state Forest Service in 1916. His priorities were by then well established there, and the implantation of eucalyptus was spreading among estate owners. The onset of war in Europe nearly eliminated coal imports, and demand for wood surged. The federal government offered subsidies for tree planting that resulted in awards for 20 million trees—though that may not signify that so large a number were in fact planted. Withal, the Atlantic Forest was by war's end only on the edge of an immense wave of eucalyptus planting. Navarro's work was praised by nearly all observers, he was entrusted with a number of other important state scientific posts, and he had won numerous honors, in Brazil and abroad, by the time of his death in 1941. Still, there were also from the beginning criticisms, most of them oddly misplaced. It was annoying to some that large swaths of the countryside were coming to be occupied by an exotic, not a native tree. This objection was never raised in the case of the coffee tree, however, or of citrus or mango trees or the dozens of other exotic crops upon which the country had come to depend. That eucalyptus dried up surface waters came to be held against it, but that complaint might have been raised against any fast-growing tree species, or even against sugarcane, for that matter.[47]

Navarro, for his part, never claimed that he was reforesting; he was merely tree farming—producing a necessary raw material by the fastest and most efficient means available. The replacement of native forest by endless kilometers of homogeneous eucalyptus groves, nevertheless, was a transformation that was causing a degree of unease among some in the middle classes who before then had not concerned themselves overmuch with the disappearance of the Atlantic Forest. It was a sign perhaps of their distrust of the new scientific imperatives that were cited to justify technocratic management of natural resources. Even though they could not articulate defensible arguments against this attempted appropriation, they sensed that the changes it might entail might not be for the better.

Navarro turned out to be the only successful Paulista conservationist of his generation. Most of the other leading figures of this group were eclipsed or destroyed by their experiences. It does not seem coincidental that they were foreigners. Loefgren was edged aside by Navarro himself. Dafert gave up trying to persuade planters to adopt more intensive farming techniques and took up the directorship of the Austrian agronomic institute. Ihering wrote an essay for the 1903 Saint Louis Exposition in which he appeared to condone the extermination of indigenes. Members of the Campinas scientific society, for whom Ihering was a less dangerous target than the landowners who were behind the massacres, then hounded him out of his directorship. Ihering, feeling disgraced, abandoned his Brazilian citizenship and retreated to European exile. The incident did, at least, help bring about the formation of the Indian Protection Service, a task that the republic had ignored for more than twenty years. Derby's superiors treated his policies and his person so ignominiously that he committed suicide. These incidents were a sign that the defense of the Brazilian natural patrimony would not be readily entrusted to outsiders, no matter how competent.[48]

Clearly, forest conservation could not be implanted by foreigners, even well-intentioned, energetic, and long-resident foreigners. A native generation of scientists and activists would have to emerge. This would indeed occur, amid the postwar crisis and breakdown of the positivist republic. This time the conservationist proposals, influenced by a growing ideology of statism and social intervention, would be clearly and determinedly political. Meanwhile, demands upon the resources of the Atlantic Forest were growing: If government action could achieve for it a respite, it would be none too soon.

11

Industrial Nomadism, Predatory Industrialism

O fogo enriquece os pais e deixa na miséria os filhos.

Fire enriches the parents and leaves the children in penury.

LUIZ PEREIRA BARRETO

The region of the Atlantic Forest continued, in the first half of the twentieth century, to experience rapid human population growth, and this remained the principal cause of accelerated forest destruction. The "grandiose line of assault on the primitive forest" each year gained hundreds of thousands of recruits. Between 1900 and 1950, the population of the Southeast, including the broad-leaved forest region of Paraná, grew from roughly 7 million to 22 million. By midcentury a distinct "pioneer front" no longer existed, even though sizable patches of what may have been undisturbed forest still stood here and there. This sudden decisive defeat of the forest had been inevitable, because farming was in most places carried on as before, with primary-forest burning followed sooner or later by cattle pasture. As the last stands of accessible primary forest were cleared, some farmers did indeed take up the plow at last, but these experiments in intensive cultivation were not sufficient to offset losses in natural fertility, as forest humus leached and eroded away. The yields of many crops, therefore, began to decline, and the demand for secondary as well as primary woodlands intensified.[1]

A regional economy dynamized by exports stimulated population growth. The inflow of European and Japanese worker-families, attracted to the coffee and cotton plantations of São Paulo and Paraná, dwindled in the depression of the 1930s, but migrants from the impoverished Brazilian Northeast and the overcrowded Southeast inundated the work force thereafter. While Brazil's population tripled from 1900 to 1950, that of São Paulo quadrupled and that of Paraná grew nearly six-and-a-half-fold. The forest became more accessible than ever to the markets of the city and the world: By midcentury the region was crisscrossed by 21,500 kilometers of railroads and 166,000 kilometers of roads. Population pressed ever more heavily on the forest, for domestic and industrial uses, for recreation and transport. One of the poignant signs of the times was the São Paulo State law (of 1927, but one of many dating back to colonial times) that forbade *balões*: During the weeks of Saint John's and Saint Joseph's days large paper balloons containing suspended wads of wax were lighted, heating the air inside and lifting them into the sky. The sight of dozens, hundreds, of luminous balões floating up into the still, wintry night is thrilling—and also frightening, because the danger of fire from these fragile, flaming globes, especially in the dry month of June, is very great. That law, and many thereafter to the same effect, were neither respected nor enforced; they did not "take," as they say, and balloons, though less common, still threaten suburban woodlands.

The usurpation of public lands on these farthest limits of the Atlantic Forest was, to the very end, a murderous business. "Land soaked in blood is good land," one successful dealer in real estate remarked. The cadavers were mostly poor men's—hired gunslingers and small farmers. The native survivors of the last, brutal ambuscades were rounded up by the Indian Protection Service, secularized successor to the empire's Capuchin missionaries. They were placed in a few tiny reserves, way stations to "acculturation" and extinction. The courts and legislatures then bestowed clear titles on the claim jumpers. The Brazilian state thus carried on, in the region of the Atlantic Forest, its heinous tradition of responsibility abdicated and villainy rewarded.[2]

The purpose of this final generation of claim jumpers was novel: It was not to establish great estates but instead to subdivide their claims into lots for sale on installments to all comers. This was characteristic of northern Espírito Santo, westernmost São Paulo, and northern and western Paraná. Of the land companies, the Northern Paraná Land Company, organized in London in 1925, was the best known and, indeed, came to be respected and admired. Its partners, led by Simon Fraser, Lord Lovat, bought 13,600 square kilometers from the state and from private owners. Tribal peoples still occupied some of this area, and there were also numerous claimants and squatters. The company formed a private police force, which, it has been claimed, did not operate differently from the gunslingers hired by less fastidious developers. The company ran a rail line along this vast holding, laying out a town every hundred kilometers. It sold thousands of rural lots, presumed suitable for coffee, to hopeful small farmers before it was obliged by the cash-strapped British government to sell out during World War II to Brazilian capitalists.[3]

The Northern Paraná company required—before any Brazilian forest code had been written—that the purchasers of its lots maintain 10 percent of their area in woodland. It does not appear, however, that the company enforced this contractual stipulation. The successor Brazilian owners established three forest reserves under an experienced forester, but these amounted to a mere 17 square kilometers, nothing more than tree nurseries for beautifying the towns. In 1975 and 1981 the company burned and cleared two large unsold tracts, the last sizable ones in its domain, totaling 140 square kilometers, to plant pasture and sugarcane. The purchasers themselves soon subdivided their holdings into parcels averaging less than 10 hectares each. Many of these *minifundia* were soon rendered treeless. The shift to smallholding thus modified the tactics, but not the strategy, of the attack on the forest. If anything, the removal of forest cover under this novel regime of undersized, undercapitalized smallholdings was very likely quicker and more thorough.

The cities of the Southeast, meanwhile, multiplied their commercial, political, and financial functions and acquired significant manufacturing capacity. Commerce and industry craved the raw materials of the Atlantic Forest. Less commonly would timber be burned carelessly to fertilize errant patches of maize or beans. By midcentury the energetic and material resources of the remaining forest were valuable stocks in trade. For the most part, merchants and manufacturers of these "modern" sectors acted no more conservatively than had the caboclos, colonists, and planters. This was a period of miserly inputs of capital and technique into raw material exploitation, an age of what one agronomist has called "industrial nomadism."[4]

It is likely that the great majority of the inhabitants of the region of the Atlantic Forest looked upon these transformations with complaisance, even satisfaction. Nearly all of those scientists and public figures who adopted conservationist positions despaired of the average citizen's indifference or hostility toward the natural environment. "Among us," said one speaker at a conference in Minas Gerais in 1924,

> null is the love for our forests, null the comprehension of what
> they represent as an economic factor, and null the comprehension
> of the unhappy consequences that flow from their impoverishment
> and of the horror that would result from their complete destruc-
> tion. To fortify the sentiment [of conservation] is a measure of
> pressing necessity.

What concerned city inhabitants more than conservation was the expansion and prosperity of the export trade that, directly or indirectly, provided their livelihood. Expressions of sympathy for the living environment that occasionally emerged from their ranks, especially from their elected representatives, seem abstract and sterile, admonitions directed to no one in particular, or at any rate not to anyone with the power to modify social behavior. There appeared a strain of children's literature designed to instill reverence for trees; like the municipal tree nurseries founded in various places at the time, its concern was for the replanting of town squares and avenues. Arbor Day came to be celebrated in some public schools, for the edification of children. One commentator complained that sometimes coffee trees were planted on these occasions, a practice he complained would be like eulogizing chickens on a day given to the celebration of wildlife.[5]

Conservationist arguments were often based on nothing more than impressionistic observations, which pro-developmentalists confronted with impressionistic observations of their own. The widely held belief that forest clearing had reduced rainfall, increased temperature extremes, and extended the dry season thus came to be a subject of extended controversy. Two of its opponents were distinguished naturalists: Âlvaro da Silveira, a Mineiro botanist, and João Barbosa Rodrigues, director of the Botanical Garden of Rio de Janeiro. The resulting public debate was probably the first on an ecological issue. Although neither side possessed convincing evidence, conventional wisdom was not shaken. Even planters showed signs of unease: In 1908 the National Agricultural Society, fearing that droughts caused by deforestation would bring about the collapse of coffee cultivation, passed a resolution recommending countermeasures.[6]

Upon their forests members of the Brazilian elite projected uncomfortably their ambiguities concerning their society and their culture. In an age of triumphant European and North American imperialism, they managed a weak, indebted state whose disease-ridden, malnourished, uneducated citizenry they could barely tax and had little hope of mobilizing, should they be faced with war. How could they not wonder whether they suffered inherent flaws, the result of the admixture of African and Native American races, whom the imperialists despised? And might not their deficiencies be induced by the tropical climate? How then could the flora and fauna of such a region be judged equal to those of Europe and North America?

These were fears repelled by Afonso Celso de Assis Figueiredo, intimate of the departed emperor and writer of one of the most frequently reprinted books of the early twentieth century, *Porque Me Ufano do Meu Paiz—Why I Take Pride in My Country,* subtitled in English "Right or Wrong, My Country." His country's resources he proclaimed inexhaustible, its natural attractions the most splendid and inspiring, its forests the most diverse, the richest in medicinal plants, endowed with the strongest and handsomest woods, and freest of dangerous beasts of all the tropical world.

But Assis Figueiredo's intent was to promote the liberal civic virtues. He stood Social Darwinism on its head, reading in the biotic diversity of Brazilian forests a "living democracy" that

> consists in the continual struggle for liberty, for air and for light. There presides over this democracy perfect equality. No family monopolizes a zone with the exclusion of other families or groups. The most diverse species vegetate conjointly, fraternizing, entwining each other. Thus the variety in unity, multiple and diverse manifestations of the beautiful.

It is clear from its context that this is an appeal for racial and social harmony, a message apparently lost upon his readers, who digested only the sugar coating, the appeal to pride, and so Assis Figueiredo has been remembered merely as the leading exponent of *ufanismo*, the Brazilian variety of jingoism.[7]

Other writers expressed openly a distaste for the nature that had been allotted to Brazil, so unlike that of far-off desired Europe, where humans were not overwhelmed by

> an orgy of forms, an unimaginable surfeit of climbing plants, a tragic disorder of trunks, of branches, of carpets of greenery and parasites, a mortal combat among trees and species, an irresistible tending toward air and light. . . . In the South American forests one sees man imprisoned in the labyrinth of demented vegetation.

The temperate forest, in contrast, offered "an aspect more grandiose than the tropical forests, where the overabundance of superfluities destroys all regularity." How unlike the Mediterranean, "the loveliest and happiest land, the true garden of refreshment. . . . The contemplation of the shores of this admirable sea moves one more than the fantastical opulence of the forests of the Tropic."[8]

Attempts were duly made to replace native flora and fauna with wild European species. The mayor of Rio de Janeiro caused house sparrows to be imported and set loose in his handsome new avenues, a final touch to the carefully copied Parisian facades. Introduced into the wild were song and game birds, freshwater fish, and mollusks, by public officials or anonymous immigrants, out of hubris and nostalgia, or simply by accident. Luckily, none of the intruders from colder climes succeeded except in completely humanized landscapes, and even there their lease was precarious. Even the persistent, noxious little sparrows were confronted by assorted competitors and restricted to a straitened niche. European racists worried that they themselves might not thrive in the tropic zone. In the 1930s geographers were sent from Hitler's universities to study the progress of the German colonies in Espírito Santo, spreading northward toward Bahia from their homesteads in the hills behind Vitória. Their findings were too embarrassing to publish under the Reich: The third generation of Aryans, having abandoned the plow for the hoe and the firebrand, was as impoverished as its mestizo neighbors. For the Brazilian elite, the distress of these invitees, whose culture and genes they had supposed might improve the natives, even as the Angus and Hereford bulls they imported might improve their creole cattle, was in a way consoling.[9]

Perhaps the rusticity of the caboclos was the best evidence of their strength: Abandoned and oppressed by a government that refused to recognize their right to land, they survived nonetheless, multiplied, and confronted the forest that terrified immigrants and city folk. The sturdy caboclo was the hero of the essayist Alberto Torres, who presented a conservationist argument from a perspective quite different from scientists like Alberto Loefgren and Hermann von Ihering. Torres, perhaps the most influential political thinker of the Republic, was a critic of the drive to export that exalted foreign values and attitudes. He considered it improvident and opportunistic, securing immediate gains at the cost of future generations. Indeed, he complained, the speculation that accompanied the spread of coffee, like earlier waves of economic expansion, had stimulated the itinerancy that interfered with the accumulation "of knowledge of the means and processes appropriate to the exploitation of our nature." In Brazil the only thought was of expansion, "to accomplish the task, as vain as it is illusory, of 'greatness' and of economic emulation—dreams of the phantasists of the materialist millennium." "Our forests," he complained, are "so frivolously devastated in this craze to go on extending populations of adventurers and capitalist enterprises, which spread like destroying plagues over all the land, without love for the soil or interest in the human future."[10]

Torres was possibly the first to employ the term conservation in the sense it had acquired in the United States. This was in his proposal for a new constitution, published in 1913, that included a provision for "defense of the soil and natural resources of the country." He thought conservation "fundamental, extraordinary." He was convinced in fact that "the hygronomic problem" was the single most important question confronting the country and that watershed protection, reforestation, and irrigation were of a higher priority than roads and railroads. He called for the "repair of ruined areas, concentration of populations in zones already opened to cultivation, the educating of men to utilize them and make them bear fruit, improving their value." Torres's conservationism was a way of resolving the conflict between his almost instinctive nativism and ideas originating in Europe of biological and geographical determinism. Conservation, along with investments in human capital, might overthrow European conceptions of the inappropriateness of the tropics for civilization and of Brazilian racial inferiority. Conservation, thus, was a strategy that might help to stave off European and American expansionism:

> Civilization has a duty to conserve the unexploited resources of the earth, reserves destined for future generations, and to defend those which are in production against improvident exploitation, just as it has a duty to protect all races and nationalities against forms of competition that might threaten their vital interests, as well as the security, property and prosperity of their posterity.[11]

Torres's economic nationalism and physiocratism resounded powerfully during the crises of supply and finance that Brazil experienced during World War I, a struggle that demonstrated the dangers of reliance on the blind forces of capitalist expansion. His jeremiads were remembered by the revolutionaries who, a decade later, were to overthrow the opportunistic Republic.

But the opportunists were quite capable of weaving their own myths, of heroic *desbravadores*—tamers—of the wilderness, "that ugly, short, uneven and unhealthy woods," as Edmundo Navarro de Andrade, eager to replace it with eucalyptus, described the forest of the Paulista northwest. Forests were increasingly coming to be characterized as unhealthy; their destruction, as an act of public sanitation. These were signs of "initiative" and evidence of the fullest exercise of "liberty." Monteiro Lobato, a major literary figure of the time, delighted in the speed with which the native forest was obliterated and a homogeneous landscape put in its place. The Paulistas had never admired, he said, the "august beauty of the jequitibás, their branches murmuring like the ocean, nor the grave aspect of millenarian perobas." Their "ferocious ambition prefers, to the beauty of natural disorder, the aligned beauty of the tree that yields gold. We confess it: The one spectacle equals the other." Even though, he admitted, the "Green Wave of Coffee"—the often-repeated phrase he originated—undulating to the horizon, "produces only at the cost of the earth's blood. It is . . . insatiable of humus."[12]

It was not on mythical terrain, however, that the struggle for forest preservation was contested. At issue were private property rights—because nearly all the public forests had already been usurped. Conservationists like Lourenço Baeta Neves and F. S. Rodrigues de Brito therefore advocated limits on private-forest exploitation. "The owner of the land is only a steward of the soil, that was entrusted to him by the past generations; . . . territorial property must have a social application, in attending to the collective interest." Ary Fontenelle suggested that property rights were relative: Owners had rights to water as it flowed through streams on their property; weren't those who cut their forest upstream harming those rights? In 1904 the state legislature of Rio de Janeiro debated, although it did not pass, a rural code that would have required private owners to petition their county councils for permission to clear their woodlands. Hunting would have required licenses. The bill also forbade logging in public forests and affirmed the state's competence to conserve forests and promote their regrowth. But measures such as this, which would have restored colonial policies, were anathema to landowners. Navarro was one of the most vigorous opponents of such proposals. If the state lacked the funds to expropriate private holdings, so much the more reason to deny it the power to legislate on land use. High land prices demonstrated the degree of potential loss to the owner. "To oblige a proprietor to conserve his forest, preventing him from exploiting it as he pleases, is vexatious, violent and brutal." Only the protection of watersheds (like the Cantareira reserve he directed) and the prevention of soil erosion could justify limits on the otherwise absolute rights of private property.[13]

To some, it appeared incongruous that the state asserted the power to prohibit the planting of coffee trees, as it did during the crisis of 1901–1907, but forswore any responsibility for the primary forests customarily cleared to plant coffee. To others, burning forest for coffee was acceptable, because coffee trees were of such great value, while only the poor caboclo was to be condemned, for practicing slash-and-burn on lands that might otherwise bear coffee. Ihering countered Navarro's arguments directly: State lands were being alienated for 15 to 20 percent of their market value, bestowing windfalls on speculators and impoverishing the state. Loggers, furthermore, were cutting trees on public land, unimpeded by any law and subject to no rents. He therefore proposed the establishment of a federal forest service to inventory forested public lands, prevent incursions into them by squatters, and regulate concessions to timber companies. The state, already despoiled of most of its forested land, would buy back forest and biotic reserves with the proceeds of a land tax that would also have the salutary effect of moderating prevailing land prices. Ideas such as these may have been the real reason why Ihering lost favor among the state's elite.[14]

Increased attention to the condition of the forests obliged the authorities to begin to survey the country's remaining resources. A forest map produced in 1910 by Gonzaga de Campos for the Ministry of Agriculture estimated that the four Southeast states (São Paulo, Rio de Janeiro, Minas Gerais, and Espírito Santo, excluding Paraná) still contained 500,000 square kilometers of forest, an evidently exaggerated figure that apparently included secondary formations and wooded savannas. Surveys of the state of São Paulo were most frequent and careful. Its 1905 agricultural census, which included half of the state's land area, found only 41,640 square kilometers of primary forest, 34 percent of the area censused. The national censuses of 1920, 1940, and 1950 and the São Paulo census of 1934 included expanded private areas but showed a declining ratio of wooded land on these holdings. The 1950 farm census of São Paulo recorded only 27,705 square kilometers of forest—no longer discriminated as primary or secondary—only 15 percent of the area surveyed. For the state as a whole, it was estimated by Mauro Victor that the period 1920 to 1934 witnessed the most rapid destruction of forest in the state—more than 3,000 square kilometers a year—and that by midcentury the forest, which had originally covered 85 percent of the state, was reduced to 18 percent. An estimate of 1947 for the four Southeast states showed only 168,000 square kilometers of forest remaining, a probable loss of about 50 percent since 1910. At the same time, only 60,000 square kilometers remained of Paraná broad-leaved forest, a loss of more than a third since 1910.[15]

In Minas Gerais, deforestation was most advanced, the legacy of gold hunting and iron working and a larger population. The 1920 census found that in Minas Gerais, forest covered only 20 percent of surveyed private properties. The state government in 1923 estimated that 41 percent of the forest remained in the East region and 22 percent in the Zona da Mata; these were the two districts that had been originally nearly entirely forest covered. The diary of the botanist Frederico Carlos Hoehne's 1927 excursion in the coffee-growing South region is a depressing account of dilapidation—towns founded in the midst of forest where none was any longer to be seen from horizon to horizon. Older residents often directed him to "virgin forest" stands that no longer existed—cut down since these pioneers had last visited them. He found that the meaning of the term "virgin forest" had significantly degraded—often it referred to surviving stands that had, indeed, never been burned but that had been used for shorter or longer periods as logging reserves and therefore contained only isolated old-growth specimens. According to other informed observers, the South region's woodlands, which once extended over perhaps half its territory, were, by the time of Hoehne's excursion, reduced to 21 percent. A 1922 report of the Ministry of Agriculture confirms that deforestation in the state of Rio de Janeiro had proceeded even farther than in Minas Gerais or São Paulo. Meanwhile, Espírito Santo, the southern panhandle of Bahia, and the broad-leaved forest region of Paraná were experiencing only the beginning of incursions into their forests.[16]

By the first decade of the century, in the prime coffee-growing areas a reversal had occurred in land values that had held steady since the beginning of plantation clearing. Although in the nineteenth century forested land had generally sold for half the price of cleared land, reflecting the cost of clearing, now forested land cost more than cleared land. In eighteen counties surveyed in the Zona da Mata of Minas Gerais in 1905, primary forest was valued 70 percent above cleared land and 220 percent above pasture. The price of primary forest in each of these counties was related not to its absolute scarcity but to the value of cleared land, suggesting that the factors determining its price were the county's soil fertility and climate, hence its potential for coffee growing. The implication of these changing ratios is that, at some early point in settlement, there was an advantage in withholding forest from the market but that this advantage faded fairly soon—the very last patches of primary forest would not continually increase in value but would accompany the market for cleared land. Speculation in these patches was thus unpromising, and therefore so were the long-run prospects for their survival.[17]

The market for coffee was a subject of considerable unease after 1900, as coffee planting began to outrun the growth of world demand—the Brazilian Southeast counted at least 1.5 billion trees by then—provoking repeated price-support schemes. The crises of world war and depression had severe consequences for trade, and by the early 1920s customers in the major markets had reached their limit of daily consumption, marking slower growth in consumption thereafter. Despite these alarms, the incorporation of frontier land neither ceased nor slowed. As long as it was believed that primary-forest soils best suited the coffee plant, speculators would advance inexorably toward the extreme limits of the Atlantic Forest to the west and southwest, until the last of it was burned and cleared. In the 1930s cotton for a time took the place of coffee as the major export of a number of counties, and cotton and sugar continued to be important staples of the internal market. But the association of coffee with primary forest remained in the Southeast the decisive factor in accelerating the advance of the agricultural frontier.

In South Bahia, meanwhile, a new plantation front opened, as the cocoa plant, transferred from the Amazon, encountered adequate soils, and growers gained a considerable share of the U.S. market. Some 1,000 square kilometers must have been wrested from the piedmont zone centered on Ilhéus by the mid-1930s. This was a somewhat more benign form of clearing than that practiced in the coffee zone. On many of the estates a certain number of the primary-forest trees were left standing, providing growing conditions like those of the plant's native understory habitat. This system, called *cabroca*, lengthened the productive life-span of the grove and may have reduced the danger of pests and parasites. It did not, however, accompany a more benign work regime. Although there were many middling and small holdings, most of the crop was produced on estates. Most of their laborers were migrant, because cocoa did not require year-round care. Recruited from an even more impoverished Northeast, their living conditions were miserable. Rarely would they return to the same estate, and meager were the savings they brought back to their hometowns.[18]

Primary-forest stands were subjected to extreme pressures of extraction that no longer resembled the subsistence activities of tribal peoples or caboclos. Although the traditional hunter's custom of stripping naked before entering the wood was still observed in remote areas as late as the 1920s, most hunters were no longer the sort that experienced a mystical identification with their prey. Indeed, the new breed destroyed the hunting stocks of indigenes and caboclos. Now they were immigrant coffee tenants, innocently putting food on the table, no doubt, but heedless of the necessity of maintaining animal stocks. Farmers who would not trouble to dynamite stumps to make possible the use of the plow found it profitable to fling dynamite into the rivers to catch fish. Because of this practice, the restocking of rivers was one of the urgent tasks that had been set for the São Paulo Forest Service. Game and bird hunting became a sport practiced by the middle classes of São Paulo and Rio de Janeiro, facilitated by the increasing use of automobiles and improved roadways. Local laws against hunting in breeding seasons went unenforced. Hunters were accused of setting fires to drive animals or merely to spite landowners who refused them passage. Observers found hunters shooting animals "just for fun." Bird mortality was said to have greatly increased along with the ubiquitousness of discarded inner tubes, appropriated by small boys for slingshots.[19]

Wildlife became the object of a considerable domestic trade. Songbirds were extremely popular—few were the town markets without their bird vendors and few the households without caged birds hanging in the windows. Birds were netted on Comprida Island in winter, when they descended from the cold highlands, killed, pickled, and sold at Iguape and Cananéia. City inhabitants also appreciated wild plants—orchids, ferns, and bromeliads—gathered in primary forests, and they consumed hearts of palm from several palm species, wild fruits, and innumerable medicinals. It was reported to the Brazilian Association of Pharmacists that, because the majority of medicinal plants formerly collected in the wild had grown extremely rare, other plants had been given their names in the market-place. (This may be a point worth considering by modern ethnobotanists who seek "traditional" folk remedies.) It is unfortunate that a center formed in 1917 by Hoehne at the Butantã Institute to domesticate medici-nals was several times transferred to other research institutions without ever finding adequate support. Rural people also extracted vines, bamboo, and rush for various purposes. The garlic tree was sometimes burned in place for its ashes, which were used to make soap. Small trees were cut down for wattle, fencing, crates, tool handles, posts, and clogs.[20]

Extractivism for export did not disappear in the twentieth century but instead gained momentum. The orchid trade continued to boom, and the trade in bird plumage and pelts, especially hummingbirds, was extensive. It was estimated that before World War I, 400,000 hummingbird skins and 360,000 skins of other birds, mainly egrets, had been sent abroad in a short space of time. There were no laws against these exports. Buyers of pelts and feathers advertised in the newspapers of small towns along the pioneer front. At midcentury commercial hunters in São Paulo were paying taxes on nearly 250,000 animal pelts a year. Evaders of game licensing may have doubled that amount.[21]

More effective in transforming unburned stands of primary forest, however, was selective removal of timber. By the late 1920s, gasoline-fueled trucks and portable steam-powered sawmills made economic an overland trade in hardwoods. The largest, most valuable trees, which usu-ally remained standing after the burn, would formerly have been left to rot in place or cut down, piled up, and burned again. Now, in São Paulo, at least, where demand was strongest, they were sold. In the valley of the Ribeira River, it was reported, Italian immigrants bought land merely to fell and clear its timber. When the best was removed, they sold out, per-haps to charcoal makers, and moved on. The potential market for hard-woods is very likely the reason why the relative prices of cleared and for-ested land reversed during this period. Timber sales could easily equal the cost of clearing. Logging of primary-forest species was extremely selective, so that relatively little of the forest biomass was exploited, and most of it continued to be burned. Primary forests that served as woodlots were gradually despoiled of their most valuable specimens and then of those less merchantable. Trail cutting, tree falls, and draglines pulled by oxen dam-aged many standing trees, until at last the degraded lots were burned for farming.[22]

Total hardwood demand is difficult to calculate, in the absence of better statistics. The scale of the trade is suggested in records of the Sorocabana Railway, which, in the 1920s and 1930s, expanded into extreme northwestern São Paulo State. In those years it loaded an average of 70,000 tons a year of timber—surpassing in value its receipts from coffee. A consumption of 0.2 cubic meters of hardwood per capita per year may be estimated for the first half of the twentieth century in the Southeast. Hardwoods of the Atlantic Forest entered very little into international trade, although, far inland, along the Paraná Valley, the remotest extension of the Atlantic Forest, timber companies had begun at the turn of the century to strip the forest of cedro and imbuia trees—lighter woods that could be floated downriver to Buenos Aires. This trade reached significant volume only in the 1950s. Araucaria, a timber similar to pine, was found in fairly dense stands in a broad swath of highlands running from Rio Grande do Sul to Paraná and was becoming at about the same time a significant export.[23]

The implications of all these extractive activities is that relict plots of primary forest were become less pristine, less complex, and less populous. Latter-day studies of forest "island" biodiversity in the Amazon put in doubt the degree of "wildness" that can be attributed to forest patches, even quite large ones preserved from extractive pressures. What could be said for those that were constantly rummaged through for every sort of useful creature and plant?

The railroad brought cattle to market more quickly and therefore may have reduced the need for forest clearing along the numerous former cattle trails that had extended all the way to Rio de Janeiro. The immense *invernadas*—wintering pastures—of the suburbs, where trail-starved steers were fattened before slaughter, were turned over to dairy cattle or occupied by the growing cities. But the urban demand for beef was now much greater, and cattle still had to be fattened at the end of long marches that brought them to the railheads. There—at Barretos in São Paulo and at Monte Carmelo, Curvelo, Patrocínio, and Vila Brasília, in Minas Gerais—more than a million head were stocked, implying the burning of some 2,500 square kilometers of primary forest in order to plant artificial pasture to feed these animals at the end of the yearly drives.[24]

Brazil entered the Industrial Age extremely deficient in one of its prerequisites, fossil hydrocarbon fuels. Like Sweden and Italy, Brazil was delayed in the fuller application of industrial techniques until the invention of the electric dynamo. The abundant rainfall of the region of the Atlantic Forest and its rugged topography offered vast hydroelectric potential, which began to be exploited at the turn of the century. But hydroelectric power was at the time difficult to apply economically to many requirements that in other countries were satisfied by fossil fuels. Coffee exports did not earn enough to import great quantities of coal or oil, much of which was applied, in any case, to maritime transport. Brazilian industry therefore continued to depend for fuel primarily on its immense standing stock of native wood resources.[25]

At the start of the twentieth century, the stock remaining in the southeastern region of the Atlantic Forest still extended over approximately 390,000 square kilometers. This was an energy reserve of immense proportions. An average hectare—a difficult and somewhat elusive concept—of primary forest may be estimated at 400 cubic meters of wood available for fuel. The woods of this forest exhibited a very high specific gravity, perhaps 750 kilograms per cubic meter on average, which would have been capable of liberating energy equivalent to 400 kilograms of coal. Thus the fuel resources of the Atlantic Forest at the turn of the century were equivalent to more than 6.2 billion tons of coal. Had the turn-of-the-century inhabitants of the Atlantic Forest region been consuming fuel at the same rate as their industrialized English contemporaries—that is, 4.7 tons of coal per capita per year—they could have fueled their economy with the contents of their primary forest for nearly 200 years.[26]

The primary forest was not, from the forester's point of view, a renewable resource, in that the secondary formation that succeeded it was much less dense and was composed of woods of about half the energy value. Nevertheless, these stands of capoeira were traditionally the primary source of domestic firewood. About 20 cubic meters of this wood per capita per year—nine times what Brazilians in fact consumed—would have assured the turn-of-the-century population of the Atlantic Forest region a rate of energy consumption equal to that of the English. Each hectare of native capoeira added about that much wood annually, so a permanent reserve of 70,000 square kilometers in the Southeast, less than 7 percent of its area, might have supplied abundant fuel reserves and ended pressure on primary reserves.

Evidently, this modest reserve was not arranged. It still existed in São Paulo in 1905, according to the farm census of that year, when 1.3 million hectares of secondary forest were found on private holdings surveyed. This implied a renewable energy reserve of 26 million cubic meters a year, or 11.3 cubic meters for each Paulista, equivalent of only half the consumption of the English but nearly five times more than the state's inhabitants then consumed.

Firewood for domestic consumption was the bulkiest item in the supply of cities. Early in the century the capital came to be supplied with it largely by rail, as local woodlands disappeared—the Paulista Railroad transported 16,000 tons of firewood a year from 1911 to 1915 and 30,000 tons a year from 1916 to 1920. City wood consumption annoyed some elite observers, of physiocratic bent and prejudiced against city dwellers, whom they saw as escapees from the plantations and a drag on the export sector. Nevertheless, firewood was a stock-in-trade of failing landlords, some of whom were chopping down in desperation their senescent coffee trees.[27]

In São Paulo, domestic consumption of firewood may have declined slightly in the first half of the twentieth century, from about 2.4 to 2.0 cubic meters per capita. However, industrial uses expanded sharply. Consumption for process heat and mechanical power grew from about 0.4 cubic meters to about 2.2 cubic meters per capita by 1950. It appears that such traditional users of firewood as brick, tile, and lime makers continued to employ traditional methods, while rapid growth of population and income per capita greatly increased demand. Breweries and distilleries probably ranked in second place as consumers of wood fuel, followed by sugar mills and refineries, cement factories, tanneries, dyeworks, coffee roasters, manioc processors, bakeries, and factories making soap, candles, food preserves, matches, ceramics, lard, glassware, and hats.[28]

No single industry had a greater impact on firewood reserves than iron and steel making. In the 1920s integrated mills were built in Minas Gerais that employed blast furnaces and were designed to be charged with charcoal. By 1950 there were twelve of these mills, and they had produced, since their installation, 4.2 million tons of pig iron. The mills bought their charcoal from itinerant contractors, who felled forest on leased land and cooked their wood for the most part in traditional earthen mounds. The yield of these *medas* was no better than one unit of charcoal by volume for three of wood. The mills themselves required 4.5 cubic meters of charcoal to produce a ton of pig iron. The forests in the area of the mills—some of it savanna, some of it secondary rain forest—yielded, according to local specialists, about 200 cubic meters of suitable woods per hectare. Thus, by midcentury, these mills had caused 2,650 square kilometers of woodland to be cleared.[29]

Meanwhile, in São Paulo, an important metalworking sector was growing up, some of it employing imported pig iron—furnaces, forges, rolling mills, stamping mills, boilermakers, and foundries, in addition to the traditional smithies. By 1942 they were transforming 30,000 tons of iron a year. Although some of the furnaces were electric powered, most required wood charges, which they obtained in the same manner as the mills of Minas Gerais. By 1950 total annual demand for woodland by the metalworking industries in these two states and in Rio de Janeiro may have amounted to 140 square kilometers.[30]

Firewood also fed steam engines, which supplied power in many factories as well as a small fraction of electric power. In 1920, perhaps 30 percent of the stationary engines in Paulista industry were steam engines, most of them stoked with wood. This estimate includes sawmills; sugar mills; cotton gins; coffee, maize, and rice hullers; flour mills; and textile mills. As late as 1950, despite the competition of the internal combustion engine and the expansion of the electric power grid, 11 percent of São Paulo's engines were steam powered and wood fired.[31]

Railroads burned even more wood than the iron and steel industry. Despite the use of a certain amount of imported coal and the beginning of electrification in the 1920s, railroads depended on wood for more than half their energy supply. By 1950, just as electric and diesel locomotives began to replace the steam fleet, regional railroads were carrying about 6 billion ton-kilometers and consuming about 12.4 million cubic meters of firewood annually, the equivalent of some 620 square kilometers of forest.[32]

Government estimates of the consumption of firewood are suspect: Official inspection of this dispersed and shadowy business was difficult and perhaps even dangerous. More telling is the number of persons occupied in wood cutting and charcoal making, which in 1950 amounted, in São Paulo, to 76,000 workers, or 7.5 percent of the rural labor force. As late as 1975, 10 percent of the rural labor force of Minas Gerais was extracting wood and charcoal. It was estimated that, in 1948, wood and charcoal represented 79 percent of all energy consumed in Brazil—although considerably less than that percentage of energy was effectively applied, because wood burning was decidedly inefficient. In the Southeast, wood and charcoal burning was certainly not less than 50 percent of fuel consumption, despite a significant amount of hydroelectric generation and the region's improved capacity to import fossil fuels.[33]

Nearly all of this wood came from native forests. Furthermore, commercial charcoal makers, unlike domestic firewood scavengers, preferred primary forest because the trees with the densest wood were to be found there and because these produced the highest yields and provided the most carbon-rich charcoal.[34]

Despite Navarro's proselytizing, tree farming was by midcentury still extremely limited. In São Paulo, where the Paulista Railroad and the state Forest Service created their own reserves and sold eucalyptus seed to farmers, there were by 1928 at most 30 million trees, possibly 250 square kilometers, in the entire state. By midcentury their extent had increased to perhaps 1,000 square kilometers, much inferior to the yearly rate of deforestation. The Paulista Railroad remained the largest planter, with 24,000 hectares of reserves. By 1957 these forests had yielded 6.6 million cubic meters of wood; nearly 10 percent of this, however, was from native forest that had been cleared to plant the eucalyptus. Not all of the wood had been used for fuel, apparently, because eucalyptus by the 1930s commanded a higher price as raw material for paper pulp and construction, and the company was selling more of its wood as lumber than it consumed as firewood. In 1935 the Paulista Railroad burned 540,000 cubic meters of firewood, but its reserves supplied less than a fifth of that amount. The rest was sold to the company by contractors. Some of this may have been eucalyptus, planted at the railroad's urging, but it is very likely that the company bought wood derived from native forest as well. Thus even the Paulista Railroad, held up as the model of reforestation, engaged in far less planting than was necessary to supply its current, much less its future, needs.[35]

The Paulista Railroad had few imitators, most of whom seemed to be planting only experimentally and mostly "to give satisfaction to the government." Of the other railroads, only the Mogiana, the Sorocabana, and the Central established reserves, none very large. In the 1930s two São Paulo paper companies began large-scale planting of pine in order to produce wood pulp, and, during the extreme fossil-fuel crisis of World War II, a few manufacturers, including the Matarazzo conglomerate, initiated some further planting. By 1930 perhaps 4.5 million trees had been planted in Minas Gerais—only 37 square kilometers. Reserves of a hundred or so hectares each were established in the 1920s by the Morro Velho gold-mining company and by the Siderúrgica Mineira iron and steel mill. The Belgo-Mineira mill started eucalyptus planting when it discovered, to its alarm, that lands it had clear-cut in the 1920s had not grown back to forest as expected, but to grass. In 1959 its reserve was still not in production, and it burned 450,000 cubic meters of native wood—22 square kilometers—a year. Replanting was thus insignificant compared to future requirements. A German forester who carried out a survey for the Ministry of Agriculture testified in the Chamber of Deputies that São Paulo alone should have been replanting 700 square kilometers a year. Between 1911 and 1953, it was estimated, only 3 hectares had been replanted for every 10,000 that had been cleared! Evidently native Atlantic forest formations, by midcentury, still provided almost all the Southeast's wood fuel.[36]

World War II caused an intense crisis in wood supply. Imported coal and petroleum were rationed, in the face of increasing demand. Diesel and gasoline engines were shut down, and abandoned steam engines were repaired and put to use again. Charcoal-burning gas generators were attached to cars and trucks. In São Paulo, the price of firewood rose by a factor of ten. Federal railways were required to double their tariffs for charcoal, in order to stimulate local forest planting—a measure whose only effect was to increase fuel prices. The Central Railroad soon exhausted its meager eucalyptus reserves. This company was also hard put to find suitable material for crossties, especially for 1.6-meter gauge. Crossties had been drawn, customarily, from the forests that were cut down as the rail line expanded. But the slower expansion of the railroads in the 1930s led to the use of less-resistant tree species and to the purchase of crosstie timber from the farthest rail frontier—Espírito Santo and northern Paraná. Despite their distress, the railroads did not preserve their crossties with creosote.[37]

Even the wartime crisis failed to persuade private landowners to plant trees on a large scale. The Belgo-Mineira mill, one of the largest users, possessed 1,500 square kilometers of native forest. The company evidently did not intend to replant on a large scale until that reserve was exhausted. The increasing demand for wood fuel, however, must be considered one of the factors that increased the value of forested land relative to cleared land, narrowing the gap between the cost of native and planted forest. The prospect of increasing demand, furthermore, offered planters of eucalyptus some hope of potential profits at a rate comparable to annual crops. Planters were reluctant, however, to take on the risks of a crop that was so vulnerable to fire and so uncertain in its yields—about a third of eucalyptus seedlings normally failed. Like nearly every other crop, eucalyptus turned out to be to the taste of leaf-cutter ants. Planters were still using unselected seedlings, and most eucalyptus species had still not been tested in all localities. For all these reasons, some further stimulus would be needed before widespread planting could occur.[38]

Scientists and technicians entrusted with the early conservation of public forests were unsuccessful in establishing sanctions against the waste or misuse of wood reserves. They made legislators aware of the conservation efforts of other countries in the hope that they would feel obliged to try to catch up. The model of Yellowstone National Park had inspired André Rebouças, who called as early as 1878 for national parks to be created at Sete Quedas and Iguaçu. Theodore Roosevelt's expansion of U.S. national parks and forests, his convocation of a national congress on conservation problems, and Gifford Pinchot's forest management were often referred to by statesmen as well as scientists. Curiously, neither Roosevelt nor his hosts seem to have raised the issue of conservation during his 1913 Brazil expedition, even though Hoehne accompanied him. Raphael Zon's critical reports on Brazilian forest practices were much commented on, and German, Italian, French and Austrian forest law and forestry were often cited. As experience accumulated abroad and as conservation organizations in the advanced countries sought international linkages, such as the International Forest Congress at Paris in 1913, Brazilian scientists and bureaucrats felt impelled to participate, even though Brazilian accomplishments were still embarrassingly lacking.[39]

The Republic was little inclined to husband natural resources. Loefgren's proposal, in 1900, for a federal forest code went unheeded. In 1907 state codes were debated in São Paulo and Minas Gerais. In Paraná one was adopted but never enforced. One of its authors later characterized it as "mere decoration . . . as though it never existed." Wartime fuel shortages temporarily fixed attention on conservation policy, and, in 1920, President Epitâcio Pessoa, pointing out to the Congress that Brazil was the only forested country without a forest code, pressed for the creation of a federal Forest Service. The decree implementing the service was issued, by his successor, in 1925. Alas, all that had been accomplished was to change the letterhead of the tree nursery of the federal capital; a decade later it was doing little more than passing out seedlings for street beautification. The service lacked a budget or a code to enforce, and even forests to maintain, because the Republican constitution had devolved all public lands upon the states. Exceptionally, the service did manage the forests that protected the water supply of the city of Rio de Janeiro, which had grown with the population of the capital to 500 square kilometers. The federal government called upon the states to donate some of their forested lands for the purpose of creating preserves, to no avail. The Forest Service was just beginning to sign accords with a few states to help them fund their own forest services when the Republic was overthrown.[40]

The "Revolution" of 1930 was led by Getúlio Vargas, political chief of the southernmost state of Rio Grande do Sul. His presidential campaign had been thwarted by the Republican party machines of São Paulo and Minas Gerais. The forces grouped around him exhibited inchoate and far from revolutionary principles, yet the new government, impelled by the world economic crisis, favored interventionist and centralizing measures. Encouraged by the rhetoric of elite revolutionists, elements of the middle and working classes prepared for a democratic future, free of electoral fraud, in which political parties and labor unions might freely form and compete. The collapse of external trade suggested to them that Torres had been correct in scorning the Republic's heedless exploitation of natural resources. Nationalism began to lure the middle class from liberalism and the working class from internationalism. In this atmosphere, natural resources were coming to be viewed as a collective stockpile to be employed efficiently in the nation's behalf.

Meanwhile, there had come of age a new generation of scientist-conservationists who linked their concerns and their careers with those of the emerging nation-state. Of these, the most active was Alberto José de Sampaio, director of the National Museum. Sampaio had been writing in favor of reforestation and nature reserves since 1912. In 1926 he presented a report on Brazilian forests at an international conference in Rome. He intended this report, published soon afterward in Brazil, as a prod to persuade the government to fund the Forest Service and create a corps of forest rangers. In it he took a position on state intervention in private forests which was halfway, as he put it, between Navarro and statism like that practiced in Finland. He offered a theory of historical stages in regard to forest policy, the dynamic of which was the increasing scarcity of natural forest. Brazil had emerged from the primitive epoch of clearing without replanting and was in the transition, heading toward a final stage of artificial forests, homogeneous and high yielding.[41]

Sampaio was frequently interviewed. He spoke often before civic groups and conventions and presented, at the National Museum, courses in biogeography for the public that were printed in books and newspapers. Public education was one of his major concerns, and he sponsored school programs in natural history and organized conservationist groups in Rio de Janeiro. By 1935, however, his views were evolving within the technocratic, elitist atmosphere of the Vargas government. He had come to believe in the efficacy of state power. Efficiency, in the application of conservationist measures as in other matters, depended on "technology, education and force." Force, the "guarantee of order," was effectively applied in Italy, where the forest service was militarized. Sampaio expressed aesthetic and moral, as well as practical, grounds for his conservationism: "We need to have forests, to defend forests, just for the simple reason that they are beautiful in their majesty." "Not by bread alone," he declared. His acceptance of his rural compatriots was less unreserved. Although he told his audience, echoing the social concerns of Torres, that the forests had to be protected because they were the habitat of the caboclos, the "marrow of our race," a little later he proposed that the caboclos be "called gradually to civilization," to improve their means of subsistence "and to prevent them from being the eternal factors of destruction of nature," a reference to their dependence on slash-and-burn farming.[42]

Hoehne, head of the São Paulo Botanical Institute, was another figure who gained public attention. Hoehne, primarily a taxonomist, was also interested in biogeography and ecology and pioneered ethnobotanical research. He was perhaps the first in Brazil to point out the necessity of genetic reserves. In 1927 he wrote: "That which nature created, once destroyed, can never be confected artificially and . . . in the wild forests and fields we still possess thousands and thousands of plants and animals which we do not know and which one day perhaps may become very important and useful to us." Echoing newly awakened middle-class nationalism, he lamented the "xenophilia" that caused interior towns to ornament their streets with European trees and called for reforestation with native species. In 1924 he had campaigned to save the Jabaquara forest, south of the city of São Paulo. His arguments, upholding the functionalist view of nature, foreshadowed the Vargas government's interventionism: "Man has every right to dispose of trees, as of everything that nature offers him, as he thinks best, but even so we cannot bestow rights upon private persons to the prejudice of the collectivity." Hoehne's preservationism was correspondingly functionalist: Preserving strips of native forest, he suggested, would provide habitats for birds, insects, and animals that might protect coffee trees and other crops from predators and parasites. His view of reforestation in the industrialized countries stripped them of their tutelary role: They were not model but doomed experiments. "Let these other countries serve as a lesson; having stripped their soil of their primitive and native forests, today they try to re-establish their biota and optimal conditions through natural forests, without ever succeeding."[43]

A truly engaging conservationist was Armando Magalhães Correa, perhaps the only contemporary observer of backwoods life who managed to view it both objectively and sympathetically. A professor at the National Museum, he was also a journalist and essayist. In 1932 he described in a series of articles in a Rio de Janeiro newspaper his excursions into the *sertão carioca*—the outback of the city of Rio de Janeiro. There he found, within a few kilometers of the city center, backwoodsmen who guarded the water supply and forest reserve and others who supplied the city with its charcoal, firewood, lumber, baskets, mats, clogs, ax handles, and dozens of other products and who caught its fish and shellfish. The articles, soon published in book form, displayed to the city middle class the toil that brought them their sustenance at the cost of devastating the environment of all. Correa closed with a ringing appeal for conservation, especially reforestation, hunting regulations, and wildlife refuges. His book persuaded several of the city's associations of the validity of conservationism, including civic clubs, the teachers' association, and the fishermen's unions.[44]

Before 1930, civic associations had played only a minor role in the few conservationist measures enacted, and specifically conservationist organizations had not existed. The Vargas regime much preferred technocracy to a self-activated citizenry, but the latter could not be suppressed in the reformist, innovative atmosphere of the moment. A Constituent Congress was elected that represented middle-class and, to some extent, working-class aspirations. A number of civic groups took up conservationist issues, notably the Rio de Janeiro–based Brazilian Excursionist Center, founded in 1919, whose guides had been issued forest-guard identification in the early days of the Forest Service. The Brazilian Federation for Feminine Progress took conservationist stands, probably in part because one of its leaders was Berta Lutz, another biologist at the National Museum.

Several organizations directly concerned with conservation appear to have influenced legislation of the early Vargas period—the Society of Friends of Alberto Torres, the Friends of Nature Clubs, the Geographical Society of Rio de Janeiro, and the Society of Friends of the Trees. A Society of the Friends of the Flora Brasilica was organized by Hoehne. Its 113 founding members included horticulturists and improving farmers. Hoehne principally desired to promote the publication of a new flora, but the society also agitated for biological reserves and reforestation. The staff of the National Museum formed a Society of Friends of the Museum, in effect a front, which purchased a biological reserve and lobbied for the museum. There were more than a thousand chapters of the Society of Friends of Alberto Torres in the late 1930s. They took active stands in local conservation issues and provided tools, seeds, and instruction to schools. The Society of Friends of the Trees, founded in 1931 by Sampaio, proselytized among the elite and lobbied for a forest law and agricultural reform—which would make possible the preservation of the remaining primary forest. The society protested deforestation in Rio de Janeiro, and it convened the first Brazilian Conference on Nature Protection in 1934.[45]

That conference brought together delegates, mostly scientists and government officials, from several states. The condition of the forest was reviewed, state by state. In Rio de Janeiro, it was estimated, no primary forest had survived—a remarkable conclusion, in view of present-day efforts to preserve what is taken to be undisturbed forest. In Espírito Santo and Minas Gerais the extent of forest destruction was "calamitous," and in São Paulo, despite reforestation, clearing was widespread. Participating institutions and organizations reported on their activities, nearly all of which were educational—apparently very little research was being carried out. A delegate from Argentina presented a report that showed how far Brazil had fallen behind in conservation. The clear purpose of the conference was to pressure the government to enforce conservationist measures just approved by the Constituent Congress and to create a national park system.[46]

The Vargas government did enact, between May 1933 and October 1934, on the advice of Sampaio, Hoehne, Andrade, and other conservationists, a series of codes regulating scientific expeditions, water use, mines, hunting and fishing, and forests. A new constitution, also promulgated in 1934, entrusted both the states and the central government with the protection of "natural beauties and monuments of historical or artistic value." Most critically, the new Forest Code denied the absolute right of property, prohibiting, even on private holdings, the cutting of trees along watercourses, trees harboring rare species, or those protecting watersheds. It forbade owners to cut more than three-quarters of the trees remaining on their property. Industries were required to replant trees sufficient to maintain their operations. A Forest Guard was mandated, and the basis of national and state park organization was laid out. The Code of Waters similarly withdrew from landowners control of water that flowed through their properties. This was a historic denial of liberalism and reversion to state control, muffled since the early days of the empire but now under the banner of a modernizing and technocratic nationalism.[47]

Before passage of the Forest Code, the only forest reserves in Brazil were those of Alto da Serra, above the town of Cubatão in São Paulo, and Itatiaia in the Serra da Mantiqueira in westernmost Rio de Janeiro State. Alto da Serra had been donated to the state by Ihering in 1909. Itatiaia had been acquired by the federal government on the advice of Loefgren. Alto da Serra, though only 500 hectares in size, contained some remarkable, nearly undisturbed montane rain forest. Itatiaia was an extraordinary spectacle, an eruptive massif that rose nearly 3,000 meters, displaying several ecological zones, including alpine rain forest and montane meadows. At Itatiaia, locale of an earlier failed colonization scheme, a research station was constructed in 1908, attached to the Botanical Garden of Rio de Janeiro. In 1937 Itatiaia was the first site to be declared a national park. Only two others were created under Vargas: Serra dos Orgãos, an ensemble of picturesque mountain peaks just north of Rio de Janeiro, and Iguaçu, a temperate rain forest bordering the immense waterfall in Paraná. These additions did not imply any quickening of government interest in forest preservation. Serra dos Orgãos appears to have received effective protection mainly because a nearby textile factory owner wanted his watercourse safeguarded, and a park at Iguaçu could hardly have been avoided because the Argentines had established one ten years before on their side of the falls. This small result must have disappointed those who had designed the code. Their proposed surveys of additional sites suitable for parks and reserves went unheeded.[48]

The states set up forest councils, in accordance with the Forest Code, and established a few reserves of their own. Minas Gerais demarcated a 36,000-hectare tract on the Doce River. This was the last large remnant of primary forest in the state. The interventor (that is, dictator-appointed governor) of São Paulo, Fernando Costa, undertook to preserve the araucaria formations at scenic Campos do Jordão, a measure that had in view the supposed benefits of an atmosphere cleansed by trees to tubercular patients of the sanatoria located in that mountainous county. He also declared, during the wartime crisis of fuel supply, the protection of seven forested areas. A large forest reserve was also delineated by Manuel Ribas, interventor of Paraná. In Espírito Santo a forest preserve at Sooretama was donated to the state by the conservationist Alvaro Aguirre. In Bahia a park was decreed at Monte Pascoal, the first landfall sighted by Cabral's fleet.[49]

Only a few counties founded municipal reserves; a survey of 848 Southeast counties found only thirty of them in the early 1950s. Almost all of these were mere tree nurseries for embellishing city streets. A remarkable exception was the reserve of Jacarepaguá, in Rio de Janeiro State, whose purpose was not scenic but ecological—to protect an endemic ornamental species then thought endangered, *Goethea alnifolia*. Few local preserves originated in scientific forecasts, however. The biologist Cândido de Melo Leitão warned that scientific commissions should be responsible for choosing sites because:

> We know that the politician, for example, who has a plantation, and wants to get rid of it at a good price, offers it and sells it to the state [as a reserve], even though it is absolutely inappropriate. . . . If the owner is a friend of the government, the sale is easily carried out.[50]

The Forest Code's defects were soon revealed. An owner might cut down valuable hardwoods and allege that he had fulfilled his obligation to replant by simply allowing capoeira to grow back. The courts decided that an owner who had reduced the forest on his land to the minimum one-quarter could then sell the forested quarter; the new owner would enjoy the right of clearing three-quarters of his purchase—and so on, down, presumably, to the last sapling. Industrial firms easily evaded their obligation to replant by hiring independent contractors, who were not affected by the code. The federal government, furthermore, was assigned insufficient means to enforce the codes. The Forest Guard that it called for was not established; instead, local police forces were expected to undertake forest protection as an additional duty. By 1953, in all of Brazil only 216 counties had set up the stipulated advisory forest delegations. The Federal Forest Council, with few preserves to guard and no police to enforce the law on private holdings, continued to busy itself with the arborization of Rio de Janeiro. The provision that landowners had to notify the Forest Service thirty days in advance of clearing forest was defeated by the bureaucracy's inability to react within thirty days. In fact, few landowners ever gave notice.[51]

In November 1937, Vargas, with the backing of the army, carried out a coup d'état that established a corporatist dictatorship. This government decreed a few additional conservationist measures made necessary by wartime fuel shortages, such as reforestation along railroad rights-of-way. Brazil took part in Pan-American Union–sponsored conservationist conferences that were part of the U.S. effort to bolster Latin American economies wracked by wartime shortages. Nevertheless, a retraction of enthusiasm for implementation of the codes may be observed, suggesting that the intervention of civilian middle-class lay conservationists had been significant in the legislative campaigns of 1933 and 1934 and that once all forms of civic political participation had been stilled, conservationist scientists no longer exercised much influence with Vargas's inner circle, composed mainly of current or former military officers. Costa and Ribas represented remarkable exceptions. The liberal Costa confronted considerable criticism for his continued loyalty to Vargas after the coup, and Ribas's successor abolished his reserve.[52]

Vargas was overthrown in 1945. The elected government that succeeded did not mark a change in conservation policy. The new president was a general who had been a mainstay of the dictatorship. The Congress that produced a new constitution the following year did not insert in it any novelties regarding the government's responsibilities toward the environment. Even so, the deficiencies of the Forest Code and the inability of the state to enforce it became again a subject of public debate. Civil society, however, was coming to be far more concerned with the issues of nationalist economic development. Nevertheless, the question of forest conservation would evolve in the postwar period from utilitarian concerns for the continued viability of commercial extraction to something approaching preservationism and environmentalism.

The first half of the twentieth century had witnessed the final envelopment of the Atlantic Forest. Private expropriation of the entire territory was complete. Tribal and backwoods peoples who had lived, if not exactly protective of the forest, at least in temporary balance with it, were reduced to laboring for those who were intent on eliminating it. Urban, industrial civilization had triumphed—its tentacles reached everywhere, its craving for fuel, wood, and other forest resources extended over the entire Atlantic Forest. Forest, even as it was reduced to smaller and smaller tracts, gained in value as these demands became more insistent. The effective critics of wastefulness and malfeasance were limited largely to the technocratic and scientific elite. Nearly all of them were servants of the state, a state that showed but slight interest in their counsels in behalf of the rational exploitation of forests. Instead, the state, still beholden to the very interests that had usurped the forest lands, left the scientists embittered and the public unserved. Only briefly did a civic, quasi-conservationist movement converge with the technocratic cadres, during crises of war and depression. The political climate was favorable to democratic aspirations for just one moment during this half century, but this was enough to see forest law made one of the government's responsibilities. This was only a temporary victory in a great struggle that was to become more and more urgent, as it became clear that defeat meant extinction.

12

The Development Imperative

Em um país de 80.000.000 de habitantes talvez apenas algumas centenas compreendem realmente a fauna indígena como um recurso patrimonial brasileiro, que merece por isso mesmo atenção.

In a country of more than 80 million inhabitants, perhaps no more than a few hundred really understand native fauna to be a Brazilian patrimonial resource, which for this very reason merits attention.

ADELMAR COIMBRA FILHO AND ALCEO MAGNANINI (1968)

In the dawn of the postwar world a terrible new threat stood revealed to the Atlantic Forest—to what remained of it. This was an idea, an obsession in fact, called "economic development": The proposition that government policies could be devised that would stimulate capital accumulation and industrialization, and thereby a rate of economic growth much faster than any historically experienced. Depression and war had brought home to the elites of Latin America how very insignificant, compared with those of the industrial countries, were their economies and their place in the world. Their expectations of comfort and consumption, depending largely upon imported novelties, had been thwarted for a generation. The rhetoric of the Allies—indeed, of the Axis powers as well—had given them to believe that the prosperity of the industrial "center" would, if invited, be readily transferred to the "periphery." The strategic necessity of propping up the Latin American economies in wartime and of preventing their "loss" to their cold war antagonists obliged the Western capitalist governments to countenance and even to encourage measures they had formerly looked upon with distaste, including the funding of industrial projects that would eventually cause the loss of part of their Latin American markets. Indeed, as companies in the United States and western Europe perfected techniques of global communications, management, and finance, they became themselves bemused with the prospects for investment that "underdeveloped" Latin America held out. The governments of the region no longer would limit themselves, however, to welcoming foreign capital to invest as it would in their territories. Now they would plan these investments and discipline them—or try to, at least. And they would go farther; they would install factories themselves when private capital was lacking or faint-hearted.[1]

Economic development implied more than the temporary growth of the economy—that had occurred in Brazil over the previous centuries, when one stockpile or another of standing resources was exploited and a momentary prosperity was experienced. These economic cycles, as they came to be called, had been regarded as inevitable, but now they were interpreted as the wages of fatalism, passivity, and colonial victimization. Development was imbued with the positive values of independence and self-realization. As a system of belief, it was millenarian: Backwardness would cease, traditionalism would give way to modernization, and the nation would attain development, an edenic plateau. Instead, disastrously, development was to become an ever-receding target.

Economic development was more than a government policy; it amounted to a social program of vast scope, energy, and originality. The idea of economic development penetrated the consciousness of the citizenry, justifying every act of government, even dictatorship, even the extinction of nature. Above all, economic development was linked in the representations of the state, the communications media, and the popular imagination to the eradication of poverty. This proved a chimera. In reality, the strategy that was deliberately pursued substituted economic growth for redistribution of wealth. Most of the gains from growth were bestowed upon those at or near the top of the social ladder, intensifying the concentration of income. Agrarian reform and the secure entitlement of land belonging to smallholders were evaded by sponsoring the expansion of colonization onto remaining patches of the Atlantic and Amazon forests. Land hunger and the continuing wasteful exploitation of forest as a nonrenewable resource made inevitable a precipitous decline in the remaining relatively undisturbed stands of the Atlantic Forest. To a significant degree, forest was bartered for economic development, an exchange that could be made to appear a brilliant stroke only by assigning to the former a trifling economic value and ignoring all other values.[2]

Nearly all of the physical and economic transformations of the 1950s through the 1970s that might be called development were confined to the region of the Atlantic Forest. Very nearly all the investment of multinational and state-owned corporations came to be concentrated in the "industrial triangle" formed by the cities of São Paulo, Belo Horizonte, and Rio de Janeiro. Industry expanded vertiginously: By the early 1960s, factories in the region produced motor vehicles, electric and electronic machinery, petrochemicals, ships, pharmaceuticals, paper pulp and paper, sheet glass, rubber tires—nearly all the appurtenants of "modernization." Population growth, historically rapid, rose even more steeply, impelled by suddenly lowered mortality and accelerated migration from north and south. By 1970 the population of the region of the Atlantic Forest stood at about 40 million, an annual rate of growth of 3 percent over twenty years. Most of this population increase occurred in the cities, but the extermination of the last tracts of forest convertible to farms and pasture intensified in a period of global prosperity and rising world demand for coffee, cotton, cocoa, and soybeans and of rising urban demand for these and other materials and foodstuffs.

The period was politically agitated; successive governments displayed contradictory policies toward forest exploitation and preservation, a circumstance that reduced still further the possibility that any of the primary forest might survive. With the overthrow of the dictator Getúlio Vargas, altogether demodé after the defeat of the Axis powers, a liberal constitutional framework was constructed that resembled the abortive government of 1934. At least incipiently representative, it permitted the free play of parties, trade unions, and civic associations. The first elected president was Vargas's chief general, partly as the representative of a middle class that found itself increasingly outnumbered and alienated by a growing labor movement. Vargas returned to power in 1951, this time elected by an odd coalition of the urban masses, whom the middle classes despised and feared, and industrialists, whom the middle classes distrusted and disliked. His populist policies led to his overthrow by the army and to his suicide, in 1954. He was followed in office, after an interregnum, by Juscelino Kubitschek, a Mineiro who reassembled Vargas's coalition in behalf of an aggressive program of economic development. His successor soon renounced office, for obscure reasons, and was replaced by the vice-president, whose exclusive reliance on the working-class wing of the regnant coalition again led, in the context of heightened but unreal expectations of revolution inspired by the Cuban example, to military intervention in 1964. This time the generals did not restore office to civilian politicians but imposed authoritarian rule to guarantee "national security." A series of general-presidents relied on civilian technocrats to accelerate economic development. They were to remain in power for twenty-one years.[3]

It might have been expected that, throughout this fevered and violent power struggle, neither industrialists, urban middle classes, labor union activists, technocrats, nor army officers could be distracted by conservationist issues. Those who struggled in behalf of environmental legislation suffered the disadvantage that native forests were not seen, for the most part, as significant by any of these actors. Nor was there much point in establishing legal prescriptions in an atmosphere in which the rule of law was regularly contravened. Nor was it practicable to spread a conservationist ideology under a regime suspicious of collective civic action, whatever form it took. After 1964, among reformist movements, the reestablishment of elected government and civil rights necessarily held the highest priority. Conservationist reformers, difficult to label politically but still for the most part lodged in the state scientific bureaucracy, meantime occupied a precarious position, unheeded by the government and disdained by its opponents.

The remaining tracts of relatively undisturbed primary forests were now commonly those less suitable, or unsuitable, for agriculture of the sort that had been traditionally practiced. Nevertheless, primary forest continued to be preferred for slash-and-burn farming, and that method continued to be preferred above all intensive methods. Slash-and-burn remained responsible, therefore, for much primary-forest destruction. Where thinly scattered populations once resided, permitting a degree of stability through the natural regrowth of forest, now denser rural populations were leading to minifundia. These units were most likely to have been entirely cleared of forest and least likely to display any reforestation, because their owners were increasingly obliged to put their time into employment off the farm. Rural population increase and minifundismo were thus increasingly part of the problem of forest extinction.[4]

Another cause of extinction was insistent and foolhardy cultivation of steep slopes. Much of the "sea of hills" region of the Serra do Mar was not arable under any conditions. Thirty percent of the county of Viçosa, in Minas Gerais, for example, exhibited grades higher than 40 percent; another 40 percent exhibited grades between 20 and 40 percent. Farming soils on these slopes, universally done uphill and downhill, not on contour, caused mud slides—ruining fields in bottomlands, silting streams, and, in the rainy season, causing deaths. Farmers pressed to increase production eliminated long-fallow practices, accelerating the erosion of the humus layer. The deep and porous loamy soils of the basaltic depression, where coffee was so admirably acclimatized, were stabilized by nothing more than the humus layer. The usual methods of coffee cultivation, however, rapidly wasted it. In northern Paraná, in groves that possessed 165 tons of humus per hectare when they were planted, 10 tons were left after twenty years. With the elimination of humus, immense voçorocas began to tear through plantations and town sites, utterly unstoppable, sometimes swallowing them whole. Soil erosion eventually revealed hardpan in the lower horizon. Even where hardpan remained hidden, it prevented the reestablishment of capoeira. Some of the forest stands of the Paraná Valley overgrew quite fine loess; when they were felled and burned, dust storms became more common—the dry winter air was thick with an orange powder that formed haloes around street lights and deposited a chalky film over everything and everyone—a fact of life so ubiquitous as to be unnoticed. It seemed to be the universal assumption that farming was an activity that destroyed soils. Here and there, however, a few of the colonies of recent immigrants from harsher, more densely populated countries managed soils so as to retain humus, minerals, and porosity—a novelty so strange as to seem miraculous.[5]

Commercial opportunity, affecting larger and more prosperous farms, was another component of forest destruction: One of the more important losses was the ribbons of gallery forest to which the Atlantic Forest was limited in the savannas of the far interior of Minas Gerais and São Paulo. The moist, fertile soils underlying gallery forest were attractive to farmers who wanted to plant rice, a staple that was replacing manioc in city diets. Industrial customers encouraged the supplanting of sugar, maize, and beans by cotton, a crop that caused far more rapid erosion.

Another of the reasons for accelerated forest loss was chronic inflation. The grand project of economic development involved the application of a much larger proportion of national product to capital formation. The government was never forthright enough to appropriate these funds through taxation; instead, it created money to pay for them through inflation. The citizenry reacted by trying to store its funds in goods that would at least offset the falling value of the currency. One of these goods was rural property, traditionally the preferred investment of the upper class, now increasingly the speculation of the urban middle class. Amazing evidence of this rush to the frontier is found in the records of the Northern Paraná Land Company: Between 1946 and 1956, 80 percent of the lots it sold were resold within three years; 50 percent of these buyers then sold again within another three years. By 1961, 50 percent of the lots were sold within two years, and 33 percent of the buyers sold out again within the space of a single year! A third to a half of the original purchasers were city people, as were a quarter of the second buyers.[6]

As this speculative wave moved westward across northern Paraná, it encountered sandier soils, where coffee trees bore less abundantly and grew senescent more quickly. The climate of the region turned out to be much riskier, too. Imagined to be susceptible to only infrequent and mild freezes, it experienced a series of severe ones in the 1960s and then a terrible freeze in 1975. Many groves were hastily uprooted and planted in annual crops or were abandoned to pasture, to the grim satisfaction of conservationist scientists who recalled the predictions of geologist Reinhard Maack that deforestation on those soils, which had once been steppe, would invite the return of a drier and colder local climate. In 1963 the entire region, having just suffered a severe frost that withered much of the cultivated area, underwent the worst drought in memory, a peril that did not inhibit farmers and ranchers from setting their usual early spring fires. The result was devastating—in numerous counties, fire escaped control and destroyed 21,000 square kilometers of forest, araucaria as well as broad-leaved, and at least 1,200 square kilometers of reforested pine. More than 100 persons died.[7]

In the wake of these failures, Brazilians proved to themselves that the burning and clearing of primary forest had never been necessary to plant coffee. Hundreds of millions of coffee trees were uprooted in marginal areas, most of them under a government-assistance program. The postwar fever of expansion had once again glutted the market, and the government sought to improve productivity in the major export crop in order to maintain competitiveness. It encouraged, through selective credit, replanting with technically advanced inputs: selected seedlings, contour-planted groves, and fertilizers. Yields per hectare soon matched historical yields from primary forest. Between 1960 and 1974, the area planted in coffee in the Southeast and Paraná was reduced from nearly 44,000 to 28,000 square kilometers, with no loss in output (see map 6). In effect, broad swaths of the Atlantic Forest had been cleared and burned for no purpose except speculation. This draconian program, furthermore, was striking evidence that the government was capable of drastic intervention in the countryside when it suited its purposes.[8]

Brazilians were culturally addicted to beef eating. In the cities, beef was consumed almost to the exclusion of other sources of animal protein. In the early 1960s, annual per capita consumption amounted in São Paulo to 51 kilograms of beef; in Rio de Janeiro, to 61 kilograms. Although these amounts were comparable to European standards of the time, they concealed enormous pent-up demand, because beef eating, a daily or twice daily habit of the well-off, was still no more than a holiday indulgence of the beans-and-rice-eating poor. As economic development added marginally to the acquisitive power of the working class, the first luxury brought into the house was beef. Cattle raising, therefore, was a business of immense potential. Landowners, who considered cattle raising a more "noble" employment of their talents than farming, were further stimulated to convert to ranching by successive governments. Populist administrations threatened land reform; then the military tried to deflect burgeoning unrest and increase productivity by extending labor laws to the

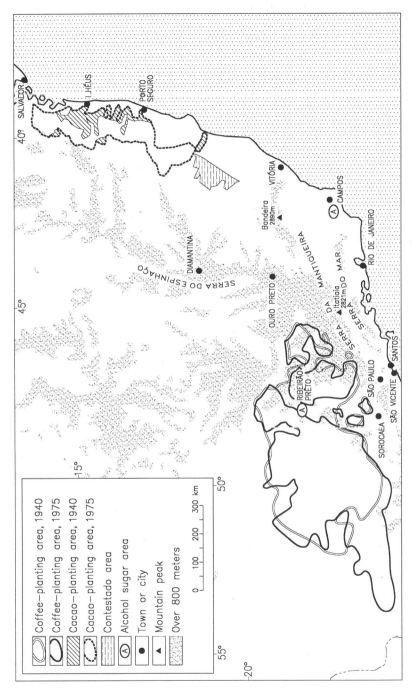

Map 6. Coffee, cacao, and alcohol sugar areas, 1940–1975

Legend:

- Coffee–planting area, 1940
- Coffee–planting area, 1975
- Cacao–planting area, 1940
- Cacao–planting area, 1975
- Contestado area
- Alcohol sugar area
- Ⓐ Town or city
- ● Town or city
- ▲ Mountain peak
- Over 800 meters

0   100   200   300 km

Places and features labeled on map:

SALVADOR
ILHÉUS
PORTO SEGURO
VITÓRIA
Bandeira 2890m
CAMPOS
Ⓐ
DIAMANTINA
SERRA DO ESPINHAÇO
OURO PRETO
SERRA DA MANTIQUEIRA
Itatiaia 2821m
SERRA DO MAR
RIO DE JANEIRO
SÃO PAULO
SÃO VICENTE
SANTOS
SOROCABA
RIBEIRÃO PRETO
Ⓐ

40°
45°
50°
55°
-15°
-20°

countryside. The response of the landowners was in many cases to set their workers to burning forest and planting guinea grass for pasture and then to send them packing.[9]

Guinea grass had its own way with the landscape. Although it was difficult to start on native grassland, it flourished on deforested soils. Itinerant loggers and charcoal makers were sometimes allowed to plant in their clearings for subsistence, but their clearings would eventually be overrun. In planted fields it became a weed uncontrollable with the hoe, driving squatters away more effectively than the ranchers' hired gunmen. Guinea grass invaded forest margins and thrived under the fire regime loosed by the ranchers. "It's common to see thousands of dead trees, where the substrate is the exuberant green of guinea grass," remarked an ecologist who observed coastal ranchlands in Espírito Santo in the late 1950s. This and other exotic grasses, part of the allied expeditionary force that had invaded the Neotropic realm hundreds of years before, were creating an environment more appropriate for themselves than for the humans who supposedly directed their implantation and reproduction. By the early 1950s, 36 percent of the land surface of São Paulo was covered with exotic pastures.[10]

The asphalting of rural roads reorganized the ranching business. Cattle bred and raised at great distances from the railheads were now trucked to railhead slaughterhouses. Improved breeding reduced time to slaughter, and improved grass varieties made possible increased grazing capacity, but management still fell far short of potential. Pastures continued to be burned, more often than even the ranchers thought prudent, and often they were overstocked. The result was degraded pasture. Less nutritious grasses proliferated, the litter layer disappeared, and topsoil washed away in sheets. On the native grasslands of Paraná, where one hectare had been sufficient to graze an animal, by the 1960s two hectares were required. The cost of converting native pasture to exotic grasses was by that time technically feasible, but still more expensive than burning forest. Primary forest therefore continued to be felled for the purpose. Gallery forests of western Minas Gerais, the mostly secondary forests of the Jequitinhonha and Doce rivers, and primary forests of northern Espírito Santo all went up in flames, not for agriculture but for cattle.[11]

Economic development relieved a few pressures on the Atlantic Forest, even while it imposed many others. The most-traveled railroad lines began to be electrified in the 1920s, but this conversion acquired significant dimensions only after the war. Between 1950 and 1953, consumption of electricity by regional railroads quintupled, to 400 million kilowatt hours. Conversion of the rest of the system to diesel began at the same time. In the same period oil consumption doubled, to 53,200 tons. Railroad use of firewood came to an end in the early 1960s. This was a relief to the companies, whose trackage was no longer expanding and whose access to abundant wood supplies was in consequence failing. It was a relief to farmers, as well, whose fields and woodlands had so long been damaged by sparks that flew from locomotive stacks. The railroads soon canceled their reforestation projects. A few, such as the reserve at Rio Claro, in São Paulo, survived into the 1980s, testimony to a brief and less-than-wholehearted commitment to self-sufficiency. Most of the others disappeared without a trace, despite some criticism from a public that had come to view these tracts as preserves rather than as woodlots.[12]

Urban households were beginning to shift to stoves fueled with bottled gas. Indeed, the introduction of this imported energy source was critical to the viability of the larger cities, which would have quickly become unlivable had tens of thousands of cubic meters of wood been burned each day in a million kitchens—had such supplies been available or transportable. By the early 1960s, more than half of the kitchen stoves in the Southeast were gas, kerosene, or electric fueled. Even so, wood fuel use was declining only relatively, not absolutely. There were more wood stoves in the region in 1980 than there had been in 1960. Wood fuel continued to be consumed in the ovens of even the most "modern" restaurants, bakeries, and pizzerias. It was estimated that such establishments daily burned 48,000 cubic meters of wood in Rio de Janeiro. Furthermore, larger and larger wooded tracts had to be cleared because as pressure upon them grew, the fertility of their soils declined, and as less time was allowed for regrowth, they yielded less wood per hectare.[13]

Wood was expected to be in the postwar world a raw material of immense value to Latin America. Wood-starved Europe was to be reconstructed, according to forestry conferences of the late 1940s, with wood supplied by the tropics. The Food and Agriculture Organization of the United Nations was enjoined to promote "rational" forestry, discourage the use of wood as fuel, and facilitate the modernization of sawmills. Indeed, international agencies carried out studies to promote these ends. But logging was not put on a sustainable basis. In Brazil, wood was the raw material of an industrial sector that mainly satisfied a growing domestic market, responsible for more than 7 percent of the value of manufactured product in 1955, not including the sizable amount of wood that was transformed in rural areas, beyond the government's ken. In the Southeast, much of this raw material was obtained not from broad-leaved trees of the Atlantic Forest but from araucaria—Paraná pine. Araucaria felling rose sharply in the 1950s and peaked a mere twenty years later, as the denser stands were exhausted. The domestic market for softwood absorbed nearly

70 percent of this windfall (many small specimens were not left to grow but were sold as Christmas trees). Even so, Paraná pine was for a time quite an important export, greater in value than sugar, in fact—another of the depressingly repeated extractive cycles that economic-development schemes were supposed to eliminate, not encourage. Unfortunately, araucaria, a relict species after all, did not prove suitable for commercial reforestation, at least not as a timber species—in plantations it was too slow-growing and branched so low that its wood was marred by knots.[14]

Hardwoods of varied species, scattered through the primary broad-leaved forests and therefore difficult to log, were exploited in a different fashion, albeit just as casual and wasteful. In northwestern São Paulo and northern Paraná there were nearly 1,500 sawmills in 1955; in the 1960s there were 1,700 in northern Espírito Santo. They were supplied by itinerant loggers who drove about the frontier areas in flatbed trucks equipped with hoists. The far frontier was prodigal of wood. Dwellings were built of it, scrap lumber went into the boilers of the sawmills and of the steam engines that produced electric light. Even so, a great deal of wood went unused and simply was left, in mountains of scrap lumber and limbs, to rot. Years later, these monuments to haste and greed could still be seen on the edges of towns in northwestern São Paulo.[15]

Even so, only a few tree species were worth cutting down; the rest were sent up in flames where they stood. Indeed, the amount of hardwood that was appropriated for some use more valuable than ashen fertilizer seems to have been minuscule. Although Maack calculated that 150,000 hectares of broad-leaved forest were cut and burned annually in northern Paraná in the 1950s, an area that might have supplied 75 million cubic meters of hardwoods and softwoods, the sawmills of the region reported processing only 300,000 cubic meters a year. The true volume would have amounted to considerably more than that, given the average mill's daily capacity of about 10 cubic meters. At the same time, official exports of hardwood timber through the river port of Foz do Iguaçu averaged a reported 18,000 cubic meters a year, perhaps half the true amount. Meanwhile, only very small quantities of raw and processed hardwoods were officially noted to have been sold in the internal market, on average less than 7,000 cubic meters a year. It is clear that extensive ranching and agriculture were overwhelmingly the causes of the disappearance of the Atlantic Forest, even in its latter days, when means were available to extract its wood. The largest and most relentless of the loggers of northern Espírito Santo, Rainol Grecco, accurately described the logger as "the foot soldier of the cattle rancher."[16]

Integrated steel mills erected at Volta Redonda, in Rio de Janeiro, and

Cubatão, in São Paulo, burned imported and domestic coking coal, but the rest of the country's iron and steel continued to be produced with charcoal. Some of the mills invested in eucalyptus, but even in the late 1970s planted forests supplied only 10 percent of the charcoal burned in the blast furnaces of Minas Gerais. Some of the native wood was obtained from the cerrado, not from the Atlantic Forest. The expanding road network, much of it now paved, made accessible that more remote and much less dense formation, alleviating the anxiety that had overcome mill managers during the war. By the late 1970s, trucking charcoal from native forests to the mills cost nearly four times as much as did transport of nearby eucalyptus-derived charcoal, but this expense continued to be offset by the higher cost of planting.

Conservationists regretted the recalcitrance of the steelmakers, not only because charcoal contractors persisted in destroying primary formations but also because their coking method—the mounds of firewood covered with grass and earth—was much less efficient than the brick ovens used by the mills on their own grounds. Mill managers sought out contractors to evade forest regulations; the contractors were too numerous and itinerant to be themselves regulated. Even the mill-owned ovens, however, were far from representing the state of the art, wasting as they did gasses and volatile by-products. The Belgo-Mineira company did install a sinterizing mill that reduced by about a quarter the energy needed to reduce its ores. Most of the other mills continued to burn as much as 5 cubic meters of charcoal—perhaps 15 cubic meters of wood—to produce a ton of pig iron. By 1974, the mills of Minas Gerais consumed 7.8 million cubic meters of charcoal from native forest, the equivalent of perhaps 1,200 square kilometers. To this must be added the demand of the mills of Rio de Janeiro, also supplied largely from Minas Gerais. Itinerant charcoal making in the Paraíba Valley stoked the Paulista mills. In São Luiz de Piraitinga, there were 2,000 woodcutters, whose reported output of 18,000 tons a year implied the annual clearing of 10 square kilometers in that county alone.[17]

In 1959 a survey was taken of 77 counties in São Paulo by the state Secretariat of Agriculture. It was found that they contained an average of less than 8 percent forest cover, which appears to have included eucalyptus. Among them were 14 counties that possessed 2 percent or less. The analysts of this survey thought that a complete census would have shown about 10 percent cover. This was followed, in 1962, by an aerial survey of a part of the southeastern region that was extrapolated to indicate that São Paulo retained between 34,000 and 35,000 square kilometers of forest, less than 14 percent of the state's territory, 81 percent of which had originally been covered by forest. Unfortunately, photo interpretation could not well distinguish between primary forest and capoeira. The broad-leaved forest cover of all the states of the Southeast and of Paraná may have amounted to 160,000 square kilometers, although there are a number of conflicting estimates. Of this amount, it is even less certain what percentage was primary. In Paraná, it was estimated that, of 53,500 square kilometers of remaining broad-leaved forest in 1955, 31,000 were primary. In Minas Gerais, of 91,000 square kilometers of forest in 1950, only 35,000 were estimated to remain in 1964, very little of it primary. In Espírito Santo, it was estimated in 1950 that half of the state's original forests were gone—a loss of 21,000 square kilometers.[18]

Preoccupied as the state had become with economic development, its role as protector of the country's remaining primary forest turned altogether problematic. Economic nationalism, as well as a shortage of private capital, led to the creation of government enterprises in mining, steelmaking, hydroelectricity, petroleum, and petrochemicals, all potentially heavily polluting. The government's proposals to expand exports of hardwoods, to transform iron ore into the raw material of machine industry, and to bestow upon all hitherto remote areas the benefits of roads and electricity were threatening in the extreme to what remained of the Atlantic Forest. For some of the technocrats, the preserves under state and federal protection were tempting resources, cheaper to exploit than resources in private hands, which they would have had to lease or expropriate. Thus the government of Minas Gerais decided to cut a road through the Rio Doce state park, which contained the last sizable stand of primary forest in Minas Gerais. The purpose, supposedly, was to facilitate access to sources of charcoal beyond the park to the state-owned Acesita steel company, but more likely it was to initiate the destruction of the park itself. The state also contemplated the installation of a sawmill there. Politicians were only too eager to facilitate this sort of exploitation, from which they benefited in the form of campaign funds and votes. The generals, who largely lacked other means of eliciting collaboration from the political elite, found that it could often be obtained in return for a concession to devastate a public resource.[19]

The exchange of state patrimony for the short-term gain of private interests is a constantly repeated theme in Brazilian history, so ingeniously and variously pursued and so ingrained as to appear the very reason for the existence of the state. Another example of the period: In 1956, the Federal University of Viçosa, in Minas Gerais, was obliged to exchange a 1,000-hectare tract of primary forest for a like amount of degraded, worthless pasture. The forest was then sold to the Belgo-Mineira steel mill for charcoal. Bureaucratic corruption, systemic and widespread, found in the environmental laws a green pasture. In the early 1950s, a professor at Viçosa went to the state capital to claim 100 hectares of public land—awarded by law to all graduates of agricultural schools. He intended to turn his grant into a forest preserve. His petition was not recognized, however, and at last he was taken aside and given to understand that his title would be awarded only on condition that he sell it immediately to a contractor, who intended to vend the timber to the Belgo-Mineira mill. Without a complete renovation in the country's political and administrative structures, additional environmental regulation portended not greater protection but less.[20]

Political as well as bureaucratic connivance was essential to the destruction of the forest in an area known as the Contestado. Between the states of Minas Gerais and Espírito Santo there had persisted since colonial times an unresolved border question, a contested zone of about 2,000 square kilometers, still almost entirely covered with primary forests. Clandestine loggers filed claims with both states for public lands in this zone, based on fraudulent allegations of prior occupation. Meanwhile, they felled forest on their claims as quickly as possible. Although state laws prohibited logging on public land, they did allow claimants to such lands to remove timber that might result from their agricultural activities. Indeed, they encouraged forest clearing by recognizing the practice to constitute effective occupation. In fact, the loggers had no intention of occupying their claims, much less farming them. Local notaries were willing to register their declarations, and local police were willing to certify that their dealings in timber were incidental to farming. The loggers, when stopped on the road by state police, claimed that the timber on their trucks originated on land they owned elsewhere. The odd chance that clandestine timber might be apprehended was not a serious risk because it would be sold at auction, and auctions could also be rigged. Loggers interdicted in the Contestado could represent their booty as originating in either state, depending on the uniform of the police who challenged them. These practices were denounced by the secretary of agriculture of Minas Gerais, Alvaro Marcílio, in a report to the legislature in 1957, but they were not interrupted, not entirely surprising because at least one member of the legislature was involved prominently. By the time the border dispute was resolved, the primary forest of the region was entirely gone.[21]

Perhaps, in the case of the Contestado, the absence of effective state action may be laid to the confusion caused by an uncertain state border. The same may not be said of another reserve, the Pontal, belonging to São Paulo, the richest and most effectively administered of the states (see map

7). Almost entirely usurped and destroyed in a space of fifteen years, the Pontal—the point of land between the Paraná and Paranapanema rivers, in the state's extreme northwest—had first been proposed as a reserve by Alberto Loefgren in 1905. Largest of the reserves decreed in 1941 and 1942 by Interventor Fernando Costa, it extended over 3,000 square kilometers. The state's capacity to assert control over this forested area seemed solid. Prior land titles in the region were all preposterously bogus, based on usurpations of public lands irregularly registered in the mid-1850s. Lacking legal grounds, pretenders to titles had tried to secure them through violence, carried out by private armies of gunslingers. Just two claimants emerged from the carnage in the area of the Pontal by 1890. Cunningly they exchanged their "properties" between them in order to solidify their claims. Effective occupation was still incipient; economic activity was limited to commercial hunting for skins and logging. In the mid-1930s, there were 36 sawmills in nearby Presidente Prudente but very few squatters within the Pontal itself. In 1936 the state declared illegitimate all titles in the Pontal and reclaimed the land for itself. Costa's wartime decrees therefore reserved a forest that was indubitably in the public domain. Unfortunately, this admirable resolve soon collapsed.[22]

In 1946 Costa died in an automobile accident while campaigning for the governorship—a tragic loss for the cause of forest conservation. Another hand came to the helm, this time a buccaneer's. Governor Adhemar de Barros, elected with the support of the mayors of the Northwest, showed his gratitude by renouncing state ownership over nearly half of the Pontal reserve, permitting a railroad to be built through it and awarding a contract to found an immigrant colony within it. The invasion of the preserve continued under his successor, accompanied by the usual violence and chicanery. Tracts of usurped land were sold and resold, even donated to municipal councils, in order to gain allies in the task of legitimation. The tax collector connived in these land grabs by assessing taxes on the claims, taxes that the usurpers were only too happy to pay. Craftier yet, with the collaboration of the public prosecutor, on occasion tracts of this public land were auctioned off for unpaid taxes to fellow conspirators! The state Forest Service was repeatedly instructed not to interfere in the activities of loggers, who were smuggling timber down the Paraná River. Migrants swarmed into the region, seeking crumbs at this banquet. Public land was much safer to squat on—after all, the state hired no gunslingers. Most disastrously, claim jumpers were burning forest in the Pontal simply to preempt the state's interest. Once the forest was gone, there would be nothing to protect![23]

In May 1954 newspapers of the state capital initiated what may have

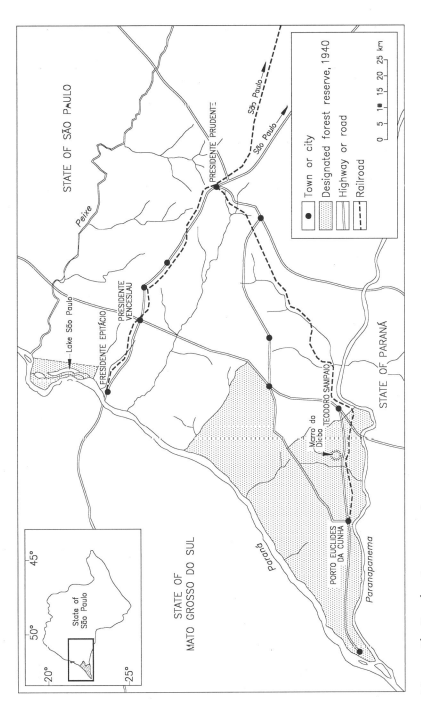

Map 7. The Pontal region, 1940–1980

Legend:
- Town or city
- Designated forest reserve, 1940
- Highway or road
- Railroad

0 5 10 15 20 25 km

STATE OF SÃO PAULO

STATE OF MATO GROSSO DO SUL

STATE OF PARANÁ

PRESIDENTE PRUDENTE
PRESIDENTE VENCESLAU
PRESIDENTE EPITÁCIO
TEODORO SAMPAIO
PORTO EUCLIDES DA CUNHA

Lake São Paulo
Morro do Diabo

Peixe
Paraná
Paranapanema

São Paulo

State of São Paulo

-20°
-25°
50°
45°

been the country's first press campaign in behalf of preservation. The *Folha da Manhã* revealed the names of numerous officials involved in illegalities in the Pontal and demanded the removal of intruders on lands declared protected. It published endorsements of numerous private persons and associations and resolutions by various county councils, all located far from the scene (and probably controlled by opposition parties). A bill was hurriedly introduced in the state legislature by Deputy Cunha Lima that would have leased the entire Pontal to private parties, on condition that each would keep a quarter of their leaseholds in forest. This, he cynically declared, would be a better guarantee of forest because the state was in competent to protect its reserves. The state legislature claimed to be hamstrung by an anomaly in the 1946 constitution, which seemed to withdraw from the states the power to legislate on land questions. The federal Congress, however, for twenty years took no action to assume its responsibilities or to restore these powers explicitly to the states.[24]

In response to public clamor, the new governor, Jânio Quadros, ordered an aerial survey, which showed that, of the inner "perimeter," or district, of the preserve, almost 90 percent remained forested. He appeared to support a substitute bill, which would relinquish the outer perimeters to squatters, while he strengthened control of the inner perimeters, dismissing a number of offending functionaries, tripling the number of forest guards, equipping them with vehicles, and installing guards' housing. The newspaper *O Estado de São Paulo* pointed out that Quadros was, in effect, acquiescing in the usurpation of state property by abandoning land that indubitably belonged to it simply because the overlying forests had been destroyed. This logging and burning was a criminal offense, the editors complained—it should certainly not have won its perpetrators any rights. *O Estado* led an excursion to the Pontal which demonstrated that the "improvements" that the claim jumpers had installed on the lands they were devastating were merely for show and all very recent: The purpose of their activities was timber extraction, not agriculture.[25]

Another of the capital's dailies, the *Correio Paulistano*, enlisted on the side of the claim jumpers. Because all land titles in Brazil were dubious, the newspaper asked, with even balder cynicism, why single out these titles? Acquiring public land through squatting, it insisted, was a national tradition—setting it aside in protected reserves evidently was not. Populism was enlisted, as it would be in future: Expelling the squatters would deprive them of their livings. The *Correio* also gave currency to a version that was resorted to repeatedly in later environmental conflicts: Foreigners were behind the conservationists, seeking to deny the country's resources to its own citizens. It chanced that the Brazilian subsidiary of Standard Oil of New Jersey had published an article in favor of forest conservation in its house magazine and was suspected of knowing of petroleum deposits that it wanted to keep off the market.[26]

The Quadros administration's defense of the Pontal was ineffectual, and his successors displayed even less concern. Gradually, with the connivance of the courts and despite the efforts of the state Forest Service, claim jumpers secured legal title to nearly all the area. Congress made no move to establish federal-land law guidelines, a not entirely surprising lapse, because Barros had been elected a senator and his own brother and son claimed property in the Pontal. The first of the perimeters to disappear was that of Lake São Paulo, a meander of the Paraná River surrounded by wetlands, which was a wildlife paradise. It had not been included in the state decrees of the 1940s but was merely declared subject to expropriation. It was therefore the easiest to invade, a process nearly completed, along with the destruction of much of the wildlife, by the early 1950s. The state's suit against the principal claim jumper dragged through the courts for more than twenty-five years—the defendant himself was murdered in 1967. On the inner perimeter, smuggling of the most valuable timber and the deliberate burning of the rest went on, uncontrolled except by forest guards, whom neighbors accused of taking a commission on clandestine wood. Their director allowed the removal of trees that had been killed by "accidental" fires. The decline in forest reserves can be charted in railroad loadings of logs and sawn wood at Presidente Prudente: In 1955 they totaled 2,062 cars; in 1959, only 538, and in 1961, just 87. In 1966 Barros, once again governor, decreed the final abolition of the Pontal reserve.[27]

Claim jumpers had asserted that they would give employment to thousands. The reality was that the workers hired to clear forest were then instructed to plant pasture grass and, having completed that chore, they were fired. As in so many formerly forested areas of the state, cattle took the place of people, this time without any interlude of cultivation. The Pontal, as it transpired, was inappropriate for farming. Its soils were sandy, retaining little of the moisture provided by irregular rainfall. For that reason, almost a third of the region had been covered with a cactus-studded savanna, not forest. When the humus that had accumulated under the forest was washed or blown away, pasture grass offered an insecure basis for exploitation. The Pontal had been destroyed more to vaunt the political power of its invaders than to swell their fortunes. These forlorn pastures, called *paliteiros*—toothpick holders—ornamented with the still-upright trunks of dead trees, were inhabited in the early 1970s by a population of squatters, former employees of the ranches, so destitute that Brazil's domestic welfare corps sent volunteers from Alagoas, one of the country's poorest states, to succor them.[28]

Miraculously, one tract of the original reserve survived, the Morro do Diabo—Devil's Hill—somewhat more than 370 square kilometers, centering on a dramatically isolated flat-topped rise, 400 meters high, and fronting on the Paranapanema River. More-or-less intact forest covered about half of this reserve, despite the repeated invasion of claim jumpers, the construction of a railroad, a highway, and a penetration road, semiannual burnings of surrounding pasture, and the open hostility of neighbors. Plans to "develop" the reserve—to plant eucalyptus, to settle families expelled from the rest of the Pontal(!)—came to nought. Through the 1970s, Morro do Diabo was menaced by an uncertain legal status, by the suits of claim jumpers, by poachers, and by a niggardly budget that supported only five guards, but its alienation from state patrimony was somehow resisted. This was a critical victory, because all the rest of the large stands of the low forest typical of the Paraná Valley meanwhile disappeared. It was in this reserve that there were discovered the last forlorn bands of the black lion tamarin, the rarest and most threatened primate of the Neotropics.[29]

São Paulo readily declared new reserves, even while it abandoned existing ones. By 1961 there were more than fifty, under the management of the state Forest Service. According to the decrees that set them up, they totaled a very modest 2,138 square kilometers. Many of them were secondary forest; some were tree plantations donated by railroads, which no longer had use for them. Few were adequately guarded, and therefore all were in danger of usurpation. In 1961 Jânio Quadros, by then president, declared the entire Serra do Mar, from Espírito Santo to Rio Grande do Sul, to be federal "protective forest"; that is, protective of watersheds and soils. The following year, Governor Carvalho Pinto declared Cardoso's Island, a relatively undisturbed site, a state park. Remarkably, like Morro do Diabo, squatters were resisted there, and in succeeding years it largely escaped depredation. Most of the other preserves, including all the larger ones, were only partly in the public domain, and even these areas were ill defined during decades of delayed surveys, court challenges, continued poaching, and clandestine logging and charcoal making, repeatedly denounced and never effectively suppressed.[30]

Across the Paranapanema River from the Pontal, the state of Paraná decreed, by the mid-1960s, eighteen reserves, totaling 5,428 square kilometers. It contained, as well, two federal parks, Iguaçu and Sete Quedas, totaling 3,010 square kilometers. However, of the state reserves, by 1969 only a minuscule 51 square kilometers had been surveyed and were effectively protected and administered. A study of four of the largest units, including the federal Sete Quedas, based on aerial mapping carried out in 1964, showed that only a little more than half of their combined area remained forested. On the assumption that these reserves had originally been entirely forested (and that all the remaining forested area was primary), it was calculated that deforestation had averaged 7.7 percent a year since their creation. Data supplied by Maack suggest that the overall rate of deforestation in Paraná did not exceed 3.2 percent. State and federal preserves were being cut down more than twice as fast as those on private properties! Indeed, most of the state reserves and Sete Quedas were later extinguished entirely.[31]

The other states hardly accompanied even these failed essays. By the early 1960s, five more reserves were decreed in Espírito Santo, comprising 370 square kilometers; in Rio de Janeiro two were created in 1970 and 1971, also totaling 370 square kilometers. Both contained undisturbed forest but were subject to constant incursions. Only two new national parks were decreed in the Southeast. Caparaó, a 162-square-kilometer tract between Minas Gerais and Espírito Santo, protected what was then thought to be Brazil's highest peak. The other was the Bocaina Range, originally enclosing 1,340 square kilometers. Bocaina's creation was debated for a decade before it was declared in 1971. The federal government struggled to achieve ownership of its minuscule park system. Even within the city of Rio de Janeiro, control was precarious: There were plans, abandoned after a struggle, to convert the Forest Service's nursery into a cemetery. In the city's watershed preserves, there were clandestine wood cutters, protected by a friend of the governor. They went about armed, and they did not hesitate to fire at forest guards. Itatiaia and Serra dos Orgãos never came entirely under effective control and were riddled with private holdings. Bocaina, only 30 percent government owned, became a paradise for charcoal makers and firewood smugglers. A survey of the national parks carried out by Alceo Magnanini and Maria Tereza Jorge Pádua in 1969 showed that the government itself was considering abandoning half of the areas that it had designated parkland.[32]

The ignominious defeat, throughout the 1950s and 1960s, of conservationist impulses within the government and in nearly all its confrontations with private interests leads one to ask why any efforts were made at all. The centuries-old detestation of the wild, expressed by most Brazilian neo-Europeans, combined with the general readiness to sack the national patrimony for private gain, as if the country were still a colony and there were some other El Dorado in some other Indies to which to repair when nothing of value remained in this temporary abode, are sufficient, perhaps, to explain in general terms why the forest was disappearing. But why did the government make repeated rhetorical efforts to save its remnants?

One of the reasons appears to be that awareness was growing among public servants that conservation, and even preservation, of nature was one of the attributes of a self-respecting state. As with many other novelties, this idea appeared over the horizon from the very countries that also provided the model of economic development toward which the state was simultaneously striving. Conservation and preservation were two more of the activities in which the state engaged in order to give credence to the proposition that it was in fact a state. To a considerable degree, these measures, like many others the state undertook, were, as a traditional saying had it, *para inglês ver*—for the Englishman to see—the eternally judging, supercilious, contemptuous, and dangerously competent Englishman, whose attitudes and technical and financial means of intervention had overspread the globe. If the technical and financial means were to be grasped, these attitudes would have to be placated, fended off, lest they be internalized. And the most glaring evidences of backwardness would have to be patched over or denied, lest the foreigners' sense of superiority turn hostile and interventionist, or worse, indifferent.

Brazilian conservationists heightened these tensions in behalf of their own budgets by pointing out how far advanced were the Americans. Wanderbilt Duarte de Barros, the able director of the Itatiaia park, claimed for the national parks an "elevated public importance" and linked together in the opening paragraph of his treatise on the subject the ideas of foreign superiority, the need to catch up, and the essential role of the government: National parks were institutions "considered an essential question in all countries that see to the conservation of nature." "Therefore," he insisted, "Brazil could not remain alienated, in its long-standing and profound indifference to or distaste for the goods of the Earth, leaving unprotected natural beauty and treasures found in its territory." These, he declared, "are questions exclusively within the sphere of the state." This was an effective syllogism, though dangerous, because it rendered the conservationists vulnerable to the charge of cosmopolitanism.[33]

Since the 1920s, American conservation organizations and U.S. government offices with responsibilities for nature conservation had occasionally displayed some concern for the struggling few in Brazil who took up these tasks. Shortly after World War I, which had prodigally consumed hardwood reserves, the U.S. Forest Service became convinced that the industrial countries would soon experience a critical shortage of hardwoods and that the United States would much increase its imports from Latin America. For this to occur, forestry research would have to be encouraged there. Forest Service officials advised the Brazilian government to send students to the Yale Forestry School, which added courses in tropical forestry. American foresters were sent to Brazil, notably the genial and curious Roy Nash, who was to write a vivid critique of Brazilian culture in its relation to nature, *The Conquest of Brazil*. He advocated the preservation of at least a third of Brazil's surface in forest and insisted that land be expropriated where necessary because private interests were "diametrically opposed" to the public interest. William A. Orton, director of the Tropical Plant Research Foundation, founded in 1925 and staffed by foresters with experience in Philippine colonial forests, was contracted by the Ministry of Agriculture to report on Brazil's timber potential. Orton, like Nash, recommended forestry scholarships abroad preparatory to the founding of a forestry school, preferably at Viçosa or Campinas—a recommendation carried out thirty-two years later. The ministry hired American foresters recommended by Orton to advise the newly organized Forest Service.[34]

American collaboration appears to have ceased thereafter, very likely because U.S. demand for hardwood slumped during the depression. A few Brazilians did train at American schools, notably Paulo Ferreira Souza, who studied at Yale and became director of the National Park Service. During World War II, a modest exchange of foresters was carried out, and films on conservation topics were distributed as part of a broad U.S. campaign to align Latin American governments, shore up their economies, and guarantee a supply of raw materials. After the war, once again, it was expected that demand for hardwoods would rise. Brazilians participated in regional and international forest conferences in the late 1940s and early 1950s, organized by the Organization of American States, the United Nations, and the International Union for the Conservation of Nature. Conservationist proposals expressed at these conferences had only rhetorical appeal for the governments of Latin America; nevertheless, they suggest the beginning, at least, of postcolonial collaboration and of regional and global perspectives on the problem of forest conservation. Even so, the colonial powers continued to dominate these forums until Latin America organized its own schools of forestry. This is hardly surprising—in 1955, the Brazilian Ministry of Agriculture employed 22 foresters; the United States employed 21,000.[35]

The government's drive for economic development paradoxically caused it to augment a cadre of public servants who upheld the cause of conservation and, indeed, in some cases offered their careers on its altar. There was a need for specialists capable of improving the efficiency with which the country's natural resources were exploited. Soil erosion, for example, was unavoidably obvious as a major cause of declining yields, obliging the creation of federal and state soil conservation units. Soil conservation experts soon turned to criticizing wasteful destruction of primary forest as well as haphazard farming methods and to demanding reforestation to safeguard watersheds. Indeed, soil engineers possessed a professional foresight steadier than most other scientists, to judge by José Setzer's 1940 jeremiad:

> We always try to maintain and improve our houses in solid comfort. But from our soils we extract the maximum, and if we concern ourselves with the future, it is limited to the next harvest, or to that of a few years more. Brazilians who live a hundred years from now will not be living in our houses, but they will have to live from our soils.[36]

Soil scientists were able to demonstrate that restriction of farming to appropriate soils, crop rotation, contour and subsurface plowing, and the addition of organic fertilizers could dramatically slow erosion, belying the traditional write-off of supposedly "tired" land.

Individuals might be thwarted within their agencies in attempts to protect the environment, but they were often backed by the scientific associations to which they belonged. These multiplied remarkably during this period, fertilized by a state corporatism that endowed them with semi-official status: the Brazilian Society for the Advancement of Science, the Brazilian Academy of Sciences, the Brazilian Botanical Society, the Association of Brazilian Geographers, and many others. Even though they subscribed in greater or lesser degree to the development thesis, they frequently voted resolutions critical of government policies and carried out studies that government offices would have found intolerable. Even the National Agricultural Society, representing large landowners, now sponsored conservationist reports, written by agronomist members. Budding professionals, traditional enemies of the status quo, banded together to promote environmental protection along with their careers. Students at the newly founded forestry school at the Federal University of Viçosa took to demanding enforcement of the forest code, enlargement and effective protection of the national and state parks, increased legal requirements for replanting, and a replanting quota for native tree species.[37]

Economic development enlarged the ranks of the middle class, a privileged group to which the government awarded free schooling, unburdensome taxes, cheap consumer credit, and domestically produced consumer durables upon which to spend it. Some few of this middling, reasonably well educated group took up interests that made them aware of the costs of economic development—birding, orchid cultivation, hiking, cave exploration—as well as the more traditional hunting and fishing, which perhaps they were beginning to practice more in accord with fish and game laws. From these interests, organizations were constructed, such as the Bandeirante Ornithological Society and the Mineiro Ornithological Society. It was apparently in response to the emerging concerns of this urban audience that the press began to publish environmentalist exposés.

A few broader-based civic environmental organizations also sprouted in this period: In 1949 the Campaign for the Protection of Nature was formed, with a directorate composed of leaders of a number of nongovernmental and professional organizations. Proposing to struggle for reforestation, defense of habitats, and preservation of species, it broadcast saccharine radio appeals to love nature:

> Do you not hear the earth tremble, poor thing, in paroxysms of desolation?
> The tree is the perfection of form consecrated to the vegetable realm!
> It is the glory of the backlands!
> It is the friendly companion, it is the beloved companion![38]

Reorganized in 1952, the campaign took up various conservationist issues and protested the destruction of the Pontal. In this it was joined by the Defense Association of Flora and Fauna, unfortunately to little effect. The Brazilian Foundation for the Conservation of Nature was founded in 1958, affiliated with the International Union for the Conservation of Nature. It took up the defense of national parks and offered a platform for scientists within the bureaucracy. These were, however, according to their own accounts, voices in the wilderness.[39]

The conservationism expressed by these few representatives of middle-class enthusiasm was unfortunately vitiated by its lack of connection to the essential political concerns of the Right or the Left. Indeed, the inability of the middle class to capture the issues that energized either camp caused it to lose all influence during this frantic period of thwarted populist "revolution" and military dictatorship. Conservationists, like other salaried and educated Brazilians, regarded both wings with hostility, infuriated as they were by the corruption and prepotence of the rich and appalled by the ignorance and volatility of the poor. Conservationists did not take part, therefore, in the national debate over agrarian reform, even though the criminal usurpation of public lands was clearly a major reason for the disappearance of the forest at such a horrendous rate. Paulo Duarte, the brilliant publisher of the influential *Anhembi* magazine, could not visualize a potential connection between reform and conservation. Instead, he considered the former merely a "demagogic preoccupation." It was "much more important," he insisted, "to put a stop to the destruction of natural resources" and "begin immediately a great campaign to recuperate or restore exhausted lands." More sympathetic and sensible was Augusto Ruschi, the Espírito Santo naturalist who proposed that the preservation of natural areas should be integrated in any agrarian reform plan, a position that would have strengthened the hand of reformers, had it been taken up generally by conservationists.[40]

The military cut short the debate over agrarian reform in 1964. It overthrew the leftist President João Goulart and proscribed hundreds of civilian politicians and labor leaders whom it considered subversive or corrupt. Existing political parties were outlawed and replaced by new, subservient ones. Much of this was in accord with the wishes of the middle class, with whom the generals shared many fears and ambitions. Conservation did not much concern the latter, yet they gave the subject some initial attention because they identified conservation, to some degree, with their legitimizing principle of "national security." This doctrine was for the generals nearly a religious imperative, no less compelling for all the unbelief of the civilians. Forest destruction was taken up several times in the army's Superior War School, where civilian scientists were invited to lecture on the subject and where student officers and civilian familiars studied the problem. The generals wanted to rationalize the timber trade in order to put exports of wood on a sustainable basis, but they also conceived of Brazil's forests as guaranteeing its "territorial integrity." This may seem odd, because armies from time immemorial have preferred treeless plains on which to perform, especially on national borders, but the generals still felt the pull of the nativist ideas of Alberto Torres, whose appeal to the "sources of life" echoed in the Superior War School.[41]

Whatever the generals' motives, during their first years in power a series of laws and decrees were passed that bore promise of real stewardship over national patrimony. Study groups had for years been drafting a replacement for the Forest Code of 1934. The code's principal defect, in fact, was that it had never been enforced: Sufficient funds were never provided, and for many years it had been policed by volunteers, many of whom were on the take. Their duties were then assigned to untrained civil police. A multiplicity of agencies was responsible for executing the code. Prosecution was undercut by a new penal code, which reduced forest crimes to misdemeanors, and by a reluctance to apply a law that was being rewritten. By 1957 there had been only one conviction under it! A principal sticking point was, once again, the question of private-property rights. Goulart's minister of agriculture had advanced the notion that it was not the government that limited property rights over certain kinds of forests but "nature itself" and that, therefore, the prohibition on cutting them down was inherently nonindemnifiable. A few months after their coup, the generals cut through this discussion with a constitutional amendment that returned public lands to the federal government. This was immediately followed with a "Land Statute" that affirmed the social role of landownership, which depended on fair distribution and appropriate use, including assurance of its conservation. The military, annoyed at the intransigence of large landowners before any sort of reform and fearful of radicalization of the strike movements that had preceded their takeover, were trying to grasp the agrarian issue for themselves and at the same time stimulate efficient land use. Thus the generals brought together the issues of landownership and conservation.[42]

In 1967 a new Forest Code was promulgated. It reaffirmed the authority of the state over private forests, restored criminal penalties for infractions, extended protection to more kinds of vegetation, including gallery forests and mangrove, and simplified forest classification. Industries that consumed wood and charcoal were required to establish, within ten years, planted forests ample enough to supply all their requirements. Forested land was exempted from all taxes, and the forest itself was excluded, for tax purposes, from assets. It abandoned the principle that landowners must protect forested watersheds without compensation and instead committed the state to their eventual expropriation. The code also contained sufficient loopholes to eliminate every native tree still standing. Although the landowner was required to keep 20 percent of his land in forest, there was, as before, no provision against his selling off his wooded tract to a buyer, who could cut down 80 percent of it—ad infinitum. The government did not itself abjure the destruction of "forests of permanent preservation," although cases of "public utility or social interest" were subjected to presidential approval. Agrarian reform was the only federal project obliged to respect standing forest. The landowner was permitted, "for the purpose of increasing economic return," to cut down his last patch of native forest as long as his purpose was to replace it with homogeneous planted stands. Mauro Victor, of the Forest Institute of São Paulo, pointed to the contrast between the government's draconian monopoly of subsoil rights—ores and hydrocarbons—and its renunciation of forest resources evident in this document.[43]

The Forest Code was followed by a law that permitted a tax deduction against costs of reforestation. To qualify, reforestation projects had to be approved by the Ministry of Agriculture, and proof had to be presented that the projects were carried out. These incentives were available only to landowners willing to plant at least 10,000 trees a year—more than 3 hectares, an area larger than the average smallholder could undertake. The military government thus heeded the warnings of forest depletion, a serious threat to an economy still so dependent on fuelwood and now striving to be self-sufficient in a raw material as basic as paper pulp. Indeed, the hope that pulp might become an important export impelled the generals as much as did their worry over domestic shortage. It had become clear that cheap seeds and easy bank credit were insufficient to persuade iron and steel mill owners to plant on sufficient scale. (It was also pointed out to the generals that Argentina, Brazil's largest customer for araucaria, was systematically planting it and someday might be Brazil's largest supplier— a galling prospect.) By the mid-1960s, perhaps 500 million trees, mostly eucalyptus, were growing in the area of the Atlantic Forest. But this was the rough equivalent of just 2,000 square kilometers, and experts were estimating that as much as 240 million trees would have to be planted each year, four times the actual rate.[44]

Tax incentives were insufficient to persuade private landowners to preserve primary forest or to plant permanent forests. Indeed, they had expressed unease at drafts of the Forest Code which implied that they would not be allowed to cut down woodlots they had planted. Forest specialists knew that the government alone possessed the resources to plant for posterity. Existing areas of planted forest in state and federal ownership, however, were very small and were designed rather to serve as seed nurseries and model exploitation forests, not as protective preserves—the forest services were expected to raise part of their budgets by sales of their wood. Tax incentives, furthermore, threw most of the burden of reforestation on the taxpaying public instead of the landowners, already obliged to keep 20 percent of their properties in forest. By excluding smallholders from the benefits of the law, furthermore, another wedge was placed between rich and poor, and an opportunity was lost to improve the viability of family farms.[45]

In 1967 the final elements in the military program were promulgated. A new hunting and fishing code was passed that authorized the creation of wildlife refuges and forbade the export of wildlife. A decree-law brought together several agencies with responsibility for parks and forest reserves under a Brazilian Institute for Forest Development. Development was indeed its overriding concern. Parks were afforded no new funding. A report written for the institute in 1969 showed that only the three oldest were effectively managed, and even these remained in part in private hands and were too short of funds to permit scientific investigations. No new parks were created for a decade. By 1970 there were three more forestry schools, attached to regional universities, at Itaguaí, Piracicaba, and Curitiba. They were expected to train the specialists needed by the reforestation enterprises.[46]

Thus had the military government confirmed Brazil on the path of conservation, firmly subordinated to the goal of economic development. Lamentably, there was little of the Atlantic Forest left to conserve, and even less of it could be described with any confidence as undisturbed or nearly so. How those remnants could be exploited and yet considered to be "conserved" was as uncertain and unexplained as ever. Preservation, much less environmentalism, was an impulse that remained beyond the consciousness of those in power. At the turn of the 1970s, the Brazilian economy embarked on five years of extremely rapid growth, the so-called economic miracle, which was paralleled by extremely harsh repression, made necessary as the military closed off all surviving independent forms of political expression. In the midst of this terrible time, the environmental costs of development began to be debated much more widely and urgently in the "developed" countries. Some of these costs were appearing at the door of urban Brazilian society, provoking shock and confusion. The Atlantic Forest might yet be saved, but only in the nick of time.

13

Unsustainable Developments

"Você já pensou seriamente nas suas consequências?"
"A consequência é o lucro."

"Have you thought seriously about the consequences?"
"The consequence is profit."

RAINOL GRECCO, "BRAZIL'S BIGGEST TIMBERMAN" (1975)

During the decade of the 1970s, the scale and velocity of the military government's development projects reached a climax that ended not only in economic crisis but also in a gathering storm of environmental disasters, discrediting its avowed concern for national security. The economic "miracle" that began in 1968 was accompanied, paradoxically, by increased reliance on arbitrary rule and military force. One of the army's climactic battles with tiny, desperate guerrilla bands took place, in fact, in the Caparaó National Park, where wrecks of the engagement still clutter the landscape. The viciousness and insecurity of the struggle made foreign investors uneasy—the formula that had been followed since the early 1950s of enticing overseas capital by offering it a tightly closed domestic market was losing its potency.

The military and its sympathizers reacted arrogantly to the issues raised at the first United Nations Conference on the Environment and Development, at Stockholm in 1972. It was suspected that the industrialized countries had invented still another obstacle to Brazil's elevation to their ranks, and it was theorized that one of Brazil's comparative advantages consisted precisely in its undiminished capacity to absorb industrial pollution. "Let pollution come, as long as the factories come with it," exulted José Sarney, a northeastern senator who was to become president a decade later. The government's representative to the conference offered an insincere populist formula that was to be repeatedly relied upon: "The worst form of pollution is poverty." The director of the ill-advised drainage works in the Campos region felt authorized to describe its lakes as "an ecological disaster, biologically unbalanced and useless" and to characterize his task

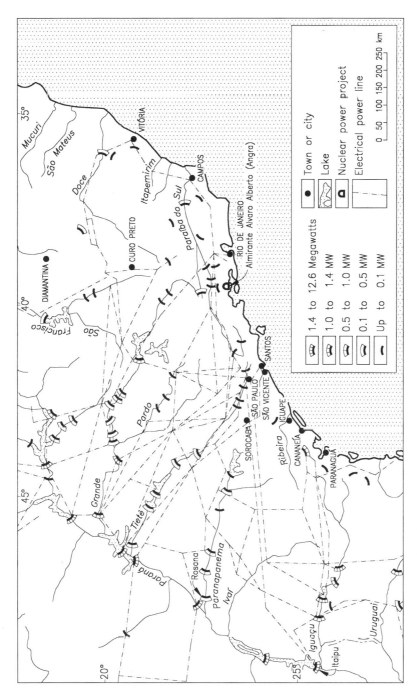

Map 8. Hydroelectric and nuclear projects, 1950–1990

as "correcting the aberrations of nature." Foreign scientists were questioning the viability of development projects in tropical forests, but Brazilian emissaries to international meetings on the subject tended to dismiss them, preferring to emphasize instead the extremely optimistic goals of these programs. Although a few critical voices were raised, among scientists and within civil society, they were isolated and often paid dearly for their dissent.[1]

Brazil's momentarily rapid economic growth rate appeared to justify technocratic heedlessness. But at the end of 1973, the "miracle" was jolted by the quadrupling of oil prices. The industrialized Southeast had become in two short decades dangerously dependent on petroleum to keep it in motion, and almost all of this fuel had to be imported. The response of the technocrats was to launch development projects ever more invasive of the environment and careless of their social effects. They obtained abundant credits from foreign banks, which were desperate to recycle funds pouring in from members of the oil cartel, and invested them in an expansion of exports to pay the petroleum bill and in a diversified program to achieve energy self-sufficiency. Offshore oil drilling, nuclear power plants, a sugarcane-to-alcohol fuel scheme, and an enormous expansion in hydroelectric development were enthusiastically and simultaneously prosecuted. These schemes, carried out for the most part in the region of the remnant Atlantic Forest, implied dangers for its survival. The alcohol program quickly became a major cause of deforestation. Dredging and filling in the Campos region was accelerated to expand canefields, nearly extinguishing its lakes. In the Ribeirão Prêto district of São Paulo, sugarcane was responsible for almost half the loss of primary forest between 1962 and 1984 and was even more damaging to savanna formations, destroying 457 square kilometers of it. Industries that burned wood as a substitute for imported petroleum were exempted from the Forest Code requirement that they replant.[2]

Perhaps most damaging of all the development schemes were the hydroelectric projects. The rugged topography and abundant rainfall of the region of the Atlantic Forest had invited entrepreneurs, civil engineers, and electrical-equipment manufacturers to collaborate, quite soon after the turn of the twentieth century, in constructing hydroelectric plants in the neighborhood of nearly every city in the Southeast. By the mid-1920s, the region's metropolises were equipped with very large installations. In São Paulo, the current of rivers circulating around the city was reversed in order to fill a reservoir, occupying 127 square kilometers, whence the flow tumbled 800 meters through tubes to the town of Cubatão, at the foot of the coastal palisade, where a 336,000-kilowatt hydroelectric plant was built. By 1950 there were 126 hydroelectric plants in the region of the Atlantic Forest. Collectively, their impact on the surviving gallery forests was limited: Only those at São Paulo, Rio de Janeiro, and Campinas dammed more than a square kilometer or so of surface.

These plants were privately owned, the largest of them by foreign companies. In the late 1950s and early 1960s, however, they were expropriated, victims of nationalist and populist pressures and their own inability to raise more capital. The new state-appointed directors confronted sharply rising demand for power in an atmosphere of crisis, marked by overloads and blackouts. They began building plants of much larger capacity and extended a network connecting the industrial triangle of Belo Horizonte, Rio de Janeiro, and São Paulo. This generation of plants occupied the most easily exploited sites on the Tietê, Paranapanema, Grande, Paraibuna, Paraíba, and Pardo rivers, backing up the flow of water for several kilometers and creating 40- to 70-square-kilometer reservoirs. The next generation of plants was already planned: high dams requiring vast quantities of concrete to span less favorable sites on the affluents of the Paraná and on the Paraná itself. These required human-made lakes of 200 to more than 1,000 square kilometers. Capping all these was Itaipu, near Foz do Iguaçu, the world's largest hydroelectric dam, 185 meters high and 7 kilometers wide, designed to generate 12.6 megawatts. Construction began in 1973, as a binational project with Paraguay, eventually to flood 1,529 square kilometers on the Brazilian side of the river and 2,260 square kilometers on the Paraguayan side. In addition, a 1,350-square-kilometer protective area would surround the impounded river.

Incredibly, the project was allowed to obliterate one of the world's natural wonders, Sete Quedas, the magnificent cataract that had long before been declared a national park. With it disappeared the uninvestigated ruins of the sixteenth-century Royal City of Guairá. Numerous tourists rushed to experience Sete Quedas before it drowned: The rickety suspension bridges could not bear their weight, and nineteen fell to their death one day. A few thousand protesters held, in honor of the dead tourists and the dying river, a *quarup*—the indigenous ceremony of grief for a defunct chieftain. Nervous relatives and neighbors sought to dissuade them; indeed, one of the dam's leading opponents was jailed for a year and a half. Octávio Marcondes Ferraz, who, as head of Eletrobrás in 1964, had planned a lower dam at Itaipu that would have left Sete Quedas intact, complained of the secrecy and arbitrariness that had made the tragedy possible: We are, he wrote, "a country of faits accomplis and submissive taxpayers."[3]

By 1992, 269 hydroelectric plants in the southeastern region of the Atlantic Forest had flooded 17,130 square kilometers, and their transmission lines occupied another 2,800 square kilometers, together an area equal to nearly half the territory of the state of Rio de Janeiro. Eighty-eight other plants had already been decommissioned. More plants were under construction, which would drown another 10,000 square kilometers. In addition, there were in the region at least 20 large water reservoirs of unreported dimensions that served city populations and provided irrigation and flood control. It is not possible to estimate the amount of forest that disappeared under the rising waters of all these dams and under the towers of the transmission lines. Certainly a considerable area under water had been previously deforested. This was the case of one of the two still formally protected areas of the Paulista Pontal, the São Paulo Lagoon, which was estimated to have lost 90 percent of its forest before flooding began. By 1992 most of this aquatic bird reserve was disappearing under the waters of the still uncompleted Primavera dam. The rest of it was divided up into lots by the electric company and passed out to colonists brought in from elsewhere on the dam site! Although it was believed that most of the area of Sete Quedas National Park had been deforested before it was drowned, the Itaipu authority stated that it had cleared 591 square kilometers of forest on the Brazilian side of the river, nearly 40 percent of the area submerged. Total tree removal was required by a law of 1960, but cutting appears to have been selective. The sale of merchantable timber from their dam sites represented, in fact, a modest source of income for the electric companies.[4]

Since the beginning of the century, thousands of square kilometers of gallery and semideciduous forest had been obliterated to produce and transmit electricity. Nevertheless, until the late 1970s, conservationists offered no dissent to the public's favorable opinion of the "harnessing" of Brazil's "white petroleum." On the contrary, they joined the chorus of praise. Brazil's coal deposits were exiguous and of poor quality, and its oil reserves were untested and largely untapped. Hydroelectric power, clean and apparently cheap and nonpolluting, therefore seemed to redeem Brazil's disappointingly nonnavigable rivers for a strategically valuable purpose. Indeed, it was hoped that hydroelectricity might reduce fuelwood extraction. Hydroelectric companies, furthermore, were expected to encourage reforestation, because their operations depended upon a regulated flow of the hydrological cycle and because their investment had to be protected from siltation.[5]

The Itaipu project, however, provoked at last severe questioning, not limited to environmentalists or ecological specialists. It caused considerable diplomatic friction with Argentina and submitted Paraguay to a treaty that none but a collusive dictatorship would have signed. It required the removal, just on the Brazilian side, of 42,000 residents, many of whom were paid only for improvements to their land, and only tardily, after inflation had reduced the awards. The farms that were submerged would have produced 600,000 tons of foodstuffs each year, a loss that would beggar the counties along the reservoir.[6]

In reaction to public murmurings, the electric companies engaged archaeologists to conduct hurried surveys of dam sites and unearth whatever traces they could find of indigenous cultures. They hired wildlife specialists to "rescue" animals trapped by the rising waters—a photogenic, if not very effective, activity. At Itaipu, the hapless "animal units" were installed in "refuges" along the lakeside, totaling 390 square kilometers—less than 10 percent of the area flooded. Meanwhile, several companies, in the hope of developing an industry that might compensate in part for lost farms, released the African tilapia fish in their reservoirs, despite repeated disasters that have followed introductions of exotic fish in other countries. The companies were required by law to reforest their margins. They did not make this a priority, even though they might have profited from it—one specialist estimated that the planting of a three-meter swath along the length of the dam-impounded Tietê River would store energy equivalent to 6,000 megawatts. Some of the companies did found tree nurseries, as much, it seems, out of a concern to demarcate the borders of their property as to reduce siltation of their reservoirs. In 1993 the Itaipu authority announced at last that it would reforest with native species its entire protective area. This effort would be by far the largest such experiment in reestablishing the Atlantic Forest and was a remarkable sign of the acceptance by state-owned enterprises of environmentalist principles. Whether this goal was realizable was another matter.[7]

The Rosana dam, whose construction began in the early 1980s on the Paranapanema River near its confluence with the Paraná, subtracted more than 30 square kilometers from the shrinking Morro do Diabo reserve, the last remnant of the Pontal. The state-owned electric company cut down more forest than was necessary to clear the rising waters—apparently it was not sure exactly how high the level would rise, a miscalculation that seems to have been common in dam construction. The company also decided to build an airstrip within the reserve, for the convenience of its staff while the dam was abuilding. Abandoned thereafter, it was discovered by drug smugglers, who further complicated the work of the beleaguered forest guards. By way of compensation for all this damage, the electric company, counseled by Maria Tereza Jorge Pádua, enlarged the forest police detachment from 11 to 70 guards, equipped them with uniforms and vehicles, and funded a biologist. Morro do Diabo thus became one of the very few preserves in the Atlantic Forest that was adequately protected.[8]

The modest efforts of the electric companies to deflect public criticism were increasingly ineffective in the face of severe social and political problems arising from these investments. The dislocation of residents, the loss of productive lands, and the abandonment of workers at the end of the phase of construction proved immensely embarrassing. It seemed altogether strange that the government was unable to expropriate latifundia for the purpose of land reform although it experienced no difficulty in expropriating smallholders for the purpose of building dams. In the Pontal, the electric company was confronted with hundreds of families camping along the roadside, in the hope of obtaining some of its lands, which the company had instead leased to large-scale ranchers—a sad finale to the drama of the forest preserve that had begun fifty years before and that by the late 1980s had been erased from the collective memory. Even worse were the scandals associated with the financing and construction of the dams. Itaipu, originally budgeted at US$10 billion, cost a reported US$20 billion. Overruns and inflation could account for only a lesser part of this staggering total—it was obvious to an enraged electorate that unrestrained corruption had increased costs of dam building, which had become a means of paying off the government's supporters and thus an end in itself. Itaipu was one of the principal reasons why Brazil's foreign debt skyrocketed and became, by the late 1970s, unpayable. Only after it became nearly impossible to contract new foreign debts did the electric companies begin to consider ways of conserving energy. Even the simplest of conservation measures remained untried by the late 1980s, however.[9]

Other tactics employed in the struggle to free the economy from the burden of imported petroleum were not without consequences for the Atlantic Forest. Alcohol fuel was criticized mainly for the cost of its subsidies and for the shift it induced from basic foodstuffs for the city populations. Complaints were raised as well against the increasing favor shown export agriculture, which was also intended to offset the petroleum bill. Both of these programs surely resulted in forest clearing, at least at second hand, as foodstuff-producing small farmers were pushed from lands coveted for canefields. This phenomenon, however, did not receive much public attention. An accord with West Germany to import, store, and reprocess that country's nuclear wastes in return for technical assistance in the building of six nuclear plants along the Southeast coast was narrowly averted, mainly because of the near financial collapse of the federal government by the end of the decade. Two of the plants were built on the coast near Angra dos Reis, in Rio de Janeiro State. Meanwhile, almost no consideration was given to restraining the growth of the automobile fleet or to improving its efficiency.

By the early 1970s, the last large, accessible stands of the Atlantic Forest were found in the panhandle of South Bahia. There, where an asphalted federal highway had just been pushed through that linked the area with Rio de Janeiro, hundreds of contractors equipped with chain saws, diesel tractors, winches, skidders, and flatbed trucks made quick work of trees that had stood unharmed since the Portuguese first landed on that very coast in 1500. In 1971 some 11,000 square kilometers of the South Bahia forest remained intact. By the early 1980s less than 2,000 square kilometers were left. Some 230 sawmills were still in operation, employing 7,000 workers and capable of sawing nearly 1.5 million cubic meters a year. When this forest was finished, it was given over to pasture. The market for these fine hardwoods was not foreign but domestic. In 1989 only 2.4 percent of Brazilian timber, native and planted, was exported. Brazilians appreciated wood, if not trees, employing it lavishly in veneers and even in solid planks in the decoration and furnishings of their homes, offices, and public buildings.[10]

Meanwhile, cacao cultivation was coming to be pursued in South Bahia in a manner considered more threatening to the Atlantic Forest. The traditional cabroca system preserved perhaps half the original forest species and so came to be looked upon by environmentalists as preferable to clear-cutting, which was insistently recommended by the regional agricultural research center. Smallholders, impelled by the need to utilize their land more intensively, were much more likely to eliminate shade, embarrassing the same environmentalists who would prefer to view smallholders as better stewards of natural patrimony. Cacao planting expanded rapidly as prices rose up to 1986, occupying 7,000 square kilometers in that year, more and more of it under a regime of clear-cutting because banks would lend only on the research center's recommendations. But if clear-cutting really doubled production, it might have been preferable to clear-cut and occupy half as much forested land as cabroca plantations. Cabroca, in any case, did not preserve remnant forest, it merely stayed its execution: As primary-forest trees aged, they did not reproduce. Shade trees on the oldest estates, some dating to the 1910s, were being cut down before they collapsed on the workers' heads.[11]

Neither in South Bahia nor elsewhere was the requirement of the 1965 Forest Code obeyed that 20 percent of the land remain in woodland, despite increased inspection by state and federal forest services. In a concerted drive in the area of São Fidelis in Rio de Janeiro in 1976, for example, dozens of landowners and contractors were fined for clearing forest without authorization, but the malefactors paid without demur, an inconvenience of small importance compared with the value of the timber. Indeed, the fines were a trifle compared with the cost of buying additional cleared land.[12]

More usually, local sawmill owners and their contractors, men of considerable wealth and political influence, had nothing to fear from the federal Forest Service, renamed the Brazilian Institute for Forest Development (IBDF). The president of this agency announced that its mandate was "precisely to promote management [*sic*] of native forests and reforestation with economic species, in behalf of rational utilization and increase of new energy sources." Forest inspection and arrests were usually carried out by a division of the state police forces. Undermanned and ill equipped, they were directed by timorous supervisors, in turn mostly ignored by the IBDF state delegates, political nominees almost never concerned with the conservation of native forest. Permits to cut forest were thus easily obtained and almost never confirmed on site. A landowner on the border of the Itatiaia National Park was therefore not only candid but also realistic in responding to an environmentalist who had threatened to report him to the forest guards: "I'm cutting trees all the same, I'm cutting them from the watershed and it's going to be the way I want it, tell that to the forest guards. Tell them—they're all in my pocket." Indeed, the federal guards, demoralized and underpaid, were quitting in legions.[13]

In São Paulo, woodcutting permits declined in number through the 1970s, because landowners were running out of native forest. The 675 sawmills operating in the state were for the most part no longer processing local timber but were buying from other states, approximately 3.4 million cubic meters a year, equivalent, perhaps, to 170 square kilometers a year of Mato Grosso's forests. Surviving stands were nibbled at by small-scale operators. Not even national and state parks and reserves were spared. Or, better said, woodcutters preferred to attack government reserves, where no owners were waiting to collect a fee. Timber poachers in the Rio de Janeiro state forest of Desengano went heavily armed, unchallenged by forest guards, who had not been issued the weapons they were authorized. The cunning and determination that were invested in these activities may be imagined: At a time when the minimum wage was the equivalent of US$60 a month, a single specimen of jacarandá, 2 meters in diameter, would bring in US$7,000. Nor did landowners hesitate to fell such giants on their properties: They could assert that they had not diminished the size of their woodlots but were merely subjecting them to "rational exploitation." The Forest Service was always there to provide seedlings of jacarandá to conscientious owners, whose great-great-grandchildren might (or more likely might not) find them grown to respectable size.[14]

One of the most lamentable and final losses was that of mangrove, greatly endangered because of its economic value and its presence in wetlands coveted for real estate development. By 1979, on Guanabara Bay, once ringed by thousands of square kilometers of mangrove, only 50 square kilometers remained, degraded and immature, ranged only a few meters wide along a few of the creeks that fed into its northeastern corner. Although protected by law, mangrove was being cut and burned by bakeries and brickworks and used in wattle-and-daub construction. Drainage and landfill operations were taking place in the area. These last stands would probably not survive long, even if protection were made effective, because the channels were transited by large vessels and were polluted with sewage. Prior deforestation caused mudbanks to form that desiccated mangrove roots.[15]

Less attention was given to rationalizing the exploitation of fuelwood than might have been expected. Firewood was no longer the principal source of energy in the industrialized Southeast, but it remained important. It was estimated that the region consumed 73.7 million cubic meters of firewood in 1970, about half of which was for domestic use, now mainly rural. The iron and steel industry of Minas Gerais still fired its furnaces with charcoal, for which it consumed annually 5 million cubic meters of wood. The government-sponsored expansion of the Mato Grosso agricultural frontier and the slowdown of the economy after 1973 kept the supply of firewood high and the prices low. The consumption of charcoal for the production of iron and steel in Minas Gerais doubled over the decade, even though the mills were becoming more efficient in its use: By 1980 the state's mills required 11 million cubic meters of wood, the equivalent of almost 9,000 square kilometers a year of planted forest. The mills' own planting could supply no more than a quarter of this amount, and some of their stocks was diverted to paper-pulp factories, which required homogeneous raw material. The mills continued to resort to contractors to obtain wood from native forests, thereby insulating themselves not only from legal difficulties but also from growing public criticism. Contractors began to practice claim jumping widely in eastern Minas Gerais, where the expulsion of poor backwoods squatters was the cheapest means of acquiring woodland. Astonishingly, the IBDF collaborated by permitting charcoal cutters to clear the minimum 20 percent of woodlot reserves, as long as they submitted replanting schedules—schedules it was far beyond the capacity of the institute to supervise. In 1988 the IBDF decreed that all commercial consumers of firewood plant sufficient trees to achieve self-sufficiency within seven years. By 1992 the iron and steel manufacturers' association admitted that they were planting only a third as much as would be needed, and it obtained a further three-year delay.[16]

Wood contractors invaded savanna formations, less dense than second-growth forest and less likely to grow back to equivalent volumes of usable fuelwood. The savanna was being put to the same pressures that had confronted the Atlantic Forest for more than a century, but it was likely to succumb in a shorter time. Suppliers of smaller industries were more likely to engage in contraband woodcutting on private properties and public reserves. In the late 1970s, cutting in the Desengano State Park was so open that wood was piled on the side of the road, awaiting loading in trucks. Truckers bringing firewood to ceramic, tile, and paper factories and bakeries in the city of Rio de Janeiro in the early 1980s refused to report the sources of their cargoes.[17]

The integrity of the remaining tracts of the Atlantic Forest was threatened by dealers in birds, plants, flowers, essences, and pelts. These lesser, more easily hidden extractive products were subjected to even less inspection than were loggers and charcoal makers. As subsistence farmers who squatted on claims at the forest edge lost them to developers, many turned to extractivism for a living. The brazilwood tree, the increasingly rare national symbol, was still being cut down to make bows for musical instruments. A giant tree fern had to be put on the endangered list even though it was widely distributed because its trunk was in great demand for the confection of flower planters. An understory tree called caxeta was used to make pencils. Orchid and bromeliad vendors experienced little difficulty in filling vans full of flowers, mostly in parks and other preserves, and selling them in the cities. Pharmaceutical companies and even the Rio de Janeiro state Vital Brasil Institute were accused of decimating native medicinal flora. The trade in hearts of palm had become industrialized—in the Ribeira Valley there were eighteen canning factories. The search for palms now extended deep into the forest, along trails guarded from competitors. Saplings were no longer spared. This was prohibited, because the palm laid seed only after ten years of growth. Indeed, as more and more of the Serra do Mar was designated protected, the entire trade became illegal. Not surprisingly, factory owners were not questioned about their sources of supply, but the displaced and desperate gatherers were subject to extortion by forest guards. Commercial hunting was finally outlawed in 1974. It had never been subject to any significant degree of regulation before then, judging from the very small number of licenses previously issued (5,650 in all of Brazil in 1973) and the even fewer fines levied thereafter. Brazil, in 1975, was one of the earliest signers of the Convention on International

Trade in Endangered Species. Live birds, monkeys, and plants continued, nevertheless, to be smuggled in immense numbers to Europe and the United States, mostly through Paraguayan and Bolivian dealers. Smuggling of pelts was common and profitable in the late 1970s and early 1980s: An ocelot skin could fetch US$100, nearly twice the monthly minimum wage.[18]

The great metropolises of Rio de Janeiro, São Paulo, and Belo Horizonte were still surrounded by wooded greenbelts, small areas of which might possibly be undisturbed. They depended heavily on their wooded uplands for water supply. Public authorities repeatedly treated these protected reserves as inexpensive sites for development rather than as an essential amenity. Their occasional efforts to prevent the invasion of these spaces by private individuals, poor or rich, were halfhearted, overruled by venal or populist interests. The swelling of the cities thus led to a number of dramatic conflicts, most of them defeats for conservationists. One of the most conflictful episodes was provoked by the state of São Paulo's plan to violate the state-owned forest reserve of Caucaia, which protected a watershed that had supplied water to the city since the beginning of the century. An airport was planned there in 1977 that would have deforested 60 square kilometers. Buffeted by "ecological hysteria," in fact the first successful environmental campaign in the state, the issue was finally resolved by converting the military air base of Cumbica. Flatlands of the bordering Tietê River were designated an "ecological park," to pacify environmentalists. The state could not be prevented, however, from scarring the Cantareira hills, on the north side of the city, with water treatment plants, electric power lines, radio and television towers, and roadways, while private interests were allowed to quarry for granite and to implant luxurious suburban developments.[19]

In Rio de Janeiro, the ecological reserve of Jacarepaguá was obliterated, as real estate interests were allowed to claim and subdivide the area. It is an exquisite irony that the convention center that was built on this site hosted, in 1992, the second United Nations Conference on the Environment and Development. Continued settlement and interference with precarious vegetation on the exceedingly steep hillsides that dominate much of the city caused repeated and increasingly severe landslides and flooding. More than a million inhabitants were clinging to the hills in shantytowns that had become permanent residences, beyond the financial resources of the city to remove. Meanwhile, the asphalting of the coastal road between Santos and Rio de Janeiro made it possible for thousands of middle-class families to realize their dream of spending their weekends on the shore.

The resulting real estate rush made numerous fortunes, obliterated an isolated rural culture of fisher folk, and destroyed a thousand square kilometers of coastal forest. As plans were drawn up to extend the road past Santos to Iguape and beyond to Paranaguá, developers anticipated a building
boom along the paradisiacal estuary of Comprida Island.[20]

Despite the extreme disfavor with which international environmentalist
concerns were received by the military government and its technocratic
aides, it was thought prudent to erect a facade that might allay foreign
criticism. In 1973 a federal Special Secretariat of the Environment (SEMA)
was created, charged with monitoring and controlling pollution. This
agency was also made responsible for the prevention of plant and animal
extinction, thereby balancing to some degree the interventionism of the
IBDF. Remarkably, committed and able environmentalists were named to
direct SEMA and the IBDF. Paulo Nogueira Neto and Maria Tereza Jorge
Pádua struggled unceasingly and increasingly effectively over the course
of a decade to enlarge and protect national parks and other reserves. These
agencies devoted nearly all their attention to the Amazon region. The Atlantic Forest seemed doomed, already degraded with little left to protect,
at best a reminder of what might happen if immediate measures were not
taken in the north. The Amazon was also immediately threatened by the
aggressive development plans of other federal agencies.[21]

The states of the Southeast, however, set up their own agencies, which
were increasingly active and somewhat more effective in persuading their
governments to declare additional protected areas. All these efforts coincided with gathering political difficulties for the military government and
its official party, whose shortcomings as environmental stewards could be
emphasized by the media with less risk of censorship than could other
sorts of malfeasance. Nogueira Neto and Jorge Pádua achieved ample and
sympathetic press coverage as environmental awareness began to bloom
among significant numbers of the urban middle class.[22]

Even more the hero of this youthful urban stratum and the press of the
metropolises was a self-taught naturalist of Espírito Santo whose disposition was entirely uncongenial to wheedling concessions from the governing elite. This was Augusto Ruschi, a descendant of Italian immigrants,
son of a land surveyor, trained in the law and agronomy. Since childhood
he had been fascinated by the forests of his native Santa Tereza. Saving all
that he could of his earnings as a surveyor, he had created an herbarium
and natural history museum at the homesite he inherited from his parents.
There he succeeded in the remarkable feat of keeping and breeding hummingbirds, his special enthusiasm and subject of study. The dependence of

these birds on the nectar of orchids and bromeliads led him to excel in these taxa as well. Ruschi published privately more than 400 papers, full of rhetoric and eccentricities yet original and insightful, based as they were on closer and longer observation of primary forest than that of any other Brazilian naturalist. He discovered more than 100 species, and he perceived the dangerous side effects of DDT as early as 1949. He experimented with biological controls of bat-spread rabies, schistosomiasis, and malaria. He studied the collections of the natural history museums of Europe and the United States, advised zoos, hosted such foreign notables as the amateur naturalist and president of Dupont, Howard Greenewalt, and corresponded with many Brazilian and foreign tropical specialists.[23]

Ruschi's mentors at the National Museum recognized his worth and offered him a research professorship, initiating a long and valuable relationship with that principal center of environmental research. In 1940 he had bought with his own funds a patch of forest in the Valssugana district of the nearby county of Nova Lombardia, to preserve it from slash-and-burn farmers. In 1953 he donated this land to the museum and persuaded it to purchase an additional tract to add to the preserve, where he then devoted much of his career. He also studied all the other surviving remnants of the Atlantic Forest in his state. In 1948 Ruschi began a parallel career as gadfly of the state government, appearing before its legislature and calling for the expropriation of Espírito Santo's remaining primary forest. He demanded the creation of a state forest service, a policy-making forest council, and a department of natural science within the state secretariat of agriculture. He denounced the introduction of coffee farming on the exceedingly rugged hillsides of the state and fulminated against the planting of the exotic eucalyptus.[24]

The remaining forest lands were fortunate to have in Ruschi so determined a defender, because the state for most of the period he was active was in the hands of an elite absolutely uncaring of its natural endowment—indeed, totally committed to wringing from it every possible immediate profit. When, in 1953, Ruschi proposed to a reform governor to turn over to the state the forest preserve he had rescued, the governor replied, "Are you loony? Don't you know what these politicians are like? Today, I'm in office, but tomorrow someone can come along who may expel even you from [Nova Lombardia]!" Unfortunately, Ruschi was almost entirely isolated within his own community; local people knew nothing of what went on within the walls of his estate, and local hunters detested him, holding him responsible for the passage of the wildlife code of 1967 that prevented them from selling their prey. They nailed hummingbirds to his gate. One night in November 1976 marauders invaded his museum,

armed with revolvers and shotguns. They killed caged monkeys and released his birds, smashed the plant nursery, and fired their guns to intimidate the staff. They left behind a written warning:

> Only the poor are arrested, while the rich hunt and kill whenever
> they want. Is that because they give certain persons assistance?
> That's why the [forest] guards are getting fatter day by day.

Those whom the marauders suspected of special privileges were named
and were accused of "parking their cars on the edge of the forest and going
to hunt as calm as you please." Apparently, Ruschi was unable to defuse
tensions arising not only from an arbitrarily conceived hunting code but
also from favoritism and corruption in its application, for which he had
become the scapegoat. The police took no action.[25]

In 1965 Ruschi fought to block the state's plan to sell timber in the state
forest reserves and plant them in eucalyptus. In the early 1970s Ruschi
carried on a campaign against the federally owned Vale do Rio Doce mining company (CVRD), which had reinforced the broad-gauge railway line
between the iron deposits of Minas Gerais and a port that it built on the
coast north of Vitória. The company owned, in the county of Linhares,
adjoining the Sooretama State Park, a forest reserve, which it was bent
on exploiting for crossties. It attempted to persuade the governor to trade
Sooretama and the other four state reserves for a piece of real estate in
downtown Vitória! Ruschi also campaigned in 1975 against Aracruz, a
paper-pulp company, and the CVRD, which wanted to expropriate the
coastal reserve of Comboios, a breeding ground of giant sea turtles. The
governor on that occasion created a state forest service for the sole purpose
of preventing the transfer of this reserve to the federal IBDF. This time
Ruschi persuaded the navy that this maneuver threatened national security, and the reserve was federalized.[26]

Ruschi's best-known struggle, however, came in 1977, when the state
governor, Élcio Alvares, tried to expropriate the Nova Lombardia reserve,
registered in the name of the National Museum since 1953. The governor's
intention was to lease the reserve to cronies, who wanted to clear it and
plant hearts-of-palm trees! The government claimed that Ruschi had no
title and was merely squatting in the area. Because he had neither cleared
the forest nor installed any "improvements," title reverted to the state.
Ruschi insisted that he had registered his title in 1953 but that it had been
stolen from the registry office by order of the governor himself. When he
reminded the press that the title had been published in the state's official
journal, the governor had every copy of the issue confiscated. Fortunately,
a sympathetic historian found the listing in the state archive. Nogueira

Neto attempted to negotiate a settlement between the state and the museum. But Ruschi refused Nogueira Neto's formula of a state donation to the museum because it implied that he had embezzled the money the museum had given him in 1953. But the rector of the Federal University of Rio de Janeiro, to which the museum was subordinate, refused any compromise regarding its ownership. And public support was building for Ruschi. A caravan, organized by environmentalists in Rio de Janeiro, drove to Vitória and delivered a petition signed by 12,000 citizens. There were 2,000 signatures in Vitória as well, even though the city's newspapers had buried the story. At last, Ruschi and the museum got their title confirmed. At a legislative hearing called by the opposition party, during which numerous other land grabs were recalled, Ruschi testified that he had met the state's surveyors with a gun and that he would have shot them if he had to. Indeed, one could read on a plaque in his garden, "These plants are worth more than my own life."[27]

What sort of polity was it that placed intelligent and dedicated men in such a position? What sort of government was it that was willing to deal so sordidly with its own institutions? A jurist friend of Ruschi suggested one reply: "I hope that Brazil won't go on persecuting its savants and celebrating its mediocrities. Mediocrities detest science, and economic interests are destroying Brazil's worth and wealth." For all the energy invested in it, this was only a skirmish in an endless war. During this same decade half of the reserve of Comboios was lost, and the Itaúna reserve disappeared altogether. What was left of protected primary forest in Espírito Santo, settled by European immigrants who had supposedly brought a superior culture to its benighted natives, was the magnificent total of 319 square kilometers, 0.7 percent of its land surface.[28]

The environmentalists placed in charge of the newly created agencies had to persuade influential members of the military of the economic and strategic advisability of increased nature protection. It is difficult to imagine a tactic that would have gained them more, as little as they did gain at the time, yet it required the enunciation of ideological positions that were better forgotten when democratic government was reinstalled. Economic nationalism was a stance that appealed to military self-esteem, and so it was employed by a few environmental activists. João José Bigarella, consummate defender of the Paraná Serra do Mar, advanced the notion of "environmental security" in a course he offered in 1974 at the Superior War School (ESG). This was the military's prestigious and influential think tank. Invitations to its seminars were greatly prized by civilians of conservative or opportunistic stripe. Only in 1980, as its influence was waning, did it undertake a major analysis of environmental questions. The directors of all the principal environmental agencies and nongovernmental organizations were heard, and an extensive review of current policies was drawn up that displayed an awareness of the agencies' principal problems.[29]

Conservation held some appeal for the generals, not only because it enhanced their sense of possessing a clearer vision of the national interest but also because it offered a chance to bash the bourgeoisie for its sloth and fecklessness. This theme was irresistible for the major-brigadier who was subcommandant of the ESG: He lamented the destruction of forests, soils, and wildlife and the contamination of water and atmosphere, and he pointed out that the coastline was "in an accelerated state of degradation" because of real estate speculation, "a source of income," he remarked drily, echoing Ruschi's supporters, "for those who have no competence for other more rational activities."[30]

Civilian conservationists were capable of exacerbating their hosts' enduring suspicion of foreign interests, as one environmental agency official demonstrated: "Supra-national forces . . . exert every pressure to maintain the undeveloped countries in this stage," an idea axiomatic at the school, to which he annexed the corollary that this was accomplished "through environmental control"—influencing their governments in the direction of no controls or of excessively sophisticated controls. His agency, evidently, stood ready to define for the nation the golden mean. He was also capable of propping up the army in its resistance to a return to direct elections. Noting that opinion polls showed that the environment was already the second greatest concern of youth in the larger cities, he warned that "this is coming to be noticed and exploited by so-called 'renovative' forces as an argument for agitation. Given the long shadow of this age group and its potential political importance, this is a subject that merits careful thought." The government would have to pay "attention to the fact that the environmental defense campaigns, if not absorbed and even anticipated by the Government, can be used against certain National Objectives. Look, for example, at how the nuclear installations are being subject to exploitation abroad."[31] These were counterproductive arguments. The speaker was certainly aware that the government was indeed paying close attention to the environmental association that opposed the nuclear facility on the Espírito Santo coast—many of its members were frightened off when they were labeled Communists and blacklisted. Military nativism had already interfered with attempts at cooperation with international agencies. Nogueira Neto, who presided over the Brazilian section of the United Nations–organized Man and the Biosphere program, was prevented from accepting its assistance to establish biosphere reserves because the military thought it part of the international conspiracy.[32]

The military appeared unable to formulate more effective solutions, or, indeed, to impose obedience of the laws that they had devised fifteen years before. "What is needed," exclaimed the major-brigadier, "is the definitive law, the one that orders that all the others be respected!" This was hardly an original bon mot, yet he may have been the first to admit the systematic failure of the military's environmental codes. Military power was already faltering; this last attempt to puzzle out what to make of the environmental argument came when the inner circle of the generals had already decided to "return to the barracks."[33]

Little more of the Atlantic Forest was taken under federal protection during the 1970s. In 1971 the Bocaina National Park was decreed, supposedly 1,340 square kilometers in extent, along the Serra do Mar between São Paulo and Rio de Janeiro. Two federal biological stations were authorized in Rio de Janeiro and South Bahia, to protect species of lion tamarin in extreme danger of extinction. Nogueira Neto implanted another category of preserve—ecological stations, where preservation was to be linked to research. SEMA situated one of them at Juréia, on the Paulista coast, as a security zone around nuclear plants yet to be constructed—another intromission of environmentalist projects into the blueprints of the military. At the time this mutualism was much criticized by environmentalists, yet it might have been foreseen that the ecological station, securely implanted, would survive the grandiose and unrealizable nuclear project. The army and navy during this period took over several reserves for their own purposes, carrying out antiguerrilla exercises. The resulting exclusion of all civilian activities may well have preserved the Mendanha and Cicuta forests, respectively near Volta Redonda and Nova Iguaçu, in Rio de Janeiro State. Indeed, military reserves, alone of all government properties, were, as one naturalist pointed out, "inviolable."[34]

The states created only a few more parks and "equivalent reserves" during the decade after the first oil crisis. Minas Gerais authorized nine, totaling a mere 69 square kilometers. Rio de Janeiro had decreed somewhat earlier the state parks of Desengano and Ilha Grande, totaling nearly 500 square kilometers, along with a number of other smaller preservation units. São Paulo during this period added 940 square kilometers to its protected areas, although it appears to have lost entirely three reserves containing 370 square kilometers.[35]

This extremely modest expansion in protected area was entirely too slow a response to the destruction of the last primary stands of the Atlantic Forest during the decade of the 1970s. Many tracts containing endangered species or representing unique assemblages of species were not included among these projects—for example, the semideciduous forest of the South Bahia panhandle. Furthermore, the official lists of existing protected areas masked enormous problems in maintaining their integrity. Most important, the decrees proclaiming the parks and other sorts of reserves were almost never accompanied by the appropriation of funds to expropriate inholdings or even to delineate their borders. Even the earliest national parks, decreed in the 1930s, were, as late as 1988, still not definitively owned by the federal government. Of the 100 square kilometers included in the decree establishing the Serra dos Orgãos National Park, by 1979— 42 years later—only 23.5 square kilometers were actually under park administration, and the Park Service could prove ownership of only 8.4 square kilometers, none of which had ever been registered in the office of the National Patrimony. The Bocaina National Park was soon scaled back to 1,140 square kilometers. The Park Service failed to claim 165 square kilometers within its bounds that already belonged to other government agencies. By the late 1980s it owned only 55 square kilometers of the park's declared area. Although official maps of Bocaina still displayed an impressive patch of green, the reality was that it contained more than 3,000 inholders, brandishing conflicting titles, and countless charcoal burners, clandestine loggers, and other intruders. The park staff was but a skeleton, and no funds for expropriation had yet appeared.[36]

Some of the reserves created at the time amounted to nothing more than pious pronouncements by state or municipal authorities, visible nowhere but in the yellowing pages of the official gazette. José Augusto Drummond, who studied the reserves of the state of Rio de Janeiro, called several of them "mysterious," lacking declared boundaries, locations, or areas. A few reserves possessed no identifiable legislative authority. Sometimes, successive decrees reaffirmed or reassigned the protected status of a reserve, a sign of the ineffectiveness of the original decree or of the intention of later administrations to take credit at no budgetary cost. Numerous agencies competed in exercising authority over these reserves, even though, in the end, federal, state, and county executives overruled environmental agencies whenever some more immediate purpose intervened. Throughout the period, budgets for park staff continued to decline. At Itatiaia, where there were 120 employees in the 1950s, only 44 were left in 1982.[37]

Fire was allowed to ravage the reserves. Those located in the drier interior at the interface with savanna may have been, at great intervals in the past, subject to natural fires, but now, isolated amid farmlands and pasture, they were in much greater danger. The state park at Vassununga, São Paulo, showed no sign of fire disturbance since at least the turn of the century and had not been damaged during the widespread fires of the drought year of 1963. Yet half its forested area was destroyed in 1975. Itatiaia National Park was invaded repeatedly by fire. In 1981, 7,000 hectares of it burned in a fire that broke out at numerous points simultaneously. The suspicion was strong that it was the work of neighboring ranchers. Some of them had lost lands to park expansion (probably without receiving compensation); others of them saw a chance to convert the park to grassland that could be invaded by their herds. That was a drought year, but arson was suspected in many of the fires that broke out all over Paraná and São Paulo, where reforestation companies coveted forested lands that might not have been liberated by the IBDF for clearing, had fires not already destroyed the vegetation.[38]

It was evident that constant poaching, unpunished and sometimes even protected, was wearing the reserves away. Studies carried out in 1962 and 1977 of the forest cover of the São Paulo county of Campos do Jordão, where the long-established and popular state park of the same name was located, showed a loss in the park of 2 percent, exactly the same as the loss, during the same period, in the county as a whole. Evidently government protection in this case had no effect. In other cases, government protection was worse than no protection: The mere presentation of a plan to preserve the forest of Marumbi, in the coastal escarpment of Paraná, was the signal to local landowners to accelerate their logging to the utmost.[39]

These were the realities that provoked Mauro Victor, director of the São Paulo Forest Institute, demoted for opposing a road through the Jacupiranga State Park, to remark bitterly:

> The action of the state was so innocuous . . . or so hostile to the field of forest defense that, save for the work carried out in the state forests and reserves, one is tempted to ask—what would have happened had the state adopted a policy of "laissez-faire" in this area? Perhaps the results would have been identical.[40]

Beginning in 1966, federal tax incentives were conceded to prospective planters of eucalyptus and pine. They proved only moderately successful. By 1975 the government's program had implanted some 14,400 square kilometers of various species of these two exotic genera in the Southeast and Paraná. Unfortunately, these incentives allowed much leeway for speculation, low productivity, and unsalable wood. Therefore in that year a new directive was issued: Forested land was once again taxable, although tax

abatements were offered to industrial consumers of wood, in order to stimulate the integration of tree planting and manufacturing. These measures
were mainly intended to benefit paper-pulp manufacture, because growing
domestic and world demand for that product was forecast. The decree also
encouraged iron and steel makers to engage directly in charcoal manufacture. Thus the planners were narrowing the definition of the potential
value of planted forests, despite the IBDF's promotion of wood for fuel. By
limiting these incentives to a minimum planting of 200 hectares, they were
also causing eucalyptus investments to become more concentrated and
more attractive to foreign investors.[41]

The company that took greatest advantage of these new rules—and that
probably had a hand in shaping them—was Aracruz Celulose. Organized
in 1967, it bought more than 1,000 square kilometers of coastal lands in
Espírito Santo. In 1973 it began to build a pulping plant of 400,000-ton
capacity. The company introduced an extraordinarily high level of technical skill: When eucalyptus clones obtained in São Paulo proved susceptible
to diseases and insufficiently productive, others were procured from South
Africa and Zimbabwe. Still not satisfied, the company mounted its own
expedition to Papua New Guinea and Australia to obtain wild materials.
These were cloned and field tested. Resistant varieties yielding a remarkable 55 cubic meters per hectare of denser wood were obtained, reducing
considerably the company's need for additional land. These experiences
and materials were made available to forest institutes in Brazil and abroad.
Most of the pulp, of high quality, was sold in the world market. Aracruz
earned 26 percent on capital in 1988, thanks in part to generous tax abatements.[42]

Aracruz proclaimed "nature as its partner" and achieved international
press coverage as a model of "sustainable" economic development. The
company followed the Forest Code and even exceeded it somewhat—230
square kilometers, mostly along the margins of its streams and indented
shoreline, were left in native forest, some of it possibly primary, and hundreds of thousands of native trees were added to attract wildlife, which was
protected from hunters. It claimed to have installed antipollution devices
in accordance with Scandinavian and North American standards (because
none existed at the time in Brazil). Most of the potentially polluting by-
products of the pulp-making process were recycled within the system. The
plant was fueled almost entirely with waste products of the pulp-making
process. According to the company's publications, the resistant clones it
had developed and the biological controls its entomologists had promoted
obviated the need for all but very small amounts of biocides. All in all,
Aracruz appeared to have established standards equaled by few companies,

even in the developed countries. Its directors pointed out that planted forest monoculture was the only economically feasible alternative to destruction of what remained of Brazil's native forest.

Despite this record, Aracruz was from its very beginning highly controversial. It was claimed by Augusto Ruschi, and repeated by others, that all the lands acquired by Aracruz had been in primary forest. In fact, part of its original tract had been bought from a steel company that had already begun to plant it in eucalyptus. Aracruz insisted that nearly all its lands had been logged, burned for charcoal, farmed, and turned over to cattle years before and that consequently there had been very little left to clear. Ruschi had already denounced Aracruz for its attempted acquisition of the remnant Comboios giant sea turtle–breeding reserve. More grievous still, part of the Aracruz acquisitions had been a reservation of Mbyá tribespeople. They had been forced by the state government to accept a settlement that was not to their liking, and they had been evicted from the site. Ruschi detested eucalyptus and saw no point in planting it anywhere in Brazil, believing that native species would perform equally well. He was indignant that so large a project could have been installed without an analysis of its potential environmental impact. He charged that the factory would "sterilize all the region around it." Ruschi complained of Aracruz's 1,700-meter-long sewer outlet, which discharged the factory's effluents into the ocean at only 17 meters of depth. Although he admitted lacking empirical data, he predicted that all marine flora and fauna would be destroyed and that damage would be done as far as Vitória, 65 kilometers to the south.[43]

These charges did not prevent Aracruz from doubling its capacity to a million tons. This phase was completed in 1991, at which point it was the largest such installation in the world. The company nevertheless may well have felt itself on the defensive. An accord was reached with the former occupants of its properties, and, according to the company's accounts, another US$66 million was expended (out of a total US$1.1 billion for the added plant) to improve its environmental controls, principally to switch from chlorine to chlorine dioxide–oxygen bleaching and to build 45 hectares of settling and aerating basins in order to reduce the volume and toxicity of its effluents.[44]

The company was vulnerable on several other counts which suggest that environmental issues were to some degree pretexts. The largest of more than fifty Brazilian cellulose plants, it was mainly foreign owned, in a country where distrust of foreign investment has historically been widespread and intense. Furthermore, Aracruz produced principally for overseas markets, and many Brazilians considered foreign trade to be antinational per se. In the case of bleached paper pulp it was certainly evidence of insufficient recycling abroad. Opposition to exports was intensified during the 1980s when a great part of them were applied to paying interest on the country's immense foreign debt. Aracruz represented a vast concentration of capital in a small state whose political elite, already ferociously divided into angry moieties, made Aracruz another point of issue. Thus, when the company sought additional lands to supply the projected doubling of output, the governor blocked the sale, and Aracruz was obliged to purchase a tract of 760 square kilometers in South Bahia. Higher transport cost was another price it would have to pay for its success. It is not surprising that Aracruz, with all these debilities, was chosen by Greenpeace, during the Rio de Janeiro environmental conference of 1992, to be the object of a sea "blockade" to dramatize and condemn what it considered the company's hypocrisy. This was also a deliberate riposte to the company's president, Erling Lorentzen, who was presented, and presented himself, to the gathering as a paladin of environmental sensibility. Reality probably lay somewhere in between.[45]

For planters unconnected to the paper pulp or iron and steel industries, eucalyptus and pine became a good deal less attractive under the revised rules. The area of planted forest therefore began to shrink in the Southeast, as harvesting of mature trees soon outran replacements. In São Paulo, where 12,746 square kilometers were in eucalyptus and pine in 1980, there were only 8,451 a decade later. By 1989 native forest still supplied about 60 percent of the charcoal and firewood consumed in the Southeast. Eucalyptus planting remained extensive except among industrial planters. Overall yields improved little, to an average of about 22 cubic meters per hectare per year. Apparently, few companies were capable or willing to replicate Aracruz's labors. Thus it was that native forests still provided 80 percent of the charcoal burned in the iron and steel mills of Minas Gerais as late as 1988, despite repeated targets set by the government for the mills' self-sufficiency in charcoal. Meanwhile, land suitable for planting eucalyptus was becoming more expensive. Land values in Rio de Janeiro had already risen too high to admit of any significant amount of reforestation even under the first of the incentive decrees. The hope that wood from planted forests might substitute more widely for wood from remaining native forest thus seemed to fade.[46]

This misdirection of extractive activity might have been avoided. By 1975 there were perhaps 20,000 square kilometers of planted trees in the region of the Atlantic Forest. These woodlots would have immediately doubled or tripled in value had all further clearing of native forest been prohibited. Owners of eucalyptus and pine stands might well have given some thought to backing the most stringent interpretations of the Forest

Code and to pressuring the IBDF to reconsider its belief that native forests represented a resource no different from planted forest.

Instead, the cultivation of eucalyptus and pine was consistently carried out in a fashion that conflicted with the goal of preserving the Atlantic Forest. Even though prospective planters were advised by the IBDF to avoid lands suitable for agriculture and to plant on eroded hillsides already denuded of tree cover, they were well aware that eucalyptus grows better on flatlands with good soil not yet subject to erosion—on land, that is, that might, if left untended and free of cattle, grow back to forest. Most coveted of all were tracts still covered with timber, the sale of which would help offset the cost of planting eucalyptus. Soils only recently cleared of forest were not yet biologically dead. Surviving microbes, fungi, and worms might nourish the seedlings and protect them from disease, making possible a much higher survival rate. Reforestation was therefore paradoxically a major cause of continued deforestation. Because it was also a form of production most profitably carried out on a large scale, it was identified with the latifundia and the most retrograde tactics of claim jumping, monopolization of lands along roads, and the denial of easements to inholders. Reforestation was less labor intensive than any other form of cultivation and therefore contributed to the exodus to city slums.[47]

Doubtless, the term reforestation, ideologically convenient in some contexts, was a source of public confusion, because eucalyptus planting was merely another sort of monoculture whose product happened to be cellulose. Just like agriculture, rationalized eucalyptus or pine planting involved considerable costs of implantation and cultivation, including improved seeds, fertilizers, and biocides. Eucalyptus was vulnerable to the attacks of several species of leaf-cutting ants and other native insects that had acquired a taste for this exotic. A few of the pests that had coevolved with eucalyptus and pine in their native habitats had also caught up with the trees. The means of combat most often wielded, biocides like chlordane and mirex, were expensive and, as environmentalists pointed out, dangerous to handle and release. Eucalyptus was also vulnerable to fire, which imposed added costs of insurance and fire brigades. Thus, when tax incentives expired, many landowners abandoned tree planting.[48]

Some specialists suggested that this cost profile favored a return to the management of native woodlands, which involved almost no initial capital input. Even though capoeira was considerably less productive of wood and of no use to the pulp factories, it offered additional moderate rewards as extractive and game reserves. It was also pointed out that landowners were subject to fines if they did not replant woodlots they had cleared, in order to bring their properties up to the 20 percent minimum stipulated in the

Forest Code. Obliging them at last to do so could re-create an immense stock of biomass fuel. But the ending of the tax exemption on forested land, along with the increasing injections of credit into agriculture, had the pernicious effect of making it extremely expensive for even the most conscientious farmers to preserve the minimum 20 percent in forest and entirely beyond their means to set aside any tracts, save steep hillsides or ravines, for the regrowth of native trees. The greatest cost of the wasteful destruction of forest of the preceding century turned out to be the economic impossibility of replacing it.[49]

There persisted, among recent recruits to the incipient environmental movement, rejection of eucalyptus almost as determined as that confronted by Edmundo Navarro de Andrade seventy years before. A curious sort of xenophobia was directed against this "foreign invader"—a sobriquet never applied to coffee or citrus trees, or even to pine. By the early 1980s, however, field and experimental data had accumulated in Brazil and abroad which demonstrated that none of the popular prejudices about eucalyptus was true. It did not require any more water than any other fast-growing species. It did not impoverish the soil but rather, like other tree species, recycled nutrients, accumulated humus, increased exchangeable cations, and improved soil-mechanical qualities. Nutrients were indeed removed from eucalyptus plantations by fast-rotation harvesting, but that was true of any monoculture. Eucalyptus, like many other species, emitted substances—terpenes and phenolics—that inhibited the growth of competitors, but underbrush did grow in eucalyptus groves. Little wildlife was to be found in eucalyptus groves, again mainly because it was a monoculture. When underbrush was allowed to appear, so did wildlife.[50]

In 1962 scientists at the Agronomic Institute of São Paulo at Campinas had for the first time in Brazil made an estimate of deforestation based on aerial photography. Almost no attention had been paid to that pioneering work, but in 1973 the task was repeated by a team at the state Forest Institute, joined by Campinas staff. Their conclusion was that there remained in the state only 20,700 square kilometers of dense forest. This was 10 percent of the area forested in 1500, and it represented a loss of 40 percent of the dense forest that had been surveyed ten years before. Because aerial photography could not distinguish precisely between primary forest and long-established capoeira, it was likely that less than 10 percent of the original Atlantic Forest survived. In 1976 Mauro Victor, then director of the Forest Institute, published a popular version of this study that included a series of maps showing in dramatic form the disappearance of the state's forests. Although this edition had but a limited circulation, these maps were reprinted hundreds of times in the succeeding years, whenever the subject of deforestation was raised in print, achieving an extraordinary public impact. This was, however, only the beginning of painful and controversial labors that were to assess the damage done to the Atlantic Forest.[51]

This widespread erosion of the nation's substrate of natural capital did not yet receive governmental attention. The official measures taken during the 1970s to defend the style of economic development adopted in the 1950s had managed to stave off economic crisis, a consideration of more immediate political importance. Industrial and agricultural production outpaced the continued rapid growth in population. Regional life expectancy and nutritional standards improved slightly though unsteadily. The human population in great majority now resided in immense urban agglomerations, which were kept viable, if precariously, through the vast investments in infrastructure of the development drive. The quest for development had not come any closer to its goal. Concentration of income and wealth was increasing, the direct and indirect result of the government's economic policies. Meanwhile, the definition of development had to be constantly revised upward. There was effectively no forecast of a plateau upon which the felicity and well-being of the citizenry might be considered secured. The ideology of economic development did not offer any such resting place: The "developed" economy was a receding target because the "developed countries" also continued to grow, and Brazilian developmentalists intended to catch up in rates of production and consumption. Moreover, the dynamic of social relations of the authoritarian state required that inequalities be maintained and even intensified, so that still more rapid growth in economic product was necessary to prevent the collapse of the mass of the population into misery, despair, and perhaps revolution.

At the beginning of the 1980s, the government's frantically stitched together economic schemes came unraveled quite suddenly. The loans it had contracted in the wake of the oil-price rises became unpayable when the United States steeply raised its interest rates in order to cap an inflationary spiral. Brazil came close to bankruptcy as new money stopped flowing into the country. This was fatal to the military government, all of whose legitimacy was by then grounded upon its record of economic development. Exhausted by internal divisions, confused by economic failures, embarrassed by scandals, and besieged by burgeoning political and civic opposition, the generals gradually shut down their repressive machinery and extracted themselves from power. Parties were allowed to reorganize, labor unions were released from subjection, and a civilian president was installed at last in 1985. The retreat of the military—a continentwide phenomenon, in fact—put in question the model of economic development followed for thirty years and stimulated debate on its environmental consequences. The reestablishment of civil rights, an uncensored press, and freedom of association made possible the reanalysis of these policies, including their inherent environmental dimensions. The citizenry was resuming, in effect, full responsibility for its national patrimony.

14

Getting It off the Paper

Cada comunidade tem o controle de poluição que merece.

Every community has the pollution control it deserves.

NELSON NEFUSSI, CETESB

The retreat of the military was long-drawn-out and rancorous. The mandate of the last general-president expired in 1985. The Congress, packed with appointed members, managed to fend off a popular campaign for the direct election of a civilian president. Instead, it carried out its own election. The winner died as he was about to take office and was succeeded by the vice-president-elect, a politician of limited range and vision. Bound by the traditional politics of regional favoritism and cronyism and committed above all to preventing a leftist candidate from succeeding him, he subscribed to the military view of national security and depended not a little on the generals for political support. At the national level, then, the political climate thawed only slowly, and the executive continued to regard environmental issues with suspicion and incomprehension.

Nevertheless, in the shadow of this tattered canopy, a democratized political culture was gathering strength. Civil society, at first limited in expression to lay church activism and neighborhood-improvement associations, had taken up issues of human rights. Professional associations and labor unions at considerable cost acquired independence from the state. Political parties were freed of military containment and multiplied. In several of the states, especially those of the Southeast, administrations came into office that in some measure represented popular aspirations. A modest organizational base for the pursuit of self-government had been formed, including a number of environmental organizations. A constitutional assembly was convened that fostered the widest possible debate on the foundations of the state and its purposes. This was not exactly a return to democracy—Brazil had never before experienced such broad political participation or such confidence in principles of equality and citizenship and of responsible government. Nor was it in any sense a revolution—the conservative civilian political elite had cast itself loose from an alliance that was no longer advantageous, but it was not much embarrassed by its longtime dependence on the generals. The social hierarchy was still in place, and the elite was confident that customary methods of social control could be resumed, now reinforced by the ubiquitous and effective media of communications.

Lamentably, all this ferment was taking place in the midst of economic depression. Throughout the 1980s, the burden of foreign debt loomed over every government initiative. In order to mobilize the resources needed to keep up interest payments, the government was forced to favor numerous export schemes that proved environmentally destructive. The governments of the 1980s were not strong enough to expropriate the foreign-exchange earnings of the private sector via taxation and therefore resorted to confiscation in the form of inflation. Inflation also paid the cost of political favors, great and small. The resumption of electoral politics and the formation of numerous parties favored influence peddling, the stuffing of public offices with excessive employees, and the expansion of unaffordable services to a newly empowered electorate that suffered rising unemployment. The lack of funds for capital expenditures, on the other hand, offered the environment some slight respite—hydropower and nuclear projects, roads, and bridges all had to be delayed in execution. Ominously, investment in education, communications, and science fell behind growth in population and the needs of an urban, industrial society. Brazil ended the 1980s with 20 million illiterates. The average factory worker had less than four years of schooling.

The realistic insertion of environmental issues in this maelstrom of economic difficulties and political reconstruction proved, to say the least, challenging to those who devoted themselves to the task. They were favored by a world climate of environmental crisis that even the xenophobic federal government could no longer ignore. The growing concern that deforestation was contributing to increasing levels of carbon dioxide in the atmosphere caused public attention in the industrialized countries to focus on the Amazon Forest, where government planning had for a decade stimulated ill-considered colonization projects, vast speculative cattle ranches, and intrusive mining enterprises. Brazilian environmentalists who had struggled through the 1970s to delimit forest reserves in that region suddenly gained international attention and even a degree of support. Some small part of this attention was diverted to consideration of the plight of the Atlantic Forest, which was, it came to be recognized, along with the Madagascar forests, the most endangered in the world.[1]

The survival of the Atlantic Forest, thus elevated to a world concern,

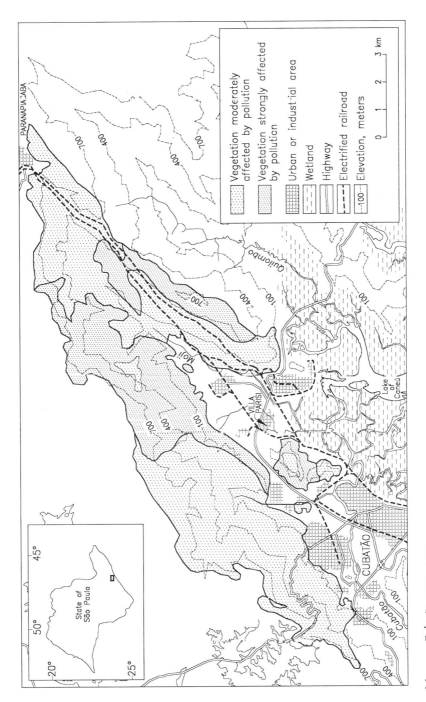

Map 9. Cubatão, 1970–1990

Legend:
- Vegetation moderately affected by pollution
- Vegetation strongly affected by pollution
- Urban or industrial area
- Wetland
- Highway
- Electrified railroad
- —100— Elevation, meters

PARANAPIACABA

Quilombo

Moji

VILLA PARISI

Lake of Caneú

CUBATÃO

Cubatão

State of São Paulo

0 1 2 3 km

did not cease being a question inherently local, soluble only by those who surrounded and exploited it.

The demands of the cities for materials, energy, and space were imperious, threatening to exhaust all that the forest had left to offer. São Paulo had become the world's fourth-largest city; its industries absorbed almost half the country's raw materials, including forest products. Rio de Janeiro was the world's tenth-largest city. Within the region of the Atlantic Forest there were two other cities of more than a million population, Curitiba and Belo Horizonte. By 1990 the urban population of the region of the Atlantic Forest stood at 62 million—an increase of 15 million in ten years. The last of the standing primary forest, protected or not, was being cut and sold. In South Bahia, the saying was that wherever a tree still stood, there was nearby a migrant *Capixaba*—as natives of the by now denuded state of Espírito Santo are called—with a chain saw in his hand. Apprehensions of trucks laden with logs, charcoal, and firewood of unexplainable provenance that were reported almost daily in the press represented only a fraction of the true extent of the traffic. By the end of the 1980s, Brazilian forests were insufficient to supply domestic demand: 600,000 cubic meters of Paraguayan wood, a quarter of that country's output, was being smuggled yearly to Southeast Brazilian markets.[2]

The city of São Paulo was unable to prevent shantytown squatters and their middle-class equivalent, the buyers of lots offered by clandestine developers, from invading land surrounding the suburban reservoirs that fed the hydroelectric plants at the base of the sea cliff and that supplied water to its southern suburbs. By 1992 there were more than 600,000 residents in the basin, nearly all of whom depended on wells and latrines, an invitation to cholera, by then firmly established in northern Brazil. The century-old national park of Tijuca and the nearly two-century-old Botanical Garden were increasingly besieged by the surrounding population of Rio de Janeiro. Forest guards continuously dislodged squatters, some of them affluent, from the park's edges. Meanwhile, the attempts of the city's parks and gardens office to reforest the barest and steepest hillsides of Rio de Janeiro—the inveterate cause of landslides and deaths during each rainy season—were being thwarted by the presence of hundreds of goats. Breeding stock of these voracious animals had been introduced in 1985 by a governor seeking to improve the diets of the shantytown dwellers. The city's authorities were only partly successful in reducing its enormous consumption of firewood—in 1989 bakeries were forbidden to burn wood, but brickworks were exempted. Nearly all of their supply was illegally cut, subjecting them to repeated fines and court appearances. They paid all this with little complaint, because it cost less than fuel oil. Hardly any of this wood was produced within the state—it was estimated that 90 percent of the 6 million cubic meters of wood consumed by Rio de Janeiro in 1987 was brought in from Minas Gerais.[3]

Extractive activities were intensified along the Serra do Mar, convenient to the factories, warehouses, and markets of the cities that nested among its promontories. Construction companies needed sand, limestone, and granite, dug out of the beaches and cliffs. Along the Espírito Santo shoreline monazitic sand, a valuable radioactive product, was mined, nearly all of it from federal property, some of it protected. Gold prospectors worked the headwaters of the Paranapanema River, an activity more than three hundred years old, but now the ore was refined with mercury, cast senselessly into streams. Each gram of gold signified a gram of mercury that poisoned the waters and wildlife of the river.[4]

The environmental costs of these destructive activities were nearly everywhere diffuse, difficult to measure and trace, and differentially burdensome to the poor and the powerless. The military government had refused to discuss these costs and had discouraged analysis of them, cutting off funding of research that might have embarrassing effects and treating scientific critics as pariahs or subversives. At last, however, a disaster emerged so large and undeniable that it could not be hidden or temporized. The destruction of the Atlantic Forest might yet have consequences catastrophic for the government's dream of development.[5]

The oldest of Brazil's state parks is Alto da Serra, on the forested rim of the Serra do Mar, only a short distance from the city of São Paulo. In its midst, set on a low rise, is a small guardhouse. Inside, it is cool and bare, just a few chairs and a table, and on the table is a large ledger. The ledger contains the remarks of visitors to the park, dating from the 1920s. At one time, this park, donated to the state by Hermann von Ihering, was a way station on the spectacular rail line up the coastal palisade, obligatory for the most illustrious of the state's guests. One finds there, among the first signatures, that of Marie Curie and of distinguished naturalists of the era—Auguste Chevalier, Konrad Gruenther, Jean Massart, Mulford and Racine Foster, and the great N. I. Vavilov. Gruenther called it "one of the loveliest jewels of Brazil." Vavilov must have pleased his hosts immensely when he wrote, "The creation of the station is the best proof of the progress of Estados Unidos do Brasil."

How remarkable that the guest book has survived the petty thieves who have broken into the park over the years to carry off orchids and parrots— they could never have conceived the worth of Madame Curie's autograph.

The park's latter-day curators seem not to care, either. Turning back into the harsh sunlight, the modern visitor is surrounded by a dying nature. Trees stripped of leaves, of bark, bleached and shattered. Hillsides ravined and subsided, bearing off trees, bushes, and lianas with them. Grasses invading the naked earth, streams stagnant and lifeless. The epitaph of the park is to be found on one of the later pages of the book—an entry of 17 April 1980: "Alto da Serra will never again be worthy of the eulogies consigned to this book. . . . It is already irremediably asphyxiated by the 'progress' exhaled by Cubatão."[6]

Cubatão was not yet a world famous synonym for ecological catastrophe, but soon it would be. In the 1950s that village, nestled at the base of the coastal palisade, was chosen by the federal and state governments to be a major industrial site. Convenient to the port of Santos and endowed with abundant hydroelectricity generated by São Paulo's cliffside reservoirs, it was easily adapted to the requirements of steel, petroleum, cement, and chemical manufacturing. Its mangroves were cut down, its lowlands were drained and filled, and pipelines were laid to the port and up the cliff to related industries and consumers in the capital. The steady jobs of the factories attracted thousands of desperate migrants, many more than the factories could hire. The village swelled to perhaps 100,000, almost half of them shanty squatters, perched everywhere, on the margins of the estuary, up the hillsides, and over the pipelines. Water supply, sewer lines, electricity, and telephones were all inadequate, even hazardous. Far from being failures of planning, these were settled features of Brazilian industrialization, which was based solidly and prosperously on the misery of its workers.[7]

One of the "poles" of development was the federally owned Petrobrás oil refinery, which attracted petrochemical, pharmaceutical, natural gas, and fertilizer plants. There was also a steel-rolling mill, built by the state government, and a paper mill. By the mid-1970s there were more than 100 factories in Cubatão, almost half of them state owned. The municipality generated a remarkable 3 percent of Brazil's gross national product and 7 percent of its tax revenues. The generals were extremely protective of this immense investment of capital and Brazilian technical skill. They worried that it might be attacked by their guerrilla adversaries, even by foreign enemies. Cubatão was therefore declared a strategic municipality, and its mayor was appointed from Brasília.

The technical integration of this vast complex had been helter-skelter. One very large difficulty had been entirely overlooked: Cubatão was located at the base of a cliff that experienced perhaps the heaviest precipitation in Brazil. Even the deepest recesses of the Amazon Forest could not match the nearly 4,500 millimeters of average annual rainfall, rising in very wet years to 5,500 millimeters, recorded at Itapanhaú, towering above Cubatão. Even in the drier winter months, at least 200 millimeters fell, and in the summer months that much and more could fall in a day. Relative humidity in the valley was rarely less than 50 percent and could remain at 100 percent for weeks. The cliffside during most months was perpetually drenched in mists. Indeed, the vegetation of Alto da Serra, rooted in a thin and impoverished soil, derived part of its nutrients from this moisture.

Cubatão, furthermore, was set at the entrance of a 40-kilometer-long gore in the coastal palisade, down which flowed the Mogi River. Wind and rain that blew over Cubatão almost invariably flowed into this sleeve, where they were trapped. The cliffside, rising to nearly 1,000 meters, was in most places extremely steep. Declivities of 40 percent were not uncommon. The potential erosive effects of the torrential rains were held in check only by the tenacity of the forest vegetation. Over the centuries, this barrier could not always hold the cliffs in place: Their bases, piled with great mounds of rubble and earth, attested to repeated slides in earlier epochs. When the ducts were laid down that fed the hydroelectric plant at the foot of the palisade, the electric company solved the problem of landslides by dousing a swath of forest with gasoline, setting fire to it, and encasing the bare cliffside in concrete.[8]

In February 1967 a tremendous landslide had occurred at Caraguatatuba, some 150 kilometers east of Santos. Days of soft, steady showers had soaked into the forest soils, burdening them with thousands of tons of extra weight. Next came two days of unremitting torrents, surpassing 220 millimeters each day. An estimated 250,000 tons of rock and earth were dislodged, damaging a hydroelectric plant and killing nearly 100 persons. This was not entirely a natural phenomenon—small farmers had cleared part of the hillsides to grow bananas, a plant with shallow roots.

At Cubatão, still larger disasters loomed. The factories of the basin were emitting from their smokestacks, unfitted with any control devices, a daily 1,000 tons of particulates and gases. The plants experienced frequent accidents that, in addition to the usual output of sulphur dioxides, iron oxides, nitrous oxide, and carbon monoxide, released ammonia, chlorine, and organic and inorganic acids. Solid wastes, some of them toxic, were being used for landfill. Industrial sewage poured into the estuaries, killing the mangrove and contaminating the food chain. By 1974, when the city's health officer mimeographed a report containing data he had been collecting for several years, air pollution was already relentless and dense in the valley. Respiratory ailments were unusually common, as were sales of remedies in the local pharmacies. Obstetricians were beginning to take notice of what seemed to them an unusual number of congenital birth defects, including anencephaly. These reports were given wide circulation but were not subjected to careful analysis. Even so, the press began to refer to Cubatão as the "Valley of Death."[9]

The city also began to suffer much greater damage from summer rains. In 1975, 750 residents lost their houses, water lines were cut, and three electric towers collapsed, cutting off services. The next year, a week of steady rains caused landslides, along with widespread flooding. This time 18,000 were left homeless, and at least one person died. Although down in the valley no connection was yet posited between these events and the degradation of vegetation, botanists were observing worrisome signs of collapse. A field study in the late 1970s showed extreme depression in populations of lichens, which are especially susceptible to air pollution, all along the valley of the Mogi. In late 1980, the press printed a University of São Paulo botanist's denunciation of the critical state of Alto da Serra. The state railroad and road authorities were already quite aware that dying vegetation was widespread and were quietly trying to defend their roadbeds from landslides—unfortunately, they were covering cuts and fills with pitch, thereby rendering the hillsides even less permeable.[10]

State and federal authorities tried to ignore the problem. Worse, they seemed unable to conceptualize it. The governor blamed the shanty squatters, who obviously had put themselves in harm's way. Authorities would soon begin to issue directives to remove these offending persons, as a way of resolving the problem of the floods. Evidently, CETESB, the state sanitation agency, was on notice not to annoy the polluting factories. CETESB's 1978 report offered information on the effluents of only fifteen of them, noting that just one had installed antipollution devices and that half of the rest had apparently not even heard the subject raised. The state legislature formed, only after great delay, an investigative committee and then tabled its furious recommendation that CETESB be extinguished and a real environmental agency be created. CETESB had, meanwhile, installed automatic monitoring devices and began investigating the volume and effects of Cubatão's pollutant agents, but it kept the results confidential. In January 1983 the agency, to demonstrate its openness to academic criticism, sponsored a conference at which the directors heard themselves accused of corruption and incompetence and were told that landslides were imminent.[11]

CETESB's aerial surveys showed that Cubatão had lost 49 of its 62 square kilometers of dense forest to buildings, high-tension lines, quarries, and roads or, as it suspected, to air pollution. CETESB's directors testified to the committee that their agency was on top of the situation but was "not assuming, however, radical attitudes that might possibly lead the state to industrial stagnation." One of them opined that "every community gets the pollution control it deserves." A federal investigative committee formed early in 1982 deliberated for a year and a half and also found its recommendations ignored. Meanwhile, a few of the companies were themselves beginning to consider installing pollution-control devices, as silently as possible, so as to avoid the conclusion that they might have acted earlier—or that they could have afforded to do so all along. In 1975 a Japanese salesman of antipollution equipment had returned home in dismay when the factories showed themselves uninterested and the federal government refused to waive import duties.[12]

All this was before Cubatão was rocked by two horrifying and clearly avoidable disasters, of a scale that advanced the city to the ranks of Minamata, Bhopal, and Savesio: On 25 February 1984, a leak occurred in a gasoline pipeline that had been laid in a ditch running through one of the most miserable of the squatter settlements. Householders who had built their shacks over the ditch did not notice the odor, because it normally reeked of a rich broth of effluents. Finally, inevitably, one of the neighbors flicked a live cigarette butt out a window. The number of dead was never ascertained. Two hundred persons may have been incinerated that day. At last, CETESB announced emergency actions to be taken during winter temperature inversions and presented the factories with time limits for the reduction of emissions.[13]

Less than a year later, after a week of not unusually heavy rains, the industrial park and the shanties of Cubatão were struck by floods and mud slides. This time 4,000 residents lost their homes. Higher up in the valley of the Mogi, the railroad lines were cut at numerous points, stalling traffic for twenty-two days at a cost of more than US$3 million. Still worse, the flooding caused a pressurized ammonia pipeline to break, releasing nearly 40 tons of the highly toxic chemical. This was the largest leak of ammonia to occur in fifteen years of global monitoring. Six thousand persons were evacuated; 65 of them were hospitalized. A representative of Ultrafertil, the company that owned the pipeline, blamed the event on the rains and philosophized that "risks exist in any industrial activity."[14]

This evaluation did not calm the terrified survivors. It was abundantly clear to them that the floods and mud slides could do tremendous damage to the valley's crazy quilt of pipelines and holding tanks. The prospect of leaks of even more dangerous gases, such as chlorine and benzene, or of explosions of hydrogen or liquid petroleum gas, was revived when, a few weeks later, a landslide tore away a section of the coastal highway at Angra dos Reis, reaching within 800 meters of the nuclear plant there. Still, the state authorities seemed unable to contain the drive for "development." In the midst of this crisis permits were granted for the construction of another ammonia plant and a coking plant. The authorities might have temporized for a few more years, had not the director of the state Forest Institute commandeered a helicopter and a video camera on a providentially sunny day soon after the latest accident and taped a view of the Mogi Valley unavailable to the authorities at ground level—40 kilometers of mountainsides gashed by immense gullies, a protective forest murdered by acid rain. The riverbed, formerly only 10 meters wide, now charged with hundreds of thousands of tons of silt, extended over 120 meters. State authorities took no notice of the director's report, until the videotape was displayed on the news program of Brazil's largest television network.[15]

Régis Guillaumon's videotape was confirmed by a quantitative study based on aerial photography: The annual number of landslides in the area had increased from 165 to 525 between 1971 and 1985. It was obvious that, in the long run, pollution would have to be severely contained. Unfortunately, time seemed to be running out. Another of the Forest Institute's scientists showed the governor a CETESB report of 1981, long buried, that predicted that 1986 would be a year of much heavier rains and catastrophic landslides. Worried chemical-plant executives built dikes around their holding tanks, formulated plans for the emergency shutoff of pipelines, and demanded that the Mogi and Perequê riverbeds be dredged. Residents of some of the more precarious squatter settlements were uprooted, and more committees were formed. CETESB, finally aware that, as one state deputy put it, "If the Serra do Mar gives way, the government goes with it," contracted for the planting of an exotic grass, brachiaria, to stop the spread of gullies. Unfortunately, this plant was to prove as susceptible as the dying forest, a lucky happenstance, because otherwise it might have prevented the return of woody species. After some confusion, a number of native plants were identified as resistant and were spread in nutrient-bathed seed pellets by helicopter. Although this campaign presented a spirit-lifting television spectacle, it was far from effective. Luckily, CETESB's prediction of flooding did not come to pass in 1986, or in the next few years.[16]

At length the industrialists acceded to what had become a deafening clamor for control of Cubatão's pollution. As the head of the environmental department of the state's trade association put it, they were "receptive to whatever plan might be realized for society's benefit [*sic*] and disposed to contribute, but within Brazilian reality." By 1988 the factories, awarded low-cost loans, had reduced their release of the most easily scrubbed pollutants. Very little improvement was undertaken thereafter. The state-owned steel mill was fined in late 1992 because it had carried out only half its stated plan. Enough had been achieved, nevertheless, to permit the regrowth of tolerant native invasive plants, so that many of the unsightly gashes were masked. It was unlikely, however, that a deeply rooted forest would return as long as particulates, sulphur dioxide, nitrous and nitric oxides, and hydrocarbons continued to be released. Although states of emergency during rainy periods and temperature inversions were less frequently declared, they were still necessary. Monitoring of roadbeds and pipelines detected continued slides, and the newly sprouted scrub vegetation, unlike the primary forest, was subject to fires. As the decomposition of tree roots progressed, the potential for further disasters remained real, even though the government and the factories pretended otherwise.[17]

Meanwhile, other sectors of the Atlantic Forest were threatened by air pollution: The greenbelts around the metropolitan areas of Rio de Janeiro and São Paulo were quite likely heavily affected by automobile and industrial effluents, although this was barely studied. The Rio Doce State Park, containing the last sizable tract of primary forest in Minas Gerais, was located in the midst of the state's charcoal-oven and iron-mill complex and was also suspected of air-pollution damage. Despite the fright and embarrassment endured at Cubatão, Petrobrás, the state oil monopoly, in the meantime built an additional deepwater port nearby at São Sebastião. Natural gas from a new offshore deposit was shipped there and piped up the Serra do Mar and to Cubatão. At this point the littoral is so narrow that there is almost no room for storage tanks, so it was planned to place them in caverns bored into the mountainside.

The disaster at Cubatão took place as Brazilian society was emerging from a long tunnel of secretiveness, abuse of authority, and repression of the rights of association and citizenship. Accumulated rage and despair were released when the United Nations commission led by Gro Harlem Brundtland visited Cubatão shortly after the events of January 1985. The factories shut down while they toured the site, a maneuver that did not go unnoticed. At CETESB's headquarters in São Paulo, the committee confronted hundreds of frightened, angry citizens from all over southern Brazil—they had never seen such crowds anxious to "protest what had been done with their world." When a representative of Mato Grosso reported that the state had been allotted the equivalent of US$2,000 that year to protect its rivers, the audience broke out in laughter. An anguished committee member remarked, "In the end, the tragi-comic picture of a country that makes believe it is preserving itself becomes painfully funny."[18]

Cubatão was influential in the development of a modest environmental movement in the region of the Atlantic Forest in the mid-1980s. In 1984 a revived Brazilian Foundation for Nature Conservation (FBCN) sponsored a Second Brazilian Conference on Nature Protection—fifty years after the first! At the time, SEMA, the federal environmental agency, had notice of only 55 nongovernmental organizations concerned with the environment in all of Brazil. The FBCN had a mailing list of about 120 such organizations active in the region of the Atlantic Forest. By 1992, 809 Brazilian environmental organizations joined in signing a statement at the Rio de Janeiro conference on the environment—possibly another 1,500 existed. At the time of the 1984 conference, the FBCN was the largest Brazilian association, though it counted fewer than 1,000 members. By 1992 the largest was probably Fundação S.O.S. Mata Atlântica, with 5,000 members. The average was very much less, probably fewer than 100. Activist members were still fewer—often, as was traditional, university and research-center scientists. This exceedingly fragmented movement consisted mostly of ephemeral associations, appearing on only one or another of the lists. Many were neighborhood exclusionary groups seeking merely to avoid the lowering of property values. Probably there were, in all of Brazil in the late 1980s, no more than 75,000 persons involved in the struggle in any substantive way.[19]

This sudden growth may be seen as a triumph, considering the minimal participation of the Brazilian middle class in civic associations of any sort, or it may be seen as insignificant compared with the size of the challenge or of the middle class itself. By way of comparison, in Greater São Paulo alone, some 2.5 million private automobiles were registered. Membership was far below S.O.S. Mata Atlântica's own projections at the time of its founding in 1986; its minimum membership fee amounted to US$3—the cost of 4 liters of gasoline. It is not surprising that fees covered only 15 percent of this organization's budget and that many of the projects it had hoped to fund were abandoned.

The environmental movement was becoming, if not a mass movement, at least more political. At the 1984 conference, a group of conservationist organizations that had first gathered in 1978 issued its own proposals, in disagreement with the FBCN's anodyne final declaration and in implicit disapproval of its semiofficial attitudes. They emphasized the necessity of politicizing the movement, creating a bloc of environmentalist congressional representatives, and proposed eventually to form a Green party. Such a bloc was formed in the Constituent Assembly; it was responsible for the clauses declaring the right of the citizenry to a viable natural environment and declaring the Atlantic Forest part of the national patrimony. A small Green party was formed soon after. Politicians who had derided the movement only a few years before were now eager to pick up the banner, if only at election time.[20]

Environmentalism came increasingly to be lodged within the parties of the Left. Although the political Left at first regarded the issue to be a diversion from the class struggle or an "infantile disorder" of conservationism, events such as those at Cubatão led at least some of its activists to incorporate environmentalist views into its conventional ideological structure. It took rather a long time to perceive that environmental pollution represented a transfer of costs from the owners of capital to society in general, but especially to the hapless work force and dwellers in places like Cubatão. It was belatedly recognized that most forest clearing was done by large landowners and that the lesser damage done by the poor were acts of desperation. Even so, these more enlightened positions were not necessarily relevant to the Left's presumed lower-class constituencies. There were many more votes to be gained by parceling out to the poor what was left of the national patrimony than by preserving it. Governor Leonel Brizola of Rio de Janeiro, he of the introduced goats, a classically populist politician, ruined a ceremony at which he was presented the latest survey of forest destruction in his state by asking belligerently, "Which is more important: Preserving the Atlantic Forest or resolving the extremely grave problem of homeless children?"[21]

The rise of populist politics revived the issue of land reform, with potential harm to the forest. Because the reforestation schemes of the 1970s had commonly expelled smallholders fraudulently and even violently—indeed, in some cases, the entire purpose of reforesting was to justify claim jumping and speculation—it was inevitable that the endless groves of eucalyptus and pine should become the target of land reformers. Unfortunately, no distinction was made between native and planted forest. The National Colonization and Land Reform Institute (INCRA) perversely classified forested land as "underutilized." Landowners who had preserved more than the minimum 20 percent of forest were thus especially singled out for expropriation. In more than one case, private forests that had been declared "private preserves" were parceled out to grateful beneficiaries, who immediately began hunting and fishing on their new homesteads. On the other hand, many landowners obtained the status of private reserve who had no idea of preserving their woodlands but merely sought to escape taxes. In São Paulo, the governor ordered a study of the state's parks and reserves, with the end in view of settling the jobless on them.

Not surprisingly, landowners confronted with the threat of expropriation hastened to sign contracts with timber dealers. This tactic was unavailable to reforestation companies, who sometimes found all of their lands classified as "unproductive"—in Paraná, almost half of all expropriations were reforested lands. The prospect that the Constituent Assembly would strengthen the agrarian reform program was enough to exacerbate land conflicts throughout Brazil. Invasions of latifundia were organized as the debate grew more heated in Brasília. Not uncommonly they ended in murder: 600 rural workers and labor leaders were killed in 1986 and 1987. In South Bahia, the landowners took stern measures—they burned down what remained of their forests, to prevent intruders from clearing patches unobserved. They were careful, however, first to sell off the best timber to sawmills. "This year," boasted one of the timber merchants, "there hasn't been anything better for us than this talk of agrarian reform." In the end, all it amounted to was talk. The assembly caved in to organized latifundists and passed a land-reform clause weaker than the one the generals had decreed.[22]

Environmentalism could also be made to serve ideological purposes of broader traditional appeal. It was claimed that forest destruction was the direct result of the country's immense burden of foreign debt: The urgent necessity of paying interest charges in hard currencies obliged Brazil to ransack its natural endowment for exports. While this served anti-imperialist rhetoric on the Left, it also served to justify conservative politicians in staying an environmentally destructive course. Both Left and Right clung to economic developmentalism as the essence of public policy. Poverty was held to be the ultimate cause of environmental destruction; effective environmental measures were not possible until economic development had been achieved. Contradictorily, the most-developed countries were rightly charged with responsibility for most of the world's pollution. The concept of "sustainable development" was increasingly invoked as a means of squaring the circle, even as "rational" and "modern" had earlier justified the inevitable breaking of eggs. "Sustainable" was often translated as "sustained" development, a sinister truncation, albeit more descriptive of intent. Even more questionable was "self-sustained development," which suggested a reversion to the autarkical economic policies long preferred by the military and corporatist trade unions. In 1992, delegates to an environmental conference, evidently uncertain, resolved to carry out research to find out if such a thing as sustainable development had ever occurred.[23]

With few members, environmental organizations had to depend on other sources of income. Most of the larger environmental organizations obtained funding from private industry. Indeed, the larger environmental organizations achieved their status through the patronage of business leaders, who in some cases directed them. A few of these persons were evidently personally and genuinely concerned with the fate of their country's natural endowment. Their presence in the movement was no small victory—it represented a breach in the wall of impassivity that the bourgeoisie had eternally raised against environmental reality. Indeed, the heedlessness and incapacity of the government suggested to some environmentalists the necessity of greater dependence on private enterprise.[24]

It is likely that, for the majority of entrepreneurs, less admissible motives were more determinant. Even though superficial, public concern for nature preservation was by now lively enough to generate profits. "When you manage to associate your product with an ecological message," one marketing executive explained, "the return, in sales as well as image, is fantastic." More defensively, companies that had already had image problems might salvage them with a green campaign. "It's like putting honey in the mouth of a bear." Such campaigns became more critical when a federal law was passed in 1986, largely as the result of the Cubatão disaster, that gave standing in court to environmental organizations. A suit was quickly filed by an association called OIKOS against twenty-four of the Cubatão factories for damages to the Serra do Mar. These were obviously irreparable and nearly incalculable, but the companies fought the suit to a standstill. Another law of the same year that permitted tax deductions to cultural and environmental organizations greatly facilitated image building. Unfortunately, much of this investment was foolishly spent on hastily designed research, cocktail-table books of photographs, and excursions. Goggle-eyed reporters described a field trip to Desengano State Forest in 1989 that resembled a military exercise. Various companies provided trucks, motorcycles, hovercraft, field telephones, portable computers, and even a hot-air balloon. Food came in a refrigerated van, cooked and packed by one of Rio de Janeiro's best restaurants. Local residents, who had been connected to the electric network only a few weeks before, were present at the creation of designer environmentalism.[25]

The larger environmental organizations were vulnerable in another way: Most of them depended, for nearly all their field projects, on foreign funding. Well-meaning European and North American environmental organizations sought to strengthen their Brazilian counterparts while preserving exotic locales and saving indigenous peoples. Because the press of these same countries was simultaneously expressing horror at Brazil's garish environmental disasters, among them Cubatão and the burning of the Amazon Forest, this dependence made Brazilian environmental organizations vulnerable to ferocious criticism from the nationalist Right. They were accused of conspiring to slow down the country's economic development, it being a nationalist article of faith that the industrial countries did not wish Brazil to enter their ranks. The Left, meanwhile, claimed that much of the environmental damage was being done by multinational corporations, whose funding of environmental organizations would white-wash their images. The purchase, proposed by foreign environmentalists, of a part of the Brazilian foreign debt at its depressed market price and transformation of it into a fund for nature reserves was received with hostility by nationalists of all tendencies: The Left denied the legitimacy of the foreign debt and wanted simply to repudiate it; the Right saw the "swap" as a first step in the "internationalization" of the Amazon, a fear it had nursed for more than a century and which was actually being suggested by the president of France, apparently ignorant of his country's attempt to swallow the Brazilian territory of Amapá at the turn of the century.[26]

Environmental organizations also exhibited problematic relations with the government itself. Out of a need for funds and a desire to influence, some of them accepted government support. The FBCN, among others, signed contracts with federal and state environmental agencies to develop plans and carry out research in forest reserves. Doubtless, many of these were useful tasks that improved the quality of government services and that were unlikely to be carried out in any other fashion, given the government agencies' lack of technical staff and near-monopoly of financial resources. But they also blurred the distinction between civic activism and official policy, an especially unfortunate tendency during the military dictatorship and debilitating during a period of reconstruction of civil society. It is difficult to interpret, for example, research on fishing practices, sponsored by Petrobrás, as anything other than collaboration on image improvement, given that company's role in the degradation of Cubatão and São Sebastião. Involvement of this sort may also help to explain the FBCN's avoidance of political positions.[27]

Environmental organizations generally sought not to be influenced by the government but to influence it. Their principal strategy, and the most efficient use of their funds, was to press the government to assume its responsibilities. To this end their connections with foreign counterparts was critical, because they were able to apprise international development agencies of the dire results of their participation in earlier development schemes. Politically vulnerable, these agencies came to insist that part of their loans and a share of Brazilian government funds be devoted to environmental safeguards. In this way, there became available for forest preservation and recuperation hundreds of millions of dollars that the government found almost impossible to refuse. The government, through the pressure of these agencies, was also embarrassed into canceling, as part of a plan truculently entitled "Our Nature," a number of its less well thought-out resource policies, although it announced its determination to go through with others.[28]

Evidently, Brazilian environmental organizations experienced considerable difficulty in styling themselves legitimate representatives of civil society. Perhaps most problematic was their relationship to the people who actually lived in and near the Atlantic Forest. The movement consisted almost entirely of university-trained urbanites whose information regarding rural politics and conflicts was limited and whose contact with the rural lower class was distant, an inevitable consequence of the social inequality regnant in Brazilian society. Their organizations did not include representatives of this social class, which was in fact directly responsible for forest destruction, if only as the employees of others, and was therefore the only group that could ensure its safety. A movement that participated in the struggle to establish a democratic society would have to forswear the resort to authority, a strategy that had never proved effective in any case. Nor could it permit its relations with rural dwellers to descend to the hostility experienced between Augusto Ruschi and his neighbors.

Environmentalists who had thrown themselves into the saving of the Amazon Forest readily championed its indigenous inhabitants. Indeed, they had seized on the statements of a few anthropologists that forests inhabited by primitive swidden farmers exhibited higher biological diversity than those that were unoccupied. These sympathies were extended to rubber gatherers, whose occupation was not really traditional, dependent as it was on a commercial, government-subsidized market, but publicity and funding had flowed their way when one of their leaders, Chico Mendes, was identified as an "environmentalist" and subsequently, like numerous other Brazilian rural labor leaders, was killed by latifundists. This connection inspired the creation in the Amazon of a new form of conservation unit, the "extractive reserve," whose residents were expected to carry out only traditional forms of exploitation, leaving the forest in place.[29]

The Atlantic Forest certainly contained many oppressed lower-class residents, who were increasingly subject to eviction and violence, but they were difficult to identify as traditional inholders. By 1990, only twenty indigenous communities in the region of the Atlantic Forest had been granted reservations larger than 10 square kilometers, totaling at most 1,500 square kilometers and sheltering about 15,000 residents. Indeed, one of the few surviving sizable indigenous groups had an embarrassingly disastrous effect on the forest entrusted to it. These were the Pataxó, a group that had come, sometime in the second half of the nineteenth century, to reside in South Bahia, near Monte Pascoal. This historic promontory had been a state park since 1943. In 1951 the Pataxó were persuaded by mysterious strangers from Rio de Janeiro to attack and ransack a nearby town. In reprisal, police raided the Pataxó settlement, and town residents set it on fire, killing two and scattering many of the rest. In 1959 the park was transferred to the federal government, its area somewhat reduced. Even so, it was, at 225 square kilometers, the largest single stand of primary Atlantic Forest in the Northeast. In the 1970s the Pataxó, having wandered in nearby Minas Gerais, supporting themselves as farm workers, began filtering back to the site of their former settlement, which was on the lands of the federal park. During their wandering, or perhaps earlier, they lost the use of their language and other elements of their culture.[30]

The National Indian Service (FUNAI) supported the Pataxó claim to their former residence. Indigenous claims held precedence over those of the Park Service, so nearly a third of the park was ceded to them in 1980. Soon, as was their right, they cut down and sold their woodlands. Then they began to trap animals and extract piaçava palm from the park and hired out to commercial timber dealers who sold the wood cut in the park—Indians could not be jailed under Brazilian law. During the drought of 1989, members of the tribe set fires within the park and held IBDF workers hostage when they tried to extinguish them. Environmentalists reeled back in horror—here was proof that no one could be trusted with forest reserves, not even the indigenes in whom they had so emotionally invested their hopes. It went unnoticed that the land the Pataxó had been awarded had become increasingly cramped and quite inadequate for any form of what might have been defined as "traditional" economy: By 1989 there were 2,100 residents on the reserve, and the tribe was demanding more of the park's lands. Their poverty and suffering worsened as the forest disappeared: In 1992 Pataxó were dying of cholera, caused by drinking from their polluted streams.[31]

In graver state were the Guarani tribespeople who had been migrating to the forests of the São Paulo Serra do Mar since the 1830s. Rejecting government reservations and dependent on seasonal dislocations for religious and material reasons, they inhabited, pacifically and barely noticed, upland areas between Registro and the border of Paraná. These lands were never granted them by the state but remained in private hands. The presence of these transient swidden farmers was useful to the owners because the indigenes did not attempt to establish their own claims but, by providing the appearance of a tenantry, gave more weight to the titleholders. In the late 1970s, real estate speculators began buying up these holdings, with the intention of promoting vacation subdivisions, and expelled the Guarani. An indigenous rights group struggled in court to establish their rights to the land that FUNAI had failed to defend.[32]

By the 1980s neither itinerant indigenes nor those settled on reservations lived any longer as they had a century before. They engaged in commercial exchange with the outside world, so they worked part time for wages or ransacked their environment for goods to sell. Their economy approximated that of ethnically mixed and culturally largely assimilated rural dwellers. Although these more numerous peoples were also looked on as living in harmony with their environment, few of them had developed a culture in place but were, instead, smallholders whose lands had been grabbed by large-scale ranchers and reforesters. Environmental activists in the Southeast were inclined to assess the forest activities of such "traditional peoples" as benign, possessing a "profound relationship with the environment in which they live," and "conservationists by vocation," much like the image of Amazon rubber gatherers. A study of one such coastal community located within the Serra do Mar State Park, in the county of Ubatuba, São Paulo, suggested that these were pious hopes. It showed that half of the village's houses had been sold to tourists within twelve years of the park's creation and that the most persistent demand of the remaining traditional inholders was to be allowed to practice swidden farming within the park.[33]

Plans for the preservation of expanded areas of the Atlantic Forest awarded "traditional peoples" occupation of "buffer zones" that would surround "nuclear zones" in which no human activities would be permitted. Because no one was competent to define exactly what was meant by "traditional," much less to order eviction of those whose activities did not fit the definition, a third zone was devised, the "transitional," which could be drawn around those inholders judged to be at one more remove from Eden, yet not altogether "modern" or "capitalist." This was a political, as well as an ideological, design—total exclusion of local peoples, traditional or not, would turn them against the reserves. On the other hand, facilitating their permanence with legal titles might motivate them to hinder the entrance of outsiders into the nuclear zone and hopefully to refrain from doing so themselves. It was not altogether unforeseen that these special statuses were, ironically, salable—they would quite likely incite outside interests, eminently capitalist, to act through the "traditional" inholders.[34]

Whether these formulations would knit into the movement lower-class dwellers, whose eternal demand was simply to be guaranteed secure title, remained altogether problematic. The mutual alienation of the two sectors of society was captured by the linguist and poet Carlos Vogt, who remarked that

> Recent times have shown abundantly the country's two most visible faces: One showing that the consciousness of citizenship is alive, but almost always shining on the cheeks of well-fed folk; the other demonstrating the effects of misery and social injustice on

Brazilians who, having received nothing from society, owe little in return, not even involvement.[35]

The environmental movement was responsible, directly or indirectly, for a remarkable expansion in parks and reserves in the southeastern Atlantic Forest. In a single decade, from 1981 to 1990, their number doubled, reaching 205, and their area nearly quintupled, from 9,918 to 48,307 square kilometers (see map 10). Widely resorted to was the declaration of landmark status—*tombamento*. Landmark status was applied to nearly all the conservation units along the Serra do Mar, from Paraná to Espírito Santo. The first of these decrees was signed in São Paulo in 1985, the direct result of the fright occasioned by the floods at Cubatão. That state was joined by Paraná the following year. In both, a number of environmentalists and civil servants with environmental responsibilities, most notably José Pedro de Oliveira Costa and João José Bigarella, had been agitating for this measure for several years. Tombamento added another level of protection to an assortment of reserves and parks and was also intended to coordinate and consolidate existing efforts. Because most of the conservation units had not been expropriated and because there was little hope that they would be in the short term, landmark status at least restricted the activities of private inholders. Henceforth, it would be necessary to petition the state landmark commissions, as well as the agencies already in charge, for permission to make any changes within parks and reserves.[36]

The Constitution of 1988 backed this concept further by declaring the entire Atlantic Forest "national patrimony," along with the Amazon Forest and the Pantanal—the wetlands of Mato Grosso do Sul. Shortly thereafter, a consortium was formed of representatives of the states that had landmarked their sections of the Atlantic Forest. Espírito Santo and Rio de Janeiro joined after a delay, as did the northeastern states in 1992. The plan of the sponsors was to request that the landmarked Serra do Mar be declared a Biosphere Reserve by UNESCO. This status, which had been granted to hundreds of reserves worldwide, had been requested previously in behalf of only one Brazilian natural reserve, Iguaçu National Park. UNESCO recognition enhanced requests for funding of nature protection to the World Bank, foreign foundations, and international environmental organizations. This was a prospect that gladdened state governors, who readily signed the necessary documents.[37]

The installation, in 1990, of the first elected president in thirty years, Pedro Collor de Mello, appeared to give new impetus to the environmental movement. A meeting of biologists proposed, with some hope of being

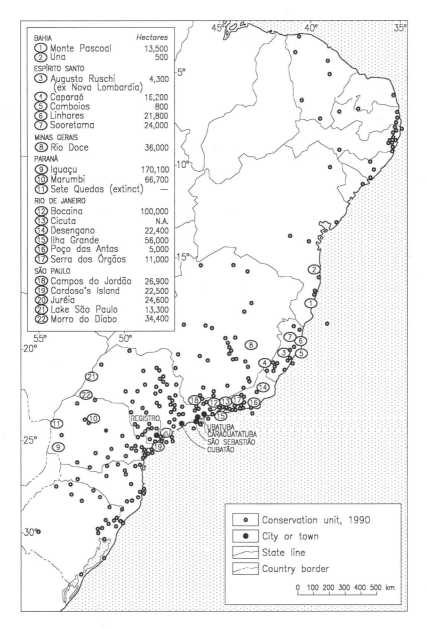

BAHIA	Hectares
① Monte Pascoal	13,500
② Una	500
ESPÍRITO SANTO	
③ Augusto Ruschi (ex Nova Lombardia)	4,300
④ Caparaó	16,200
⑤ Comboios	800
⑥ Linhares	21,800
⑦ Sooretama	24,000
MINAS GERAIS	
⑧ Rio Doce	36,000
PARANÁ	
⑨ Iguaçu	170,100
⑩ Marumbi	66,700
⑪ Sete Quedas (extinct)	—
RIO DE JANEIRO	
⑫ Bocaina	100,000
⑬ Cicuta	N.A.
⑭ Desengano	22,400
⑮ Ilha Grande	56,000
⑯ Poço das Antas	5,000
⑰ Serra dos Órgãos	11,000
SÃO PAULO	
⑱ Campos do Jordão	26,900
⑲ Cardoso's Island	22,500
⑳ Juréia	24,600
㉑ Lake São Paulo	13,300
㉒ Morro do Diabo	34,400

REGISTRO

UBATUBA
CARAGUATATUBA
SÃO SEBASTIÃO
CUBATÃO

○	Conservation unit, 1990
●	City or town
	State line
	Country border

0 100 200 300 400 500 km

Map 10.   Conservation units, 1990

heard, 145 additional reserves, in order to protect species known to be endangered and to join together already protected units in an uninterrupted chain. The recently restructured federal environmental agency—the Instituto Brasileiro do Meio Ambiente (IBAMA), which incorporated the former federal forest service (the Instituto Brasileiro do Desenvolvimento Florestal, or IBDF)—was put in the hands of an energetic director who obtained from UNESCO the declaration of the Biosphere Reserve. She also signed (in the headquarters of S.O.S. Mata Atlântica) a temporary staying order against all further clearing of native trees in the Atlantic Forest. President Collor de Mello soon signed a decree extending this order indefinitely.[38]

Declarations and prohibitions, though essential and urgent, were of no particular value unless complementary measures were taken—indeed, they were to some degree counterproductive. It was the constant refrain of environmentalists that these plans and injunctions had to "get off the paper" and into effect. Unfortunately, the governors who saw advantage in attracting high-minded foreigners with money were in no hurry to annoy their constituents with decrees that would block their path to riches. In the region of the Atlantic Forest, 70 percent of the areas of parks and reserves was still privately held. Inholdings within them became more numerous, as speculators bet that some day protection would be withdrawn. Governors were therefore urged to expropriate all inholdings as quickly as possible. Estimates of expropriation of the rest varied between US$2 billion and US$6 billion, a large but not impossible sum, equivalent to the cost of three to nine more subway stations in the capital of São Paulo. Unfortunately, it was probably well below reality, because much of this land had multiple claimants and heirs in litigation—or in blood feuds. It would take regiments of lawyers years to resolve all this even if the money were immediately appropriated. There was also the likelihood that corruption would be involved in distributing a sum of this size—already a few scandals had come to light in federal parkland purchases, dating from the early 1980s.[39]

Declarations and prohibitions were themselves found to be in need of revision before "getting off the paper." The decree that forbade all further cutting of native forest immediately caused terrible hardship: Despite their protestations of solidarity, environmentalists had given no thought to the plight of the "traditional" inholders. The canoe makers, hearts-of-palm gatherers, bamboo- and liana-basket weavers, and loggers of giant ferns and sassafras were now all outlaws. The hearts-of-palm canneries began to shut down. After hearing itself cursed in a year of demonstrations in remote coastal villages, IBAMA came forth with regulations that legitimized swidden farming in second-growth forest, along with every sort of extractivism, as long as it was practiced according to an undefined "regime of sustained management."[40]

The conservation units added in the 1980s and early 1990s were a hodgepodge: twenty different classes of reserve, under a confusion of authorizations—laws, decrees, decree-laws, regulations, orders, and others—a few under no known authorization. This was a strategic weakness: Legislatures felt little obligation to provide operating funds for reserves they had not created. Management was carried out at all three levels of government by a multiplicity of agencies—in São Paulo, on the state level alone, at least fourteen agencies were involved. Of areas reserved before 1981, 25 percent had still not been demarcated by 1990. Some had been in that state for decades, their very existence doubtful. Demarcation was also lacking for 10 percent of the area reserved between 1981 and 1990. Many of the new units were defined as "Areas of Environmental Protection" (APAs), a sort of zoning instrument that merely prohibited activities that residents within the APA itself might decide were undesirable.

The agencies responsible for these areas were unable to expand apace. The budgets of many of them did not increase proportionately, because they did not contribute directly to economic development. Their staffs were consequently ill paid—only idealists and incompetents persisted. Complex tasks were often farmed out to other agencies at a higher cost—or sometimes at no cost, when interagency bills went unpaid. The multiplication of agencies, already a problem in the 1970s, continued. Overlapping and ill-defined responsibilities caused confusion, inefficiency, and rivalries. At the federal level, IBAMA and the Ministry of the Environment, at loggerheads, were wracked by repeated changes of leadership. Sometimes counterpart funds from abroad were lost because an agency was unable to persuade the government to release its share of costs.[41]

These bureaucracies depended ultimately upon forest guards and police to enforce their numerous and mutable commands. It was the IBDF's responsibility to authorize forest cutting. Of the hundreds of thousands of permits it issued each year, some were sold to third parties who were clearing preserved areas; sometimes blank forms were sold by IBDF employees; sometimes forms were counterfeited. An authorization for clearing in one place could be modified to appear to refer to a second area, and on the open road a single permit might serve to clear numerous truckloads of hardwood. Forest rangers on duty within the parks were usually too few to do more than keep the gates. The budgets and morale of the federal Park Service continued to decline. Itatiaia National Park lost ten of its twenty-two rangers between 1982 and 1987; in 1988 lack of funds obliged the shutting down of several federal parks. Federal forest police were spread extremely thin and retreated almost entirely from the southeastern states, which funded their own forces. São Paulo's force more than doubled in size during the 1980s, to 2,400, and its vehicles increased from 130 to 280. Meanwhile, the area under preservation had increased ten times. Paraná and Rio de Janeiro were far less well served—their effectives amounted to 380 and 30, respectively.

State forest police were state police detached to forest service. State police had been subordinated to the military under the dictatorship; with the return of civilian government they operated as a law unto themselves, their brutality condoned and their incompetence overlooked by many, besieged by the insecurity and crime of the big cities. In São Paulo, the forest police formed an elite—volunteers who received six months' extra training. Most of their isolated detachments, only loosely coordinated with other environmental agencies, carried out their charge faithfully, even though they doubted the efficacy of the unrealistic laws they enforced. They suffered in consequence the detestation—and occasional death threats—of "traditional" folk, loggers, and real estate developers alike. Forest police were nevertheless frequently accused of accepting or extorting bribes from rural dwellers. Police vehicles were very commonly inoperative, prompting suspicions that spare parts were going astray. The director of S.O.S. Mata Atlântica was moved to exclaim that it was "incredible how the infrastructure for inspection—the biggest in the country—can be so expensive and so inefficient." Even though the forest police were critical to the survival of the forest, environmental organizations were apparently queasy about a closer relationship with a branch of the state repressive apparatus tainted with a reputation for corruption and brutality. Reforestation companies were not so shy: They demanded adequate protection from arsonists and timber thieves, who cut sizably into their profits. Although their influence might oblige the government to improve forest police forces, it would probably turn their attention away from public reserves.[42]

Threats to the remnants of the Atlantic Forest were not lessened merely because an environmental movement had formed or because channels of protest had been enlarged. In fact, as areas in primary forest shrank, the danger increased, no matter what the means or the will. Competing government agencies, such as the power companies, water authorities, road departments, and forest "development" institutes, presented some of the gravest challenges, because their purposes were unquestioned and their projects were funded effortlessly, regardless of potential environmental impact. The pressure of mayors, city councilmen, and state legislators to convert forest into votes through concessions to build hotels, subdivisions, social clubs, and industrial districts was relentless and virtually irresistible.[43]

Meanwhile, many reserves were coming to pieces under the assaults of thousands of "traditional" folk tempted to make a few more cruzeiros than their "sustainable" pursuits normally yielded. The Bocaina National Park was a dramatic example. In 1982 only one guard was stationed in this 1,000-square-kilometer reserve on the summit of the Serra do Mar. Astonishingly, the IBDF had allowed a sawmill to operate within the park, accepting the owner's claim that he would only process logs from outside its boundaries. Poachers roamed freely, in bands of thirty to forty. They opened clearings with fire, so that tender shoots and seedlings might sprout and attract game. They fed on their kill for weeks at a time, all the while collecting jaguar pelts and other rarities for sale abroad. In Angra dos Reis, at the foot of the park, a monthly bird fair was held openly, stocked with birds trapped in Bocaina. Worst of all, loggers were cutting roads throughout the park, with tractors and draglines, some in plain view of the main highway between Rio de Janeiro and São Paulo. The reporter who brought all this to public attention encountered, among other colorful characters, a humble farmer who had just burned a clearing in the park, to feed, as he explained, his twelve hungry children. Loungers in a downtown bar laughed and told the naive reporter that the hardworking paterfamilias was a "professional squatter" who burned clearings all over the forest in order to establish phony claims that he later sold. At the time of this report, for one such worthy reason or another, 40 percent of Bocaina had already been cleared.[44]

In contrast to the disrepair and neglect of public preserves, there extended across the breadth of the Atlantic Forest an uncounted number of private reserves and a few reserves under the control of state-owned corporations. As the frontier expanded over the course of the twentieth century, quite a few planter families had left significant areas of their estates in primary forest, sometimes out of prudence, to assure a wood supply, sometimes as a hunting reserve, or sheerly out of respect for nature. The latter sort of proprietor was very rare and tended to become, like Ruschi, embittered with age at the greed of his neighbors and the heedlessness of the government. One such was Olavo Godoy, who in the 1930s had bought with his brothers a 3,600-hectare estate in northern Paraná, not far from Londrina. Entranced at the beauty of the forest, they had, alone of all their neighbors, obeyed the Forest Code and spared 670 hectares of it from the matchbox. This forest became their obsession—over the years they paid their own forest guards, as many as fifteen during the dry season, to keep out loggers, hunters, collectors, and arsonists. During the great fires of

1963, they hired 200 men to save their trees. The reimposition of taxes on forested land was a severe blow to their finances, already reeling from the freezes of 1975 and 1981. In 1986 the assessment was greatly increased. Olavo, the surviving brother, offered his forest to the state as a preserve, but the government would accept it only as a gift. Olavo could not afford so large a benefice to a government that by then he considered incompetent and malign. At the last moment it was acquired by the University of Londrina as a research center.[45]

Environmental organizations offered support to landowners who preserved their forests, representing their interests, sometimes investing in them directly or channeling foreign funding for the purpose, sometimes buying them out, after the pattern of the North American environmental organization, the Nature Conservancy. A few landowners were persuaded to protect rare species found or introduced on their estates. A few municipal governments, aware of the touristic potential of preserved areas, collaborated with environmental organizations and academic entities in the formation of reserves. These seemed to be more secure arrangements, but companies sometimes sold out, mayors were replaced in office, heirs indifferent to nature succeeded to estates, and government curatorial agencies of all sorts underwent internal bureaucratic struggles, collapsed budgets, or even abolition. Ruschi had persuaded the Klabin paper and pulp group to sign an accord with the IBDF to leave intact a 2,700-hectare tract in the county of Conceição da Barra, just south of the Bahia state border, in order to protect several endangered bird species, but the Klabins sold out to the Monteiro Aranha group, which ignored the accord and began to cut it down. Two of the most famous private reserves fell almost immediately into disrepair and confusion after they were donated to the federal government: the botanical garden of Rio de Janeiro's internationally famous landscape artist, Roberto Burle Marx; and the museum and herbarium of Augusto Ruschi.[46]

Somewhat more solidly emplaced, seemingly, were those few reserves that had been created by state-owned companies. These entities engaged in environmentally obtrusive activities yet required public approval in order to avoid oft-threatened privatization. Those among them that accumulated monopoly profits could easily afford to set aside reserves. One such was that at Linhares, Espírito Santo, owned by the Vale do Rio Doce mining company (CVRD). This was the 217-square-kilometer tract that had been acquired to produce sleepers for the railroad CVRD rebuilt in the 1970s to transport iron ore to the coast. Probably because of Ruschi's public attacks, the company decided to leave the forest intact and hired guards and a staff of scientists to carry out a program of research. It also preserved a second tract of 61 square kilometers in South Bahia, in the county of Porto Seguro. The company's continued interest in preserving the Atlantic Forest may have been related to its decision to cut down forest along its railroad in Pará State, to make charcoal for iron smelting: The Linhares reserve, of little commercial value, might help offset the company's unfavorable image in the Amazon.[47]

Whatever their form of ownership, all the Atlantic Forest's reserves were increasingly threatened by fire. The traditional burning of pasture, convenient but wasteful of nitrogen and ultimately self-defeating, was still very common. Swidden farming was practiced wherever primary or secondary forest remained more-or-less intact. State laws were supposed to discourage burning by requiring licenses, but the practice could not be prohibited outright. As surviving forest came to be broken up into smaller patches, its soil and ambient atmosphere dried up, and it became increasingly vulnerable to wayward flames. As drought struck repeatedly in the 1980s, the Atlantic Forest was swept over and over by uncontrollable fires. In 1986, 13 percent of the woodlands of the state of Minas Gerais was burned, including part of the poverty-stricken Jequitinhonha Valley. In 1989, after two rainless months, 300 square kilometers of South Bahian forest burned down. Even if all accidental fires could be prevented, the forest would still burn: A study of incidents logged by forest police in the area of the Atlantic Forest showed that a third to a half were the result of arson.[48]

By the end of the 1980s, the extent of surviving Atlantic Forest and its condition had become critical questions. In the state of São Paulo, where photographic inventories had been carried out over the longest period, uneasiness and controversy ran the highest. The IBDF's 1982 National Forest Inventory, based on aerial photographs, indicated a loss of a quarter of the woodland found in that state only nine years before. Satellite imaging began in the mid-1970s, and resultant maps were being published by 1983. S.O.S. Mata Atlântica hired the National Space Research Institute to analyze Landsat images of the Atlantic Forest, and São Paulo's Secretariat of the Environment also began periodic monitoring, using the same images. The first data emitted by S.O.S. Mata Atlântica showed a greater extent of forest than had been found in earlier surveys, but these findings were later lowered. Its revised atlas of the state of São Paulo showed that, in 1985, 9.12 percent of the originally forested area was covered with primary and secondary forest and that five years later this cover was reduced to 8.80 percent. The state secretariat's analysis of images taken in 1988 and 1989 listed primary and secondary forest separately but found a considerably greater total, the equivalent of 14.27 percent. By late 1990, however, the secretariat lowered its estimate to 7.58 percent. These analyses were methodologically vulnerable. They suggested, nevertheless, that the alarming predictions of the 1970s were exaggerated and that the rate of destruction of undisturbed forest had slowed down in São Paulo during the 1980s. This was a pleasing result from the point of view of the state governments and newspapers that represented the development-minded elite. They also seemed to vindicate the government agencies responsible for preserving the forest. Nevertheless, the later forecasts were similar to those of the previous decade: The forest of São Paulo was continuing to disappear and would be reduced, if matters did not improve, to perhaps 3 percent of its original area by the end of the century.[49]

By late 1993, S.O.S. Mata Atlântica had completed its survey of the entire Atlantic Forest over the five-year period 1985 to 1990. It showed that 5,330 square kilometers had been lost and that by the latter date only 83,500 square kilometers—a little more than 8 percent of the forest that was presumed to have existed in 1500—remained.[50]

Although it was possible that the rate of forest destruction might be slowing, it was not certain how much of the Atlantic Forest that might still be in place in the year 2000 would be what could still be called primary or undisturbed. This was an especially worrisome question in regard to the semideciduous interior sector. Because it had grown on flatter terrain and was therefore readily cultivated by machines, it was in much greater danger of disappearing entirely, even before the turn of the century. Indeed, because this region, by far the most extensive part of the Atlantic Forest, had been subjected to every form of exploitation for centuries, it lacked baseline research. "Original area" in all these studies was theoretical, based upon soil, climate, and relief conditions, all of which might have changed in historical times along with forest clearing. Botanists often expressed doubt that any undisturbed forest still existed. Ecological studies in forest reservations exhibited numerous and unmistakable signs of disturbances. The lack of a standard against which to measure undisturbed forest had legal as well as intellectual consequences. "Traditional" peoples were permitted to cut down capoeira, but not primary forest. The regulation emitted by IBAMA defined capoeira as exhibiting a reduced number of tree species (which was not necessarily the case) less than twenty years old. In a sense, just as indigenous populations untouched by neo-European cultures had disappeared and "traditional" peoples now came to be, for lack of authentic hunter-gatherers to protect, thought worthy of "preservation," now, faute de mieux, second growth twenty years old was the subject of increasing study and concern.[51]

It was also too late to find out if the destruction had really worked climate change: Reduced and irregular rainfall, lower atmospheric humidity, and wider temperature extremes had been predicted for more than a century but were never systematically investigated. If the droughts and hard freezes of the 1970s and 1980s were in fact the result of deforestation, then their effects on forests would also have to be classified as anthropic. Judging from research carried out in the Amazon that showed that much of the rainfall in the interior consisted of water transpired from coastward forests, these misfortunes of the interior plateau of the Atlantic Forest might indeed be attributable in part to human action.[52]

An environmental consciousness was dawning in Brazilian culture nearly too late for the Atlantic Forest. The demands of rapidly growing city populations for space, water, food, raw materials, and energy wore ever more insistently on a natural realm that seemed simply to be fading away before them. As usual in the history of the human relation to the natural environment, effective countermeasures began to be taken only after an immense, undeniable disaster had occurred. The political expressions of this environmental consciousness were still uncertain, ambiguous, and tiny, compared with the tradition and coherence of other social goals and the weight of economic interests. Yet the environmental organizations of the 1980s did gain some victories and had cause to expect increasing responsiveness from elected representatives and bureaucrats. The contradiction that afflicted the movement was, after all, generic in Brazilian society—the chasm that stretched between those few who owned most of the country's forests and felt little responsibility for preserving them and the mass of the citizenry, desperately in need of relief from a social system that had denied them land, education, and justice.

The principal achievement of the environmental organizations—the expansion of a system of parks, reserves, and landmarked areas—offered some hope for the survival of a forest that was coming to be recognized as the most endangered in the world. Means of protecting what remained were slowly expanding, with financial assistance from abroad, and more members of rural communities were cooperating in these efforts. Although the extent of the remaining forest was still not entirely clear, it did appear to be disappearing at a slower rate. This was hardly reassuring because the means and the will might not accumulate rapidly enough to halt the process entirely. Indeed, it might be that no matter how lavish the means or how determined the will, the Atlantic Forest was already doomed.

15

The Value of Bare Ground

Gostaria de perguntar por onde é que vocês estão indo?

I'd like to ask where is it that you're going?

AILTON KRENAK, INDIGENOUS LEADER

By the early 1990s, the Atlantic Forest was in a critical state. If those remnants identified or presumed to be primary were to survive, drastic measures would have to be undertaken immediately, measures quite the opposite of those customary to Brazilian culture and governance. It was not clear how many of the forest's species still existed. It was still less clear whether it might be possible to re-create sections of the forest that had disappeared. What was quite evident was that, as primary forest on private holdings continued to be converted to arable and pasture, reservoirs and highways, country clubs and slums, and as more and more publicly owned lands gained ever more layers of legal protection, government agencies were becoming the last hope of the forest's salvation.

Manuel Arruda da Câmara was, in 1810, the first to envision the possibility of human-induced extinctions of plants and animals of the Atlantic Forest. It was one of the justifications he advanced for the creation of botanical gardens. Extinction was a worry that repeatedly entered Auguste de Saint-Hilaire's mind. He noted numerous incongruous place-names: Canindé, Anhumas, Guará, Arapongas, names of birds that evidently had once inhabited these locales but were no longer to be found in them. Driven in his collecting by the thought that "these virgin forests as ancient as the world" might one day perish, he reflected mournfully:

> Nothing then will remain of the primitive vegetation; a host of species will have disappeared forever and the labors, in which the savant von Martius, my friend Doctor Pohl, and I have consumed our existence, will be in large part nothing more than historical monuments.[1]

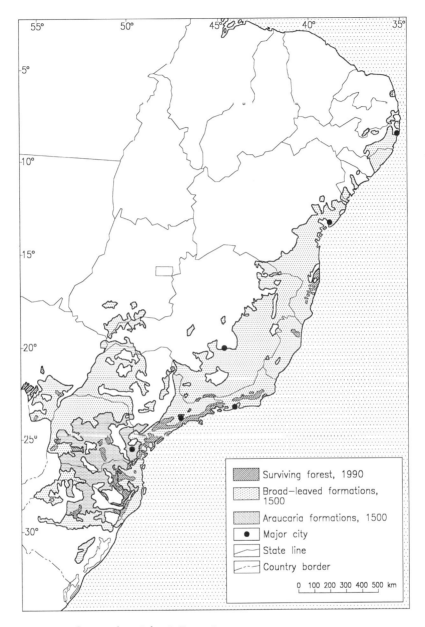

Map 11. The Brazilian Atlantic Forest in 1990

Legend:
- Surviving forest, 1990
- Broad—leaved formations, 1500
- Araucaria formations, 1500
- Major city
- State line
- Country border

0 100 200 300 400 500 km

Curiously, however, no species of the Atlantic Forest has yet been recorded, with certainty, as extinct, even though the forest has been reduced to less than 10 percent of the area it occupied in 1500 and even though most of what remains has been subjected to all sorts of extractivism and vandalism. Island biogeography theory, which relates the abundance of species to the relative size of landmasses, suggests that at least half of its species should have disappeared by now. Continental ecosystems may be expected to contain or retain more species than islands of the same size, given the greater ease of migration into and within them. The Atlantic Forest is also presumed to offer a superior haven because of its complex topography and climatic variability, which have fragmented its populations into small, viable habitats and are supposed to have accustomed them to rapid adaptation to change. Nevertheless, the physical and climatic environments of the Atlantic Forest do not appear to be so prodigiously distinctive, compared to other tropical places and climes; indeed, they might even be characterized as comparatively bland.[2]

It is therefore remarkable that so few creatures of the Atlantic Forest have even been recorded as endangered. The explanation must be in part historical: Biological collections only began three hundred years after plantation agriculture, cattle raising, and mining began. They were altogether too inadequate and skewed to represent baseline data. It is conceivable therefore that very many species of the Atlantic Forest disappeared before science was ever aware of their existence. The achievements of von Martius, Spix, Saint-Hilaire, and the other naturalists of the early nineteenth century were monumental. Their descriptions of tens of thousands of plants and animals, bound into hundreds of volumes of floral and faunal classification, their transcription into notebooks of many more thousands of pages of field observations, the kilometers of shelves they filled with specimens, dried and pressed or pickled in jars, identifications fading and uncertain, flowers crumbled into dust, tissues grey and gelatinous—a vast intellectual opus, yet tiny before the reality of still more tens of thousands of undiscovered inhabitants of the forest. Most of the collections of this classical period of botany and zoology were made on sunny beachfronts, grasslands, savannas, and secondary woodlands, not in the gloomy eternal forest, whose myriad life forms were sheltered, unsuspected, in the canopy fifty meters above the naturalists' heads. Their collecting, furthermore, was limited to the most accessible places, near the largest cities and along main roads. The 100,000-square-kilometer broad-leaved forest of northern Paraná, for example, was then terra incognita. And their collecting was only incipient—even their most often visited sites, where they persisted intact, later yielded many further discoveries.[3]

The Brazilian successors of these heroic Europeans were for a century and a half but a skeleton crew of talented, self-taught amateurs, idealists, and cranks, often lacking the means to publish their findings. The specimens they collected moldered in ill-funded and ill-kept Brazilian museums and herbaria. Whole collections disappeared. And the Atlantic Forest disappeared even faster. Freire Alemão's frantic rummaging through suburban logging sites was always interrupted when the loggers fired the slash. The irascible Augusto Ruschi identified more than a hundred new species, all in his tiny reserve, the last remnant of primary upland forest in the region. Had Espírito Santo boasted a score of Ruschis, would they not have found hundreds, thousands, more? Research has ever been an interlude before the firestorm, the rising waters of the dams, the real estate speculators' tractors. Pedro Scherer Neto, president of the Paraná birding society, complained that

> The scientists had barely a chance to cover Paraná to become familiar with it, to collect. There were some who did, but not enough, because there was too little time. The devastation was greater than the chances of the researchers to carry out the necessary studies to have, today, all the information of the flora and fauna of Paraná.[4]

It appears that what were the most biologically diverse areas were also the most drastically transformed by agriculture and cattle raising. Coffee planting devastated the western reaches of the Paraíba do Sul River valley, which Saint-Hilaire had declared the most unique and diverse that he had found in all of southern and southeastern Brazil. Furthermore, those sectors of the Atlantic Forest considered most appropriate for plantation crops, such as the Northeast coast and the highland Paulista West, have been the most thoroughly scoured of forest, so that nothing but the most insignificant patches remain of what was once a widespread flora.

As funding for biological field research became somewhat more available in the late 1970s, continuing discoveries of new species were made in remnant tall forest. Botanists at the Rio Doce State Forest found 27 between 1979 and 1986. In South Bahia, the Center for Cacao Research identified 300 new plant species and 5 new genera between 1978 and 1980. A study in 1993 of a single hectare of lowland South Bahia found dozens more unclassified tree species. Recent discoveries include others of even the most visible and striking forest life forms—trees, birds, even a primate! That the identification of new species can continue at so rapid a rate, with the enlistment of only a relatively few trained collectors and a collection rate of fewer than four specimens per ten square kilometers, indicates how much has yet to be incorporated into the database. Unfortunately, funding of inventories and monographs of known species has slackened in recent years.[5]

Even more troubling, these discoveries in quite restricted areas of still relatively undisturbed forest suggest that many life forms may have already disappeared before they could be discovered. This thought occurred to the ornithologist Helmut Sick, who considered it possible that "even species of birds as yet unidentified by science may be eradicated, as is suggested by the recent discovery of three new species of hummingbirds."[6]

As early as the 1940s, Frederico Carlos Hoehne averred that more than 300 species of orchids had already gone extinct in Brazil, because of habitat destruction. In 1975, Mauro Victor set the number of extinct plants at 3,000. These estimates are defensible, considering the uniqueness of the plants of the Atlantic Forest, limited in some cases to a single ridgeline or a single valley. Ladislau Netto noted this extreme endemism in his excursion to Minas Gerais in the 1860s. So did Hoehne, in 1927, when he collected 107 species of orchids: "Each one of the ranges of Minas has a flora more or less its own and offers different aspects for the excursionist, even though there are many species and characteristics that are common to all those of the state of Minas Gerais."[7] The local disappearance of widely distributed species has been frequently recorded: A 1974 study of bird life in Pirassununga, São Paulo, found 9 species lost of 180 formerly recorded. A 1986 census of bird species in Nova Friburgo, Rio de Janeiro, found only 184 of the 285 species collected during the nineteenth century. Such reports suggest the likelihood of concomitant total extinction of unknown species of very limited range. The extreme fragmentation of most of what is considered to be relatively undisturbed portions of the Atlantic Forest is one of the causes of this reduced diversity. The "edge effect"—the exposure of forest interiors to wind, sunlight, and invasion of grassland species by penetration roads, power lines, pipelines, motorbike trails, and such—was coming to be investigated as a major cause of degradation. The fragmented forest was no longer viable for the most free ranging of its species: A study of the probable ranges of Neotropical mammals showed that very large areas were necessary to maintain minimum breeding stocks. Carnivores are the most demanding. Jaguars would require some 5,500 square kilometers to stabilize a population of 500. Tapirs would require about 1,600; the crab-eating raccoon, 1,500.[8]

Although carnivores and other mammals represent but a trifling portion of the forest biomass, their loss or rarefaction ripples through the system incalculably. The complexity of relationships among species of the Atlantic Forest suggests the likelihood of permanent losses. In 1939 Moysés Kuhlman noted that a certain palm was becoming rare, possibly because a bee that pollinated it or perhaps a parrot that spread its seeds— this had been observed by Saint-Hilaire—was also becoming rare. The African honeybee, an exotic strain imported by a laboratory in São Paulo in the 1950s for breeding purposes, had carelessly been allowed to escape and was replacing native stingless bees throughout the forest, with effects upon flora that are incalculable. These transformations remain mysterious and uninvestigated. It has been noticed that some species of insects and birds of the chilly Serra do Mar flee to the warmer interior or to the coast in winter. It would be remarkable if all such migratory creatures have survived the degradation of two distinct habitats over the century preceding the more intensive field investigations of the last fifteen years.[9]

At the First Brazilian Conference on Nature Protection, held in 1934, a few participants made mention of species they considered rare and endangered. Alberto José de Sampaio noted some thirty plants, including *Faramea campanella*, collected once in Espírito Santo, in 1830, then only once more, in 1932, in Rio de Janeiro, and *Sanhilaria brasiliensis*, collected by Saint-Hilaire and never again. The potentiality of extinction was vague and formless, however, as long as collecting expeditions remained so infrequent and scattered. Not until the 1960s, then, did this menace gain urgency. Even so, concerns could only be expressed scientifically in regard to species that had been collected at least once, classified, and published.[10]

The assessment of the status of rare endemic species became an official object of concern with the promulgation of the Forest Code of 1967, which required the protection of threatened plants and animals. Official lists of such species therefore began to appear shortly afterward. A list of plants threatened with extinction was emitted by the Brazilian Institute for Forest Development (IBDF) in 1968. Only 12 species of the Atlantic Forest were listed, 7 of them orchids. By 1992 the Botanical Society of Brazil recommended listing 28 of the forest's species; oddly, it did not include all those already protected by the IBDF. Closer inspection of the flora of the Atlantic Forest by specialists was likely to reveal the endangerment of many hundreds more species, however. Earlier studies of three genera—*Trimezia, Griffinia,* and *Stephanopodium*—for example, had suggested that at least ten of their species endemic to the Atlantic Forest were threatened. Indeed, some of the species on these various lists are likely extinct, because a century or more had elapsed since their last collection. Graziela de Barros, one of Brazil's most distinguished taxonomists, was grimly amused by inquirers who wished to know which plants were threatened. "With so-called development, there isn't any plant that's not threatened."[11]

The potential extinction of animals was given a good deal more, though selective and similarly incomplete, official attention. Most of the scientific knowledge of Brazilian animals was concentrated on the most easily observed, spectacular, and engaging—primates, carnivores, and birds. Therefore, extremely few creatures of other orders were included on the IBDF's first list, published in 1973. It declared 11 monkeys protected; the list published in 1989 by that agency's successor, the Brazilian Institute of the Environment and Renewable Natural Resources, protected 25—half of all of the primates native to Brazil. In 1973, 8 carnivores were listed; in 1989, there were 13. The first list showed 10 birds native mainly to the Atlantic Forest; that of 1989 showed 37, two of them probably already extinct. Only a few of the smaller mammals, reptiles, amphibians, and other nonmammals were listed, along with 31 insects, nearly all butterflies. Eight of the species on the 1989 list were unknown before 1965.[12]

The rarefaction and disappearance of Atlantic Forest species and the retreat of more-or-less undisturbed patches of it to quite restricted areas gave rise to scattered attempts to reconstitute it, to replant its species and nurture it to maturity. The Energy Company of São Paulo, stung by mounting public criticism of its hydroelectric projects, gradually developed techniques for implanting native tree species along the margins of its reservoirs. Even this public company, with vast resources and a vital need to prevent siltation, planted fewer than 300 hectares a year. At that rate, it would take 150 years to reforest the 437 square kilometers with which it was entrusted! More energetic was the Vale do Rio Doce Company (CVRD), equally goaded by the press and also facing problems of erosion of its railroad trackage. In one of its projects, its staff planted a wide swath along its right-of-way connecting iron deposits in the interior of Minas Gerais and the port at Tubarão. Managerial efforts like these, however, were quite different from natural processes. The CVRD planted bushy species, not trees, and avoided economic plants that might attract humans and plants unpalatable to cattle that might spread to adjoining pasture.[13]

S.O.S. Mata Atlântica, aware that the fragmentation of preserved areas of the Atlantic Forest increased the danger of extinctions, urged the restoration of its continuity by replanting cleared intervals so as to form "natural corridors." Most of these lands would first have to be expropriated and then improvements within them demolished, foreseeably a much more costly and politically wearing affair than the buying out of inholders in existing forest. Brazilian delegates to a conference on atmospheric carbon dioxide, held at Hamburg in 1988, were challenged to devise means of reforesting their vast national territory in order to assist in the reversal of predicted global warming. In response, a plan, called FLORAM, to reforest 200,000 square kilometers within thirty years was elaborated at the Institute for Advanced Studies of the University of São Paulo. A great deal of discussion was expended on abstract parameters of such a venture and very little on incentives to private landowners. It seemed to be assumed that the same foreigners who instigated the plan would pay for its execution. To this end the planners proposed the use of "debt-for-nature swaps"—the purchase of depreciated Brazilian international debt by foreign environmental organizations or government agencies and their donation to Brazilian environmental entities to fund nature preservation. It seemed unlikely, however, that foreigners, having elicited so ambitious a plan, would actually find the means to finance it, especially since this additional forest land would consist mainly of economic species that would eventually be used for fuel, thus on balance contributing not at all to carbon dioxide storage.[14]

In 1986 the government of São Paulo created a Foundation for Forest Conservation and Production to stimulate the planting of protective as well as economic forests. It proposed reforesting 40,000 square kilometers within 25 years. This foundation was intended to service principally small businesses that consumed wood as fuel or raw material. They had been required by new regulations either to pay a tax or plant replacement forest. It was in the state government's interest that they be encouraged to choose the latter, because tax revenues simply disappeared in the craw of the federal government. Therefore it sponsored wood consumers' reforestation associations, which distributed planting materials and assistance to cooperating farmers at no cost. By 1992 the foundation was distributing sufficient seedlings to reach its goal—assuming that they were all planted and would grow to maturity. In 1991 the federal government plugged the most obvious loophole in the Forest Code by requiring that landowners whose properties lacked the required 20 percent of woodland replant trees up to that amount. It was expected that most of this replanting would be in eucalyptus or pine, thereby lessening pressure on native forest but not contributing to its restoration. Some landowners, however, would be required to replant watersheds and riversides they or their predecessors had cleared. These were supposed to be permanent forests that could be exempted from land taxes; landowners might therefore choose to plant them in native species.[15]

The technical requirements of replanting with native species were poorly understood. Very little such planting had been done, or at least reported. Traditional or indigenous lore was lost, probably irretrievably. The Botanical Garden of Rio de Janeiro began to attempt restoration in the county of Nova Friburgo, using seeds from the garden. It did not seem to be difficult to plant native species of the sort that sprang up spontaneously in capoeira. Hardwood species that normally were to be found only in primary forest were much less adaptable: When planted in such projects, they vegetated disappointingly. Even a fairly common understory tree like *Euterpe edulis*, which yields hearts of palm, took fifteen years to reach maturity—as was discovered when the government financed 150,000 hectares of it in the early 1970s, almost none of which came to market. It would apparently be necessary to follow the sequence of succession of the native forest itself. A godlike patience and persistence, and indifference to returns on capital, were called for. Even more attributes of the deity would be needed to calculate which thousands of the forest's myriad species once occupied any given location. Reestablishment of the innumerable commensal, parasitic, and epiphytic relationships of the primary forest seemed, no matter what the will or skill, a goal still less feasible, even though very likely essential to the maturation and reproduction of numberless forest species.[16]

Far more resources were devoted to a limited, unbalanced task—the reintroduction of a few endangered species of fauna into a few patches of remnant forest. The public was easily persuaded of the necessity to save species—mainly primates—that engaged its sympathies. Environmentalists and environmental agencies therefore exalted these creatures in their search for legitimacy and funding. Golden lion tamarins and woolly spider monkeys acquired a certain fame in the rich countries as international environmental organizations took up their cause and as foreign television portrayed their habits engagingly. The zoos of Brazil, like those of the rest of the world, were redefining their "primordial function" as "the preservation of species threatened with extinction" and emphasized the breeding of such animals.[17]

The most sustained, determined, and expensive of the reintroduction campaigns was the breeding in captivity and release of golden lion tamarins. The tamarin is a fierce-faced little creature, measuring about a meter in length, including its long, prehensile tail, and weighing half a kilogram. It lives on fruits, small animals such as frogs, and insects it collects in dense forest. It has been prized as a curiosity since the earliest days of the colony—many had been captured for Brazilian fanciers, and many had been exported to Europe. So much of the tamarins' lowland Rio de Janeiro habitat had been cleared that by the late 1960s only a few hundred were left in the wild. Zoos in other countries had contributed to this decline, because they had bought tamarins as long as the trade was still legal. They had been largely unsuccessful in keeping them alive, much less breeding them, so that only 70 survived in captivity, worldwide. A 1970 report by National Museum zoologists to the International Union for the Conservation of Nature inspired the World Wildlife Fund to support lion tamarin preservation. In 1974 Adelmar Coimbra Filho, director of Rio de Janeiro's Primatology Center, persuaded the IBDF to expropriate a tract of 50 square kilometers of lowland Rio de Janeiro forest at a place called Poço das Antas, in the county of Silva Jardim, about 100 kilometers east of the city of Rio de Janeiro. There, with the support of the Brazilian Foundation for the Conservation of Nature, he led research on the tamarins' diet and behavior that much improved their survival and reproductive rates, techniques that were adopted in foreign zoos. In 1983, by which time there were several hundred tamarins in captivity, he began experimental reintroduction of these animals into the forest of the Poço das Antas reserve.

Reintroduction proved exceedingly difficult. Few of the tamarins survived the shock of release until training methods were devised to assist their adaptation to the wild. It took eight years, nevertheless, to install 35 tamarins in the forest—a 30 percent survival rate. Some of these were still receiving part of their sustenance from the biologists. These animals did procreate, however: A third generation of 45 tamarins—of which 33 survived—exhausted the lebensraum of the reserve. Meanwhile, another 250 were caged on the reserve, and zoos around the world owned 550 more. A few neighboring landowners were persuaded to accept 70 tamarins—of which 70 percent survived. It is ironic that one of the animals was killed by an attack of African honeybees. The reintroduction program was costing the World Wildlife Fund, with additional help from the National Zoo of Washington and other United States, Canadian, and German organizations, US$150,000 a year. A campaign was initiated in 1991 to increase the budget to US$250,000 in order to install, by the year 2025, 2,000 tamarins—considered the minimum viable number—in forest throughout the Rio de Janeiro lowlands. This, the directors hoped, could be obtained from private Brazilian businesses, which until then had not contributed significantly. Simultaneously, they sought to enlarge potential habitat to 230 square kilometers by persuading a goodly number of planters to set aside their woodlands as permanent preserves and allow them to be stocked with tamarins in return for tax exemptions.[18]

The limiting factor in the task of reintroducing the tamarin was proving to be not money but the shrinkage of appropriate habitat. Announcement of the reserve in 1971 had stimulated inholders to sell off their timber; boundaries consequently had to be redrawn in 1975. Poço das Antas had suffered fires nearly every year thereafter. The worst occurred in 1990, when 15 square kilometers were lost in a fire that burned for more than a month. Part of the reserve had been wetland before a dam was built upstream a few years before. The underlying turf subsequently dried out and served as tinder for any carelessly thrown cigarette butt. Indeed, dried turf in the region had been known to catch fire spontaneously. There was also danger from the fire-managed fields and pastures that abutted the reserve. The suspicion of its managers, however, was that the fires were maliciously set, by hunters or fishermen, perhaps angered at their exclusion from the reserve. Fortunately, some local residents looked upon Poço das Antas with favor and had saved it numerous times by warning the staff of the outbreak of fire on its margins. Nevertheless, by 1991, 40 percent of the reserve was degraded, and US$43,000 had to be spent for two watch towers and fire-fighting equipment. The federal government, though oblivious of burnings on private lands, righteously demanded that the reserve managers replant the burned areas, as though the fires had been their doing. Restoration, in any case, was a task that was part of their program. Lamentably, another fire in 1992 ruined an ongoing replanting experiment. In worse state was the rest of the county. Its woodlands were subject to enormous pressure by woodcutters, legal and illegal, who supplied the region's tile and brick-works, sugar mills, and salt pans. Owners of these companies were buying entire farms for the sole purpose of harvesting their woodlands.[19]

By 1992 the lion tamarin program had absorbed US$817,000 of World Wildlife Fund's money, almost 40 percent of its grants within the Atlantic Forest. The budget at Poço das Antas paid for varied training programs in zoology, forestry, and environmental education; indeed, it had been turned into a sort of outsized zoo, with locked gates and firebreaks, its inmates radio monitored and marked with dyed tails. Even more had been invested in the symbolism of the golden tamarin, to the point that its survival was expected to make possible the survival of the lowland forest itself. Certainly, the disappearance of one of the closer relatives of the human species would be a great disgrace, but this was surely a mistaken formula: Nothing less than the survival of the Atlantic Forest could guarantee the survival of the golden lion tamarin. By the 1990s other tamarin species (or subspecies, biologists were not quite certain which) were in even greater danger. These were all rarer than the golden tamarin—indeed, one was so rare it had been discovered only in 1990, and then only from a contraband pelt! The reserves that served as havens for the other two—Morro do Diabo in São Paulo and Una in South Bahia—were understaffed and nearly unknown to the public. Very few specimens of either were safely housed in zoos. Foreseeably, the reproduction in captivity, reintroduction, and preservation of these creatures would at the very least quadruple the cost of the tamarin program, supposing that they had not all become extinct in the meantime.[20]

Keeping some fragment of a few animal populations living and mating in zoos—"preservation *ex situ*," as it was called—was rather more practical than preserving the genetic material of plants. The world's seed banks, even the largest, were designed for the safekeeping of the germ plasm only of varieties of economic plants and their wild antecedents. This alone was a dauntingly complicated and expensive business. Attempting to keep viable the seeds of tens of thousands of plant species for which no economic use was known was almost unimaginable. Moreover, tropical plant species were much more difficult to store—"recalcitrant," they were called. Many tree species produced seeds in pods the size and density of cannonballs, and often the intervention of specific animals or ambient conditions were necessary to provoke germination.[21]

Clearly, the government would have to stand resolutely and consistently behind whatever further efforts to catalog, preserve, and restore remnant stands of the Atlantic Forest might prove feasible. There was unfortunately altogether too much evidence that this was a duty the government found neither congenial nor suited to its talents. During the 1980s, the federal and state governments had responded to international and domestic pressures by emitting a barrage of laws and regulations, creating numberless agencies, and designating dozens of natural reserves. This was done gracelessly: President José Sarney announced his pugnaciously titled "Nossa Natureza" plan in 1989 with a blast of vituperation against the developed countries that had made Brazil the victim of an "unjust, defamatory, cruel, and vicious" campaign, designed to "turn us into slaves." Foreign and Brazilian environmentalists might congratulate themselves for the results of "the labor in solidarity of the communities in preserving the memory, the civility, and the biodiversity of the many Atlantic forests they contain"; indeed, they would have to continue to maintain this stance toward the authorities if they were to compel or embarrass them to further actions in behalf of the forest.[22]

Nevertheless, some discerned in these triumphs the workings of a traditional conservative response to the "revindications" of novel and potentially disruptive political players: Create underfunded and overlapping agencies, invest them with conflicting mandates, and staff them with corruptible loyalists. Thus the environmentalists could be mollified with the declaration of as many new phantom nature reserves as they demanded. Indeed, Mauro Victor regarded the creation of several new national parks in the last days of President-General João Figueiredo's term as "an affront,"

> because it's the consolidation among us of a Brazil of make-believe, a hallucinatory and surrealistic country that exists only in the imagination of a half-dozen authorities disconnected from reality, completely alienated from reality.

These apparently progressive edicts were never designed to "get off the paper"; on the contrary, they would be "systematically disobeyed" by the authorities themselves.[23]

Helita Barreira Custódio, who analyzed carefully and critically the flow of environmental legislation that culminated in the constitutional articles of 1988, found in it neither a transformed consciousness nor an anxiety to make amends. She came to the bitter conclusion that it represented

> the progressive execution of an anti-ecological policy, seeking only economic development, under the orientation of notorious pressure groups of national and multinational entities, with the criminal connivance of certain politicians, administrators, professionals, specialists, or unscrupulous bureaucrats.[24]

The agencies designed to enforce these contradictory decrees ballooned with political appointees and their protégés. They could be counted on to fall into the slough of confusion, inaction, and venality that had already poisoned the state's labor tribunals, social security, health care, Indian protection, land reform, and housing authorities. Environmental agencies could not be made immune to these pressures and distortions. A few have already fallen into disgrace and have been subjected to bureaucratic reshuffling or have been permitted to go on while new agencies, temporarily trustworthy, were created alongside them. These solutions have inevitably caused more confusion, excuses for malfeasance, and opportunities for graft.[25]

Clearly, the most fundamental of the government's duties was that of establishing and protecting land rights, public as well as private. Much of the loss of the Atlantic Forest had been caused simply to strengthen the pretensions of squatters and speculators. The contentious and violent practices surrounding land entitlement were nearly as intense in the cities as on the frontier, and there was no sign that the reestablished democratic government was any more willing to face up to this responsibility than had been its predecessors.[26]

The pharaonic projects of the 1980s, conceived while vast amounts of recycled international oil money flowed into the government's coffers and flowed out into the pockets of its allies in the private sector, were delayed in completion, but only because of the government's penury. Economic accounting for social patrimony was unknown. Planning for these later projects was uninfluenced by the newly required environmental impact statements, most of which were pro forma, mere afterthoughts. Planning, according to Alceo Magnanini, remained "sectoral or unilateral, seeking exclusively a single end . . . afterwards it tries to confront problems as they arise." This "mania of doing-to-see-what-happens," he complained, "had brought incalculable prejudices to the collectivity," although it was justified as necessary "at any cost. This 'any cost' is what we are being charged and what will be charged future generations." The government's justifications for this heedlessness mutated with circumstances. During the 1980s, blame was laid on the accumulated foreign debt of more than US$100 billion, which, it was alleged, made it necessary to sell off the country's natural resources at an accelerated rate.[27]

The persistence of economic stagnation and a whirlwind of inflation were leading the government, and society, to desperate and ill-conceived measures. At Angra dos Reis, the completion of the second nuclear power station was authorized. The director of the National Fuel Department proposed to reduce drastically the government subsidy on liquid natural gas, a product almost universal in cities, even in the poorest households. He therefore recommended that the public revert to cooking on wood stoves. The physicist José Goldemberg estimated that the standard 13-kilogram tank of natural gas avoided the cutting down of 13 trees—a potential increase in demand of more than 900 million trees a year! It seemed quite certain that the shortage of water confronted by the megalopolis of São Paulo would not be resolved through increased protection and extension of its watersheds, improved maintenance of its network, or instilling conservation methods among consumers but by the construction of a US$10 billion aqueduct through the Serra do Mar forest reserve, a prospect as inspirational to construction companies as it was devastating to environmentalists.[28]

The United Nations Conference on the Environment and Development, held at Rio de Janeiro in June 1992, bestowed upon posterity some of the most utilitarian, not to say mean-spirited, views of the natural world of modern times. The diversity of life was therein labeled "genetic resources," forests were characterized as a renewable resource, and preservation was subsumed under the heading of sustainable use. In the twenty years since the last conference, the leaders of the less-technified countries had become to a degree conscious of the fragility of their biotic patrimony but had nursed their resentment and suspicion of foreign intentions and were determined to exploit their resources according to their own best lights. Hidden among the conference's resolutions to the governments of the planet to extract the maximum possible sustenance from their living substrates, however, is the reflection that the forests may deserve consideration for their "spiritual functions and values." The idea seems oddly out of place, even though it does not diverge from the conference's human centeredness—if acted upon, this proposition would exempt certain biota from destruction according to their capacity to inspire elevated thoughts in the citizenry. It did not, in any case, inspire any policy recommendations. The governments of the Third World, supposedly representatives of many "traditional peoples," saw fit to embrace the most materialistic of assumptions and prescriptions.[29]

This casual admission of the existence, among some peoples at least, of sympathy, perhaps even respect and identification, with their natural environments requires nevertheless some further reflection. The readiness of Brazilians to protect what remains of the Atlantic Forest surely depends upon some motivation other than self-interest, no matter how conceived. So little of it is left that none can be spared for experiments in "sustainable development"; indeed, all such claims in reference to the Atlantic Forest must be regarded as cant and hypocrisy. Even the nurturing of spiritual values must be severely restrained: Suburban forest stands like Tijuca are in constant danger of fires spread by some practicants of African religions, who leave lighted candles under its trees to propitiate the *orixás*. The motivation for preserving the forest must be disinterested, then, and it must extend across all levels of society, especially rural society, not merely to some of the better-educated members of the urban middle class. This would be a most remarkable achievement, considering how largely the propertyless depend for their survival on stripping the land of its vegetation and how stubbornly the propertied classes maintain their holdings for the same purposes. Civil society, in nearly all of its individual, as well as private, acts, must refrain from further incursions, now and forever. The role of the Brazilian state might thereby be reduced to the more practicable one of punishing the occasional infractor; it would gain more in prestige and power by enforcing the law than by circumventing it.

Nature appreciation has had few adepts in Brazil. The prestige of urbanity, transferred by the Portuguese as a means of confirming their superior status in a strange environment, has survived nearly intact. "In Minas Gerais," commented Cláudio de Moura Castro,

> "woods" [mata] has connotations suggestive of disrespect for nature. The word is pejorative there; to say of a place that "There's only woods" is to condemn it. In the Escola Superior de Agricultura of Viçosa it was common during the forties to hear people tell a student that he came from the "woods" and obtain the reply: "No, my land is all developed." This meant that there were no more woods.[30]

A recent news report suggests the persistence of indifference even among the pious: In Rio de Janeiro, federal forest police interdicted a truck emerging from Desengano State Park. It was loaded with vinhático, the finest of all the "woods-of-law," which the Baptist congregation in São José had ordered for the fashioning of its church pews. Even the most otherworldly clergyman would have to know whence the last of Rio de Janeiro's vinhático could be fetched.[31]

A century and a half ago, the most conscious of the observers of slash-and-burn farming, that "veritable discount against the future to the profit of the present," were sure that "the descendants of contemporary Brazilians [would] feel cruelly the privation of the immense resources that so much vegetation represents, daily destroyed to no advantage." In fact, they feel nothing of the kind—they have been oblivious, and this is surely one of the reasons that the Atlantic Forest is close to disappearing. An opinion poll of 1987 showed that 90 percent of Brazilians living within the former bounds of the Atlantic Forest had never heard of it. The manner of its disappearance has been erased from the memory bank of even its middle class: Only 2.6 percent of a sample of Paraná university students in the interior city of Maringá were able, in 1983, to recall that twenty years before their region had suffered a catastrophic drought, freeze, and fires that destroyed 21,000 square kilometers of their state's forests. Should not this holocaust of human making be recounted from generation to generation? Should not the history textbook approved by the Ministry of Education begin: "Children, you live in a desert; let us tell you how you have been disinherited"?[32]

For five hundred years the Atlantic Forest has yielded easy pickings: parrots, dyewood, slaves, gold, ipecac, orchids, and timber for the profit of their colonial masters and, burned and ravaged, an immensely fertile layer of ashes that made possible an effortless, mindless, and unsustainable agriculture. Population grew and grew, capital "accumulated" while the forests disappeared; further capital was then "accumulated"—in barriers to the gullying of farmland, aqueducts, flood control and flood relief, dredging equipment, planted woodlands, and the industrialization of substitutes for hundreds of products once plucked freely in the wild. No restraint was observed during this half-millennium of gluttony, even though, almost from the beginning, solemn interdictions were intoned intermittently and, in latter days, continually and frantically.

The presence of this primary forest along the Brazilian coastline made possible the colony's uniquely dispersed settlement patterns, its bizarrely precarious land rights, its ever-renewed, ever-decadent land exploitation, and all that this brought in train—social conflict, the prepotence of a latifundist class, primitive economic relations, and poverty. "Discovery" was breathtakingly asserted to be the equivalent of conquest, "conquest" was imbued with unlimited rights over the conquered, and the forest was reduced to booty. Avarice is so pallid a word to describe this expropriation, and avarice itself is only a minor character flaw compared to the ignorance, indifference, and alienation that accompanied it. The exhaustion of the Atlantic Forest does not appear to be working a transformation in strategy. The savanna has recently been shown by modern agricultural science to be nearly as adaptable to machine-driven, integrated farming as forest land, and it is disappearing at a much faster rate. The Amazon Forest, despite the fragility and poverty of nearly all its underlying soils, has been latterly treated as though it were as stable as the "purple earth" of the Southeast. The *valor da terra nua*—value of bare ground—has become the bank manager's standard for measuring collateral. "An etymological aggression against nature," as one environmentalist has termed it.[33]

The irresponsible and spendthrift reduction of the Amazon Basin to bare ground has therefore given rise to international alarm and derision. Among those Brazilians who have studied the history of the Atlantic Forest and appreciate the presence of its remnant stands, the Amazon Forest inspires especial alarm and foreboding. The last service that the Atlantic Forest might serve, tragically and forlornly, is to demonstrate all the terrible consequences of destroying its immense western neighbor.

Notes

CHAPTER 1. THE FOREST EVOLVES

1. J.–Ch. Heusser and G. Claraz, "Des principaux produits des provinces brési-liennes de Rio-de-Janeiro et de Minas-Gerais," *Flores des Serres et des Jardins de l'Europe*, 14 (1859), 169.

2. Juan A. Saldarriaga, "Recovery Following Shifting Cultivation," in Carl F. Jordan, ed., *Amazonian Rain Forests: Ecosystem Disturbance and Recovery* (New York, 1987), pp. 24–33; Scott A. Mori, "Neotropical Floristics and Inventory: Who Will Do the Work?" *Brittonia* 44 (1992), No. 3, 372–375.

3. José Pedro de Oliveira Costa, "Toward a History of the Brazilian Forests" (M.A. thesis, University of California, Berkeley, 1979).

4. The next and succeeding paragraphs are based on Fundação Instituto Brasi-leiro de Geografia e História, *Geografia do Brasil* (Rio de Janeiro, 1977), vols. 3, 5; Henrique Pimenta Veloso, "Contribuição à Fitogeografia do Brasil," *Anuário Brasileiro de Economia Florestal*, 16 (1964), 19–41; Henrique Pimenta Veloso et al., *Classificação da Vegetação Brasileira, Adaptada a um Sistema Universal* (Rio de Janeiro, 1991); Kurt Hueck, *Carta da Vegetação da América do Sul* (Rio de Janeiro, 1972); Afrânio Gomes Fernandes and Prisco Bezerra, *Estudo Fitogeográfica do Brasil* (Fortaleza, 1990); José Setzer, *Atlas Climatológico e Ecológico do Estado de São Paulo* (São Paulo, 1966). Also, see the rainfall maps in Minoru Tanaka et al., "The Empirical Orthogonal Function Analysis of the Seasonal and Interannual Rainfall in Brazil," *Latin American Studies* (Tsukuba) (1988), No. 10, 27–46; José A. J. Hoffman, *Atlas climático de América del Sur* (Paris, 1975).

5. The next and succeeding paragraphs are based on Carlos Toledo Rizzini and Adelmar Coimbra Filho, *Ecossistemas Brasileiros* (n.p., 1988), pp. 70–96; D. J. Mabberley, *Tropical Rain Forest Ecology* (Glasgow, 1983); K. A. Longman and J. Jeník, *Tropical Forest and Its Environment* (2d ed.; Harlow, England, 1987); Paul W. Richards, *The Tropical Rain Forest* (Cambridge, MA, 1952); Jordan, *Amazonian Rain Forests*; Ghillean T. Prance and Thomas Lovejoy, eds., *Amazonia* (Oxford, 1985); Ernst Josef Fittkau et al., eds., *Biogeography and Ecology in South America* (2 vols.; The Hague, 1969); Norman Myers, *The Primary Source: Tropical Forests and Our Future* (New York, 1984); John Terborgh, *Diversity and the Tropical Rain Forest* (New York, 1992); Scott A. Mori, "Eastern, Extra-Amazonian Brazil," in

D. C. Campbell and H. D. Drummond, eds., *Floristic Inventory of Tropical Countries* (New York, 1989), pp. 427–454; M. P. Godoy, *Contribuição à História Natural e Geral de Pirassununga* (Pirassununga, Brazil, 1974); Augusto Ruschi, "Fitogeografia do Estado do Espírito Santo, 1," *Boletim do Museu de Biologia Prof. Mello Leitão, Série Botânica* (16 January 1950), No. 1; Henrique Pimenta Veloso et al., *Vegetação do Estado do Rio de Janeiro, Radambrasil* (Rio de Janeiro, 1983); Alceo Magnanini, "Area das Grandes Formações Vegetais no Brasil," *Anuário Brasileiro de Economia Florestal*, 11 (1959), 295–303; George Eiten, "A Vegetação do Estado de São Paulo," *Boletim do Instituto de Botânica*, 7 (January 1970), 98–99; Francis Dov Por, *Sooretama: The Atlantic Rain Forest of Brazil* (The Hague, 1992); Thomas Stadtmüller, *Cloud Forests in the Humid Tropics: A Bibliographical Review* (Tokyo, 1987). Restinga is also called *jundu* or *nhundu*.

6. atlantic forest soils are classified under the orders spodosols (restingas), Oxisols, Ultisols, and Alfisols, the latter two being more leached. See Armand van Wambeke, *Soils of the Tropics: Properties and Appraisal* (New York, 1992). On biogenesis, see N. van Breemen, "Soils: Biotic Constructions in a Gaian Sense?" in A. Teller et al., *Responses of Forest Ecosystems to Environmental Changes* (London, 1992), pp. 189–207.

7. Hamlet Clark, *Letters from Spain, Algeria and Brazil during Past Etymological Rambles* (London, 1867), p. 142. A brilliant description of the rain forest and the emotions it evokes is to be found in H. M. Tomlinson, *The Sea and the Jungle* (New York, 1964 [1912]), pp. 265–270. The phrase "plastic solidity" is Konrad Guenther's, in *A Naturalist in Brazil* (London, 1931), pp. 69, 75.

8. Armando Magalhães Correa describes the forest dweller's flight from storms in *O Sertão Carioca* (Rio de Janeiro, 1936), p. 41.

9. Charles Darwin, *Charles Darwin's Beagle Diary* (Cambridge, England, 1988 [1832]), pp. 59, 64; Karl Friedrich Philipp von Martius, *Die Physiognomie des Pflanzenreiches in Brasilien* (Munich, 1824), pp. 8, 11. See also Hermann von Burmeister, *Viagem ao Brasil através das Províncias do Rio de Janeiro e Minas Gerais* (São Paulo, 1952 [1853]), pp. 170–172; Alfred Russel Wallace, *A Narrative of Travels on the Amazon and Rio Negro* (London, 1889 [1853]), pp. 305–308; Francisco Freire Allemão, "Apontamentos que Poderão Servir para a Historia das Arvores Florestais do Brasil, Particularmente Das do Rio de Janeiro," *Trabalhos da Sociedade Vellosiana*, 1 (1851), 55. The last citation is from Francisco Foot Hardman, *O Trem Fantasma: A Modernidade na Selva* (São Paulo, 1988), p. 100.

10. The families mentioned are, in order, Leguminosae, Myrtaceae, Meliaceae, and Sapotaceae.

11. "New in the Botanical Book of Records: Highest Tree Diversity in the World," *Field Notes for the New York Botanical Garden*, 2 (Spring 1993), 1–2; James Brooke, "Brazilian Rain Forest Yields Most Diversity for Species of Trees," *New York Times*, 30 March 1993. The species count was at 10 centimeters, at chest height. At 5 centimeters the count was 450 species.

12. Mori, "Eastern, Extra-Amazonian Brazil," p. 438; John C. Kricher, *A Neotropical Companion* (Princeton, NJ, 1989); Louise H. Emmons, *Neotropical Rainforest Mammals: A Field Guide* (Chicago, 1990); Robert S. Ridgely and Guy Tudor, *The Birds of South America* (Austin, TX, 1989); José Cândido de Melo Carvalho, coord., *Atlas da Fauna Brasileira* (São Paulo, 1978); Fittkau et al., *Biogeography and Ecology in South America*.

13. The volume of tropical forest biomass has become controversial because of concerns over the potential harmful effects of the release of its carbon as carbon dioxide into the atmosphere. See Sandra Brown and Ariel E. Lugo, "Aboveground Biomass Estimates for Tropical Moist Forests of the Brazilian Amazon," and Philip M. Fearnside, "Forest Biomass in Brazilian Amazônia: Comments on the Estimate by Brown and Lugo," both in *Interciencia*, 17 (January-February 1992), 8–27. This estimate of 600 tons includes belowground biomass and is an extrapolation of Fearnside's highest estimate (for Amapá), of 541 tons, taking into account Brown and Lugo's thesis that all tropical forests have been to some degree degraded by human action.

14. The next and succeeding paragraphs are based on Fernando F. M. de Almeida and Yociteru Hasui, coords., *O Pre-Cambriano no Brasil* (São Paulo, 1984), pp. 282–384; Karl J. Niklas, ed., *Paleobotany, Paleoecology, and Evolution* (2 vols.; New York, 1981); Else Marie Friis et al., eds., *The Origins of Angiosperms and Their Biological Consequences* (Cambridge, England, 1987); Thomas Barry and Robert A. Spicer, *The Evolution and Palaeobiology of Land Plants* (London, 1987); Wilson N. Stewart, *Paleobotany and the Evolution of Plants* (Cambridge, England, 1983); Prance and Lovejoy, *Amazonia*; John R. Flenley, *The Equatorial Rainforest: A Geological History* (London, 1979); Brian John, ed., *The Winters of the World* (New York, 1979).

15. Anna K. Behrensmeyer et al., eds., *Terrestrial Ecosystems through Time* (Chicago, 1992); George Simpson, *Splendid Isolation: The Curious History of South American Mammals* (New Haven, CT, 1980).

16. The next and succeeding paragraphs are based on Andrew Goudie, *Environmental Change* (2d ed.; Oxford, 1983); Henry J. and Hilary H. Birks, *Quaternary Paleoecology* (Baltimore, MD, 1980); Paul S. Martin and Richard G. Klein, *Quaternary Extinctions* (Tucson, AZ, 1967); Flenley, *The Equatorial Rainforest*. Also, see André Cailleux and J. Tricart, "Zonas Fitogeográficas e Morfoclimáticas Quaternárias no Brasil," *Boletim Geográfico*, 20 (March-April 1962), 206–209; D. Walker and Y. Chen, "Palynological Light on Tropical Rainforest Dynamics," *Quaternary Science Reviews*, 6 (1987), No. 2, 77–92; Alan Graham, ed., *Vegetation and Vegetational History of Northern Latin America* (Amsterdam, 1973).

17. A discussion of refugium theory, first propounded by Jürgen Haffer in 1969, and of other explanations of diversity is to be found in Terborgh, *Diversity*, pp. 143–145.

CHAPTER 2. HUMANS INVADE: THE FIRST WAVE

1. Walter Alves Neves posits these questions in "O Meio Ambiente e a Definição de Padrões de Establecimento e Subsistência de Grupos Caçadores-Coletores: O Caso da Bacia do Alto Guareí, São Paulo," *Pré-História*, 6 (1984), 175–180. On the arrival of the first humans in South America, see Donald Lathrop, "The 'Hunting' Economies of the Tropical Forest Zone of South America: An Attempt at Historical Perspective," in Daniel Gross, ed., *Peoples and Cultures of Native South America* (Garden City, NY, 1973), pp. 83–97.

2. André Prous, *Arqueologia Brasileira* (Brasília, 1991), pp. 119, 145, 334; Pedro Ignácio Schmitz, "Prehistoric Hunters and Gatherers of Brazil," *Journal of World*

Prehistory, 1 (March 1987), 53–126; Wesley R. Hunt and Oldemar Blasi, "O Projeto Arqueológico Lagoa Santa, Minas Gerais, Brasil," *Arquivos do Museu Paranaense, Nova Série, Arqueologia*, 1 (April 1969), No. 4, 1–15; Annette Laming-Emperaire et al., *Grottes et abris de la région de Lagoa Santa, Minas Gerais, Brasil* (Cahiers d'Archeologie d'Amérique du Sud, No. 1; Paris, 1975), pp. 160–161; Fausto Luiz de Souza Cunha and Martha Locks Guimarães, "Posição Geológica do Homem de Lagoa Santa no Grande Abrigo da Lapa Vermelha, Estado de Minas Gerais," in *Colectânea de Estudos em Homenagem a Annette Laming-Emperaire* (São Paulo, 1978), pp. 275–305.

3. Arno Alvarez Kern, "Paleo-Paisagens e Povoamento Pre-Histórico do Rio Grande do Sul," *Estudos Ibero-Americanos* [Porto Alegre], 8 (December 1982), 153–208; Altair Sales Barbosa, "O Período Arqueológico 'Arcaico' em Goiás," *Anuário de Divulgação Científica, Instituto Goiano de Pré-História e Antropologia*, 10 (1981–1984), 85–97. See also the essays in Paul S. Martin and Richard G. Klein, eds., *Quaternary Extinctions: A Prehistoric Revolution* (Tucson, AZ, 1984), which weigh the available evidence from several continents.

4. M. P. de Godoy, "Antique Forest, and Primitive and Civilized Men at Pirassununga County, S. Paulo State, Brazil," *Anais da Academia Brasileira de Ciências*, 35 (1963), 86–87.

5. João Ferreira de Oliveira Bueno, "Simples Narração da Viagem Que Fez ao Rio Paraná," *Revista do Instituto Histórico e Geográfico Brasileiro* [hereafter *RIHGB*], 1 (1839), No. 3, 191; Fausto Ribeiro de Barros, "A Transformação Florística dos Campos de Avanhandava pela Ação das Queimadas," in Congresso Brasileiro de Geografia, 10 Rio de Janeiro, 1944, *Anais* (Rio de Janeiro, 1952), 2:621–626; A. Brandão Joly, "Estudo Fitogeográfico dos Campos de Butantã (São Paulo)," *Boletim da FFCL-USP*, Botânica No. 8 (1950), No. 109, 59–61; Prous, *Arqueologia*, p. 147. On the vulnerability of primary forest, see Paul Richards, *The Tropical Rain Forest* (New York, 1979), pp. 385–386; Christopher Uhl et al., "Os Caminhos do Fogo na Amazônia," *Ciência Hoje*, 11 (August 1990), 24–32; José Luiz de Moraes, "Inserção Topomorfológico das Aldeias do Médio Paranapanema Paulista," *Revista de Pré-História* [hereafter *RPH*], 6 (1984), 181–184; Carl O. Sauer, "Man's Dominance by Use of Fire," *Geoscience and Man*, 10 (20 April 1975), 1–13. For evidence of human-set fires in more southerly latitudes, see Calvin J. Heusser, "Fire History of Fuego Patagonia," *Quaternary of South America and Antarctic Peninsula*, 5 (1987), 93–109.

6. Oscar Schmieder, "The Pampa, a Naturally or Culturally Induced Phenomenon?" *University of California Publications in Geography*, 2 (1927), No. 8, 255–270. Igor Chmyz, "Estado Atual das Pesquisas Arqueológicas na Margem Esquerda do Rio Paraná (Projeto Arqueológico Itaipu)," *Estudos Brasileiros*, 8 (1982), No. 13, 4–40.

7. On sambaquis, see Prous, *Arqueologia*, pp. 204–254; Dorath Pinto Uchôa, "Coletores-Pescadores do Litoral Meridional Brasileiro," *RPH*, 6 (1984), 104–106; Lina Maria Kneip, "Ocupação Pré-Histórica das Restingas do Litoral de Cabo Frio e Niterói, Rio de Janeiro," *Revista do Museu Paulista* [hereafter *RMP*], 29 (1983–84), 143–150; Maria da Conceição Beltrão, *Documentos sobre a Pré-História dos Estados do Rio de Janeiro e Guanabara* (Coleção Museu Paulista, Série de Arqueologia, vol. 2; São Paulo, 1976); Rhodes W. Fairbridge, "Shellfish-eating Pre-ceramic Indians in Coastal Brazil," *Science*, 191 (30 January 1976), 353–359; Dorath Pinto

Uchôa and Caio del Rio Garcia, "Cadastramento dos Sítios Arqueológicos da Baixada Cananéia-Iguape," *Revista de Arqueologia* [Museu Goeldi], 1 (July-December 1983), 19–29; Ondemar Dias Junior, "Dados para o Povoamento Não Tupiguarani do Estado do Rio de Janeiro," *Boletim do Instituto Arqueológico Brasileiro* [hereafter *BIAB*] (June 1979), No. 8, 28–33; Ondemar Dias Junior, "Pesquisas Arqueológicas no Sudeste Brasileiro," *BIAB*, Série Especial (1975), No. 1, 7–8; Annette Laming and J. Emperaire, "Bilan de trois campagnes de fouilles archéologiques au Brésil méridional," *Journal de la Société des Américanistes*, 47 (1958), 199–212; Uchôa and Garcia, "Ilha do Casqueirinho, Estado de São Paulo, Brasil; Dados Arqueológicos Preliminares," *Arqueologia: Revista do Centro de Estudos e Pesquisas Arqueológicos*, 5 (1986), 43–54; Tânia Andrade Lima, "Pesquisas Zooarqueológicas em Sambaquis da Baía da Ribeira, Angra dos Reis, Rio de Janeiro," *Boletim da FBCN*, 22 (1987), 126–132; Walter Alves Neves, "Antropologia Física e Padrões de Subsistência no Litoral Norte de Santa Catarina, Brasil (Projeto)," *RPH*, 6 (1984), 467–477.

8. Karl Friedrich Philipp von Martius, *Die Physiognomie der Pflanzenreiches in Brasilien* (Munich, 1824), p. 22; Pierre Denis, *Amérique du Sud* (Paris, 1927), p. 183. Anthony Anderson and Darrell Posey have studied the *apetê*, or mixed planted woodlots, of the Kayapó of southern Pará State. These are fertilized and even provided with introduced ants to lessen pest infestation: "Reflorestamento Indígena," *Ciência Hoje*, 6 (May 1987), 44–50. See also William Balée, "Indigenous Adaptation to Amazonian Palm Forests," *Principes*, 32 (1988), No. 2, 47–54.

9. Ondemar Dias Junior et al., "Pesquisas Arqueológicas em Minas Gerais (Brasil): O Propevale (Programa de Pesquisas no Vale do São Francisco)," in *Congrès International des Americanistes*, 42, Paris, 1976, *Actes*, IX-A (Paris, 1976), pp. 24–25; Celso Perota, "Resultados Preliminares sobre a Arqueologia da Região Central do Estado do Espírito Santo," in *Programa Nacional de Pesquisas Arqueológicas* (Museu Paraense Emílio Goeldi, Publicações Avulsas [hereafter MPEG–PA], No. 26; Belém, 1971), pp. 124–127; Mário Simões, *Indice das Fases Arqueológicas Brasileiras* (MPEG-PA, No. 18; Belém, 1972), pp. 104–108. Igor Chmyz has reported ceramic phases in sites west of Curitiba, Paraná, at 1,500 years before the present, in *Relatório das Pesquisas Arqueológicas Realizadas na Area da Usina Hidrelétrica de Salto Santiago (1979–80)* (Florianópolis, 1981), pp. 1–15. Dias and a collaborator have inferred much earlier, but uncorroborated, dates for a site in highland Rio de Janeiro: Eliane Teixeira de Carvalho, *Estudo Arqueológico do Sítio Corondó: Missão de 1978* (Rio de Janeiro, 1984), pp. 1–20.

10. Dias Junior, "Dados," p. 28. On agricultural origins, see Ester Boserup, *The Conditions of Agricultural Growth* (Chicago, 1966); Kent V. Flannery, *Guila Naquitz* (New York, 1986), pp. 3–17. On manioc, see David G. Rogers and S. G. Appan, *Manihot manihotoides* (Flora Neotropica, Monograph No. 13; New York, 1973). There are 98 species, all New World; *M. esculenta* is not known in the wild state.

11. Hans Ruthenberg et al., *Farming Systems in the Tropics* (3d ed.; Oxford, 1980), pp. 31–47; Raymond F. Watters, *Shifting Cultivation in Latin America* (Rome, 1971); William M. Denevan, "The Causes and Consequences of Shifting Cultivation in Relation to Tropical Forest Survival," in idem, ed., *The Role of Geographical Research in Latin America* (Muncie, IN, 1978); Edison Paulo Chu and Rita C. L. Figueiredo-Ribeiro, "Importância Alimentar do Gênero *Dioscorea* do

Brasil," in Congresso Brasileiro de Botânica, 40, Cuiabá, 1989, *Resumos* (Cuiabá, 1989), 2:409. On modern swidden farmers, see William M. Denevan and Christine Padoch, eds., *Swidden-Fallow Agroforestry in the Peruvian Amazon* (Bronx, NY, 1987).

12. The botanical names of the untranslatable species are:

jabuticaba *Myrciaria cauliflora* cambucá *Marlierea edulis*
grumixama *Eugenia brasiliensis* sapucaia *Lecithys zabucajo*
araçá *Psidium littorale* pacova *Swartzia langsdorfii*
cambuçi *Paivaea langsdorfii*

13. John Hemming, *Red Gold: The Conquest of the Brazilian Indians, 1500–1760* (Cambridge, MA, 1978), pp. 487–501. Densities of 0.2 per square kilometer were found in modern populations by Marcos Magalhães Rubinger, "O Desaparecimento das Tribos Indígenas em Minas Gerais e a Sobrevivência dos Indios Maxacali," *RMP*, n.s., 14 (1963), 252 (nineteenth century); and William T. Vickers, "Game Depletion Hypotheses of Amazonian Adaptation," *Science*, 239 (25 March 1988), 1521–1522.

14. Prous, *Arqueologia*, p. 337; Walter Alves Neves, "Estilo de Vida e Osteobiografia: A Reconstituição do Comportamento pelos Ossos Humanos," *RPH*, 6 (1984), 287–291; idem, "Incidência de Cáries e Padrões de Subsistência no Litoral Norte de Santa Catarina, Brasil," *RPH*, 6 (1984), 371–380. See also Marília Carvalho de Mello e Alvim et al., "Traços Não-Métricos Cranianos e Distâncias Biológicas em Grupos Indígenas do Brasil—Botocudos e Construtores de Sambaquis," *RPH*, 6 (1984), 107–117.

15. On Tupi-Guarani origins, see Branislava Susnik, *Dispersión Tupí-Guaraní prehistórica: Ensayo analítico* (Asunción, 1975); Donald W. Lathrap, *The Upper Amazon* (New York, 1970). On earliest Tupi in the Atlantic Forest area, see Ondemar Dias Junior, "Evolução da Cultura em Minas Gerais e no Rio de Janeiro," *Anuario de Divulgação Científica, Universidade Católica de Goiás* (1976–1977), 124–125; Carlos Fausto, "Fragmentos de História e Cultura Tupinambá: Da Etnologia Como Instrumento Crítico de Conhecimento Etno-Histórico," in Manuela Carneiro da Cunha, ed., *História dos Indios no Brasil* (São Paulo, 1992), pp. 381–396.

16. Maria da Conceição da M. C. Beltrão, *Os Tupinambá no Rio de Janeiro (1.200 anos de ocupação)* (Brasília, 1972), pp. 3–6; Fernando Altenfelder Silva, "Arqueologia Pré-Histórica da Região de Rio Claro," in Paulo Duarte, ed., *Pré-História Brasileira* (São Paulo, 1968), pp. 157–166; Solange Bezerra Caldarelli, "Aldeias Tupi-Guanarís no Vale do Rio Mogi-Guaçu, Estado de São Paulo," *RPH*, 5 (1983), 37–124. Among sixteenth-century observers, see Gabriel Soares da Souza, *Tratado Descritivo do Brasil em 1587* (4th ed.; São Paulo, 1971 [1851]); [Francisco Soares], *Coisas Notáveis do Brasil* (Rio de Janeiro, 1966); Fernão Cardim, *Tratados da Terra e Gente do Brasil* (3d ed.; São Paulo, 1978 [1583–1580]); and the extraordinary Jean de Léry, *Histoire d'un voyage fait en la terre du Brésil* (La Rochelle, France, 1578). Classic analyses of Tupi culture are those of Florestan Fernandes, *Organização Social dos Tupinambá* (2d ed., rev. and corr.; São Paulo, 1963); and Alfred Métraux, *La civilisation matérielle des tribus Tupi-Guarani* (Paris, 1928).

17. Manuel da Nóbrega, "Informação das Terras do Brasil," *RIHGB*, 6 (1844),

No. 21, 91–94. On the introduction of maize in South America, see Anna Curtenius Roosevelt, *Parmana: Prehistoric Maize and Manioc Subsistence along the Amazon and Orinoco* (New York, 1980). On whales, see [Soares], *Coisas Notáveis*, pp. 183, 185. Paulo B. Cavalcante found 192 fruits collected in the Amazon, and he supposed the true number to be more than 300: "Frutas Silvestres da Amazônia," in Congresso Brasileiro de Botânica, 39, Belém, 1988, *Resumos* (Belém, 1988), 2:148.

18. Robert L. Carneiro, "Slash-and-Burn Agriculture: A Closer Look at Its Implications for Settlement Patterns," in A. Wallace, ed., *Men and Cultures: Selected Papers of the Fifth International Congress of Anthropological and Ethnological Sciences* (Philadelphia, 1960), pp. 229–234. On the trails, or *peabirus*, see João Baptista de Freitas, "A Pré-História Passou por Aqui," *Jornal do Brasil* (25 October 1988), 6, a report on research by Carlos Otávio de Andrade.

19. Pamela Lancaster and D. G. Coursey, *Traditional Post-Harvest Technology of Perishable Tropical Staples* (FAO Agricultural Services Bulletin, No. 59; Rome, 1984), pp. 25–34; Soares de Souza, *Tratado*, p. 177.

20. Compare Marvin Harris, *Cannibals and Kings* (New York, 1977), pp. 102–110, citing Michael Harner, "The Ecological Basis for Aztec Sacrifice," *American Ethnologist*, 4 (February 1977), 117–135; with W. Arens, *The Man-Eating Myth: Anthropology and Anthropophagy* (New York, 1979), and Anthony Pagden, *The Fall of Natural Man* (Cambridge, England, 1982). No archaeological field study seems yet to have been undertaken to confirm Tupi cannibalism, although archaeologists seem to accept it. The Jesuit letters are reviewed in great detail by Donald W. Forsyth, "The Beginnings of Brazilian Anthropology: Jesuits and Tupinamba Cannibalism," *Journal of Anthropological Research*, 39 (Summer 1983), 147–178, who notes that Arens seems not to have read any of the abundant and easily available Jesuit reports, published in Italian, Latin, Spanish, and Portuguese. See, for example, Nóbrega, "Informação," p. 193. Among the secular reports of cannibalism, the most striking is that of Hans Staden, *The Captivity of Hans Staden of Hesse* (New York, 1963 [1557]). On interpretation of the Jesuit reports, see Bartolomeu Meliá, "El 'modo de ser' Guaraní en la primera documentación jesuítica (1594–1639)," *Revista de Antropologia*, 24 (1981), 1–24. On jaguar eating, see Sérgio Buarque de Holanda, *Caminhos e Fronteiras* (Rio de Janeiro, 1957), pp. 105–111.

21. William Balée, "The Ecology of Ancient Tupi Warfare," in R. Brian Ferguson, ed., *Warfare, Culture and Environment* (Orlando, FL, 1984), pp. 241–265; R. Brian Ferguson, "Ecological Consequences of Amazonian Warfare," *Ethnology*, 28 (July 1989), 249–264. See also Florestan Fernandes, *A Função Social da Guerra na Sociedade Tupinambá* (São Paulo, 1951).

22. Nunes, no receiver noted, São Vicente, 24 August 1551, and Bras, no receiver noted, Espírito Santo, both in *Avisi particulari delle Indie di Portugallo* (Rome, 1552), pp. 148, 133; Cardim, *Tratados*, p. 118. On Tupi physiognomy, see also Léry, *Histoire*, p. 101.

23. On the lack of population estimates, note Zulmara C. S. Posse, "A População Pré-Histórica," in *Colectânea de Estudos*, pp. 369–381; Warren Dean, "Indigenous Populations of the São Paulo–Rio de Janeiro Coast: Trade, Aldeamento, Slavery and Extinction," *Revista de História*, 58 (October-December 1984), 18. Compare the discussions of village size and density in Balée, "Ecology," and Lina Maria Kneip,

"Projeto Sítio Arqueológico de Três Vendas, Araruama, Estado do Rio de Janeiro," in *Colectânea de Estudos*, p. 161.

24. [Soares], *Coisas Notáveis*, p. 101.

25. José Carneiro da Silva, *Memoria Topographica e Historica sobre os Campos dos Goytacazes* (2d ed.; Rio de Janeiro, 1907 [1819]), p. 17.

26. João de Azpilcueta Navarro, 28 March 1550, Salvador, *Diversi nuovi avisi particolari dall'India di Portogallo* (Venice, 1562), translated in Afrânio Peixoto, ed., *Cartas Avulsas de Jesuitas, 1550–1568* (Rio de Janeiro, 1931), pp. 49–51.

27. José de Anchieta, *Cartas, Informações, Fragmentos Históricos e Sermões, 1554–1594* (Rio de Janeiro, 1933), pp. 74, 75; Staden, *Captivity*, pp. 82–83 on fish meal. Balée puts a different interpretation on the fish catch in "Ecology," pp. 24–25.

28. Ghillean T. Prance, David G. Campbell, and Bruce W. Nelson, "The Ethnobotany of the Paumari Indians," *Economic Botany*, 31 (April-June 1977), 129. The warfare practiced against both groups by neo-Europeans might be seen as a cause of this isolation in recent times, though it should be noted that several of the varieties of manioc known to the Paumari have evidently come to them through contact with neo-Europeans.

29. Vespucci stated (1501) that "the country is a very thick jungle full of ferocious wild beasts"; see Frederick Pohl's translation in *Amerigo Vespucci, Pilot Major* (New York, 1944), p. 133; Brazil, Arquivo Nacional, *Tombos das Cartas das Sesmarias do Rio de Janeiro, 1594–1595, 1602–1605* (Rio de Janeiro, 1967).

30. On these issues, see J. Baird Callicut, "American Indian Land Wisdom? Sorting out the Issues," *Journal of Forest History*, 33 (January 1989), 35–42.

31. Luis da Câmara Cascudo, *Geografia dos Mitos Brasileiros* (Belo Horizonte, 1983 [1948]), pp. 51–91; Antônio Geraldo da Cunha, *Dicionário Histórico das Palavras Portuguesas de Origem Tupi* (São Paulo, 1978); Alfred Métraux, *A Religião dos Tupinambás e suas Relações com a das Demais Tribos Tupi-Guarani* (2d ed.; São Paulo, 1979), pp. 45–50, and notes by Estévão Pinto, p. 52. On menstruation, see Holanda, *Caminhos*, p. 127. In another version of the creation myth the first woman is killed by her own twin hero-sons, who lure her into the jaguars' lair while they are still in the womb; the jaguars then raise them: Curt Nimuendaju Unkel, *As Lendas da Criação e Destruição do Mundo Como Fundamentos da Religião dos Apapocuva-Guarani* (São Paulo, 1987), pp. 143–151.

32. José de Anchieta, "Carta sobre as Coisas Naturais de São Vicente," 31 May 1560, *Cartas: Correspondência Ativa e Passiva* (São Paulo, 1984), 6:123–145; Manuel da Nóbrega, *Cartas do Brasil e Mais Escritos* (Coimbra, 1955), pp. 83, 377.

33. Couto de Magalhães, *O Selvagem* (Rio de Janeiro, 1876), pp. 138–139; Câmara Cascudo, *Geografia*, pp. 84–91; idem, *Dicionário do Folclore Brasileiro* (3d ed.; Brasília, 1972), 1:91, 144, 152. The Fundação Brasileira para Conservação da Natureza employs Curupira as its logo.

34. Carlos Estévão de Oliveira, "Uma Lenda Tupina [Arawak]," *RMP*, 17 (1931), Part 1, 523, cited by Cascudo, p. 73n; Soares de Souza, *Tratado*, pp. 184–185.

35. On native American self-denial, see William Cronon, *Changes in the Land* (New York, 1983), pp. 34–53.

36. Andrew Vayda, comp., *Environment and Cultural Behavior* (Austin, TX, 1977). For a discussion and review of vegetation changes caused by North American Indians, see Hazel R. Delcourt, "The Impact of Prehistoric Agriculture and

Land Occupation on Natural Vegetation," *Trends in Ecology,* 2 (February 1987), 39–44.

CHAPTER 3. HUMANS INVADE: THE SECOND WAVE

1. Critical editions of the Vaz de Caminha letter include Silvio Castro, *A Carta de Pero Vaz de Caminha: O Descobrimento do Brasil* (2d ed.; Porto Alegre, 1985); José Augusto Vaz Valente, *A Carta de Pero Vaz de Caminha* (Coleção Museu Paulista, Série de História, 3; São Paulo, 1975); Leonardo Arroyo, *A Carta de Pero Vaz de Caminha: Ensaios de Informação à Procura de Constantes Válidas de Método* (São Paulo, 1971). For a historiographic study of the colonial chronicles, see José Honório Rodrigues, *História da História do Brasil* (São Paulo, 1979). Meirelles's work is at the Museu Nacional de Belas Artes, Rio de Janeiro.

2. On the biological implications of the discoveries, see Alfred Crosby, *The Columbian Exchange: Biological and Cultural Consequences of 1492* (Westport, CT, 1972).

3. On intentionality and possible earlier discovery, see Manuel Nunes Dias, *O Descobrimento do Brasil (Subsídios para o Estudo da Integração do Atlântico Sul)* (São Paulo, 1967), pp. 150–177.

4. Sérgio Buarque de Holanda, *Visão do Paraíso (Os Motivos Edénicos no Descobrimento e Colonização do Brasil)* (2d ed., rev. and aug.; São Paulo, 1969), pp. 1–33.

5. Castro, *Carta,* pp. 44.

6. Simão de Vasconcellos, *Chronica da Companhia de Jesu do Estado do Brasil* (Lisbon, 1663), 1:126. This calculation of logging output by the Portuguese is from Bernardo José de Souza, *O Pau-brasil na História Nacional* (2d ed.; São Paulo, 1978 [1938]), pp. 107–112. Unfortunately, I presented much lower and incorrect figures in "Indigenous Populations of the São Paulo–Rio de Janeiro Coast: Trade, Aldeamento, Slavery and Extinction," *Revista de História,* 58 (October–December 1984), 25. See also Carlos Henrique R. Liberalli, "Nossa Flora, Nossa História," *Estudos Históricos* (1971), No. 10, 43–63; Calvino Mainieri, *Estudo Macro e Microscópico de Madeiras Conhecidas por Pau-brasil* (IPT, Publicação No. 612; São Paulo, 1960), pp. 7–11; Francisco Freire Alemão, "Apontamentos sobre a Conservação e Corte das Madeiras de Construção Civil," and "Carta a von Martius, Rio de Janeiro 30 Novembro 1849," both in *Anais da Biblioteca Nacional,* 81 (1961), 135, 185; Pierre Dansereau, "The Distribution and Structure of Brazilian Forests," *Bulletin du Service de Biogéographie* (March 1948), No. 3, 13. The lack of historical investigation of the brazilwood trade filled Artur Neiva with melancholy in 1938, and still surprises this author; see his introduction to Souza, *O Pau-brasil,* p. 32. It remains a historical gap.

7. Frederick Pohl, *Amerigo Vespucci, Pilot Major* (New York, 1944). Souza, *O Pau-brasil,* pp. 107–117. On the period of barter, see Alexander Marchant, *From Barter to Slavery* (Baltimore, MD, 1942). On French interlopers, see Michel Mollat, "Premières relations entre la France et le Brésil: des Verrazani à Villegagnon," *Cahiers de l'Institut des Hautes Etudes de l'Amérique Latine,* 6 (1964), 62–67.

8. On smuggling and the regulation of 12 December 1605, see Joaquim Veríssimo Serrão, *Do Brasil Filipino ao Brasil de 1640* (São Paulo, 1968), pp. 110–114;

Souza, *O Pau-brasil*, pp. 70, 97; André Thevet, *Cosmographie Universelle* (Paris, 1575), 2:949v; Antônio Leôncio Pereira Ferraz, *Terra da Ibirapitanga* (Rio de Janeiro, 1939), pp. 48–49, 62, 67–73; Orlando Valverde, *Geografia Agrária do Brasil* (Rio de Janeiro, 1964), 1:346–348. On numbers of trees: Accepting the cargo of the ship *Bretoa* as an average one, taking the specific gravity of brazilwood at 0.9, and supposing that the logs were cut into sections about 75 centimeters long, then the resulting core wood would be about 22 centimeters in diameter, assuming that about 10 centimeters of bark and cortex had been stripped off. The average tree selected for logging would then have been not very large, perhaps 12 meters high to its lowest branches, therefore yielding about 16 segments each. The *Bretoa's* cargo of 125 tons would then have been derived from a few more than 300 trees. See Paul Gaffarel, *Histoire du Brésil français* (Paris, 1878), cited by Souza, *O Pau-brasil*, pp. 129–131.

9. Pero Lopes de Souza, *Diario de Navegação . . . pela Costa de Brasil até o Rio Uruguay . . . e Livro da Viagem da Nao Bretoa ao Cabo Frio* (Rio de Janeiro, 1867), p. 98–109; Vivaldo Coaracy, *O Rio de Janeiro no Século Dezessete* (Rio de Janeiro, 1965), p. 30; Joaquim Veríssimo Serrão, *O Rio de Janeiro no Século XVI* (Lisbon, 1965), 1:25. See the encyclopedic works of John Hemming on Brazilian slavery: *Red Gold: The Conquest of the Brazilian Indians, 1500–1760* (Cambridge, MA, 1978), and *Amazon Frontier: The Defeat of the Brazilian Indians* (Cambridge, MA, 1987).

10. Hermann von Ihering experimented with the use of stone axes; see "Os Machados de Pedra do Brasil e o seu Emprego na Derrubada das Matas," *Revista do Instituto Histórico e Geográfico de São Paulo*, 12 (1907), 426. See also Jules Henry, *Jungle People: A Kaingang Tribe of the Highlands of Brazil* (New York, 1964 [1941]), pp. 161–162; Jesuíno Felicíssimo Junior, "História da Siderurgia de São Paulo, seus Personagens, seus Feitos," *Boletim do Instituto Geológico e Geográfico* (1969), No. 49, 3; Alfred Métraux, "The Revolution of the Ax," *Diogenes* (Spring 1959), No. 25, 28–40.

11. Jean de Léry, *Histoire d'un voyage fait en la terre du Brésil* (Paris, 1972 [1557]): translation here is from the English edition, *History of a Voyage to the Land of Brazil, Otherwise Called America* (Berkeley, CA, 1990), p. 102.

12. Jaime Cortesão, *A Fundação do São Paulo* (Rio de Janeiro, 1955), pp. 130–134.

13. João Capistrano de Abreu, *O Descobrimento do Brasil* (2d ed.; Rio de Janeiro, 1976), pp. 44, 52; Alfred Métraux, *A Religião dos Tupinambás e suas Relações com a das Demais Tribos Tupi-Guaranis* (2d ed.; São Paulo, 1979 [1925]), p. 150, citing André Thevet.

14. Holanda, *Visão*, p. 206; Fernão Cardim, *Tratados da Terra e Gente do Brasil* (3d ed.; São Paulo, 1978 [1583]), p. 34; Pero de Magalhães Gandavo, *História da Província de Santa Cruz* (Coimbra, 1955 [1576]), p. 32; [Francisco Soares], *Coisas Notáveis do Brasil* (Rio de Janeiro, 1966), 1:128–129; Antonio Geraldo da Cunha, *Dicionário Histórico das Palavras Portugueses de Origem Tupi* (São Paulo, 1978), p. 63.

15. Vasconcellos, *Chronica*, 1:133.

16. The brazilwood trade did not eliminate the tree in Rio de Janeiro—the botanist Freire Alemão found them common in the mid-nineteenth century as far as

Cape Frio, "Carta," p. 135. See also Mário Neme, *Notas de Revisão da História de São Paulo: Século XVI* (São Paulo, 1959), pp. 23–34, 65, 160.

17. Cortesão, *Fundação*, p. 43; Sérgio Buarque de Holanda, *Expansão Paulista em Fins do Século XVI e Princípio do Século XVII* (São Paulo, 1948), p. 14. The quotation is from Lopes de Souza, *Diario de Navegação*, p. 31–34.

18. Lopes de Souza, *Diario de Navegação*, pp. 35–36; João de Souza Campos and Luiz Emgydio de Mello Filho, "Observações Biológicas sobre a Ilha da Queimada Grande," *A Folha Médica*, 52 (May 1966), 11–26. For a map, see *Diario* (Rio de Janeiro) (1927), 2:map 8.

19. Alfred Crosby, *Ecological Imperialism* (New York, 1986).

20. Holanda, *Visão*, pp. 190–192, 217, 227; Gandavo, *História*, p. 5; Manuel da Nóbrega, "Informações das Terras do Brasil" ([August?] 1549), in Manuel da Nóbrega, *Cartas do Brasil e Mais Escritos* (Coimbra, 1955), pp. 57–67; J. F. de Almeida Prado, *Primeiros Povoadores do Brasil* (5th ed., rev. and aug.; São Paulo, 1976), p. 78. The most detailed lists of native flora and fauna are those of José de Anchieta (1 September 1554), in Serafim Leite, ed., *Monumenta Brasiliae* (Rome, 1956), 2:112; Gabriel Soares de Souza, who lists medicinals in *Tratado Descritivo do Brasil em 1587* (4th ed.; São Paulo, 1971 [1851]), p. 206; and Francisco Soares, who noted, in *Coisas Notáveis*, pp. 183–185, 193–203, "herbs that Dioscoredes had no notice of" and offered a list of the fish and shellfish resources of Guanabara Bay—he appears to have been a fisherman. Trout, salmon, and other exotic fish have lately been introduced to South America. Dutch studies of Brazilian natural history date from the second century of the invasion; see Gugliemus Piso, *De indiae utriusque re naturali et medica* (Amsterdam, 1658), and Kaspar van Baerle, *Historia dos Feitos Recentemente Praticados durante Oito Anos no Brasil* (Rio de Janeiro, 1940 [1640]).

21. Cardim, *Tratados*, pp. 67–68, 209, 210; Soares de Souza, *Tratado*, pp. 167–168, 188; Francisco Freire Alemão, "Apontamentos sobre a Obra de Gabriel Soares de Souza," 4 October 1851, Manuscript Collection, Biblioteca Nacional, Rio de Janeiro.

22. Basílio de Magalhães, *O Açúcar nos Primórdios do Brasil Colonial* (Rio de Janeiro, 1953), p. 25; Eddy Stols, "Um dos Primeiros Documentos sobre o Engenho dos Schatz em São Vicente," *Revista de História*, 37 (1968) No. 74, 407–420; Francisco Freire Alemão, *Memoria . . . Quais São as Principais Plantas Que Hoje se Acham Aclimatizadas no Brasil?* (n.p., 1856), an offprint, pp. numbered 539–578.

23. Manuel da Nóbrega, *Cartas do Brasil, 1549–1560* (Rio de Janeiro, 1931), pp. 131, 134.

24. Stuart B. Schwartz, "Indian Labor and New World Plantations," *American Historical Review*, 83 (February 1978), 57, 60; Alcântara Machado, *Vida e Morte do Bandeirante* (São Paulo, 1965), pp. 176–177. For coastal slave trade, see Leite, *Monumenta*, 1:220. On slave policy, see Manuel Tavares da Costa Miranda and Alípio Bandeira, "Memorial Acerca da Antiga e Moderna Legislação Indígena," in L. Humberto de Oliveira, ed., *Coletânea de Leis, Atos e Memorias Referentes ao Indígena Brasileiro* (Rio de Janeiro, 1947), p. 55.

25. Serafim Leite, *História da Companhia de Jesus no Brasil* (Lisbon, 1938–1950), 2:194, 207; Walter Albert Engler, "A Zona Pioneira no Norte do Rio Doce," *Revista Brasileira de Geografia*, 13 (April-June 1951), 231; Afonso d'Escragnolle

Taunay, *Ensaios de Carta Geral das Bandeiras Paulistas* (2d ed.; São Paulo, 1937); Abreu, *Descobrimento*, p. 63; Branislava Susnik, *Dispersión Tupi-Guaraní prehistórico: Ensayo analítico* (Asunción, 1975), pp. 53–54. For pretexts, see São Paulo (City), Arquivo Municipal, *Atas da Câmara Municipal* (São Paulo, 1914), 1:171, 276, 388–404, 417–418; (São Paulo, 1915), 2:12–13, 46–47.

26. Luiz Felipe Baeta Neves, *O Combate dos Soldados de Cristo na Terra dos Papagaios* (Rio de Janeiro, 1978), pp. 51, 63.

27. Afrânio Peixoto, ed., *Cartas Avulsas de Jesuitas, 1550–1568* (Rio de Janeiro, 1931), letter dated 1552, p. 103; Leite, *História*, 1:239, 245, 2:42; Nóbrega, *Cartas*, pp. 166–167, 196–197; Leite, *Monumenta*, 1:447; 3:464; Fernão Guerreiro, *Relação Annual das Cousas que Fezeram os Padres da Companhia de Iesus nas Partes da India Oriental, & em Algũas Outras da Conquista deste Reyno no Anno de 606 & 607* (Lisbon, 1609), pp. 118–119v, 196–196v. See also David Sweet, "Indian Amazonia and the Frontier Mission" (paper presented to the American Historical Association meeting, New York, December 1990).

28. Leite, *Monumenta*, 3:464; idem, *História*, 2:92–94; Venâncio Willeke, *Missões Franciscanas no Brasil (1500–1975)* (Petrópolis, 1974), pp. 126–127. For an analysis of the aldeias, see Pasquale Petrone, "Os Aldeamentos Paulistas e a sua Função na Valorização da Região Paulistana" (2 vols.; Livre-Docência thesis, University of São Paulo, 1964), 1:1–12, 2:39. Stuart B. Schwartz takes pains to absolve the Tupi of the charge of laziness, evidently a tendentious accusation by whites. One imagines, had the indigenes maintained their independence, how difficult it would have been for a Tupi ethnohistorian to explain that Portuguese who evaded the honor of being sacrificed as ceremonial victims ought not to be considered cowards. See Stuart B. Schwartz, "Indian Labor and New World Plantations," *American Historical Review*, 83 (February 1978), 43–79.

29. Nóbrega, *Cartas* (2 September 1557), pp. 278–279; (8 May 1558), pp. 282–283; (5 July 1559), p. 351; Leite, *Monumenta* (10 March 1553), 1:444–445; (1 June 1560), 3:255.

30. Leite, *Monumenta* (August 1567), 4:401–414; Peixoto, *Cartas* (Espírito Santo, 13 June 1559), p. 216; Basílio de Magalhães, *Expansão Geographica do Brasil Colonial* (São Paulo, 1935), p. 109.

31. Crosby, *Columbian Exchange*, pp. 35–63; Dauril Alden and Joseph C. Miller, "Out of Africa: The Slave Trade and the Transmission of Smallpox to Brazil, 1560–1831," *Journal of Interdisciplinary History*, 18 (Autumn 1987), 195–224.

32. Gandavo, *História*, p. 5. Contrast Fr. Pedro da Costa, who was tending the ill (Espírito Santo, 27 July 1565): "This land is sickly, and there are always the sick," Peixoto, *Cartas*, p. 456.

33. Leite, *História*, 1:235–236, 302; 2:42; *Atas da Câmara Municipal*, 1:275; Leite, *Monumenta*, 1:220; 2:107, 108; *Lettres du Iappon, Peru et Brasil, envoyées au R. P. General de la Societé de Iesus* (Paris, 1578), pp. 101; Peixoto, *Cartas* (Espírito Santo, 1559), p. 207, 214–216; Dean, "Indigenous Populations," pp. 21–23. On the effect of epidemics throughout the New World, see William M. Denevan, ed., *The Native Population of the Americas in 1492* (Madison, WI, 1976). On the impact of contemporary epidemics on Brazilian Indian populations, offering some insight into the effect on sixteenth-century villages, see Darcy Ribeiro, "Convívio e Contaminação: Efeitos Dissociativos e Depopulação Provocada por Epidemias em Grupos Indígenas," *Sociologia*, 18 (March 1956), 4–41.

34. Gandavo, *História*, p. 60.

35. Daisy Bizzochi de Lacerda Abreu, "A Terra e a Lei—Estudo de Comportamento Sócio-Econômico em São Paulo nos Séculos XVI e XVII" (Ph.D. dissertation, University of São Paulo, 1981), pp. 1–25; Leite, *História*, 2:85; Brazil, Arquivo Nacional, *Tombos das Cartas das Sesmarias do Rio de Janeiro, 1594–1595; 1602–1605* (Rio de Janeiro, 1967).

36. José Carneiro da Silva, *Memoria Topographica e Historica sobre os Campos dos Goytacazes* (2d ed.; Rio de Janeiro, 1907 [1819]), pp. 28–29; Florestan Fernandes, *Aspectos do Povoamento de São Paulo no Século XVI* (São Paulo, 1948), p. 24; [Soares], *Coisas Notáveis*, p. 11.

37. Petrone, "Aldeamentos," 3:71, 106–107; Leite, *História*, 1:229–243, 304, 316; Benedito Calixto, *A Vila de Itanhaem* (Santos, 1895), pp. 16, 17; [Soares], *Coisas Notáveis*, p. 11.

38. Abreu, *Descobrimento*, p. 79. Other estimates are to be found in [Soares], *Coisas Notáveis*, p. 11. Another contemporary source is Cardim, *Tratados*, pp. 204–215. Fernandes cross-lists all estimates then available: see *Aspectos*, pp. 13–15. See also Serrão, *Rio de Janeiro*, pp. 180–182; Machado, *Vida e Morte*, p. 45. On the disappearance of the indigenes, see Afonso A. de Freitas, *Os Guayanás de Piratininga* (São Paulo, 1910), p. 26; Willem Glimmer, full text published in Abreu, *Descobrimento*, p. 73.

39. São Paulo (City), Arquivo Municipal, *Actas da Camara da Vila de São Paulo* (São Paulo, 1914), 1:311; João Barbosa Rodrigues, "A Diminuição das Aguas no Brasil," in Congresso Científico Latino-Americano, Rio de Janeiro, 1905, *Relatório Geral* (Rio de Janeiro, 1905), vol. 3A:175–180. R. M. Keogh believes Costa Rican forests similarly expanded after the native demographic collapse; see "Changes in the Forest Cover of Costa Rica through History," *Turrialba*, 34 (July-September 1984), 325–331.

CHAPTER 4. ESTRANGEMENT: DEPOPULATION
AND THE REGROWN FOREST

1. Fernão Cardim, *Tratados da Terra e Gente do Brasil* (3d ed.; São Paulo, 1978 [1583]), p. 113; Hans Staden, *Viagem ao Brasil* (Salvador, 1955 [1555]), pp. 139, 139n. See also Manuel da Nóbrega, *Cartas do Brasil e Mais Escritos* (Coimbra, 1955), p. 283; Jaime Cortesão, *A Fundação de São Paulo, Capital Geográfico do Brasil* (Rio de Janeiro, 1955), p. 135; "Relation of Master Thomas Turner who lived the best part of two yeeres in Brasill, &c," in Richard Hakluyt, *Hakluytus Posthumus or Purchas his Pilgims* (Glasgow, 1906), 4:1243. *Pombeiro* may derive from Kimbundu *pombelu*—backlands—according to Waldemar de Almeida Barbosa, *Negros e Quilombos em Minas Gerais* (Belo Horizonte, 1972), p. 135.

2. João Capistrano de Abreu, *O Descobrimento de Brasil* (2d ed.; Rio de Janeiro, 1976), p. 54.

3. Maria Luiza Marcílio, "Crescimento Demográfico e Evolução Agrária Paulista, 1700–1836" (Livre Docência thesis, University of São Paulo, 1974), p. 249; Afonso A. de Freitas, *Os Guayanás de Piratininga* (São Paulo, 1910), p. 24; Nelson Coelho de Senna, *Chorographia de Minas Gerais* (Rio de Janeiro, 1922), p. 222; Afrânio Peixoto, ed., *Cartas Avulsas de Jesuitas, 1550–1568* (Rio de Janeiro, 1931), p. 197 (see also p. 67).

4. Simão de Vasconcellos, *Chronica da Companhia de Jesu do Estado do Brasil* (Lisbon, 1663), p. 61; [Nicolas Barré], *Copie de quelques lettres sur la navigation du Chevalier de Villegagnon es terres de l'Amerique oultre l'Aequinoctial* (Paris, 1557), p. 26.

5. On squaw men, see Serafim Leite, *Monumenta Brasiliae* (Rome, 1956), 1:250–251; Peixoto, *Cartas*, p. 67; Serafim Leite, *Paginas da Historia do Brasil* (São Paulo, 1937), p. 17. Florestan Fernandes, *Aspectos do Povoamento de São Paulo no Século XVI* (São Paulo, 1948), pp. 19, 21, states that the first white woman arrived in São Vicente in 1538, but there were very few before 1600. For more on white women, see Luiza Volpato, *Entradas e Bandeiras* (2d ed.; São Paulo, 1985), pp. 25–26. John Monteiro, "São Paulo in the Seventeenth Century: Economy and Society" (Ph.D. dissertation, University of Chicago, 1985), chap. 6.

6. Maria da Conceição da M. C. Beltrão, *Os Tupinambá no Rio de Janeiro (1.200 Anos da Ocupação)* (Brasília, 1972), p. 5; São Paulo, Arquivo Municipal, *Actas da Câmara Municipal de São Paulo* [hereafter SP–ACM], (São Paulo, 1914), 1:211, 201.

7. Pasquale Petrone, "Os Aldeamentos Paulistas e sua Função na Valorização da Região Paulistana" (2 vols.; Livre-Docência thesis, University of São Paulo, 1964), 3:64–65.

8. On indigenes and property, see Fernão Guerreiro, *Relação Annual das Cousas que Fezeram os Padres da Companhia de Iesus nas Partes da India Oriental & no Brasil* (Lisbon, 1605), p. 116v.

9. Serafim Leite, *Novas Páginas de História do Brasil* (Lisbon, 1962), pp. 321, 324, 334–338; Venâncio Willeke, *Missões Franciscanas no Brasil (1500–1975)* (Petrópolis, 1974), pp. 119–122.

10. Cassiano Ricardo, *A Floresta e a Agricultura em nossa Expansão Geográfica* (Rio de Janeiro, 1964), pp. 17–18; Vivaldo Coaracy, *O Rio de Janeiro no Século Dezessete* (Rio de Janeiro, 1965), pp. 132–133, 177; Sérgio Buarque de Holanda, "Movimentos da População em São Paulo no Século XVIII," *Revista do Instituto de Estudos Brasileiros*, 1 (1966), 96–97.

11. Renato Barbosa, "A Sesmaria e a Floresta na Formação de Rio de Janeiro," *Anuário Brasileiro de Economia Florestal*, 3 (1950), 39–44. On sesmaria legislation, see Raimundo José da Cunha Matos, *Corografia Histórica da Província de Minas Gerais* (Belo Horizonte, 1979 [1837]), p. 267: he lists five sixteenth-century decrees and twenty-five eighteenth-century decrees.

12. On urban food supply in 1646, see Rio de Janeiro, Prefeitura, Diretoria Geral do Patrimônio, Estatística e Arquivo, *O Rio de Janeiro do Seculo XVII* (Rio de Janeiro, 1935), p. 109.

13. Felisberto C. de Camargo, "Agricultura na América do Sul," in E. J. Fittkau et al., eds., *Biogeography and Ecology in South America* (The Hague, 1968), p. 320; John E. Rouse, *The Criollo: Spanish Cattle in the Americas* (Norman, OK, 1977), pp. 291–293; Elizabeth J. Reitz, "Some Consequences of Introducing Animals to the New World" (paper presented at a conference "Rethinking the Encounter: New Perspectives on Conquest and Colonization, 1450–1550," Gainesville, FL, April 1988); Baltasar Fernandes, São Vicente, 5 December 1567, in Peixoto, *Cartas*, p. 483; Alcântara Machado, *Vida e Morte do Bandeirante* (São Paulo, 1965), p. 62.

14. SP–ACM, various complaints, 1576–1580: see 1:99, 119, 122–123, 159, 181, 185; Serafim Leite, *História da Companhia de Jesus no Brasil* (Rio de Janeiro, 1945), 6:57; Richard Flecknoe, *A Relation of Ten Years Travells in Europe, Asia,*

Affrique, and America (London, [1656]), p. 72; André João Antonil [João Antônio Andreoni], *Cultura e Opulência do Brasil* (3d ed.; Belo Horizonte, 1982 [1711]), pp. 200–201; Renato da Silveira Martins, "Paisagens Culturais da Baixada Fluminense," *Boletim da Faculdade de Filosofia, Ciencias e Letras, 110 Geografia* (1950), No. 4, 49.

15. Victor Magalhães Godinho, *Os Descobrimentos e a Economia Mundial* (2d ed.; Lisbon, 1983), 4:107.

16. Sérgio Buarque de Holanda, *O Extremo Oeste* (São Paulo, 1986), pp. 31–36.

17. Buarque de Holanda, "Movimentos," p. 57. Luis Lisanti, "La productivité agricole dans l'Etat de São Paulo, XIXe-XXe siècles" (n.p., September 1971), mimeog., estimated the cultivated area at 1.8 hectares per male worker for later centuries.

18. Gabriel Soares de Souza, *Tratado Descritivo do Brasil em 1587* (4th ed.; São Paulo, 1971 [1851]), p. 163. João Luís Ribeiro Fragoso, "A Roça e as Propostas de Modernização na Agricultura Fluminense do Século XIX," *Revista Brasileira de História*, 6 (March-August 1986), 125–150, defends these practices from foreign criticisms.

19. On the adequacy of sesmarias, see the discussions in Joaquim Caetano da Silva Guimarães, *A Agricultura em Minas Gerais* (Rio de Janeiro, 1865), pp. 6–7, and in Coaracy, *Rio de Janeiro*, p. 239. In 1583 the municipal council of São Paulo prohibited the building of homesteads closer than 660 meters apart, suggesting plots of as little as 43.56 hectares each or, assuming 30 persons per household, 68 persons per square kilometer. The author, assuming a lower household size, interpreted this order to suggest a maximum rural density, but it seems more likely that this may be an indicator of urban density. See Warren Dean, "Indigenous Populations of the São Paulo–Rio de Janeiro Coast: Trade, Aldeamento, Slavery and Extinction," *Revista de História*, 58 (1984), No. 117, 26. See also John Monteiro, "Celeiro do Brasil: Escravidão Indígena e a Agricultura Paulista no Século XVII," *História*, 7 (1988), 10–11; Gov. Pimentel, Consulta to the Conselho Ultramarino, São Paulo, 1730, from the Arquivo Histórico Ultramarino, São Paulo, cod. 760, cited in Marcílio, "Crescimento Demográfico," p. 260.

20. On this complex transition, see Charles Boxer, *The Portuguese Seaborne Empire* (London, 1969).

21. Stuart Schwartz, "Colonial Brazil, c. 1580–c. 1750: Plantations and Peripheries," in Leslie Bethell, ed., *Cambridge History of Latin America* (Cambridge, England, 1984), 2:427; J. H. Galloway, *The Sugar Cane Industry: An Historical Geography from Its Origins to 1914* (Cambridge, England, 1989), p. 77; Antonil, *Cultura*, p. 140; Mario Aristides Freire, *A Capitania de Espírito Santo* (Vitória, 1945), p. 75. Dyewood trees are mentioned as "innumerable" in 1694, according to a royal permit obtained in 1700; see *Documentos Históricos*, 93 (1951), 54, 101. See also Rio de Janeiro, Prefeitura, Diretoria Geral do Patrimônio, *O Rio de Janeiro no século XVII* (Rio de Janeiro, 1935), p. 137; Silveira Mendes, "Paisagens," pp. 45–47; Dídima de Castro Peixoto, "Fatos ocorridos nos sécuos XVI e XVII," in Congresso de História Fluminense, *Anais* (Petrópolis, 1963), 1:78–81; Coaracy, *Rio de Janeiro*, pp. 204–205; Thales de Azevedo, *Povoamento da Cidade do Salvador* (2d ed.; Rio de Janeiro, 1955), pp. 289–98.

22. Miguel Costa Filho, *A Cana de Açucar em Minas Gerais* (Rio de Janeiro, 1963), p. 380; Elysio de Oliveira Belchior, *Conquistadores e povoadores do Rio de Janeiro* (Rio de Janeiro, 1965), p. 79.

23. Sérgio Buarque de Holanda, *Caminhos e Fronteiras* (Rio de Janeiro, 1957), pp. 205–214; Machado, *Vida e Morte*, p. 60; Monteiro, "Celeiro," pp. 1–12.

24. Romário Martins, *Bandeiras e Bandeirantes em Terras do Paraná* (Curitiba, n.d.), pp. 16–23; Luiz Gonzaga Jaeger, "La Compañía de Jesús en el antiguo Guayra (1585–1631)," *Pesquisas*, 1 (1957), 105–106, 120; Antonio Ruiz de Montoya, *Senhor Antonio Ruiz de Montoya de la Compañía de Jesus . . . dize* ([Madrid, 1639 or 1640]); Antonio Ruiz de Montoya, *Haseme Mãdado, Q̃ Asi Como Representè . . .* [Madrid, 1639 or 1640]; Afonso d'Escragnolle Taunay, *Ensaio de Carta Geral das Bandeiras Paulistas* (São Paulo, 1922); Carlos Davidoff, *Bandeirantes, Verso e Reverso* (3d ed.; São Paulo, 1986), pp. 26–37; Jaime Cortesão, ed., *Manuscritos da Coleção de Angelis, I: Jesuitas e Bandeirantes no Guairá (1549 [sic—1594]–1604)* (Rio de Janeiro, 1951), 131–173; and Igor Chmyz, "Arqueologia e História da Villa Espanhola de Ciudad Real de Guairá," *Cadernos de Arqueologia*, 1 (1976), No. 1, 78–80.

25. See the letter from Manuel José de Morales in Cortesão, *Manuscritos*, pp. 183–193. Varnhagen's estimate of 300,000 is often cited; see Cassiano Ricardo, *Marcha para o Oeste* (Rio de Janeiro, 1940), 1:104–105, and Davidoff, *Bandeirantes*, pp. 60–61.

26. Regina Maria A. Gadelha, *As Missões Jesuíticas do Itatim* (Rio de Janeiro, 1980), pp. 255–294; Jaeger, "La Compañia," p. 108; Machado, *Vida e Morte*, p. 179.

27. Morales, in Cortesão, *Manuscritos*, p. 187.

28. On Jesuit labor demands, see José Arouche de Toledo Rendon, *Memoria sobre as Aldeas de Indios da Provincia de S. Paulo Segundo as Observações Feitas no Anno de 1793* (Rio de Janeiro, 1824), p. 19, who also reports on indigenous flight on pp. 12–13, 21, 32. See also Machado, *Vida e Morte*, pp. 170–174.

29. Leite, *História*, 2:92–93, citing a manuscript source but with no details.

30. Pero de Magalhães Gandavo, *Tratado de Terra do Brasil* (Belo Horizonte, 1980 [1570?]), p. 43.

31. Luis de Pina, *As Ciências na História do Império Colonial Português* (Porto, 1945); Carlos França, "Os Portugueses do Século XVI e a História Natural do Brasil," *Revista de História* (Lisbon), 15 (1926): No. 57, 35–74; No. 58, 81–152; No. 59, 161–166. See also Frei Cristóvão de Lisboa, *História dos Animais e Árvores de Maranhão* (Lisbon, 1967). The drawings surfaced only in 1934; see Luiza da Fonseca, "Frei Cristóvão de Lisboa, OFM, Missionary and Natural Historian of Brazil," *The Americas*, 8 (January 1952), 289–303, 357–359.

32. Vasconcellos, *Chronica*, pp. 44–45, 142–143, 145, 147–148, 163.

33. Ibid., pp. 45, 88, 147, 161–162. The fruits, most lacking English equivalents, are:

mocuguê (also itapeuá) *Eugenia flavescans*	juá *Ziziphus joazeiro*
sapucaia *Lecythis zabucajo*	maçaranduba *Manilkara elata*
pitomba *Eugenia luschnathiana*	murici *Byrsonima* spp.
araçá *Psidium littorale*—"strawberry guava"	ibaraé (avará?) *Astrocaryum* sp.?
imbu *Spondias tuberosa*	guabiraba *Cordia rotundifolia*
araticum *Annona crasiflora*	guabiroba (also araça-felpudo) *Psidium incandescans*
ingá *Inga* spp.	

The other fruits are unidentified—possibly they have disappeared from rural diets.

34. See the accounts of Gugliemus Piso, *História Natural e Médica da India Occidental* (Rio de Janeiro, 1957 [1648]); Georg Marggraf, *História Natural do Brasil* (São Paulo, 1941 [1648]); Kaspar van Baerle, *História dos Feitos Recentemente Praticados durante Oito Anos no Brasil* (Rio de Janeiro, 1940 [1647]); Johan Nieuhof, *Gedenkwaerdige brasiliaense zee- en lant-Reize* (Amsterdam, 1682). Nancy Leys Stepan, *Beginnings of Brazilian Science* (New York, 1981), pp. 17–23, points out the contrast between Spanish and Portuguese efforts to reconnoiter their respective empires. Phillip II, for example, ordered minutely detailed "Geographical Reports" between 1577 and 1586. Curiously, the same monarch, once he had acquired the crown of Portugal in 1580, does not appear to have ordered any similar census of Brazil.

35. Augusto de Lima Junior, *Notícias Históricas (de norte a sul)* (Rio de Janeiro, 1953), pp. 9–24; Manoel Jacinto Nogueira da Gama, *Memoria sobre o Loureiro Cinnamomo, Vulgo Caneleira de Ceylão . . . para Acompanhar a Remessa das Plantas que pelas Reaes Ordens Vão Ser Transportadas ao Brasil* (Lisbon, 1797), pp. 12–13, 14.

36. Baltasar da Silva Lisboa, *Anais do Rio de Janeiro* (Rio de Janeiro, 1973 [1834–1835]), 4:247–249.

37. Nogueira da Gama, *Memoria*, pp. 4–11; Luis Ferrand de Almeida, "Aclimação de Plantas do Oriente no Brasil durante os Séculos XVII e XVIII," *Revista Portuguesa de História*, 15 (1975), 339–395; José Roberto do Amaral Lapa, *O Brasil e as Drogas do Oriente* (Rio de Janeiro, 1966), pp. 34–38; Azevedo, *Povoamento*, p. 293.

38. Toledo Rendon, *Memoria*, p. 33; Leite, *História*, 1:239; Egon Schaden, *Aculturação Indígena* (São Paulo, 1969), pp. 179, 185, 187–188; J. Resende Silva, "A Formação Territorial de Minas Gerais," in Congresso Sul-Riograndense de História e Geografia, 3, Porto Alegre, 1940, *Anais* (Porto Alegre, 1940), 2:696; Fernandes, *Aspectos*, p. 31.

39. Sérgio Buarque de Holanda, *Visão do Paraíso* (23d ed., rev. and aug.; São Paulo, 1982 [1936]), pp. 88–96.

40. Buarque de Holanda, *Visão*, pp. 54–56; Cortesão, *Fundação*, p. 126; Vasconcellos, *Chronica*, pp. 61–62. See also Monteiro, "São Paulo," chap. 4, for a different interpretation of native influences.

41. John Hemming, "Indians and the Frontier," in Bethell, *Cambridge History*, 2:512.

42. Sérgio Buarque de Holanda, "Movimentos," 98–101, thought the fracturing of Paulista municipalities "a little in the manner of the ancient inhabitants." In 1556 the Jesuit Luis de Grã noted that both natives and neo-Europeans constantly moved on and burned the forest; see Leite, *Monumenta*, 2:292. On the imposition of colonial cultures, see George M. Foster, *Culture and Conquest* (New York, 1960).

43. Flecknoe, *Relation*, p. 7.

CHAPTER 5. GOLD AND DIAMONDS, ANTS AND CATTLE

1. Virgílio Noya Pinto, *O Ouro Brasileiro e o Comércio Anglo-Português* (São Paulo, 1979), pp. 59–117, estimated 876,629 kilograms of officially counted gold,

except for Bahian output (and perhaps that of Rio de Janeiro). To this it seems reasonable to add another 124,000 kilograms, assuming official records are themselves incomplete. Because Pinto found twice as much gold entering Lisbon between 1725 and 1750 as was officially counted in Brazil and showed some quantity remaining in Brazil, traded with smugglers on the coast, or sent to Africa, this estimate of untaxed gold may be conservative. See also Dauril Alden, "The Population of Brazil in the Late Eighteenth Century: A Preliminary Study," *Hispanic American Historical Review*, 43 (May 1963), 173–205; Thomas W. Merrick and Douglas H. Graham, *Population and Economic Development in Brazil, 1800 to the Present* (Baltimore, MD, 1979), pp. 29–30.

2. "Projecto, ou Plano Ajustado por Ordem de S. M. F. entre o Governador & Capm. Geral. de S. Paulo D. Luis Anto. de Souza e o Brigadeiro José Custodio de Sá e Faria . . . 1772," *Monumenta* (Curitiba), 1 (Summer 1987), 11–148.

3. According to Serafim Leite, *Monumenta Brasiliae* (Rome, 1956), 2:196, the Jesuit José de Anchieta thought gold reports would rouse the king to send a fleet to destroy the "wicked who resist the preaching of the Gospel and subject them to the yoke of slavery." See also Paulo Florêncio da Silveira Camargo, *História de Santana de Parnaíba* (São Paulo, 1971), p. 16; Theodoro Knecht, "Ouro no Estado de São Paulo," *Boletim do Instituto Geográfico e Geológico* (1939), No. 26, 1–97; Lucy de Abreu Maffei and Arlinda Rocha Nogueira, "O Ouro na Capitania de São Vicente nos Séculos XVI e XVII," *Anais do Museu Paulista* [hereafter *AMP*], 20 (1966), 7–136.

4. Aurélio Buarque de Holanda Ferreira, *Novo Dicionário da Lingua Portuguesa* (2d ed., rev. and aug.; Rio de Janeiro, 1986), derives garimpeiro from *grimpar*, to climb mountains.

5. Pedro Taques de Almeida Paes Leme, *Notícias das Minas de São Paulo e dos Sertões da Mesma Capitania* (Belo Horizonte, 1980 [1772]), pp. 34, 43, 50–52.

6. Pinto, *Ouro Brasileiro*, p. 52; José João Teixeira Coelho, "Instrucção para o Governo da Capitania de Minas Gerais [1780]," *Revista do Instituto Histórico e Geográfico Brasileiro* [hereafter *RIHGB*], 15 (1852), 317–324, 363; José Matol, *Notícia Prática que dá ao R. Diogo Soares . . . sobre o Famoso Rio das Mortes* (Juiz de Fora, Brazil, 1975 [1740?]), pp. 1–3.

7. Pinto, *Ouro Brasileiro*, p. 52.

8. Waldemar de Almeida Barbosa, *Negros e Quilombos em Minas Gerais* (Belo Horizonte, 1972), pp. 8–11, 59; Iraci del Nero da Costa, "Fundamentos Econômicos da Ocupação e Povoamento de Minas Gerais," *Revista do Instituto de Estudos Brasileiros* [herefter *RIEB*] (1982), No. 24, 41–52; Sérgio Buarque de Holanda, "Metais e Pedras Preciosas," in idem, *História Geral da Civilização Brasileira* (São Paulo, 1960), 2:274–275; transcription of a report by Francisco Tavares de Brito [Diogo Soares?], in Augusto de Lima Junior, *A Capitania das Minas Gerais* (3d ed.; Belo Horizonte, 1965), p. 227; J. Resende Silva, "A Formação Territorial de Minas Gerais," in Congresso Sul-Riograndense de História e Geografia, 3, Porto Alegre, 1940, *Anais* (Porto Alegre, 1940), 2:686; John Mawe, *Travels in the Interior of Brazil* (2d ed., rev.; London, 1823), 1:77–78, 273, 277.

9. Martim Francisco Ribeiro de Andrada, "Jornal de Viagem até Curitiba," in *Roteiro e Notícias de São Paulo Colonial* (São Paulo, 1977), p. 152, reports a stream diversion 13.2 km long; [José Joaquim da Rocha], "Geographia historica da Capitania de Minas Gerais [1780?]," *Publicações do Arquivo Público Nacional*, 9 (1909),

24; Wilhelm von Eschwege, *Pluto Brasiliensis* (São Paulo, 1944 [1832]), pp. 316–320; Alvaro Astolfo da Silveira, *Memorias Corograficas* (Belo Horizonte, 1921), 1:229; Jose Vieira Couto, "Memoria sobre a Capitania de Minas Gerais," *RIHGB*, 11 (1848), Supplement, 300–306; Report of Tavares de Brito, pp. 70, 227–228. See also Roberto Simonsen, *História Econômica do Brasil (1500/1820)* (4th ed.; São Paulo, 1962), p. 275.

10. Couto, "Memoria," p. 307.

11. Saint-Hilaire, a botanist, repeatedly referred to removal of plant cover by miners in *Voyage dans les provinces de Rio de Janeiro et Minas Gerais* (Paris, 1830), 1:131, 133, 135, 153, 158, 165, 187, 216. See also Johann Emanuel Pohl, *Viagem no Interior do Brasil* (Belo Horizonte, 1976 [1832]), pp. 86, 88, 89, 380, 384; Alexander Caldcleugh, *Travels in South America during the Years 1819–20–21* (London, 1825), 2:279, 237. On flooding, see "Resumo da Memoria do Segundo Vereador da Camara do Sabará Offerecida no Anno de 1807," *RIHGB*, 6 (1844), No. 21, 280–282; Simonsen, *História*, p. 276.

12. Tristão de Alencar Araripe, "O Ciclo de Ouro em Castelo," *UFES-Revista de Cultura*, 1 (First Semester, 1979), 42–43; Ney Strauch, *A Bacia do Rio Doce* (Rio de Janeiro, 1955), p. 3; Mawe, *Travels*, p. 190. On clearing in Cantagallo, see Francisco Duarte Malha, "Oficio do Conde de Arcos Sobre as Minas de Cantagallo," 7 October 1805, Instituto de Estudos Brasileiros, Coleção Lamego [hereafter IEB–CL]. See also Simonsen, *História*, pp. 286, 286n. Wilhelm von Eschwege, "Noticias, e Reflexões Estadisticas a Respeito da Provincia de Minas Gerais," *Memórias da Academia Real das Sciencias de Lisboa*, 9 (1825), 9, estimated the (official) work force at midcentury at 80,000.

13. A. J. R. Russell-Wood, "Colonial Brazil: The Gold Cycle, c. 1690–1750," in Leslie Bethell, ed., *Cambridge History of Latin America* (Cambridge, England, 1984), 2:579.

14. Dauril Alden, "Late Colonial Brazil, 1750–1808," in Bethell, *Cambridge History*, 2:604–607; Alden, "Population," pp. 173–205; Merrick and Graham, *Population*, pp. 29–30; Saint-Hilaire, *Voyage dans les provinces de Saint Paul et de Sainte Catherine* (Paris, 1851), 1:133; D. de Alencar Araripe, *História da Estrada de Ferro Vitória a Minas* (Rio de Janeiro, 1954); Maria Manuela Ramos de Souza Silva, "Os Produtos Coloniais e a Economia Européia do Século XVII" (M.A. thesis, Federal University of Rio de Janeiro, 1981), pp. 79, 80; Maria Luiza Marcílio, *A Cidade de São Paulo* (São Paulo, 1974), p. 99.

15. [Rocha], "Geographia historica," p. 25; Miriam Ellis, *Contribuição ao Estudo do Abastecimento das Areas Mineradoras do Brasil no Século XVIII* (Rio de Janeiro, 1961). Farmed area is calculated at 1.8 hectares per farm worker, an average work force of 100,000, and an average shift of fields of three years.

16. Mário Neme, "Um Governador Reformista no São Paulo Colonial," *AMP*, 24 (1970), 5–54; Ordem Circular, 29 April 1772, *Documentos Interessantes*, 33 (1901), 57–58; Luiz Lisanti, "Comércio e Capitalismo: O Brasil e a Europa entre o Fim do Século XVIII e o Início do Século XIX" (Ph.D. dissertation, University of São Paulo, 1962), pp. 83–84.

17. Carlos Borges Schmidt, "A Vida Rural no Brasil: A Area do Paraitinga," *Boletim da Agricultura*, 1 (1951), Número Unico, 11–13, 31–32; Mário Neme, "Apossamento do Solo e Evolução da Propriedade Rural na Zona de Piracicaba," *Coleção Museu Paulista, Série de História*, 1 (1974), 31, 46–48; Sérgio Buarque de

Holanda, "Movimentos da População em São Paulo no Século XVIII," *RIEB*, 1 (1966), 59. See also Maria Luiza Marcílio, "Crescimento Demográfico e Evolução Agrária Paulista, 1700–1836" (Livre Docência thesis, University of São Paulo, 1974); São Paulo (State), Arquivo Público do Estado de São Paulo, *Documentos Interessantes*, 73 (1952), 20.

18. Heloísa Liberalli Bellotto, "O Presídio do Iguatemi: Função e Circunstâncias," *RIEB*, 21 (1979), 33–57; Antônio Rodrigues Veloso de Oliveira, *Memória sobre o Melhoramento da Provincia de São Paulo* (2d ed.; São Paulo, 1978 [1810]), p. 59, 59n. A gem of colonial reportage is Teotônio José Juzarte's account of his expedition to Iguatemi, "Diario de Navegação do Rio Tietê, Rio Grande, Paraná e Rio Iguatemi," *AMP*, 1 (1922), 41–118. An elegant shopping mall in São Paulo now bears the ill-fated outpost's name, a curious memorial.

19. João Mariano de Deus e Souza, "Chronologia, ou Serie de Tempos das Duas Freguesias de Nossa Senhora da Conceição de Campo Alegre da Paraíba Nova e São João Marcos" (31 August 1797), IEB–CL. On degredo, see Manuel Eufrâzio de Azevedo Marques, *Apontamentos Historicos, Geograficos, Estatisticos e Noticiosos da Provincia de S. Paulo* (Rio de Janeiro, 1879), 1:198–199. The quotation is from J. J. Teixeira Coelho, "Instrucção para o Governo da Capitania de Minas Gerais [1780]," *RIHGB*, 15 (1852), No. 7, 347, 358–360. See also Resende Silva, "Formação," 2:694; Laura de Mello e Souza, *Os Desclassificados do Ouro: A Pobreza Mineira no Século XVIII* (Rio de Janeiro, 1982), pp. 64–69, 72–73.

20. Max H. Boudin, *Dicionário de Tupi Moderno* (São Paulo, 1978), p. 94; Antônio Geraldo da Cunha, *Dicionário Histórico das Palavras Portuguesas de Origem Tupi* (São Paulo, 1978), pp. 83, 79–81. Buarque de Holanda, *Novo Dicionário*, p. 314, lists 65 synonyms for caipira, mostly pejoratives.

21. João Ferreira de Oliveira Bueno, "Simples Narração da Viagem Que Fez ao Rio Paraná," *RIHGB*, 1 (1839), No. 3, 179–193; Inácio Accioli de Vasconcellos, *Memoria Statistica da Provincia do Espirito Santo Escrito no Anno de 1828* (Vitória, 1978), p. A [*sic*]; Murilo Mendes, "O Reflorestamento," in Congresso Florestal Brasileiro, 1, Curitiba, 1953, *Anais* (Curitiba, 1954), p. 74; "Memoria Dirigida ao Ilmo. Exmo. Snr. Conde de Linhares" [post 1807], Manuscript Collection, Biblioteca Nacional, Rio de Janeiro [hereafter BN–RJ]; Marcos Magalhães Rubinger, "O Desaparecimento das Tribos Indígenas em Minas Gerais e a Sobrevivência dos Indios Maxacali," *RMP*, n.s., 14 (1963), 238.

22. Almeida Barbosa, *Negros*, pp. 33–34, 46–49, 59–77, 85–86; Resende Silva, "Formação," p. 694. Kimbundu vocabulary derived from J. D. Cordeiro da Matta, *Ensaio de Diccionario Kimbundu-Portuguez* (Lisbon, 1895). See also Baltasar da Silva Lisboa, *Anais do Rio de Janeiro* (Rio de Janeiro, 1973 [1834–1835]), 3:295, 307.

23. Manuscript map of Paraná River [1750s], and Henrique Guilherme de Oliveira, "Demonstracao Topographica do Curso do Rio Tietê desde a Cidade de S. Paulo" [1750?], manuscript map, watercolor, both in the Pimenta Bueno Collection, BN–RJ; Antônio Pires de Campos, "Breve Noticia de Gentio Bárbaro [1723]," in Afonso d'Escragnolle Taunay, ed., *Relatos Sertanistas* (São Paulo, 1953), p. 181; "Digressão que Fez João Caetano da Silva em 1817 para Descobrir a Nova Navegação entre a Capitania de Goiaz e de São Paulo pelo Rio dos Bois até ao do Rio Grande," *RIHGB*, 74 (1978), 192; Robert Southey, *History of Brazil* (London, 1819), 3:802, 807; José Joaquim de Azeredo Coutinho, *Ensaio Econômico sobre*

o Commercio de Portugal e suas Colonias (Lisbon, 1794), pp. 62–3, 65; Neme, "Apossamento," p. 8.

24. Manuel Tavares da Costa Miranda and Alípio Bandeira, "Memorial acerca da Antiga e Moderna Legislação Indígena," in L. Humberto de Oliveira, ed., *Coletânea de Leis, Atos e Memórias Referentes ao Indígena Brasileiro* (Rio de Janeiro, 1947), pp. 64–65; Venâncio Willeke, *Missões Franciscanas no Brasil, 1500–1975* (Petrópolis, 1975), p. 123; Souza Botelho to Joaquim Peres de Oliveira, 2 May and 16 May 1771, *Documentos Interessantes*, 92 (1978), 156–157, 159. José Joaquim da Rocha, "Mappa da Capitania de Minas Gerais, 1777," manuscript map, BN–RJ, shows seven aldeias. See also Joaquim Norberto de Souza e Silva, "Memoria Historica e Documentada das Aldeias de Indios da Provincia do Rio de Janeiro," *RIHGB*, 17 (April-June, 1854), 142–220; José Carneiro da Silva, *Memoria Topographica e Historica sobre os Campos dos Goytacazes* (2d ed.; Rio de Janeiro, 1907 [1819]), pp. 21–26; Heloísa Liberalli Bellotto, "Política Indigenista no Brasil Colonial," *RIEB*, 29 (1988), 57.

25. Almeida Barbosa, *Negros*, pp. 89–90; "Guido Thomaz Marlière [Documents]," *Revista do Arquivo Público Mineiro*, 10 (1905), 610; Souza e Silva, "Memoria," pp. 184–185; Joaquim Ferreira Moutinho, *Noticia sobre a Provincia de Matto Grosso, seguido d'um Roteiro da Viagem da sua Capital á São Paulo* (São Paulo, 1867), p. 321.

26. Neme, "Apossamento," pp. 8, 48. See also Luiz dos Santos Vilhena, *Recopilação de Noticias da Capitania de S. Paulo* (Salvador, 1935 [1802]), pp. 39, 41–42; Populacao Mogi-Mirim, 1766–1771, Lata 116, Arquivo Público do Estado de São Paulo.

27. Pohl, *Viagem*, p. 326; Paulo Mercadante, *Os Sertões do Leste* (Rio de Janeiro, 1973), pp. 67–68; Sérgio Buarque de Holanda, *Caminhos e Fronteiras* (Rio de Janeiro, 1957), p. 129; José Ribeiro do Valle, "A Propósito das Observações Botânico-Medicais de Bernardino Antônio Gomes," in Bernardino Antônio Gomes, *Plantas Medicinais do Brasil* (São Paulo, 1972), p. 23; Arsène V. Pierre-Noél, *Nomenclature polyglotte des plantes haïtiennes et tropicales* (Port-au-Prince, 1971), p. 217; Maria Tereza Lemos de Arruda Camargo, *Plantas Medicinais e de Rituais Afro-Brasileiros* (São Paulo, 1988).

28. Nelson Coelho de Senna, *Chorographia de Minas Gerais* (Rio de Janeiro, 1922), pp. 182–199, found some 250 indigenous toponyms in Minas Gerais in 1922. See also Almeida Barbosa, *Negros*, pp. 133–135. On African-indigenous relations, see Antônio Muniz de Souza, *Viagens e Observações de hum Brasileiro* (Rio de Janeiro, 1834), 1:92–93.

29. Neme, "Governador," p. 28; Mawe, *Travels*, p. 207.

30. On rodents, see Moysés Kuhlmann and Eduardo Kühn, *A Flora do Distrito de Ibiti (ex Monte Alegre) Municipio de Amparo* (São Paulo, 1947), p. 145. On pests generally, see "Memoria dirigida ao Illmo. Excellmo. Senhor Conde de Linhares D. Rodrigo de Souza Coutinho," n.d., BN–RJ; Gabriel Soares de Souza, *Tratado Descritivo do Brasil em 1587* (4th ed.; São Paulo, 1971 [1851]), pp. 166–168. Mawe, *Travels*, p. 197, notes the rat problem.

31. Soares de Souza, *Tratado*, pp. 173, 269; Neal A. Weber, *Gardening Ants: The Attines* (Philadelphia, 1972), pp. 1–146.

32. Soares de Souza, *Tratado*, p. 269.

33. Francisco A. M. Mariconi, *As Saúvas* (São Paulo, 1970); Francisco H.

Schade, "The Ecology and Control of the Leaf-Cutting Ants," in J. Richard Gorham, ed., *Paraguay: Ecological Essays* (Miami, 1973), pp. 77–95; Jonas Machado da Costa et al., "As Formigas Cortadeiras e Métodos de Controle," *Circular Técnico da Empresa de Pesquisa Agropecuária da Bahia* (April 1983), No. 3, pp. 5–28. The Atlantic Forest–area species are *A. sexdens, A. capiguara, A. bisphaerica, A. robusta,* and *A. laevigata*. The fungus is *Rozites gonglyophora* [Pholiota gongylophora] Moeller. There are also subspecies and a related genus, *Acromyrmex*, called *quenquens* in Portuguese. Each occupies a somewhat different niche and prefers different plant foods.

34. José Arouche de Toledo Rendon, "Reflexões sobre o Estado em Que se Acha a Agricultura na Capitania de S. Paulo [1788]," in his *Obras* (São Paulo, 1978), p. 7. For modern estimates, see E. Amante, "A Formiga Saúva *Atta capiguara*, Praga das Pastagens," *O Biólogo*, 33 (1967), No. 6, 113–120, cited by Machado da Costa et al., "Formigas."

35. Yael D. Lubin, "Eating Ants Is No Picnic," *Natural History*, 92 (October 1983), 55–59. The cuiabana is *Paratrechina fulva*. On ant predators, see Ana Primavesi, *Manejo Ecológico de Pastagens* (2d ed.; São Paulo, 1986), p. 125. On ant eating, see Carlos Augusto Taunay, *Manual do Agricultor Brazileiro* (Rio de Janeiro, 1839), pp. 164–165. Auguste de Saint-Hilaire, *Voyage dans le district de diamants et sur le littoral du Brésil* (Paris, 1833), 2:181, records townspeople's derision. See also Neme, "Governador," p. 30.

36. Konrad Guenther, *A Naturalist in Brazil: The Flora and Fauna and the People of Brazil* (London, 1931), p. 304. On countermeasures, see João Caetano da Gama Araujo Azevedo, "Informações sobre o Augmento da Agricultura e Lavoura do Brazil," Rio de Janeiro, 7 September 1811, manuscript, Instituto Histórico e Geográfico Brasileiro.

37. Muniz de Souza, *Viagens*, 1:137.

38. Soares de Souza, *Tratado*, p. 173; Silva Lisboa, "[Corte de Madeiras]" [post-1804?], Boston Public Library; idem, *Anais*, 5:180. See also Taunay, *Manual*, pp. 104–105; Araujo Azevedo, "Informações."

39. Buarque de Holanda, "Movimentos," pp. 106–107; Altiva Pilatti Balhanna et al., *Campos Gerais: Estruturas Agrárias* (Curitiba, 1968), p. 30; Antônio Rodrigues Veloso de Oliveira, *Memoria sobre o Melhoramento da Provincia de São Paulo* (Rio de Janeiro, 1822), p. 7; Agueda Vilhena de Moraes, "Bandeirantes et indiens dans la région de Lagoa Santa," in Annette Laming-Emperaire et al., *Grottes et abris de la région de Lagoa Santa, Minas Gerais, Brésil* (Cahiers d'Archeologie d'Amérique du Sud, No. 1; Paris, [1975]), p. 19.

40. José Vieira Couto, "Considerações sobre as Duas Classes Mais Importantes de Povoadores da Capitania de Minas Gerais," *RIHGB*, 25 (1862), No. 8, 430–431; Simonsen, *História*, pp. 180, 181, 184; Vivaldo Coaracy, *O Rio de Janeiro no Século Dezessete* (Rio de Janeiro, 1965), p. 22; José Joaquim da Cunha de Azeredo Coutinho, *Ensaio Economico Sobre o Commercio de Portugal e suas Colonias* (Lisbon, 1794), pp. 6–8; Mawe, *Travels*, pp. 74, 180, 216; Joaquim Caetano da Silva Guimarães, *A Agricultura em Minas Gerais* (Rio de Janeiro, 1865), p. 46. See also Roy Nash, *The Conquest of Brazil* (New York, 1926), p. 265.

41. On cattle parasites, see S. V. Vigneron Jousselandière, *Novo Manual Pratico de Agricultura Intertropical* (Rio de Janeiro, 1860), pp. 190–191; Muniz de Souza, *Viagens*, pp. 124–125; José da Cunha Mattos, *Itinerario do Rio de Janeiro*

ao Pará e Maranhão pelas Provincias de Minas Gerais e Goiás (Rio de Janeiro, 1836), 1:34, 46; idem, *Corografia Histórica da Província de Minas Gerais* (2d ed.; Belo Horizonte, 1979 [1837]), 1:263.

42. Alberto Loefgren, "Ensaio para uma Distribuição dos Vegetaes nos Diversos Grupos Floristicos do Estado de S. Paulo," *Boletim do Instituto Geológico e Geográfico*, 11 (1896), 31, 48; George Eiten, "A Vegetação do Estado de São Paulo," *Boletim do Instituto de Botânica*, 7 (January, 1970), 106; Carneiro da Silva, *Memoria*, pp. 16–17. On fire, see Primavesi, *Manejo*, pp. 44–48.

43. Botanical and Brazilian equivalents of these grasses are: Guinea grass, *Panicum maximum*, capim colonião; Pará grass, *Brachiaria mutica*, capim Angola; Molasses grass, *Melinis minutiflora*, capim gordura, capim melado; Jaragua grass, *Hyparrhenia rufa*, capim Jaraguá. Also, *Digitaria decumbens* is capim pangola. See James J. Parsons, "Spread of African Pasture Grasses to the American Tropics," *Journal of Range Management*, 25 (January 1972), 12–14. Guinea grass was probably deliberately introduced, via the Caribbean; see Carneiro da Silva, *Memoria*, p. 71. For classification, see Karl Friedrich Philipp von Martius, *Flora Brasiliensis, Gramineae I* (Munich, 1871–1877), 2,2:241–242. See also Auguste de Saint-Hilaire, "Mémoire sur le systhème d'agriculture adopté par les Brésiliens et les résultats qu'il a eus dans la province de Minas Gerais," *Mémoires du Museum d'Histoire Naturelle*, 14 (1827), 88n, 91, 92; Jousselandière, *Novo Manual*, pp. 151–152; Muniz de Souza, *Viagens*, pp. 124–125. On native versus exotic grasses, see Primavesi, *Manejo*, pp. 12–14, 24, 34, 38, 42.

44. Tarciso de Souza Filgueiras, "Africanas no Brasil: Gramineas Introduzidas da Africa," *Cadernos de Geociências* (1990), No. 5, 57–63.

45. Soares de Souza, *Tratado*, pp. 164–165; Simão de Vasconcellos, *Chronica da Companhia de Jesu do Estado do Brasil* (Lisbon, 1663), p. 147; Fernão Cardim, *Tratados da Terra e Gente do Brasil* (3d ed.; São Paulo, 1978), p. 66. On range capacity, see Auguste de Saint-Hilaire, *Voyage aux sources do Rio de S. Francisco et dans la province de Goyaz* (Paris, 1847–48), 1:70, 76; Carneiro da Silva, *Memoria*, pp. 14, 52–53; Henry Hill, *Uma Visão do Comércio do Brasil em 1808* ([Salvador], 1964), appendix. On pasture transformation, see Eiten, "Vegetação," p. 106.

46. José Ferreira Carrato, "O Primeiro Polo de Criação de Gado que Houve no Triângulo Mineiro," *Estudos Históricos*, 12 (1973), 1; Parsons, "Spread," p. 12.

47. Kurt Hueck, "Sobre a Origem dos Campos Cerrados no Brasil e Algumas Novas Observações no seu Límite Meridional," *Revista Brasileira de Geografia*, 19 (January-March 1957), 68–80.

48. Here 4,000 square kilometers are estimated to have been destroyed by gold prospecting, 22,000 by swidden farming, 1,000 by invernadas, and 3,000 out of fright, malice, and carelessness. See Thomas Lindley, *Narrative of a Voyage to Brazil* (London, 1805), pp. 219–220; Mawe, *Travels*, pp. 358–361.

CHAPTER 6. SCIENCE DISCOVERS THE FOREST

1. Luis Ferrand de Almeida, "Aclimação de Plantas do Oriente no Brasil durante os Séculos XVII e XVIII," *Revista Portuguesa de História*, 15 (1975), 395–413; William J. Simon, *Scientific Expeditions in the Portuguese Overseas Territories (1783–1808)* (Lisbon, 1983), pp. 5–15; idem, "A Forgotten Eighteenth-Century Scientific Expedition to the Amazon," *Camões Center Quarterly*, 2 (Autumn-Winter

1990), 1–13; Domenico Vandelli, *Memoria sobre a Utilidade dos Jardins Botânicos a Respeito da Agricultura e Principalmente da Cultivação das Charnecas* (Coimbra, 1770).

2. Augusto da Silva Carvalho, "As Academias Científicas do Brasil no Século XVIII," *Memorias da Academia das Ciências de Lisboa, Classe de Ciências*, 2 (1939), 4–8; Baltasar da Silva Lisboa, *Discurso Historico, Politico e Economico dos Progressos, e Estado Actual da Philosophia Natural Portuguesa Acompanhado de Algumas Reflexões sobre o Estado do Brasil* (Lisbon, 1786), pp. 39–40; "Sumario da Historia do Descobrimento da Cochonilha no Brasil, e das Observaçoens, Que sobre Ella Fez no Rio de Janeiro o Dr. José Henriques Ferreira," *O Patriota: Jornal Litterario, Politico, Mercantil, etc., do Rio de Janeiro* [hereafter *Patriota*], 3 (January-February 1814), 3–4.

3. Dauril Alden, *Royal Government in Colonial Brazil* (Berkeley, CA, 1968), pp. 377, 380.

4. Simon, *Scientific Expeditions*, p. 58.

5. Kenneth R. Maxwell, *Conflicts and Conspiracies: Brazil and Portugal, 1750–1808* (Cambridge, England, 1973), p. 187.

6. Moreira de Azevedo, "Sociedades Fundadas no Brasil desde os Tempos Coloniais," *Revista do Instituto Histórico e Geográfico Brasileiro* [hereafter *RIHGB*], 48 (1885), Pt. 2, 271; Simon, *Scientific Expeditions*, p. 111.

7. Kenneth Maxwell and Maria Beatriz Nizza da Silva, "A Política," in M. B. Nizza da Silva, coord., *O Império Luso-Brasileiro, 1750–1822* (Lisbon, 1986), p. 374. Simon, *Scientific Expeditions*, pp. 112, 115, 117; José Correa da Serra, "Cartas . . . a um Destinatario não Declarado [Rodrigo de Souza Coutinho] Referindo-se a Assuntos Nauticos, Botanicos e Agricultura," 1797–1798, Manuscript Collection, Biblioteca Nacional, Rio de Janeiro [hereafter BN–RJ]; Hipólito José da Costa Pereira, "Memoria sobre a Viagem aos Estados Unidos [1801]," *RIHGB*, 21 (1858), Pt. 3, 361–365; Francisco Adolfo Varnhagen, "Os Dois Vellosos," *Gazeta Medica da Bahia*, 12 (1881), 72–78.

8. Manuel Ferreira Lagos, "Elogio Historico do Padre Mestre Fr. José Mariano da Conceição Velloso," *RIHGB*, 2 (1840), Pt. 8, supplement, 596; Varnhagen, "Dois Vellosos," pp. 72–78; José Mariano da Conceição Velloso, *O Fazendeiro do Brasil* (Lisbon, 1798–1805); Rodrigo de Souza Coutinho, "Aviso de . . . que se Publique uma Flora Completa e Geral do Brasil e de Todos os Dominios de Portugal, BN–RJ; Anyda Marchant, "Dom João's Botanical Garden," *Hispanic American Historical Review* [hereafter *HAHR*], 41 (May 1941), 265; Luis de Pina, *As Ciências na História do Império Colonial Português (Séculos XV a XIX)* (Porto, 1945), p. 178; Souza Coutinho to Francisco da Cunha e Menezes, Queluz, 5 June 1802, BN–RJ; Daniel Pedro Müller, *Ensaio d'um Quadro Estatistico da Provincia de S. Paulo* (2d ed.; São Paulo, 1923 [1837]), p. 260.

9. José Jobson de A. Arruda, *O Brasil no Comércio Colonial* (São Paulo, 1980); Maxwell, *Conflicts and Conspiracies*, pp. 232–235.

10. Leslie Bethell, "The Independence of Brazil," in idem, ed., *Cambridge History of Latin America* (Cambridge, England, 1985), 3:157–174; Decree of 28 April 1809, *Codigo Brasiliense, ou Collecção das Leis, Alvarás, Decretos, Cartas Régias, &c. Promulgadas no Brasil* (Rio de Janeiro, 1811), 1:n.p.

11. José Vieira Couto, *Memoria sobre as Salitreiras Naturaes de Monte Rodrigo* (Rio de Janeiro, 1809 [1803]); João Manso Pereira, *Copia de huma Carta sobre a Nitreira Artificial, Estabelecida na Villa de Santos* (Lisbon, 1800); Silva

Lisboa, *Discurso*, pp. 56–62. Preserved fish were consumed when whales wintered in Guanabara Bay and fish were scarce. On potash and salt, see Antônio Rodrigues Veloso de Oliveira, *Memória sobre o Melhoramento da Provincia de São Paulo* (São Paulo, 1978 [1810]), p. 18. John Mawe, *Travels in the Interior of Brazil* (2d ed.; London, 1823), p. 271, found potash from giant fern (*Pteris caudata*) ashes, but potash was still imported in the 1850s; see I.–Ch. Heusser and G. Claraz, "Des principaux produits des provinces brésiliennes de Rio-de-Janeiro et de Minas-Gerais," *Flores des Serres et des Jardins de l'Europe*, 14 (1859), 192. On "black soap" from ashes of pau d'alho (*Gallesia gorazema*), see Ezechias Paulo Heringer, *Contribuição ao Conhecimento da Flora da Zona da Mata de Minas Gerais* (Rio de Janeiro, 1947), p. 148; Maria Paes de Barros, *No Tempo de Dantes* (São Paulo, 1946).

12. Maria Odila Silva Dias, "The Establishment of the Royal Court in Brazil," in A. J. R. Russell-Wood, ed., *From Colony to Nation: Essays on the Independence of Brazil* (Baltimore, MD, 1975), p. 107; Larissa Brown, "Internal Commerce in a Colonial Economy: Rio de Janeiro and Its Hinterland, 1790–1822" (Ph.D. dissertation, University of Virginia, 1986). On salt, see Baltasar da Silva Lisboa, *Anais do Rio de Janeiro* (Rio de Janeiro, 1973 [1834–1835]), 1:371; João Rodrigues de Brito, *Cartas Economico-Politicas sobre a Agricultura e Commercio da Bahia* (Lisbon, 1821), pp. 62–64. On barrel making, see Veloso de Oliveira, *Memoria . . . São Paulo*, p. 32; John Luccock, *Notes on Rio de Janeiro and the Southern Parts of Brazil Taken during a Residence of Ten Years in the Country from 1808 to 1818* (London, 1820), p. 311.

13. Silva Carvalho, "Academias Científicas," pp. 23–24; Simon, *Scientific Expeditions*, p. 128.

14. [José Feliciano Castilho], *Instrucção para os Viajantes e Empregados nas Colonias, . . . Precedida de Algumas Reflexões sobre a Historia Natural do Brazil* (Rio de Janeiro, 1819), p. xxix; João Barbosa Rodrigues, *Hortus Fluminensis ou Breve Noticia sobre as Plantas Cultivadas no Jardim Botanico do Rio de Janeiro* (Rio de Janeiro, 1894); Ladislau Netto, *Le Muséum National de Rio-de-Janeiro et son influence sur les sciences naturelles au Brésil* (Paris, 1889). On botanical gardens, see Lucile Brockway, *Science and Colonial Expansion* (New York, 1979).

15. On foreign exclusion, see Louis de Bouganville, *Voyage autour du monde, par la frigate du roi La Boudeuse* (Neuchatel, 1773), 1:58. Auguste de Saint-Hilaire, *Histoire des plantes les plus remarquables du Brésil et du Paraguay* (Paris, 1824), p. lxvii.

16. Silvia Figueroa, "German-Brazilian Relations in the Field of Geological Sciences During the Nineteenth Century," *Earth Sciences History*, 9 (1990), No. 2, 132–137; Manuel Ferreira da Câmara, *Ensaio de Descripção Fizica e Economica da Comarca dos Ilheus na America* (Lisbon, 1789). Domenico Vandelli referred to the Ribeiro de Macedo letters: see "Memoria sobre Algumas Produçõens Naturaes das Conquistas e Dominios de Portugal," n.d., BN–RJ, p. 197. On the history of transfers, see also B*** [Domingos Borges de Barros], "Memoria sobre o Café, sua Historia, Cultura e Amanhos," *Patriota*, 1 (May 1813), p. 11.

17. Manuel Arruda da Câmara, *Discurso sobre a Utilidade da Instituição de Jardins nas Principais Provincias do Brazil* (Rio de Janeiro, 1810), pp. 7–9.

18. Correa da Serra, "Cartas . . . a [Rodrigo de Souza Coutinho]," *Codigo Brasiliense*, 1:n.p.; Ferrand de Almeida, "Aclimação," p. 404; "Nota sobre Plantas Exoticas," Lagôa de Freitas [Rio de Janeiro], 4 October 1811, BN–RJ. The director of the Rio de Janeiro botanical garden gave seeds freely to visitors; see Maria Graham,

Journal of a Voyage to Brazil and Residence There during Part of the Years 1821, 1822, 1823 (London, 1824), pp. 163–164, 299.

19. Arthur Cézar Ferreira Reis, "A Ocupação de Caiena," in Sérgio Buarque de Holanda, ed., *História Geral da Civilização Brasileira, Tomo 2, O Brasil Monárquico* (São Paulo, 1962), 1:281–295, passim; Ciro F. C. Cardoso, "La Guyane française (1700–1817); Aspects économiques et sociaux" (Ph.D. dissertation, University of Paris X, 1971), pp. 349–355; Barbosa Rodrigues, *Hortus*, p. xxiii; [Castilho], *Instrucção*, pp. xxxiv–xxxv. J. Mabberley, *The Plant-Book: A Portable Dictionary of the Higher Plants* (Cambridge, England, 1987), p. 54, is uncertain whether starfruit and bilimbi (*Averrhoa carambola* and *A. bilimbi*) are Asian or Neotropical. Jalap (*Ipomoea purga*) was another transfer from Meso-America. Quassia is *Quassia amara*.

20. Luiz d'Abreu, "Relação das Plantas Exoticas e de Especiarias, Cultivadas no Real Jardim da Lagoa de Freitas," *Patriota*, 1 (March 1813), 19–22; João Conrado Niemeyer de Lavor, *Histórico do Jardim Botânico do Rio de Janeiro* (Rio de Janeiro, 1983), p. 6.

21. Barbosa Rodrigues, *Hortus*, p. iv; Abreu, "Relação," pp. 19–22; Felix de Avellar Brotero, *Compendio de Botanica* (Lisbon, 1788), 1:362–427; Johann Emanuel Pohl, *Viagem no Interior do Brasil* (Belo Horizonte, 1976 [1832]), pp. 55–56, 69. Tea was introduced to Charleston, South Carolina, in 1813; see William Saunders, *Tea-Culture as a Probable American Industry* (Washington, DC, 1879), pp. 3–5. On Indian tea, see Samuel Ball, *An Account of the Cultivation and Manufacture of Tea in China* (London, 1848); D. M. Guillemin, *Rapport sur sa mission au Brésil, ayant pour objet principal des récherches sur . . . le thé* (Paris [1839?]).

22. Edgar Valles, "Introdução da Cultura das Plantas de Especiarias do Oriente no Brasil," *Garcia da Horta*, 6 (1958), 711–718; Manoel Jacinto Nogueira da Gama, *Memoria sobre o Loureiro Cinnamomo vulgo Caneleira de Ceylão* (Lisbon, 1797), p. 7; José Roberto do Amaral Lapa, "O Brasil e as Drogas do Oriente," *Studia*, 18 (August 1966), 27–33, 37–38.

23. Auguste de Saint-Hilaire, *Voyage dans les provinces de Saint Paul et de Sainte Catherine* (Paris, 1851), 2:93; Pohl, *Viagem*, pp. 49–50; Arruda da Câmara, *Discurso*, p. 12; "Provincia de Rio de Janeiro [1814]" *Publicações do Arquivo Público Nacional*, 9 (1909), 111. Figs require a wasp for their development; it would be interesting to learn how that relationship was re-created in Brazil; see [Castilho], *Instrucção*, p. x.

24. Henry N. Ridley, *Spices* (London, 1912), pp. 158–159, 161, 206–208, 250–252; Barbosa Rodrigues, *Hortus*, p. vii; Ferrand de Almeida, "Aclimação," p. 408.

25. Dauril Alden, "Late Colonial Brazil, 1750–1808," in Bethell, *Cambridge History*, 2:640–641; idem, "Manoel Luís Vieira: Entrepreneur in Rio de Janeiro During Brazil's Eighteenth-Century Renaissance," *HAHR*, 39 (August 1959), 521–537; idem, *Royal Government*, p. 364; Maria Manuela Ramos de Souza Silva, "Os Produtos Coloniais e a Economia Européia do Século XVII; Uma Análise do Movimento de Exportação do Rio de Janeiro" (M.A. thesis, Federal University of Rio de Janeiro, 1981), pp. 106–109; Vandelli, "Memoria sobre Algumas Produçoens," p. 189; Alexandre Rodrigues Ferreira, "Memoria sobre a Introdução de Arroz Branca no Estado de Gram-Pará," *RIHGB*, 48 (1885), Pt. 1, 79–84.

26. Wilson Popenoe, *Manual of Tropical and Subtropical Fruits* (New York, 1974 [1920]), pp. 148, 286–290.

27. Decree of 1 March 1811, in Paulo Ferreira de Souza, *Legislação Florestal* (Rio de Janeiro, 1934–1935), 2:67; Arruda da Câmara, *Discurso*, p. 11; Auguste de Saint-Hilaire, *Plantes usuelles des Brésiliens* (Paris, 1824). Veloso de Oliveira partly denied inferiority; see *Memoria* . . . *São Paulo*, pp. 18–19; Silva Lisboa, *Discurso*, p. 42.

28. Mary C. Karasch, *Slave Life in Rio de Janeiro, 1808–1850* (Princeton, NJ, 1987), pp. 187–188; Vandelli, "Memoria sobre Algumas Produçõens," pp. 187–206; idem, "Catalogo de Varios Generos do Brazil, e Mais Colonias Portuguesas Que Ainda Não Estão no Ordinario Commercio," [ca. 1800?], BN–RJ; Jobson de A. Arruda, *Brasil*, pp. 163–164; Baltasar da Silva Lisboa, *Riqueza do Brasil em Madeiras de Construcção e Carpintaria* (Rio de Janeiro, 1823), p. 8.

29. Francisco Antônio de Sampaio, "Historia dos Reinos Vegetal, Animal e Mineral do Brasil, Pertencente à Medecina [1782, 1789]," *Anais da Biblioteca Nacional*, 89 (1969), 5–95), 1–91; Luis José de Godoy Torres, "Plantas Medicinais Indigenas de Minas Gerais," *Patriota*, 3 (March 1814), 62–73. Frederico W. Freise, *Plantas Medicinais Brasileiras* (São Paulo, 1934), lists more than 400 such plants. See also Saint-Hilaire, *Plantes usuelles*; idem, *Voyage dans les provinces de Rio de Janeiro et Minas Gerais* (Paris, 1830), 1:64.

30. Ipecac is *Psychotria ipecacuanha*; see Bernardino Antônio Gomes, "Memoria sobre a Ipecacuanha Fusca do Brasil; ou Cipó das Nossas Boticas [1801]," in idem, *Plantas Medicinais do Brasil* (São Paulo, 1972); Jobson de A. Arruda, *Brasil*, pp. 484–485; João Mariano de Deus e Souza, "Descripção do Districto da Parepetinga da Banda do Norte do Rio Paraiba," 31 August 1797, Manuscript Collection, Instituto Histórico e Geográfico Brasileiro.

31. Sarsaparilla is *Smilax* spp.; hemp, *Cannabis sativa*; cinchona, *Cinchona officinalis, C. calisaya*. See Alden, *Royal Government*, pp. 367, 369n, 370–372; José Roberto do Amaral Lapa, *A Bahia e a Carreira da India* (São Paulo, 1968), pp. 86–90, 95, 102; Manuel Arruda da Câmara, *Dissertação sobre as Plantas do Brazil que Podem Dar Linhos Proprios para Muitos Usos da Sociedade, e Suprir a Falta do Canhamo* (Rio de Janeiro, 1810); idem, "Memoria sobre a Cultura dos Algodoeiros," *Patriota*, 2 (January 1813), 32–33. Guaxima is *Urena lobata*; piassava, *Attalea funifera*. See Robert A. Voeks, "The Brazilian Fiber Belt: Harvest and Management of Piassava Palm," *Advances in Economic Botany*, 6 (1988), 254–267.

32. Theodor and Gustav Peckholt, *Historia das Plantas Medicinaes e Uteis no Brasil* (Rio de Janeiro, 1888), p. 107; Domenico Vandelli, Memoria sobre Alguns Generos das Colonias, n.d., BN–RJ; idem, "Memoria sobre Algumas Produçõens," pp. 187–206; [Castilho], *Instrucção*, p. xxxviii–xlii; Ferreira de Souza, *Legislação*, 2:62, 109. On quinine, see Daniel Headrick, *Tools of Empire* (New York, 1981), pp. 58–79.

33. Alexandre Rodrigues Ferreira, "Diario da Viagem Philosophica pela Capitania de São José do Rio Negro," *RIHGB*, 48 (1885), Pt. 1, 66; Ferreira da Câmara, *Ensaio*, p. 19.

34. "Sumario da Historia do Descobrimento da Cochonilha," pp. 3–13. Augusto da Silva Carvalho refers to a fuller unpublished version in "Academias Científicas," pp. 16–19.

35. Robert Southey, *History of Brazil* (London, 1810–1819), 3:813.

36. Conceição Velloso, "Tinturaria, Parte I, Cultura do Indigo e Extracção da sua Fecula," *O Fazendeiro do Brazil* (Lisbon, 1798), p. v; B. de Barros, "Noções

sobre a Cultura e Fabrica do Anil," *Patriota,* 2 (February 1813), 15–43; Dauril Alden, "The Growth and Decline of Indigo Production in Colonial Brazil: A Study in Comparative Economic History," *Journal of Economic History,* 25 (March 1965), 35–60; idem, *Royal Government,* pp. 372–376; Ramos de Souza Silva, "Produtos Coloniais," p. 110.

37. Luccock, *Notes,* pp. 318–319; Southey, *History,* 3:817; Luís de Pina, "Materiais para a Historia das Ciencias no Brasil (Medicina e Historia Natural)," in Congresso Luso-Brasileiro de História, *Anais* (Lisbon, 1940), 3:407–443; Alden, "Growth and Decline," cites "Memoria Historica da Cidade de Cabo Frio," *RIHGB,* 46 (1883), Pt. 1, 219; and Jerônimo Vieira de Abreu [brother of Manuel Luís Vieira], "Brevissima Instrucção para Uso dos Fabricantes de Anil," BN–RJ. See also "Mappa Geral dos Distr[it]os Que Estão de Hũa e Outra Banda do Rio Parahyba Relativos a Freguesia de Nossa Senhora da Conceição de Campo Alegre, 31 August 1797, Manuscript Collection, Instituto de Estudos Brasileiros, shows fourteen indigo works in this town. On plague, see Inácio Accioli de Vasconcellos, *Memoria Statistica da Provincia do Espirito Santo Escrito no Anno de 1828* (Vitória, 1978), p. F [sic].

38. Conceição Velloso, "Cultura do Indigo," p. vi.

39. Robert C. Smith, "The Wood-Beach at Recife," *The Americas,* 6 (October 1949), 215–233; Luci Maffei Hutter, "A Madeira do Brasil na Construção e Reparos de Embarcações," *Revista do Instituto de Estudos Brasileiros,* 26 (1986), 47–64; Alden, *Royal Government,* p. 358; Amaral Lapa, *Bahia,* p. 42. An exception, the building in Rio de Janeiro in 1665 of what was then the largest galleon ever seen, was noted by Charles Boxer, *Salvador de Sá and the Struggle for Brazil and Angola, 1602–1686* (2d ed.; Westport, CT, 1975).

40. The next paragraphs owe much to F. W. O. Morton's "The Royal Timber Trade in Colonial Brazil," *HAHR,* 58 (February 1978), 42–47. See also A. J. R. Russell-Wood, "Ports of Colonial Brazil," in Franklin Knight and Peggy Liss, eds., *Atlantic Port Cities* (Knoxville, TN, 1991), pp. 206–207; Amaral Lapa, *Bahia,* pp. 31–36; "Carta Regia do 13 de Março de 1797, em que S. Magestade Declara ser da Propriedade da sua Real Coroa Todas as Matas, e Arvoredos, que Estão á Borda da Costa ou Rios Navegaveis," *RIHGB,* 6 (1844), No. 24, 497; Ferreira de Souza, *Legislação,* 2:17–18; Decree of 19 March 1810, *Codigo Brasiliense,* 1:n.p.

41. Antônio Manuel de Mello Castro, "Providencias Interinas para a Conservação das Mattas e Paos Reaes da Costa desta Capitania [1799]," *Documentos Interessantes para a Historia e Costumes de S. Paulo,* 44 (1915), 172. The author thanks Robert Wilcox for this reference.

42. José de Mendonça de Matos Moraeira, "Das Matas das Alagoas, [1809]" *RIHGB,* 7 (October 1845), 483–492. Francisco Freire Alemão transcribed a 1792 document, "Inventario Geral das Madeiras de Construção do Brasil," *Estudos Botanicos,* vol. 12, BN–RJ, listing prices. The botanical names were: tapinhoá, *Mezilaurus* spp.; sucupira, *Ormosia* spp.; canela, *Ocotea* spp., *Nectandra* spp.; canjarana, *Cabralea canjerana*; jacarandá, *Dahlbergia* spp., *Maecherium* spp.; araribá, *Centrolobium robusta*; maçaranduba, *Manilkara elata*; pequi, *Caryocar brasiliensis*; genipap, *Genipa americana*; peroba, *Aspidosperma polyneuron*; urucurana, *Hieronyma alchorneoides*; vinhático, *Platymenia reticulata*. Silva Lisboa listed 268 species or varieties of merchantable timber and their uses in "Corte de Madeira," [post-1804], Manuscript Collection, Boston Public Library, pp. 134–144v.

43. Mello Castro, "Providencias Interinas," pp. 161–187; João da Costa Ferreira, "Copia do Plano que foi Aprovado, e Adoptado pello Exmo General Antônio Manuel de Mello Castro, e Mendonça . . . sobre os Rios, e Mattos q̃ Deverão Ficar Conservados pa. os Cortes Reais em a Costa do Mar da Capitania de S. Paulo," Rio de Janeiro, 17 September 1808, BN–RJ; idem, "Relação das Madeiras q̃ com Mais Facilidade se Achão nos Mattos q̃ Fazem Barra na Costa do Mar da Capitania de S. Paulo," 1808, BN–RJ; José Caetano de Barcellos Caetano to Viceroy, Campos, 14 June 1798, Arquivo Nacional, Rio de Janeiro, Caixa 746 (the latter kindly supplied by Larissa Brown); Thomas Lindley, *Narrative of a Voyage to Brazil* (London, 1805), p. 225–226. M. V. G. Fraga, "A Questão Florestal ao Tempo do Brasil Colonia," *Anuário Brasileiro de Economia Florestal* [hereafter ABEF], 3 (1950), 89–96, on Alagoas forests, exploited for curved wood shapes.

44. Silva Lisboa, "Corte de Madeira," pp. 26v–29, 31v, 44. On Silva Lisboa's career, see Pedro de Alcântara Bellegarde, "Elogio Historico do Fallecido Socio Honorario o Conselheiro Balthazar da Silva Lisboa," *RIHGB*, 2 (1840), Pt. 8, Supplement, 590–595. Another active judge conservator was José de Mendonça Matos Moreira; see Fraga, "Questão Florestal," pp. 89–96.

45. On enforcement, see Captain Antônio Muniz Vilaforte to Colonel Inacio de Andrade Soutomaior Rendon, Guaratiba, 22 August 1805, Arquivo Nacional, Ex 484, 2/260 (document kindly supplied by Sueann Caulfield); Mello Castro, "Providencias Interinas," p. 186n; Antônio Rodrigues Veloso de Oliveira, "Memoria sobre a Agricultura no Brasil [1810]," *RIHGB* (1873), Pt. 1, 101; "Observações sobre o Plano Feito para Conservação das Matas da Capitania de Bahia," Lisbon, 24 June 1799, BN–RJ; Morton, "Royal Timber," pp. 42–47; Costa Ferreira, "Copia do Plano"; Manuel Botelho de Almeida, "As Grandes Utilidades que Pode a Fazenda Real Receber em se Estabelecer no Rio de São Mateus Hoje o Assim Chamado Cortes de Madeiras," [1737], BN–RJ; Silva Lisboa, *Riqueza*, p. 11. By the 1790s recorded brazilwood exports were Northeastern; see Jobson de A. Arruda, *Brasil*, pp. 479–480; Manuel Moreira de Figueiredo, "Oficio de . . . Secretario da Junta do Commercio . . . sobre o Corte, Destruição e Extravio do Pau Brasil," [Rio de Janeiro], 1811, BN–RJ.

46. José Joaquim de Azeredo Coutinho, *Obras Econômicas* (São Paulo, 1966), p. 129.

47. Wilhelm von Eschwege, *Pluto Brasiliensis* (São Paulo, 1944 [1833]), p. 437. Veloso de Oliveira, *Memoria . . . São Paulo*, p. 17, proposed sawmills. Cf. Thomas R. Cox et al., *This Well-Wooded Land: Americans and Their Forests from Colonial Times to the Present* (Lincoln, NE, 1985), pp. 14–16. See also Silva Lisboa, "Corte de Madeira," p. 30; Ministry of Foreign Affairs and War report, "Nossa Situação Madeireira em 1811," *ABEF*, 5 (1952), 36–38.

48. Auguste de Saint-Hilaire, *Voyage dans le District des Diamans et sur le littoral du Brésil* (Paris, 1833), 2:133–134, 1:153.

49. José Vieira Couto, "Memoria sobre a Capitania de Minas Gerais [1799]," *RIHGB*, 11 (1849), Supplement, 319.

50. Silva Lisboa, "Corte de Madeira," pp. 3v, 26v, 28.

51. Saint-Hilaire, *Rio de Janeiro et Minas Gerais*, 2:287. Ferreira da Câmara letter in Rodrigues de Brito, *Cartas Economico-Politicas*, pp. 80–81. João Severiano Maciel da Costa, *Memorial sobre a Necessidade de Abolir a Introdução dos Escravos Africanos no Brasil* (Coimbra, 1821), pp. 42–43.

52. Observações sobre o Plano; Luccock, *Notes*, p. 296; Silva Lisboa, *Riqueza*, pp. 60–61; Decisão da Marinha, 11 January 1813, in Brazil, Ferreira da Souza, *Legislação Florestal*, 1:71; Edital, 26 January 1813, in *Codigo Brasiliense*, 2:n.p.

53. Saint-Hilaire, *District des Diamans*, 2:69, 71; James R. Wells, *Exploring and Travelling Three Thousand Miles through Brazil* (London, 1886), 1:70; Alfred Russel Wallace, *A Narrative of Travels on the Amazon and Rio Negro* (London, 1889 [1853]), p. 305; Hermann von Burmeister, *Viagem ao Brasil através das Províncias do Rio de Janeiro e Minas Gerais* (São Paulo, 1952 [1853]), p. 107. See also Louis d'Alincourt, *Memoria sobre a Viagem do Porto de Santos à Cidade de Cuiabá* (Belo Horizonte, 1975), p. 72.

54. Luccock, *Notes*, p. 300.

55. Eschwege, *Pluto*, p. 67; Accioli de Vasconcellos, *Memoria*, pp. Dv, E [sic].

56. Pohl, *Viagem*, p. 88; Auguste de Saint-Hilaire, *Tableau générale de la Province de Saint-Paul* (Paris, 1851), p. 75; idem, *Rio de Janeiro et Minas Gerais*, 2:182–184.

57. Silva Lisboa, *Anais*, 1:371; Veloso de Oliveira, *Memoria . . . São Paulo*, pp. 11, 18, 76–77, 82–84.

CHAPTER 7. THE FOREST UNDER BRAZILIAN RULE

1. Emílio Joaquim da Silva Maia, *Discurso sobre os Males que Tem Produzido no Brasil o Corte das Matas e sobre os Meios de os Remediar* (Rio de Janeiro, 1835).

2. Roderick J. Barman, *Brazil: The Forging of a Nation* (Stanford, CA, 1988), analyzes state building before and after independence.

3. Leslie Bethell, *The Abolition of the Brazilian Slave Trade* (Cambridge, England, 1970), pp. 1–61. Bethell shows that the British were disposed to allow Brazil to retain its conquest in the south, to pay an indemnity for the loss of the trade, and possibly to have assigned it a lesser share of the Portuguese debt. Olga Pantaleão discusses Pedro's hesitations over the British demands in "O Reconhecimento do Império; Mediação Inglesa," in Sérgio Buarque de Holanda, ed., *História Geral da Civilização Brasileira*, Tomo 2, *O Brasil Monárquico* (São Paulo, 1962), 1:342–346.

4. Fernando A. Novais, *Portugal e Brasil na Crise do Antigo Sistema Colonial (1777–1808)* (São Paulo, 1979), pp. 108–109.

5. José João Teixeira Coelho, "Instrucção para o Governo da Capitania de Minas Gerais [1780]," *Revista do Instituto Histórico e Geográfico Brasileiro* [hereafter *RIHGB*], 15 (1852), No. 7, 452. Johann Emanuel Pohl, *Viagem no Interior do Brasil* (Belo Horizonte, 1976 [1832]), pp. 335, 337.

6. Francisco José de Lacerda e Almeida (1790), quoted in Alice P. Canabrava, "A Repartição da Terra na Capitania de São Paulo, 1818," *Estudos Econômicos*, 2 (December 1972), 109.

7. Brazil, Ministério de Agricultura, *Legislação Florestal* (Rio de Janeiro, 1934), 1:16; *Codigo Brasiliense, ou Collecção das Leis, Alvarás, Decretos, Cartas Regias, & c., Promulgadas no Brasil* (Rio de Janeiro, 1811), 1:n.p. Decrees requiring surveys had been issued in 1713, 1731, 1748, 1753, 1763, and 1793. See Nanci Leonzo, "A Propriedade," in Maria Beatriz Nizza da Silva, coord., *O Império Luso-Brasileiro (1750–1822)* (São Paulo, 1986), pp. 66–73; Teixeira Coelho, "Instrucção," p. 451;

Raimundo José da Cunha Matos, *Corografia Histórica da Província de Minas Gerais* (2d ed.; Belo Horizonte, 1979 [1837]), 1:266. On sesmaria reform, see Antônio Rodrigues Veloso de Oliveira, "Memoria sobre a Agricultura no Brasil [1810]," *RIHGB,* 36 (1873), Pt. 1, 96–101.

8. José Arouche de Toledo Piza blamed rural instability on the failure to survey; see Leonzo, "Propriedade," pp. 66–67. On connivance and fraud, see Cunha Matos, *Corografia,* 1:264–265; Paulo Mercadante, *Os Sertões do Leste; Estudo de uma Região: A Mata Mineira* (Rio de Janeiro, 1973), pp. 79, 82. Inácio Accioli de Vasconcellos counted unoccupied sesmarias in Espírito Santo in *Memoria Statistica da Provincia do Espirito Santo Escrito no Anno de 1828* (Vitória, 1978), pp. D, E [*sic*]. See also Auguste de Saint-Hilaire, *Voyage dans les provinces de Rio de Janeiro et Minas Gerais* (Paris, 1830), 1:239.

9. *Codigo Brasiliense,* 1:n.p.

10. Law of 27 October 1823, Paulo Ferreira de Souza, *Legislação Florestal* (Rio de Janeiro, 1934–35), 1:101; Leopoldo Collor Jobim, "Um Estudo sobre o Reformismo Agrário no Brasil do Século XVIII," in Sociedade Brasileira de Pesquisa Histórica, Reunião, 2, *Anais* (São Paulo, 1983), pp. 93–94; Antônio Rodrigues Veloso de Oliveira, "Memoria sobre a Agricultura no Brasil [1810]," *RIHGB,* 36 (1873), Pt. 1, 104–106; José Bonifâcio de Andrada e Silva, *Obras Científicas, Políticas e Sociais* (São Paulo, n.d.), 2:95–114, 3:20. The quotation is cited by Alberto José de Sampaio, *Phytogeographia do Brasil* (2d ed. rev. and enl.; São Paulo, 1938), p. 23. The 1823 Constituent Assembly's report on land law was lost; see Brazil, Câmara de Deputados, *Arquivo da Assembléia Geral Constituinte e Legislativo do Império do Brasil; Inventário Analítico Arquivístico e Sinopse de Tramitação* (Brasília, 1987), p. 149 (Sueann Caulfield's assistance in searching for this report is appreciated).

11. Administrative decision of 11 June 1829, Ministério de Agricultura, *Legislação,* p. 105.

12. Paulino José Soares de Souza, President of Province, *Mensagem á Assembleia Legislativa Provincial, 1 de Março de 1840* (Rio de Janeiro, 1840), p. 23.

13. José Murilo de Carvalho, "Modernização Frustrada: A Política de Terras no Império," *Revista Brasileira de História,* 1 (March 1981), 39–57; Vilma Paraíso Ferreira de Almada, *Escravismo e Transição; Espírito Santo, 1850–1888* (Rio de Janeiro, 1984), p. 82; Warren Dean, "Latifundia and Land Policy in Nineteenth-Century Brazil," *Hispanic American Historical Review* [hereafter *HAHR*], 51 (November 1971), 606–625; County Council to President of Province, Rio Claro, São Paulo, 13 March 1847 and 7 December 1857, TI–OD 396, Arquivo Público do Estado de São Paulo [hereafter APESP].

14. Cunha Matos, *Corografia,* 1:266.

15. Warren Dean, *Rio Claro: A Brazilian Plantation System, 1820–1920* (Stanford, 1976), p. 130.

16. Alida C. Metcalf, "Fathers and Sons: The Politics of Inheritance in a Colonial Brazilian Township," *HAHR,* 66 (August 1986), 455–484.

17. John Hemming, *Red Gold: The Conquest of the Brazilian Indians, 1500–1760* (Cambridge, MA, 1978), pp. 475–482; Auguste de Saint-Hilaire, *Voyage dans le district des Diamans et sur le littoral du Brésil* (Paris, 1833), 2:216; idem, *Voyage dans les provinces de Rio de Janeiro et Minas Gerais* (Paris, 1830), 2:148; Luiz Thomaz de Navarro, "Itinerario da Viagem que Fez por Terra da Bahia ao Rio de

Janeiro," *RIHGB*, 7 (1845), No. 28, 446–449; *Codigo Brasiliense*, 1:n.p.; Manuel Tavares da Costa Miranda and Alípio Bandeira, "Memorial acerca da Antiga e Moderna Legislação Indígena," in L. Humberto de Oliveira, ed., *Coletânea de Leis, Atos e Memórias Referentes ao Indígena Brasileiro* (Rio de Janeiro, 1947), pp. 66–68.

18. Cunha Matos, *Corografia*, 2:63–65; Tavares and Bandeira, "Memorial," pp. 66–68; Laura de Mello e Souza, *Os Desclassificados do Ouro: A Pobreza Mineira no Século XVIII* (Rio de Janeiro, 1982), pp. 80, 83; Marcos Magalhães Rubinger, "O Desaparecimento das Tribos Indígenas em Minas Gerais e a Sobrevivência dos Indios Maxacali," *Revista do Museu Paulista* [hereafter *RMP*], n.s., 14 (1963), 240.

19. See the case of indigenes, Campinas, 1810, and São Carlos, 1826, in TI–OD 849, APESP; Auguste de Saint-Hilaire, *Voyage dans les provinces de Saint Paul et de Sainte Catherine* (Paris, 1851), 1:454; Joaquim Antonio Pinto Junior, *Memoria sobre a Cathechese e Civilisação dos Indigenas da Provincia de S. Paulo* (Santos, 1862), p. 24; Teófilo Otóni, "Noticia sobre os selvagens do Mucuri," *RIHGB*, 21 (1858), No. 2, 196, 199; Georg W. Freyreiss, "Viagem a Varios Tribus de Selvagens na Capitania de Minas Gerais," *Revista do Instituto Histórico e Geográfico de São Paulo* [hereafter *RIHGSP*], 6 (1900–1901), 280.

20. Oiliam José, *Marlière, o Civilizador* (Belo Horizonte, 1958), pp. 34–39, 85, 89; "Guido Thomaz Marlière [Documents]," *Revista do Arquivo Público Mineiro*, 10 (1905), 424–425; Saint-Hilaire, *District des Diamans*, 2:337–340; João Severiano Maciel da Costa, letter to Governor of Espirito Santo, Rio de Janeiro, 28 January 1824, *RIHGB*, 6 (1844), No. 24, 488–489.

21. "Guido Thomaz Marlière," pp. 509–510, 609; Freyreiss, "Viagem," p. 238.

22. "Guido Thomaz Marlière," pp. 520, 595, 610, 612; letter, signed by 154 residents, Ponte Nova, 8 April 1826, and another signed by 166 residents, Ribeira de Santa Anna da Onça Pequena, 17 October 1827, to President of Province of Minas Gerais, Manuscript Collection, Biblioteca Nacional, Rio de Janeiro [hereafter BN–RJ].

23. J. Resende Silva, "A Formação Territorial de Minas Gerais," in Congresso Sul-Riograndense de História e Geografia, 3, Porto Alegre, 1940, *Anais* (Porto Alegre, 1940), 2:686; José, *Marlière*, pp. 55, 137–140, 240, 533; Antonio Muniz de Souza, *Viagens e Observações de hum Brasileiro* (Rio de Janeiro, 1834), pp. 94, 139, 141; José Marcelino Pereira de Vasconcelos, *Ensaio sobre a Historia e Estatistica da Provincia de Espirito Santo* (Vitória, 1858), pp. 130–132, 154–155; Saint-Hilaire, *Rio de Janeiro et Minas Gerais*, 1:38; idem, *District des Diamans*, p. 340.

24. Miranda and Bandeira, "Memorial," pp. 66–68; José Bonifâcio de Andrada e Silva, *Apontamentos para a Civilização dos Indios Bravos do Império do Brasil* (Santos, 1965 [1823]); Carlos de Araujo Moreira Neto, "A Política Indigenista Brasileira durante o Século XIX" (Ph.D. dissertation, University of the State of São Paulo–Rio Claro, 1971), p. 355.

25. Moreira Neto, "Política," pp. 360–365, 370–372; Miranda and Bandeira, "Memorial," pp. 30–31; Pinto Junior, *Memoria*, pp. 1–3; Jacinto de Palazzolo, *Nas Selvas do Mucuri e do Rio Doce* (Petrópolis, 1945), pp. 34–35. Palazzolo, *Selvas*, p. 66, records Brother Angelo de Sassoferrato's fright when led into the forest. See also Ary França, *A Marcha do Café e as Frentes Pioneiras* (Rio de Janeiro, 1960), p. 181; Manuel Francisco Ferreira Correia, *Noticia sobre o Estado do Paraná* (Curitiba, 1893), pp. 9–10.

26. Otóni, "Noticia," pp. 192–194; Egon Schaden, "Os Primitivos Habitantes

do Território Paulista," in *Ensaios Paulistas* (São Paulo, 1958), pp. 756–757; John Henry Elliot, "Resumo do Itinerario de uma Viagem Exploradora pelos Rios Verde, Itararé, Paranapanema e seus Affluentes," *RIHGB*, 9 (1847), No. 1, pp. 17–42. Curt Nimuendaju reconstructs oral traditions of a migrating Guarani group in the 1830s in "Apontamentos sobre os Guarani," *RMP*, n.s., 8 (1954), 1–33. See also Maria Inês Ladeira and Gilberto Aranha, *Os Indios da Serra do Mar: A Presença Mbyá-Guarani em São Paulo* (São Paulo, 1988), pp. 7–8, 13, citing R. Kione, "O Aldeamento do Rio Itariry," *Revista de Sciencia, Letras e Artes* (1909), p. 57.

27. Otóni, "Noticia," pp. 193, 197–198; João Francisco Tidei Lima, "A Ocupação da Terra e a Destruição dos Indios na Região de Bauru" (M.A. thesis, University of São Paulo, 1978), pp. 85, 89.

28. Otóni, "Noticia," pp. 201–204, 210, 221; idem, *A Colonização do Mucuri* (Rio de Janeiro, 1859), pp. 4, 57–58; Paulo Pinheiro Chagas, *Teófilo Otóni, O Ministro do Povo* (3d ed.; Belo Horizonte, 1978), pp. 137–241. Hermenegildo Antônio Barbosa d'Almeida, "Viagem ás Villas de Caravellas, Viçosa, Porto Alegre, de Mucury, e aos Rios Mucury e Peruipe," *RIHGB*, 8 (1846), No. 4, 437.

29. Palazzolo, *Selvas*, pp. 64, 191, 195; Instituto Brasileiro de Geografia e Estatística, *Enciclopédia dos Municípios Brasileiros* (Rio de Janeiro, 1959), 27:347–348.

30. Antonina's arms were a lion rampant, presenting a Bible and rosary to an indigene; see Baron of Antonina to President of Province, n.d., APESP, Polícia, No. 110, 1872. Saint-Hilaire, *Saint Paul et Sainte Catherine*, 1:460–461; José da Matta Cardim, *Memorial Apresentado ao Exm. Sr. Dr. Rodolpho Miranda, Ministro de Agricultura, Industria e Commercio* (São Paulo, 1910).

31. José Joaquim Machado de Oliveira, "Apontamentos sobre a Provincia do Espirito Santo," *RIHGB*, 19 (1856), No. 2, 254–255; Palazzolo, *Selvas*, p. 197; Pinto Junior, *Memoria*, p. 4. In 1878 the director of Minas Gerais's Service of Catechesis and Civilization estimated the native population outside aldeias at 4,000, all north of the Doce River; see Oiliam José, *Indígenas de Minas Gerais* (Belo Horizonte, 1961), p. 16; William John Steains, "O Valle do Rio Doce," *Revista da Sociedade de Geografia do Rio de Janeiro*, 4 (1888), 213–226.

32. Muniz de Souza, *Viagens*, pp. 24–27, 29, 30.

33. Thomas Flory, *Judge and Jury in Imperial Brazil, 1808–1871: Social Control and Political Stability in the New State* (Austin, TX, 1981), pp. 49–68; Osny Duarte Pereira, *Direito Florestal Brasileiro* (Rio de Janeiro, 1950), pp. 96–101.

34. Antônio Leôncio Pereira Ferraz, *Terra da Ibirapitanga* (Rio de Janeiro, 1939), pp. 76n, 77n, 81–83, chart opposite p. 84; Marquis of Baependi to Director, Museu Nacional, 26 October 1826, Museu Nacional, Rio de Janeiro, Letter Book 1.

35. Saint-Hilaire, *Rio de Janeiro et Minas Gerais*, 2:174; "Guido Thomaz Marlière," pp. 425, 492–493; Paulo Mercadante, *Os Sertões do Leste: Estudo de uma Região, A Mata Mineira* (Rio de Janeiro, 1973), pp. 42, 44; Arnaldo Augusto Addor, *Considerações acerca de Poaia* (Rio de Janeiro, 1947), p. 3. Addor also mentions *Ornithion cinerascans*, not confirmed in Helmut Sick, *Ornitologia Brasileira* (3d ed.; Brasília, 1984), 2:551. See also Heinrich Wilhelm Schott, *Tagebücher des k. k. Gärtners, Hrn. H. Schott in Brasilien* (Brünn, 1822), p. 22; Muniz de Souza, *Viagens*, p. 176; United Nations, Food and Agriculture Organization, Forestry Department, *Some Medicinal Forest Plants of Africa and Latin America* (Rome, n.d.), pp. 2, 167–169.

36. Muniz de Souza, *Viagens*, p. 24; Charles James Fox Bunbury, *Botanical*

Fragments (London, 1883), p. 32; Georg W. Freyreiss, "Viagem ao Interior do Brasil nos Annos de 1814–1815," *RIHGSP*, 11 (1906), 188; Hermann von Burmeister, *Viagem ao Brasil através das Províncias do Rio de Janeiro e Minas Gerais* (São Paulo, 1952 [1853]), p. 117; José Ferreira Carrato, "O Primeiro Polo de Criação de Gado que Houve no Triângulo Mineiro," *Estudos Históricos*, 12 (1973), 99.

37. Eddy Stols, "A Flora Brasileira e os Naturalistas e Horticultores Belgas no Século XIX," *Revista de História*, 44 (1972), No. 89, 155–172; Louis van Houtte, "Notice sur quelques plantes nouvelles, cultivées au Jardin Botanique de Bruxelles," *L'Horticulture Belge*, 3 (August 1836), 247–251.

38. José da Saldanha da Gama, *Discours prononcé au Congrés* [sic] *International des Economes Forestiers à Vienna en 1873* (Rio de Janeiro, 1874), pp. 9–10.

39. Burmeister, *Viagem*, pp. 131, 133; Frederico C. Hoehne, *Excursão Botanica Feita pelo Sul do Estado de Minas Gerais e Regiões Limítrofes do Estado de São Paulo* (São Paulo, 1939 [1927]), pp. 40, 46; Álvaro Astolfo da Silveira, *Flora e Serras Mineiras* (Belo Horizonte, 1908), p. 155; Hermann von Ihering, "A Devastação e Conservação das Mattas," *RMP*, 8 (1911), 485. The county was Capanema.

40. Muniz de Souza, *Viagens*, pp. 78–79; Charles Darwin, *Charles Darwin's Beagle Diary* (Cambridge, England, 1988 [1832]), pp. 70–71; Burmeister, *Viagem*, p. 117; Mulford B. and Racine Sarasy Foster, *Brazil* (Lancaster, PA, 1945), p. 122.

41. Daniel Pedro Müller, *Ensaio d'um Quadro Estatistico da Provincia de S. Paulo* (2d ed.; São Paulo, 1923 [1837]), p. 56. Information on exports is in Sebastião Ferreira Soares, *Estatistica do Commerico Maritimo do Brazil do Exercicio de 1869–1870* (Rio de Janeiro, 1874). See also Martim Francisco Ribeiro de Andrada, "Diario de uma Viagem Mineralogica, pela Provincia de S. Paulo no Anno de 1805," *RIHGB*, 9 (1847), No. 4, 527; Burmeister, *Viagem*, p. 131; Muniz de Souza, *Viagens*, p. 128; Darwin, *Beagle Diary*, p. 57; Construction contract, 26 August 1877, Rio Claro, São Paulo, Segundo Cartório de Notas, Livro de Notas, No. 13; Francisco P. de Lacerda Werneck, *Memoria sobre a Fundação e Custeio de uma Fazenda na Provincia do Rio de Janeiro* (Rio de Janeiro, 1847), p. 13.

42. Cícero Moraes, *Geografia do Espírito Santo* (Vitória, 1974), p. 127; José de Saldanha da Gama, "Relatorio: Botanica Industrial no Brasil," in *Relatorio sobre a Exposição Universal de 1867* (Paris, 1868), 1:161–163. Cf. S. V. Vigneron Jousselandière, *Novo Manual Pratico de Agricultura Intertropical* (Rio de Janeiro, 1860), p. 50.

43. Muniz de Souza, *Viagens*, p. 149; Burmeister, *Viagem*, p. 171; Saint-Hilaire, *District des Diamans*, 2:17, 21, 289–290; Machado de Oliveira, "Apontamentos," p. 255; Schott, *Tagebucher*, pp. 51–52.

44. Lacerda Werneck, *Memoria*, pp. 13–14.

45. José de Saldanha da Gama, *Configuração e Estudo Botanico dos Vegetaes Seculares da Provincia do Rio de Janeiro e de Outros Pontos do Brasil, Segunda Parte* (Rio de Janeiro, 1872), pp. 34–35.

46. José Gregorio de Moraes Navarro, *Discurso sobre o Melhoramento de Economia Rustica do Brasil* (Lisbon, 1799), p. 13.

CHAPTER 8. COFFEE DISPOSSESSES THE FOREST

1. Wilhelm von Eschwege, *Pluto Brasiliensis* (São Paulo, 1944 [1832]), 1:72–77).

2. Marshall C. Eakin, *British Enterprise in Brazil: The St. John d'el Rey Mining Company and the Morro Velho Gold Mine, 1830–1960* (Durham, NC, 1989), pp. 12–18.

3. Andrada e Silva to Guarda, 25 November 1822, Archive of the Museu Nacional, Rio de Janeiro, Book 1. Helmut Sick also noticed this episode in *Ornitologia Brasileira* (Rio de Janeiro, 1988), 1:110.

4. Charles Darwin, *Charles Darwin's* Beagle *Diary* (Cambridge, England, 1988 [1832]), p. 68.

5. Leandro do Sacramento, *Memoria Economica sobre a Plantação, Cultura, e Preparação do Chá* (Rio de Janeiro, 1825); Alexander Caldcleugh, *Travels in South America during the Years 1819–20–21* (London, 1825), 1:29; Luís de Almeida Nogueira Porto, "Chineses no Bananal," *D.O. Leitura,* 10 (May 1992), 5; José Arouche de Toledo Rondon, "Pequena Memoria de Plantação e Cultura do Cha," *Auxiliador da Indústria Nacional,* 2 (May 1834), 145–152; (June 1834), 179–184. See also Januário da Cunha Barbosa, "Memoria sobre a Vantagem, Necessidade, e Meio Mais Prompto de Propagar a Cultura e Manipulação do Cha," *Auxiliador da Indústria Nacional,* 2 (September 1834), 262–273; João Barbosa Rodrigues, *Hortus Fluminensis, ou Breve Noticia sobre as Plantas Cultivadas no Jardim Botanico do Rio de Janeiro* (Rio de Janeiro, 1894), p. xxiii; Samuel Ball, *An Account of the Cultivation and Manufacture of Tea in China* (London, 1848), p. 361; J.–Ch. Heusser and G. Claraz, "Des principaux produits des provinces brésiliennes de Rio-de-Janeiro et de Minas Gerais," *Flores des Serres et des Jardins de l'Europe,* 14 (1859), 183–189.

6. Barbosa Rodrigues, *Hortus,* p. xxiii; D. M. Guillemin, *Rapport sur sa mission au Brésil, ayant pour objet principal des récherches sur . . . le thé* (Paris, 1839); John M. Baker, *A View of the Commerce between the United States and Rio de Janeiro, Brazil* (Washington, DC, 1838), p. 1.

7. Virgílio Noya Pinto, *O Ouro Brasileiro e o Comêrcio Anglo-Português* (São Paulo, 1979), pp. 191, 196–198; José Jobson de A. Arruda, *O Brasil no Comêrcio Colonial* (São Paulo, 1980), pp. 361–362, 375–376.

8. José de Souza Azevedo Pizarro e Araujo mentions ubiquitous engenhos and engenhocas; see, for example, his *Memórias Históricas do Rio de Janeiro e das Províncias Anexas* (Rio de Janeiro, 1945 [1820–1822]), 2:67. See also Gabriel Bittencourt, *A Formação Econômica do Espírito Santo (O Roteiro da Industrialização)* (Vitória, 1987), p. 53; Antonio Muniz de Souza, *Viagens e Observações de hum Brasileiro* (Rio de Janeiro, 1834), pp. 127–129; João José Carneiro da Silva, *Estudos Agricolas* (Rio de Janeiro, 1872), pp. 4, 5; José Carneiro da Silva, *Memoria Topographica e Historica sobre os Campos dos Goytacazes* (2d ed.; Rio de Janeiro, 1907 [1819]), p. 57; João Oscar, *Escravidão e Engenhos* (Rio de Janeiro, 1985), pp. 44, 46–48, 55; John Luccock, *Notes on Rio de Janeiro and the Southern Parts of Brazil Taken during a Residence of Ten Years in the Country from 1808 to 1818* (London, 1820), p. 294; Renato da Silveira Martins, "Paisagens Culturais da Baixada Fluminense," *Boletim da Faculdade de Filosofia, Ciências e Letras,* 110 *Geografia* (1950), No. 4, 50–51; Robert Southey, *History of Brazil* (London, 1819), 3:817; Auguste de Saint-Hilaire, *Voyage dans le District des Diamans et sur le littoral du Brésil* (Paris, 1833), 2:128.

9. Corcino Medeiros dos Santos, "Algumas Notas para o Estudo da Economia de São Paulo no Final do Século XVIII," *Estudos Históricos* (1975), No. 13, 95;

Daniel Pedro Müller, *Ensaio d'um Quadro Estatistico da Provincia de S. Paulo* (São Paulo, 1837); Maria Thereza Schorer Petrone, *A Lavoura Canavieira em São Paulo* (São Paulo, 1968), pp. 43–44.

10. Ministério de Agricultura, *Legislação Florestal* (Rio de Janeiro, 1934), 1:57–59; Raimundo José de Cunha Matos, *Corografia Histórica da Província de Minas Gerais* (Belo Horizonte, 1979 [1837]), p. 272; Miguel Costa Filho, *A Cana-de-Açucar em Minas Gerais* (Rio de Janeiro, 1963), pp. 143, 103–118, 169–170; João Rodrigues de Brito, *Cartas Economico-Politicas sobre a Agricultura e Comercio da Bahia* (Lisbon, 1821), p. 6.

11. *Codigo Brasiliense, ou Collecção das Leis, Alvarás, Decretos, Cartas Regias, &c., Promulgadas no Brasil* (Rio de Janeiro, 1811), 1:n.p.; Cunha Matos, *Corografia*, 2:272.

12. Johann Emanuel Pohl, *Viagem no Interior do Brasil* (Belo Horizonte, 1976 [1832]), pp. 69, 72; Muniz de Souza, *Viagens*, p. 178; Caldcleugh, *Travels*, 1:52; Luccock, *Notes*, p. 350; Cunha Matos, *Corografia*, 2:272; Oscar, *Escravidão*, pp. 105, 112. On Bourbon cane, see J. H. Galloway, *The Sugar Cane Industry: An Historical Geography from Its Origins to 1914* (Cambridge, England, 1989), pp. 96–97; Stuart B. Schwartz, *Sugar Plantations in the Formation of Brazilian Society: Bahia, 1550–1835* (Cambridge, England, 1985), p. 431.

13. Saint-Hilaire noted planting cycles in various places: *Voyage dans les provinces de Saint Paul et de Sainte Catherine* (Paris, 1851), 1: 329, 348, 362; idem, *District des Diamans*, 2:236.

14. Muniz de Souza, *Viagens*, p. 123.

15. See tables in Stuart Schwartz, "Colonial Brazil, c. 1580–c. 1750: Plantationas and Peripheries," 2:431, and Dauril Alden, "Late Colonial Brazil, 1750–1808," 2:631, both in Leslie Bethell, ed., *Cambridge History of Latin America* (Cambridge, England, 1984). See also Jobson de A. Arruda, *Brasil*, pp. 361–362, 375–376; Sebastião Ferreira Soares, *Notas Estatísticas sobre a Produção Agricola e a Carestia dos Géneros Alimentícios no Império do Brasil* (2d ed.; Rio de Janeiro, 1977 [1860]), pp. 215, 216. For São Paulo estimates, see Peter Eisenberg, *Homens Esquecidos: Escravos e Trabalhadores Livres no Brasil, Séculos XVIII e XIX* (Campinas, Brazil, 1989), p. 328; Schorer Petrone, *Lavoura*, pp. 48, 166; and Medeiros dos Santos, "Algumas Notas." "Industria Saccharina do Brazil," *Revista do Imperial Instituto Fluminense de Agricultura* [hereafter *RIIFA*, 8 (September 1877), 87–98, provides yield and conversion data. The modern conversion rate is about 9 to 1; see Instituto Interamericano de Cooperación para la Agricultura [hereafter IICA], *Compendio de Agronomia Tropical* (San José, Costa Rica, 1989), 2:529–531. João Rodrigues de Brito et al., *A Economia Brasileira no Alvorecer do Século XIX* (Salvador, n.d.), cite use of new ovens, which reduced wood consumption from 12 to 4 kilograms per kilogram of sugar; cited by Ruy Gama, *Engenho e Tecnologia* (São Paulo 1983), pp. 167–168.

16. There are few exact references to firewood requirements: see Schorer Petrone, *Lavoura*, p. 78. Costa Filho, *Cana-de-Açucar*, p. 380, shows 3.4 kg wood per kg sugar obtained in a modern central in 1887. It seems doubtful that earlier mills would have achieved better than 5:1. Modern small producers, the equivalent of engenhocas, in Costa Rica achieve 1:1. See Humberto Labarthe F. and Carlos Reiche C., *Consumo de leña y otros combustibles en los trapiches de San Ramón, Costa*

Rica (Turrialba, Costa Rica, 1989); Francisco Peixoto de Lacerda Werneck, *Memória sobre a Fundação de uma Fazenda na Província do Rio de Janeiro* (Brasília and Rio de Janeiro, 1985 [1847]), p. 74; Carneiro da Silva, *Estudos*, p. 28.

17. Schorer Petrone, *Lavoura*, pp. 80, 82.

18. Júlio Brandão Sobrinho, *A Lavoura de Canna e a Indústria Assucareira dos Estados Paulista e Fluminense* (São Paulo, 1912), p. 8. On bagasse, see Arcângelo de Ancora, "Memoria sobre as Novas Fornalhas para Cozer o Assucar com o Bagaço," *O Patriota: Jornal Litterario, Politico, Mercantil, etc., do Rio de Janeiro* [hereafter *Patriota*], 1 (May 1813), 32, 36. On caiena, see Heusser and Claraz, "Principaux produits," p. 191; Carneiro da Silva, *Estudos*, p. 28.

19. Saint-Hilaire, *District des Diamans*, 2:131; Muniz de Souza, *Viagens*, p. 127.

20. Galloway, *Sugar Cane Industry*, pp. 139–141.

21. Augusto de Lima Junior, *Notícias Históricas (de norte a sul)* (Rio de Janeiro, 1953), pp. 23–24; Manuel Barata, *A Antiga Produção e Exportação do Pará* (Belém, 1915). The Brazilian officer was Francisco de Melo Palheta. See also Joaquim Eduardo Leite Brandão, *Dissertação sobre o Cafeseiro* (Rio de Janeiro, 1842), p. 8; Francisco Freire Alemão, "Memoria; Quais São as Principais Plantas Que Hoje se Acham Aclimatizadas no Brasil?" *RIHGB* 19 (1856), No. 4, 563–570; "Os Portugueses e a Flora do Brasil," *Documentos dos Arquivos Portugueses Que Importam ao Brasil* (September 1946), No. 15, p. 3. The judge was João Alberto Castello Branco. There are alternate versions. Domingos Borges de Barros had been told by José Correa da Serra that Hopman had introduced coffee himself; see B*** [Domingos Borges de Barros], "Memoria sobre o Café, sua Historia, Cultura e Amanhos," *Patriota*, 1 (May 1813), 11. Domenico Vandelli implied that Hopman had obtained planting material directly from Asia: "Memoria sobre Alguns Generos das Colonias," n.d., Manuscript Collection, Biblioteca Nacional, Rio de Janeiro [hereafter BN–RJ]. Francis Castelnau was told by an aged monk that he had seen the first plants from Cayenne some sixty years before; see *Expedição à Regiões Centrais da América do Sul* (São Paulo, 1949 [1843]), 1:87. See also Manuel Ferreira da Câmara, *Ensaio de Descripção Fizica e Economica da Comarca dos Ilheus na America* (Lisbon, 1789), p. 21.

22. [Borges de Barros], "Memoria," p. 11.

23. On growing conditions and botany of *Coffea arabica*, see José Setzer, *Sobre a Ecologia do Café* (São Paulo, 1949), pp. 4–18; M. N. Clifford and K. C. Willson, eds., *Coffee: Botany, Biochemistry and Production of Beans and Beverage* (Westport, CT, 1985), pp. 13–156; IICA, *Compendio*, 2:495–515.

24. Lacerda Werneck, *Memoria*, p. 29. See also Frederico Leopoldo César Burlámaqui, *Monografia do Cafeseiro e do Café* (Rio de Janeiro, 1858), pp. 42–43.

25. Lacerda Werneck, *Memoria*, p. 59. For a longer, ranked list of padrões, see Theodor and Gustav Peckholt, *Historia das Plantas Alimentares e de Gozo do Brasil* (Rio de Janeiro, 1871), 1:32–33; Stanley J. Stein, *Vassouras: A Brazilian Coffee County, 1850–1900* (Cambridge, MA, 1957), p. 32. On the humus layer, Charles James Fox Bunbury, *Narrativa de Viagem de um Naturalista Inglês ao Rio de Janeiro e Minas Gerais (1833–1835)* (Rio de Janeiro, 1943), p. 91; Inácio Accioli de Vasconcellos, *Memoria Statística da Província do Espírito Santo Escrito no Anno de 1828* (Vitória, 1978), pp. D, E [*sic*].

26. Garlic tree is *Gallesia goarzema*. Borges de Barros vaunted, in his "Memoria," *Patriota*, 1 (June 1813), 31–35, a familiarity with French agricultural and botanical authors, but he does not appear to have attempted to plant coffee: He was wary of uncritically applying techniques tried elsewhere. The survival of *padrões* may be seen in nineteenth-century plantation portraits: Acervo Galeria de Arte, *O Grupo Grimm; Paisagens Brasileiras no Século XIX* (Rio de Janeiro, 1980).

27. Socrates Alvim and L. F. Clerot, "A Cultura," in *Minas e o Bicentenario do Cafeeiro no Brasil, 1727–1927* (Belo Horizonte, 1929), 1:104–105. The quotation is from Joaquim Caetano da Silva Guimarães, *A Agricultura em Minas Gerais* (Rio de Janeiro, 1865), pp. 21–22. See also Stein, *Vassouras*, pp. 30–31.

28. Alvim and Clerot, "Cultura," 1:105.

29. Luccock, *Notes*, pp. 357–358.

30. Rio de Janeiro (Province), *Legislação Provincial do Rio de Janeiro de 1835 a 1850* (Niterói, 1851), p. 495; Rio de Janeiro (Province), *Collecção de Leis, Decretos e Regulamentos . . . 1852* (Rio de Janeiro, 1852), p. 140; S. V. Vigneron Jousselandière, *Novo Manual Pratico de Agricultura Intertropical* (Rio de Janeiro, 1860), p. 46. Alexandre José de Melo Moraes, *Phytographia; ou Botanica Brasileira, Applicada á Medicina, ás Artes e á Industria* (Rio de Janeiro, 1881), p. xxxii. Luccock, *Notes*, p. 358. M. R. Lezé, "Culture et industrie du café," *Annales Agronomiques*, 18 (1892), 50. Georg W. Freyreiss noted numerous such fires in the drought year 1814–15: "Viagem ao Interior do Brasil nos Annos de 1814–1815," *Revista do Instituto Historico e Geografico de São Paulo*, 11 (1906), 180; Bunbury saw a large burned tract in Minas Gerais in another drought, 1834, *Narrativa*, p. 91.

31. Hermann von Burmeister, *Viagem ao Brasil através das Províncias do Rio de Janeiro e Minas Gerais* (São Paulo, 1952 [1853]), p. 151.

32. Lourenço Granato, *A Queima e seus Efeitos na Fertilidade do Solo* (São Paulo, 1918), p. 59. Both were scientists; Granato, an Italian émigré, was a director of the Secretariat of Agriculture of the state of São Paulo.

33. Adolphe d'Assier, *Le Brésil contemporaine* (Paris, 1867), pp. 124–125; J. Barbosa Rodrigues, "A Diminuição das Aguas no Brasil," in Congresso Científico Latino-Americano, 3, Rio de Janeiro, 1909, *Relatorio Geral* (Rio de Janeiro, 1905), 3A:206; "Questões Propostas para Serem Discutidas por Escripto," and "Questão do Nevoeiro, ou Enfumaçado," *Trabalhos da Sociedade Vellosiana*, 1 (1851), 77–84; 2 (1852), 106–108.

34. Besides Werneck, *Memoria*, other contemporary planters' manuals include João Joaquim Ferreira de Aguiar, *Pequena Memoria sobre a Plantação, Cultura e Colheita de Café* (Rio de Janeiro, 1836); Carlos Augusto Taunay, *Manual do Agricultor Brasileiro* (Rio de Janeiro, 1839); Joaquim Eduardo Leite Brandão, *Dissertação sobre o Cafeseiro* (Rio de Janeiro, 1842); Agostinho Rodrigues Cunha, *Arte da Cultura e Preparação do Café* (Rio de Janeiro, 1844); Burlamáqui, *Monografia*; Jousselandière, *Novo Manual*, p. 48.

35. Emílio Augusto Goeldi, "Resumo do Relatorio sobre a Molestia do Cafeeiro na Provincia do Rio de Janeiro," *RIIFA*, 19 (March 1868), 43.

36. Carlos Conceição, "A Decadencia dos Cafezais Fluminenses e os Fatores de sua Degradação Fisiologica," *Revista do Departamento Nacional do Café*, 2 (August 1934), 249–253. On roots and nutrition, see International Atomic Energy Commission, *Root Activity Patterns of Some Tree Crops* (Vienna, 1975), p. 62.

37. Stein, *Vassouras*, pp. 35–38.

38. Burmeister, *Viagem*, p. 155.

39. Lacerda Werneck, *Memoria*, p. 31, from the 1858 edition. His son was Manuel Peixoto de Lacerda Werneck. See Eduardo Silva's valuable introduction to the 1985 edition.

40. Export volume shown in Brazil, Fundação Instituto Brasileiro de Geografia e Estatística, *Estatísticas Históricas do Brasil* (2d ed.; Rio de Janeiro, 1990), p. 350. See also Soares, *Notas*, p. 212.

41. Francisco Freire Alemão to Karl Friedrich Philipp von Martius, Rio de Janeiro, 20 December 1845, *Anuis da Biblioteca Nacional*, 81 (1961), 118–120. Freire Alemão's notebooks, preserved in the Biblioteca Nacional, Rio de Janeiro, are mute testimony to a life of solitary struggle.

42. Augusto Ruschi, "O Café e o Estado do Espírito Santo," *Boletim do Museu de Biologia Prof. Mello Leitão, Série Divulgação* (25 July 1974), No. 42, 12.

CHAPTER 9. INSTRUMENTS OF DEVASTATION

1. Fundação Instituto Brasileiro de Geografia e Estatística [hereafter FIBGE], *Estatísticas Históricas do Brasil* (2d ed.; Rio de Janeiro, 1990), pp. 30–35; Mary C. Karasch, *Slave Life in Rio de Janeiro, 1808–1850* (Princeton, NJ, 1987), pp. 62, 63; Eulalia Maria Lahmeyer Lobo, *História do Rio de Janeiro* (Rio de Janeiro, 1978), 1:121–123, 226–227; 2:469.

2. See Herbert Klein, "Tráfico de Escravos," in FIBGE, *Estatísticas*, pp. 55–61; Luis Lisanti, "Comércio e Capitalismo; O Brasil e a Europa entre o Fim do Século XVIII e o Início do Século XIX" (Ph.D. dissertation, University of São Paulo, 1962), p. 57.

3. Lobo, *História*, 1:83–90, 92–99; Larissa Brown, "Internal Commerce in a Colonial Economy: Rio de Janeiro and Its Hinterland, 1790–1822" (Ph.D. dissertation, University of Virginia, 1986).

4. Maitacas are *Pionus* sp.; blackbirds (*pássaro preto*) are *Gnorimopsar chopi*; oropendolas are *Psarocolius* (possibly *P. bifasciatus*, although that species is now limited to the Amazon; either it has become extinct in the Atlantic Forest or the vulgar name "João Congo" was once applied to some other bird); see Helmut Sick, *Ornitologia Brasileira* (3d ed.; Brasília, 1984), 2:659, 660; Robert S. Ridgely and Guy Tudor, *The Birds of South America* (Austin, TX, 1989), 1:378–379; Joaquim Caetano da Silva Guimarães, *A Agricultura em Minas Gerais* (Rio de Janeiro, 1865), p. 22. On shorter fallows, see J.–Ch. Heusser and G. Claraz, "Des principaux produits des provinces brésiliennes de Rio-de-Janeiro et de Minas-Gerais," *Flores des Serres et des Jardins de l'Europe*, 14 (1859), 174. Márcia Maria Menendes Motta's data suggest one slave per 3.4 to 4 hectares on farm units up to 100 hectares; see "Proprietários de Terra e Arrendatários-Escravistas em uma Região Produtora de Gêneros Alimentícios (São Gonçalo, 1808–1892)," *Revista Arrabaldes*, 1 (September-December 1988), 87–99.

5. C. F. van Delden Laerne, *Brazil and Java* (London, 1885), p. 291.

6. [Anonymous], Memoria Dirigida ao Ilmo. Exmo. Sr. Conde de Linhares [Minas Novas, 1807?], Manuscript Collection, Biblioteca Nacional, Rio de Janeiro; Wilhelm von Eschwege, "Noticias, e Reflexões Estatisticas a Respeito da Provincia de Minas Gerais," *Memorias da Academia Real das Sciencias de Lisboa*, 9 (1825), 4; Charles James Fox Bunbury, "Narrativa de Viagem de um Naturalista Inglês ao Rio

de Janeiro e Minas Gerais (1833–1835)," *Anais da Biblioteca Nacional*, 62 (1940), 35; *Revista de Horticultura*, 1 (January, 1876), 21.

7. Silva Guimarães, *Agricultura*, pp. 24, 32; Francisco Peixoto de Lacerda Werneck, *Memoria sobre a Fundação de uma Fazenda na Provincia do Rio de Janeiro* (Rio de Janeiro, 1847), pp. 9–10; Auguste de Saint-Hilaire, *Voyage aux sources du Rio de S. Francisco et dans la province de Goyaz* (Paris, 1847–48), 1:24; Carlos Borges Schmidt, *A Vida Rural no Brasil: A Area do Paraítinga* (São Paulo, 1951), pp. 43–44. On native cattle raising, see "Guido Thomaz Marlière [Documents]," *Revista do Arquivo Público Mineiro*, 10 (1905), 496.

8. Lobo, *História*, 1:99–100, 169; John Luccock, *Notes on Rio de Janeiro and the Southern Parts of Brazil Taken during a Residence of Ten Years in the Country from 1808 to 1818* (London, 1820), pp. 295–296.

9. Frederico Carlos Hoehne, *Excursão Botanica Feita pelo Sul do Estado de Minas Gerais e Regiões Limitrofes do Estado de São Paulo . . . 1927* (São Paulo, 1939), p. 14; Silva Guimarães, *Agricultura*, p. 16; Gustavo Schuch de Capanema, "Agricultura; Fragmentos do Relatorio dos Commissarios Brasileiros à Exposição Universal de Paris em 1855," *Arquivos da Palestra Scientifica do Rio de Janeiro*, 1 (1858), 152.

10. Teresa Maria Baker Botelho, *Tecnologia Popular e Energia no Setor Residencial Rural: Um Estudo sobre Fogão a Lenha* (Rio de Janeiro, 1986), pp. 214–216; Luiz Pinguelli Rosa, coord., *Relatório de Pesquisa: O Uso de Lenha no Setor Doméstico Rural do Estado do Rio de Janeiro* (Rio de Janeiro, 1987), pp. 50–60, 80–85, 11; "Consumo y abastecimento de leña en Costa Rica," *Silvo-Energía* (March 1986), No. 14. On manioc drying, see L. F. Raposo Fontenelle, *Rotina e Fome em uma Região Cearense* (Fortaleza, 1969), p. 51; Álvaro Astolfo da Silveira, *Flora e Serras Mineiras* (Belo Horizonte, 1908), p. 128.

11. Paulo Ferraz Vianna to Count of Linhares, Registro do Officio Expedido ao Ministro de Estado dos Negocios da Guerra, 11 July 1809, Arquivo Nacional, Rio de Janeiro, Cod. 323, vol. 1, pp. 100v–102v (this reference provided by Larissa Brown); Antonio Cândido do Amaral, *Questões de Silvicultura: Noticia sobre as Mattas do Municipio Neutro e sua Explicação* (Rio de Janeiro, 1890), pp. 35, 62, 64–69; Capanema, "Agricultura," p. 20; Lobo, *História*, 1:106–121, 279, 301–3.

12. Amaral, *Questões*, pp. 30, 35, 41–42, 77; Brown, "Internal Commerce," pp. 180, 352–353; Pedro Soares Caldeira, *O Corte do Mangue: Breves Considerações sobre o Antigo e Actual Estado da Bahia do Rio de Janeiro* (Rio de Janeiro, 1884), p. 45; Armando Magalhães Correa, *O Sertão Carioca* (Rio de Janeiro, 1936), p. 74; John Mawe, *Travels in the Interior of Brazil* (2d ed.; London, 1823), p. 98; José Praxedes Pereira Pacheco, *O Util Cultivador* (Rio de Janeiro, 1855), pp. 57, 59. On mangrove extinction on the bay, see Dorothy Sue Dunn de Araújo and Norma Crud Maciel, "Os Manguezais do Recôncavo da Baía de Guanabara," *Cadernos FEEMA*, Série Técnica 10/79 (October 1979).

13. On brickworks, see Magalhães Correa, *Sertão Carioca*, p. 134. Raquel Rolnik provided data on bricks and tiles in a personal communication, São Paulo, 31 August 1989. For conversion of volume to weight of lime (1 m³ = 640 kg), see Harold B. Olin et al., *Construction Principles, Materials & Methods* (Chicago, 1983), p. 205/26 (this source provided by Thomas Dean). On modern brickmaking, see Hugo Zamberra, "Muestreo de consumo de leña en ladrilleras en El Salvador"

(paper presented to the Simposio sobre Técnicas de Producción de Leña en Fincas Pequeñas y Recuperación de Sitios Degradados por Medio de la Silvicultura Intensiva, CATIE, Turrialba, Costa Rica, 1985). On lime making, see Luccock, *Notes*, p. 364; Mawe, *Travels*, p. 127; Auguste de Saint-Hilaire, *Voyage dans les provinces de Rio de Janeiro et Minas Gerais* (Paris, 1830), 1:29; Caldeira, *Corte*, p. 8. Raúl A. Montenegro calculates a modern ratio of up to three tons of wood per ton of lime; see his "La ciudad como ecosistema," in Jorge Wilheim, ed., *Medio ambiente y urbanización* (Buenos Aires, 1982), p. 119. Here 1 cubic meter of stacked wood (*estere*) is estimated at 500 kilograms. Baked bricks are estimated in half of all city construction by the end of the nineteenth century.

14. Douglas Cole Libby, *Transformação e Trabalho em uma Economia Escravista: Minas Gerais no Século XIX* (São Paulo, 1988), p. 179f., cites Beatriz Ricardina de Magalhães, "La société ouropretaine dans les inventaires post-mortem (1740–1770)" (Ph.D. dissertation, University of Paris, 1986), pp. 168–181. See also Wilhelm von Eschwege, *Pluto Brasiliensis* (São Paulo, 1944 [1833]), 2:360–361, 336, 337, 341; Joaquim Feliciano dos Santos, *Memórias do Distrito Diamantino* (5th ed.; Petrópolis, 1978), pp. 292–294, 299–300; Jesuíno Felicíssimo Junior, "História da Siderurgia de São Paulo, seus Personagens, seus Feitos," *Boletim do Instituto Geológico e Geográfico* (1969), No. 49, 4, 6; Mário Neme, *Notas de Revisão da História de São Paulo, Século XVI* (São Paulo, 1959), p. 341; "7 Sessão em 5 de Julho de 1857," *Archivos da Palestra Scientifica do Rio de Janeiro*, 1 (1858), 237–238.

15. Libby, *Transformação*, p. 154; João Antônio de Monlevade, "Resposta aos Pedidos abaixo do Presidente o Exmo. Sr. Dr. Francisco Diogo Pereira de Vasconcellos (12 December 1853)," in Rodolfo Jacob, *Minas Gerais no Século XX* (Rio de Janeiro, 1911), pp. 242–243; Henri Gorceix, *O Ferro e os Mestres de Forja na Provincia de Minas Gerais* (Ouro Preto, 1880), pp. 4–5; Luccock, *Notes*, p. 396. Modern ratios of yield and density are from Walter Emrich, *Handbook of Charcoal Making* (Dordrecht, 1985), pp. 19–33; David R. Lida, ed., *CRC Handbook of Chemistry and Physics* (Boca Raton, FL, 1990), p. 15/40. See also Gerald Foley, *Charcoal Making in Developing Countries* (London, 1986), pp. 78–79, 98–99; José Tabacow et al., "Von Martius 1985: Viagem através do Sertão até ao Rio São Francisco" (n.p., [1987?]), xerog., pp. 70–71.

16. Foley, *Charcoal*, p. 108.

17. Francisco Magalhães Gomes, *História da Siderurgia no Brasil* (São Paulo, 1983), p. 93.

18. Juscelino Barbosa, "These II, Conservação e Replantio de Mattas," in Congresso das Municipalidades Mineiras, Belo Horizonte, 1923, *Annaes* (Belo Horizonte, 1924), p. 83.

19. Heusser and Claraz, "Principaux produits," pp. 172–173; Theodor Peckholt, *Historia das Plantas Alimentares e de Gozo no Brazil* (Rio de Janeiro, 1871), 1:52–53, 56, 64. On the rarity of capoeirão, see Saint-Hilaire, *Rio de Janeiro et Minas Gerais*, 1:319–320.

20. Carlos Augusto Taunay, *Manual do Agricultor Brasileiro* (Rio de Janeiro, 1839), pp. 49, 98; João José Carneiro da Silva, *Estudos Agrícolas* (Rio de Janeiro, 1872), p. 59; Philippe Aristide Caire, *Cultura de Mandioca* (4th ed.; Rio de Janeiro, 1919), p. 11; Raposo Fontenelle, *Rotina*, pp. 45–51. See also Carlos Borges

Schmidt, "Lavoura Caiçara," *Documentos da Vida Rural* (Rio de Janeiro, 1958), 14:28; S. V. Vigneron Jousselandière, *Novo Manual Pratico de Agricultura Intertropical* (Rio de Janeiro, 1860), pp. 34–35, 37, 110. On floodplain cultivation, see Antonio Muniz de Souza, *Viagens e Observações de hum Brasileiro* (Rio de Janeiro, 1834), pp. 130, 133.

21. Muniz de Souza, *Viagens*, pp. 41–44.

22. Raimundo José da Cunha Mattos, *Itinerario do Rio de Janeiro, Pará e Maranhão pelas Provincias de Minas Gerais e Goiás* (Rio de Janeiro, 1836), 1:57; André Rebouças, *Agricultura Nacional* (Rio de Janeiro, 1883), pp. 97–98; Michael C. McBeth, "The Brazilian Recruit during the First Empire: Slave or Soldier?" in Dauril Alden and Warren Dean, eds., *Essays Concerning the Socioeconomic History of Brazil and Portuguese India* (Gainesville, FL, 1977), pp. 71–76.

23. "Guido Thomaz Marlière," pp. 536–538; Maria Silvia Carvalho Franco, *Homens Livres na Ordem Escravocrata* (São Paulo, 1969), p. 92; Silva Guimarães, *Agricultura*, p. 16.

24. *Informação sobre o Estado da Lavoura* (Rio de Janeiro, 1874), p. 113.

25. Luccock, *Notes*, p. 294; Hebe Maria Mattos de Castro, "Beyond Masters and Slaves: Subsistence Agriculture as a Survival Strategy in Brazil during the Second Half of the Nineteenth Century," *Hispanic American Historical Review*, 68 (August 1988), 461–489.

26. Muniz de Souza, *Viagens*, p. 77; Gorceix, *Ferro*, p. 6; Edmundo Navarro de Andrade and Octâvio Vecchi, *Os Eucaliptos e sua Cultura e Exploração* (São Paulo, 1918), pp. 98–99.

27. Ladislau Netto, *Additions à la flore brésilienne: Itineraire botanique dans la Province de Minas Gerais* (Paris, 1866), p. 22; João Henrique Elliot, "Itinerario das Viagens Exploradoras Emprehendidas pelo Sr. Barão de Antonina para Descubrir uma via de Communicação entre o Porto da Villa de Antonina e o Baixo Paraguay," *Revista do Instituto Histórico e Geográfico Brasileira* [hereafter *RIHGB*], 10 (1848), No. 2, 156–158.

28. William Sanford and Elizabeth Wangari, "Tropical Grasslands: Dynamics and Utilization," *Nature and Resources*, 21 (July-September 1985), 12–27; Ana Primavesi, *Manejo Ecológico de Pastagens* (2d ed.; São Paulo, 1986), pp. 70–76, 127; Karl Friedrich Philipp von Martius, *Die Physiognamie des Pflanzenreiches in Brasilien* (Munich, 1824), p. 23; Auguste de Saint-Hilaire, "Tableau de la végétation primitive dans la Province de Minas Gerais," *Annales des Sciences Naturelles*, ser. 1, 24 (1831), 64–65.

29. Hermann von Burmeister, *Viagem ao Brasil através das Províncias do Rio de Janeiro e Minas Gerais* (São Paulo, 1952 [1853]), p. 120; Carlos Pereira de Sá Fortes, *Industria Pastoril: Relatorio Apresentado á Commissão Fundamental do Congresso Agricola, Commercial e Industrial de Minas* (Belo Horizonte, 1903), p. 84; Auguste de Saint-Hilaire, *Voyage dans les provinces de Saint Paul et de Sainte Catherine* (Paris, 1851), 1:168, 373; Arthur Getúlio das Neves, *Noticia sobre o Estado da Agricultura e da Zootecnia no Brasil* (Rio de Janeiro, 1888), p. 44.

30. Sérgio Buarque de Holanda, *Monções* (2d ed.; São Paulo, 1976), pp. 36–38.;Teotônio José Juzarte, "Diario da Navegação do Rio Tietê, Rio Grande, Paraná e Rio Iguatemi," *Anais do Museu Paulista*, 1 (1922), 41–118; Antônio Rolim, Count of Azambuja, "Relação da Viagem que Fez . . . da Cidade de S. Paulo para a Vila do Cuyabá em 1751," *RIHGB*, 7 (1845), No. 28, 469; "Digressão que Fez João

Caetano da Silva em 1817 para Descobrir a Nova Navegação entre a Capitania de Goiaz e de São Paulo pelo Rio dos Bois até ao do Rio Grande," *Revista do Instituto Histórico e Geográfico de São Paulo* [hereafter *RIHGSP*], 74 (1978), 193. Peroba is *Aspidosperma polyneuron*; tamburi is *Enterolobium contortisiliquum*.

31. W. A. Engler, "A Zona Pioneira ao Norte do Rio Doce," *Revista Brasileira de Economia,* 13 (April–June 1951), 233–234; Luis de Alincourt to Jos Lino Coutinho, Vitória, 18 June 1832 [Report on the Rio Doce], *RIHGB*, 7 (1845), No. 27, 351–382; E. Alchorne to Limpo de Abreu, n.p., 30 January 1835, in Luis Amaral, *Aspectos Fundamentais da Vida Rural Brasileira* (São Paulo, 1936), p. 14; Manuel Vieira de Albuquerque Tovar, "Informação . . . sobre a Navegação importantissima do Rio Doce," *RIHGB*, 1 (1839), No. 3, 173–178.

32. Orville Darby, "O Roteiro de uma das Primeiras Bandeiras Paulistas," *RIHGSP*, 4 (1899), 343, cited in Sérgio Buarque de Holanda, *Caminhos e Fronteiras* (Rio de Janeiro, 1957), pp. 33–34; Ceciliano Abel de Almeida, *O Desbravamento das Selvas do Rio Doce* (Rio de Janeiro, 1959), p. 10; Teófilo de Carvalho, *Caminhos e Roteiros nas Capitanias do Rio de Janeiro, São Paulo e Minas Gerais* (São Paulo, 1931), p. 24.

33. Mawe, *Travels*, p. 100; Bento José Labre, *Memoria Offerecida ao Illustrissimo e Excellentissimo Senhor Senador José Joaquim Fernandes Torres, Presidente da Provincia de S. Paulo* (São Paulo, 1859), pp. 11–12; Bernardino José de Souza, *Ciclo do Carro de Bois no Brasil* (Rio de Janeiro, 1958), pp. 493, 500, 502; Richard P. Momsen, Jr., *Routes over the Serra do Mar* (Rio de Janeiro, 1964), pp. 37, 43, 54; Ezequiel Ubatuba, *Da Zona da Mata, das Margens do Pomba às do Parahyba* (Belo Horizonte, 1918), p. 48; João Rodrigues de Brito, *Cartas Economico-Politicas sobre a Agricultura e Commercio da Bahia* (Lisbon, 1821 [1807?]), p. 64.

34. André João Antonil [João Antônio Andreoni], *Cultura e Opulência do Brasil* (2d ed.; São Paulo, 1976 [1711]), pp. 285–290; Mawe, *Travels*, p. 100; Mafalda Zemella, *O Abastecimento da Capitania das Minas Gerais* (São Paulo, 1951), pp. 122 150; Myriam Ellis, *Contribuição ao Estudo do Abastecimento das Areas Mineradoras do Brasil no Século XVIII* (Rio de Janeiro, 1961), pp. 48–58; Bunbury, "Narrativa," p. 41; Alexander Caldcleugh, *Travels in South America during the Years 1819–20–21* (London, 1825), 2:182–192, 207, 208. Detailed maps of roads can be found in Momsen, *Routes*.

35. Momsen, *Routes*, pp. 34, 37–38; Mário Neme, "Apossamento do Solo e Evolução da Propriedade Rural na Zona de Piracicaba," *Coleção Museu Paulista, Série de História*, 1 (1974), 26–27; Ellis, *Contribuição*, p. 86; Maria Odila Silva Dias, "The Establishment of the Royal Court in Brazil," in A. J. R. Russell-Wood, ed., *From Colony to Nation: Essays on the Independence of Brazil* (Baltimore, MD, 1975), pp. 107–108; Moacir M. F. Silva, *Geografia dos Transportes no Brasil* (Rio de Janeiro, 1949), pp. 76–89; Francisco Vidal Luna and Iraci del Nero da Costa, "A Estrada e o Desenvolvimento Económico: A Estrada São Paulo–Santos," in Simpósio Nacional da Associação dos Professores Universitários de História, 9, Florianópolis, 1977, *Anais* (São Paulo, 1979), 2:551–556; Adolpho Augusto Pinto, *História da Viação Pública de S. Paulo (Brasil)* (São Paulo, 1976 [1903]), pp. 14–16.

36. Carta Regia, 4 December 1816, *Codigo Brasiliense* (Rio de Janeiro, 1817), 2; "Guido Thomaz Marlière," p. 521; Gabriel Getúlio de Mendonça to Visconde d'Alcântara, Vitória, 9 March 1831, *RIHGB*, 19 (1856), No. 2, 244–246; José Marcelino Pereira de Vasconcelos, *Ensaio sobre a Historia e Estatistica da Provincia do*

Espirito Santo (Vitória, 1858), pp. 125–127; Auguste de Saint-Hilaire, *Voyage dans le District des Diamans et sur le littoral du Brésil* (Paris, 1833), 2:217; José Joaquim Machado de Oliveira, *Noticia sobre a Estrada, que da Provincia de Espirito Santo Segue para a de Minas, através da Serra Geral* (Rio de Janeiro, 1841), pp. 8–9; Bunbury, "Narrativa," p. 41.

37. Getúlio Bittencourt, *A Formação Económica do Espírito Santo* (Vitória, 1987), pp. 75–80; Momsen, *Routes,* pp. 39, 42, 44, 46, 60, 69, 73; *Geografia,* pp. 76–84; Luna and da Costa, "Estrada," 2:557–558; Francisco Soares Franco, *Ensaio sobre os Melhoramentos de Portugal e do Brazil* (Lisbon, 1820–1821), p. 41; Saint-Hilaire, *Rio de Janeiro et Minas Gerais,* 1:70–71, 158; *Revista Agricola do Imperial Instituto Fluminense de Agricultura,* 8 (September, 1877), 108n. Luccock, *Notes,* p. 304, mentioned corduroy roads, which seem to have been rare.

38. Almeida, *Desbravamento,* p. 10; Francisco Agenor Noronha Santos, *Meios de Transporte no Rio de Janeiro* (Rio de Janeiro, 1934), 2:216; Momsen, *Routes,* pp. 67, 81; João Martins da Silva Coutinho, *Relatorio da Comissão Encarregada do Reconhecimento da Região do Oeste da Provincia de S. Paulo* (Rio de Janeiro, 1872), p. ii.

39. Momsen, *Routes,* pp. 71–77; Pinto, *Historia,* pp. 21–31; Robert H. Mattoon, Jr., "The Companhia Paulista de Estradas de Ferro, 1868–1900" (Ph.D. dissertation, Yale University, 1971), pp. 41, 57, 65; Jaime Antônio Cardoso and Cecília Maria Westphalen, *Atlas Histórico do Paraná* (2d ed.; Curitiba, 1986), pp. 60–61; Bittencourt, *Formação,* p. 86.

40. Capanema, "Agricultura," p. 4.

CHAPTER 10. SPECULATION AND CONSERVATION

1. São Paulo (State), Secretaria de Agricultura, Comêrcio e Obras Públicas, *Relatorio* (São Paulo, 1896), Law 323, 22 June 1895; João Pedro da Veiga Filho, *Estudo Econômico e Financeiro sobre o Estado de S. Paulo* (São Paulo, 1896), p. 30; Célia de Carvalho Ferreira Penço, "A 'Evaporação' das Terras Devolutas no Vale do Paranapanema" (Ph.D. dissertation, University of São Paulo, 1980), pp. 141, 142.

2. Pierre Monbeig, *Pionniers et planteurs* (Paris, 1952), pp. 125–126; Monteiro Lobato, *A Onda Verde* (12th ed.; São Paulo, 1967); Diores Santos Abreu, "Os Medeiros: Uma Família Pioneira na Ocupação do Sertão do Paranapanema," *Ciência e Cultura,* 31 (August, 1979), 862.

3. Antônio Mariano Azevedo, *Relatorio sobre os Exames de que Foi Incumbido no Interior da Provincia de São Paulo* (Rio de Janeiro, 1858), p. 45. Amador Nogueira Cobra, *Em um Recanto do Sertão Paulista* (São Paulo, 1923), is a scarifying exposé of public land theft by an incorruptible public servant.

4. On obsolescence of the posseiros, see Darrell Levi, *A Família Prado* (São Paulo, 1977), pp. 165–166. On more recent frontier expropriation, see Joe Foweraker, *Brazil: The Struggle for Land* (Cambridge, England, 1983).

5. Peter Blasinheim, "A Regional History of the Zona da Mata in Minas Gerais, Brazil, 1870–1906" (Ph.D. dissertation, Stanford University, 1982), p. 216; Cláudio de Moura Castro, "Ecology—Gunpowder Rediscovered" (Rio de Janeiro, [1980]), mimeog. p. 31.

6. Azevedo, *Relatorio,* pp. 20–21. André Rebouças, engineer and entrepreneur, was an abolitionist and land-reform and conservation advocate; see his *Ao Itatiaya*

(Rio de Janeiro, 1878), p. 11; and *Agricultura Nacional* (Rio de Janeiro, 1883), pp. 117–122.

7. Subdelegate to President of Province, Report on costs of production and wages, Itaqueri, São Paulo, [Day illegible] January, 1856, TI–OD, 397, Arquivo Público do Estado de São Paulo; João Caetano da Silva Guimarães, *A Agricultura em Minas Gerais* (Rio de Janeiro, 1865), pp. 21–22; João Martins da Silva Coutinho, *Relatorio da Comissão Encarregada do Reconhecimento da Região do Oeste da Provincia de S. Paulo* (Rio de Janeiro, 1872), p. 20. On land speculation, see Thomas Holloway, *Immigrants on the Land* (Chapel Hill, NC, 180), pp. 113–121.

8. Afonso d'Escragnolle Taunay, "Os Primeiros Cafesais do Oeste de S. Paulo," *Revista do Instituto de Café*, 2 (March 1935), 626–631; Teodoro Sampaio, *São Paulo no Século XIX e Outros Ciclos Históricos* (Petrópolis, 1978 [1892]), p. 87; *Almanach de Campinas para 1908* (Campinas, 1908), pp. 35–36.

9. Pierre Denis, *Le Brésil au XXe Siècle* (Paris, 1909), p. 138; Preston E. James, "Coffee Lands of Southeastern Brazil," *Geographical Review*, 22 (April 1932), 235; José Setzer, *Sobre a Ecologia do Café* (São Paulo, 1949), pp. 4–5.

10. A. Lalière, *Le café dans l'Etat de Saint Paul (Brésil)* (Paris, 1909), pp. 39, 59, 63–65, 82–83, 86; José Vergueiro, *Memorial acerca de Colonização e Cultivo de Café* (Campinas, 1874), p. 17; Theodor Peckholt, *Historia das Plantas Alimentares e de Gozo no Brasil* (Rio de Janeiro, 1871), 1:53–54; Monbeig, *Pionniers*, pp. 78–79; Setzer, *Sobre a Ecologia*, pp. 10, 15.

11. Rogério de Camargo, *Rincões dos Andes* ([São Paulo], 1939), pp. 74–76; Rogério de Camargo and Adalberto Queiroz Telles, Jr., *O Café no Brasil: Sua Aclimatação e Industrialização* (Rio de Janeiro, 1951), 1:319, 327, 329–377; Mário Guimarães Ferri, "A Botânica em S. Paulo desde a Criação de sua Universidade," in *Ensaios Paulistas* (São Paulo, 1958), pp. 16–17; M. G. R. Cannell, "Physiology of the Coffee Crop," in Michael N. Clifford and Ken C. Willson, eds., *Coffee: Botany, Biochemistry, and Production of Beans and Beverage* (Westport, CT, 1985), p. 128.

12. A. Carrier and J. Berthaud, "Botanical Classification," in Clifford and Willson, *Coffee*, p. 28.

13. José Bonifâcio de Andrada e Silva, *Memoria sobre a Necessidade e Utilidade do Plantio de Novos Bosques* (2d ed.; Rio de Janeiro, 1925 [1815]), pp. 17, 18; idem, *Obras Científicas, Políticas e Sociais* (Santos, 1965), 2:95–114, 3:20.

14. José Praxedes Pereira Pacheco, *Minha Tentativa Dirigida para Remediar a Maior Necessidade do Brasil* (Rio de Janeiro, [1855]); *Trabalhos da Sociedade Vellosiana*, 1 (1851); Actas da Sociedade Vellosiana no Periodo de 1851 a 1871, Manuscript Archive, Museu Nacional, Rio de Janeiro [hereafter MN–RJ]; *Arquivos da Palestra Scientifica do Rio de Janeiro* [hereafter APSRJ], 1 (1858), 1–3.

15. Guilherme Schuch de Capanema, "Agricultura: Fragmentos do Relatorio dos Comissarios Brasileiros á Exposição Universal de Paris," *APSRJ*, 1 (1858), 21, 170–171. Antonio Cândido do Amaral compared observations made in 1781–1785 with observations made in 1851–1870 and found a $1°$ F increase; see his *Questões de Silvicultura: Notícia sobre as Mattas do Municipio Neutro e sua Exploração* (Rio de Janeiro, 1890), p. 24.

16. José Gregorio de Moraes Navarro, *Discurso sobre o Melhoramento da Economia Rustica do Brasil pela Introducção do Arado* (Lisbon, 1799), pp. 17–19; Silva Guimarães, *Agricultura*, p. 30. Replanting noted in *Memoria sobre a Agricultura e a Impugnação do Sistema de Derribar as Matas* (Rio de Janeiro, 1823), p. 3. See

also Jesuíno Felicíssimo Junior, "História da Siderurgia de São Paulo, seus Personagens, seus Feitos," *Boletim do Instituto Geológico e Geográfico* (1969), No. 49, 83; Januário da Cunha Barbosa, "Discurso sobre o Abuzo das Derrubadas de Arvores em Lugares Superiores de Vales," *Auxiliador da Indústria Nacional*, 1 (October 1833), 17–25; Raimundo José da Cunha Matos, *Corografia Histórica da Província de Minas Gerais* (2d ed.; Belo Horizonte, 1979 [1837]), 1:263.

17. Francisco Freire Alemão, Caça que existiu, ou que ainda existe, nos matos virgens do Campo Grande, etc. [Campo Grande], 1845, Manuscript Collection, Biblioteca Nacional, Rio de Janeiro. Among the prescient, often foreigners, were: J.–Ch. Heusser and G. Claraz, "Des principaux produits des provinces brésiliennes de Rio-de-Janeiro et de Minas-Gerais," *Flores des Serres et des Jardins de l'Europe*, 14 (1859), 172; S. V. Vigneron Jousselandière, *Novo Manual Pratico de Agricultura Intertropical* (Rio de Janeiro, 1860), p. 189; Salvador José Correa Coelho, *Passeio á minha Terra* (São Paulo, 1860), p. 76; Ladislau Netto, *Appontamentos Relativos á Botanica Applicada no Brasil* (Rio de Janeiro, 1871), p. 9.

18. Diretoria Central, 1a. Secção, Ministério de Agricultura, Comêrcio e Obras Públicas to J. A. Moreira Guimarães, Rio de Janeiro, 21 November 1861, MN–RJ, book 9, no. 151; Pedro d'Alcântara Bellegarde to Director Frederico Leopoldo Cezar Burlamaque, National Museum, Rio de Janeiro, 5 May 1863, MN–RJ, 1863, book 10, no. 62; Emílio Augusto Goeldi, *Relatorio sobre a Molestia do Cafeeiro na Provincia do Rio de Janeiro* (Rio de Janeiro, 1887). The butterfly was *Leucoptera coffeella*; the nematode was *Meloidogyne exigua*. See also Carlos Conceição, "A Decadencia dos Cafezais Fluminenses e os Fatores de sua Degradação Fisiologica," *Revista do Departamento Nacional do Café*, 2 (August 1934), 249–253; idem, *História da Irradiação e Decadencia do Café no Estado do Rio de Janeiro* (Rio de Janeiro, 1927), pp. 19–22; Richard Bardner, "Pest Control," in Clifford and Willson, *Coffee*, pp. 208–219. In 1870 the minister of agriculture hired American entomologist Benjamin Pickman Mann to survey insect pests; see Mann to Minister of Agriculture, Rio de Janeiro, 19 October 1870, MN–RJ, book 10, no. 52.

19. Emílio Joaquim da Silva Maia, *Discurso sobre os Males que Tem Produzido no Brasil o Corte das Matas e sobre os Meios de os Remediar* (Rio de Janeiro, 1835), pp. 8, 9; Nicolau Moreira, "Economia Rural," *Revista Agricola do Imperial Instituto Fluminense de Agricultura* [hereafter *RAIIFA*], 13 (December 1882), 184.

20. Miguel Antônio da Silva, "Silvicultura Brasileira, Trabalhos" *RAIIFA*, 5 (September 1870), 29–33; Armando Magalhães Correa, *O Sertão Carioca* (Rio de Janeiro, 1936), pp. 119–122, 202; Fuad Atala, *Floresta de Tijuca* (Rio de Janeiro, 1966), pp. 20–45; Raymundo Ottoni de Castro Maia, *A Floresta da Tijuca* (Rio de Janeiro, 1967), pp. 19–29; José Augusto Drummond, "National Parks in Brazil: A Study of 50 Years of Environmental Policy (With Case Studies of the National Parks of the State of Rio de Janeiro)" (M.A. thesis, Evergreen State College, 1988), pp. 345–363.

21. Atala, *Floresta*, and Drummond, "National Parks," note the real estate dimension of the restoration. Details of administration may be glimpsed in Arquivo Nacional (Brazil), *Floresta da Tijuca: Inventário dos Documentos Doados pelo Mosteiro de São Bento* (Rio de Janeiro, 1991).

22. Amaral, *Questões*, pp. 13, 13n. Charles James Fox Bunbury found second growth in abandoned coffee groves on Corcovado in 1835; see his "Narrativa de Viagem de um Naturalista Inglês ao Rio de Janeiro e Minas Gerais (1833–1835)," *Anais da Biblioteca Nacional*, 62 (1940), 27.

23. Schuch de Capanema, "Agricultura; Fragmentos," p. 158; Miguel A. da Silva, "Do Solo Agricola," *RAIIFA*, 1 (January 1869), 37; José de Saldanha da Gama, report as delegate to the International Congress of Agronomists and Forest Economists, Vienna, 1873, *RAIIFA*, 5 (June 1874), 5; José Marcelina Pereira Vasconcelos, *Ensaio sobre a Historia e Estatistica da Provincia de Espirito Santo* (Vitória, 1858), p. 47.

24. José Bonifácio de Andrada e Silva to Guarda, Museu Nacional, 15 and 19 February 1823, MN–RJ, book 1; Auguste de Saint-Hilaire, *Voyage dans le District des Diamans et sur le littoral du Brésil* (Paris, 1833), 2:278; Joao Francisco Souza, *Freire Alemão, o Botânico* (Rio de Janeiro, 1948), p. 82; Arthur Neiva, *Esboço Histórico sobre a Botânica e Zoologia no Brasil* (São Paulo, 1929), pp. 16–23; *APSRJ*, 1 (1858), pp. 56–58.

25. Auguste François Marie Glaziou to Karl Friedrich Philipp von Martius, Rio de Janeiro, 22 June 1868, manuscript copy (original in Ministério de Relações Exteriores), Instituto Histórico e Geográfico; Outwards Book, 30 April 1869, Royal Botanic Gardens, Kew (this reference kindly provided by Leonore G. Thompson, Assistant Librarian, Kew).

26. Director Museu Nacional to Minister of the Interior, 7 May 1859, MN–RJ, book 6.

27. Teófilo Benedito Ottoni, "Noticia sobre os Selvagens do Mucuri," *Revista do Instituto Histórico e Geográfico Brasileiro*, 21 (1858), No. 2, 200. Schott noted that Johann Emanuel Pohl took a Botocudo couple to Europe with him; see Heinrich Wilhelm Schott, *Tagebücher des k. k. Gartners, Hrn. H. Schott in Brasilien* (Brünn, 1822), p. 101. See also Auguste de Saint-Hilaire, *Plantes usuelles des Brésiliens* (Paris, 1824–1828).

28. Françoise Massa, *Alexandre Brethel: Pharmacien et planteur à Carangola* (Paris, 1977), pp. 336–358.

29. The bird is *Furnarius rufus*. See Hermann von Burmeister, *Viagem ao Brasil através das Províncias do Rio de Janeiro e Minas Gerais* (São Paulo, 1952 [1853]), p. 204; Alferes Eusébio José Gonzaga, Relatorio Apresentado ao Presidente de Minas Gerais, n.p., n.d., MN–RJ, book 10, no. 32; Alvaro Astolfo da Silveira, *Narrativas e Memorias* (Belo Horizonte, 1924), 1:316; Luiz da Câmara Cascudo, *Dicionario do Folklore Brasileiro* (3d ed.; Brasília, 1972), 1:90–92, 143.

30. *Estatutos da Associação Brasileira de Acclimação Fundada na Cidade do Rio de Janeiro sob a Immediata Protecção de S. M. I. O Senhor Dom Pedro II* (Rio de Janeiro, 1873); *Revista Trimestral da Associação Brasileira de Acclimação* 1 (1873), 1–6.

31. See correspondence of the National Museum, MN–RJ, books 1 to 9, 1810–1869, and Relatorios dos Trabalhos e Acquisições feitas no Museu Nacional, 1845, 1846, 1848, 1855. Ladislau Netto transmitted a translation of Agassiz's published remarks to the minister of agriculture with the comment that, had anyone been indiscreet enough to have told the visitor the size of the museum's budget, those thoughts would never have entered his mind. See Considerações Apresentadas pelo Dr. Ladislau Netto ao Ministro de Agricultura [Rio de Janeiro], 18 June 1868, MN–RJ, 1868, No. 138. Also Ladislau Netto, *Investigações Historicas e Scientificas sobre o Museu Nacional* (Rio de Janeiro, 1870); idem, *Le Muséum National de Rio-de-Janeiro et son influence sur les sciences naturelles au Brésil* (Paris, 1889).

32. *Relatorio do Museu Nacional*, 1 (1874), 1–5; Netto, *Muséum*, p. 14; idem, *Appontamentos Relativos á Botanica Applicada no Brasil* (Rio de Janeiro, 1871),

pp. 1, 2, 13, 15, 32–33, 34; Programma do Dr. Nicolau Moreira a Seguir, em seu Curso Oral de Agricultura, Rio de Janeiro, 1877, MN–RJ, book 16, no. 35; Netto, *Additions à la flore brésilienne: Itinéraire botanique dans la province de Minas Gerais* (Paris, 1866), p. 4; idem, *Breve Noticia sobre a Colecção de Madeiras no Brasil* (Rio de Janeiro, 1867).

33. "Da Utilidade dos Jardins Botanicos," *RAIIFA*, 10 (May 1879), 54–58; J. M. Leitão da Cunha, "Instituições Agricolas," in F. J. de Santa-Anna Nery, ed., *Le Brésil en 1889* (Paris, 1889), pp. 299–302; Francisco Peixoto de Lacerda Werneck, *Memoria sobre a Fundação de uma Fazenda na Provincia do Rio de Janeiro* (Brasília and Rio de Janeiro, 1985 [1847]), pp. 186–226; John James Aubertin, *O Norte da Provincia de S. Paulo, 1866: Carta Dirigida ao Ilmo. Snr. João Ribeiro dos Santos Camargo* (São Paulo, 1866).

34. João José Carneiro da Silva, *Estudos Agricolas* (Rio de Janeiro, 1872); Theodor Peckholt, *Historia das Plantas Alimentares e de Gozo no Brasil* (Rio de Janeiro, 1871), 1:56; Francisco Freire Alemão, "Apontamentos [sobre a Conservação e Corte das Madeiras de Construção Civil]," *Anais da Biblioteca Nacional*, 81 (1961), 184, 185. The National Museum held few of Darwin's works, as of 1877, perhaps because nearly all its purchases were in French or of French translations; see Relação Obras Compradas pr a Bibliotheca, 1877, MN–RJ, book 16, no. 158B.

35. Ezequiel Correa Souza Brito, "A Devastação das Florestas," *Revista Medica de São Paulo*, 5 (1902), 25–31; idem, *A Distribuição dos Vegetaes Como Factor Biologico: Trabalho Apresentado ao 1° Congresso de Geographia [1909]* (Rio de Janeiro, 1911), p. 59; Gustavo Konigswald, *São Paulo* (São Paulo, 1895), p. 24; Hermann von Ihering, *Os Mammiferos de S. Paulo* (São Paulo, 1894), p. 17.

36. Euclides da Cunha, *Contrastes e Confrontos: Obras Completas* (Rio de Janeiro, 1966), 1:183, 185.

37. Silvia F. M. de Figueroa, *Um Século de Pesquisa em Geociências* (São Paulo, 1985); Warren Dean, "The Green Wave of Coffee: Beginnings of Tropical Agricultural Research in Brazil," *Hispanic American Historical Review*, 69 (February 1989), 91–115; Nancy Leys Stepan, *Beginnings of Brazilian Science* (New York, 1981).

38. "Alberto Loefgren, um Pioneiro da Silvicultura Brasileira," *Anuário Brasileiro da Economia Florestal* [hereafter *ABEF*], 3 (1950), 115–117; São Paulo (Province), President of Province, *Relatorio, 10 January 1888* (São Paulo, 1888), annex: report of the Comissão Geográfico e Geológico, 1887; "Codigo Florestal," *Boletim da Agricultura* [hereafter *BA*], 2 (1901), No. 6, 479; Alberto Loefgren, "Serviço Florestal no Estado de S. Paulo," *BA*, 3 (August 1902), 533–539, (September 1902), 583–590.

39. Loefgren had been inspired by reports of Arbor Day in the United States, first celebrated in 1882; see Loefgren, "Serviço Florestal," pp. 538, 586, 590. The organizer of this celebration was João Pedroso Cardoso. In 1976 its last surviving witnesses were a 91-year-old former sawmill owner and his wife, who saw no irony in this, because he had "only sawn forest trees that didn't bear any fruits, nor serve to make teas." He had retired a few years before because by then logs had to be fetched all the way from Mato Grosso. See "Quando Plantar e Serrar Não se Antagonizam," *Silvicultura*, 1 (July-August 1976), 38–39. Paulo Ferreira de Souza, *Legislação Florestal: Segunda Parte, Leis Florestais dos Estados* (Rio de Janeiro, 1934–35), pp. 179–181, reproduces a bill proffered in Rio de Janeiro State in 1904. See also Carlos Borges Schmidt and José Reis, *Rasgando Horizontes* (São Paulo, 1942), p. 156.

40. Alberto Loefgren, "Conservação dos Mattos," *BA*, 4 (March 1903), 134–139; idem, *Serviço Florestal de Particulares* (São Paulo, 1903). See also Rebouças, *Agricultura*, p. 142.

41. See Júlio Brandão Sobrinho, *Apreciação da Situação Agricola, Zootechnica, Industrial e Commercial do 3° Districto Agronomico do Estado de S. Paulo com Sede em Ribeirão Preto* (São Paulo, 1903), on the economics of woodlots.

42. Loefgren, "Serviço Florestal," p. 537; Warren Dean, "Forest Conservation in Southeastern Brazil, 1900–1955," *Environmental History Review*, 9 (Spring 1985), 54–69; Mauro Antônio Moraes Victor, *A Devastação Florestal* (São Paulo, n.d.), p. 19; Brandão Sobrinho, *Apreciação*, p. 82; Gertrudes Luiza Gonzaga et al., to President of State, n.p., 20 September 1894, Arquivo Público do Estado de São Paulo, Secretaria de Agricultura, TR–OD, 41, 65/45.

43. Victor, *Devastação*, p. 19; Edmundo Navarro de Andrade, *Utilidade das Florestas* (São Paulo, 1912), pp. 74, 76–79, 81; idem, *Questões Florestais* (São Paulo, 1915), p. 51.

44. Armando Navarro Sampaio, "Edmundo Navarro de Andrade: Um Pouco de sua Vida e do seu Trabalho," *ABEF*, 2 (1949), 51–62; Congresso de Ensino Agrícola, 1, São Paulo, 1911, *Primeiro Congresso de Ensino Agricola* (São Paulo, 1911), p. 144.

45. Alberto Loefgren, "A Lenha," *BA*, 4 (January 1903), 19–23; João Barbosa Rodrigues, *Hortus Fluminensis, ou Breve Noticia sobre as Plantas Cultivadas no Jardim Botanico do Rio de Janeiro* (Rio de Janeiro, 1894), p. xxiii; Joaquim Antônio de Azevedo, "Eucalyptus globulus," *RAIIFA*, 5 (March 1874), 14–39. Portugal acquired *E. globulus* in 1839, and a treatise was published on it there in 1876; see Lars Kardell et al., "Eucalyptus in Portugal—A Threat or a Promise," *Ambio*, 15 (1986), No. 1, 7. See also Mariano Berro, *La agricultura colonial* (Montevideo, 1975 [1914]); José de Saldanha da Gama, *Relatório sobre a Exposição Universal de Vienna d'Austria em 1873* (Rio de Janeiro, 1874), p. 63; Netto, *Apontamentos*, pp. 23–29; J. Remedios Monteiro, "Eucalyptus Globulus," *RAIIFA*, 7 (December 1876), 151–157; "Eucalyptus," *Revista de Horticultura*, 1 (January 1876), 2, 3 (July 1878), 134–135.

46. Zoraide Martins, *Agricultura Paulista: Uma História Maior Que Cem Anos* (São Paulo, 1991), p. 181; Brazil, Serviço de Inspecção e Defesa Agrícolas, *Questionarios sobre as Condições de Agricultura . . . de São Paulo . . . 1910–1912* (Rio de Janeiro, 1913), p. 450; Georg Eiten, *A Vegetação do Estado de São Paulo* (São Paulo, 1970), p. 115.

47. Armando Navarro Sampaio, "Os Eucaliptos no Reflorestamento do Brasil," *ABEF*, 9 (1957), 81–89.

48. Régis Guillaumon, "Como el Hombre Blanco se Aposó de la Tierra Indígena en el Pontal de Paranapanema en el Estado de São Paulo," in Harold P. Steen and Richard P. Tucker, eds., *Changing Tropical Forests* (Durham, NC, 1992), pp. 198–216; Hermann von Ihering, *The Anthropology of the State of São Paulo, Brazil* (2d ed.; São Paulo, 1906).

CHAPTER 11. INDUSTRIAL NOMADISM, PREDATORY INDUSTRIALISM

1. Wanderbilt Duarte de Barros, citing Oliveira Vianna, in *Parques Nacionais do Brasil* (Rio de Janeiro, 1952), p. 18. Some of the material in this chapter is

adapted from the author's "Forest Conservation in Southeastern Brazil, 1900–1955," *Environmental History Review,* 9 (Spring 1985), 55–69.

2. José Ferrari Leite, "A Ocupação do Pontal do Paranapanema" (Livre Docência thesis, State University of São Paulo at Presidente Prudente, 1981), p. 59n; João Francisco Tidei Lima, "A Ocupação da Terra e a Destruição dos Indios na Região de Bauru" (M.A. thesis, University of São Paulo, 1978); Cecília Maria Westphalen et al., "Nota Prévia ao Estudo da Ocupação da Terra no Paraná Moderno," *Boletim da Universidade Federal do Paraná, Departamento de História,* 7 (1968), 1–52; Célia de Carvalho Ferreira Penço, "A 'Evaporação' das Terras Públicas no Vale do Paranapanema" (Ph.D. dissertation, University of São Paulo, 1980), pp. 43–48.

3. Companhia Melhoramentos Norte do Paraná, *Colonização e Desenvolvimento do Norte do Paraná* (São Paulo, 1975), pp. 49–56, 60, 77–78, 83, 89, 97, 120–124, 261. Reinhard Maack mentions a 15 percent reserve in "O Ritmo da Devastação das Matas no Estado do Paraná," *Ciência e Cultura,* 15 (1963), No. 1, 29. See also N. D. Tomazi, "Certeza de Lucro e Direito de Propriedade: O Mito da Companhia de Terras Norte do Paraná" (M.A. thesis, State University of São Paulo, 1989), cited in Francisco das Chagas e Silva and Lúcia Helena Soares-Silva, "Povoamento do Norte do Paraná e seus Reflexos na Devastação da Cobertura Vegetal" (n.p., n.d.), xerog., p. 15; Ulisses Capozou, "Norte do Paraná Está Perdendo sua Ultima Floresta Natural," *Folha de São Paulo,* 13 September 1981.

4. G. Kuhnholtz-Lordat, *La terre incendiée: Essai d'agronomie comparée* (Nîmes, 1939), p. 19, refers to wood-fired smelters.

5. The quotation is by Aristides Milton, Congresso das Municipalidades Mineiras, Belo Horizonte, 1923, *Annaes* (Belo Horizonte, 1924), p. 147. The children's books are: Tales C. de Andrade, *Encanto e Verdade e A Filha da Floresta (Contra a Devastação das Matas)* (Caieiras, 1921); and Júlia and Afonso Lopes de Almeida, *A Arvore* (Rio de Janeiro, 1916). See also João Pedro Cardoso, "Festa das Arvores em Araras," *Boletim da Agricultura* [hereafter *BA*], 3 (1902), 343–346.

6. Lourenço Baeta Neves, *Seccas e Florestas: O Estado e a Floresta Particular* (Belo Horizonte, 1911); João Barbosa Rodrigues, "A Diminuição das Aguas no Brasil," in Congresso Científico Latino-Americano, Rio de Janeiro, 1905, *Relatorio Geral* (Rio de Janeiro, 1905), vol. 3A; Álvaro Astolfo da Silveira, *Flora e Serras Mineiras* (Belo Horizonte, 1908), p. 112, an early conservationist position, which he contradicts in *Consultor Agricola* (2d ed., aug.; Belo Horizonte, 1917), pp. 182–183. See also Sociedade Nacional de Agricultura, Congresso Nacional de Agricultura, 2, Rio de Janeiro, 1908, *Conclusões* (Rio de Janeiro, 1909); Ezequiel Correa de Souza Brito, "A Devastação das Florestas," *Revista Médica de São Paulo,* 5 (1902), 25–31.

7. Afonso Celso de Assis Figueiredo, *Porque Me Ufano do meu Paiz* (2d ed., rev.; Rio de Janeiro, 1901).

8. Camilo Loureiro Bento, *These escripta . . . das Verdadeiras e Legitimas Causas do Clima e seus Effeitos* (Vitória, 1917), pp. 24–25.

9. Georg W. Freyreiss, "Viagem ao Interior do Brasil nos Annos de 1814–1815," *Revista do Instituto Histórico e Geográfico de São Paulo,* 11 (1906), 184; Zoraide Martins, *Agricultura Paulista: Uma História Maior Que Cem Anos* (São Paulo, 1991), p. 123; Antonio Serrano, "Los Sambaquis y Otros Ensayos," in Congresso Sul-Riograndense de História e Geografia, 3, *Anais* (Porto Alegre, 1940), 2:358; Ernst Wagemann, "A Colonização Alemã no Espírito Santo," *Boletim Geográfico,*

6 (November 1948), 905–932; Gustav Giemsa and Ernst G. Nauck, "Uma Viagem de Estudos ao Espírito Santo," *Boletim Geográfico*, 8 (July 1950), 451–470, (August 1950), 560–575, (September 1950), 653–701.

10. Alberto Torres, *As Fontes da Vida no Brasil* (Rio de Janeiro, 1915), pp. 10–14; idem, *O Problema Nacional Brasileiro* (3d ed.; São Paulo, 1938 [1914]), p. 213; Barros, *Parques*, p. 15.

11. Torres, *Fontes*, pp. 19–22; idem, *Problema*, pp. 31, 213.

12. Edmundo Navarro de Andrade, *Utilidade das Florestas* (São Paulo, 1912), p. 100; Monteiro Lobato, *A Onda Verde* (12th ed.; São Paulo, 1967 [1921]), pp. 3, 5.

13. Lourenço Baeta Neves quotes Rodrigues de Brito: *Preservation of Forests and Irrigation in Brazil* (Albuquerque, NM, 1908), pp. 28–29; Ary Fontenelle, *A Devastação das Mattas: Discurso Pronunciado na Assembleia Fluminense* (Rio de Janeiro, 1912), p. 11; Navarro de Andrade, *Utilidade*, p. 101; idem, *Questões Florestais* (São Paulo, 1915), pp. 44–46; São Paulo, Secretaria de Agricultura, Comêrcio e Obras Públicas, *Relatorio, 1900* (São Paulo, 1901), p. 46.

14. Edmundo Krug, "Sessão de 25 de Junho," *Revista da Sociedade Scientifica de São Paulo*, 3 (June 1908), p. 73; Hermann von Ihering, "A Devastação e Conservação das Mattas," *Revista do Museu Paulista* [hereafter *RMP*], 8 (1911), 485–500.

15. Gonzaga de Campos, "Mappa Florestal do Brasil," in Brazil, Ministério de Agricultura, *Relatorio* (Rio de Janeiro, 1910–1911), p. 75; São Paulo, Secretaria de Agricultura, Comêrcio e Obras Públicas, *Estatistica Agricola e Zootechnico do Anno 1904–1905* (São Paulo, 1907–1911); Mauro Antônio Moraes Victor, *A Devastação Florestal* (São Paulo, n.d.); Wanderbilt Duarte de Barros, *A Erosão no Brasil* (Rio de Janeiro, 1956), p. 224.

16. Afrânio de Carvalho, *A Actualidade Mineira* (Belo Horizonte, 1929), pp. 16–17; Frederico Carlos Hoehne, *Excursão Botânica Feita pelo Sul do Estado de Minas Gerais* (São Paulo, 1939 [1927]), pp. 8–67; Sócrates Alvim et al., "O Meio Agricola e as Reservas de Terras Cafeeiras," in *Minas e o Bicentenario do Cafeeiro no Brasil, 1727–1927* (Belo Horizonte, 1929), 1:150–151; Brazil, Directoria do Serviço de Inspecção e Fomento Agrícolas [hereafter SIFA], *Aspectos da Economia Rural Brasileira* (Rio de Janeiro, 1922), 1:517.

17. Carlos Prates, *A Lavoura e a Industria da Zona da Mata* (Belo Horizonte, 1906), table 1.

18. Pierre Monbeig, "Colonisation, peuplement et plantation de cacao dans le sud de l'état de Bahia," *Annales de Géographie*, 46 (1937), 278–299.

19. On naked hunters, see Silveira, *Flora e Serras Mineiras*, p. 103; idem, *Narrativas e Memorias* (Belo Horizonte, 1924), 2:373. See also Marcos Magalhães Rubinger, "O Desaparecimento das Tribos Indígenas em Minas Gerais," *RMP*, n.s. 14 (1963), 248; Congresso das Municipalidades Mineiras, *Annaes*, p. 111; Olivério M. de Oliveira Pinto, "Resultados Ornitologicos de uma Excursão pelo Oeste de São Paulo e Sul de Matto-Grosso," *RMP*, 17 (1932), Part 2, 4–5; Ihering, "Devastação," pp. 485–486; Konrad Guenther, *A Naturalist in Brazil* (London, 1931), p. 182.

20. Armando Magalhães Correa, *O Sertão Carioca* (Rio de Janeiro, 1936); Ezechias Paulo Heringer, *Contribuição ao Conhecimento da Flora da Zona da Mata de Minas Gerais* (Rio de Janeiro, 1947), p. 148.

21. Ihering, "Devastação," p. 485; Guenther, *Naturalist*, pp. 180–181; Alberto José de Sampaio, *Phytogeographia do Brazil* (2d ed.; São Paulo, 1938), p. 169; Alceo Magnanini, "Fauna Selvagem, Vegetação e Conservação dos Recursos Naturais,"

Anuário Brasileiro de Economia Florestal [hereafter *ABEF*], 9 (1957), 235; idem, "A Ação do Homem na Extinção das Espécies Selvagens," *Vellozia*, 1 (15 December 1961), 50; Ferrari Leite, "Ocupação," p. 26; Congresso das Municipalidades Mineiras, *Annaes*, p. 575.

22. Pierre Monbeig, *Pionniers et planteurs* (Paris, 1952), pp. 221–225; Gustav Stutzer, *The Ribeira Valley* (London, 1911), pp. 44, 68; Brazil, SIFA, *Estudo dos Factores de Producção nos Municipios Brasileiros e Condições Economicas de Cada Um* (Rio de Janeiro, 1921), No. 1.

23. José Guimarães Duque, *Silvicultura: Os Problemas das Florestas Mineiras* (Belo Horizonte, 1932), p. 13; Juiz de Fora, Prefeitura Municipal, *Relatorio, 1931* (Juiz de Fora, 1932), pp. 14–15; Flávio Azevedo Marques de Saes, *As Ferrovias de São Paulo, 1870–1940* (São Paulo, 1981), pp. 93, 115. Cedro is *Cedrela* spp.; imbuia is *Ocotea porosa*.

24. Brazil, Ministério de Agricultura, Indústria e Comércio, Diretoria Geral de Estatística, *Estimativa do Gado Existente no Brasil em 1916* (Rio de Janeiro, 1917); Roy Nash, *The Conquest of Brazil* (New York, 1926), p. 262; Hoehne, *Excursão*, p. 512.

25. This paragraph and the next are adapted from Warren Dean, "A Floresta como Fonte de Energia na Urbanização e na Industrialização de São Paulo, 1900–1950," in Seminário Nacional de História e Energia, 1, São Paulo, 1987, *Anais* (São Paulo, 1987), pp. 41–55. This was also presented to the Seminar on Forests, Habitats, and Resources, Duke University, April, 1987, whose members are thanked for their comments.

26. Densities of various species are found in Huascar Pereira, *The Timber Trees of the State of São Paulo, Brazil* (Antwerp, 1919). Energetic values are from R. Summitt and A. Silker, eds., *CRC Handbook of Materials Science*, vol. 4, *Wood* (Boca Raton, FL, 1980). These calculations are improved over those in Dean, "Floresta."

27. "Devastação das Mattas," *BA*, 2 (1901), 467–468.

28. Alberto José de Sampaio, cited by Magalhães Correa, *Sertão*, p. 71; Brazil, Ministério de Agricultura, *Estatística de Produção de Lenha* (Rio de Janeiro, [1956?]); Arlindo de Paula Gonçalves, "Estudo da Questão Florestal no Município de Viçosa" (thesis for the Chair of General and Special Forestry, Federal University of Viçosa, 1959); Mansueto Koscinski, "O Problema da Lenha," *BA*, 38 (1937), 507. Júlio Brandão Sobrinho counted 317 brickworks in the Third Agricultural District of São Paulo, which contained a quarter of the state's farms: *Apreciação da Situação Agricola, Zootechnica, Industrial e Commercial do 3º Districto Agronomico do Estado de S. Paulo com Sede em Ribeirão Preto* (São Paulo, 1903).

29. Horâcio Peres Sampaio de Mattos, *Proteção Florestal no Brasil* (Rio de Janeiro, 1953), p. 33; "Reflorestamento," *O Estado de São Paulo*, 15 November 1961; Octâvio de Castro Oliveira, "Situação e Política Florestal no Estado de Minas Gerais" (Trabalho Prático, Forestry School, Federal University of Paraná, 1968), mimeog., pp. 8–9; Laércio Osse, "Reflorestamento para Siderurgia em Minas," *Revista Orientação Agrícola*, 1 (September-October 1959), 31–37; Eudoro H. Lins de Barros, *Recursos Florestais da Bacia Paraná-Uruguai* (São Paulo, 1956), p. 92.

30. Brazil, Serviço Florestal, *Plano de Reflorestamento para as Usinas do Centro do País* (Rio de Janeiro, 1951); Minas Gerais, SEPLAN, *Ensaios sobre a Economia Mineira*, Livro 6, *O Setor Siderúrgica no Estado de Minas Gerais* (Belo Horizonte, 1978); Jesuíno Felicíssimo Junior, "História da Siderurgia de São Paulo,

seus Personagens, seus Feitos," *Boletim do Instituto Geológico e Geográfico* (1969), No. 49, 116; Laércio Osse, "Lenha, Carvão e Carvoejamento," *Brasil Florestal*, 2 (July 1971), 32–80.

31. Brazil, Serviço Nacional de Recenseamento [hereafter SNR], *VI Recenseamento Geral do Brasil [1950], Censo Industrial* (Rio de Janeiro, 1956), 3:1.

32. Data in Castro Oliveira, "Situação," p. 10, and in William W. Coelho de Souza, "A Derrubada das Matas em S. Paulo," *Revista Florestal*, 6 (1947), 18–24, were extrapolated.

33. Brazil, SNR, *Recenseamento [1950]*, 3:1; José do Carmo Neves, "Areas e Recursos Florestais do Estado de Minas Gerais," in Brazil, Superintendência de Recursos Naturais, *Recursos Naturais, Meio Ambiente e Poluição* (Rio de Janeiro, 1977), 2:39. On charcoal, see Carlos Borges Schmidt, *A Vida Rural no Brasil: A Area de Paraitinga* (São Paulo, 1951), p. 25; Sampaio de Mattos, *Proteção*, pp. 33–34; Kurt Hueck, *Wandlungen im Antlitz der Landschaft um São Paulo* (Bremen, 1958), p. 34.

34. Osse, "Lenha," p. 55.

35. Companhia Paulista de Estradas de Ferro, *Relatorio da Directoria, 1928* (São Paulo, 1928); idem, *Relatório da Directoria, 1935* (São Paulo, 1935); Companhia Paulista de Estradas de Ferro, Serviço Florestal, *Ligeiras Notas Históricas e Estatísticas* (Rio Claro, 1958), pp. 6–7. In the museum of the Horto Florestal at Rio Claro a plaque records the extraction of 425,500 cubic meters of native woods by 1938. Five of its eighteen reserves were founded after that date.

36. Sampaio de Mattos, *Proteção*, p. 7; C. R. Cameron, São Paulo Forestry Service, São Paulo, 27 December 1927, MS, U.S. National Archives, Washington, RG 166, Foreign Agricultural Reports, Forestry Reports, Box 531; Lins de Barros, *Recursos*, p. 90; José Guimarães Duque, "Os Problemas Florestais Mineiros," *Boletim de Agricultura, Zootecnia e Veterinaria*, 5 (October 1932), 261–270; Alvaro Astolfo da Silveira, *Agricultura e Pecuaria* (Belo Horizonte, 1919), p. 345; Brazil, SIFA, *Estudo dos Factores*, entry titled Santa Luzia do Rio das Velhas; Murilo Mendes, "O Reflorestamento," in Congresso Florestal Brasileiro, 1, Curitiba, 1953, *Anais* (Curitiba, 1954); "Ameaça ao Futuro do Brasil: A Destruição da Florestas," *Tribuna da Imprensa*, 21 January 1955; André Aubréville, "As Florestas do Brasil," *ABEF*, 11 (1959), 215; Paulo Erichsen de Oliveira, "O Problema das Reservas Florestais e do Reflorestamento" (lecture presented in the Curso Superior de Guerra, Escola Superior de Guerra, Rio de Janeiro, 1960).

37. Sampaio, *Phytogeographia*, p. 161; Henry W. Spielman, U.S. Consulate-General, São Paulo, 9 January 1943, 12 October 1944, U.S. National Archives, Foreign Agricultural Reports, Narrative Reports, RG 166, Entry 5, Box 75; Paulo de Souza, "Impressionante a Devastação das Nossas Matas," *A Noite*, 10 May 1946; Adalberto Mário Ribeiro, *O Problema Florestal e a Ação do Presidente Getulio Vargas* (Rio de Janeiro, 1941), pp. 26–29; Tito Guedes Costa, "Produção de Dormentes Ferroviários," *ABEF*, 10 (1958), 135–149.

38. Brazil, Instituto Brasileiro de Desenvolvimento Florestal, *Reflorestamento, Rio de Janeiro/Espírito Santo* (Brasília, 1983), p. 93; Juscelino Barbosa, "These II, Conservação e Replantio de Mattas," in Congresso das Municipalidades Mineiras, Belo Horizonte, 1923, *Annaes* (Belo Horizonte, 1924), pp. 85, 86.

39. On Baeta Neves's travels, see his *Seccas*. See also Alberto Loefgren, "Conservação dos Mattos," *BA*, 4 (1903), 134; Fontenelle, *Devastação*; Theodore Roosevelt, *Through the Brazilian Wilderness* (New York, 1914); Raphael Zon, "South

American Forest Resources and Their Relation to the World's Timber Supply," in Pan American Scientific Congress, 2, Washington, 1915–1916, *Proceedings* (Washington, DC, 1917), 3:483–492; Raphael Zon and William N. Sparhawk, *Forest Resources of the World* (New York, 1923), 2:692–727.

40. Brazil, Ministério de Agricultura, *Legislação Florestal* (Rio de Janeiro, 1934–1935), 2:179–181, 194; Romario Martins, *Livro das Arvores do Paraná* (Curitiba, 1944), p. 101; Fontenelle, *Devastação*, p. 34; Sociedade Nacional de Agricultura, *Situação Florestal Brasileira* (Rio de Janeiro, 1956), pp. 13–15; Osny Duarte Pereira, *Direito Florestal Brasileiro, Ensaio* (Rio de Janeiro, 1950), p. 104; Luís Simões Lopes, "Acordos com os Estados para Execução dos Serviços Florestaes," *Revista Florestal*, 2 (July-August 1930), 31.

41. Alberto José de Sampaio, "Pela Conservação e Renovação das Mattas Indigenas," *Chácaras e Quintais*, 5 (March 1912), 3–6; "O Problema Florestal no Brasil em 1926," *Arquivo do Museu Nacional*, 28 (1926), 134–137.

42. Alberto José de Sampaio, ed., "Primeira Conferencia Brasileira de Proteção á Natureza," *Boletim do Museu Nacional*, 11 (March 1935), 13; idem, *Biogeografia Dinamica: A Natureza e o Homem no Brasil* (São Paulo, 1935), pp. 7–8, 111–112, 210; idem, *Phytogeographia do Brasil*, p. 15–17, 165; José Mariano Filho, *Aspectos do Problema Florestal Brasileiro* (Rio de Janeiro, 1934).

43. Federico Carlos Hoehne, "Em Defesa da Flora Indigena," *O Estado de São Paulo*, 10 February 1924, 15 February 1924. For Hoehne's remarks on genetic reserves, see his *Excursão*, pp. 27, 98, 101. See also Moysés Kuhlmann, *A Flora do Distrito de Ibiti* (São Paulo, 1947).

44. Correa, *Sertão*, pp. 79, 81, 174–175, 287.

45. *Boletim do Centro Excursionista Brasileiro* (November, 1978), No. 319; Sampaio, *Biogeographia*, pp. 86–89; Correa, *Sertão*, p. 79; Sociedade dos Amigos das Arvores, *Postulados sobre o Problema Florestal* (Rio de Janeiro, 1933); Cristóvão Ferreira de Sá, *O Eucalipto e o Reflorestamento do Brasil no Quadro da Natureza* (São Paulo, 1952), p. 22; Cándido de Mello Leitão, *A Vida na Selva* (São Paulo, 1940), p. 195; Ribeiro, *Problema Florestal*, pp. 24–25.

46. Sampaio, "Primeira Conferencia," pp. 10–11, 48–55.

47. The codes are in Duarte de Barros, *Parques Nacionais*; the legislation from 1934 is in David F. Cavalcanti, *Legislação de Conservação da Natureza* (2d ed.; Rio de Janeiro, 1978).

48. Ribeiro, *Problema Florestal*, pp. 3, 7, 8, 13; *o Estado de São Paulo*, 5 June 1941; Augusto Ruschi, *O Problema Florestal no Estado de Espírito Santo* (Espírito Santo, 1948); Reinhard Maack, "A Modificação da Paisagem Natural pela Colonização e suas Conseqüências no Norte do Paraná," *Boletim Paranaense de Geografia*, 1 (1961), No. 2/3, 42.

49. "Este Parque Exige Apenas Paz," *Estado de Minas Gerais*, 4 November 1979; E. Roquette-Pinto, "Parques Nacionais," *Boletim do Museu Nacional*, 11 (March 1935), 1–20; Duarte de Barros, *Parques Nacionais*, pp. 38–39; Wallace W. Atwood, *La protección de la naturaleza en las Américas* (Mexico City, 1941); Mário de Sampaio Ferraz, "Campos do Jordão—Derrubada de Pinheiros," *Boletim de Agricultura*, série 38 (1937), No. único, 744.

50. Sociedade Nacional de Agricultura, *Situação Florestal Brasileira* (Rio de Janeiro, 1956), p. 24; Sampaio, *Phytogeographia*, p. 169; idem, *Biogeographia*, p. 78; Cândido de Melo Leitão, comments in Reunião Sul-Americana de Botânica, 1, Rio de Janeiro, 1938, *Annaes* (Rio de Janeiro, 1938), 1:112

51. Osny Duarte Pereira, *Relações do Problema Florestal com a Reforma Agrária* (Rio de Janeiro, 1959), p. 5; Roberto dos Santos Vieira, "Legislação Florestal e Conservação de Recursos Naturais" (paper presented to the II Curso Internacional de Direito Comparado do Meio Ambiente: Legislação Ambiente e Desenvolvimento Econômico, Salvador[?], 1981), mimeog., pp. 5–6; Sampaio de Mattos, *Proteção*, p. 33; Mariano Filho, *Aspectos*, pp. 21–22; Mário Marcondes Loureiro, "Necessidade da Revisão do Código Florestal," in Congresso Florestal Brasileiro, Curitiba, 1953, *Anais* (Curitiba, 1954), pp. 315, 472; Brazil, Câmara dos Deputados, Comissão Especial de Defesa dos Recursos Naturais do Pais, *Sugestões dos Técnicos do Ministério de Agricultura à Nova Legislação Florestal* (Rio de Janeiro, 1954); Ferreira de Sá, *Eucalipto*, p. 36; José Mariano Filho, "Memorial do Conselho Florestal Federal ao Ministro de Agricultura," *Diário Oficial*, 10 December 1945; Ribeiro, *Problema Florestal*, pp. 4–5, 38–39.

52. José Augusto Drummond, "National Parks in Brazil: A Study of 50 Years of Environmental Policy (With Case Studies of the National Parks of the State of Rio de Janeiro)" (M.A. thesis, Evergreen State College, 1988), p. 42; Maack, "Modificação," pp. 29–45.

CHAPTER 12. THE DEVELOPMENT IMPERATIVE

1. The literature of economic development is vast. For an introduction to the Brazilian case, see Celso Furtado, *Perspectiva da Economia Brasileira* (Rio de Janeiro, 1958); idem, *Uma Economia Dependente* (Rio de Janeiro, 1956); João Paulo de Almeida Magalhães, *A Controvérsia sobre o Desenvolvimento Econômico* (Rio de Janeiro, 1966); Nathaniel Leff, *Economic Policy Making and Development in Brazil* (Rio de Janeiro, 1966).

2. On forest destruction and development, see Mauro Antônio Moraes Victor, *A Devastação Florestal* (São Paulo, n.d.), p. 36.

3. On postwar political struggles, see Thomas Skidmore, *Politics in Brazil, 1930–1964* (New York, 1967); idem, *The Politics of Military Rule in Brazil, 1964–1985* (New York, 1988).

4. Arlindo de Paula Gonçalves, "Estudo da Questão Florestal no Município de Viçosa" (thesis for the Chair in General and Special Forestry, Federal University of Viçosa, 1959), pp. 80–81; J. C. G. Camargo et al., "Estudo Fitogeográfico da Vegetação Ciliar do Rio Corumbataí, São Paulo," *Biogeografia*, 3 (1971), 30.

5. Gonçalves, "Estudo," p. 52; Hilgard O'Reilly Sternberg, "Floods and Landslides in the Paraíba Valley," in International Geographical Congress, 16, Lisbon, 1949, *Compte Rendu* (Lisbon, 1951), pp. 335–364; Louis Papy, "En marge de l'empire du café: la façade atlantique de São Paulo," *Cahiers d'Outre-Mer*, 5 (October-December 1952), 374; Reinhard Maack, "A Modificação da Paisagem Natural pela Colonização e suas Conseqüências no Norte do Paraná," *Boletim Paranaense de Geografia*, 1 (1961), Nos. 2/3, 41, 42; José Setzer, "O Reflorestamento em Face do Estudo Moderno do Solo," *Boletim de Agricultura*, 42 (July 1941), 385–396.

6. Raymond Pébayle et al., *Le Bassin Moyen du Parana Brésilien: L'homme et son milieu* (Talence, France, 1977), p. 45.

7. Reinhard Maack, "As Conseqüências da Devastação das Matas no Estado do Paraná," *Arquivos de Biologia e Tecnologia*, 8 (1953), 437–457, 439; idem, "Modificação," pp. 43–44; Paraná, Assessoria da Imprensa, *Paraná, Do Flagelo à Recuperação* (Curitiba, 1964), pp. 54–56.

8. Augusto Ruschi, "O Café e o Estado do Espírito Santo," *Boletim do Museu de Biologia Prof. Mello Leitão*, Série Divulgação (25 July 1974), No. 42, 27–45.

9. Bertha K. Becker, "Expansão do Mercado Urbano e Transformação da Economia Pastoril," *Revista Brasileira de Geografia*, 28 (October-December 1966), 297, 300, 302, 303, 305; Alisson P. Guimarães, *Estudo Geográfico do Vale do Médio Jequitinhonha* (Belo Horizonte, 1960), pp. 157, 201, 202; Harold C. Clements, Sr., *The Mechanization of Agriculture in Brazil* (Gainesville, FL, 1969), pp. 13–15. Guinea grass is *capim colonião*. See also Maria Elisa Linhares Borges, "A Recriação de uma Fronteira: A Luta pela Terra no Leste de Minas Gerais," *Revista Brasileira de Estudos Políticos* (July 1991), No. 73, 180, 197.

10. G. Glaser, "Neue Aspekte der Rinderweide-Wirtschaft in Zentralbrasilien," *Beitrage zur Geographie Brasiliens* (Heidelberg, 1971), pp. 19–38; Hermógenes de Freitas Leitão Filho et al., *Plantas Invasoras de Culturas no Estado de São Paulo* (São Paulo, 1972), vol. 1; [Fernando Segadas Vieira], "Espírito Santo à Beira de Ser um Deserto," *Correio da Manhã*, 13 February 1959; Geraldo Leme da Rocha and Dinival Martinelli, "Levantamento Sumário da Cobertura do Solo nas Pastagens do Estado de São Paulo," in Congresso Nacional de Conservação do Solo, 1, Campinas, 1960, *Anais* (Campinas, 1960), pp. 389–390.

11. Reinhard Maack, "O Ritmo da Devastação das Matas no Estado do Paraná," *Ciência e Cultura*, 15 (1963), No. 1, 25–33.

12. Companhia Paulista de Estradas de Ferro, "Histórico" (n.p., n.d.), mimeog.; "O Oleo Diesel e a Energia Elétrica Salvam as Nossas Florestas," *Diário Popular* (São Paulo), 23 May 1956; "Reserva Florestal e Reflorestamento Econômico," *O Estado de São Paulo* [hereafter *ESP*], 2 December 1958.

13. Maurício Andrés Ribeiro and Delly Oliveira Filho, "Florestas Sociais: Problemas, Perspectivas, e Tarefas," *Fundação JP*, 10 (January 1980), 2–18; Orlando Valverde, *Geografia Agrária do Brasil* (Rio de Janeiro, 1964), 1:362; Aníbal Pinto de Souza, "A Lenha como Base do Progresso Industrial," *Anuário Brasileiro de Economia Florestal* [hereafter *ABEF*], 3 (1950), 263–282.

14. José Alves, ed., *Conferencia Latino-Americana de Florestas e Produtos Florestais, Organizado pela FAO, Teresópolis, . . . Relatório* (Lisbon, 1948), pp. 57–77; William McNeill, "Deforestation in the Araucaria Zone of Southern Brazil, 1900–1983" in John F. Richards and Richard P. Tucker, eds., *World Deforestation in the Twentieth Century* (Durham, NC, 1988), pp. 15–32; Aida Mansani Lavalle, *A Madeira na Economia Paranaense* (Curitiba, 1981), pp. 17–18, 21, 23, 69, 74; Valverde, *Geografia*, 1:352–353; Maack, "Conseqüências," p. 452.

15. José Ferrari Leite, "As Reservas Ecológicas do Sudoeste Paulista" (thesis presented to the Congresso Estadual de Municípios, 23, Praia Grande, São Paulo, 1979), p. 8; Paulo Fraga, interview with the author, Vitória, 15 June 1983.

16. Lavalle, *Madeira*, pp. 69, 74; Eudoro H. Lins de Barros, *Recursos Florestais da Bacia Paraná-Uruguai* (São Paulo, 1956), pp. 80–82; Reinhard Maack, "Ritmo," pp. 25–33; Rogério Medeiros, "Maior Madereiro do País se Diz Assassino de Arvores," *Jornal do Brasil*, 11 November 1979.

17. Companhia Siderúrgica Belgo-Mineira, *Carvão Vegetal para Siderurgia* (n.p., 1955); Laércio Osse, "Lenha, Carvão e Carvoejamento," *Brasil Florestal*, 2 (July 1971), 32–80; José do Carmo Neves, "Areas e Recursos Florestais do Estado de Minas Gerais," in Brazil, Superintendência de Recursos Naturais, *Recursos Naturais, Meio Ambiente e Poluição* (Rio de Janeiro, 1977), 2:38; Alceo Magnanini et

al., *Atlas de Elementos Ambientais do Estado do Rio de Janeiro,* Cadernos FEEMA, Série Congressos 06/81 (Rio de Janeiro, 1981), p. 20.

18. "Municípios do Estado com menos de 1% de Superfície Florestada," *Folha da Manhã,* 5 April 1959. Differing interpretations of aerial data appear in J. V. Chiarini and Arnaldo Guido de Souza Coelho, "Cobertura Vegetal Natural e Areas Reflorestadas do Estado de São Paulo," in Simpósio sobre Conservação da Natureza e Restauração do Ambiente Natural do Homem, *Anais da Academia Brasileira das Ciências,* 41 Suplemento (1969), 46; Mário Borgonovi et al., "Cobertura Vegetal do Estado de São Paulo," *Bragantina,* 26 (March 1967), 93; Victor, *Devastação,* p. 14; Maack, "Modificação," pp. 35–39; Minas Gerais, Instituto de Desenvolvimento Industrial, *Reservas Florestais em Minas Gerais,* Relatório Agri-011 (Belo Horizonte, 1972), mimeog.; Octávio de Castro Oliveira, *Situação e Política Florestal do Estado de Minas Gerais* (Belo Horizonte, 1968), p. 15; Miguel A. Kill, *Geografia e História do Espírito Santo* (Vitória, 1974), p. 41.

19. Material in this and following paragraphs is adapted from the author's "Forest Conservation in Southeastern Brazil, 1900–1955," *Environmental History Review,* 9 (Spring 1985), 55–69. See also "Este Parque Exige Apenas Paz," *Estado de Minas Gerais,* 4 November 1979; Castro Oliveira, *Situação,* p. 16; Mulford B. and Racine Sarasy Foster, *Brazil* (Lancaster, PA, 1945), pp. 225, 230, found charcoal making on the edge of the Doce River park in 1944.

20. Arlindo de Paula Gonçalves, interview with the author, Department of Forestry, Federal University of Viçosa, August 24, 1981.

21. Alvaro Marcílio, *O Problema das Terras Devolutas e suas Matas no Estado de Minas Gerais* (Belo Horizonte, 1961). On land struggles, see Linhares Borges, "Recriação," pp. 173–201.

22. José Ferrari Leite provided much of the information in this and next paragraphs; see his "Reservas," and "A Ocupação do Pontal do Paranapanema" (Livre-Docência thesis, State University of São Paulo at Presidente Prudente, 1981). See also "O Pontal de Paranapanema, O Histórico da Questão," *ESP,* 4 July 1955.

23. "6 Capítulos Negros da Escandalosa História das Reservas Florestais da Alta Sorocabana," *Folha da Manhã,* 9 June 1954.

24. *Folha da Manhã,* 5 May–7 August 1954, especially "'O Panamá Florestal' da Alta Sorocabana," 30 May; "A Afirmação desse Matutino É a Afirmação de Que Nem Tudo É Perdido em Nossa Pátria," 9 June; "Insiste o Deputado Cunha Lima na Tese de Que o Estado É Incapaz de Manter Reservas Florestais," 2 July. See also "O Desalojamento de Intrusos da Reserva Florestal de P. Venceslau," *ESP,* 18 June 1954; "O Pontal de Paranapanema; Tentativas para Resolver a Questão," *ESP,* 7 August 1954.

25. "Inteiramente de Acordo o Governo do Estado com o Projeto Camarinha," *Folha da Manhã,* 6 September 1955; "O Pontal do Paranapanema: Os Deputados Estaduais e as Reservas do Pontal," *ESP,* 21 September 1955; "O Pontal de Paranapanema: A Verdade sobre as Bemfeitorias," *ESP,* 26 October 1955; "O Apelo ao Governador," *ESP,* 13 December 1955.

26. "Sereias da 'Reserva,'" *Correio Paulistano,* 24 August 1956; "O Caso das Reservas Florestais, Pinhões para os 'Nativos,'" *Correio Paulistano,* 8 September 1956.

27. "O Pontal do Paranapanema," *ESP,* 13 June 1956; "O Pontal do Paranapanema," *ESP,* 10 August 1956; "O Caso das Reservas Florestais," *ESP,* 26 October

1956; "Pontal do Paranapanema," *ESP,* 1 November 1960; "Dúvida: Nossas Matas Têm Algum Futuro?" *Jornal da Tarde,* 7 December 1977; Ferrari Leite, "Ocupação," pp. 73–84; "O Estado as Protegia, mas Foram Destruidas," *Jornal da Tarde,* 3 September 1969; Ferrari Leite, "Reservas," pp. 8–9, 34–35; "Mais Uma," *ESP,* 22 January 1966.

28. See the following articles in *ESP:* "Esperança para o Pontal," 9 March 1973; "Ainda ao Abandono o Pontal do Paranapanema," 11 March 1973; "Despejo Continua, Mais 57 Famílias Deixarão o Pontal," 18 September 1973; "Posseiros Despejados no Pontal," 10 January 1974; "Despejo Gera Clima de Tensão no Pontal," 13 July 1977.

29. João C. Chagas Campos and Dammis Heinsdijk, "A Floresta do Morro do Diabo," *Silvicultura em São Paulo,* 7 (1970), 43–58; William O. Deshler, *Recomendações para o Manejo do Morro do Diabo* (Publicação No. 6, Instituto Florestal; São Paulo, 1975 [1973]); Ferrari Leite, "Reservas," pp. 25, 27; "Advertências Não Impedem o Dematamento no Pontal," *ESP,* 11 March 1976; "Só Planos contra a Devastação do Morro do Diabo," *ESP,* 3 January 1978.

30. São Paulo, Serviço Florestal, "Dependências do Serviço Florestal: Denominação, Localização e Area" (n.p., [1961?]); "Florestas Protetoras" *ESP,* 18 June 1961; "Dúvida"; "Já no Ano 1950 o Próprio Serviço Florestal Encarecia a Necessidade de Concretizar-se a Reserva de Caraguatatuba," *Folha de Manhã,* 13 June 1956.

31. A. Albino Ramos, "A Situação Atual das Reservas Florestais do Paraná," *Revista Florestal,* 1 (June 1969), 71–100; Maack, "Ritmo," pp. 25–33.

32. Paulo França, "Berço de Mudas, Horto Quase Virou um Cemitério," *O Globo,* 1 March 1987; "Desmatamento no Estado do Rio Alcança Proporções Absurdas," *Jornal do Brasil,* 8 July 1962; José Augusto Drummond, "National Parks in Brazil: A Study of 50 Years of Environmental Policy (With Case Studies of the National Parks of the State of Rio de Janeiro)" (M.A. thesis, Evergreen State College, 1988), p. 140, cites Magnanini and Pádua's report in the *Boletim Informativo* of the Fundação Brasileira pela Conservação da Natureza, 4 (1969), 28–58.

33. Wanderbilt Duarte de Barros, *Parques Nacionais do Brasil* (Rio de Janeiro, 1952), p. 9.

34. G. P. Ahern and Gifford Pinchot, *Pan American Cooperation in Forestry Cooperation* (Serie de Selvicultura de la Unión Panamericana; Washington, DC, 1925); Raphael Zon and William N. Sparhawk, *Forest Resources of the World* (New York, 1923). The U.S. Forest Service distributed a pamphlet at the 1922 Brazilian Centennial: Henry S. Graves, *O Estudo da Silvicultura* (1922). See also Roy Nash, *The Conquest of Brazil* (New York, 1926); idem, "Brazilian Forest Policy," *Bulletin of the Pan-American Union,* 58 (July 1924), 688–706; William Allen Orton, *A Riqueza Florestal do Brasil* (Rio de Janeiro, 1929), pp. 1–6; W. T. Cox and Donald M. Mathews, reports in U.S. National Archives [hereafter NARS], Record Group 166, Foreign Agricultural Relations, Forestry Reports, Entry 3, Box 531, 1929. Paulo Ferreira Souza was instrumental in the forestry school's foundation; see his *Escola Nacional de Florestas; Necessidade de sua Criação* (Rio de Janeiro, 1958).

35. NARS, Record Group 79, National Park Service, Central Classified File, 1933–1949, Foreign Parks (0–30); International Union for the Conservation of Nature, *Campaña latinoamericana para la protección a la naturaleza y la conserva-*

ción de los recurses naturales (Buenos Aires, 1952); Inter-American Conference on Conservation of Renewable Natural Resources, Denver, Colorado, 1948, *Proceedings* (Washington, DC, 1949); Paulo Erichsen de Oliveira, "O Problema das Reservas Florestais e do Reflorestamento" (lecture presented in the Curso Superior de Guerra, Escola Superior de Guerra, Rio de Janeiro, 1960).

36. Setzer, "Reflorestamento," p. 396. Wanderbilt Duarte de Barros connected soil conservation and forest preservation in *A Erosão no Brasil* (Rio de Janeiro, 1956). See also J. Q. A. Marques et al., "As Perdas por Erosão no Estado de São Paulo," in Congresso Nacional de Conservação do Solo, 1, Campinas, 1960, *Anais* (São Paulo, 1963), pp. 77–91.

37. Nilson Cortez Crocia de Barros, "Desenvolvimento e Meio Ambiente nas Revistas Geográficas Brasileiras" (paper presented in a course in the history of conservationism in Brazil, Department of History, University of São Paulo, 1985); "Manifesta-se a Sociedade Botânica do Brasil Favorável ao Projeto Camarinha," *Folha de Manhã*, 17 September 1955; Itagiba Berçante, *Situação Florestal Brasileira* (Rio de Janeiro, 1956); Congresso Brasileiro dos Estudantes de Engenharia Florestal, 1, Rio de Janeiro, 1968, *Anais* (Rio de Janeiro, 1968), pp. 35–37.

38. Campanha de Proteção à Natureza, *Sete Palestras Irradiadas em Comemoração do Primeiro Aniversário da Campanha* (São Paulo, 1950), p. 18.

39. Adelmar Coimbra Filho and Alceo Magnanini, "Animais Raros ou em Vias de Desaparecimento no Brasil," *ABEF*, 19 (1968), 174.

40. Paulo Duarte, "Jornal de 30 Dias," *Anhembi*, 11 (July 1953), 307; José Setzer, "O Caboclo como Formador do Solo," *Boletim Geográfico*, 8 (March 1951), 1441–1442; Augusto Ruschi, "Fitogeografia do Estado de Espírito Santo, I," *Boletim do Museu de Biologia*, Série Botânica, 1 (16 January 1950), 76.

41. José Eurico Dias Martins, "Capacidade de Produção: Reflorestamento e Erosão" (lecture given at the Escola Superior de Guerra, Rio de Janeiro, 1951), mimeog., marked "Confidential," Manuscript, Escola Superior de Guerra, Rio de Janeiro [hereafter ESG–RJ]; Erichsen de Oliveira, "Problema"; Fernando Lustoza Garcia do Aragão, "A Exploração, Proteção e o Desenvolvimento de Nossas Riquezas Florestais" (term paper, Curso Superior de Guerra, Escola Superior de Guerra, 1970), ESG RJ; Associação dos Diplomados da Escola Superior de Guerra, Delegacia de São Paulo, Grupo de Trabalho da ADESG, *Floresta e Segurança Nacional* (2d ed.; São Paulo, 1974); Drummond, "National Parks," pp. 215–216. In 1929, W. A. Orton put forward "national security" as a reason for protecting forests in his advice to the Brazilian government: *Riqueza*, pp. 7–8.

42. Ramos, "A Situação," p. 90; Berçante, *Situação*, p. 160; Victor, *Devastação*, p. 7; Brasil, Câmara dos Deputados, Comissão Especial de Defesa dos Recursos Naturais do País, *Sugestões dos Técnicos do Ministério de Agricultura à Nova Legislação Florestal* (Rio de Janeiro, 1954); Brazil, Ministério de Agricultura, *Política Florestal Brasileira: Relatório do Grupo de Trabalho Instituído pelo Memorando GP/MA–42 de 5/iv/61* [hereafter MinAgr, *Política*] (Rio de Janeiro, 1961); Armando Monteiro Filho, *Anteprojeto de Lei Florestal*, Serviço de Informação Agrícola, Série Documentária, No. 23 (Rio de Janeiro, 1962), see quotation, p. 9; Osny Duarte Pereira, *Relações do Problema Florestal com a Reforma Agrária* (Rio de Janeiro, 1961), pp. 18–19; "Análise da Situação Florestal Brasileira," *ABEF*, 15 (1963), 89–90; "Grave a Situação das Reservas Florestais," *ESP*, 27 February 1962; Drummond, "National Parks," pp. 39–40.

43. Brazil, Instituto Brasileiro de Geografia e Estatística, *Código Florestal* (Rio de Janeiro, 1967); Victor, *Devastação*, p. 39.

44. "Breve Execução do Grande Plano de Reflorestamento," *O Jornal* (Rio de Janeiro), 17 August 1951; David de Azambuja, *Medidas Fundamentais para o Equacionamento do Problema Florestal Brasileiro* (Rio de Janeiro, 1959); Léa Goldenstein, "Aspectos da Reorganização do Espaço Brasileiro face a Novas Relações de Intercâmbio" (Livre Docência thesis, University of São Paulo, 1975); "Lançada a Campanha do Reflorestamento," *ESP*, 24 August 1966; Valverde, *Geografia*, 1:361; "Reflorestamento Reclama Plantio Mínimo de 50 Milhões de Arvores," *Diário de São Paulo*, 8 June 1963; MinAgr, *Política*, pp. 16–17.

45. "Novos Rumos para a Política Florestal," *ESP*, 16 November 1958; Vice Consul John F. Root, "São Paulo Forestry Service Plans Reforestation Program of 100.000.000 Pine Trees," São Paulo, 5 April 1949, NARS, Foreign Agricultural Reports, Narrative Reports, RG 166, Box 527; Luiz de Toledo Filho et al., "Estratégia para Utilização das Floresas Nacionais das Regiões Sul e Sudeste," *Brasil Florestal*, 13 (April-June 1983), 5–12. Planting along roadsides, a hoary suggestion, seems to have been done at least once on a large scale, in São Paulo, in 1960; see "Cruzada Florestal," *ESP*, 9 March 1962. The plight of the smallholder is documented in Gonçalves, "Estudo," pp. 118–143.

46. Drummond, "National Parks," pp. 72–73, citing Harald Edgard Strong and Henrique Pimenta Velloso, "Parques Nacionais e Reservas Equivalentes no Brasil" (Rio de Janeiro, 1969), mimeog.

CHAPTER 13. UNSUSTAINABLE DEVELOPMENTS

1. José Sarney, quoted by Paulo R. Schilling and Richard Canese, *Itaipu: Geopolítica e Corrupção* (São Paulo, 1991), p. 19. See also Arístides Arthur Soffiati Netto, "A Agonia das Lagoas do Norte Fluminense," *Ciência e Cultura*, 37 (October 1985), 16–31; United Nations, UNESCO, Programme on Man and the Biosphere, *Expert Panel on Project No. 1: Ecological Effects of Increasing Human Activities on Tropical and Sub-Tropical Forest Ecosystems, Final Report* (Paris, 1972); idem, *International Working Group on Project 1: Ecological Effects of Increasing Human Activities in Tropical and Sub-Tropical Forest Ecosystems, Final Report* (Paris, 1974), pp. 57–60.

2. Soffiati Netto, "Agonia," pp. 27–31; Régis Guillaumon, "A Crise Energética e a Destruição da Cobertura Vegetal na Região de Ribeirão Preto," in Congresso Brasileiro de Defesa do Meio Ambiente, 3, Rio de Janeiro, 1988, *Anais* (Rio de Janeiro, 1988), 2:762–791.

3. Sistema de Informações Empresáriais do Setor de Energia Elétrica [hereafter SIESEE], "Sumário das Usinas Ativas, 31 Março 1992" (printout); Denise Natali, "Milhares de Pessoas Participam da Ultima Homenagem a 7 Quedas," *Folha de São Paulo* [hereafter *FSP*], 24 July 1982; Octávio Marcondes Ferraz, "Adeus, Salto de Sete Quedas," *Jornal Ilha Grande* (Guaíra), 24 July 1982. The jailed activist was Juvêncio Mazarollo.

4. SIESEE, Sumário; idem, *Linhas de Transmissão em Operação por Concessionária; Tensão Nominal e Extensão* (Rio de Janeiro, 1992). Widths of transmission lines are derived from Companhia Energética de São Paulo, *Travessia de Linha de Transmissão*, CESP Instrução TM 005/82 (São Paulo, 1982). See also Programa

de Pesquisa e Conservação de Areas Umidas no Brasil, *Inventário de Areas Umidas do Brasil, Versão Preliminar* (São Paulo, 1990), pp. 50–53; International Commission on Large Dams, *World Register of Dams, 1988* (Paris, 1988), pp. 153–157; C. A. Facetti, "Ações da Itaipu no Meio Ambiente," in Seminário Nacional de Produção e Transmissão de Energia Elétrica, 9, Belo Horizonte, 1987, *Sub-Grupo VI–01: Estudos de Impactos Ambientais (SGA)* (Belo Horizonte, 1987);"Aos Poucos, Vai Desaparecendo a Reserva Florestal," *O Estado de São Paulo* [hereafter OESP], 21 November 1978; Luciana Pallestrini, "Sítio Arqueológico da Lagoa São Paulo," *Pré-História*, 6 (1984), 381; "Aqui, Alguns Dados dos Projetos," *São Paulo Energia*, 1 (May 1984), 32; Melquiades Pinto Paiva, *Grandes Represas do Brasil* (Brasília, 1982), p. 192.

5. Carlos Augusto de Figueiredo Monteiro, *O Clima e a Organização do Espaço no Estado de São Paulo* (São Paulo, 1976), pp. 33–34; Mulford B. and Racine Sarasy Foster, *Brazil* (Lancaster, PA, 1945), p. 169; João de Vasconcelos Sobrinho, *As Regiões Naturais de Pernambuco, o Meio e a Civilização* (Rio de Janeiro, 1949), p. 173; Rubem de Mello, "Em Que Consiste o Problema Florestal," *Folha de Manhã*, 30 May 1954.

6. Ricardo Kotscho, "Em um Ano, Desaparecerão as Sete Quedas," *OESP*, 25 October 1981; Sônia Barbosa Magalhães, "Campesinato e Hidrelétricas: Uma Visão sobre o 1° Encontro Nacional de Trabalhadores Atingidos por Barragens," in Ana Luiza B. Martins Costa et al., *Hidrelétricas, Ecologia e Progresso* (Rio de Janeiro, 1990), pp. 45–68.

7. Pinto Paiva, *Grandes Represas*, pp. 195, 199; Facetti, "Ações"; Carlos Dias Brosch, "Carvão Vegetal como Fonte de Energia," in Instituto Brasileiro de Gás, Seminário Energia de Biomassas, São Paulo, 1978, *Anais* (São Paulo, n.d.), p. 72; F. Reichman Neto, "Revegetalização de Areas Marginais a Reservatórios de Hidrelétricas," Congresso Florestal Brasileiro, 3, Manáus, 1978, *Anais* (São Paulo, 1978), 2:215–217; Brazil, Eletrobrás, *Informações sobre Atividades de Meio Ambiente nas Empresas do Setor Elétrico* (Rio de Janeiro, 1983), pp. 40–62; Carlos Eduardo Torloni et al. *Reprodução de Peixes Autóctones Reófilos no Reservatório de Promissão, Estado de São Paulo* (3d ed.; São Paulo, 1988); "Reflorestamento em Itaipu," *Jornal Verde*, August 1993, p. 8.

8. "Pontal do Paranpanema Ameaçado de Devastação," *FSP*, 10 April 1984; Luis Carlos Lopes and Valderi dos Santos, "Violência contra Mico-Leão, em Rosana," *OESP*, 4 December 1986; Cláudio Pádua, interview with the author, Morro do Diabo, 17 May 1989.

9. "Os Compromissos da CESP no Pontal," *São Paulo Energia*, 1 (May 1984), 27–29; Valderi dos Santos, "Região do Pontal Enfrenta Nova Crise," *OESP*, 15 November 1988; idem, "Teodoro Sampaio Cria Incentivo para Indústrias," *OESP*, 15 March 1990; Barbosa Magalhães, "Campesinato," pp. 45–68; Howard S. Geller, "The Potential for Electricity Conservation in Brazil" (draft report presented to the Companhia Energética de São Paulo, February, 1984); "Planalto Quer Conservar Energia," *São Paulo Energia*, 7 (November-December 1990), 32–33.

10. Máximo Hori, "Inventário Florestal das Matas Remanescentes do Sul da Bahia," in Simpósio Florestal da Bahia, 1, *Anais* [Salvador?], offprint (n.p., n.d.); Salim Jordy Filho et al., "Vegetação," in Brazil, Ministério das Minas E Energia, *Projeto Radam Brasil: Levantamento de Recursos Naturais*, vol. 34, *Folha SE.24 Rio Doce* (Rio de Janeiro, 1987), p. 385; Paulo Fraga, interview with the author,

Vitória, 15 June 1983; Mauro Antônio Moraes Victor, lecture presented at the meeting of the Sociedade Brasileira para o Progresso da Ciência, Manaus, 12 July 1983; Brazil, Fundação Instituto Brasileiro de Geografia e Estatística, *Anuário Estatístico do Brasil, 1991* (Rio de Janeiro, 1991), pp. 528, 958. Cubic meters here are converted to tons at 500 kilograms per cubic meter.

11. Keith Alger and Marcellos Caldas, "The Crisis of the Cocoa Economy and the Future of the Bahian Atlantic Forest" (paper presented at the Latin American Studies Association Conference, Los Angeles, September 1992); Angus Wright, "Land Tenure, Agrarian Policy, and Forest Conservation in Southern Bahia, Brazil" (paper presented at the Latin American Studies Association Conference, Los Angeles, September 1992).

12. "IBDF Não Detém Devastação no Rio," *OESP*, 25 January 1976.

13. Paulo de Azevedo Berutti, "Contribuição Energético das Florestas Brasileiras," *Silvicultura*, 1 (July-August 1976), 25. The second quotation is secondhand, from the person who threatened to tell the IBDF; see Norma Couri, "A Briga entre Ecologistas e Fazendeiros em Bocaina de Minas; Uma Ameaça ao Parque de Itatiaia," *Jornal do Brasil* [hereafter *JdB*], 30 November 1980.

14. Fraga, interview; Victor, lecture; Albert Alcouloumbre, Jr., "Desmatamentos Ilegais Destroem Unica Reserva Florestal Primitiva do Norte Fluminense," *O Globo*, 7 September 1982; São Paulo (State), Instituto Florestal, "Distrito Florestal do Vale da Ribeira," pamphlet (São Paulo, [1982?]).

15. Dorothy Sue Dunn de Araújo and Norma Crud Maciel, "Os Manguezais do Recôncavo da Baía de Guanabara," *Cadernos FEEMA*, Série Técnica 10/79 (October 1979).

16. Brazil, Instituto Brasileiro de Desenvolvimento Florestal, *O Setor Florestal Brasileiro, 1979/85* (Brasília, [1986?]), pp. 9, 11; Fundação João Pinheiro, *Perspectivas para a Siderurgia a Carvão Vegetal* (Belo Horizonte, 1978), pp. 2–6; Brazil, Ministério de Minas e Energia, *Matriz Energética Brasileira* (Brasília, 1973); "Matas Nativas Fornecem 80% do Carvão da Siderurgia Mineira," *JdB*, 9 October 1988; Rio de Janeiro, Secretaria de Estado de Obras e Meio Ambiente, "Desmatamento: Propostas para o Controle" (Rio de Janeiro, 1984), xerog.; Rio de Janeiro (State), Secretaria de Estado de Agricultura e Abastecimento, Departamento Geral de Economia Rural, "Estimativa do Consumo de Combustiveis no Estado do Rio de Janeiro: Subsídios para uma Política de Reflorestamento" (Rio de Janeiro, [1981?]), xerog., pp. 8–10; Carlos Eugênio Thibau, "Potencial Leheiro e Perspectivas da Economia Carvoeira" (paper presented at the Consulta sobre Economia Florestal no Brasil, 1, Rio de Janeiro, 1972), mimeog.; Maria Elisa Linhares Borges, "A Recriação de uma Fronteira: A Luta pela Terra no Leste de Minas Gerais," *Revista Brasileira de Estudos Políticos*, Special Number (July 1991), p. 184.

17. "Reserva Florestal Devastada," *OESP*, 7 December 1977; Luiz Pinguelli Rosa, coord., *Relatório de Pesquisa: O Uso da Lenha no Setor Doméstico Rural do Estado do Rio de Janeiro* (Rio de Janeiro, 1987), pp. 114, 116.

18. Sociedade Botânica do Brasil, *Centuria Plantarum Brasiliensium Exstintionis Minitata* (n.p., 1992), p. 26. The fern is *Dicksonia sellowia*; caxeta is *Tabebuia cassinoides*. See also Cory T. de Carvalho, "Esboço de uma Introdução ao Levantamento de Mamíferos Silvestres," in *Recursos Naturais, Meio Ambiente e Poluição* (Rio de Janeiro, 1977), 1:235; "Plantas Ameaçadas de Extinção; Os Botânicos Reclamam: Não Há Verba," *O Globo*, 3 April 1981; Luiz Fernando Emediato,

"Faltam Recursos para Conter a Devastação," *OESP*, 23 January 1979; Fraga, interview; "Reserva Florestal Devastada"; Léa Goldenstein, "Aspectos da Reorganização do Espaço Brasileiro face a Novas Relações de Intercâmbio" (Livre Docência thesis, University of São Paulo, 1975), pp. 113, 113n; Célia Maria Romano, "A Rede Clandestina dos Palmitos," *OESP*, 15 January 1984; Sarah Fitzgerald, *International Wildlife Trade: Whose Business Is It?* (Washington, DC, 1989), pp. 52–54, 158, 164.

19. São Paulo (State), Secretaria dos Negócios Metropolitanos, *Proteção das Mananciais na Grande São Paulo* ([São Paulo, n.d.]); Cecília Pires, "Ameaça à Rica Natureza do Morro Grande," *FSP*, 22 January 1978; Sebastião Fonseca César, "Pressões Urbanas sobre Areas Silvestres: Reserva da Cantareira, Um Exemplo," in Congresso Florestal Brasileiro, 3, Manáus, 1978, *Anais* (São Paulo, 1978), 2:220–221.

20. Norma Crud Maciel, "Praias, Dunas e Restingas," in Simpósio de Ecossistemas da Costa Sul e Sudeste Brasileira, 2, Aguas de Lindóia, 1990, *Anais* (São Paulo, 1990), 3:328; "Helicópteros para Evitar Derrubadas," *FSP*, 30 October 1981; São Paulo, Superintendência do Desenvolvimento do Litoral Paulista, *Plano Básico de Desenvolvimento Auto-Sustentado para a Região Lagunar de Iguape e Cananéia* (São Paulo, 1987), pp. 15, 20.

21. For a thorough study of the environmental politics of the period, see Ronald A. Foresta, *Amazon Conservation in the Age of Development: The Limits of Providence* (Gainesville, FL, 1991).

22. Ricardo Lisboa da Cunha, "Resumo das Principais Implicações na Segurança e Desenvolvimento Nacionais Decorrentes da Necessidade da Preservação do Meio Ambiente" (lecture delivered at the Escola Superior de Guerra [hereafter ESG], Rio de Janeiro, 16 June 1980).

23. Foster and Foster, *Brazil*, pp. 155–158; "Augusto Ruschi," *OESP*, 7 October 1966; Hitoshi Namura, "Da Captura ao Alimento é Complexo Criar Beija-Flores," *OESP*, Suplemento Agrícola, 15 November 1978

24. Augusto Ruschi, "O Problema Florestal no Estado de Espírito Santo, 1948" (thesis Presented to the Conferência de Florestas e Produtos Florestais, Teresópolis, 1948).

25. "Ruschi Depõe no Senado e Acusa Governador Capixaba de Corrupto e Mentiroso," *JdB*, 28 October 1977. The governor who had defended Ruschi's reserve was Santos Neves; Augusto Ruschi, interview with the author, Santa Tereza, 14 June, 1983. See also "Augusto Ruschi, o Apóstolo Que Prega na Floresta," *OESP*, 26 January 1977; "Este Homem Está Disposto a Morrer," *Jornal da Tarde*, 12 September 1977. Ruschi was not the only naturalist to be targeted; cf. the invasion of Giuseppe Rossi della Riva's farmstead in the Ribeira valley in "Devastação Ameaça Serra do Mar," *OESP*, 7 May 1972.

26. "Augusto Ruschi, o Apóstolo"; "Ocupação da Reserva de Comboios," *OESP*, 25 August 1977.

27. Rogério Medeiros, "Na Guerra AntiBeija-Flor, Todos os Cartuchos contra Ruschi," *JdB*, 7 September 1977; Rosenthal Calmon Alves, "Enfim, a Resistência," *JdB*, 15 September 1977; "Ruschi a Promessa Oficial: O Cientista Terá sua Reserva Assegurada, *JdB*, 20 September 1977; Fernando Achiamé, interview with the author, Vitória, 13 June 1981; "Para Ruschi, Pior Ainda Pode Vir," *JdB*, 28 September 1977; "O Caso Ruschi: A Universidade Fecha Questão e Não Abre," *JdB*, 29 Sep-

tember 1977; "O Meio-Ambiente Quer um Final Feliz," *JdB*, 28 September 1977; "Ruschi na Floresta Encantada," *JdB*, 15 October 1977; "Homenageado, Ruschi Critica Alvares," *OESP*, 5 October 1977.

28. Calmon Alves, "Enfim."

29. João José Bigarella, *Segurança Ambiental: Uma Questão de Consciência . . . e Muitas Vezes de Segurança Nacional* (Curitiba, 1974).

30. Lisboa da Cunha, "Resumo." See also Paulo Nogueira Neto, "Ação Governamental na Preservação do Meio Ambiente" (lecture delivered at the ESG, 18 June 1980), xerog.; José Cândido de Mello Carvalho, "A Preservação do Meio Ambiente e as Implicações na Segurança e Desenvolvimento Nacionais" (lecture delivered at the ESG, 16 June 1980), xerog.; "Subcomandante da ESG [Pedro Frazão de Medeiros Lima] Vê Areas Florestais em Processo de Extinção," *Boletim da FEEMA*, 7 (January 1981), 38.

31. Lisboa da Cunha, "Resumo."

32. Fraga, interview; Jaime Larica, quoted in "Técnico Denuncia Indústria do ES por Poluir Litoral," *OESP*, 2 December 1979; Consórcio Mata Atlântica–Universidade Estadual de Campinas, Seminário Nacional Reserva da Biosfera da Mata Atlântica, Campinas, December 1991, *Anais* ([Campinas, 1992?]), p. 55.

33. "A Ciência Ambiental e seus Reflexos na Segurança e Desenvolvimento Nacionais" (14 vols.; class report, ESG, Rio de Janeiro, 1980), xerog.

34. José Augusto Drummond, "National Parks in Brazil: A Study of 50 Years of Environmental Policy (With Case Studies of the National Parks of the State of Rio de Janeiro)" (M.A. thesis, Evergreen State College, 1988); Carlos A. Girotti, *Estado Nuclear no Brasil* (São Paulo, 1984), pp. 213–236; Statement of Paulo Nogueira Neto in Brasil, SEMA, *Encontro sobre Areas Naturais Preservadas na Região Neo-Tropical, Porto Alegre, 1980* (Brasília, 1980), pp. 183–207; Francisco Luiz Noel, "A Mata Que Resiste," *JdB*, 10 February 1992; "Floresta do Mendanha Tem Armadilhas," *JdB*, 22 April 1992; Helmut Sick, *Ornitologia Brasileira* (3d ed.; Brasília, 1984), 1:93.

35. Drummond, "National Parks," pp. 140, 291–297, 392; São Paulo (State), Instituto Florestal, *Projeto de Pesquisas Florestais no Estado de São Paulo* (São Paulo, 1979), quadro 3 (xerog.); São Paulo (State), Conselho Estadual do Meio Ambiente, *Areas Naturais do Estado de São Paulo* (São Paulo, 1985); Cory T. de Carvalho, "Mamíferos dos Parques e Reservas de São Paulo," *Silvicultura em São Paulo*, 13–14 (1979–1980), 51–52.

36. Scott A. Mori, "Southern Bahian Moist Forests," *Botanical Review*, 49 (April-June 1983), p. 168; Drummond, "National Parks," pp. 147–149, 340, 392, 395.

37. Drummond, "National Parks," pp. 97, 119, 188–189, 290, 298; "Devastação Avança e Governo Preserva Só 3% das Reservas," *OESP*, 22 January 1978. On interagency competition, see Aziz N. Ab'Saber, "Diretrizes para uma Política de Preservação de Reservas Naturais no Estado de São Paulo," *Geografia e Planejamento* (1977), No. 30, 3–4.

38. Fernando Roberto Martins, *Estrutura de uma Floresta Mesófila* (Campinas, 1991), pp. 69–71; "Itatiaia Fora de Perigo, Mas Danos São Grandes," *OESP*, 15 September 1981; "Nossas Matas em Chamas," *Jornal da Tarde*, 11 September 1981; "A Grande Queimada," *Veja*, 23 September 1981.

39. Leandro José Bellix Favrin, "Levantamento da Cobertura Vegetal do Município de Campos do Jordão no Período de 1962 a 1977, Através de Fotografias Aé-

reas," *Silvicultura em São Paulo*, 17–19 (1983–1985), 39–45; "Preservação Começa Timidamente," *OESP*, 18 August 1974.

40. Mauro Antônio Moraes Victor, *A Devastação Florestal* (São Paulo, n.d.), p. 7; "Araújo Dias Alega Indisciplina do Instituto Florestal," *OESP*, 8 January 1975.

41. J. G. Rivelli Magalhães, "O Desenvolvimento da Engenharia Florestal no Brasil," in Congresso Brasileiro de Florestas Tropicais, 2, Mossoró, 1976, *Anais* (São Paulo, 1976), p. 293; "IBDF Ampliou Prazos para Florestal," *JdB*, 9 October 1988; Goldenstein, "Aspectos," pp. 136–162, 168–170.

42. Companhia Souza Cruz Indústria e Comércio, "Perfil" (n.p., [1988?]); Aracruz Celulose, S.A., "Meio Ambiente" ([Rio de Janeiro, 1988]); idem, "Relatório Anual" (Rio de Janeiro, 1988]); idem, "Demonstrações Financeiras em 31 de Dezembro de 1988 e de 1987" ([Rio de Janeiro, 1989]); idem, "Aracruz Celulose" ([Rio de Janeiro, 1988]); idem, "Aracruz Project" (Aracruz, 1989), xerog.; Edgard Campinhos Junior, Luiz Soresini, and Francisco Valério, Aracruz managers, and Luis Pellegrini, Banco Safra, interviews with the author, Aracruz, 9 November 1989; Goldenstein, "Aspectos," pp. 198–201; International Task Force, *Tropical Forests: A Call for Action* (Washington, DC, 1985), 2:49–50; "Aracruz Investe US$1.2 Bilhão em Nova Fábrica," *FSP*, 25 May 1991; James Brooke, "High Profile on Environment for Brazilian Company," *New York Times*, 1 June 1992.

43. "Ruschi Depõe"; Programa de Pesquisa e Conservação de Areas Umidas do Brasil, *Inventário*, pp. 307–308; Ecotec—Economia e Engenharia Industrial, S.A., *Potencial Florestal e Silvicultura no Estado do Espírito Santo* (Rio de Janeiro, 1967); Maria Inês Ladeira and Gilberto Azanha, *Os Indios da Serra do Mar: A Presença Mbyá-Guarani em São Paulo* (São Paulo, 1988), p. 37. "Biólogo Aponta Dano Trazido pela Aracruz," *OESP*, 13 December 1978; "Cientista Denuncia Governo," *JdB*, 10 December 1978; Augusto Ruschi, "O Eucalipto e a Ecologia," *Boletim do Museu de Biologia Prof. Mello Leitão*, Série Divulgação (31 May 1976), No. 44.

44. "Empresa Quer Reduzir Poluição," *FSP*, 25 May 1991.

45. The foreign owners, with equal shares in 84 percent of the company, were Banco Safra, Companhia Souza Cruz, and Lorentzen. See *The Greenpeace Book of Greenwash* ([Washington, DC, 1992]), pp. 27–28.

46. Mário Capp Filho, "Avaliação Econômico do Reflorestamento no Estado de Minas Gerais: Efeitos do Incentivo Florestal" (M.A. thesis, Federal University of Viçosa, 1976), pp. 1–80; Brazil, IBDF, Seminário sobre o Planejamento do Desenvolvimento Florestal e do Uso da Terra, Rio de Janeiro, 1977, *Anais* (Rio de Janeiro, 1978), 2:56–65.

47. "A Utilização de Terras Marginais para o Reflorestamento," *Silvicultura*, 2 (September-October 1976), 10–12; Dammis Heinsdijk, *Forestry in Southern Brazil* (n.p., [1970?]), pp. 65, 68.

48. José Cándido de Melo Carvalho, *Entomologia e Meio Ambiente* (Rio de Janeiro, 1979), p. 36; Francisco A. M. Mariconi, *As saúvas* (São Paulo, 1970), pp. 103–111; Francisco Schade, "The Ecology of Leaf-Cutting Ants in Paraguay," in J. Richard Gorham, ed., *Paraguay: Ecological Essays* (Miami, FL, 1973), pp. 89–90; Minas Gerais, Instituto Estadual Florestal, *Prodemata: Programa de Desenvolvimento Integrado da Zona da Mata* (Belo Horizonte, 1976), p. 60.

49. Alceo Magnanini, "Situação, Legislação e Política Florestais, Algumas Sugestões" (Rio de Janeiro, 1979), xerog., p. 3; Godofredo N. Tinoco, *Sugestões para o Reflorestamento* (Campos, 1940), 6; Marco Takao Inoue, *Regeneração Natural:*

Seus Problemas e Perspectivas para as Florestas Brasileiras (Curitiba, 1979); José Ferrari Leite, *Desmatamento e Erosão em Presidente Prudente*, Caderno No. 2, Geografia Regional (Presidente Prudente, 1965).

50. Cristóvão Ferreira de Sá, *O Eucalipto e o Reflorestamento do Brasil no Quadro da Natureza* (São Paulo, 1952), p. 26; Walter de Paula Lima, *O Reflorestamento com Eucalipto e os seus Impactos Ambientais* (São Paulo, 1987), pp. 44–67, 78, 80, 85, 87–91, 93; Germi Porto Santos, "Eucalipto versus Ecologia," *Revista da Madeira*, 25 (October 1976), 21–25; Helládio do Amaral Mello, "Florestas Naturais e Implantadas: Uma Discussão Irrelevante," *Silvicultura*, 1 (July-August 1976), 13–16.

51. Mário Borgonovi et al., "Cobertura Vegetal do Estado de São Paulo, II Levantamento por Fotointerpretação das Areas Cobertas com Floresta Natural e Reflorestamento," *Bragantia*, 26 (1967), No. 6, 93–117; J. V. Chiarini and Arnaldo Guido de Souza Coelho, "Cobertura Vegetal Natural e Areas Reflorestadas do Estado de São Paulo," *Boletim do Instituto Agronômico* (August 1969), No. 193, pp. 1–28; São Paulo, Instituto Florestal, *Levantamento da Cobertura Natural e do Reflorestamento no Estado de São Paulo*, Boletim Técnico No. 11 (August 1974); Victor, *Devastação*. Similar maps have been published for Paraná and South Bahia: Fundação Araucária [brochure without title] (Curitiba, n.d.); Projeto Mata Atlântica Nordeste, "45 Anos de Desmatamento no Sul da Bahia" (Ilhéus, Brazil, 1994).

CHAPTER 14. GETTING IT OFF THE PAPER

1. See Ronald A. Foresta, *Amazon Conservation in the Age of Development: The Limits of Providence* (Gainesville, FL, 1991).

2. Demóstenes Teixeira, "Devastação 50 Hectares por Dia," *Jornal da Tarde* [hereafter *JdT*], 2 September 1987; Bruno Casotti, "A Repetida Agressão às Matas," *Jornal do Brasil* [hereafter *JdB*], 8 March 1989; José Antônio Vera, "Paraguai Corre Risco de Ficar sem Arvores," *JdB*, 27 January 1992.

3. "Juiz Absolve Mulher que Loteou a Billings," *JdT*, 12 January 1991; Denise Pires Vaz, "Mata Atlântica: O Milagre do Verde no Rio de Janeiro," *Revista Geográfica Universal* (July 1990), No. 188, 86, 90; Celina Côrtes, "Jardim Botânico Vai Expulsar Ocupantes Clandestinos," *JdB*, 27 April 1986; Paulo Roberto Araújo, "Cabritos Impedem Reflorestamento," *O Globo*, 23 October 1991; Vicente Moreira Conti, "A Questão das Florestas no Estado de São Paulo" (Rio de Janeiro, 1987), xerog.

4. "Os Matadores da Serra do Mar," *JdT*, 18 October 1990; "Garimpo Prejudica Meio Ambiente em S.P.," *A Crítica* (Manaus), 10 October 1990.

5. Aziz Ab'Saber, *A Serra do Mar na Região de Cubatão*, Coleção Documentos, Série Ciências Ambientais, No. 6, Instituto de Estudos Avançados (São Paulo, 1991), p. 33.

6. The 1980 entry was written by Randau Azevedo Marques, then representing the Brazilian Foundation for the Conservation of Nature. The most distressing entries are by schoolteachers and their charges, sunnily oblivious of the disaster they were witnessing: For the city child, Alto da Serra was by comparison still edenic!

7. Léa Goldenstein, *A Industrialização na Baixada Santista: Estudo de um*

Centro Industrial Satélite, Monografia No. 7, Instituto de Geografia, University of São Paulo (São Paulo, 1972); Samuel M. Branco, *O Fenómeno Cubatão* (São Paulo, 1984).

8. Kurt Hueck, *Wandlungen im Antlitz der Landschaft um São Paulo (Brasilien)* (Bremen, 1958), pp. 2–4; Leopoldo Magno Coutinho, "Contribuição ao Conhecimento da Ecologia da Mata Pluvial Tropical," *Boletim FFCL–USP,* Botânica, No. 18 (1962), No. 257, 1–35; Moysés Kuhlman, "Aspectos e Problemas da Conservação da Natureza no Brasil," *ABEF, Anuário Brasileiro de Economia Florestal* 7 (1954), 300; Ab'Saber, *Serra do Mar,* pp. 3–4; Pierre Gourou, *Les pays tropicaux* (Paris, 1947), pp. 15–23; Olga Cruz, *A Serra do Mar e o Litoral na Area de Caraguatatuba* (São Paulo, 1974), pp. 155–161.

9. University of São Paulo, Grupo de Estudos de Poluição do Ar [Celso M.–Q. Orsini, coord.], "Relatório Final; Avaliação Preliminar da Qualidade do Ar de Cubatão" (São Paulo, July 1982); Cubatão, Coordenadoria de Saúde e Promoção Social, "Poluição Ambiental na Baixada Santista" (Cubatão, 1974), mimeog.; Faculdade de Ciências Médicas de Santos, *Estudo Epidemiológico de Asma Brónquica, Rinite, e Bronquite Crónica, na Cidade de Cubatão em Dois Períodos, 1982 e 1988* (n.p., n.d.); "Crianças Deformadas pela Poluição em Vila Parisi," *O Estado de São Paulo* [hereafter *OESP*], 4 February 1981.

10. "Chuva Desabriga 750 em Cubatão," *OESP,* 21 January 1975; Nivaldo Lemes da Silva Filho, *Recomposição da Cobertura Vegetal de um Trecho Degradado da Serra do Mar, Cubatão, SP* (Campinas, 1988), p. 20; Maria Eugênia M.–C. Ferreira, "Estudo Biogeográfica de Líquens com Indicadores de Poluição do Ar em Cubatão," *Boletim de Geografia* (Maringá), 2 (January 1984), 52–75. The botanist was Nanusa Luísa Meneses; see José Ortiz, "A Serra do Mar Está Morrendo," *Folha de São Paulo* [hereafter *FSP*], 16 November 1980. She led a tour of environmentalists to the Serra do Mar; see "Uma Reserva Ecológica Está Morrendo (Envenenado)," *OESP,* 1 December 1981; "A Serra do Mar: Que Beleza,"*JdT,* 17 December 1981.

11. São Paulo, Companhia Estadual de Tecnologia de Saneamento Básico [hereafter CETESB], *Relatório Anual: Controle de Fontes Poluidores* (São Paulo, 1978); São Paulo, Assembléia Legislativa, Comissão Especial de Inquérito para Apurar Possíveis Irregularidades no Município de Cubatão e Dar Soluções aos Problemas da Poluição Ambiental, *Relatório Final* (São Paulo, May 1981); CETESB, *Avaliação das Emissões de Poluentes Atmosféricos de Origem Industrial na Região de Cubatão: Subsídios para uma Política de Ação* (São Paulo, [November 1980]); "O Segredo da Cidade Envenenada," *OESP,* 4 March 1982; "E a Cetesb Diz: Há Poluição em Cubatão," *JdT,* 11 January 1983.

12. CETESB, *Degradação da Cobertura Vegetal da Serra do Mar em Cubatão: Avaliação Preliminar* (São Paulo, January 1981); idem, *Degradação . . ., Anexo: Complementação—Levantamento Aerofotogramétrico do Ano de 1980* (São Paulo, May 1982); CETESB, *Baixada Santista: Memorial Descritivo e Carta do Meio Ambiente e de sua Dinâmica* (São Paulo, 1985), pp. 12–13; Leda Mondin, "Na Visão Aérea, as Terras Nuas das Encostas," *A Tribuna* (Santos), 6 June 1985; "Governador Vai Receber Relatório Secreto da Poluição de Cubatão," *OESP,* 9 May 1980; "Estado da Poluição em Cubatão Já Não Desperta Interesse," *OESP,* 31 October 1975.

13. Sílvia Levi-Moreira, "Cubatão: Crescimento e Devastação" (term paper presented in a graduate course in environmental history, University of São Paulo, April 1985).

14. "A Enchente: Vila Parisi: 2,500 Desabrigados," *OESP*, 24 January 1985; "Zulauf Foi Ver Devastação e Não Viu Nada," *Folha da Tarde*, 3 August 1985; Élio Lopes dos Santos et al., "Vazamento de Amônia em Cubatão" (paper presented at the Congresso Brasileiro de Engenharia Sanitária e Ambiental, 13, Maceió, 1985), xerog.; "Vazamento de Amônia Gera Novo Pânico em Cubatão," *OESP*, 27 January 1985.

15. "A Usina Ameaçada" [27 February], *Visão*, 25 March 1985, pp. 32–34. The director was Régis Guillaumon, accompanied by Hélio Ogawa and Russell Mittermaier; Guillaumon, personal communication, 4 January 1991; "A Morte Desce a Serra," *Visão*, 11 March 1985, pp. 25–29.

16. Helmut Troppmaier and Maria Eugênia M. C. Ferreira, "Cobertura Vegetal, Poluição Aerea e Deslizamentos na Serra do Mar," *Geografia* (Rio Claro), 12 (April 1987), 117–128. The scientist was Mauro Victor; see Lane Valiengo, "Catástrofe na Serra do Mar em 86," *A Tribuna*, 29 May 1985; Leda Mondin, "E Zulauf Diz Que Não Conhecia o Relatório," *A Tribuna*, 31 May 1985; Rachel Melamet, "Obras de Emergência na Serra Só Ficarão Prontas em Janeiro," *FSP*, 6 October 1985; São Paulo, Secretaria do Meio Ambiente, *A Serra do Mar: Degredação e Recuperação*, Série Documentos (São Paulo, 1990).

17. "Serra do Mar Terá Plano de Emergência," *FSP*, 20 April 1985; CETESB, *Ação da CETESB em Cubatão: Situação em Junho de 1992* (São Paulo, 1992); idem, *Aspectos Fitossociológicos da Vegetação da Serra do Mar Degradada pela Poluição Atmosférica de Cubatão* (São Paulo, June 1989); Luiza S. J. Aguiar and Roney P. Santos, "Mapeamento da Cobertura Vegetal e das Cicatrizes de Escorregamentos na Serra do Mar-Cubatão," in Seminário de Integração Técnica sobre Poluição e a Serra do Mar, São Paulo, December 1988, *Seminário . . .* (São Paulo, 1989), pp. 37–44; Nivaldo Lemes da Silva Filho, *Recomposição de Cobertura Vegetal de um Trecho Degradado da Serra do Mar, Cubatão, SP* (Campinas, 1988); "IPT Fará Estudo na Serra do Mar," *OESP*, 24 May 1991.

18. "Ambiente: Protestos, Desabafos, Choro," *JdT*, 29 October 1985.

19. Brazil, Secretaria Especial do Meio Ambiente, *Catálogo Nacional das Instituições Que Atuam na Area do Meio Ambiente* (Brasília, 1982); Forum de ONGs Brasileiros, *Meio Ambiente e Desenvolvimento: Uma Visão das ONGs e dos Movimentos Sociais Brasileiros* (Rio de Janeiro, 1992); *Boletim S.O.S. Mata Atlântica*, 4 (June-July 1992), 3; *Jornal Verde*, 1 (13 May 1988), 4.

20. Fundação Brasileira para a Conservação da Natureza, Conferência Brasileira de Proteção à Natureza, 2, Rio de Janeiro, July 1984, "Relatório Preliminar" (xerog.); Encontro Nacional das Organizações Não-Governamentais Conservacionistas, 4, Rio de Janeiro, July, 1984, "Declaração" xerog.; "FBCN—Esta Sigla Defende a Natureza," *JdT*, 29 August 1978; Eduardo Viola, *O Movimento Ecológico no Brasil, 1974–1986: Do Ambientalismo à Ecopolítica* (Notre Dame, IN, 1987); Mauro Victor, "Raizes Históricas do Movimento Conservacionista Brasileiro," *Ciência e Cultura*, 31 (June 1978), 644–651.

21. Frederico Fuellgraf, "Quarup, A Fórmula Mágica para os Ecologistas Brasileiros," *FSP*, 8 August 1982; *Boletim S.O.S. Mata Atlântica* 4 (May 1992), 2.

22. Jair Borin, "Deixam-nos em Paz em Nossas Terras," *FSP*, 11 February 1979;

"Reforma Agrária Agora Ameaça a Reserva de Ribeirão," *OESP*, 4 December 1986; "Relatório Acusa Colonos de Devastar Area em Minas Gerais," *FSP*, 4 July 1990; Angus Wright, "Land Tenure, Agrarian Policy, and Forest Conservation in Southern Bahia, Brazil" (paper presented at the Latin American Studies Association Conference, Los Angeles, September 1992); "A Reforma Agrária Ilegal," *O Compensado* 1 (May 1987), 7; Teixeira, "Devastação"; Mauro Victor, lecture presented at the meeting of the Sociedade Brasileira para o Progresso da Ciencia, Belém, July 1983; Paulo França, "Berço de Mudas, Horto Quase Virou um Cemitério," *O Globo*, 1 March 1987. Surprisingly, landscaper and environmentalist Roberto Burle Marx was associated with this plan.

23. The literature of sustainable development, or ecodevelopment, is vast; see Ignacy Sachs, *Strategies de l'écodeveloppement* (Paris, 1980). A useful synthesis is W. M. Adams, *Green Development: Environment and Sustainability in the Third World* (London, 1990). See also Consórcio Mata Atlântica and Universidade Estadual de Campinas [hereafter CMA–UNICAMP], *Reserva da Biosfera da Mata Atlântica: Plano de Ação* (São Paulo, 1992), 1:65.

24. The most visible environmentalist-entrepreneur was Rodrigo Lara Mesquita, heir and editor of São Paulo's most important media company, a founder of S.O.S. Mata Atlântica, and severe critic of development policies; see Rodrigo L. Mesquita, "A Ocupação Selvagem Continua," *Jornal Verde*, 1 (13 May 1988), 1; José Ruy Gandra, "A Mancha Verde Se Espalha," *EXAME VIP*, 27 June 1990, p. 28; Regina Pessoa, "Preservação das Espésies," *Jornal Verde*, 1 (13 May 1988), 3.

25. Gandra, "Mancha Verde," p. 27; Thomas E. Lacher et al., "National and International Cooperation in Wildlife Management and Conservation at a Brazilian University," in M. J. Mares and D. J. Schmidly, eds., *Latin American Mammalogy: History, Biodiversity and Conservation* (Norman, OK, 1991), p. 370; Édis Milaré and Ronald Magri, "Cubatão: Um Modelo de Desenvolvimento Não Sustentável," *São Paulo em Perspectiva*, 6 (January-June 1992), 99–105; Bruno Casotti, "Os Exploradores do Desengano," *JdB*, 20 May 1989. Nira Worcman concluded that "to a considerable extent" environmentalism was a "fad"; see "Brazil's Thriving Environmental Movement," *Technology Review*, 93 (October 1990), 42–51.

26. Lacher et al., "National and International," p. 370. Among contributors to Brazilian environmental organizations were the World Wildlife Fund, the Nature Conservancy, and the National Wildlife Federation. See Fernando Homem de Mello, "O 'Times,' a Dívida e a Ecologia," *FSP*, 11 March 1989; Caio Túlio Costa, "Itamaraty Exclui a Amazônia da Declaração de Haia," *FSP*, 11 March 1989. Privileged media access of foreign environmentalists like Jacques Cousteau caused some to worry that so many dashing foreign models might further alienate national consciousness; see Edilson Martins, "A Natureza e Ainda Jacques Cousteau e o Xingu," *Jornal do País*, 3 June 1985.

27. "Piquet Carneiro Substituído; Mas Ainda Falta Verba," *OESP*, 21 May 1974); Fundação Brasileira para a Conservação da Natureza–FBCN [a description of past and current projects] (n.p., [1991?]), xerog.

28. A. Paulo M. Galvão, *International Cooperation on Forestry Research and Development* (Curitiba, 1991), pp. 68, 93–94; CMA–UNICAMP, *Reserva*, 1:69; "Mata Atlântica e Tietê Vão Ter Investimento de Banco Alemão," *JdB*, 6 August 1992; Mônica Falcone, "Brasil Recusa Verbas para Proteger as suas Florestas," *O Globo*, 20 February 1988.

29. The best source on Chico Mendes is Andrew Revkin, *The Burning Season* (Boston, 1990).

30. Brazil, Departamento de Recursos Naturais e Estudos Ambientais, "Cadastro de Areas Especiais" ([Brasília], October 1990), printout; Brazil, Fundação Instituto Brasileiro de Geografia e Estatística, *Anuário Estatístico do Brasil, 1991* (Brasília, 1991), pp. 56–57.

31. Edilson Martins, "Resurreição de uma Tribo," *Isto É*, 4 May 1977, pp. 36–40; Mitico Yoshijima, "Madereiros Usam Indios para Devastar Parque," *O Globo*, 7 January 1989; "Pataxós Não São os Unicos Culpados," *JdT*, 15 March 1989; K. H. Redford, "Monte Pascoal: Indigenous Rights and Conservation in Conflict," *Oryx*, 23 (January 1989), 33–36; Sérgio Brant Rocha, "Parque Nacional de Monte Pascoal," in Amend, Stephen and Thora, eds., *Espacios sin habituntes? Parques nacionales en América do Sul* (Caracas, 1992), pp. 125–135; "Técnicos Dizem Que Indios Impedem o Combate ao Incéndio," *JdB*, 7 March 1989; "Surto de Cólera Atinge Reserva de Indios Pataxós," *OESP*, 20 October 1992; "Chuva em Porto Seguro Não Acaba com o Fogo na Reserva dos Pataxó," *JdB*, 8 March 1989. Another logging tribe was the Caiapó, in Pará State; see "Floresta de Contradições," *Veja* (3 March 1993), p. 51.

32. Maria Inês Ladeira and Gilberto Azanha, *Os Indios da Serra do Mar: A Presença Mbyá-Guarani em São Paulo* (São Paulo, 1988), pp. 7–27.

33. L. P. Vianna and M. C. W. Brito, "Vila de Picinguaba: O Caso de uma Comunidade Caiçara no Interior de uma Area Protegida," in Congresso Nacional sobre Essências Nativas, 2, São Paulo, *Anais*, special edition of *Revista do Instituto Florestal* (March 1992), 1067–1073.

34. CMA–UNICAMP, *Reserva*, 1:27–28; idem, Seminário Nacional—Reserva da Biosfera da Mata Atlântica, Campinas, December 1991, *Anais* ([Campinas, 1992]), 8–11, 13–18, 104–106; Paulo Nogueira Neto, comments, in Brazil, Secretaria Especial do Meio Ambiente, *Encontro sobre Areas Naturais Preservadas na Regiao Neo-Tropical, Porto Alegre, 1980* (Brasília, 1980), p. 206.

35. Carlos Vogt [rector of the University of Campinas], "O Brasil do Arrastão e dos Caras-Pintadas," *FSP*, 28 October 1992.

36. CMA–UNICAMP, *Reserva*, 1:33; São Paulo, Secretaria de Cultura, Conselho de Defesa do Patrimônio Histórico, Arqueológico, Artístico e Turístico [CONDEPHAAT], Resolução No. 40, 6 June 1985, mimeog.; Paraná, Secretaria de Cultura e do Esporte, Coordenadoria do Patrimônio Cultural, *Tombamento da Serra do Mar* (Curitiba, 1987).

37. Consórcio Mata Atlântica, *Proposta de Reconhecimento dos Remanescentes da Mata Atlântica Como Reserva da Biosfera da UNESCO* (n.p., n.d.); Encontro Nacional das Organizações Não-Governamentais Conservacionistas, "Declaração," p. 2; José Pedro de Oliveira Costa, Secretary of Environment (São Paulo) to Maria Tereza Jorge Pádua, Councillor to International Union for the Conservation of Nature, São Paulo, 18 June 1986, xerog.

38. Fundação S.O.S. Mata Atlântica [hereafter SOS–MA], Reunião Nacional sobre a Proteção dos Ecossistemas Naturais da Mata Atlântica, Workshop Mata Atlântica, Atibaia, March-April 1990, *Anais* (São Paulo, [1990]); Brazil, President, Decree 99,547, 22 September 1990, xerog.

39. CMA–UNICAMP, *Reserva*, 1:63, 70; Carlos Alfredo Joly, "A Preservação da

Serra do Japi," in L. Patrícia Morellato, org., *História Natural da Serra do Japi* (Campinas, 1992), pp. 315–316; "Mata Atlântica Quer Mais Investimento," *JdB*, 22 April 1990; Eduardo Pires de Castanho et al. estimated the cost of expropriation of 341,493 hectares in São Paulo at US$176 million in June 1984; see their *Proposta de Política Florestal para o Estado de São Paulo*, Publicação Instituto Florestal, No. 24 (São Paulo, June 1984), xerog. See also Florência Costa and Ricardo Miranda Filho, "IBAMA Manda Investigar Compra Irregular de Terras," *JdB*, 27 July 1989.

40. Teresa Furtado, "A Lei Protege a Arvore: E Acaba com uma Arte," *JdT*, 24 August 1991; Rosemeiry Tardivo, "Norma Permite Exploração no Paraná," *Gazeta Mercantil*, 28 September 1991; Brasil, Instituto Brasileiro do Meio Ambiente e Recursos Naturais Renováveis—IBAMA, "Instrução Normativa No. 78," 25 September 1991 (xerog.).

41. José Augusto Drummond, "National Parks in Brazil: A Study of 50 Years of Environmental Policy (With Case Studies of the National Parks of the State of Rio de Janeiro)" (M.A. thesis, Evergreen State College, 1988), pp. 97, 188–189; "No Desenvolvimento Florestal, a Maior Falha do IBDF," *O Compensado*, 1 (May 1987), 4; "Proposta do Corpo Técnico-Administrativo do Instituto Florestal ao Senhor Coordenador da Coordenadoria da Pesquisa de Recursos Naturais" ([São Paulo, 1983]), xerog.; Paulo Nogueira Neto, "É Preciso Liberar Recursos Existentes para os Parques," *Jornal Verde* (March 1990), No. 20, 3; Werner Zulauf [ex-president of IBAMA], "IBAMA—Oitava Diretoria," *FSP*, 31 October 1992.

42. Drummond, "National Parks," p. 322; "IBDF Aponta Uso Doloso de Guias de Exploração," *FSP*, 20 November 1987; Antônio S. Tozzi, "Falta de Verbas, o Maior Desafio para a Polícia Florestal," *JdT*, 28 February 1985; Elaine Saboya, "Polícia Florestal, Só Dificuldade no Ribeira," *OESP*, 9 October 1985; "Ataque ao Corte Clandestino de Madeira," *JdT*, 17 October 1986; Milton Abrucio, Jr., "São Paulo Tem Menos de 5% de suas Florestas Nativas," *JdT*, 5 April 1987; Célia Maria Romano, "A Rede Clandestina dos Palmitos," *OESP*, 15 January 1984; Lt. P. M. Wagner, 1st Battalion, Forest Police, interview with the author, São Paulo, 2 November 1992; *Tietê* [Bulletin of the Forest Police], 1 (September 1992), 6; "As Dúvidas do Policial Florestal," *JornalECO*, 1 (December 1989), 7; "Em Defesa da Mata," *JornalECO*, 2 (October 1990), 6; "Atlas Revela: São Paulo Destrói a Mata Atlântica a um Ritmo Alucinante," *Boletim S.O.S. Mata Atlântica*, 4 (August 1992), 1. Only one police participant was found among the seminars promoted by environmentalists; see CMA–UNICAMP, *Reserva*, p. 73. See also "Reflorestadoras Querem Policiamento," *FSP*, 3 February 1986.

43. Pedro Fávaro, Jr., "Japi, uma Floresta Milenar Agredida," *OESP*, 29 May 1988; "As Ameaças às Nossas Últimas Florestas," *JdT*, 18 June 1985.

44. "Parque Nacional de Bocaina Está Sendo Devastado," *O Globo*, 23 May 1982; "Parque da Serra da Bocaina Vem Sendo Desmatado Até com Máquinas," *O Globo*, 16 August 1983.

45. Germano de Oliveira, "Ameaça a uma das Ultimas Florestas," *JdT*, 15 November 1982; Rosemeiry Tardivo, "Trincheira na Mata," *Isto É*, 20 August 1986, pp. 86–88; "Imposto Ameaça Mata Nativa no Paraná," *FSP*, 20 December 1987.

46. "A Terra para os Macacos," *Isto É*, 25 April 1984, p. 45; "A Invasão Ecológica," *Veja*, 26 (8 September 1993), 68; Sérgio Pugliese, "Em Defesa da Mata Atlântica," *JdB*, 12 January 1990; Sônia Regina Pereira, "Espírito Santo Perde suas

Últimas Reservas Florestais," *Jornal do País*, 18 March 1988; "Plantas de Burle Marx Poderão Vir a Morrer," *Jornal Verde* (December 1991–January 1992), p. 2; Andréia Curry, "A Briga pelo Museu Ruschi," *JdB*, 16 March 1992.

47. Mario Borgonovi, "Reserva Florestal da Companhia Vale do Rio Doce em Linhares, ES—Fonte Inesgotável de Produtos Florestais," *Brasil Florestal*, 5 (July-September 1975), 40; Renato Moraes de Jesus, "Mata Atlântica de Linhares: Aspectos Florestais," in Seminário sobre Desenvolvimento Econômico e Impacto Ambiental em Areas de Trópico Húmido Brasileiro, 1, Belém, 1986, *A Experiência da CVRD* (Rio de Janeiro, 1987), pp. 35–71; idem, "A Reserva Florestal da CVRD" (n.p., [1988]), xerog.; Vera Lex Engel and Renato Moraes de Jesus, "A Relíquia Florestal de Porto Seguro," in Simpósio sobre Recursos Naturais e Meio Ambiente, Rio de Janeiro, June 1987, *Resumos* (Rio de Janeiro, 1989), p. 19.

48. "As Leis Que Apagam o Fogo," *JdT*, 19 August 1988; "Minas: Um Prejuízo de US$12 Milhões com as Queimadas," *JdT*, 19 September 1987; "Fogo Destroi Metade da Mata Atlântica na Bahia," *O Globo*, 24 February 1989; "Incéndios Florestais, *Informativo da FBCN*, 13 (July-September 1989), 3.

49. Brasil, Instituto Brasileiro de Desenvolvimento Florestal, *Inventário Florestal Nacional (Síntese dos Resultados)* (n.p., 1983); José Cláudio Cardoso Uruahy et al., "Vegetação," in Brasil, Ministério de Minas e Energia, *Projeto Radam Brasil: Levantamento de Recursos Naturais*, vol. 32, *Folhas SF.23/24 Rio de Janeiro/Vitória* (Rio de Janeiro, 1983), pp. 578–579; SOS–MA, Instituto Nacional de Pesquisas Espaciais (INPE), and Instituto Brasileiro de Meio Ambiente e Recursos Naturais Renováveis, "Atlas dos Remanescentes Florestais do Domínio Mata Atlântica" (n.p., n.d.), xerog.; SOS–MA and INPE, "Atlas da Evolução dos Remanescentes Florestais e Ecossistemas Associados do Domínio da Mata Atlântica no Estado de São Paulo no Período 1985–1990" (São Paulo, 1992), xerog.; São Paulo, Secretaria do Meio Ambiente, Departamento Estadual de Proteção de Recursos Naturais, "Vegetação Nativa do Estado de São Paulo—Olho Verde" (n.p., [1990]), printout (images dated 1988 and 1989); Alberto Brant et al., "O Fim da Mata Atlântica Paulista: Uma Análise Quantitativa," in Sociedade Brasileira pelo Progresso da Ciência, Reunião Anual, 43, Rio de Janeiro, 1991, *Anais* (São Paulo, 1991), p. 629–630; "Olho Verde—Sorpresa via Satélite," *JornalECO*, 2 (January 1991), 5; Hideyo Aoki, "Quanto Sobrou das Nossas Matas," *JornalECO*, 2 (March 1991), 2; Mauro Victor, "A Devastação em São Paulo Revisitada 16 Anos Depois" ([São Paulo, June 1992]), xerog.; Mauro Victor to Hélio Ogawa, Secretary of Environment, São Paulo, 28 July 1992, xerog. On methodology, see Alan Grainger, "Rates of Deforestation in the Humid Tropics: Estimates and Measurements," *Geographical Journal*, 159 (March 1993), 33–44.

50. Patrícia Ferraz, "Mata Atlântica Perdeu 53 Mil Hectares em 5 Anos," *OESP*, 24 November 1993; SOS–MA, *Atlas da Evolução dos Remanescentes da Mata Atlântica* (São Paulo, 1993).

51. George Eiten, "A Vegetação do Estado de São Paulo," *Boletim do Instituto de Botânica*, 7 (January, 1970), cited by Fernando Roberto Martins, *Estrutura de uma Floresta Mesófila* (Campinas, 1991), p. 200; Uruahy et al., "Vegetação," p. 572; Tardivo, "Norma Permite Exploração."

52. Mário Borgonovi, "Sugestões para Pesquisa Tendo em Vista a Defesa da Flora e da Fauna," in *Recursos Naturais, Meio Ambiente e Poluição* (Rio de Janeiro,

1977), 1:217–219; Alceo Magnanini, "Situação, Legislação e Política Florestais, Algumas Sugestões" (Rio de Janeiro, 1979), xerog.; Rubens Leite Vianello, "Indícios de Mudança Climática Causada por Desmatamento, Município de Juiz de Fora, Minas Gerais," *Ciência e Cultura,* 33 (May 1981), 665–666; V. M. Meher-Homji, "Probable Impact of Deforestation on Hydrological Processes," in Norman Myers, ed., *Tropical Forests and Climate* (Dordrecht, 1992), pp. 163–173.

CHAPTER 15. THE VALUE OF BARE GROUND

1. Manuel Arruda da Câmara, *Discurso sobre a Utilidade da Instituição de Jardins nas Principais Provincias do Brazil* (Rio de Janeiro, 1810), p. 3; Auguste de Saint-Hilaire, *Voyage dans le District des Diamans et sur le littoral du Brésil* (Paris, 1833), 1:51, 2:64–65; idem, *Voyage dans les provinces de Rio de Janeiro et Minas Gerais* (Paris, 1830), 2:96, 97; idem, *Voyage dans les provinces de Saint Paul et de Sainte Catherine* (Paris, 1851), 1:92; "Memoire sur le systhème d'agriculture adopté par les Brésiliens et les résultats qu'il a eu dans la Province de Minas Gerais," *Memoires du Muséum d'Histoire Naturelle,* 14 (1827), 89.

2. Robert MacArthur and Edward O. Wilson, *The Theory of Island Biogeography* (Princeton, NJ, 1967), pp. 8–18; C. Barry Cox and Peter D. Moore, *Biogeography: An Ecological and Evolutionary Approach* (4th ed.; Oxford, 1985), pp. 112–116; Keith S. and G. G. Brown, "Habitat Alteration and Species Loss in Brazilian Forests," in T. C. Whitmore and J. A. Sayer, eds., *Tropical Deforestation and Species Extinction* (London, 1992), 119–142.

3. The bromeliad collectors Mulford B. and Racine Sarasy Foster, *Brazil* (Lancaster, PA, 1945), could not collect specimens in Aimoré State Park because its trees were too tall; note also their discovery, p. 230, of a new species in the long-culled Itatiaia park.

4. Paraná, Coordenadoria do Patrimônio Cultural, *Tombamento da Serra do Mar* (Curitiba, 1987), p. 35.

5. Rogério Medeiros, "A Ultima Memória," *Jornal da Vale,* June 1986, p. 9; "Devastação: 50 Hectares por Dia," *Jornal da Tarde,* 2 September 1987; Maria do Carmo Mendes Marques, "Botânicos Investigam a Antiga Flora Fluminense," *Ciência Hoje,* 12 (October 1990), 60–61; Scott A. Mori, "Eastern, Extra-Amazonian Brazil," in D. C. Campbell and H. D. Drummond, eds., *Floristic Inventory of Tropical Countries* (New York, 1989), p. 445.

6. Helmut Sick, *Ornitologia Brasileira* (3d ed.; Brasília, 1984), 1:100.

7. Foster and Foster, *Brazil,* p. 122; Mauro Antônio Moraes Victor, *A Devastação Florestal* (São Paulo, n.d.), p. 37; Ladislau Netto, *Additions à la flore brésilienne: itineraire botanique dans la province de Minas Gerais* (Paris, 1866), pp. 5–6, 7. The quotation is from Frederico Carlos Hoehne, *Excursão Botânica Feito ao Sul de Minas e Regiões Limitrofes do Estado de São Paulo* (São Paulo, 1939), p. 9; see also pp. 13, 111.

8. Manuel Pereira de Godoy, *Contribuição à História Natural e Geral de Pirassununga* (Pirassununga, 1974); L. F. Weinberg, "Nova Colectânea e Listagem das Aves de Nova Friburgo, Cantagalo e Trajano de Moraes," *Boletim da FBCN,* 21 (1986), 172–190, 22 (1987), 133–134; Kent H. Redford and John G. Robinson, "Park Size and the Conservation of Forest Mammals in Latin America," in Michael A.

Mares and David J. Schmidly, *Latin American Mammalogy: History, Biodiversity and Conservation* (Norman, OK, 1991), pp. 227–234.

9. Moysés Kuhlman and Eduardo Kühn, *A Flora do Distrito de Ibiti (ex Monte Alegre)* (São Paulo, 1947), p. 146. The palm was *Syagrus oleracea*. See Francis Dov Por, *Sooretama: The Atlantic Rain Forest of Brazil* (The Hague, 1992), p. 50; Keith S. Brown, "Borboletas da Serra do Japi," in L. Patricia C. Morellato, org., *História Natural da Serra do Japi* (Campinas, 1992), pp. 145–146.

10. Alberto José de Sampaio, ed., "Primeira Conferencia Brasileira de Proteção á Natureza," *Boletim do Museu Nacional*, 11 (1935), No. 2, 37–38. See also idem, *Biogeografia Dinamica: A Natureza e o Homem no Brasil* (São Paulo, 1935), p. 204.

11. Brazil, Instituto Brasileiro do Desenvolvimento Florestal [hereafter IBDF], "Espécies de Plantas Brasileiras Ameaçadas de Extinção," Portaria No. 303/68, xerog.; Sociedade Botânica do Brasil, *Centuria Plantarum Brasiliensium Exstintionis Minitata* (n.p., 1992); Pierfelice Ravenna, "Neotropical Species Threatened and Endangered by Human Activity in the Iridaceae, Amaryllidaceae, and Allied Bulbous Families," in Ghillean T. Prance and Thomas Elias, eds., *Extinction Is Forever* (New York, 1977), pp. 257–282; Ghillean T. Prance, *Dichapetalaceae*, Flora Neotropica Monograph No. 10 (New York, 1972). The de Barros quotation is in "Plantas Ameaçadas de Extinção; Os Botânicos Reclamam: Não Há Verba," *O Globo*, 3 April 1981.

12. Brazil, IBDF, Portaria No. 348I–DN, 31 May 1973, xerog.; Instituto Brasileiro do Meio Ambiente e dos Recursos Naturais Renováveis, Portaria No. 1522, 19 December 1989; Academia Brasileira de Ciências, *Espécies da Fauna Brasileira Ameaçada de Extinção* (Rio de Janeiro, 1972). See also Sick, *Ornitologia*, pp. 100–102.

13. Luis Octávio da Silva, "Recomposição de Matas Nativas Empreendida pela CESP," in Congresso Nacional sobre Essências Nativas, 2, São Paulo, *Anais*, special edition of *Revista do Instituto Florestal*, 4 (March 1992) [hereafter CNEN, *Anais*], 1054–1060.

14. Consórcio Mata Atlântica–Universidade Estadual de Campinas, *Reserva da Biosfera Mata Atlântica* (São Paulo, 1992), 1:64; "Memória do Projeto FLORAM," *Estudos Avançados*, 4 (May-August 1990).

15. Brazil, IBDF, *Plano de Manejo: Reserva Biológica de Poço das Antas* (Brasília, 1981), pp. 11–12; São Paulo (State), Fundação para a Conservação e Produção Florestal, *Fundação Florestal: Uma Maneira Realista de Conservar* (São Paulo, 1990); Antônio Carlos Macedo, Fundação Florestal, interview with the author, São Paulo, 26 October 1992; Wantuelfer Gonçalves and Vanderlei José Ventura, "Uma Política para Manutenção da Biodiversidade no Estado de São Paulo," CNEN, *Anais*, 1063–1066; Congresso "Produtor Rural Tem de Reflorestar Parte do Que Desmatou," *O Estado de São Paulo* [hereafter *OESP*], Suplemento Agrícola, 30 September 1993.

16. José Carlos Bolliger Nogueira, *Reflorestamento Heterogéneo com Essências Indígenas*, Instituto Florestal Boletim Técnico, No. 25 (São Paulo, 1977); "Desvio de Bilhões no Golpe do Palmito," *OESP*, 15 December 1983.

17. Adayr Mafuz Saliba, director of the São Paulo Zoo, quoted in Marina Caldeira, "Mais Que Lazer, Zôo Trabalha na Preservação de Espécies," *Folha de São Paulo* [hereafter *FSP*], 3 January 1988.

18. World Wildlife Fund, *Yearbook, 1970–1971* (Washington, DC, 1971), p. 165; James Brooke, "Golden Monkeys Learn How to Live in Wild in Brazilian Preserve," *New York Times*, 7 October 1989; Diane Ackerman, "A Reporter at Large: Golden Monkeys," *New Yorker*, 21 June 1991, 35–51; Adelmar Coimbra Filho, lecture at the Confederação Nacional de Comércio, Rio de Janeiro, 24 October 1991; "Proteção para o Mico-Leão," *Jornal do Brasil* [hereafter *JdB*], 29 May 1991; Golden Lion Tamarin Conservation Program, "Countdown 2025" (pamphlet; n.p., [1991]); "FEEMA Exporta Conhecimento em Primatologia," *Revista FEEMA*, 1 (July-August, 1992), 41; "Centro de Primatologia Defende a Vida," *Revista FEEMA*, 1 (January-February 1992), 20–23; "Prestígio Internacional Leva Centro a Ampliar Atividades," *Revista FEEMA*, 1 (January-February 1992), 24–25.

19. "Fernanda Pedrosa, "Poço das Antas em Chamas," *JdB*, 5 February 1990; "IBAMA Condenada por Incêndio em Reserva," *O Globo*, 9 April 1990; "Proteção para o Mico-Leão," *JdB*, 29 May 1991; "Diretor Acusa Caçadores," *JdB*, 27 October 1991; "Fogo Atinge 10% de Poço das Antas," *O Globo*, 27 October 1991; "Desmatamentos Ameaçam Secar os Mananciais Que Abastecem Toda a Região dos Lagos," *O Globo*, 30 January 1984.

20. World Wildlife Fund, *Yearbook* (1987–1988), project 3215; idem, Latin America/Caribbean Projects, FY88–FY93 (Washington, DC, 31 May 1993), printout.

21. Maria del Carmen Rodríguez-Hernández and Carlos Vásquez-Yanes, "La conservación de plantas en peligro de extinción a través del almacenamiento," *Interciência*, 17 (September-October 1992), 293–297.

22. "Sarney Lança 'Nossa Natureza,'" *JdB*, 7 April 1989; see also "Desmatamento da Amazônia é Maior do Que Diz Sarney," *JdB*, 8 April 1989; José Pedro de Oliveira Costa and Fredman Corrêa, "A Reserva da Mata Atlântica," *São Paulo em Perspectiva*, 6 (January-June, 1992), 111.

23. Randáu Marques, "Destruição: O Brasil Perde Dois Milhões de Arvores Todos os Dias," *JdT*, 26 September 1984; Mauro Antônio Moraes Victor, "Floresta Amazônica e Mata Atlântica: Começo e Fim" (paper presented at the International Assembly on Deforestation, Geneva, April 1989), p. 10.

24. Helita Barreira Custódio, "Legislação Brasileira do Estudo de Impacto Ambiental," in Sámia Maria Tauk et al., orgs., *Análise Ambiental: Uma Visão Multidisciplinar* (São Paulo, 1991), p. 46.

25. Keith Alger and Marcellos Caldas, "The Crisis of the Cocoa Economy and the Future of the Bahian Atlantic Forest" (paper presented at the Latin American Studies Association Conference, Los Angeles, September 1992), p. 13.

26. James Holston, "The Misrule of Law: Land and Usurpation in Brazil," *Comparative Studies in Society and History*, 33 (October 1991), 695–725.

27. United Nations, Economic Commission for Latin America, and United Nations Environment Programme, *Expansión de la frontera agrícola y medio ambiente en América Latina* (Madrid, 1983), pp. 15–16; Alceo Magnanini, "Situação, Legislação e Política Florestais; Algumas Sugestões" (Rio de Janeiro, 1979), xerog., p. 2.

28. Tânia Malheiros, "Obra de Angra 2 Pode Começar em 93," *OESP*, 25 October 1992; "De Volta ao Mato," *O Globo*, 12 March 1993.

29. United Nations Conference on Environment and Development, Rio de Janeiro, 1992, *Report* (New York, 1992), 2:24–33, 2:103; 3:111–116.

30. Cláudio de Moura Castro, "Ecology—Gunpowder Rediscovered" (Rio de Janeiro, [1980]), mimeog., p. 31.

31. "Começa a Operação Salva Mata Atlântica," *O Globo*, 23 February 1990.

32. V. L. Baril, Comte de la Hure, *L'Empire du Brésil* (Paris, 1862), p. 234; Carlos E. Quintela, "An SOS for Brazil's Beleaguered Atlantic Forest," *Nature Conservancy Magazine*, 40 (March-April 1990), 14 (by 1989, 20 percent had heard of it); Antônio Giacomini Ribeiro, "Seca, Geada e Incéndios no Ano de 1963," *Boletim de Geografia* (Maringá), 2 (January 1984), 24–33.

33. S.O.S. Mata Atlântica, Seminário Internacional "Manejo Racional de Florestas Tropicais," Rio de Janeiro, 20–21 June 1988, *Seminário . . .* (São Paulo, 1988), p. 98.

Pronouncing Glossary

This list omits words and phrases used only once or twice in the text. The pronunciation guide is approximate. A tilde, ~, indicates nasalization.

a favor	*ah fah-VOHR*	precarious form of tenantry
administrado	*ahd-mee-nee-STRAH-doo*	native slave (euphemism)
agregado	*ah-greh-GAH-doo*	poor farmer "attached" to owner's household; tenant
aldeia	*ahl-DAY-ah*	village, specifically native village resettled by colonial authorities
bandeira	*bãn-DAY-rah*	slave- and gold-hunting expedition
Botocudo	*boh-toh-KOO-doh*	Gê-speaking indigenous groups
bugre	*BOO-grih*	indigene (pejorative)
caá-etê	*kah-AH eh-TAY*	primary forest
caatinga	*kah-ah-TEẼN-ga*	dry scrub forest
caboclo	*kah-BOH-kloo*	backwoodsman, mestizo
cabroca	*kah-BROH-ka*	cacao-planting regime that leaves native forest partly intact
cachaça	*kuh-SHAH-su*	rum
campo	*KÃM-poo*	prairie, grassland
capão de mato	*ka-PÃOO dih MA-too*	wooded islet in prairie

441

capitão do mato	*ka-pee-TÃOO doo MA-too*	slave catcher
capoeira	*ka-poo-AY-ra*	secondary forest
cerrado	*seh-HAH-doo*	savanna
Coroado	*koh-roh-AH-doh*	Gê-speaking indigenous groups
degredado	*deh-greh-DAH-doo*	banished convict
engenho	*ẽn-ZHE-nyoo*	sugar mill
engenhoca	*ẽn-zhẽn-NYOH-kah*	small sugar or rum mill
entrada	*ẽn-TRA-da*	slave-catching expedition
garimpeiro	*ga-reẽm-PAY-roo*	gold prospector
grilo, grilagem	*GREE-loo, gree-LAH-zhẽm*	claim jumping, land theft
jacarandá	*zhah-ka-rãn-DAH*	name of a number of trees, several of which are valued as hardwoods
jequitibá	*zheh-kee-tee-BAH*	forest tree prized for wood
Kimbundu	*kim-BUN-doo*	West African language
latifundia	*lah-tee-FOON-dee-ah*	very large landed estate
lavoura	*lah-VOH-rah*	farming
madeira de lei	*ma-DAY-ra dih LAY*	hardwood species, reserved by crown for naval construction
mameluco	*ma-meh-LOO-koo*	mestizo
mata, mato	*MAH-tah, MAH-too*	woods, woodlands, forest
mata virgem, mato verdadeiro	*MA-ta VEER-zhem, MA-to vehr-da-DAY-roo*	primary forest
meda	*MEH-dah*	earthen-mound charcoal kiln
minifundia	*mee-nee-FOON-dee-ah*	undersized farmstead
padrão, padrões	*pa-DRÃOO, pa-DRÕ-es*	tree species presumed to indicate the presence of superior soils
pagé	*pa-ZHEH*	shaman

pau-brasil	*paoo bra-ZEEL*	brazilwood
pau real	*paoo hey-AHL*	*see* madeira de lei
Paulista	*paoo-LEES-tah*	resident of São Paulo
Pontal	*pohn-TAHL*	point of land between the Paraná and Paranapanema rivers
posse	*POH-see*	squatter's claim
posseiro	*poh-SAY-roo*	squatter
quilombo	*kee-LOHM-boo*	community of escaped slaves
restinga	*hes-TEẼN-gah*	coastal forest vegetation
salto	*SAHL-too*	*see* entrada
sambaqui	*sãm-bah-KEE*	kitchen midden of extinct coastal tribal culture
saúva	*sa-OO-vah*	leaf-cutting ants
sertão	*sehr-TÃO*	backlands, interior
sesmaria	*sez-mah-REE-ah*	royal land grant (literally, "portion")
tapera	*ta-PEH-rah*	abandoned village, homestead
tapinhoá	*tah-pee-nyoh-AH*	forest tree prized for wood
terra devoluta	*TEH-ha deh-voh-LOO-tah*	crown land (literally, "reverted land")
terra roxa	*TEH-ha HOH-shah*	a type of fertile soil (literally, "purple land")
tombamento	*tõm-bah-MEN-too*	declaration of landmark status
voçoroca	*voh-soh-ROH-kah*	gully
Zona da Mata	*ZOH-nah dah MAH-tah*	southeastern district of Minas Gerais

Index

Index:	Paul Spragens
Maps:	Tom Dean
Composition:	Graphic Composition, Inc.
Text:	10/13 Aldus
Display:	Aldus
Printing and Binding:	Thomson-Shore